PERSUASION
FORCE
-The Complete Edition

Containing All 23 E-Book Releases of This Course in a
Single Collected Edition

KENRICK
CLEVELAND

Table of Contents

BOOK ONE

INTENTION AND RAPPORT

INTRODUCTION

Introducing Your Newfound Skills

Welcome to the first book of **Persuasion Force**. My name is Kenrick Cleveland. For just a moment I want you to imagine something with me. I want you to imagine that you're not simply reading a book, but that you just came for your first appointment to meet with me and begin your studies.

As you sit there, waiting to see me, your mind begins to think back about why you decided to come. You think about all the areas where, if you could only persuade better, things would be different for you. Then, your mind begins to zero in on one area that is most important – the area where you'll immediately begin applying your newfound skills.

And as you think about it, many things flood your consciousness. There's some regret that you didn't do this earlier but that quickly fades as you begin to imagine what your life will be like with these new skills. You lose yourself in one incredible thought after another, indulging for a moment and letting your deepest desires overtake you. Next thing you know, you feel the gentle touch on your arm and you look up to see that I've joined you. It's time to begin and as we do, I want you to stay focused on the desires you have for learning to persuade better. These will become your **focus** – the things you will aim your skills and efforts at and with each book of this series, first thing as you are preparing to read, imagine that you have come for your next live session and magically transport yourself to sitting and studying with me.

This is going to be a very exciting journey that we'll be taking together. So let's go over now the best way to study and learn this material. If possible, read the entire book from start to finish. There's a *lot* there. If you can do it all in one sitting, that's fine. The goal is to read through the entire book each time, before digging in and putting things into practice.

And use the QR code or link provided to obtain to the **audiobook** version. This contains more of my insights on the material and some bang up to date observations. You'll be able to actually **listen** to some of the practices being put into use, and this will make a whole world of difference. Don't neglect this really powerful tool which can be used alongside the book.

CHAPTER ONE

Integrating the Skills into Your Life

Study the principles in the book every day. As you progress, read the book again chapter by chapter. *Wrestle* with the material and *use* it constantly. It's not enough to read through this one time and expect your results to skyrocket. You must **integrate the skills into your life** so they are a natural part of what you do.

This program will provide all you need to make this happen and you must do it. One of my favorite sayings is "**The only time the skills don't work is when you don't use them**." To get to the point of using them all the time, you need to *make them a part of your ongoing behavior* so they are as much a part of you and your skill set as shaking hands or smiling. So read the material in each module over and over again..

If you follow these suggestions, you will see dramatic results.

As we prepare to jump in, let me just tell you a little bit about how I'm going to be structuring the content at least in this book.

The book is going to be a **very packed read**. We're going to cover a tremendous amount of information and so as we do that, the idea here is that you're going to read it *from start to finish* first. So, for example, let's say right now is the first time you're reading. Go ahead and just read all the way through.

However, I want you to stop and go back and re-read each of the different major sections that we will be covering and talking about. It's really not meant to be *ingested* in one read or *behavioralized* in one read.

This is the part of the process where your job is to be open – to open up your mind and engage your brain and really look, think and learn, okay? It's to get the **concept**. It's to begin to get the *idea* of exactly what you're going to be *doing* and how it's going to be *working*.

Then, you're going to go back and go through it again and again. The idea is to pick sections of it that you want to learn better, or just read it from start to finish again, but the *best* thing you could do after you've read it from start to finish the first time all the way through is then go back *section by section* and really work with each part of it.

CHAPTER TWO

Read With a Beginner's Eyes

Now, as we start, I want to tell you something. I know that there's going to be some who as they read this are going to go, "Ah! I've heard this. I know a little bit about this." or "I know a lot about that," and that's okay. What I want you to do is to **read with a beginner's eyes**. If you think you know some of this, that's great. Just *pretend you don't* because when you read with new eyes, what you're going to find is that all of a sudden you'll *see things in a new way.*

And there is an important point that I need to make that's really, really helpful for you and that is that **what I teach has a purpose**. It has a **structure** and it has an **overall goal** and as we go through this program with these books, my goal is *to install that in you.*

You see, the power isn't in any one book. In other words, this book in and of itself is by no means sufficient nor will be book number three or book number 12 or book number 15. It's the way in which this *works together*. It's the **synergy** and the way in which I teach these *strategies* and the way in which *you'll integrate them into your life.*

That's what makes them powerful and that's what my top students, those that are absolutely setting records in their industries, that's what they're getting.

It's the way in which you *integrate these skills together.* That's where you'll find the power. It's that you can do **all** of them, all of the skills and they're **behavioralized** and that's what this program, **Persuasion Force**, is all about. It's helping you to *behavioralize these skills* and make them *yours.*

So, it's real important that you read with a beginner's eyes, so that you can really understand the depths of which we'll be speaking about as we go through the process.

CHAPTER THREE

Setting Your Intention

Okay, now let's jump into the next section I want to talk about and that's **setting your intention**. I just want to touch on it here in this part of the program. It's important that you begin to get an understanding of the *power of intention* and what it'll do for you as you begin to implement it. So, first of all, what is intention? Let's just talk about that for a little bit.

Intention is like a decision. That's an easy way to look at it. *Intention is like making a decision* but it's a decision that is fully supported with *all of who you are*. It's a decision that you intend to carry out, that you are setting in motion at that moment. It's more important than a decision like, "Well, should I stop off at the bookstore on the way home; or should I just go on by?"

So, intention is what you use to help guide yourself and it's also a way of *turning over to your unconscious mind* what it is that you want to do as you begin. In other words, it's like *giving instructions to your unconscious* for you to start and for you to follow through in a very particular way.

You can make **the setting of your intention** the first step in your process before your meeting with, say, a client or if you're going out on a sales call, to make sure everything is *lined up and headed towards your outcome* or your intention.

For example, if you have a multi-step process where you have to find out information first, make sure that's your *intention* for that appointment. In other words, you're gonna go out and *get all the information you need*. It is much stronger to set your intention first than it is to show up and say, "Hmm. So, what do we want to do today?"

In fact, I set little mini intentions as I go. I start off, my overriding intention of course is to get the sale, and along the way I know I need to **establish rapport** and so I have a little *mini intention* to make sure I've got it and I have little *checkpoints* along the way that I'm using to make sure that I'm doing each of these steps as we proceed. And we'll talk about those steps and how you can incorporate them with each book so that you're understanding that part of it.

So what you're really doing here is - we're talking about making a decision right now and I'm going to go much more in depth with this but, for this section, I just want to simply say it's making a decision about what's going to happen – so I'd recommend you get into the habit, especially in the beginning, of actually **having a discussion with yourself** in which you are going to **set the rules for your unconscious mind**.

Let's define conscious and unconscious real quick. I keep it real simple. Your conscious mind is that part of you that is aware and your unconscious or subconscious mind is that part of you that takes care of all the things that happen automatically for you. It makes you breathe. It controls the myriad of muscles that you use when you turn your neck as an example. I mean, imagine if you had to *think* about all the muscles involved and *make* each one work. Now, when you're a little baby, that was exactly what you had to do but basically your unconscious mind is capable of dealing with *huge quantities of data very, very fast* – like a very efficient giant computer system.

Now, I also consider that the unconscious mind is that part of you that *processes* all these things and it's the part of you that *you're not aware of*. It exists but you're not aware of it. Now, you can shift your attention to inner parts of it and *become more aware*.

So it is really easy to think about this because your conscious mind, I'll define, is that which you are aware of and that's what processes the things that you're aware of. So, in essence, we're going to have a discussion in which we're instructing it to go to work – the unconscious mind – and *accomplish a result*. And that's what I'm talking about when I tell you to **set your intention**: you're going to *make a decision inside yourself*.

So let's talk about the first level of **intention** that we're going to use and the first level is that we want you to *set the overall intention*. So let's say you say "The overall intention here today is for me to make a sale in this upcoming interaction and the next intention I'm going to do is I'm going to gain rapport real quick and I'm going to know that I have rapport. In other words, I'm not going to guess about this. I'm going to know it."

And so the first thing I want you to do as you're beginning to practice these skills is to practice **setting your intention**. Tell yourself *exactly* what you expect to have happen and give yourself *a way to measure it*.

For example, I'll know I have rapport because I'll see them moving like I do. I'll feel a *connection* with them as if they trust me.

And there'll be a number of things as we go through this book and it's important that you **start setting your intention purposefully for what you want to accomplish**. That's a real key and you'll understand this much more as we progress.

CHAPTER FOUR

Rhythmic Speaking

Alright, now I'm going to jump away from the things we've been talking about into another section right now. And it's a section on **rhythmic speaking**. Now this is going to be something we're going to come back to over and over again. But for now I want to give you a briefing on it and I want you to *do* a few things so that you can put this into place and *begin to practice*. This is something that requires practice so that you can implement it really powerfully.

When you launch into a real strong *rhythm*, people will *lock on* to everything that you're saying. It's as if the words out of your mouth are causing them to stop and pay close attention to all the things that you're doing and it can have a dramatic impact in the way in which you're received as you go through the presentation.

Now, try reading that last paragraph out loud, adding a rhythm to the words, as if you were reciting poetry. I want you to get really good at *rhythmic speaking*.

To that end I want you to go get yourself a tool to help you. Here's a recommendation for tool number one. You're not going to have to get many things but I definitely recommend you get this and it's very inexpensive. I want you to go get a **metronome**. Now, the cheaper, the better on this, okay? These days you can simply get an app for your iPhone or Android and turn it on, and that will be perfectly good enough. But I do want you to go get a metronome. It's important to have it.

Set it at about 45 beats a minute and as you do this you'll have a **tool** that you can begin practicing with. Now, it's really *important*, okay? It really is, so please **do this**. We're also going to provide an audio file with the audiobook of this chapter which you can listen to via the QR code or link provided, but you can get an app for only about a dollar.

And what I really want you to do is to spend at least 5 minutes a day, if not 10, practicing *speaking in a rhythm*. Now, what'll happen is when you first get the metronome and the thing starts ticking away at you, it goes *<tick-tick-tick>* and what's going to happen is you're going to go "I-have-to-speak-like-this-with-one-word-per-beat.".

Now, you'll get over it real fast, especially with a little practice; but here's the thing. When you start off that's probably the best you can do. You'll just put one word down on each beat and that's fine, okay?

Now, what you want to do is to start to put more words down with each beat so you could then realize you can *skip a beat* if you have to. Pretty soon you'll find that you can just speak with the number of words that stop on each of the beats that you find *important* to stop upon. And when you do that kind of thing you can even just use your **accents** on the words that you're using so that *occasionally* your words are *right in line* with the beat.

So you'll learn to **emphasize** a word when the beat is happening and *that's* how you can do this. It's just that simple. Let me share three great ways to practice this.

First, and you have to have your metronome app for this, so let's hope you've already got it, and if not, please do so...

First look at the light on your metronome flash, and speak in time with it. Second, turn off or cover the light or turn the metronome around so you can only hear it and talk with the sound of it beating. And, by the way, that's a very important one, okay? And, three, set your metronome so you're listening to it and start *walking* at the same rate of the beat. So every step is a beat on the metronome. And what you'll find is: you can start to walk, and as you walk you'll naturally begin to *get in the rhythm* with each and every step.

So now you'll have all three pieces: you can hear the metronome; you can see the metronome, and you can feel the pace of the metronome as you're walking.

What I'm going to recommend is, once you have this metronome in your possession, that you *play it all the time*. You're going to practice *at least* 5 minutes per day speaking with it, but if you can *listen* to it for several hours a day in the background, all the better. You wanna **burn that beat into your brain**! About 45 beats a minute is really, really good.

Now, when you're driving, you can even put it on but I want you to be careful doing that so you don't zone off. If you think you have an issue with that then just *don't do it while you're driving*, but I have students who carry the thing around with them and they have it going even when they go into stores. People would think they're crazy, but they were determined to really **master the rhythmic speaking**.

So let's get into more details, because this is one of those skills that is going to require *a whole lot of effort and work over time*. You're not going to probably get this right off the bat. Not at the level I want you to. Not if you're also going to be able to maintain awareness of the other things that are important at the same time.

What I want is for this to be kind of like walking. At first, you are going to teeter and totter around, and stumble about a little bit, and fall, and all those kinds of things. But pretty soon you're going to be able to walk without too much difficulty and, before you know it, you're running down the road and you don't even give a second thought to walking.

So *that's* the way speaking to a beat is going to be; and to that end I want you to **drill this beat into your brain** and I mean *really* drill it into your brain. Listen to it *all the time* whenever you can. So, for me, I can hear this beat all the time in my brain. All I have to do is **focus** on it for a second and I can immediately begin hearing it.

Another trick to learning this is to *read* to the beat of the metronome. So, just open a book and start *reading aloud* and get to the point where you can read really smoothly as the metronome is playing. Remember, *you don't have to stop on each beat*. You can let several beats go by and you can also just sort of pause a little at each of the beats or a few of the beats, or you can also *adjust your tone* when the beat happens. You can *accent* it a bit or you can *deepen* it a bit. There are all kinds of things you can do.

So when you're talking along and the metronome is beating, you're sort of *adjusting your tone* to be pretty much in alignment with what the metronome is doing.

And the idea is that you can jump into this at a moment's notice. You may be asking at this point, why are we going to do this and what in the heck are we spending time learning this for? Well, I'll tell you...

Have you ever seen a televangelist deliver their sermon? Have you? This brings me to another part of the homework for this book and that is I want you to tune in to a televangelist and *watch them*. And it should be the more *impassioned* kind of televangelist when they're really into their speaking, that's all the better still. These are the people that are speaking with great **passion** about whatever they're talking about and I want you just to **listen** because it'll really, really *teach you how to do this* because they're *great* at it. I think, by nature, they're good at it.

You're going to hear some other interesting things when you watch them or listen to them and that is **repetition in three**. By the way, let me make it very clear as I bring up these example:. I want you to know that I'm doing so with huge respect. I'm not making value judgments about any group or anyone. It's not about value judgments. It's about **observation** and it's about *learning how to deal with human nature more effectively* and to *become more persuasive*.

I was watching one who began to read from Scripture. He was reading something that expressed emotions. Something in the Bible that expressed emotions.This isn't an exact quote, but he was saying something like, "and Jesus seeing the crowd was joyful", and *he smiled as he said it*. And so, he **expressed the emotion very fully in his voice and very much in beat**. Always in a rhythm and I want you to watch this.

I want you to *listen for and see what they're doing* and I'm going to tell you what it does. Now they might explain it in all sorts of ways – all of which can be accurate. If you were to ask a minister why they do that, they may say, "Well, I'm not aware of doing it," and they may not be and yet they're very clearly doing it. They may also say, "Well, I just feel the Lord and I speak with the power of his passion," or something. However they want to explain it is fine. It might just be something they've inherited by listening to the elders in their church doing the same thing. *They've learned that over many years of doing what they do*, but ultimately, when you think about it, what's a minister or pastor or priest or elder's job in front of a crowd when they're giving a sermon or speech like that? It's to **influence the crowd**.

You call it influence, you call it sharing, whatever. Again, I'm not making value judgments. I'm teaching you how to persuade. And so as they do this, what they're really doing is *they're opening your mind*. They're *setting aside your habitual frame of reference*. Let me say that again because it's really important. They're setting aside your habitual frame of reference and *they're causing you to think in a different way to enter a different state*, a different emotional state. So you hear them with new ears.

That's why they do this and that's why I want you to **learn to do this** and all you have to do is practice and you're going to be blown away at what this will do for you as we'll discover, as we continue through our books. It actually **alters your state**.

Now, when you scan the QR code or click the link to listen to the audiobook version of this chapter, you're going to find it to be absolutely invaluable. Because you're going to be able to **listen** to me speaking rhythmically in this section. You'll be able to hear an actual **spoken example** of how this is done and how it sounds, and that will make it so very clear and will save you so much trial and error to *get it right*. This will really help you to understand how this works.

So, you might be asking, "So, Kenrick, are you saying we should speak like this all the time?" And the answer is, *absolutely not*! No way! That is not what you want to do! Notice even in a church environment, there's all kinds of things that go on before the minister steps up and starts doing this. There's a whole song service, their Scripture readings, there's all kinds of things are going on prior to the minister coming in and beginning a rhythmic speech like this and even they often times are not doing it right off the bat. They kind of *warm up to it.*

I started to mention *speaking in threes* and if I remember a little later on I'll try to catch on that a little bit as well and the power that it contains because it's not just a reminder about the tri-fold godhead, you know, God, Jesus and the Holy Spirit. Of course, it does do that, especially for those who are Christians, but **repetition in three** has long been known to *make it easier to install things*. And again we'll talk a little bit more about it because there's some powerful things you can do when you repeat like that, and you can *repeat in rhythm* because that makes a big difference – in rhythm, things can be repeated and people will lock on to them and they'll get it, and they'll stop, and they'll hear you in a new way.

Now you see I just did it. I just repeated. So you can do this on and on and on. You can just lock into the rhythm and do it.

So the question is do we do it all the time? The answer is no. Let me explain when we do do it. We do it *every once in a while*. Now, we're going to be talking more about this and I'm going to show you how to use it and we'll do more and more with it in later books in the series. This is going to become more important as we continue so I want you to start practicing with it **now** because the better you are with it the more you're going to see how it fits right into this whole persuasion process. It is going to really amplify what you're doing hugely and I also promise you – you can absolutely *switch into this* and do it so *covertly* that people won't even really know that you're doing it.

When you do it like that all that will happen is *it'll just start to alter their consciousness*. They'll start to fade away a little bit and when you notice that, you'll be able to *change the way in which are talking* and you'll be able to **directly install what you want them to do.**

Alright, let me review the three steps that I mentioned earlier. First off, *get the metronome going* at about 45 beats per minute so you can hear the click going; and, by the way, once you choose like, let's say 45, just leave it at 45. Don't adjust it, alright? In reality, it could be anywhere from 45 to 60 but 45 is much, much better and easier to practice with, and it's a better beat, I believe. Also, what you want to do once you get it going is stare at the light on your metronome (if it's electric, of course) or the little square ball at the top of the metal part that swings if you have a manual metronome. Also, *walk to the beat* to help you put it all together.

Next, I want you to *listen to the metronome all the time* as much as is possible, especially for extended time periods. Now, it might drive you a bit crazy at first but you will get used to it, I promise, then you'll find you can just drop into it while speaking at will.

Third, I want you to practice a *minimum of 5 minutes per day*, no less. You should also practice *reading aloud* in rhythm. Get used to dropping into a rhythm at will and pretty soon you'll be able to just shift into it any time you want to.

Okay, now when you go into rhythmic speaking, be very careful **not** to also talk in a monotone. The fact is people do really *get engaged* in what you're saying when you do this and you do it *right* and because it's only a short time they don't even realize that anything really changed consciously. **Being engaged** is a lot of what we're going to be talking about.

In fact, the whole section on telling stories persuasively is exactly that – *how we engage people*. I mean, engage them like a movie and get them to understand and shift their consciousness, literally, *take control of their consciousness*. In other words, guide what they're paying attention to and where they're going in their brain, and do it in a way that's *enjoyable* so that they're really having fun and yet we're getting tremendous **leverage** from this from a persuasion standpoint.

That whole section will teach you how to do it and imagine if you could add **rhythmic speaking** to be able to tell stories like that. It is really amazing. Rhythmic speaking really amps up what's going to be able to take place for you.

So, I'm starting off with these pieces that you need to know and understand and as we build throughout the books, we'll be fitting them all in. We're going to be coming back to them over and over. I'm giving you right now a flyby, okay, and then I'm going to give you a very detailed look.

CHAPTER FIVE

Just Do It

So, we're going to go back and look at what we've talked about and then we're going to go through with a magnifying glass and show you how to **tweak it to make it better**.

Pay close attention, I'm going to tell you this right now. Here is a really important truism. **Persuasion is not about the big strokes. It's about the small strokes.** Anybody can say "Oh yeah! Rapport, pace, lead, uh-huh, rhythmic speaking, yup sure. Altered people's consciousness, yup sure uh-huh." Few can really **do it**.

The ones that work with me can **do it** and if you go through these books, and give me your attention, and put this to work the way I tell you, you will *have the result that you're looking to get*. You'll be **far more persuasive** and that's my goal for you and that's where we're headed.

Alright, there is rhythmic speaking. We're going to deal with that much, much more but start into it. Do the things I've suggested and away you go.

We're going to keep coming back and coming back and perfecting this and taking it to higher levels and the key to you reading right now is just *be relaxed and enjoy it*, okay? Because there's so much here. Going through it once, the first time, is great, but you've got to *go back through each part*. Stop and re-read it. Stop and re-read it again and again and again and then *practice*.

The idea here is not that you're knowledgeable. I don't care how knowledgeable you are. I care *how much of it you can incorporate into your **behavior***. For example, how many times in the last 5 minutes as you've been reading this, how many times did you have to stop and remind yourself to breathe? Probably not at all, and that's good, that's a good thing, because that means you're pretty well solidly with me. Otherwise, I'd worry that maybe you should get yourself to a hospital or something, right?

So in other words, *you didn't really have to think about that*. You don't have to *remind* yourself to process your food and separate the good part of it from the bad and eliminate what you don't need and keep what you do. I mean, that all just kind of happens for you, thank goodness – and *that's how persuasion needs to be*.

It all just happens for you, and you will install it a section at a time and that's what we're doing – installing a section at a time.

CHAPTER SIX

Rapport: Creating Trust

Moving on. We're going to talk about **rapport** now because, let me tell you right now, without rapport nothing as it relates to persuading, at least that you want, will happen. *Nothing will happen without rapport.*

I suppose I should put that a little differently. Let me put it this way: if you're out in the middle of a desert and you've gone three days without water and you're dying and your archenemy shows up in an air-conditioned limo and offers you a glass of water, you don't have to necessarily like the guy to take it, right? In fact, it might even change your mind a little. You may even like him a little bit afterwards.

So, there are some places where rapport isn't all that necessary. For example, you have a flat tire, you're in the middle of a really bad section of town and you don't really belong there. Well, you may accept almost *any* help to get out of there – that kind of thing. But for business to transpire, where people have a choice, that requires rapport and it requires trust and so the first stage of anything to do with rapport needs to be a very profound understanding of **trust**, of rapport, of what creates it, of how it works, and why it works, and how you can do it, and how exactly you're going to doing it *each and every time* you talk to people.

So, I'm going to lay down some basic concepts and some basic ideas of rapport. Rapport, the way I'll teach you to understand it and do it, *creates trust* and that's what we want. That's what we're going after.

So let's talk about the kind of people who are so *clumsy* and *obvious* about this. In fact, the chances are, you have probably at one point done this, admit it, even if only to yourself, even quietly. You'll probably start cracking up and laughing when I say it, because you'll have seen the salespeople who go into someone's house or they going into an office and they say, "Hey Bill! How's it going? I'm Joe. How are you?" And Bill says, "Oh, I'm doing great. Good to see you today. Great." Then Joe says, "Hey that's a beautiful marlin fish there on the wall, are you a fisherman?"

Have you done that? Come on!

How about if there's nothing on the wall but there's a picture on the desk? "Hey, Dave, is that a picture the wife and kids?" What do you think it is? What do you think they're going to say? "No, it's my mistress. Why do you ask?" I mean, but really, in your heart, don't you *know* that that's what these guys are thinking? That this is really *stupid*? They're thinking something like, "What an idiot!"

You know that they're literally going in with a sign blazing above their forehead: Salesperson! Salesperson! Salesperson! It's an air raid warning going up. Everyone's going to run for shelter! I mean, can you imagine? *Think* about it for a minute. Your first seconds of interaction with somebody and they're already wanting to run for shelter. Is that what you want? I think not. I wouldn't want people thinking that way about me, that's for sure.

The problem is most people learn to do it this way first. Guys learn that rapport is being *pushy*. They do too hard of a handshake and they look you in the eye. They're supposed to be someone assertive. They do this kind of thing to overcome a feeling of fear or insecurity. Sometimes they do it as a defense mechanism. You know they don't want to be told, "We don't have time for you today," or "We're not interested." So sometimes they are also being tricky to get the person to see them. They can also be overcompensating, so people will not think that they're a "salesperson." Now, you can guarantee that when you think that way and behave that way that that's *exactly* how they'll see you. You're literally advertising it, like I said, as if you had neon signs flashing on your forehead.

The bottom line is when people see you that way it's because *that's what you are*. Got it?

So first, **stop and think about what you are**. Are you a salesperson? In reality, *everyone* is selling which is another way to say **persuading**. Everyone is selling or persuading something, right? So what's the mindset, in your opinion? What is your *mindset of a salesperson*? Are they **honest** people? Are they **good**? Are they **necessary**? Are they **honorable**? Do they **contribute**? It's time to do a real evaluation of yourself. It's time to uncover what *you* think about people who persuade or who sell. **The beliefs *you* have about this are what you are projecting** and if you're projecting something negative, it's hurting you. So are your beliefs, are they helping you or are they hurting you? That's the real question.

So I'd recommend that you stop right now and you really do an analysis. What is a persuader? What is a salesperson? What does it mean to you?

Write it down because if you want to work on anything that's negative, you'll want to *reframe* it, you'll want to *change* it, as the case may be, and I'll show you in future books how to start doing that. But for right now it's really important that you begin to *look at it and understand*. So please stop now and do this part and then continue on once you've gotten it done.

Okay, next, rapport suffers when there are **incongruities**. Remember Zig Ziglar? When he started out, he started selling pots and pans. Now Zig wouldn't let anyone sell for him who didn't own a set of the pots and pans and use them regularly. Think about that for a moment. Now, today we might not be able to get away with that, with today's rules and all, but think about *why* he did that. Can you imagine actually selling pots and pans that you *didn't* use? Why would you think that they were valuable enough for other people to buy if you, yourself, wouldn't buy them?

For example, do you sell life insurance but only own a little bit or none, or only own term-life? Do you sell Mercedes but you drive an old Ford?

So what do these things tell us? What it says is *you don't believe in what you're selling*. I mean, we all have to start somewhere and if you're going to be selling Mercedes and they hire you and you don't drive one, well then, you'll get to the point where you will be *able* to buy one. One of the things I would do is see if you can't get a used one right away. The bottom line is that you must *believe in what you're selling* through and through, right? You don't just sell something because it's available to do it. It's because you *believe in what you're selling*. You *believe in what the service is*. You *believe in your ability to help people*. And the more this is true for you, the easier it's going to be to persuade people to do what you want.

So the first step to rapport is: **Walk a mile in your customers' moccasins**. It's a wise statement. Put yourself in the role of the customer. That's really important and when you're there, how did you want to be treated? Do you want to buy from someone who's a con artist? Or from someone who doesn't believe in their own product or service? Of course not!

So let me give you a real persuasion secret, and I'm not kidding when I say that. This is **a real persuasion secret**. You might have had to study for years and years and years on your own to discover this and I'm going to tell it to you right now. The best thing you could ever do is believe that when you see your client, what they say to you when you first begin interacting, **what's true for them in their world is 100% correct**. Assume that, whatever they've experienced in their life, whatever they believe to be true, whatever values they hold, have gotten them to the place of now, where you now find them, and this now where they are is *absolutely correct for them*.

Now, **you** know that there may be something better but **they don't**. So, with everything they know, where they are is exactly where they should be: with the *questions* they have, with the *concerns* they have, with the *worldview* that they have, et cetera.

So we talked about what the client *doesn't want*. Now let's contrast that with what they *do want*. So I want you to imagine for a moment that you're the person being sold something and doing the selling is the salesperson of your dreams. Imagine that this is an expert. The person knows what they're doing and they love it. They love the company they work for and it shows. They know their product inside and out and they are a genius at *figuring out what and where the fit is between their product and you*. Think about it because **this** is the kind of person I want you to identify with and morph into.

Now, the best way to do that is to imagine time after time what this perfect salesman who comes to sell you is and does. How do they talk? How do they present themselves? How do they demonstrate caring to you? How do they demonstrate expertise to you? And it's those basic concepts that you begin to express through these skills that you're going to be learning as you go through this program, so that you'll find that you have rapport nailed down, easily able to do at a moment's notice.

22

I told you to walk a mile in their moccasins earlier. Let's explore that a little bit more now. Let's talk about some of the basic core elements of this. The first core element is simply *observing people*. Observe how they interact when they see people they know and when they see people that they don't know. What are the tiny, subtle differences in their physical bodies when interacting with someone they know, and what are the differences between that and when they're interacting with someone they don't know?

Let me give you a little bit of history for a moment. Back in the beginning, when some of the social scientists began studying in the realm of NLP and other related sciences; they began studying courting, and they began observing how people dance. And what did they find? Well, they found that for successful interactions to take place there were always a number of elements that seem to be there.

They witnessed, for example, when something didn't work very well, the guy might go out and approach the girl and he might start up a conversation or maybe even just directly approach and ask to dance. Assuming the girl says yes, they watched *how* they danced. If there wasn't much synchronization between the two, it generally ended poorly. It generally ended with one saying to the other, "Thank you," and off the floor they went, not to be repeated. If they were asked again to dance, it would be a "No thank you".

The opposite then also held true: in this example, a guy would approach a girl and ask her to dance. She'd say yes and they begin dancing and immediately they would notice a tremendous *synchronization*. You know, he'd move forward, she'd move back. She'd move forward, he'd move back. They'd both go to one side or the other simultaneously and there was tremendous *synchronization* between the two. In fact, the more synchronization that was witnessed, the more *successful* that interaction tended to be.

So they had a really bright idea. They thought, "We're observing this. I wonder if we could *artificially simulate it* and it would work?"

So they gathered a small group of researchers and they taught the researchers to do this. So they sent the people out one night into bars and these researchers literally just replicated the success actions. So they went and asked someone to dance and they simply did as much synchronization as they possibly could. The results were **mind-blowing**! Researcher after researcher had more fun than they'd experienced in ages. They had more successful social interaction that night than they could remember. Many of them had **real successes**: phone numbers, dates set up and more!

It was an amazing success and one of the first times that they discovered the real **power** of what this is.

CHAPTER SEVEN

Pacing

Alright, we're building. Let's move now to talk about a core element called **pacing**. Pacing can be split into two categories called **mirroring** and **matching**. Now, these words are thrown about a lot with few *understanding what they really mean*. So here is what they *really* mean, are you ready?

Mirroring is the better to use for a few technical reasons so, in general, I'm just gonna call it mirroring for the most part – mirroring our pacing; but mirroring is simple. The point is to *look like the other person is looking in the mirror*, okay? So what does that mean? Let's say that they raise their right hand. You, if you are facing them, would raise your *left* hand. That would make the client look like they're looking in the mirror. Got it?

So they lean forward, *you* lean forward. Again, it looks like they're looking in a mirror. There's real power in this *synchronization*. **People don't resist themselves**. So the more they *look* like they're looking in a mirror, the more *it feels to them* like they're looking in a mirror, the better it is for you.

So when you hear people saying, "Oh, I was mirroring and matching," well let me give you the definition of *matching* real quick. Matching would be the client raises their left hand, and you raise your left hand. In other words, if you're standing facing each other, you both have the opposite hand raised, or so it looks. If the client were looking in the mirror, the person in the mirror has the *opposite* hand raised. So if they're looking in a mirror; it would look like you'd raised your *right* hand. In other words, if they raise their left hand and you raise your left hand, you're *matching* them but you're not *mirroring* them.

You cannot be both mirroring and matching at the same time. That's really the point. The point is, when you hear people saying, "Well, you've got to do mirroring and matching." *No!* **You've gotta do *pacing***. Mirroring and matching are part of the category called **pacing**, okay?

And just to make it simple, we're going to stick with the *mirroring* side of it. For various technical reasons, it's the better way to go for most things and certainly for business interactions.

So we do pacing, mirroring, to *create trust* and that's where we're headed with this. Remember, let's go back to your definition: to our picture in our mind, of the perfect person that's doing what you do. That perfect salesperson or persuader, right? That person that, when they walk in the door, you're *immediately put at ease*. You immediately feeling like you want to talk with them. You immediately feel that this is a good guy that's going to help you and if there's not a fit, they're going to go on their way and there's not going to be any difficulty. They'll leave and it'll have been an interesting interaction. In other words, a feeling that this person is **a real pro**.

One of the first things this expert person his done behind-the-scenes is they've **set their intention** and that's the first thing I want you to do. Your *intention* is set before you walk in the door – that you're going to do *rapport* with whoever you meet for the point of getting them to *trust you* and buy from you or go along with your proposal or whatever you're wanting them to do. You're going to *create trust* and so you're going to do this by *pacing the other person's behavior.*

And as you pace their behavior, you're going to have *evidence* that what you're doing is *working* and I'm going to tell you about what that evidence is in just a little bit.

But before we go any further, let's say that you're doing rapport now and you've got the basic concept. Well, there are also *problems* with rapport and I want to talk with you about those before we continue.

CHAPTER EIGHT

The Double-Edged Sword of Rapport

Just imagine for a moment that you sit down with a client and, wow, it's just amazing. You get into rapport with them and they're just so friendly. You really feel like you've just met a new friend and you talk and you talk - probably much longer than you should have - and you share examples and you just go on and on together, and it's just really an interesting time. Finally, you get around to talking about what you really came there to talk about and you told them the price and they just look at you and their face falls and they go, "Man, I just can't afford it," and *immediately you agree with them*. You say something like "You know, I know. I understand."

You know what's really sad? You *do* understand and you really *are* in agreement with them!

I have a student that runs a real estate office. He teaches his people, his agents, how to do rapport. Now, he says that many of his new people come back when they first start out and he'll ask, "So, how was that appointment you just went on?" and they'll say, "Oh wow! It was really good! We had good rapport!" and he'd say, "Excellent! So, where's the listing?" and they go "Well… uhm-hmm… You know, the guy said he wants to think about it. But you know, we had really good rapport and he really liked me so I'm sure that he's going to want to give me the listing."

Beginning to see an issue here?

How about when a persuader gets strong rapport while selling and the client says, "I have to think it over," and the persuader immediately understands and agrees and that became the persuader's problem. You see, *he took it on* and that is absolutely what happens within rapport.

I really want you to stop and think about this. *This is what happens within rapport*. You begin to feel a bond with the other person and what bothers *them* will bother *you*. By the way, what bothers *you* will bother *them*. So that's why it's so important to **have your intention set**. It will help you to be able to work around this.

Rapport is much more than just liking somebody. Sometimes people think that's what rapport is. In reality, what's missing is the real *purpose* of rapport. The meaning of rapport is that *they trust you*. They trust you. They value you and *they want to do what you think is right and good*, provided that it equals what they think is right and good; and by the way, we're going to have a section of that in the next book in this series, in which we're going to cover that every which way but loose.

What we're talking about is what I call **the double-edged sword of rapport**. What I mean by that is that rapport affects *everybody*, not just the person you're persuading. When you jump into rapport with someone *you* are also trusting *them*.

Now, think about those examples I just gave you. When you jump into rapport with somebody, you are also trusting them, liking them and if you don't, you're not doing rapport right. So let me tell you right now, I'm not suggesting you don't jump in rapport with them. It's far different.

So here is a big secret to help you jump-start the rapport process. If you want someone to have rapport with you, if you want them to trust you: then *you* have rapport with *them* first, trust *them* first, like *them* first. Make sense?

How do you just have rapport with them? Well, you **pace** them. We'll talk more about this. So, if you'll just use that secret alone, it'll start this whole process working for you *right now*. If you didn't learn anything else about rapport, but you just knew, when you want someone else to have rapport with you then you begin by liking them, by trusting them and by pacing them. And before you do any of that, before you even get out your car at the appointment or before they come into your office, you **set your intention** so that you are going to, first of all, get into rapport with them and then use that to get them to understand why you, your service, your products, your company is the only possible choice for them to make.

Now, once you've done this, once you've jumped into rapport, imagine if you *didn't* have your intention set. Let me give you an example. I had a couple many years ago… I won't go too much into the story at length, because today I'd probably handle it differently than I did back then… I was selling books. I was really young, about 18 years old, maybe 19 or something like that. I was selling books and I went to their house. It was a very long way away and the people were listening very politely to what I had to say. They were actually a young Christian couple with young children. They listened to everything I had to say and when I was done, they said to me, "You know, Kenrick, we really appreciate you taking your time to come all the way out here," and they really were out in the middle of nowhere, and they said, "You know, before we do anything, we always talk to the Lord and if you would, let's all kneel in prayer," and off they go, getting down on the floor. So I followed them and they began praying.

In the prayer, the gentleman says "Lord, we need you to move in Kenrick's heart so that he understands that I'm without work right now and we don't have the means to do anything right now and that, as much as we are really wanting to help our children, Lord now is not the time; and Lord we know there's no accidents. We hope that you move in Kenrick's heart for him to experience all the love and success in his life and business that he's looking for and pray that everything goes really well for him."

Now, that's really a prayer in the form of an objection, right? It's just said via prayer. Today, I might have handled that somewhat differently, but back then here's what happened. He started to get up after he was done and he looked like we were all just going to get off the floor, so I quickly interrupted and I said, "Wait, I'd like, too, to talk and tell the Lord what's on my mind," and I stayed kneeling and he immediately knelt back down and the guy said "Absolutely."

And I prayed, "Our dear heavenly father. I give great thanks today for bringing me here. I know that you know, Lord, that there are no accidents. I being one of your children recognize that all of us are your children and I'm in one of your children's homes and, Lord, you wouldn't have sent me out here for no reason. If there weren't a need here, Lord, you wouldn't have put me here. And I ask now that you move in the hearts of the people that are hearing this prayer and you help them to understand exactly why you brought me here. I ask that you help them to understand the importance of what it is that their children need, and I pray they're able to hear your words of wisdom, Lord, and act upon those today in the appropriate way."

Now, I have to say, I would probably not have gotten in that position today with all that I know. I would never ever have had to deal with that. I wouldn't have made that lengthy presentation only to have them want to pray a prayer of objection. But back then that's what I did and, boy, you should have seen the red faces when I got up.

The husband and wife were stammering and stuttering. They didn't know what to say for themselves other than, "Uhh-uhh-uhh… Well, we just don't have work."

Now, I explored that with them a little bit. It comes to light, they really weren't so much out of work. There was a seasonal layoff that happened, but there's still income during that seasonal layoff and the other member of the family was working. So, yes, it was a little bit less of an income than normal but there were a lot of reasons that they could have gone ahead.

So what I did by that prayer that I made is I *alienated myself* and that wasn't smart. Funny, maybe, depending on your position, but it wasn't very smart.

Let me tell you where the *real* problem came in. The real problem was that **I didn't hear or ask for or get their criteria early on** and I'm going to show you how to never ever make that mistake – ever! Had I determined their criteria in the first five or ten minutes of being in that house, I would have left. I would never have had to go through that.

What I did, I want to tell you, I wouldn't ever have done today. Now the prayer itself, I think it was effective in the sense that maybe they got that using Jesus as an objection as a "No" isn't probably the wisest choice, especially on someone who considers themselves very spiritual and probably doesn't really appreciate that tactic. I don't know. I wonder if they ever did it again? I suspect not but I don't know. I think they thought themselves to be pretty darn tricky and I think that really caused them a little bit of grief.

Alright, I found that to be a very interesting situation. What I can tell you is that if I had just bought into their objection, into their stuff, I would've just said goodbye, and so I would have simply wasted $20 in gas, plus the three hour drive it took me to get there, and a whole night of my time.

But it *wasn't* a waste of time. You see, there *is* a reason for it and I'll tell you what the reason is for my failure so *you* don't have to experience it for yourself. *I didn't do my job up front right*, and had I done that, that was the real lesson. There was no other real lesson. It was a learning lesson for me. *I didn't do right.*

I had rapport and I had it powerfully. Now, rapport is so very powerful because *it can be used against you*. When you trust them, you also believe what they say. Now, wait. *Turn it around.* When they trust you, they believe what you say and that's where we're headed. We've gotta get them to trust you fast, quick and immediately, alright? To do that, you better have **set your intention first** so you can *keep right on going* and not have the rapport turned back as a double-edged sword and cut you.

CHAPTER NINE

Saying Hello to the Unconscious

This brings us to **unconscious recognition and greeting**. The first thing we need to do when we're looking to gain rapport is you have to be in **uptime**. Now, what do I mean by that? Well, if there's an uptime there's probably a downtime, right? So let's look at the reverse of uptime. Downtime is when you're going, "I feel good inside. I'm paying attention to myself. Does my hair look good? My clothes look fine? Do I have anything in my throat? I'm thinking about tomorrow. I'm thinking about today." That's *downtime*. I'm in my own head, thinking about what's going on with me. It's not bad. It is just *not okay for persuasion*.

Uptime is when **your five senses are focused externally**. That means you are looking into your environment and paying attention to it. You're listening to what's going on externally. Everything is oriented and orchestrated to hear what's happening, to sense what's happening, to see what's happening externally. So you have to go there first. If you don't, you're never going to get what's going to come next.

In other words, you've got to *orient your five senses externally*. That'd put you in **uptime**.

The second step is, when people greet each other, they do it *way before* the actual place and time when they stop and stick out their hands and shake them.

So if you're approaching someonethat you know at a distance, at a mall for example, as you get nearer to them, you'll notice that you recognize them and this often happens around 30 feet; or you'll be recognized, either way. So you'll see that maybe if they recognize you first, you'll see them maybe raise an eyebrow, or smile, or look at you in some way that acknowledges you.

Here's some of the ways that they can recognize you. They tilt their head down a little bit or maybe they tilt it back in recognition. Maybe they raise their eyebrows. It could be their lips pursing a little bit or a smile. It could be the eyes widening or narrowing or even a wink. These things and more people do, and you do, when you recognize somebody.

Now, before you read any further than this section, I want you to do the following. I really would like you to just **stop everything** and I want you to go *right now* to a restaurant or to a mall or to a grocery store. I don't care which. Just stop this and turn it off after I give you these quick little instructions, and *go right now* to one of those places. And I want you to **watch people interact with each other**. Watch them as they see people they don't know. See what happens. And what you're going to find is that spark of recognition isn't there. It just isn't there. They look. They pass by each other and they might as well be passing by a rock on the ground. It just doesn't matter. Notice how oblivious they are to each other. That's the first thing. Watch what people do when there is no recognition. They just walk by each other like they don't exist.

Next, **notice how they interact with someone they know**. Notice the *difference* in the way they're dealing with each of the different people. For example, the people they recognize and those they don't, the people they're close to and those they aren't.

Now, based on what I've said so far, do you think it would be true if you initiated the behavior of what the other person does when they see someone they recognize, or if you played back what they do when they recognize someone, do you think it would have *an instant immediate effect* on what they think of you? If you said yes, you're absolutely right! It does.

And so what you want to do is you want to start to *see it*. This is the easiest thing in the world to do and it can also be the most difficult. So what I need you to do is to **go out and see it**. Go out and look *right now*.

So, why do I say it could be the most difficult? Well, it actually *seems* pretty easy. It's because this is something we have become *conditioned sociologically to ignore*. We say that meeting someone, acknowledging them for example, is when we say, "Hi!" or when we stick our hands and shake them. That's the moment of the greeting ... but it's not. The moment of greeting comes *much earlier* in the interaction, but *you are trained not to see it*.

Since you are little, you've learned that if a person is friendly towards you, there is recognition before you're even close enough to shake your hand, give them a hug or say hi with your words. Now, I want you to **see** this. I need you to go out and watch this. If you haven't already stopped this and done it, please do so now. If you need to read to the end of the book because you just can't stand stopping right now, alright go ahead. I understand. Do it. **But you *must* get out to see what I'm talking about**.

It's not enough to just *think* about this in your head. You must *see* it. In fact, I really want you to go out and look at, at least, twenty people interacting or not interacting. I'd rather it be 30 people and, really, I'd rather you spend about half a day, two or three or four times watching this.

Each time you do it, you're going to get better, but I want you to really see it.

By the way, another place that I personally really like to go and watch this is an airport. Now for me, airports aren't nearly as fun as it used to be when I was a kid, but they used to be a lot of fun. I used to just go and watch people. Now, you'd better not try to get all the way in there without a ticket like I used to do when I was little; but if you get a chance, you can go to an airport. You go to the arrivals area. There's usually a door right near the baggage claim area that people have to go through and that's where they're going to meet their family or their friends. That's the place to go.

You want to watch people coming there to find someone who's just flown in, or you want to watch the people that have just flown: they get off the plane, they come in, they walk down to the baggage claim area and they're doing what? They're *searching*. They're *looking*. They're trying to see if there's a friendly face there – a loved one, a family member, a friend – and watch what happens when they see this person. Watch that *look of recognition* cross their face.

Another thing you can watch for, when you're watching both sides: watch how one looks for the other. You'll see them scanning the crowd trying to figure out where they are, right there, looking for these friendlies. They're looking for the people that they recognize and love; and watch when they see them. Look at the glow that comes over their face.

And again I ask you, if you *did this* to people when you meet them, would it have an impact positively? And I'm telling you the answer is yes! 100% yes. And it is powerful beyond your wildest dreams.

So can you just go around acting like you recognize people? No. That's not as helpful and it's not as powerful. So let's talk about looking for friendlies, okay? So what that really means is looking for that spark of recognition. For example, have you ever found that there's a certain store you really like going to? Then maybe the reason that you like going to it is because there's someone at that store that *recognizes* you. He is always especially kind and nice to you.

Let me tell you, there was a time in my life when I was going through a year-long spiritual experience and I had a lot of things I needed to do and it was a difficult time – a beautiful, lovely time but it was also very difficult. And I went into this kind of holistic, earthy store where I'd buy whole foods and stuff like that. I'd go there and the people there were so accommodating to the things I needed. You know, I needed to have certain things and they just were absolutely helpful, and every time I came in, I'd pass through the door and one of them would look at me. They'd say "Oh hi! How are you? How's everything going? Can I help you today? What do you need?" I mean, they'd literally single me out from all of their other customers to find out what I needed.

Now, let me tell you, buying from that store cost half as much again compared to what other, nearer stores were charging, but I always went there because I knew that I would have a very pleasant experience. It was that sense of *being recognized* that was so profound for me, and this is what people are looking for. Deep in our core, we want to be recognized. We want to feel important. That's true for all human beings, and to the extent that we can *make somebody feel recognized and important* in a flash of an eye – I mean, not spending a year to do it – I mean, **instantly**, what does it cost us? Nothing, and yet what's the benefit? Huge!

So let's talk about what we're looking for and here's the easiest way to do it. What we're looking for is *the way they do it*. That's the answer. That's the million-dollar answer right there. What are we looking for? We're looking for **the way they recognize others**, because if we recognize them the way they recognize others, we're doing precisely what they do and it's just that simple.

Here's the problem. You're probably not going to see it at first. You're going to go out and you're going to go and look and you're probably going to go, "I don't see anything, you know. People are people. They're doing what they're doing!" And I say, if that's true for you, *you're looking too big*. Look smaller. *Look for smaller details*. Look for the most subtle of nods. Look for the most subtle of head shifts. Look for the most subtle of the squinting of the eyes, of a smile, of a head nod, or head lift.

When you say something to someone, they respond, right? And so, watch how these people respond. Now, if you go around doing this, saying something first, believe it or not, people try to be respectful. As a general rule, people try to be respectful in the way they respond. So what they're going to do is *imitate back* your way of saying hello, and that's not what you want. You want to find theirs.

So you want to **go into uptime** when you're about to meet somebody, okay? And by the way, this is where the problem is, because if you're walking around in **downtime** and you meet somebody, *you've already missed it*. In other words, if the point comes where they go, "Hey! Hey! Hey Julie! How are you?" "Oh, hey John. I didn't see you there. How's it going?" "Oh good!" There, you've already missed it.

See, it happened 30 feet away when the other person saw you. It happened at a great distance.

Now, *this subtle thing that I'm telling you to watch for happens at some distance out*. So the key is you want to watch them. So you're watching and you're waiting for them to acknowledge you and, *the minute you see it*, you're going to do it right back *exactly* like they just did for you.

So maybe it's goning to be that they're going to look at you and they're going to do a head raise. You know, they're gonna raise their head like "Hey!" You can imagine it, right? And you're going to go, "Hey!" alright?

Or maybe it's that they're going to look at you and a little smile goes across the right side of their face. Well, let that same little smile go across yours. You're going to do the way they say hello right back to them. So, you're going to wait for *them* to do it and then *you're* going to do it.

Now in most situations where you have to address somebody, this will always take place; however, let me tell you the difficult thing. If you've been out doing what I just told you to do and you've been looking for this out in a mall or in a restaurant or whatever, and you try to do it then you'll notice that everybody just walks by you and nobody responds. Nobody does their hello – or at least not very many.

Now, why do you think that is? *Because they're not here to interact with you*. That's not what they're here to do, so you have to be in a position in which *they're going to interact with you*.

When the waitress comes up to you, *that's* the time to make this happen – when she's on her way over to you. Maybe she's looking down at her pad on the way over, or maybe she's looking at you as she comes over; but as she adjusts herself to doing that, to looking at you, *you want to do the same thing*. You want to **fire back that hello** and you want to watch for this. Whatever she does, you do.

When you're standing in line at the supermarket, in the same way, the teller's going to have to acknowledge you sooner or later and when it happens, do it the same way. You want to play back what they're doing.

So, you're going to start to be able to **detect the person's unconscious greeting**. You just have to put yourself out there where they need to interact with you.

Now, let's talk about what we can *do* with that information once we get it, and the first thing is you could *remember it* because you can always use it in the future; but I don't really bother to remember too much because I just see it again every time I'm with somebody.

That's how I get so good at doing it, so that I just *do it automatically* and you should too. I don't really have to think about it anymore and that's ultimately what you're going to do too. But for now, this takes some conscious thought. So *think, think, think* about this all the time. I want you to spend at least one week working like crazy every day on perfecting your unconscious greeting and I'm serious – one week, okay? The week will fly by before you know it and just *focus* on this one strategy. If you do, I promise it will change your life. It's really important.

And as you do this, what you're going to find is that you get *better and better and better and better* at it. I mean, you're really going to get good and that's important because when you get good, the better you get, the more powerfully you'll be able to make people trust you, and bond with you, and the bond that you do get will be stronger. You'll make it happen faster, and you're creating a more powerful rapport that you'll be able to use as leverage and that's going to make a huge difference!

Let's go to the process to do the unconscious greeting. Are you ready? **First**, you see it and as you see it, **second**, you then do it immediately back to them. **Third**, when you do it back to them, (in other words, they did it to you and now you're doing it to them), what will happen is they will immediately *smile*. It happens almost every time. They'll do it, you'll do it back. They smile and then of course you smile. **Lastly**, at the same moment you smile, look over their left ear and just adjust your gaze from their eyes to over their left ear. (I mean, really, it doesn't make any difference which side, left or right). I'm just suggesting that you pair that smile that you've just gotten from them and that you've just returned with a look in which are going to *kind of look past them*, is a good way to explain it. You're going to look at their ear.

CHAPTER TEN

Taking It From "Knowledge" to Behavior

It's a kind of a strange feeling. When you do that, it's working with the principle of **anchoring** and **operant conditioning**. Now, we're gonna talk later in the books about all kinds of ways you can set and maneuver anchors and use conditioning strategies. I'm going to show you more ways to do this than you can shake a stick at. You're going to be so good at it, you're going to be scary good, I promise you; but right now, I just want you to *look at their ear*. I don't care which ear. I'm going to say their left ear because that's what I do. The key is to pick one and use it all the time.

Why, you ask? That's a good question. Because, in the future, you can just look over their ear and *it will immediately bring back all the feelings of connection, of being recognized*.

For now, just practice looking over at one ear and make it the same ear for each person.

Okay, so let me go through this process again a little quicker. Just imagine, I'm looking at Tim and he's a little distance away and I see Tim recognize me with his unconscious greeting. I do it back and as I do it back, Tim smiles. When he smiles, I smile, and then he's going to smile bigger and, as he does that, I'm going to look over his left ear. And at that point I'm probably within handshaking distance and I'm going to say "Hey Tim!" and shake his hand.

Now, let's just suppose, if I don't see the other person's unconscious greeting, what will I do? Well, that's okay. I may miss the opportunity. It's possible that it gets missed. Now, the better you get, the less you'll miss it. So, more than anything, the key with this is **remembering to do it**. I like to say "When this doesn't work, it's when you don't use it." You know, it can't help you if you don't use it. *You have to make using it a habit*.

So, what you need to do, you need to do this *over and over* and *think about it now* so that you've got this step under control and you *do it all the time*. The goal is to help you to take this *from knowledge to behavior*. That's the point – knowledge to behavior.

Now, I want you read this and soak it up. If you have the audiobook, I want you to listen through the link provided. I want you to *learn*. I want you to *grapple and wrestle* with this. I want you to think about the ways it'll work. I want you to imagine it working. I want you to role-play it in your own mind and I want you to role-play it with people around you. Do it with your husband, your wife, your partner, your kids. I don't care. I really want you to do this with everybody you can get your hands. on and I want you to **get it**. I

As I said, I wish I could have been fortunate enough to have this when I was just starting out. It is a game changer as you'll experience.

So, occasionally, you're going to miss with the unconscious greeting and that's okay. Don't worry about it, because the next step of what you're going to learn is the *other* things you'll be doing physically as you work with a person. And we'll be looking at those things in the next book in this series.

BOOK TWO

PACING AND LEADING

INTRODUCTION

Building On Your Skills

You've learned a whole lot of things so far in **Book One: Intention and Rapport**, and we're going to keep right on adding to that here in **Book Two**. You've learned the importance of **rhythmic speaking** and of having your **intention set**. You've learned why **pacing** is important and you've learned what **uptime** is. You know how to do the **unconscious greeting** and that's what you're going to do in every single situation that you come into, right?

Except *sometimes*.

You're going to *wish* that you could do it but you probably won't have been able to and why might that be? Let's look at it. Say that you're facing one direction and, all of a sudden, someone comes and taps you on the shoulder and says, "Hey Mark! How are you?" . . . and guess what? How are you going to see the **unconscious greeting** then? Or maybe you didn't observe someone coming up to you, or maybe, for whatever reason, you weren't watching and so you *missed* it.

Remember what I told you and that is that **the only time this doesn't work is when you don't use it**. So it's really *incumbent upon you* as you progress to *work at this* and get *better* and *better* and *better* at staying watchful for those things all the time. You have to *train yourself* to look for this and you have to *train yourself* to **see** this kind of thing and then **use** it. So, **set your intention** right now to *begin seeing it all the time*. You have to **set your intention**.

For *every single thing you want to do*, **set your intention**, because you're going to see as you develop it, it's going to be able to *guide* you to the success that you really want to have. It will *engage the persuasion strategies* that I'm teaching you.

When you start *mastering these skills,* you really are **moving into a different league**. You know you're not just a salesperson running around trying to sell some real estate, or some financial services or whatever it is that you're selling. *You're not like that*. You're a person that is like a *fine tuned machine*. You're going to use, as the base of your operation, **persuasion** and *that's* what you're looking to do and *that's* what you're always looking to do. At the bottom of everything, powering you forward is **persuasion**. And so as you *focus on that*, you'll make it more and more your **reality** and that's what you'll find.

CHAPTER ONE

Physical Pacing

We've gone over lots and lots of things you can do, but now let's just say that *you missed the* **unconscious greeting**. You *missed* the ability to gain **instant rapport**. What do you do now? Well, it's *easy*. You go to **physical pacing**. Remember that **physical pacing** is where *you're* going to do with *your* body what *they're* doing with *theirs*.

Now, in the **unconscious greeting**, you're looking for a *very specific type* of **physical pacing**. You're looking for the way in which they *signal hello*, the way in which they *signal they're friendly*. For *this* type of **physical pacing**, what we're looking for is *every way* they do *anything. Anything* and *everything* can be **paced**. You can even pace someone from across the room.

In fact, *regardless* of whether or not you did their **unconscious greeting**, you should do the **pacing** that I'm going to cover now with you. In other words, one doesn't *replace* the other. One *adds* to the other; and, by the way, that's how *everything* I'm going to be teaching you works. *Everything* works exactly like that. What's going to happen is, you're going to learn how to do, for example, **physical pacing**, but you'll *also* be doing the **unconscious greeting** that we've been talking about, and you're *also* going to be doing the criteria that we'll learn next after this, and you're *also* going to be telling **persuasive stories**, and you're going to be **following the overall persuasion format**. And, by the way, as we move on through the books and learn new things, you're *still* going to be doing everything you're learning in *this* book.

Imagine if you're six years old, you've never been on a bike and I bring you over to a bike and say "Here! Guess what? We're all going to go on a two day long bike ride. Hop on. No training wheels. I'm going to shove you down the hill, and by the way, here's a radio. I'd like you to tune it to the radio station that we're all going to listen to and just take your hands off the bars while you're riding."

So, bottom line, what happens is you've got to **start**. You've got to *crawl* before you walk. And, by the way, this is crawling, but *at hyper-speed*. But **this is what underlies everything**. It's **the ability to get people to trust us**.

Now, we're going to **build the trust**. We're going to *lock in* the trust and here's another little secret. I'm constantly looking at the **rapport** I've developed as *a measurement of how I'm doing*. I'm using the **strength of the rapport** as a *measuring stick* at all times. I'm constantly *looking* and *listening* and *feeling* the rapport I have with the other individual, and I'm constantly knowing if it's *stronger*, if it's *weaker* and if I need to *make* it stronger, what do I need to **do** to make that happen? Does that make sense?

Let me again remind you of something. I don't care how much of this you think you *heard* or you think you *know*. It's the *way in which* I'm going to go through it with you that's going to make **all the difference in the world**. I have taught people that have been selling and persuading for 30 or 40 years. They're absolutely *expert*, they *teach* it and they get this material and are *blown away* with it because what happens is they start making the *finer* and *finer distinctions* that make them *more capable* and make them earn *more money* quick.

So, here's the thing we're doing. When anything happens in the presentation, you're constantly **checking for that level of trust** so you know it. You're *alerted* to it far in advance, even advance of the clients; meaning, they may not even be completely *conscious* of what they're doing because you're so good, you're using these skills so well, that *you're* becoming conscious of whatever's going on before *they* are. And do you think if you're conscious of something that's possibly going on before they are, you can *head it off*, you could *fix* it or you could *change* it? You bet you could!

CHAPTER TWO

Sensory Acuity

Before we can do **physical pacing** really, we need to talk more about **sensory acuity** – being able to *know what's going on*. So let's talk about what **sensory acuity** is. What I mean is *being acutely aware*. And aware of what? Well, aware of what the person you're persuading, or the group you're persuading, is *doing*. What I'm talking about is **shifting your attention externally**. Now, if I'm sitting here thinking, "Does my hair look right?" and things like that, then I'm doing it *wrong*. I need to *shift my attention **externally*** so I'm *watching*.

Let me give you an example of this. Let's say that you and your family are in the car and you're on your way to a music event or something fun and you're all talking, you're having a lively conversation and you're really having a good time. You're cruising along and, all of a sudden, you look up in your mirror and there are flashing lights coming up behind you and you see they're on a police car, then what happens? You're going, "Oh no!" and you wonder, "Is this for me?", you wonder "Hey, are they going to give me a ticket? What's going on?" . . . or are you thinking, "Wow! How nice! Here is a nice person who is helping me look out for my safety." Yeah right! So, the cop comes behind you and he pulls into the lane by you. He's going slightly faster than you. He's driving by. He looks at you but he keeps right on driving and you realize that he wasn't there to pull you over. *Now* how do you feel? Relieved, right? "Phew!"

But what happened in the car *the minute you saw the cops*? You probably said, "Shut up! Shut up everyone! Let me *pay attention* here." And all of a sudden, you go on *heightened alert*. **Heightened awareness** – "What's going on? What's wrong?" How does it apply to *selling* and *persuading*?

So many times, a salesperson is there waiting to see the person they're going to talk to. Maybe they're sitting there and they're rehearsing what they're going to say: "Hello Mr. Smith! I'm Kenrick Cleveland and I'm with so and so. We're here today, blah, blah, blah, blah, blah," and they're trying to rehearse this whole process.

Now that is a *bad time* to be worried about *that*! You'd you better *already know* what you're going to be saying. Really, you need to *know* what you're going to be doing. Worse yet, if you're talking in the presentation, and you find yourself talking, but you're *thinking about something else*. You're often kind of *in your own head*. You're saying, "Hmm, I wonder what my wife's doing for dinner. Hmm, I wonder what my kids are doing and when they're going to show up. Ah, you know I wonder if that bank deposit was made on time" . . . And then the guy you're talking to goes, "Well, let me ask you about this." And you're like, "About what?" And you try to recover but you know it doesn't look good. Now, you can *never* afford for that to happen.

When you're *persuading*, you're *doing what you do better than anyone else*. You're doing the very thing that requires you that you **can't shift off** to an assistant, that you **can't shift off** to some temp help. You're doing the very thing that *makes you money* and, for that reason, **you must pay attention**. You have to pay **strong attention** and not just *any old attention*, **attention with heightened awareness**, okay?

Now, as you do this, there's a certain thing that I want you to *start paying attention to*. I want you to *zoom in* with your visual and I want you to *look at the person or persons' facial expressions* and I want you to *notice when they're laughing*. What do they look like? Because that's obviously a pretty *positive* state, right? When they're *skeptical*, what do they look like, then? So that as you're talking along to them, you're going to *notice that* as you perceive them *going into* different emotional states: you're going to *see their body adjust* right along with it.

Now, let me give you a *basic rule of persuasion*. **Anytime someone's emotional state changes their body will too.** The *emotional state* changes, usually, first and the *body* immediately thereafter. Alright, so *thoughts* come first and then *the things that they involve* come next. So, you want to **watch for this**. Really pay **close attention**. Look at their *facial gestures*. Look at their *eye raises*. Look at their *face coloration changes*. Notice the amount that their *lips* are parted or not.

Now, we're not going to make *value judgments* as we see these things. What we're going to be doing is we're just using these as **indicators of where we are** in the *process* with them and of our *trust* and our *bond* between them and us. That's what we're doing.

Now, I'm *constantly monitoring* these both *consciously* and *unconsciously* and I know I've trained myself so well that if I stop paying attention *consciously*, my *unconscious* mind is so *thoroughly trained* that it's doing it *automatically*. Moreover, if there's any *disruption* in this **trust** or it's not progressing the way it should, it *alerts* me to start *paying conscious attention* and **do** the things that I might have missed.

Now, there's a real **key** in what I just said for you. Here are some *specific* things I'm looking for, *specific indicators* that you can look for to signal that there is some **trust** happening. All we can do is make general guidelines here. Each situation is unique. And if the person is *opening up* toward you, and I mean **physically**, if they're standing more *in front* of you, they are *opening* their hands and their arms, they're *uncrossing* their legs, they're *leaning forward*, they're *smiling* . . .

If you think for a moment about any social setting; let's say that you're at a seminar, and you don't want to be bothered, what could you do? You could *cross your leg*s. You could *cross your arms*. You could *slump over*. You could *stare at the paper* down in front of you at your desk. In essence, what you're communicating to the world is, "I'm busy," or "I'm not interested. I'm closed off. Leave me alone."

Now, if you want to indicate **openness** and the *desire to interact* you could *sit up* in your chair, you could *uncross* your arms, you could *smile* invitingly at people, you could *walk up to* a group of people and you could stand a couple of feet away, but you could *begin nodding* with the speakers, you could *smile*, you could indicate that you're *open* and *available*.

So we're talking *generalities* here, but I still want you to **get specific with these generalities** by noticing the *small, tiny **changes** in behavior* – a slight *frown* or *smile*, the slight *tension* or *lack* thereof in the face. But I'm telling you to *especially* notice the **changes** in these small details. Wherever their face is right this minute doesn't matter. I care more about over the *next* two or three minutes, how is it **changing**? What am I noticing in their *body*? And am I paying attention to their *entire* body? You want to pay attention to *all* of it.

Another thing that you wanna pay attention to is their **breathing**, in particular the *speed* and *depth* of their breathing. Now, to do this you don't want to stare straight at their chest especially if you're staring at a member of the opposite sex, or a woman in particular. It won't be received very well, most likely. So what you can do is you'll notice the *speed of the breathing* with your **peripheral vision**. As you're looking at them, you can look at their eyes or right at their face, your peripheral vision will pick up *movement* and movement is the biggest thing that is seen with peripheral vision. That's how you're going to see the *speed* at which they're *breathing*. You are not looking to really see clearly as in *focus*, like you're focusing on their eyes. You're looking to *detect movement*. Have you ever seen, out of the corner of your eye, something move? You don't really know necessarily what it was, you just know that it did. So, you're looking, really, for the **changes in the movement**. So in other words, if you're talking to them and their breathing starts to *speed up* and they *smile* and they *lean forward* and they *uncross* their arms and their legs, guess what? You're seeing some *indication* and most likely it would be of *interest*.

Here's the next thing I want you to do. Check out **how you feel**. Do you feel like they're becoming *closer* to you? Or do you feel like they're *not*, because the way you **feel** is probably 100% accurate. And that's especially true because you're in **rapport** with them and, with these things, you can *gauge how they are responding to you*.

Here's something I do that you should also practice so you can easily do it. Every few minutes or so I really try to **concentrate** and I've trained myself to *accurately gauge my rapport* and I take a moment just to check, "Am I sitting with the *same posture* they are? Am I at the *same energy level* that they are, the same *speaking rate*? All those types of things that are done in rapport, am I *doing* them?" And what it does is it allows me to often *check* during a conversation to make sure I'm *getting* and *staying* in **rapport** with the person. I recommend you take that to heart. **Practice** that, because that's going to really help you considerably, and the key again is you want to **behavioralize** this. Your goal is to **behavioralize all these rapport skills** so that you can get into the *overall flow of things* and how to *present* and all the different things we're going to go through.

So let's talk about some things you can practice to **gain acuity**. The first thing is *how long they maintain eye contact* with you or even with others; and if you notice that **changing**, you can determine what's going on. Now, as an example, if a person is going to be *objecting*, if they're formulating an *objection* in their mind, the odds are, they're probably going to *look away* from you a little bit more or you'll find the *pattern of eye contact changing* anyway. So if you notice that start happening, you might want to just evaluate *what else is going on*. Does it *lead* to them objecting? And if it *does*, if all of a sudden they've *crossed their arms*, they've *crossed their legs*, they *leaned away* from you, they're *closing down* and now they're also *looking away* from you, so these are the things to start **watching for** in general.

CHAPTER THREE

Pacing Someone's Breathing

You can also watch for the *speed* and *depth* of breathing. That's a very important one. In fact, let's do an exercise. Here's what I want you to do. I want you to sit down with a partner – it could be your spouse or your kids, it could be someone you work with, it doesn't make any difference. Just sit down with them; and I want you to do this: tell them you're going to do or you need to do a special exercise, and this exercise involves them and that you're going to *observe* them for about two minutes and just ask them if they'd let you do it. They'll probably say 'sure,' and you say, "Okay, look. All I want you to do is nothing. Just think about whatever you do and whatever you want. I'm not even going to talk for little bit. I'm just going to sit here quietly and I'm going to observe several things and I'll tell you what I was observing after we get done with the exercise, alright?"

Then, as you watch them, look them in the face, or you can look all over the place, whatever you want, but notice their *breathing*. What's the *speed* of their breathing? How about the *depth* of their breathing?

That's **exercise one** and I'd like you to do it with *ten people*, if you can, at least ten; you might do it much, much more, if you can. You'll find it to be extremely helpful.

Let me tell you another place you can do this really easily. Go to a restaurant and see if you can find someone in the restaurant that you can see who is maybe sitting there alone, because it's real easy to **pace their breathing** in that environment, and you can **pace their breathing** even at a distance, clear across the room!

Now, what *else* can you pace? Well, when they lift their glass to drink, *you* could do the same thing. When they eat, *you* could take a bite every time *they* do. By the way, don't be surprised if they come over and talk with you if you do that. It's really interesting.

So **learn to start pacing someone's breathing**. It's just that *simple* and yet it's just that *difficult*. It takes a little bit of *getting used to*. As you do this a number of times, I want you to start to *instruct yourself at the unconscious level* that you're going to begin to *track the* **changes** that the breathing *represents* in everybody that you talk to from here on out. It's a great suggestion to give yourself. By the way, what do you do if the other person is *not* just sitting there quietly? What do you do if you're *talking to someone* and you want to **pace their breathing**? Well, it's a little bit more advanced but here's one interesting thing you could do: when they're *talking*, they're clearly breathing *out*, right? So they have to stop and *inhale*, they *breathe in*, at which point, *you* can breathe in at that same moment.

Another thing you could do is called **crossover pacing**, where you could simply *rise up on your heels slightly* when they *breathe in* and *lower back down* as they *breathe out*, or you could *move one finger* as long as they can see it, if you have your hand in a visible position. You could move your index finger *up* as they breathe *in* and *down* as they breathe *out*. You could pick anything. The key is that you just have to **keep doing it**. You can't *change up* in midstream. You have to *keep doing the same thing as they do* in order for it to really work, but it is a really great suggestion to give yourself that, from now on, you're going to begin to **track the changes that the breathing represents** in *everybody* you talk to from here on out; so do that, alright?

Now you're going to start looking for the **changes in people's behavior**. It's the *changes* that are important and you're going to **track where they look**. You're going to track *what they look at*. You're going to track *attention* or *lack* thereof in their face. You're going to track the *speed at which they breathe* and the *depth* at which they breathe. You're going to do *all* those things.

Alright, I know. It is not going to happen instantly. You're just going to put *piece* after *piece* together until you're finding that you're *better* at it. Even after just hearing what I'm saying right now, you're going to be better at it. But please *don't let that be enough*. I want you to really *get* this, to become an *expert* at it. I want you to become more *proficient* at this than you've ever dreamed possible. This is going to form a **very powerful foundation** for you.

Let's talk more now about **things you can pace**. So you can pace their *mood*, head *nodding* including how *fast* or *slow* they nod, facial *expressions*, how they *lean* as they sit; meaning, if they lean a little to one side or the other, or if they lean forwards or backwards, then you can **pace** all those things. You can pace their *eyebrows*. You can pace their *smile* or *lack* thereof. You can pace their overall *stance*. You could pace the *speed* of their *speaking*, their *tone* as much as possible and their *cadence* of speaking. And again you should listen to the ministers as I mentioned in **Book One**. What you want to do is **learn to talk like** *they* do. Also, listen and practice talking with an FM morning drive disc jockey. They're incredible and it would really be helpful for you to practice with both of these types of people. It'll help you to have a lot more *flexibility* and *capability* in your voice.

After you're doing it with people that you can see, you can also use the same *gestures* they use when you speak. Now, you wouldn't want to use their gestures at the same time *they're* doing them but, when you speak, you could use their gestures. You literally want to **pace it all** and, as you do, you've got to **keep your outcome in mind**.

CHAPTER FOUR

The Law of Reciprocity

Now, you might be thinking, "Good grief, Kenrick! This just sounds like trying to learn to ride a bike and chew bubblegum and do the times tables and everything all at once. It's just too much!" Well no, it's not! **You can do it**. I'm telling you. But *what* I'm telling you is **you must keep your outcome in mind** and that's the use of your **intention**. Just because you feel really good about the person you're persuading, you can't all of a sudden say, "Oh well. You know their objections must be right and their feelings of concern must be right for them." What you have to do is to **use that trust** that you're building to keep *moving you forward*.

Again, I want to reiterate the point. The point is you will establish **rapport** extremely fast if you'll simply *believe* and *trust* in them because it will show *immediately* and *they'll* want to do the same thing right back. You know, the **law of reciprocity** says they'll want to *reciprocate* in kind, if not even more, and *trust* and *like* you right back, and that's really, really important.

So let's talk about how we can do this **pacing**. We talked about pacing their *whole* body, a *part* of their body, the way in which they're *standing*, the *speed* at which they're *breathing*. We could pace the way in which they're *speaking*, the *speed* at which they're speaking. You can pace when they *cross* and *uncross* their legs, when they *fold* and *unfold* their hands, when they lean *forward* or *backwards* or to the sides. I mean, wow, you can **pace everything**! You can pace the way their head is *cocked* or *tilted* to the side or not. I mean, literally, look at the *smallest of behaviors* and you can **pace** these things and here's what I want to tell you: **Pace them all!** Be just like them! Do your level best so that they look like they're looking in a *mirror* and, guess what? **That mirror is you** – looking like them, okay? Let me say it again. That mirror is *you* looking like *them*.

For the sake of getting started, do the *same* doggone thing *they're* doing. If *they* pick up their coffee, *you* pick up your coffee. If *they* pick up their pen, *you* pick up your pen. If *they* move forward, *you* move forward. If *they* sit back, what are *you* going to do? That's right, *you* sit back. If *they* lean their head to the side, lean *your* head to the side. I don't care *what in the heck* they do, *you* do it, and here's the rule: when *they* move *you* move. When *they* move *you* move. When *they* move *you* move.

Now, at this point, you might be wondering if you can **overdo all this pacing**. I know, in the back of your head, somebody right now reading this, maybe you're thinking, "Kenrick, if did I everything they did, if I moved exactly like they moved, well heck, if somebody did that to me, I'd *recognize* it." "Oh yeah? I doubt it."

But I'm going to show you exactly what to do. I'm going to tell you what to say in the event anyone ever says, "Hey, are you imitating me?" Actually, I'll tell you in just a bit. Let's deal a little bit more with this first. One of the Chinese stratagems says *"Hide in the open."* In other words, persuasion is about **getting the job done**, not about being *subtle* and when people try to get *subtle* with these skills, they do *so little* of the skill that they're **not being effective**. And that's where you hear people that had been trained in this going, "Well, you know I was mirroring their eyebrows and I was subtly influencing them." Great! Did you get the order? "Well, no, but they like me." Thanks. I'll take the order over the like any day and I bet you would too; but, frankly, *if they like you they'll give you the order*, everything else being equal.

So when you get right down to it, we're talking about **persuasion in the trenches**, the get-down-and-dirty, make-it-happen persuasion, *not* the report-back-that-someone-likes-you-and-that-they-feel-good-about-you.

This all great and, of course, it's going to *happen naturally* as a result of what I'm teaching you here, but I'm telling you right now this is about **getting the job done** so **stop trying to hide**. You will *not* get caught, I guarantee you. You will *not* get caught. It isn't going to happen. Just take my word for it.

Want to go one better? In fact, I dare you! *I **dare** you to try and go get caught*. I *dare* you to follow someone so closely that they say, "Hey, what are you doing? How come you're imitating me?" I'm serious about this. Take me up on this dare and post your results to the community on the **Power Ark**, please.

Here's the thing. Let me tell you how you *will*, in fact, get caught if you try this. If you don't just *do what they do* but you **exaggerate** *their gestures* then you're going to get caught. And if you imitate their *speaking* and *gestures that they use when they speak*, if you do it **while they're speaking**, *right along with them* as I mentioned a minute ago; in other words, for example, if I say, "There's one thing I want to tell you today," and I hold up my number one finger, "so that we can learn all," and I spread my arms open wide and I say, "all the things that we want to cover," . . . and *while I do that*, while my finger number one is up, you put *your* finger number one up right by mine, in other words, *you're gesturing just like I do right back at me* and then when I gesture spreading my arms open wide and say, "all," if *you* then spread *your* arms open wide and do the same thing and, while doing this, you look me in the eye with a *big grin on your face* like you're doing exactly like I'm doing, **then *you will get caught*.**

That's about the **only** thing that'll get you caught. If you simply move like I do; in other words, you're *leaning forward* like I am or *back* like I am, if you're *crossing your legs* or *uncrossing* your legs when I do, if your head's *tilted* like mine, et cetera, you will *not* get caught. (Well, maybe if you try it with *me*, but you won't in the real world.)

CHAPTER FIVE

Insurance

Now let me give you some **insurance**. Want some insurance? Everybody would like insurance on this, right? I know in the back your mind you're going, "Alright, Kenrick, you may have been doing this for 30 years or more or whatever but I'm not convinced." I'm going to give you some **insurance**. Here's what you do. What you do is you *allow a mental count of three* between *their* movement and *yours* when you first meet them and you first begin.

Let's **put it all together**. You've done the **unconscious greeting**. You've **looked over their ear** so you've been able to **anchor** it, and as you've gotten within range of them, you begin **doing every single thing they do** other than their speaking gestures *except*, when you started, *they* crossed their legs and you went **1…2…3** and *then* you cross *yours*. And after a while *they* shifted in their chair and you went **1…2** and then *you* shifted. Another minute or so goes by and *they* pick something up and you go **1** and then *you* pick up, and another few seconds or whatever goes by and *they* put it down or do something else and, **bam!** *you* put it down *right with them* at that same moment.

So you *start* with a **mental count of three** and you *zero it out* over the period of maybe two or three minutes and that's your **insurance**. I *guarantee* you, the *only* way they will ever know that you know this is if they've also been through my training! I'm the one that came up with that.

But even then, most of the people that *know* how to do this are not worrying about what happens three seconds *later*. How are you really *engaged in the conversation* **and** following what the other guy's doing three seconds later? That takes a *large amount of training* to get anywhere *near* the ability to do that. In other words, after you *zero this out*, it's as if you've been their friend their whole life, and that's *exactly* the kind of comments you may start getting. And *please* **watch your intention** and **stay with your outcome** or else *you're* going to go to *theirs*.

You've heard it said I'm sure, that **in every persuasion situation a sale is made**. Either *you* buy into *their* reasons why they *can't* or *they* buy into *your* reasons why they *should*. So it's true and here's where it happens and here's where to correct it.

We're really digging down deep because I want you to **get this**. I want you to get *all the details*, all the *nuances*, because you see *that's* where the **power** is. The power is *not* in the *big broad strokes*. That's *not* where the power in persuasion comes from. It comes from the *details* and *perfecting them* at every level.

We've talked about **pacing what it is that they do** and we've talked about a **lag of 3-to-1** and we've talked about **sensory acuity**.

Do you now get why **sensory acuity** is so *powerful*? For example, if you're allowing a *mental lag of three*, you're having to *pay attention to what they did* and then *a few seconds later you do it* until, over the period of a few minutes, you've *zeroed out the lag* and now you're doing it *exactly* when they do it. But that again is causing you to **pay attention** in the right way to your client. You're *monitoring the changes* and that's what you want to pay attention to.

CHAPTER SIX

Leading

Now let's talk about **leading**. So what do we do when we've been **pacing** for a few minutes? Think about it. In other words, is our **goal** to go and *hang out* with someone and *become* them and *be* them and *do* them and *be exactly like them* indefinitely? No! The **goal** is to show them *consciously* and *unconsciously* that you **understand** where they live. You **understand** them. You **believe** in them. You **like** them and you **trust** them and, by that same way, they therefore know where **you** live. *They* like *you*. *They* trust *you*. Got it? What now? Well, at this point, it's time to **lead**.

In fact, we could easily say that the *entire point of **pacing*** is to quickly get to being able to **lead** and to do so in a way that they will **follow**. If we just started leading first, *it wouldn't work*. There'd be no **rapport**. First, you have to **pace** and then, when you **lead**, they'll **follow**.

Now, you're not going to be **pacing** for long – maybe three to five minutes on average. You're going to quickly move to **leading**. Now, I'm going to ask you *a trick question*, alright? And that is: what's more *powerful*, **pacing** or **leading**? Think about it for moment. What's more *powerful*?

Some might say **pacing** because if you don't do it, you can't ever get to the point of **leading** and you'd be right. Some might say **leading**, and those that do would go *right to the head of the class*. If all you do is **pace**, you set them into their position even *stronger*. But when you begin to **lead**, you create *independence* from your prospect to your *next word* and your *next behavior* because *they're* **following** *you*. When you learn to do this well, and I mean *really* well, what you'll find is that you're literally going to **lead** them in *thought* and *deed* right where you want them to go. **Leading** is much more powerful in the end because **leading** fosters *dependence on you as the persuader* and isn't that what you want? You want them *hanging on your every word* and *following* you through the process going, "Yeah, yeah. This is great. Oh yeah, I want this. How do I do it?

What do I do? How do I make it happen?" We want *that* to happen and we *make* that happen by **leading**.

So *when* do we **lead**? Well, we lead after we **pace**. In other words, we **pace** for a few, sometimes even just a few seconds, that's all, and then we **lead** them to *new behavior*. Now, what is the new behavior we lead? Well, maybe we've sat with our legs crossed. If so, we're going to *uncross* them. Maybe we've been talking at the emotional level and now we *raise our emotion*. We start putting a little more *excitement* in. Here's a rule. *How do you know when it's working?* And here's the answer. **When you lead, they follow** and you *notice their energy following right along with you*.

I want to give this to you in a really *easy to do* way and this is a secret I finally figured out how to do. You'll know this is happening not just by what you *see* and what you *hear*, but I've trained myself to do it by what I *feel* as well, and you should do the same. In other words, the **small cues** that I'm watching for, the **subtle behaviors** that I'm watching and the **subtle sounds** I'm hearing all add up to a *feeling* within me and, like a head of steam, I feel it *building* and I feel myself *moving in the right direction* and *everything is on track*, **or** I feel like it's *not* – one or the other.

Now, when I've been **pacing** for period of time then I want to get to the point of **leading**. In other words, maybe I *sit forward* at that point as I begin to *talk about something different* and away we go. And if I find them **following** me, even up to as much as 45 seconds or so later, it's *working* and I just keep on *working* and **leading** and they'll keep on **following**. But if I have led to some *new behavior* and, by the way, they don't have to follow it *exactly*. Let's say the person I'm persuading is you and your legs are *crossed* and my legs are *crossed* and I want to start **leading** after about 62 seconds, so I *sit forward* and *uncross* my legs and, after about 15 or 20 seconds later or so, you *shift* in your chair significantly but you keep your legs *crossed*. Well, you're *still* **following**. In other words, it doesn't have to be *exact*.

So, you're going to *watch* to see if a *shift* happens with you when you move. And if you bring up a *new subject* or you start talking about something a little bit *new* and they're *right in step* with you, they're *right along* with you. Everything *feels* good. Now, that's how I trained myself.

One of the neat things you can do here, by the way, as well, is that if you're talking along with someone and you're in a presentation mode so to speak and everything is going really, really good, guess what? If you find that they **stop following** you, if there is a *break*, if they'd done something *else*, guess what? There was a *break* and the **rapport** has probably been *lost*. It can be fickle. So, if that happens, here's what you do. You want to **stop immediately** and say something to them like this, "Mary, just a moment ago we were talking about how I can help you to get this property and get it sold and accomplish your bottom-line results. And I noticed that you sort of looked away there for a moment and seemed to, maybe, be thinking about something. I don't know. Would you mind sharing with me what it was?" Now, you can then *head off the issue* before it becomes a full-blown **objection**. You can hardly *imagine* how **powerful** this is until you *experience* it. It's as if you have **superpowers** or something. You'll learn how to *head the problem off*.

Now, many people are *afraid to do this*. They're *afraid* to bring up something that they think the client has as a *problem*. I'm telling you right now that's not right. I'm not afraid is a persuader to bring up these little things when I see them happen. In other words, I'm not going to be like a steamroller that rolls over the top of somebody while we're doing a presentation. If I sense a *problem*, I *sense* what's going on, I *see* that they're **not following me** and I wait like a lot of sales people do who have the attitude of, "Okay, I'm going to present nonstop like I'm a tape recorder on play, and when you get to the end then that's when the real salesmanship comes to play and I'm going to close them." I have this to say that: **no**, **no** and **hell no**. **That is** *not* **the way to do it**.

The way to present with **power** as a real **persuader**, as an **expert**, not as someone who thinks they're a tough closer and thus is going to *alienate* the customer, is completely different. The way to do this is to **gain rapport up front** and to *monitor* that rapport by constantly **leading** as long as they're *what*? **Constantly following**. And the *second* that they **stop**, *you* **stop** and find out *why* and, if they can't tell you, okay, don't worry about it. You go back to **pacing** them which you'll do, by the way, either way until you can begin **leading** again.

CHAPTER SEVEN

The 100+1% Rule

Let's take it another step. You can **pace people's attitudes**, and lead to *another one* that's *better*. You can also **pace their energy** and you can start to *increase your energy* and **lead** them to higher energy and more *excitement*.

Let's say you've got someone with a *bad attitude*. What do you do with that? Believe it or not, I **pace** it. So even when someone has a bad attitude, I don't *fear* it and I don't *confront* it. As a general rule, I simply **pace** it. It's just that simple.   Let's talk about the *strategy*. I heard this ages ago and I love it and I've gotten really good at it, and I'd like to suggest you do the same. It's called the **100+1% Rule**.

Supposing you go to somebody's house and, let's just say, you're a …   pick a political party… you're one or the other, okay? For the sake of discussion let's say you're a *Republican* and you're going to see a *Democrat*. If you're from a different country, by the way, I don't care. Just pick whatever party you want and *fill in the blanks* here as I go through this. Basically, you go to the other person's house and they're going, "Wow! I'm so excited about the Democratic Party and these upcoming elections. I just think this is going to be great! I can't wait for them to start…" and you're thinking to yourself, "Oh my God!" And they carry on, "In fact, wasn't so-and-so the best president ever?" referring to someone from the past, "I mean, wasn't he amazing? I mean, yeah, he had his share of problems and everything but, you know, the guy was charismatic and he was great, wasn't he?" And let's say that *you* just think he was *rotten to the core*.

Now, you **don't lie** and you don't **pace** them by lying. You *don't* do that. What you have to do is you have to find the **1%** of what they say that you can *agree* with and then back it **100%**. That's the **100+1% Rule**.

So you say, "Well, I'll tell you this. He *was* charismatic." Now, they may then jump in and say "Boy, was he ever charismatic! Yeah, you know, it's just great when I find somebody like that who understands. He is probably the greatest president ever. So-and-so from the opposing party, boy, I just can't stand him." You're going, "Uh-huh," because I'm assuming you *like* the guy from the opposing party. You say, "You know what? I think charisma plays *such an important role* in politics and I think more people could really learn how to be charismatic from those that have gone before that are."

So, you see? You continue to have **integrity** with what you do. You continue to **do the right thing** with your words. You're not *bashing them* and you're not *imposing your way of thinking* on them either, and so they feel *supported* and if they were to say to you, "Oh well, so you're a Democrat too!" . . . Look, you need to be **honest** either way. I believe it would be best to say, and do so in a very *non-offensive* way, but you say, "You know, I've always voted Republican. I've always voted for the Republican Party, but I'll tell you this. So-and-so was *so charismatic*. He was so, so *powerful* that way that I've always dreamed of a Republican president that could do just as good."

You know what? They're probably going to laugh, they're probably going to *agree* with you and you've got a basis to *continue your discussion*. You've acted with **integrity** and they *feel heard*, and I really like that rule. It's a great rule and I highly recommend you find ways and means of using it.

CHAPTER EIGHT

The <u>Feeling</u> of Leading

I want to cover two more things in this book. First, I want to talk about the ***feeling* of leading** and what it's like, and I'm going to teach you a *strategy* in an upcoming section that will show you how to take what I've given you in this book and do it with *words* as well, and I'm going to show you some *formats* you can use some ways of doing it.

What I'm going to say right now will make even more sense then, but I want you to begin to think of **leading**, and I want you to begin to not only **do** it but **experience a particular feeling** and the **feeling** is one of, "*This is working. They're* trusting *me* and *I'm* trusting *them* and I'm *monitoring this constantly* to make sure that we're together *going in the same direction*." And you want to have a ***feeling* that equals those things**. **Feel** it, and I want you to *train yourself* to have the **feeling** that, when you're *doing* it, you *know*, because if something goes wrong, you can be *alerted* this way. Your feelings will *change* and you'll go, "Oh, something's wrong!"

Now, you can *see* it. You can *hear* it. And all of those are great ways to do it, but it's *easy* to hear what someone says, and it's *easy* to see what they're doing, and you're going to find that, on top of that, you're going to train yourself to *feel* it. And that **feeling**, if it ever **changes**, you need to *pay attention*, because something is going *wrong*, and you'll learn to *listen* to that small voice within and you'll learn to *trust* it. You're going to find, with each book, I'm going to give you *more* and *more* and *more* that it'll *fill your consciousness,* okay, and so I just turned over my **feeling**. And I let it *warn* me when things aren't quite going *right*.

So you can be *totally focused* on what you're saying to someone, or *focused* on what I've been teaching you, and you're using it and practicing with it, but when that **feeling** *warns…*

For me, I actually *train it to be a **feeling***, and I imagine a *red flag* immediately flying and *waving* in front of me and I hear *warning bells*. I see all those things happen, but it's primarily my **feeling** that makes me immediately **stop**. If you'll do that, you'll make that *happen for you* by really *locking in* this lesson – what it **feels like** as you begin to **lead** successfully.

So you're **pacing** first for a few minutes. Usually, that's about all it takes, usually for me just a couple. And then I'm immediately beginning that process of **leading**. When I begin the presentation and I notice that I'm **pacing** them and they're *right with me*, I may try to do some **leading** real quick, meaning, I *shift* the subject or I *move* or something and, if they **follow** me, guess what? I keep **leading**, right? The general rule is you **pace** until they **follow** you. How do they *know* they follow you? Because you try to do a little bit of a **lead** and *they* do it and, if *they* do it, *you* just keep **leading, leading, leading, leading, leading** and so on until they *buy* or you have to *stop* and *find out what went wrong*. So do that and it's going to make a big difference. It's really going to help you.

CHAPTER NINE

Energetic Aspects of Rapport

Let's cover one more thing. I'd like to go over a couple of the **energetic aspects of rapport**. As you have been reading this, there are some of you reading that would probably like to know how to this with *groups*. Before you can do it with groups, you need to be *good* at doing it with individuals. At least, I think that's certainly the best way to learn and the best way to do this, so I'd like you to *master* this with *individuals*.

But I'm also going to give you a **strategy** that'll help you be able to use it with *groups* as well. It also, of course, applies to individuals. So, let's talk about the **energetic aspects of rapport**. If **rapport** is gained in part by *doing* what the other person *does*, *being* like they're *being*, we're going to **pace** their overall *behavior*. We're going to *stand* like they *stand*. We're going to *sit* like they *sit*. We're going to *move* like they *move*. When they use *speaking gestures*… that's right, we do *nothing*, we just *stop*. But we can use *their gestures* when *we* begin speaking, can't we?

But **what else** can we do? How about we look at their overall **energy** and we start *maneuvering* that too? So let's think of *energy* as *vibration* for a moment. Let's imagine that I'm with you and we can both see each other. We're talking together and I'm going to imagine, in my mind, a **vibration**, and you can do this *visually* or *auditorily*. I like to do it *auditorily*, usually. So I might hear your vibration as a hum, like <hmm>. Now I'm just *auditorily* **imagining** that, right? But, based on everything I see with you as I *look* at you, *that's* your **vibration**. I *hear* it. I imagine it, okay? And I might hear *mine* as a <hmm>.

Now, there's a bit of a **difference**. *You* seem to be a little *higher*, going a little *faster*. So, in my mind, I'm going to make mine *speed up*. So I'm going to **imagine** that I can *see* and *hear* my **vibration** like a *note*, like my body is *resonating to a note*, and it's going to start beating *faster* and *speeding up*. It's going to *resonate faster*. Mine's going to *increase in pitch* <hmm> till it's right up there with you, and as I do that, I'm imagining my **energy** speeding up, my *words* speeding up slightly, if need be my *muscle tension* becoming a little more, I'm going to move my **energy** up to *match yours*.

Alright, let's keep that in mind because that's another major thing you can do to **pace**, but let's go beyond. Let's go to **thought energy**. What I want to talk about now is how we can affect people with the **energy of thought**. And before you go too far into saying, "Well, now we're really getting out there into this woo-woo thing," listen up and listen close because I'm going to *show you how to do this*. I'm going to *show* you how it isn't nearly as *woo-woo* as you might think it is.

Let's first talk about the power of *joy* and *love* for just a moment. So, when you're thinking about *love* and you're thinking about *joy* in your life, what do you think about when you *feel* those things? Is it maybe *lightness*, or a sense of *well-being* and maybe an *infusion of power*? Now focus a little differently. Is joy and love a *higher* or *lower* feeling than depression? Well, for most it's much *higher*, and I imagine it is for you too. *Joy* and *love* are **very fast vibrational energies** – much, much faster than *depression* or *anger* or something like that. Well, you know anger can get fast, but it's a *lower-level* vibration.

CHAPTER TEN

The Pink Bubble

So, supposing that we could feel *joy* and *love* for our prospects, supposing that we could get them to *move faster* into that energy field and *feel* that too, would it make a difference? I believe it would and, to that end, there's an age-old technique that people have used. This goes back to the dawn of the ages. I mean, literally, back to before time started practically, where people practiced a few energetic techniques and they did so with real effectiveness. Let's call this **the pink bubble**.

Let's say we're going to go in and talk with someone and we're going to make a presentation. Now, as we begin that presentation, what if we *surrounded* them and us with an **imaginary pink bubble**? Now, I can just imagine some of you right now howling with laughter and saying, "Okay, Kenrick, now you've gone too far. Surely, you flipped your lid if you think I'm going to go putting pink bubbles around people!" Alright. Listen up. Let's just say, for sake of argument, that this has absolutely *no effect* on anybody and I'm absolutely willing to believe that. I personally think it *does* have an effect, but I'm willing to believe you if you want me to that it has absolutely *no effect* on anyone under any condition whatsoever. But what it *will* have an effect on is *you*.

If you are *consciously* saying, *I choose to experience joy and love* and express this towards my client, and I'm going to make a mental construct of a beautiful **pink bubble** that surrounds us, that fills us with *love* and *acceptance* and *joy*, then guess what? It is *affecting* **you**, the **persuader**. And if that's *all it did* and if that's *all it's done* since the dawn of time when people started using this, then so be it. Let it be *just like that* and **use** it for all it's worth because it'll have a **dramatic impact** for you. Remember, what your *prospect* experiences while you are in **rapport** with them, *you* will experience and the same is true *in reverse* as well. What *you* experience while in **rapport** with your client, *they* will too. That alone makes the **pink bubble** worth employing.

I'll now give a few **major secrets** about **rapport**. One of them is that if you want them to *love* and *trust* and *believe* in you, then *you* love and trust and believe in *them* first. **You go first**. *You* do it first. *You* love. *You* trust. *You* believe. Don't ask *them* to come to *you*. *You* go to *them*, which is the whole point of **rapport**. *We're* going to where *they* live. *We're* showing *them* we **understand their**

world and then we ask *them* to come to *a better one* where *we* live, where our products and services live – one they don't even know about or didn't know about until we got there.

So the **pink bubble**, I believe, will affect them, but let's say it doesn't. Let's just simply say *I don't care* whether it affects them or not. It affects *me* and if it makes *me* feel more of those things, then that rule that I just gave you is in play. *I'm* trusting, loving and believing in *them* and, therefore, *they're* doing it back with *me* even more.

Now, how does this help us keep our **intention**? I want you to think for a moment of this **pink bubble** being somewhat like the *matrix*. So in other words, let's say you and I are talking and, in my mind, I throw a big **pink bubble** - like a big pink blanket but it's translucent - and I throw it *around us* and it looks like a big igloo around us. And running through this are lines of **energy** – you know, some yellow lines and pink lines, and all of these things are glimmering, glistening – and I can *see* the bubble as we talk.

Now, from time to time, I might want to *change* how you're *perceiving* certain things. So what I do is I'll throw into this bubble that's over us the **emotional states** I want you to *experience*. Maybe I want you to feel *excitement*, or maybe I want you to feel that this is *profound*. So I *seed* that into the bubble, I allow it to *radiate* throughout the bubble and, as it does, it's *infusing all of that inner space* that the bubble is covering with that energy. So you see how I make the **mental construct** in my mind? It's really pretty simple.

When I do that, it's **affecting *me* first** because I'm saying, "This is what I want," and so if it's affecting *me* and that's *all* it's doing. But it's **affecting *them* through *me*** as long as I have **rapport**.

Let me give you an example. Let's take the world of **hypnosis** for a minute. One of the most profound ways that Dr. Milton H. Erickson demonstrated hypnosis to groups of people – he was a psychiatrist, a medical doctor that specialized in brief therapy, and he was the world's greatest living hypnotist prior to his death in the early 80s – he takes somebody that he's *worked with before* and who understood his brand of therapy and the way he did things and he'd bring them on stage. Then he'd bring somebody up that he wanted to *demonstrate* with, somebody that had *not* worked with him before and he'd have them sit right by the person that he'd been working with for a long time and he'd start talking to the person who he'd been hypnotizing over this long period of time and he'd say to them, "Okay. Now, as you begin to just relax and drift into your own world and blah, blah, blah," he'd go through his thing. The person next to them was instructed to *watch* the long-term client of Erickson very closely. As they would watch Erickson's client sitting right next to them, what Erickson was doing would rub off on *them* and *they'd* go right into a trance along with Erickson's client. It's just amazing. By *watching* them, *they* were affected. You see what I mean? Even if the **pink bubble** only affects *me*, it's *still* doing its job because, as *they* watch *me*, as *they* feel *my* excitement, **they too will be feeling it.** As they feel my *love*, my *trust* and my *respect*, they're going to feel that *too* and *who* will they obviously be aiming those great feelings of *trust* and *respect* at? Yup, *me*!

So you can use this in one-on-one presentations, one-on-two presentations, one-on-many presentations. You can *do* this and it works *very, very effectively.*

CHAPTER ELEVEN

Mental Construct

Alright, I want to give you one more thing. I'd like to talk to you about something I discovered as a result of doing a presentation many years ago for Jay Abraham, the famous marketing consultant. Jay asked me to come into his seminar and we made this big elaborate deal, because Jay doesn't generally pay the people that present for him, and I don't generally do anything without getting paid. Funny how that works, right?

So Jay calls me up on the phone and he says, "Well, you know, I don't really pay people. I mean, you'll get all these wonderful things if you do what I want."
And I said, "No! Hell, no. If you want someone to work for free, go find someone else! If you want the best then come to me, okay? It's like I come to you, Jay, and you're one of the very best in marketing, I don't think I'm going to get you to work for me for free. So, no, I'm not doing that."
And he said, "Well, alright. How about I do this? How about let's do this in this way. I'll pay you half of your fee and, if everybody loves you, then I'll give you the other half."
I said, "Well, now we're talking." I continued, "Of course, if we're going to negotiate, then if they love me, you're going to have to bring me in to everything else you do in this series you said that you are putting together, and pay my entire fee each and every day for each of the ones that you do."
And he says, "Alright. That's fair enough."
And I said and, actually, I don't know that he really expected that I could do it but, anyway, I said, "Well, alright, let's just *define* how we're going to know when people love me. A standing ovation, would that be good?"
He said, "Oh yeah. That'd be good."
So I said, "Well, how about, if afterwards, they come out of the seminar room and stand in lines to speak with me, would that be good?"
He said, "Oh yeah, man. That'd be really good."
And so I said, "Alright, if those things happen…"
He says "Look, man, I'm a real guy, okay? And I'm an honest guy. If that happens, I'll pay."
I said, "Alright, I'm just making sure. So, if these things happen, you're going to be excited, impressed and you're going to pay me my whole fee and you're going to do all the other things that we've agreed?"
And Jay said, "Absolutely!"
I said, "Alright, you're on! I'm up for that."

So what happens is I show up at the seminar, I give two hours of presentation unlike anything you've ever heard. I mean, I *rocked* the house. I'm standing up and I'm exerting myself like crazy in front of an audience of several hundred people. I literally *poured out all the energy I had* because, back then, I didn't know how to *control* it very well. At the end of that time, because I **programmed** it and **made it happen**, everyone *stood up, cheered* and *screamed* and *hollered* and *loved* me. Then they followed me outside the room and they all *stood in line to talk with me* – a line to talk with me and *another* line to talk with my wife. Everybody was out of the seminar room.

Now, after a little bit of time, Jay wanted to start back up again, and guess what? Nobody went back inside because they were still standing in line to talk to me. I was talking with them as fast as I could, but there was still a long line. So Jay came back out and he said, "Okay, okay, okay. You made your point. Make them come back in." It was great! So I said, "Okay, we got a deal then, right?" and he said, "Man, the check's on its way!" I said, "Alright. Well then, we got a deal." So I sent them all back in the room.

Now, about 20 minutes later, I'm *exhausted* – I mean, literally *exhausted*! And I'm thinking, "Thank God I'm done!" Jay says, "Where's Kenrick? Someone get him and have him come in." So someone ran out and got me and I came in and he said, "You know, Kenrick? Everyone loves you *so* much, they want you to *keep talking*. They're asking for you." He said, "Would you do another couple of hours?" and the audience burst into applause and I thought "Oh my goodness. How am I ever going to do this? I'm absolutely wiped out," but I did. I went ahead and did it. If any of you are public speakers or have ever done any public speaking, you can probably relate. When I was finished, I was *so tired*. I went to bed and I couldn't get out. I slept for the better part of a week, literally sleeping for days. I was completely spent.

Fortunately for me, I came upon a **strategy** that made all that **change**. So, if you happen to present, you're going to love this, you're really going to love it. I learned that what I was doing is I was *influencing* people in part through **putting out my own energy**. Meaning, I was **exerting my own energy** and I was *feeding* the audience with it. The audience was *loving* it. They were *taking the energy*. Now, if you just looked at this from an **energy** standpoint, *I* was the one feeding the *audience* with my material.

Well, the problem is, if you have 200 people in a room, it'll *drain* you and it'll drain you *real quick*. And, hey, I've got news for you: if you have *20* people in the room it'll drain you, even *10*! So what I learned to do is I learned to make the following **mental construct**: I'd put this in my mind *before* I walk on stage. I put a big **snow shovel** at the back of the room that was as wide as the room and it was taller than the heads of everyone sitting, and the way I do this is the snow shovel was clear at the back and was on the ground four or five feet high, something like that.

What I do is, as I'd speak, I'd *beam out of my eyes* and I'd *imagine a blanket of energy* that was covering the entire audience with *love*. I'd cover them with *acceptance* and with *honor* and with *respect* and with *absolute evangelical belief* in my message. And, whereas before it would pass over the heads of the audience, I would just *beam it out* and it would be going from *me* to *them* and that's it, now, I'd beam it out and, as it would travel across the room, I'd imagine it traveling slowly and then it would *hit the snow shovel*. As it hit the snow shovel, the snow shovel did a number of things. First, it spat it up, as you know the shovel curves like a dish, and it *curved around* and went down and under everybody's feet and it *came right back to me*. And then when it got to me, it *entered* me and it went *back through me* and then it went out my eyes and it went over the top of the audience and hit the shovel and went *around again* underneath their feet. And I imagine this going *faster*, the cycle *speeding up* and *speeding up* and going *faster* and *faster* and *faster* and *faster* until, finally, it's going *so fast* that I could let it go on its own. I didn't have to think about it anymore. I could *watch* it spinning at high speed. And by the way, that's the real **key**, I just *step out of myself* and then *watch it spin* and when I did that, my sales went through the roof. The persuasion was unbelievable! I believe it communicated a message very profoundly that I *love* my audience, I *trusted* them and I *believe* them. Furthermore, I figured it was really going to help me not be so tired. And it did, but I found there was a **problem**.

And the **problem** was I kind of felt all these *strange weird feelings* afterwards. Almost like feeling *dirty*, like I'd taken on everybody's problems. Now, I realized as I was doing this that somehow the *metaphor in my mind* was, as it came under everybody's feet, actually *picking up their dirt!* So I thought, "Okay, well, this is easy. Since I've done this with a *mental construct*, I'm going to build *another* mental construct."

So what I did is I built a little electronic box and it sits out in front of me. As the energy comes from my eyes, goes over the audience like a blanket, it hits the snow shovel, it comes back underneath them and, as it comes towards me, it all goes into that box. Now, the box is a big *cleaner* and an *amplifier*. An *imaginary* box. So what it does is it *strips out* all the *negative emotions* from all the people. I would imagine that there are *crystals* in the box in my imagination, and it *amplifies the energy*. Then the cleansed, amplified energy comes out of the box and through the soles of my feet and it *powers* me. It gives me all the *power of the audience* times ten or even a thousand. It radiates up through my body and out through my eyes and now we're talking about a much greater power that's going out over the audience. And as it hits the snow shovel, it cycles round again through the box, then comes back through me and I'd do the same thing again. I just *speeded up* and *speeded up* until I can stand aside and watch it happening.

So, what's happening is there's a **power ball** *building* and *building* and *building* that I can watch and I can just let it go on *autopilot* and I can **seed this** with any *emotion* or *outcome* that I want.

And I tell you right now, if you'll do it, if you present to large numbers of people, even ten or twenty, you're going to find that it will *really* help you. Now, you'll have to *perfect* it. You'll have to *think it through*, you'll have to *work with it* a little bit. It might take a while to get really good at it but if, for any reason, you're saying right now, "Ah, Kenrick. That's out of this world. That's wild, man. I don't know about that stuff." Alright, fine. You don't have to *believe* it. *Try* it. *See if it works*. If it doesn't work, who cares? I mean, you *tried* something. It didn't work, big deal! It took five minutes to learn it and 10 minutes to try it and there you go. But I'll tell you that if you *do it*, if you present to groups, you will leave those presentations *energized* and you'll feel much, much *better* and you'll also find that your ability to **persuade** them **climbs dramatically**.

Now, when you're done with the presentation, *slow* the energy speed down, jump back in, notice that it's spinning at high-speed all by itself and say, "Alright, we're done now. It's time to *slow down*," and you'll see it go *slowing* and then it *stops* and it all comes back into you and stays there and you're left *energized*. The audience is left **motivated** and **persuaded** and *you* feel **fantastic**. You've *got* to try it!

Well, this book was *jam-packed* full of **strategies**, wasn't it? It's an amazing amount of material – more than you often get in entire products!

So, now it's time to go back through the book section by section and start **working** with it to *make it your own*. Now, you won't perfect this overnight. In fact, I'm still working on perfecting it but you *can* get *good* very fast. And the more you practice, the better you'll get!

BOOK THREE

DEFINING CRITERIA

INTRODUCTION

Eliciting Criteria

Welcome to **Book Three** of **Persuasion Force**. We have a tremendous amount of incredibly exciting and powerful material to get through. And to that end, let's just jump right in.

To begin with, I'd like to focus on an *entirely different aspect* of **persuasion**. And I want to concentrate at this point on **becoming the only solution** to whatever it is that you sell, or in your industry, or for the kind of product that you represent. So, that's where we're going to be turning our attention on now.

All right, let's review and talk about **criteria**, because we're going to take **criteria** to levels that I don't think you've probably *dreamed* of. It is *phenomenal*, and I'm so excited to bring you this. First of all, **criteria**, as you know, it **focuses all you say at their *sweet spot***.

How? Because you're going to tie *your **product*** and/or *service* to *their* **criteria**. In other words, *everything you say about your product* or your *service* or *yourself* or *whatever* you're talking about **must make sense**, in light of *what*? That's right, *in light of their* **criteria**!

Always, you're going to *use* criteria to *tie* their criteria to *your product or service*. And this starts the process of *making you the **only*** solution in their mind. But, it isn't yet enough, at least, in my book.

I want it to be so slam dunk *powerful*, so overwhelmingly *compelling* and *persuasive* that literally, they turn to you as *their only possible solution*. When *you* talk about *their* **criteria**, you are **constantly pushing their hot buttons**, juicing them up to move forward.

I remember that when I was first starting, my manager used to tell me, "Now, come on, when you're talking with someone, just *find their hot buttons* and then, *push* them, *push* and *push* and *push* and push!" I was like, "Yeah, but how do you **do** that?"

He goes, "Well, you know, you just *talk about things* and you *get to know* them and you *find it*." I'm like, "Yeah, but I *hear* you do it, but I'm not quite sure *how you identify them as a hot button*." And that just ticked me off.

I have to tell you right now, that *upset* me, because I could *see* and *hear* him do it, but I *didn't get* how to **identify** when I was hearing **criteria**. So, I'd do it and then he'd listen to me and he'd say, "No, look, man, *here's* where they told you about it and you *missed* it. *This* and *this* and *this*, remember? And you *missed* it. You didn't really *hit* that." I'd go, "Agh! All right!"

So, this **criteria**, when you *elicit their criteria*, you've elicited their **hot buttons**. It couldn't be any simpler than that. I mean, really, I've given you the *exact code*, the *exact sequence* to get their **hot buttons**, plain, period and simple.

CHAPTER ONE

Defining Criteria

And now, let's *ratchet this thing way on up*. Remember, all **criteria** serves to *move* people *towards* something they want or *away* from something they don't want. So, given that that's the case, and you're already using that, I'm certain, let's jump it up.

Let's talk about **changing their criteria**. Now, this is also known as **adding to their criteria**. I want you to think of this process as the way to *craft the way that your prospect thinks* about your class of products or industry, such that you are **their only possible solution**.

And this process isn't really *possible* by the *untrained*, it's not. You'd be *luckier than heck* if you could figure this out all by yourself. And I'll tell you, it's one person in 1,000 that does. And that's why this gives you such a *tremendous advantage*.

The process is *simple to do* and *incredibly effective*, but it does take practice, like all elements of persuasion. You really have to practice it and get good at it. So let's go on to look at **criteria** and *getting the definition*.

The first step in this process, and one that will make your persuasion far more powerful, is to get them to **define their criteria**. So, let's consider this criteria for someone moving to a new home, for example, if you're a realtor. Let's say you ask the question, "What's important about moving?"

Or, better still, and more conversationally, you ask, "Why did you want to chat with me today?" And they say, "Well, I need to move." And you say, "Okay, what's *important* about moving?" And their answer is, "We want a bigger home in a nicer neighborhood."

Then you respond, "What's *important* about having a bigger home in a nicer neighborhood?" And they say, "We'd like it to *reflect what we've accomplished*, and we can *do better* now." And you say, "Excellent, that's wonderful! Glad to hear things are going better. Can I ask real quick what did you do to improve things?"

"Oh, business is good, things are just doing good. I mean, that's what it is." And you say, "Okay, well out of curiosity, *what's important* about wanting to reflect what you've accomplished and that you can do things better now?" The person says, "Well, you know, it *affirms our success both to ourselves and others*. Our home is where we live, it's where we are. And so, every day, we get up in it, it *reaffirms to us the success* that we've accomplished to date. It also is kind of the external thing that people see about us. And so, it also *affirms our success to others*. And we think that's pretty cool."

So you're going to ask the question, "**What does it mean?**" That will enable you to **find the definition** and here's what you get.

Staying with the same criteria for moving, their **highest criteria** was, *it affirms our success both to ourselves and others*. You ask, "**What does that mean to you?**" And they say, "Well, I can *see* the new house around me, it's *nicer*, it's *bigger*, the *property* is *bigger* too and *better manicured* and *I feel rich* and *successful* and *prosperous* as I experience it."

Now, the **middle criteria** was "we'd like to reflect what we've accomplished and we can do better now." The **first criteria** is, "it's a bigger home and a nicer neighborhood." Now let's say you decide to ask the **definition question** about *that* as well, so you say, "When you say it's *bigger*, **what does that mean? A** *nicer neighborhood*, **what do you mean?**"

"Well, it's five thousand or more square feet from what we can tell, and we'd like to have at least an acre or more in property, and all the homes in the neighborhood should cost more than a million dollars."

There you have the **definition!** Now you might ask, "Kenrick, why did you not get definition on the second one?" Well. because the second one says, "we'd like to reflect what we've accomplished and we can do better now." When I ask, "**What's important about that?**", they say, "it affirms our success both to ourselves and others."

So really I just *went along with that*, I just used that one. That comes from **experience**, you'll get it as well as time goes on. And I asked for **definitions** on the bigger home because 'bigger' *demands* or *implies* the question "bigger *than what?*", "nicer *than what?*", so I wanted to find out, **what do they mean** 'bigger'?

Now let's take a good look at these **definitions**.

So for the one "*affirms our success both to ourselves and others*", that **means** "I can *see* the new house around me, it's *nicer* and *bigger*, the *property* is *bigger too* and *better manicured*. I feel *rich* and *successful* and *prosperous* as I experience it."

And "*a bigger home in a nicer neighborhood*" **means** "five thousand or more square feet on a one acre or larger lot, all homes in the neighborhood cost more than a million dollars."

Now does that make sense? I hope so! In other words, **you have the criteria** and there **you have the definition** as well.

CHAPTER TWO

Leveraging Criteria

Now **what to do** with that information? There's two things that you can do, you can **fulfill** it or you can **leverage** it. I'll show you exactly how these work.

So, first you can *give them precisely what they've asked for.* That's **fulfilling** it! What's an example of that? . . .

"Well, let me show you a few homes today, we're going to start in the first neighborhood. *Every home here is at least a million dollars or more* and the house I'm going to show you is *fifty five hundred square feet* on *one point one acres.*" See? You're just *giving them precisely what they said they want.* Alright, that's **fulfilling** it.

Or, you can **leverage** it. So you can tell them that what you're showing them seems *just like what they've asked for, **only better**.* So, for example, you can say "Okay, I'm going to show you now a neighborhood, and let me tell you up front that all the homes in this neighborhood are *not* valued over a million dollars, *however* that's only because the neighborhood is *rapidly increasing in value.* When you buy here, you'll end up with *equity* in your home *very, very fast* but the evaluations have yet to catch up with how fast the property, the neighborhood, is *increasing in value.* This is something I know because I research properties and what you said really touched me, because it triggers something that's important to me. I like my clients to be able to get *precisely what they want*, better still if they can do it *and have a tremendous advantage. Equity.* So in this neighborhood, houses are on average of eight hundred thousand dollars and up to as high as about one point six million. The house I'm going to show you is just *a hair under* a million dollars, it also is *a hair under* five thousand square feet.

"And you may be saying, 'Wait a minute now, I want five thousand square feet.' Well, let me tell you something, the house I'm going to show you is written up in one of the region's local papers. Here's a quote from it, it says, '*This house feels like houses that have six thousand or more square feet with just forty five hundred square feet.*' The key is this, it's *open construction*, it's created in such a way that is extremely sophisticated and *takes advantage of the space* very, very well. So you could have a five thousand square foot home that is designed *poorly* or a forty five hundred square foot home that is designed *incredibly well.* The smaller one will *feel bigger.*

"I want you to look at it and tell me what you think, alright? I could have just shown you the home and told you, 'This house fits what you're talking about, but I want you to know, I'm always going to tell you *exactly like it is*, but I think this one's gonna really surprise you, let's go check it out."

See what I'm doing? I'm **leveraging, leveraging, leveraging.** Okay, so I'm not giving them *exactly* what they said they wanted, on the one hand, but I'm **leveraging** it by telling them *this really is exactly what you wanted **and more**.*

CHAPTER THREE

Eliciting the Definition

Here are some ways of **getting people to define their criteria**. *First* thing I usually do is ask, **"What does that mean?"** That'll usually do it.

The *second* thing I'll ask is, "If you *had* that, **how would you know**?" For example, if I ask "What does that mean?" and they go, "Well, what do you mean, what does that mean, I don't understand your question?" Then I immediately say, "Well, if you *had* it how would you *know*? You know, what would be *true* for you, what would be *going on around you*?" And I'm looking for **specifics** here, I want **specific things** they're going to tell me.

The *third* thing I might do, is I might then ask, if they really *still* don't get it, I'll say, "Well **what would you be experiencing that lets you know?**" And if they're *still* looking confused I might say, "You know, what would you be *seeing* or *hearing* or *feeling* that *lets you know you're experiencing*?" and then **name their criteria**.

Now, I don't like that last one, it's a bit more clumsy than the other methods, but you can resort to it if worst comes to worst. The other thing is, you don't have to get the definition for *all* their criteria but you *must* get it for the **highest criteria** they've given you. And that's a real important distinction.

Let's go to some *examples* of **definitions**. Here are some to consider:

"I'd feel I was doing good as a father and husband." That's the **criteria**. And you say, **"What does it mean** to be doing good as a father and husband?'"

And they say, "It means seeing my kids graduate from college, and it means making sure my wife is safe financially if I should pass away." That's the **definition**.

Okay, here's another example. Here's the **criteria**: *"I'd feel like my money was working as hard as possible on my behalf."*

Here's the question that will elicit the **definition**: **"What would you be experiencing** that lets you know that your money is working as hard as possible on your behalf?" See? *What does it mean* or *what would you be experiencing* and then **name their criteria**. And their response?

"I'd be getting regular reports letting me know what you were doing, I'd see it was increasing in value, not decreasing. You'd respond to me within a few days of receiving a call or an email from me which let's me know you're on top of things." You see how that **defines the criteria**?

The **criteria** was *"I'd feel like my money was working as hard as possible"*. But the **definition** is, *regular reports*, seeing it *increase* and *not decrease*, and *responding within a few days* of a call or email. See? That's the **definition** of what it *means*, of what their **criteria** *means*.

Now, I know I'm just jamming it in this book and so I really fully expect you to *stop* occasionally, *think*, let this *settle in*, come back, *review* it, over and over. This is very dense material and a ton of it, so read and re-read as much as you need to really get it.

CHAPTER FOUR

Only You Can Deliver!

Here's why it's important to **get the definition**. I want you to imagine two people in the context of a training. They both said that learning what was being taught in the training is *important* to them yet each one has *different* **criteria**. This is really going to make a difference.

They *both* said that learning what was being taught in the training is important. But *person one* has the **criteria** to *learn new skills*. In other words, *what's being taught* is important. Why? Because *they want to learn new skills*.

The *second person* also says what's being taught in the training is important to them. Why? Because *they want to be recognized.*

Then you go on to, let's imagine, after a month of working together, you've learned *eight new tools* that you're putting to work every day of your life. Now you just talked about it being *fundamental tools to build their success and foundation.*

Now you're naming *eight* of them, there are eight tools. Imagine how *successful* you'll feel and here you're **leveraging their criteria**. That word *successful*, you're **leveraging** that to say, *you feel what you want* because *you've learned eight new tools*. In other words, not that you've doubled your earnings but *you've learned eight new tools*. Imagine *how successful you'll feel.*

See? And *success* is even more than that, isn't it? It's *prospecting more effectively*. You're saying to them, "Hey, it's not just doubling your income, it's *learning to prospect better*. It's *closing more confidently*, so in other words, they need more *confidence* there."

And being able to *size up your prospects instantly* so you spend your time where it returns the most amount of profit. Wow! Sizing up your prospects, closing more confidently, prospecting more effectively, spending your time where it returns the most amount of profit. Now *that's* **success**, isn't it?

And then you're asking him or her to *agree* with you that **success equals this definition**, not just earning double. There are two things you can do. You can *add more* if you want to **change their criteria**, do these things, add more.

The easiest way to do this is to simply add more to the **meaning** or **definition** of their **criteria**, but here's the kicker. Add it about things that **only you** can *produce* or *deliver*. So you're going to **add more** to their **definition** that **only you can deliver!**

Now you can **reframe** it as well, so if they *resist what you add*, or they *resist* you changing the meaning, you can bring the skills of **reframing** or **magical objection mastery** to bear, and we're going to cover all of those skills together in this series of books, so for many of you who don't yet know what I'm talking about, that's fine. But we're going to cover them all in these **Persuasion Force** books. So right now we're going to focus on **adding more**.

It's *easy*, *fun* and *powerful*. Here are the steps:

- First, you **elicit the criteria** and you should be getting pretty *good* at that by now.
- Second, you **get the definitions**. Big, powerful thing to do.
- Then, you **add to the definitions**, such that **you are the only one that can possibly deliver that to the customer** (or your company's the only one, or your product's the only one, etc.)

This is how you can give yourself *a significant competitive advantage* over all your competitors and make yourself *the only possible and the highest desired provider*. Best of all, your competition will *never understand* why you walk away with the order. They won't get it.

They'll wonder how is it that *you always win* and they can't seem to outdo you even if they're cheaper. Amazing! That's the *power* of this, that is truly the power of this. So, think about it. The goal is, you're going to **elicit the criteria**, what's *important* about X.

Whatever they say, you're going to get to the *highest level* and then you're going to ask, **what does that highest level *mean* to you?** Whatever they answer, you're going to **add additional meanings** to it, things that **only you can deliver**. And that's really the key to what I call **changing criteria**, Is you're **adding** to it.

Remember always, keep the **label** of their **criteria** the *same*, just **change the meaning** or the **definition** of it. That's *critical*, if they say it means they're going to be *successful* then by golly keep it *successful*. You're just going to tell them what *successful* means.

It means *everything that they said*, but doesn't it **also** mean *this* and *this* and *that* and *this* and *that*? Yes, it sure does! Great! Now, guess what? **You're the only company that provides it.** That's the **key** to this. I hope I have been sufficiently *jamming this in* throughout this book.

CHAPTER FIVE

Putting It Into Practice

And I fully expect, you're going to need to read through this many times, go back over it and over it again and really get it, okay? This is a heavy duty lesson, very, very thought provoking and it's very stimulating, but it also is heavy duty, reading through this book once is not all it's going to take.

So what I'd like you to do to really get to grips with this material is this: **Elicit the criteria** from twenty people. And this needs to preferably be people that you are wanting to *persuade* and **get their definitions** for their criteria. You'll find this very, very useful and very, very powerful. Get their definitions.

Then I want you to practice **changing the meaning** or **adding to their definitions**.

Now this is a powerful thing I want you to do. **Raise your vibration** about what you're learning. Literally *imagine* your vibration getting *faster* as you think about what you're learning. *Project into the future* and **experience your life changing** as you **implement these skills**.

Just do exactly that, **project into the future** and *imagine your life*, your energy is *sped up*, your vibration is beating *faster*. Feel the excitement as you imagine your energy speeding further still and notice what your future becomes.

And take a few moments several times a day to be *grateful* for what you have, and for this learning. It's that attitude of *gratitude* that will help you to continue to *prosper* and move ahead powerfully. One of the greatest secrets I've ever learned is the power of **gratitude**.

So, take a few moments every day and just remind yourself of how *grateful* you are. Just stop and focus on gratitude for all that you've accomplished in life, for where you are right now and for all the fulfillment of the things that you've most wanted as they continue to come into your life.

Well this was a very fast paced book and a *lot* of information was crammed into a small amount of space. But we're on a roll and I want you to get it and so I'm hoping you'll read it back over several times from start to finish so everything sinks in and you really get it.

Go back through and *carefully* go over all of these steps and *work like crazy* to perfect **criteria**, **definitions** and then **adding** to those definitions. Add to that the **two stratagems**, wow, you've got a power packed book full of information that will, I promise you, take you to levels you've barely even imagined yet.

Criteria is the cornerstone and we are going to be working with it in so many ways it'll blow your mind as we continue. Right now, it's important you figure out that **criteria is *malleable***, it's *not locked in stone* and you can *change* it easily simply by **adding to the definition** that they give you of what their criteria means.

That is *tremendous power*. I'll bet you you hadn't thought about it like that before. I'm telling you, as you *implement* this, your *money*, your *fame*, your *abilities* will *skyrocket* and I can't wait to hear about it. So with that, we'll close this book.

And get busy now and go through and do the homework and I'll see you in the next book!

BOOK FOUR

PRECISION WITH LANGUAGE

INTRODUCTION

Increasing Your Precision With Language

Welcome to **Book Four** of **Persuasion Force**. In this book we're going to be covering **precision with language**. How to use *visual, auditory* and *kinesthetic* or *sensory* based words. Let's jump right in, shall we?

We have a lot of things to cover and even more for you to do. This is a lot to learn and to work with, so pay attention and get ready to do some work to **integrate** all of these skills and have a whole lot of fun doing it.

In this section we're going to be studying how to **increase your precision with language**. And you're going to learn how to create **rapport** *verbally*. You'll also learn how to begin the process of **training your prospects to follow your ideas and suggestions**. Now to do all this you must first develop a few skills that will give you far more *flexibility in your language* as well as laying the groundwork for powerful strategies to come.

This material is a bit different from some of the material you've been doing up to this point. This material will take *practice* and quite a bit of it. In particular, it's *not enough* to simply read me talking about this material. The more you **do** with this the better you are going to get, so apply yourself this month to *strongly increasing your skills* using this material. It is profound material. For some of you, you may *think* it's simple, but I'm going to give you exercises and if you'll do them your skills will rocket forward, and I mean *rocket* forward. It's really important that you **do** them and you **do them until you get it**.

Even after doing all the exercises I'm going to give you, I promise you, you will not have gotten it yet to the point where I'd *like* you to have it, but you'll have gotten it enough to the point that I can proceed forward in the next book.

CHAPTER ONE

Perception Filters

I want to talk to you about **reality v. thought**. What is the *difference* between **reality** and our **thoughts** of reality? What is the *difference* between **experience**, and by that I mean, that which is *happening* around us, and what we **remember** about what *happened* around us? And to get into this, let's talk a little bit about *how we perceive the world around us*.

We perceive our world through our **five senses**. Our five senses of course are *visual, auditory, kinesthetic*, which means feeling, *taste* and *smell*. Let me ask you this question, I want you to think this through really carefully. If something happens in the world around you, let's say within your ability to *see, hear* or *feel* it, let's say within ten feet of you, your eyes are open and you're watching it, do you perceive it happened *as fast as* it happened? Think about it for a minute.

The answer is *no*, you *don't*. It actually happens a split second *before* you can perceive it. Why? Because the information is being filtered through your five senses. In other words, how do you become aware that there even is an experience going on around you? Another way to look at this is, if a pencil were in a room and something happened but you weren't there, would the pencil know that it happened? There are some who argue, yes the pencil knows and if someone tunes into the pencil, it will tell them. Well, alright, maybe so, but let's just say, I doubt it.

It takes an **observer** to be there in the room to know that something happened. And *how* do we observe? By what takes place coming into our mind through our five senses. That's how it happens. And once the information comes into our five senses, we can remember it and talk about it.

We perceive our world through our five senses. Now most people think, when they first start their study of this, before they actually consider it thoroughly, "Well, my *perception* of what happened and *reality* are the same thing." Well if that's true, how is it that *no two people experienced things the same*? Good question, isn't it?

There are **filters** that *change our perception of things*. First of all, let's just be clear about the fact that *our five senses are distorted*. In fact, they go through three basic processes, basic to all human beings. NLP figured this out, many, many years ago. What comes in is *distorted*, or *generalized* and/or *deleted*. Distorted, deleted or generalized.

In other words, there are *so many things happening* every second around us that if you could possibly pay attention to all of those things, it would pretty much drive you crazy and *nothing* would make sense. So we learn to *tune* our senses to pick up the things that we believe are important. Oh, so you mean **beliefs enter into what we perceive**? You bet!

We **distort** the things that we see. This is how people make sense of art. In other words, we see something and we go, "Wow. That reminds me of _____." Or "That looks like_____." Or "That says to me _____." And we change our perception slightly to *gain new meaning*.

Or we **generalize**. Which part of what I just said was generalization? "That reminds me of

_____." Or "That's like _____." These are ways to generalize.

We **delete** it. We say, "Well, you know, the information comes in and we pick *two* things to notice and hear or feel instead of the *one hundred* that actually were available."

What dictates this? Well, for each person it's different, but there are some **general filters** that *change our perception of "reality"*. And I put "reality" in quotes because not any one person has a lock on what that is. Every person's reality quote is different. So what are some of these filters?

Well, **beliefs**, we've mentioned. **Values**, in other words, high level beliefs. How about *what your parents gave you and taught you was right*? This would be **beliefs** or **values** but coming from parents. How about *what you were conditioned socially to believe*? How about what you were conditioned socially to accept is true *about yourself*? Your *place* in the world? Your *ability to interact with others*? Your *status* or *position*? Your *desirability*? All of these, a lot of these, are affected in part by **your parents** and **your social condition**. How about the affect of **religion** on yourself or others? That can be profound.

And there are many, many more things like this that can affect our **values** and **beliefs** and our **concepts of reality**. Your interaction with *siblings*, if any, and *other family members*, if any, etc., etc. All of these are **filters that change our perception**. So through our five senses comes **data**. The **data** also *interacts* with our **beliefs** and our **values** and our **conditioning**. And what's dumped into our *memory system* is an **amalgam** of *what actually happened* and what we *think* about what actually happened, which is why no two people experience things the same.

Now are you beginning to understand why I put "reality" in quotes?

CHAPTER TWO

The Five Senses

This is kind of heavy duty and I highly recommend you go over this and over this. Read what I have to say on this numerous times. It will start to make sense. And what can happen to you as you do, is as you read it over and over, is you can *begin to feel like your reality is slipping away*, like reality itself is becoming *slippery*. And if that happens, **good**. That's *exactly* what I want. Because **reality *is* slippery.** Reality is what we make of it. And *we can choose to direct people's attention* any way we want to direct it. And that's the whole point of what we're learning.

To do that we have to learn *how* people construct and make their reality. And we have to learn how they *interact* with that reality. Here are a number of entry points: **the five senses**. NLP calls the five senses **your representational system**. Now why do they call it that? Well because our five senses are the *input mechanisms*, also the *output mechanisms*, but the *input mechanisms* that *bring data in* that allow us to *represent* that data by way of our memory to ourselves.

In other words, I just said something to you. *Remember* what it is. Something about representational systems, something about five senses and NLP, right? That's something like what I just said. What *was* it? Think about it. And you go, "Okay, I kind of remember." But you're remembering it *different* than I am. And I'm remembering it *differently* than someone else is. In other words, we're **re**-*presenting* what I said to ourselves but we can't re-present that information to ourselves *exactly* like it came, even though we *think* we can. We still have our inherent **feelings** associated, **concepts** associated. For example, this is crystal clear to me, but as you hear it, it may *not* be as crystal clear, or maybe it *is*. Maybe you understand it slightly *differently*, in fact I guarantee you. And the difference between us is *the way we represent this to ourselves*. In other words, the way *I* took in the information and made sense of it versus the way *you* took in the information and made sense of it.

I will refer to these things from time to time as **VAK**, **sensory systems**, **representational systems**. I don't use much jargon, as you know, in what I do, but you'll hear other people using it now, so you'll know kind of what they're talking about. And it's far more *profound* than most people recognize, or realize, and I hope you're starting to get a taste of that as you read what I'm saying to you.

CHAPTER THREE

The Visual System

Each of these sensual representational systems has its own associated descriptive words, and I want you to accustom yourself to how these are used. Aim in fact, to *master* them. Let's lift the **clouds** of difficulty from it and just really **focus**, if you will, on a **beautiful vision** of you understanding these words and using them to your advantage. I'll **show** you how to do it. As you **focus**, I think you're going to find that the **images** are **clear** and **bright** and you begin to **see** yourself using these kinds of sensory systems powerfully and effectively. Now *what am I doing?* I'm just choosing and picking my words and I am *aligning* them such that I'm primarily **using visual words**. Look back at the bold words in this paragraph and you'll **notice** it clearly.

I used a bunch of them there, didn't I? I'm not trying to give you an exhaustive list. Obviously there's a tremendous number of additional words that will equal **the visual system**. However, this will get you going in the right direction in a big way. If you want to *write a whole bunch more*, go ahead. That will be kind of fun and a really good exercise. See how many **visual-oriented words** you can come up with.

You'll then have *a list of visual words* that you can use around you any time you want. And it will make it much easier for you to go throughout your day and start to gain access to the **visual words** that are around you all the time.

What happens when a person is using **visual words**? Well, they're **remembering** and **processing information visually** in their mind. If you hear them do it *a lot*, it may be their **dominant sensory system**. It may be the one they're most *conscious* of.

What kind of behaviors might we expect from someone who's using predominantly **visual** words? This will help you to *recognize* people that are *predominantly visually oriented*.

Well, have you heard it said *a picture is worth a thousand words*? If you have a *picture* in your mind and you're trying to *describe* it to me, you may really get off on a roll here with your words, you're trying like crazy to describe it and you're talking really fast, even a little higher than usual. The pictures are *flipping through their mind at high speed* and they're trying to give you all the information that they're seeing and they can't quite keep up with it even.

That's a **visually oriented person** oftentimes. And you'll often see them, or hear them, I should say, *talking rather fast*. There are a few other things that you'll notice. They may often *breathe higher in their chest*. You may notice that they need *distance* between you as they speak. They don't like to stand real close to people, because what happens is you'll be *in their pictures* if you stand too close.

In fact, if you want to try something, if you think someone is very **visually oriented** when you're talking to them, just **move real close**, so you're standing real close to them and see if they don't get *uncomfortable*. Because what's happening is *you're standing in their pictures* and they don't like that and so they'll try to move away a little bit so they can *still see their pictures.*

You can also do some other interesting things. If you notice them *looking off into space* at particular areas while they talk, you could **point to that space** and **slide it around**. In other words, **point to the space** and then **move** it to some other space and watch them get confused. It's kind of funny. Just play around a little bit with it. You're not going to hurt anybody doing that. It's not like you're going to cause trauma or anything, contrary to what others might lead you to believe. But it will start to help you *understand what happens* when someone is highly **visually oriented**.

When someone is very **visually oriented** they're going to use a lot of **visual words**. Obviously. And they may *talk a little faster*. And they may *breathe higher in their chest*. They may *stand a little farther apart* from you. All these things will help you *recognize* a **visually oriented** person.

Suppose, though, you hear a person that uses a lot of **visual** words but they're *prefaced* with **feeling words**. "I **feel** like, you just have to **look** at the **situation** and understand how it will **affect** you so you know what's going to **happen**." What about those kind of people? Well, the odds are, you're experiencing someone whose **visual** system may be somewhat out of **awareness**, they're probably **feeling** and describing their **feeling** in terms of what they **see**. We'll get into that in future books, but these kinds of people can be **very powerfully persuaded**. When you find them, you'll learn to *love* what you can do with them. For now, recognize that, and people by the way are not just *one* of these. It's not like you're a Gemini or a Capricorn or an Aquarius, you're not only one thing.

People will use all kinds of *different* words when they speak. They'll talk about a **picture** that they want you to understand and they'll talk about all kinds of things. They'll tell you about **pictures** they want to understand. They'll tell you about how it makes them **feel** when they **watched** it. They'll tell you about what they were **thinking** and **saying** to themselves. *People aren't just one sensory system.* That's what makes this a little confusing, because you have to try to figure out what is the *predominant* kind of words they're using. And we're going to get into some *specific ways* you can start to do that as we continue.

CHAPTER FOUR

The Auditory System

Let's move on and consider **auditory words**. I recommend **listening** to this section with your audiobook. As you **listen** to what I'm going to **tell** you, you'll begin to **hear** the way in which you can use these words to **describe** most anything. You can orient your **phrases** and the way in which you **talk** such that people will **resonate** with what you're **saying** very well. If you make your **voice calm** and **smooth** you'll probably have an even greater appeal as you **verbalize** your **message** you're wanting to get across. You can **tune** into what people are **telling** you as well, becoming more empathic with them and helping them to understand exactly you're meaning through all the **words** that you have.

What am I doing there? I'm stringing together **auditory words.** I'm doing it so you can **hear** what a bunch of them **sound** like when you put them all together. You can make a list of these **auditory** words too. And you're going to have a list of words that you can refer to all the time that will help you to come up with them all you want. The idea is that you learn very quickly how to come up with them in every system. Just like we talked about ways to understand the **visual** person, let's talk about ways to understand and recognize an **auditory** person.

First of all, an **auditory** person can have *several vocal characteristics* that are just dead giveaways. They may have a very **sing-songy** voice and you may hear them talk a bit like you would a radio disc jockey.

Sometimes they'll have a lot of *effect* to their words and you'll hear them **rising** and **falling** in their **pitch**. Now that is a dead giveaway, **auditory** all day long.

You'll also hear what appears to be *the exact opposite* of this. However you'll learn to discover it *also* as a dead giveaway for **auditory** and that is a person who talks in a **monotone**, sometimes they'll just talk completely flatly and robotically. And they'll expect you to listen to what they're saying and they're going to *carefully phrase their words* to make the point they're trying to get across and they'll *describe things very thoroughly and carefully* and this kind of a **speaking pattern** is a dead giveaway that the person is very much into the **auditory** system.

I've got to admit, it drives me insane, but this is what you'll hear sometimes.

If you hear *either of those two things* you know that the person is going very **auditory**. They're very much into the **auditory** system. And of course, like always, you'll hear them use a lot of **auditory words** in their language.

Where will their eyes go? If a **visual** person's eyes often go *up* while they're visualizing, and they frequently do, where will an **auditory** person's eyes go? Well they'll go *level, side-to-side*. Like they'll go towards their *ears*. Let me give you another behavior that will absolutely identify the person as an **auditory**. *They cock their head to the side*, as if they're talking on the phone. Just think back and remember a time when you watched a person talk on the phone and they cranked their head to the side while they're talking. Now think of times when you've been talking with someone face-to-face and they do the same thing. They're often *leaning an ear in* to try to *hear* *better* what you're saying and to try to understand. And when you see that, bingo, you've got an **auditory** person all day long.

Auditory people are much less concerned with how close you stand to them. They're really not making pictures and it doesn't really matter, or at least not in their conscious awareness enough. Therefore they're not nearly as affected by that.

Now when I say **auditory** people, again, this *isn't* like a birth sign. It's not like astrology. **Everybody** is **all** of these, so you just have to learn to tell *which one* they're *zeroing in on* at that time.

CHAPTER FIVE

The Kinesthetic System

Let's move on to talk about **kinesthetic** or **feeling words**.

The way you know that you're interacting with a **kinesthetic** or **feeling** oriented person is that they tend to **grasp** for the way in which things are going to **come across**. They'll want to **bend** with you and **walk**, **step** by **step**. They'll often want to **stick** with things and **grasp hold** of the kinds of things you're **going over** with them. Sometimes they'll even **strain** and **work hard** to **tackle** the **task** at **hand**. This is what **kinesthetic** oriented people do and sometimes they'll even **touch** their **arm** or their **leg** and **rub** it while they talk. They're kind of **getting in touch** with the way they **feel** about what's going on. They also sometimes talk about **balance** and **merging together** and **catching up**, all these kinds of things.

I've shifted in to a way you'll often hear **kinesthetic** people talk. If a **visual** person speaks *pretty quick* and they're *zipping* right along and an **auditory** person speaks *a little slower* and sometimes in a very *sing-songy* voice or in a flat *monotone* that you can easily detect they're doing, then a **kinesthetic** person, in contrast, often speaks **much slower** and *they struggle for the next thought.*

Now you're starting to understand how to recognize this and that's my whole point.

Kinesthetic people obviously use **kinesthetic words**. Another thing they do, they love to **stand close**, in fact, you can reach out and **touch** these people. You can **touch** them on the shoulder, you can give them a **hug**, within the realm of being respectful. But you can be right in their face. They *love* it. They don't care. They're not using their pictures anyway, at least consciously.

That's another major difference between the three groups that will help you to identify them. One of the biggest ways though, for me, is that they . . . struggle . . . for their words. . . Just like the pauses illustrated there.

They, in contrast to **visual** people who look *up*, and **auditory** people look *side-to-side*, *level*, **kinesthetic** oriented people will look, you guessed it, *down*, in general. Not always, you're going to see somebody that's looking up and talking about feelings. We'll get into that. That's sort of a separate way of doing things altogether, but beyond the scope of where we're at right now.

You're going to see all kinds of things, but just focus in on what is it that you're basically *experiencing* when you talk with someone. What are they *doing*? And that will help you significantly.

CHAPTER SIX

The Unspecified System

Moving on, let's deal with what I term "the **unspecified**", which is a separate thing altogether. **Unspecified** is *not* a system. However, I'm going to treat it like it is, and I want you to do the same. It's not a sensory system. It is, in fact, an attempt at **disguising the sensory system**. It often comes from the **visual**. In fact, have you ever heard an engineer type say, "The logical way to reward a person who plans and relates well with others is to explain the overall company policies and gain feedback from them, such that the evaluation that can take place accordingly can be useful and helpful to all the people concerned, and of course the decision that comes about from that can hopefully be used in a way to help move the organization forward appropriately."

I'll tell you why else people do that. They want to **hide their true intention** and they're used to *talking in a fog* and they're used to, even worse, *thinking* in one. Thus you need to be careful. If they're *used to* thinking or talking in a fog, guess what? You're going to see all sorts of issues in their life. You just will. Start watching for this. You're going to see them **disconnecting from reality** in many, many important ways. Not all ways, but I'm just giving you broad rules of thumb.

When you hear people use words that end in *'tion'* that's almost always an **unspecified** word. Also, *'ive'*, like *adaptive*. How are you *adapting*, by what you see, hear, feel, taste or smell? Which one? Any **nominalization**, by the way, qualifies here. Let me define that. A **nominalization** is a noun that doesn't fit into a wheelbarrow.

Let me give you an example. A rock. Can you put a *rock* into a *wheelbarrow*? Of course you can. Can you put a *concept* into a *wheelbarrow*? Nope. So *concept, conceptual, conception*, these words *don't* fit into the wheelbarrow. Can you put a *verbal agreement* into a wheelbarrow? Nope. But you can certainly put something *tangible*, dirt, for example.

The way in which a person communicates, now you could say that communication could be **auditory**, right? I say it's **unspecified** because, can you communicate **visually**? You bet, I can *write words down* which you can read. I can do it by *sign language*. Can you communicate with your **words**? You bet. Could you communicate by **touch**? You bet. Therefore, it is **unspecified**.

Any word that can *fit into more than one category*, by definition, is **unspecified**. Oftentimes, when you talk with people and they're talking in **unspecified** words, you'll see them sort of *de-focus* and *stare straight ahead*. This is indicative of a **visual** system, however, off they go into their **unspecified** words. It's better if you learn how to speak in **unspecified** words so that you can *equal* that. However, *our* unspecified words, that I'm going to be teaching you, the way in which *we're* going to *use* them, go far beyond simply trying to **pace** and gain **rapport** with somebody.

These words allow us to choose to *fog the mind* of the people that we're wanting to influence. Get that? These words cause us to be able to *fog the mind* of the people we want to influence.

I could say to you, for example, "As you go through this lesson and you begin to **reflect** back on some of the many ways that you can **evaluate** what it is that you're **learning** in these sessions, in ways that point you towards **ultimately** understanding a deeper **value**, a deeper way of really impressing upon you at many levels **simultaneously**, the way in which you're moving in the direction of **success** and **opportunity**. As you begin to **relate** in a way that is **profound** at **one level or another** or even **all of them**, you can begin to have the **experience** of **organizing** these ideas in your mind in a very **profound** way such that simply going through this little exercise, right now, with me, enables you to come to **some learning** and **some understandings** that even though you might not yet be **aware** of it, are **sowing the seeds of success** and greater use of **persuasion skills** in your life. And as that happens, just enjoy the **process** and work **diligently**, just like the duck, calm on the surface but paddling like heck beneath. Because that's the answer to really **moving forward** and enjoying the **process** while gaining **benefits** that you have yet to even imagine."

Now, make sure that as you read along with this, you're beginning to *go back through it* in your mind and also in reality many times. It would be my preference if you **listen** to these sections via the Audiobook provided via the link at the back of the book. And as you **listen** I want you to be *aware* of a few things. So if you just stop and do that, great. Now remember a few things I just did.

If you're following this on the Audiobook, you'll notice I **changed the tone** of my voice. I **dropped down** my voice. And I began to speak in a **rhythm**, a rather pronounced **rhythm**. So my **voice tone** changed, my **rhythm** changed and I began to use a *whole bunch* of **unspecified** words. I started adding a few **language patterns**, **commands** and **sentence structure ambiguity** and all kinds of things I began to add in.

Go back through this a couple of times, right now. If you're reading, you'll see all those **unspecified** words, but if you're listening along with the Audiobook, you're going to hear a **lot**. *How long would you do this* in real life? As long as *I* just did? Hey, in groups I do it like this *all the time*.

But I'll tell you this, you can *go into* it and then *come back out* of it. You can *shift into it* and *come back out* of it. And one of the *shifts* I'm making is by **shifting into the use of unspecified words**. In other words, every time you use an **unspecified** word, it *forces* the person you're talking to, to figure out *which sensory system is the one being used*.

So I say, "You organize your thoughts." And they go, "Okay, my **visual** thoughts? My **auditory** thoughts? My **auditory** thoughts? My **taste** or **smell** thoughts? *What thoughts?*" And they don't do this *consciously*, but their *unconscious* mind is *constantly seeking understanding of what's being said* and it's trying to figure it out. And the **effect** is, when you string a bunch of these words together, that they just *zone right out*. It **overloads their conscious mind**.

I want you to begin to learn *how to do this* and thus we're covering the **unspecified** words.

CHAPTER SEVEN

Smell and Taste

Let's move on and talk about the remaining two senses, **smell** and **taste**. Let's first talk about **smell**. **Smell** is one of the most *profound* things that happens to human beings. Here's why: **smell takes us back**. It has *direct access* in the mind to **memory**. If you go back and *remember* the way your grandma *smelled*, you may be shocked at what images come to mind. Maybe the **smell** of your mother baking bread in your home when you were little.

These have **instant access** to your **feelings** and to **memory**. And when people talk about **smell**, when you hear **smell** words, **olfactory** words, that should alert you to ways that you can *enter into their mind*. They talk about the **fragrant** opportunities that are available to everyone. Or working with that person left a bad **smell**. Or, that was a **nosy** person. Or, what an **odor** emanated from that meeting. Or aren't they a **stinker**. Or, **perfume** or **fumigate** or all these different words that can indicate **smell**.

We don't have nearly as many words to indicate **smell** and **taste** as we do the other senses but they're *very powerful* when you hear them and you should learn how to *use them back* when you hear other people using them.

Similarly with **taste**, and by the way, **smell** and **taste** are *linked*. So if you're **smelling** something, the odds are you're **tasting** it. If you're **tasting** it, you're also **smelling** it. Most likely, for most people.

And, by the way, you notice that if people have lost some of their taste buds, if they *lose* their smell, they often *also* lose their ability to taste. The two are very *connected*.

So words indicating **taste**—**salty**, **sour**, **hungry**, **sated**, **digest**—these are all sort of **taste** words. That will help you as you start to learn those things.

CHAPTER EIGHT

Three Exercises

Here we come to the **exercise section** and let me tell you folks, I'm going to give you a *lot*. And I really need you to *dive in and do these*. Okay?

Exercise number one: I want you to *write ten sentences* in *each sensory system* about what you do. So this is really simple. You're going to back up, starting with the **visual** system, look at that page. Imagine you're talking to a *prospect* or a *customer* and I want you to *write ten sentences* about what you do, using the **visual** sense.

When you start, just like anybody, you're going to use too many and it's going to start stilted and stupid. That's okay. The whole idea is that you *become flexible and powerful* with this. Demand of yourself that you only use **visual** words. So after you're done writing your sentences, look at them and go, "Are all those only **visual**? Have I only used **visual** words there?" And if you find any that use *other* words, and you might, then stop and *re-do that sentence* until you get it to where it's only **visual** words and nothing else. Well, not nothing else, you can have other content in there, but the **sensory** words need to be **visual**. Then I want you to do this for **visual**, **auditory**, **kinesthetic** and **unspecified**. You *don't* need to do it for **taste** and **smell**.

Look at the two senses you had *most trouble* with and write twenty more sentences for each of those senses. That's really important, that you look at the one where you had the most amount of trouble and then you write sentences, twenty sentences for each system you had the most amount of problems with.

Exercise number two: Now go back to the sentences you just wrote and start with the **visual** sense. And here's where your *real* work begins. *Translate* those sentences into the **auditory**, **kinesthetic** and **unspecified** systems.

So you're going to take a **visual** sentence like, "**Look** at him go." Now, I'm going to *translate* that into the **auditory** system, "**Listen** to him go." And the **kinesthetic** system, "**Feel** him go." And the **unspecified** system, "**Experience** him go."

You're going to take *every sentence* you wrote in the first exercise, now remember that's forty to begin with, ten **visual**, ten **auditory**, ten **kinesthetic**, ten **unspecified**, and then twenty *more* for each of the two systems you didn't do well in, so that's eighty sentences your now going to go back and *translate*.

You say, "Well, that's a lot, Kenrick." Yes, it is. But if you just give a few minutes every day you'll get them with no problem. I promise you something and this is what it is, you *will not get this* unless you *spend the time* to get it.

You'll go from a wannabe to a real pro and you'll go there *fast*. Please do the work. You're going to be *using* this and *working* with it from here on out. It will *transform* your persuasion. I know you don't understand how yet, but I'm telling you it will. Take my word for it, this is what you're asking me to give you, the best of the best, and here it is.

This is a small part but an important part.

Next, I want you to take the **auditory** sense and *translate* those sentences into **visual**, **kinesthetic** and **unspecified** that you did in your first lesson. In other words, you're taking *each* of the senses and you're doing it the same, you're *translating* them into the *other* senses. You're going to do the same to the **kinesthetic** sense and *translate* those into the **auditory**, **visual** and **unspecified**. In this case you *don't* need to translate the **unspecified** sentences you wrote into sensory sentences. You *don't* need to go that direction with it.

Stop reading right here, by the way, and just get this done. Please. Don't keep going forward. Don't read on even to the next exercise. It doesn't *matter* what the next exercise is. If you're unwilling to do what I've told you so far, it isn't going to matter. Just **stop** and do it. Do the work. I don't really want you to know what's coming up until you've done what I've asked you to do so far. It's not that hard to do. You can do it.

73

Exercise number three: I want you now to write *ten words* from each of the senses *by memory* on a piece of paper. See if you can't come up with ten **visual** words by memory, ten **auditory** words by memory, ten **kinesthetic** words by memory, ten **unspecified** words by memory. You *don't* need to do the **taste** and **smell**. Just do visual, auditory, kinesthetic and unspecified. Then I want you to start with the **visual** sense and write ten sentences that use *two words* of *that* sense, then *end* the sentence with *one* from the **kinesthetic** sense.

Here's an example, "I **see** you brought your paperwork for me to **look** over, which is great because as I do, you'll begin to **feel** a sense of confidence growing within you about us working together." So I used two **visual** words, 'see' and 'look over', and then I ended with a **feeling** word, a **kinesthetic** word, "you'll begin to **feel** a sense of confidence growing." Do you understand what I'm doing there?

I'm actually beginning to teach you the concepts of **pacing** and **leading**. I am not only teaching you that concept, I'm also teaching you how to **switch sensory systems** on people as you go, again causing a greater *openness of their mind* to receive your ideas and suggestions. You're going to be able to do this without a second thought if you practice what I'm telling you to do.

You started with the **visual** sense, now do this same exercise starting with two **auditory** words and ending with one **kinesthetic**, and finally starting with two **kinesthetic**, but for those sentences you're going to end with one **visual**.

This is a very powerful exercise. I'm only asking for thirty sentences here. It's not that many. However, it's a powerful exercise and it does take time, so give it the time it takes so you can really do it well.

CHAPTER NINE

"Brain Fade"

I'm going to tell you here what you're going to experience. I almost don't care how good you are at this. I don't care if you've heard this before. I don't care how good you are. The odds are, if you do this, if you do it right, just like I'm telling you, you're going to get to the point where you have real *brain fade*. What do I mean by that? You're going to get to the point of just literally, it's going to be *unbelievable* is what's going to happen.

Your brain will just throw up its hands and say, "I give up, I don't get any of this." That's fine. When that happens, *stop*. And come back and do it again a few hours later if you're feeling more clearheaded. As quickly as you feel clear-headed again, come and do it again. When you hit that wall again, that same *brain fade*, push through it, just a little bit, see if you can spend another two or three minutes pushing through it, and then *stop*.

I'm telling you how to *break through* this. Please understand, I'm giving you these exercises to **create** this wall. Because when you **reach** it and **break through it** you're going to be *far superior as a persuader* than you are today. And you're going to *keep* reaching a wall and you're going to *know how* to break through it.

It's profound. When you reach it, push two or three minutes through it, try to see if you can get through the wall and then *stop* and come back the next day or hours later after you're much more clear, usually it will take till the next day. Usually you'll have to *sleep* on what you did. And pretty soon, after doing this a couple of times, you'll sit down to start the work again and you'll say, "**I get it**. Why was this hard?" That is how you'll know *you broke through the wall*. And I'm giving you exercises difficult enough in increased gradience that you will *reach* this wall and probably just reading about it you're reaching the wall.

Perfect. Take a break. It's *not meant* to be digested in one fell swoop. So stop. When you're feeling more clear-headed, do the exercise, do it again, do it again and keep doing it. And you're going to *get it* very quickly. By the time you've completed it and you've done it well, you'll get it.

Most of the people that teach this, teach it *the other way around*. Now I'm going to tell you how most people start off learning this, because you've already learned it *a much superior way*. I want you now to start *listening* as you talk to people for the **sensory words** they use most and I want you to **use back** the *same* sensory system of words that *they're* using as you talk with them.

For example, "**Listen** as I **tell** you how to **see** the direction we're heading **clearly**." Two **auditory**. Two **visual**. You might say, "I **hear** exactly what you're **telling** me to do, Kenrick, and it's exciting for me as I **visualize** our future that it's becoming so much **clearer** how I'm able to use this to my advantage as a persuader."

You're going to track back *exactly* what you're hearing from others. You can even use *their exact words*, that way you know for sure you're in their **sensory system**. However, if you do that *too* much you're going to sound silly and insincere.

In this exercise, as you're listening to people, I want you to then begin experimenting with the following: try **repeating back** two of their words, two of their **sensory words** and then **shifting** to a *new* sense. In particular, I want you to try **shifting** either to **kinesthetic** or **visual** and watch how it throws them into a little bit of an *altered state* just a bit. What do I mean by an *altered state*? Well they *slow down*, or they *pause* a little, or they look a little *unclear*, not as in, "What are you saying, stupid?" Not like that, but as in, "Yeah." Like they sort of *relax* a little. So, don't do it too much because they're going to look at you like you're crazy but just occasionally, throw something like this in and just start to *become aware of what happens*. This will make them more *receptive* to what you're saying as you perfect it.

There's a lot more to doing this well, but this is a start and we'll be covering more and more ways to do it powerfully as we continue on. I just want to introduce this concept so you begin to get it. This is a very powerful way to learn it. By working with the skill, you're going to experience it increasing in your life much more powerfully than if you just read me writing about it. I can do this stuff all day long, but I want *you* to be able to do it all day long.

BOOK FIVE

LEARNING TO LEAD

INTRODUCTION

An Introduction You'll Want To Come Back To

Welcome to **Book Five** of **Kenrick Cleveland's Persuasion Force**. In this book, we'll be covering **verbal pacing and leading**.

If you've been working your way through this series of books, you're really making tremendous progress in becoming a **master persuader**. In just this short period of time, look at all that we've covered. You've learned how to *gain rapport*, how to *direct your message*, how to *elicit your prospect's criteria*, how to *change their criteria* making you the *only solution*, how to know whether to use the *carrot* or the *boot* in motivating your customer to buy, how to use the *five senses* to your advantage, and so much more besides.

All this and we're only just beginning Book Five. That really says a lot. You are really making tremendous progress towards becoming a **master persuader**. And I hope you're really *enjoying* the journey. I think you'll always be happy that you did, and that you're realizing that **mastering persuasion is a lifetime journey**. It's not something that you *accomplish* and then go, "Well, now that I am a master persuader, let me look back on what I did. Good thing I chose to do it. I have made tremendous money as a result and helped myself. . ."

Sure, you'll say those things, but *it's always a journey*. I always look to *master even further* these skills, so, I'm really glad you're reading this book and I want to thank you for being with me in this project. This truly is a *groundbreaking* set of books.

With that, I want you to stop a moment and begin to think about a few things. I have listed a lot of what you've been learning up to this point. And as you think about what you've been learning, you probably have a sense that **you would like to actually know how to do what we've talked about even better**. And you will.

In fact, thinking about that with me now will enable you to begin to gain some *perspective* on the way in which, not only I'm teaching this, but you're *learning* it. You're probably beginning to *see a bigger picture* and maybe you don't have all the pieces filled in but you can probably begin to imagine what life will be like as a result of being able to implement these skills.

As you imagine that, just enjoy thinking about what you've learned so far. The tremendous amount of information that has been conveyed to you. Information that you're *wrestling* with, *grappling* with, and *working* to make your own.

And remember that a lot of *making this your own* doesn't have to be wrestling or grappling at all, it can just be relaxing. So I want to encourage you just to relax. And enjoy allowing your other-than-conscious mind to *integrate* these skills for you.

It's a lot of fun. And it's really something that will last your entire lifetime. You'll continue to be able to take this with you and when you least expect it, up will pop my voice into your mind suggesting another way that you can use these skills profoundly to help yourself.

Let's proceed with this book's lesson and I'd like you to review this introduction at the end of this book, to come back to it. There's a *reason* that I'm telling you to do that right now. Okay?

And I know that you'll know what that is by the time we finish. I want you to **come back and review** what we've just done up to this point after you finish the book. Will you remember to do that? I hope so.

CHAPTER ONE

Pacing and Leading: Definitions

Let's move on to talk about **verbal pacing and leading**.

This, you are going to love. This is just about one of my most *favorite* of all **persuasion patterns**. I'm teaching it to you a little earlier than I thought I might, but I wanted to give you something really *profound* to sink your teeth into here as we enter **Book Five**, and a way to have **a pattern** that you can use **to help integrate and organize all the *other* patterns** that are going to be coming. Almost every pattern that you're going to be learning can be *integrated* into and around and through **verbal pacing and leading**. This is an incredible pattern.

We're going to go through some simple *definitions*. I'm going to make this really easy for you to understand, go through some good examples of this, and I think, as I do those things, you'll begin to figure out *exactly what this is and how to use it in your life*. If you're reading along with this while listening to the **audiobook**, as I recommend you should, you'll see that I've given *clear definitions* and *clear examples*. Each time you see one of these, you know how they say when you read, don't subvocalize, but this time, I want you to **subvocalize**. So as you read it, I want you to **subvocalize** right along with what you hear me reading. And I want you to imagine it's **you** saying this. And further, I want you to imagine that **you feel really good saying it**.

You're going to run it through your **filters of integrity**, obviously, but I want you to just *feel really good*. Notice how **this kind of pattern creates a flow**, not only in your mind, but in the mind of the *listener* even more importantly.

Let's start with the *definition* of **pacing**, and **pacing** is **talking about either what is true or what is verifiable in a person's ongoing sensory experience**. It can also be talking about what is **commonly accepted as true**. For example, if I said, a doorway leads in or out of a home. Okay.

That's *commonly accepted as true*, isn't it? Pretty much we all have that experience and I'm not asking you to take any leap of faith. In fact, probably as I said that, you went, yeah, okay. *True*.

Just to kind of put perspective on this, talking about *what's commonly accepted as true* is also called **using truisms**. **Pacing** then, more concisely is talking about **what's true and verifiable in a person's ongoing sensory experience**. For example, right now you're reading my words, and perhaps also listening to my voice via the audiobook. You're breathing. And you are thinking about all kinds of things, perhaps, hopefully at least what I'm saying as well. Maybe because I'm calling attention to your thoughts, what I'm saying is rising to the surface, meaning you're diverting more of your attention to me at this moment.

As you begin to pay more attention to what it is you're reading, you're probably beginning to also question, "Okay, and what do I *do* with this? How do I *use* it?" And that would be very appropriate.

Let's talk about the other side. The one side is **pacing**. And it uses statements that are **true and verifiable in a person's ongoing sensory experience**, like I just did with you. Those were **pacing** statements that you can **verify** right this second as **true**. You're *breathing*, right? And you're *reading* these words, or *listening* to them, right? Therefore, it's **true**. It's **verifiable**. That's what I mean by **verifiable in your ongoing experience**.

And/or you're using **truisms**. Meaning, it isn't *necessarily* verifiable *right this second* in your ongoing experience, but it's still **true** nonetheless.

For example, unless you're walking in or out of your home *right now*, then maybe you can't verify in your **sensory experience** *at this moment* that a door is used to go in and out of your home. But in your *memory*, in your *mind*, you sure as heck have this **experience**. All of us do. That would be called a **truism**.

Let's go to the other side: **leading**. **Leading is talking about what you *want* the other person to *believe* that as yet is *not* established as *true*.**

It's quite simple. **Pacing** is talking about things that are **true** and **verifiable** in a person's ongoing sensory experience or talking about things that are commonly accepted as true, which are **truisms**, and **leading** is talking about what you **want** the other person to **believe** that **as yet is not** established as **true**.

So for example, as I speak there is a **pace**. I just said, "As I speak," you can tell that I'm speaking (on Audiobook; or writing in e-book); it's **true** and **verifiable** in your ongoing sensory **experience**. And you think about *other times* that you've heard me talk or read my writing. That's a **truism**. You've heard me talk or read my writing *at other times*. At this point in time, in this fifth book in this series, I know for sure that's a *fact*.

If you're doing the recommended practice and listening to the Audiobook while reading the e-book along with it, you probably can remember *a specific tone* that I was using when I spoke. Maybe you've associated *a tone in my voice* as one that is helpful to you to really learn quickly and if you were to think about what that *feels* like and *attach it even stronger* to my voice right now, you'd begin to *feel a sense of comfort*, would you not? Knowing that as I speak, you're *learning at even faster rates* than you might otherwise if you were talking with someone who didn't know how to use these skills.

I just **did** what I'm talking about **teaching you to do** here. And I've been doing it since you began reading or listening to this book (and this book in particular *really benefits* from that pro-tip at the beginning, to listen to the Audiobook *at the same time* as you read the e-book, for maximum good effect). As I do it I want you to *pay close attention* and I'm going to *suggest* to you that you're probably *feeling a particular way.* I'm going to tell you what that is in a minute, but I don't want to tell you because I actually want to build a little *response potential* on it. If you haven't thought it through yet, you'll go, "Ahhhh. That's what I was feeling," in a moment when I tell it to you, okay?

CHAPTER TWO

The Format To Follow

Leading. Talking about **what you want the other person to believe that as yet is not established as true**. I'm going to give you here the **verbal pacing and leading format** and here it is.

Pace, pace, pace, lead, pace, pace, lead, pace, lead, lead, lead, lead, indefinitely until . ..*what*? Well, I'll tell you in a second.

Alright. So, there's a little bit more to this format than just that and let me explain what it is. When I say, "*Pace, pace, pace, lead*," what are the paces? Again, they're going to be something that's **true** and **verifiable** in your **ongoing sensory experience**, or a **truism**.

Most likely you have a television in your home, or certainly you know people that do. That would be a **truism**. If you're not watching your TV right at this minute, then you *don't* have *sensory experience* to know that, to verify it right this second, but you *know* that you have one or you *know* that there are many people near you that have one.

So there's the **pace**. The **lead** is, now I'm going to *use **three** of those paces*, first of all, actually. You know, since I brought up the subject of televisions, we often have a favorite show that we really enjoy, that we like a lot, you probably have one too. Each season that the show is new, you probably look forward to seeing it again and having it come out. And maybe there's a show that you're hoping will come out in this next season that you can identify in your mind right now.

Well, I've just *done* that. I've just *done* **pacing** and I just *did* a **lead**. Before I did those things, you weren't thinking of television and you weren't thinking of a show you wanted to see, you were thinking of what I was talking about.

And yet, when I begin **pacing** and **leading** your mind *went right there* and with *how* much resistance? That's right. *None.* Interesting, isn't it?

The format **pace, pace, pace, lead**, then goes to the *next step* which is **pace, pace, lead**, but . . . and this is a *big* but . . . in that *next step* where it begins with a **pace**, the **lead** from the *previous step* becomes the **pace** of the *next step* and *that's what you must hold in mind*. So as you look at the formula, you'll see it says, '**pace, pace, pace, lead**,' then it says, '**pace, pace, lead**', but this first new 'pace' is a *reiteration* that the **lead** that you *wanted someone to believe* is **now true**.

Then you're therefore *stating a truth combined with another truth,* which is a **pace**, and then you're **leading** again towards where you want them to go. But if you notice the *third step*, it says, '**pace, lead**.' Well, what's the **pace**? The **pace** should be a *reaffirmation* that the **lead** that you just said is **now true**. In other words, it's gone from a *future event* to something that's *already happening*.

And then you **lead** again to another **lead**. And then you just keep right on going. The *fourth step* is, '**lead, lead, lead, lead**'. And my question to you is, *until what?* Right. Until they *buy*. Until you get what you want. Or, until **rapport** is broken. At which point you must go back to **pacing**. That's the basic rule for all of this.

That's how **verbal pacing and leading** works. It is profound, to say the least.

CHAPTER THREE

Dissecting An Example

Let's go to an example.

Here we go: As you sit there, reading this information or listening to me read it, letting your eyes follow each word, you can begin to discover how this information will allow you to increase your persuasion power. And as you think about how that might happen, and listen to what those ideas are inside your own thoughts, you may find yourself getting excited at how much easier this makes the process of convincing someone to do what you want.

In fact, feeling that excitement beginning to build now causes you to begin to want to practice to perfect this technique. The technique is strong enough to get people to go along with whatever you say, so much so, that utilizing it will dramatically increase your sales. This also establishes your credibility and furthers the rapport you were building.

Alright. That's the example. Now, I want you to *review* this example and *pick out* the **paces** and **leads**. Okay?

So the first one, '*As you sit there.*' What is that? Well, let's assume you're sitting. If you're not then it doesn't qualify, does it? But if I were saying this to you I would *know* you're sitting. If I asked you to read along with me I would *know* you're reading. So, assuming you're sitting and reading, all this works, right?

What is '*as you sit there*'? That's a **pace**. '*(R)eading this information.*' What's that? Well, if you're *doing* it, it's a **pace**, right? '*(L)etting your eyes follow each word.*' Well, if you're reading it, I guess that's what you're *doing* pretty much, right? What would that be? Correct. A **pace**. So there's **three paces**, right? '*You can begin to discover.*' Now when does that happen? Begin, I guess, now, to discover, like it's present heading towards the future, '*how this information will allow you to increase your persuasion power.*'

Is it a *fact* that you will discover how you can increase your persuasion power? Well, yeah you've bought the book so I guess in a way it is, but I mean, *really*, it's not. That's a **lead**. You see what I mean? The *difference* between **true** and **verifiable** and this is *significant*. So I'm saying to you that there's a **relationship** between sitting, reading, and letting your eyes follow each word and beginning to discover how this will allow you to increase your persuasion power.

There's also a *cause and effect* going on there. Don't worry about that. We'll get into that kind of stuff later.

There is the **lead**. The **lead** is that you'll begin to discover.

Let's go to the next sentence, '*And as you think about how that might happen. . .*' Ohhh. What just happened? Well. . .what just happened is, I took the **lead** '*begin to discover*' and *turned it into* a **pace**. '*And as you think about how that might happen*'. So now, instead of '*You'll begin now to discover*,' I guess some time in the *future*, now it's *already happening*, it's already **true**. You see how that's a subtle but profound *shift*?

So, '*And as you think about how that might happen. . .*' That's a **pace**. '*And listen to what those ideas are inside your own thoughts. . .*' Well, if you're thinking about how that will happen then there will be ideas you could listen to, again a **pace**. '*You may find yourself getting excited at how much easier this makes the process of convincing someone to do what you want.*' What's that? That's a **lead**. Isn't that cool? You see what I'm doing?

Now, what are we going to *do* with that **lead**? We're going to **turn it back into a pace**, aren't we? '*In fact, feeling that excitement beginning to build now . . .*' So what did I just say? I said, '*As you think about how that might happen, you may find yourself getting excited. . .*' Well *now* I'm saying that it's *already happening*. In fact, feeling that excitement, you're *already doing it*, '*beginning to build now.*' See, I'm **pacing** again. '*Causes you*', to what? Here I'm again using a **causal linkage statement** with the word *causes*. '*Causes you to want to begin to practice to perfect this technique.*' What's that? A **lead**. Why? Because it *didn't exist* just a moment ago, not until I *suggested* it.

My *suggestion* makes it a **lead**.

I am now in the process of the final stretch in which I'm just going to **lead**. '*The technique is strong enough to get people to go along with whatever you say, so much so that utilizing it will dramatically increase your sales.*' **Lead, lead, lead**. '*This also establishes your credibility,*' **lead,** '*and furthers the rapport you were building,*' **lead, lead, lead, lead, lead**.

Now, I want you just to sit back and read this, listening along with me reading it simultaneously in the Audiobook if possible, but just kind of **relax** as you do it, alright? And *just let my words flow* as they would naturally if I were saying this to you, okay? I want you to **experience** this now, now that I've torn it apart, let's go back and get the **experience** of *what this is like*.

'As you sit there, reading this information or listening to me read it, letting your eyes follow each word, you can begin to discover how this information will allow you to increase your persuasion power. And as you think about how that might happen, and listen to what those ideas are inside your own thoughts, you may find yourself getting excited at how much easier this makes the process of convincing someone to do what you want.

'In fact, feeling that excitement beginning to build now causes you to begin to want to practice to perfect this technique. The technique is strong enough to get people to go along with whatever you say, so much so, that utilizing it will dramatically increase your sales. This also establishes your credibility and furthers the rapport you were building.'

CHAPTER FOUR

Applying The Pattern In Other Ways

Here's a question. Could this be modified slightly and used all over the place? Absolutely. Maybe you've sent someone a letter about a conversation you had with them. Maybe you had a sales call and you couldn't close it right then and there and so you sent them a letter. And the letter says: *"Dear Mr. Smith, Thank you so much for spending a little bit if time with me yesterday. I really enjoyed talking with you. And it dawned on me that as you sit there reading this letter, letting your eyes follow each word that I've written, you can begin to discover how what we talked about will allow you to increase the profits that you are perceiving in your company. And as you think about how that might happen and listen to what those ideas are inside your own thoughts, you may find yourself getting excited at how much easier working with me makes the process of building profit into your company quickly. In fact, feeling that excitement beginning to build now causes you to want to get back together again and to implement my strategies and ideas. My strategies and ideas are strong enough to get profit to increase quickly. So much so that utilizing them will increase your sales, they will make your marketing more effective and this also gives you a greater profit margin all the way around. It makes sense to me that we get back together at your earliest convenience. I will be calling you in the next 24 hours to schedule a time. And if you can't wait, and you need to reach me immediately to set a time up, then feel free to call my assistant at this number. Looking forward to talking to you soon."*

Now, could that *work*? Sure. How about an *infomercial*? How about if I were selling my stuff on an infomercial.

"As you sit there watching this program, listening to each word that I say, you can begin to discover how this information will allow you to increase your persuasion power. And as you think about how that might happen and listen to what those ideas are inside your own thoughts you may find yourself getting excited at how much easier these concepts that I'm sharing with you here on this show makes the process of convincing someone to do what you want. In fact, feeling that excitement beginning to build now causes you to want to begin to practice to perfect the techniques I'm talking about. To get them into your home so you can study them for yourself. These techniques are strong enough to get people to go along with whatever you say, so much so that utilizing them will dramatically increase your sales and that's why you're watching this program, isn't it?"

Wow. Pretty good, huh? Now, let me point out something else. Another thing to notice in the above example is how it moves someone from the *external environment* to the *internal world of their mind*. Read it again and see if you can determine how it does that.

CHAPTER FIVE

Shifting From External To Internal

Hopefully you've done that and I'm going to go over this with you.

'As you sit there. . .' What are we talking about? Are we talking about his thoughts yet? Or her thoughts? No. We're talking about external things, aren't we? *'. . .(R)eading this information. . .'* Are we talking about the person's thoughts? No. What are we talking about? Well, we're just talking about what's going on in their external environment.

'. . .(L)etting your eyes follow each word. . ' Now we're starting to kind of go a little bit internal, but not much. *'. . .you can begin to discover how this information will allow you to increase your persuasion power.'* What is the process of discovery? Is that an internal process or an external process? Ahhh. . . .that's internal, isn't it?

So what's happening is, you start off talking about the *external world* around them and you begin to **shift** them to the *internal world of their thinking.*

'As you think about how that might happen,' now what have I done? I've now directly **shifted** them internal. Here I am shifting them to their internal thoughts, in fact, I say, *'. . . and listen to what those ideas are inside your own thoughts. . .'* My goodness, I'm telling them, in essence, what? That **they are doing exactly what I'm saying.** These words are **causing them to discover** how this information will allow them to increase their persuasion power and to **think** about how that might happen and as they do to **think** about what those ideas are. Already they're supposed to be **having these ideas.** Well, *why* will they have them? Because I *told* them to. Because it's a *suggestion.* It's a **lead.** And it's *predicated upon*, or follows, a **pace.**

Already their mind went, "Yup. Yup. Yup." You see? So that's how this has such **power**, the power of this is now we're **shifting** them to their *internal world* and as I said to them here, *'. . .think about how that might happen and listen to what those ideas are inside your own thoughts.'* Well now *whose* idea is this? *Mine* or *theirs?* Well if it's inside their own thoughts, then *they're* starting to take ownership for *my* words. It's as if **my words are literally guiding their thoughts.** Does that make sense?

This is profound. By the way, I've never heard anyone describe it like this, so I'm showing you literally *the inside working of what makes this work.* And you're going to be thrilled as you begin to implement it in all that you do. I'm telling you, this is one of those **knock out punches.** This is one of the money punches. This is one of the money techniques that you'll begin implementing more and more and more and more effectively as you go on, because I'm going to keep *building* on this process of **pacing** and **leading** as we go throughout.

So now it's *their* idea and now I'm going to tell them how to even go *further* inside their own head to tell them, *'You may find yourself getting excited,'* blah, blah, blah, blah, blah, what I want them to be excited about. Now it's *their* idea.

And then I put it into there deeper, *'in fact, feeling that excitement beginning to build now.'* What's happening? I'm really **taking control of their thoughts** and I'm going to tell you more about that in a minute.

And I then just start **leading** them. But I want you to see how I am **moving someone from the external world, to the internal world**.

CHAPTER SIX

An Unconscious 'Yes Set'

One of the reasons that makes this technique so powerful is that it uses **an unconscious 'yes set'**. Alright, so if it uses an *unconscious* 'yes set', what's a plain old 'yes set'?

A '**yes set**' is where a person is *compelled to say yes* to a question you ask because it's pretty much *only answerable with a yes*. But it gets them **in the habit of agreeing with you**. This is like the old-fashioned, manipulative, con-artistry like sales process that sounds something like this:
"Mrs. Smith?"
"Yes."
"Mrs. Smith, my records indicate that you're the owner of the XYZ business, is that correct?"
"Yes."
"Mrs. Smith, I understand that you've been in business here for five years. Is that right?"
"Yes."
"Well, Mrs. Smith, if I can show you a way to save money on your phone bill and your phone system each and every month and I can do it without taking hardly any time of yours at all and none once the process is started, you would be interested in taking a look at it, wouldn't you?"

"Uhhhhh .. . No."

But what *happens* there? Well, what happens is, that you're trying to **box them into a corner**. But I'll hold off on that for now and go to what the **unconscious 'yes set'** is.

The **unconscious 'yes set'** in *contrast* to the conscious, manipulative 'yes set' is where a person is *compelled* to **say yes inside their mind**. It's a big difference.

Let me give you a good example of this. This is more an example of just a '**yes set**' period. It is the *disgusting* use of this kind of skill and it disgusts me, but it's a good example just to show you the power of it.

There's a show that I love to hate. Maybe some of you do too, it's called '*Cops*'. I don't know if they have that outside the U.S., but basically it's a show of cops all around the country, of police forces, that are stopping people and going throughout their shift, arresting people, basically, and it's live, I mean, it's not transmitted live, it's shown at a later point after it was recorded, but I mean it was *recorded* live, on the spot, and you can see exactly what takes place and hear exactly what takes place as they go through their arrests and things like that.

Let me give you a very typical example of what they do. I call this the, '**no set**' and it's *identical* to the '**yes set**' just in reverse. Same effect though. This is every incident on the show of '*Cops*'. I'm going to boil down *every single incident* to this. Pretty much. All driving incidences anyway.

So here's what happens. The scene begins with a cop driving down the road and in front of him is a car. And the car may be driving a bit erratically. The cop radios in he's going to pull them over, he pulls them over, the cop approaches the car cautiously, where the person in the car then begins berating the cop or saying some excuse and basically looking a bit nuts or high or drunk or something. And so the cop says, "*Okay. Well, listen, do you have your driver's license and registration please?*" Generally speaking they do and they find it and they give it to the police officer.

The cop already knows exactly what he's going to do and it goes like this. I just hate this. The cop says, "*Okay. Would you please get out of your car for me?*" And the person says, "*Alright.*" So that at this point they're realizing there's probably going to be trouble, so they try to be cooperative.

Now the cop says, "*Let me ask, because I've asked you to get out, I need to search you here. You don't have any dangerous weapons on you do you? You don't have any knives? You don't have any needles? You don't have any explosives of any kind? You don't have anything like that, do you?*" "*No. No, I don't.*"

And so the cop searches him. And he says, "*Now, I'm going to ask you to sit over here on the curb for a minute. You don't have any dangerous weapons in the car, do you? You don't have any explosives or guns or drugs or anything like that, right?*" "*No, no, no. Not at all.*"

"*Okay, so you don't mind if I search you, do you?*" "*No. Go ahead.*" Idiot. And so now the cop goes and searches the car and sure enough they come out with a bag of something, heroin, coke, crack, pot, something. **Every single time**. Oh my goodness. At this point it's so predictable, it cracks me up and by the same token I think to myself, "What idiots!" First of all, here they are on the receiving end of the '**no set**' or the '**yes set**', however you want to look at it.

The cop says, "*You don't have anything illegal on you, do you?*" And then they usually kind of go to the extreme. "*You don't have any guns or explosives or needles?*" And the answer to that question is, "**No.**"

Now, what could the person do *instead*? "*I reserve my right to **remain silent**. Thank you for informing me of that in advance.*" If the cop did or didn't, doesn't make any difference.

"*Well, I'm going to search you and I need to know if you have anything on you.*" "*Well, I reserve my right to remain silent. I choose **not to speak**.*"

Okay. Now what? Now the cop goes on. "*Well, you don't have anything illegal in your car, do you? You don't have any explosives or guns or this or that?*"

"*I'm not speaking. I'm not speaking.*"

"*Okay. You don't mind if I search you, do you?*" "**Yes**, *I do. I absolutely mind that you search my car.*" "*Well, I'll just go get a warrant.*" "*Knock yourself out. Go get a warrant. But before you do, I'll ask you this question. What **articulable evidence** do you have that gives you **probable cause** to search my car? And, I caution you that my driving erratic does **not** give you a right to search my* *car. It may give you probable cause to give me a breath test or a blood alcohol test or a drug test. But it does **not** give you the right to search my car and I maintain all of my rights.*"

Now would that change the event of these shows? Oh heck yes. Cops are **done** right there. They **cannot proceed**, at least in the U.S. they're basically screwed. So how do they *trick* people, who know good and well that their car is full of drugs, or full of weapons, or full of whatever they're trying to get away with, how do they *trick* these people into saying, "*Yes, you can search my car*"?

It's through this **profound persuasion technique** that works absolute wonders even in situations like this. Can you believe it? Can you believe it?

Even when a person *knows* they're wrong and guilty, they *still* fall victim of this pattern because it has such profound abilities to persuade.

I believe it also *plays into a desire of the person being searched* that says, "Hey, if I agree to do this maybe the cop won't do it . . . he'll say, oh the guy's cooperating, I'll just let him go."

Fat chance.

So that's a good example of how powerful this pattern is. Now, one of the main reasons to use **verbal pacing and leading** is that it automatically sets up an **unconscious 'yes set'**. And this is *very desirable* to be able to do to become a master persuader. You want to *easily* be able to do this any time and every time you want, at the drop of a hat. And you *will* with just a little bit of practice.

CHAPTER SEVEN

Zoning Out

And here's an even *bigger* power behind this strategy. You're going to really be blown away with this. This strategy **covertly encourages your prospect to *stop thinking* and become *dependent* on your words to guide their thoughts**.

A little bit ago I asked you to just kind of *sit back and relax* and let me do that **pattern** again to you, let me read you the example on the audiobook, or read it yourself in the e-book. How did you *feel*? Well I'll bet you, your brain began to *shift into slow* and it just *listened* or *observed the words*, like a lullaby. **Verbal pacing and leading** begins to have a **rhythm** to it and that **rhythm** *lullabies* the brain and because you're taking a **pace** and turning it into a **lead** and then using that **lead** as the next **pace**, and you do that a few times, you get the person's brain into the mode of *simply listening to your words to have their next thought.*

Yes. It really *is* this powerful and it really *does* do exactly this. Each **pace** that your prospect says **yes** to inside their mind makes them *more willing* to accept your next **lead**. And pretty soon, *you're thinking for them*.

Did you notice when I did this **pattern** to you that you got *zoned out* a little bit? Well, if so, you're just like everybody else. This pattern does zone people out. So, don't let them zone too far. However there's tremendous power in zoning them out a little bit. But if they *become aware* that they're zoned out, it'll backfire.

What do we do to keep it from backfiring? Let me point out exactly what to do, let me have your full attention for a minute. Let me show you exactly what to do, okay? Alright. *That's* what you do. Notice how I just changed the tone of my speech if you were listening with the Audiobook? Or if you were just reading in the e-book, notice how I just **redirected your attention really strongly** to me for a minute? In other words, I asked you, in essence, without saying it in so many words, I said, "Quit being zoned out and listen to me." That's basically what I just did.

If I were talking to you about something that I wanted to *sell* you, maybe I'm a realtor, a financial adviser, anything like that, and I'm sitting there, I might say to you, "Look, let me just show you something here," and then point to papers in front of you. Or say, "Now, think back about what you said. You told me you wanted to accomplish . . ." then **name their criteria**, name their criteria, name their criteria. Notice how with this particular strategy that I'm using, and you're pointing to a paper, you're going to begin to have even more of what you want.

If you're not already reading while listening to the Audiobook, be sure to access the app and listen to it as soon as you're able, so you can **hear my tone begin to change**. Hear my **pacing** begin to get **rhythmic**. Now I'm being obvious so that you'll hear it but . . . hear what I'm doing? When we first started, I had you begin practicing with a *metronome*. Now you're beginning to understand why.

As you can tell, the **pattern** is really powerful. Again, please use this with *integrity*. Yes, you can zone people right through the floor and get them to follow you right off a cliff. Is that the way to use it? No. Use it in a way that **both parties win**. I almost want to apologize for bringing this up so much but I'm not going to because for those of you that don't need a reminder, you probably appreciate the fact that I'm reminding everybody. And for those of you that need a reminder, well, you'll appreciate the fact that you've heard this explained this well and in a way that will continue to enforce and reinforce inside your mind that using this with *integrity* is important because this has huge power to influence.

CHAPTER EIGHT

Keeping It Smooth: Why The Old-Fashioned 'Yes Set' Doesn't Work

Let's talk about the old-fashioned, ineffective, manipulative, repulsive, '**yes set**'. And here I've just listed one that I was directly trained, I was directly trained on this. This is exactly word-for-word what I learned to say when I was much, much, much younger.

Salesperson to prospect: Mr. Smith?

Prospect: Yes.

Sales person: Mr. John Smith?

Prospect: Yes.

Salesperson: Thank you, Mr. Smith. My records indicate that you're the vice-president of purchasing. Is that right?

Prospect: Yes.

Salesperson: Great. May I ask you a question?

Prospect: Of course, yes.

Salesperson: If I can show you a way to save costs on your inventory, you would be interested in taking a look, wouldn't you?

That just sounds like *nails on a chalkboard* to me. And I hope it does to you. What are the '*yeses*' here? Let's just identify them just in case they aren't bluntly and painfully obvious.

First question. *Mr. Smith?* What are we going to get there? *Yup.* And then we put the first name in there so we can get them to say *yes* again. *Mr. John Smith?* Yes. Thank you, Mr. Smith. My records indicate that you're the vice-president of purchasing. *Is that right?* Well of course you *know* he's the vice-president of purchasing so that's the title you're using. Yes.

Salesperson: Great. *May I ask you a question?* You mean *another* one? The prospect's going to go, "Yes." Now after *yes, yes, yes*, the salesperson throws the curve, doesn't he. Here comes the curve ball. "*If I can show you a way to save costs on your inventory, you would be interested in taking a look, wouldn't you?*"

Even if you could trick someone these days into saying yes, would you feel good about yourself doing that? Man, I wouldn't. I would shut someone down so fast that did this to me it'd make your head swim.

Believe it or not, this is *still* being taught out there in old-fashioned sales training. I can't get over it, but it is. And if you're using this, **Stop**! Immediately. And shift to what I'm teaching you. It's so elegant. It's so powerful. Nobody can catch you, not in a million years, not even people trained in this stuff. You'd have to be really clumsy to get caught, even by people that are trained in it. That is where the beauty is. Yes, *I'll* catch you if you do it to *me*, but nonetheless. I'd have to be alert for you doing it. If you were real smooth at it . . . Actually, if you started putting three **paces** together with a **lead**, it'd probably alert me.

I can tell you 99.9% of the population, it would go right by.

Verbal pacing and leading, as I'm teaching you, does what they *hope* this old-fashioned, ineffective, manipulative, '**yes set**' would do. Only it does it *effectively* and *elegantly* and with *far greater power* than the old way ever hoped to be able to use.

The old way attempts to *corner* the prospect and it doesn't feel good. This way, it just feels good. It feels comfortable. It feels kind. It doesn't feel manipulative, like a ploy is being used. It just feels like you've put someone into a grease shoot and it's just easier to slide down. All the way, into the zone. No. I'm just kidding. Just playing with you.

By the way, you can do that, any time you want, that's a **sentence structure ambiguity** there, you might say, "*You know, it's useful to begin to have a particular feeling of tremendous, positive good feelings, as you think about what we've been talking about. Because, look, what you're hearing is helping you and you know that to be true. It's not even something I have to say, but sitting there, listening to what I'm telling you today, thinking about these things in your own mind, the way you will, can absolutely encourage you to see light maybe where you hadn't seen it before. And seeing that light can enable you to begin to realize there's more there than you've ever thought there was before. And what's there can be used by you now to help you get ahead. So I'm really excited that we're going through this together.*"

See, I'm doing it left and right and now I'm sure you're catching me. That's my hope.

CHAPTER NINE

Pacing Statements

Let's get down to the nitty and the gritty. These are statements that qualify as **pacing statements**.

"*You are reading this.*" Now that is **true** since you are reading this, right? Or, "*You're sitting there,*" or, "*You're standing there,*" or, "**You're there.**" It doesn't have to even be all that creative folks. "*You can feel the temperature around you.*"

"*On the news last night ...*" Now is that **true** and **verifiable**? No. Probably not. However, will they *argue* with you? Well, probably not. You're **quoting a trustworthy source**. "*On CNN last night, they said ...*" you see? So now you're talking about something that's **generally accepted as true and verifiable**.

"*As you participate in this learning experience. . .*" That's **probably true** for you, right? "*Before I wrote this down for you I was thinking. . .*" Now, how can you argue with the fact that I was thinking? Or that I wrote this down for you if you're now reading it?

So, now what I want you to do is to **write three of your own pacing statements**. And yes, your brain will probably run crazy at this point going, "Wow. I don't need to just write three, I could write three hundred." Yes, you sure can, and it's really easy. "*I was thinking just a moment ago. . .*" Is that a **pace**? You bet. "*On my way in here today. . .*" **Pace**. "*As I walked through the door of your office. . .*" **Pace**. "*As you sat in that chair today looking where your eyes focused next. . .*" **Pace, pace**.

See. You can literally structure almost *anything* to be a **pace**, do you understand? It's very simple. I want you to write three of them right now. So stop reading and write three of your own, or else continue on if you're not in a position to be able to write, but if you can, just stop and write three of your own so you have it written down right there for you.

Each of what you've written needs to be **true** or **commonly accepted as true** and you should now have three or thirty **paces** there for you to look at.

CHAPTER TEN

Leading Statements

Leads are *anything that you want people to believe*. So here are some examples of things that could be considered **leads**. "*You are excited about this information.*" Well, how do you *know* they're excited? This is what you *want* them to be, right? Right. So it's a **lead**. "*You are becoming committed to learning more about this.*" Really? Well, that's a **lead**. That's what you *want* them to do. That's why it's a **lead**, it's not an **established fact** or a **commonly accepted truth**, like a **truism**.

"*Verbal pacing and leading makes persuasion easier.*" I *want* you to *believe* that. It's also **true**, by the way. "*Verbal pacing and leading creates a lullaby type of effect.*" Now since I *already told* you that, it's now more of a **pace**. However, if I *hadn't* said that you could see how this would be a **lead**. "*This training will have ongoing benefits that you haven't even become aware of yet.*" What a great thing to install in somebody's mind, right? And could you do the same thing for everything that you sell? Or everything that you want to influence someone to do? You bet!

So now I want you to write three things that would be considered **leading statements**. These would be things *you want someone to believe* but you're probably going to state it in the *present tense*. So it would be something like, "*You are feeling convinced that this is absolutely right for you.*" Or, "*You're getting ready to act on your belief that this is going to create exactly what you need and want.*" Or, "*You're going to act on your belief that you've already begun to experience what it is you hoped to be able to experience and probably much faster than you thought you would as a result of talking with me today.*"

Anything like that is a **lead**. And by the way, the last one was rather sophisticated. Pull that one apart. Okay? So, stop now and write three of your own **leading statements** if you would.

CHAPTER ELEVEN

Understanding The Difference

Let me ask you *what's the difference?* Can you begin to see the *difference* between **pacing** and **leading**? So **pacing** statements are statements that are **true**. The listener cannot take exception to them. That's what makes them so powerful for our purposes. And to expand on that a little bit, think of it this way, **pacing** statements are either **true** and **verifiable** in *their ongoing sensory experience*, meaning *they can tell right then and there* that they're true, or they're *commonly accepted as true*, in the form of **truisms**.

Either way, here's the deal. **Pacing** statements create an **unconscious agreement**. In other words, they don't have to say it out loud, but a "Yes, yes, yes." So if I said to you, "*You're reading my words.*" Your unconscious mind, or a part of you goes, "Yes." "*And you can see my words in the book.*" "Yes." "*And I'm telling you several strategies that you can begin to work with.*" "Yes." "*But because I already did a few* **paces** *you'll probably start to keep going along with that.*"

Now I'm going to use that next **lead** as a **pace**. "*And as you begin to work with these, you can feel really good,*" here's the **pace** part, "*that you can see how to apply these, and in fact,*" now here comes a bunch of **leads**, "*your unconscious mind can find many ways to use these that you haven't even dreamed of yet or that I haven't even suggested yet. And maybe it'll be my voice that will pop into your mind and give you exactly the idea you were looking for or maybe it will be something that I have said to you today that will be triggered within your own mind and deep within your own thoughts. That will immediately enable you to come up with what it is that you need at the time when you need it. And you can be thankful for that because you are learning. Each time that happens you can be assured you are learning. And I am absolutely certain you have had a number of those experiences already in reading these books. Isn't this exciting?*"

And off I am running, doing it *again* and *again* and *again* and *again*, right?

Leading statements are what you *want* the person you're persuading to *believe*. You see how I just did that to you? They aren't necessarily *proven* yet, but they are what you want your prospect to *believe* and they're stated generally in the *present tense*.

Here's another example for you. Just relax, by the way. And just kind of follow along with me, preferably you're reading this and listening to the Audiobook at the same time, as recommended.

"*As you review what you've read so far, allowing the seconds to pass while you think about this in your own way, you can begin to understand the value of using this technique to get more of what you want when you want it. And as you begin to understand the value of this, thinking back to a time when this might have made the difference, you can begin to anticipate the benefits that will be yours as you begin to use it.*

"*While that anticipation builds, you might just take a second to tell yourself how thrilled you are to have found this at a time when you can really use it. Now, as the realization begins to sink in, perhaps even outside your awareness that the real key to persuasion is having skills like this that you can use. Have you already started to wonder who you will first share this new skill of yours with?*"

Isn't that fun?

So let's go back over this passage and analyze it. First, I want you to read it one more time and I'd like you to do that right now.

Okay. Can you understand how the **pacing** and **leading** creates a powerful influence that literally **compels your experience**? You see how that works? Can you *feel* it in that example? Read it again if you need to, because you'll easily be able to feel it.

I want you to again mark those statements that are **paces** and those that are **leads**. And I want you to do that now before you go on, because I'm going to go over it with you, but I want you to have done it first.

"Review what you've read." **Pace**. *"Allowing seconds to pass."* **Pace**. It took seconds just for you to read that, right? *"While you think about this in your own way."* **Pace**. It's your way. **Truism**. What do we have here? Yes. **Three paces**. Pace, pace, pace. And then what do we have? A **lead**. *"Understand the value of using this."* And we're going to go back to what? **Pacing**. Right. *"Understand the value of using this,"* huh. What is that? That was the **lead** I just used wasn't it? And now I've *turned* it into the **pace**, the next **pace**. Then I **pace** again because the pattern is, **pace, pace, pace, lead. Pace, pace, lead. Pace, lead. Lead, lead, lead, lead.** That's the **pattern**.

So I go back to **pacing**. *"Understand the value of using this."* **Pace**. *"Thinking back to a time it could have made a difference."* Also a **pace**. Then we're going to **lead** again, right? And the **lead** is, *"Anticipate the benefits and use it."* That's the **lead**. Now, what do we do again? We're going to **pace**. *"Anticipation builds."* It could be *considered* a **lead**, but basically at this point, when I say, *"Anticipate the benefits,"* because I've turned around and said it again like that, it *becomes* a **pace**. You see what I'm doing every time?

Now, *everything else* is a **lead**. *"So, tell yourself how thrilled you are to have found this."* That's a **lead**. Because it *wasn't true* until I *said it*. *"Realization begins to sink in."* Again, it wasn't true until I said it and that also is a **lead**. *"The real key to persuasion is having skills like this."* That's a **lead** because it wasn't true until I said it. *"Wonder who you will share this new skill with first."* That also is a **lead**.

Don't be compelled to do that immediately. I'm just playing with you.

How did you do? Did you get them right?

Let's do something fun. I want you to read aloud *just the leads* above. So just read the **leads** above. Do that now.

"Understand the value of using this. Anticipate the benefits and use it. Tell yourself how thrilled you are to have found it. You'll have a realization and it will begin to sink in. The real value to persuasion is having skills like this. And wonder who you will share this new skill with first." Do you see how that doesn't really provide a smooth, slippery slope? It doesn't really provide a smooth, slippery funnel for people to just slide down. It doesn't do it, does it? It's sort of jarring. But when we go back and do it like this: *"As you review what you've read so far, allowing the seconds to pass, while you think about this in your own way, you can begin to understand the value of using this technique to get more of what you want when you want it. And as you begin to understand the value of this, thinking back to a time when this might have made the difference, you can begin to anticipate the benefits that will be yours as you begin to use it. While that anticipation builds, you might just take a second to tell yourself how thrilled you are to have found this at a time when you can really use it. Now, as the realization begins to sink in, perhaps even outside your awareness that the real key to persuasion is having skills like this that you can use. Have you already started to wonder who you will first share this new skill of yours with?"'*

Brilliant. If I do say so myself.

See how this **leads** people *smoothly*? It's so *comfortable*. Notice how I **shifted** the experience of my listener to the *inner world*? To understanding and to their own inner thoughts to thinking back in time? Notice how I've made this an *internal experience* as well?

Here's yet another example. "*As you sit there reading this information, letting your eyes follow each word, you can begin to discover how this information will allow you to increase your persuasion power. And as you think about how that might happen and listen to what those ideas are inside your own thoughts, you may find yourself getting excited at how much easier this makes the process of convincing someone to do what you want. In fact, feeling that excitement beginning to build now causes you to want to begin to practice more to perfect this technique. This technique is strong enough to get people to go along with whatever you say. It also establishes your credibility and furthers the rapport you are building.*"

That was an example I gave you earlier, but notice how it just *smoothly* slides right in. Notice again how it is an *external* orientation moving to an *internal* orientation. Even when you read it again, notice how smooth it is. Just letting it zoom right into your mind.

Let me give you some tips on using this strategy.

Get good at *prefacing* your **leads** with **paces**. This is one of the biggest tips I can possibly give you on using this skill.

CHAPTER TWELVE

Varying The Format

Now, here's another interesting one. It's not necessary to follow the format I've given you precisely all the time. Here's what I suggest. Try to get it in once early on using the format **pace, pace, pace, lead, pace, pace, lead, pace, lead, lead, lead, lead,** where each of the **leads** in the process, or each of the next **pace** after a **lead**, is a reiteration of the lead.

Try to get that format in once. However, if you've *done* that format once, you should *not* use it again. You shouldn't, especially, use it *repeatedly*, or it's going to sound stilted and alert your prospect that something is going on and that's the last thing you want to do.

What you can do is go *back and forth* using **paces** and **leads**. You can remember, for example, the way what you just read *sounds* when read aloud, and as you remember you can remember too that this is what you want to also begin to do. You want to begin to **pace** and then **lead**. Now notice I *did* that, *there it was again*. I just *did* it. I didn't have to go **pace, lead, pace, pace, lead, lead, lead**, on and on. I just do it *whenever I want*. In fact, as you think about it as you'll do it, you can find yourself just letting this roll out of your mouth. Like I just did there *yet again*!

Now you can often use *what your prospect just said* as your **pace**. Couple that with a **connecting word**, like 'so' or 'and', 'causes', 'therefore' and then your **lead**, which is very powerful. So let's say someone says, "*Well, I'm interested in what you are here to tell me today.*" You'll say, "*You know, I appreciate you saying that. You're interested in what I have to tell you today and as a result of that, you'll begin to discover how very much this applies to everything you would hope that this would be and even more. And as you begin to discover that that's exactly the case, I think* *it will form the basis, the cradle, if you will, of the reason for us to work together. It's as if a young child is rocked in a cradle and feels so comforted and you know, I think talking with me will give you that same kind of feeling. At least that's certainly my goal today, so let's go through and analyze a little bit about what it is that you were looking to accomplish and I could do that best by asking you a few questions."*

Off you go. So you can simply **repeat back** what your prospect just said as the **pace**, use a **connecting word**, a **cause and affect language pattern**, if you will, and jump right into your **lead**.

Now you *don't* do that all the time, but you can certainly do it a *lot*.

The next tip on using this strategy is it does take **practice** to use this strategy with skill. So . . . what are you waiting for? **Practice**, alright?

Here's how I want you to do it. **Write out ten paces and leads following the full format**. That means follow the full **pace, pace, pace, lead, pace, pace, lead, pace, lead, lead, lead, lead**. Write out *ten* of those full examples. Once you've done it, then I want you to **write fifty paces followed by a lead**. It'll be fifty little mini examples where you'll have just a **pace** and a **lead**.

No, I don't think you're going to get through that really quick. And no, you don't have to finish it all before the next book comes out. But I *do* want you to at least *start* on it. Most importantly, *use* this **pattern** *lots* and *lots* and *lots*. The more you do it, the more you'll get comfortable with it. And I'm going to tell you right now, don't worry if it feels a little foreign and a little difficult because we're going to use this over and over and embed all kinds of other persuasion strategies that we're going to be learning within this format.

We can use this format in **metaphors**. We can use other **language patterns** within this format. So you're going to see this **pattern** being used *over* and *over* and *over* again. I hinted at it when we went through the material on the **five senses**. Now, could you, for example, use **pacing and leading** to **pace** someone from the **visual** portion of their experience to the **kinesthetic** portion of their experience? The answer is *absolutely*.

You begin to see the point.

BOOK SIX

TELLING PERSUASIVE STORIES

CHAPTER ONE

Synesthesia and Unspecified Language

Welcome to **Book Six** of **Persuasion Force**.

We're going to get started today with some of the questions that I've been asked. Generally, is one person asks a question, a number of other people have also thought of it, so this may help clarify a few things for many of you. And here we go with the first one.

"Now that we've gone into language more extensively, let me get back to the VAK language words and ask you to clarify some of the questions I have. I don't think I fully understand the difference between **Kinesthetic** and **Unspecified**. When explaining **kinesthetic** you say it refers to *feel* or *do*, but several of the *do* words are then classified as **Unspecified**. For example, *'move back'*. This seems like something one actively *does* but is termed **Unspecified**. *'Blows me away'*. This is **Unspecified** but couldn't it be **Kinesthetic**, after all it is both a *do* and can be *felt* physically?"

Let me stop right there and go through some of this with you one step at a time. You answered your own question there in essence with that last one when you said, "after all it is both a *do* and can be *felt* physically."

Also you can *see* somebody being blown away or you can even see *yourself* being blown away? There are a few things here that I'll point out. First of all, **don't take this to too big of an extreme**. Try to **keep it simple**. And the second thing is, if it qualifies as fitting into *more than two* sensory systems, it *automatically* becomes **unspecified**.

If you can **see** it *and* **feel** it, it's **unspecified**. That's why it sounds like it would be a doing, but it actually is **unspecified**. For example 'move back'. Could you *see* me move back? You bet. Could you *see* Joe Blow 'move back'? Sure. Could you *see* your arm 'move back'? You bet. Could you *feel* yourself 'move back'? You bet. Could you *feel* someone 'move back' away from you? Most likely. Could you *hear* somebody 'move back'? Certainly, if they were talking and you heard their voice grow distant. So it actually fits into *three* main systems and therefore it's absolutely **unspecified**.

So **unspecified** means that *it can't fit into one and only one*. All right?

"'*Bright*', one can certainly *see* something as bright. It rates as a **Visual** but I can also *hear* that a *sound* is 'bright' or not. Isn't it therefore also an **Auditory**?"

Yes. Sort of. *Bright* is really quite plain and simple, just simply **Visual**. People often do what's called a *synesthesia* kind of thing with their brain which means, very simply, that **you use one system to *interpret* another one with**. For example, you might say, "She's really hot." Well, do you mean literally she's burning up or has a temperature? No. Probably not. That's using **synesthesia**. In other words, she *looks* in a particular way that you're *saying* is hot and therefore you're using a **kinesthetic** term for it. That's a **synesthesia** kind of example.

In this case, audio is described as being a 'bright' sound. However, in my opinion that's somewhat of a **synesthesia** kind of thing. In other words, it's *still* 'bright like a light bulb'. Now it's *possible* that it is just an **Auditory** and if that's the case, this would be an example where it could be an **Unspecified**. It could literally fit into *both* **visual** and **auditory** and therefore we would have to call it **unspecified** because it fits into more than one.

"A *solid idea*'. Something can *feel* solid but can *look* solid, impossible to see through which would be **Visual**. 'Bells and whistles', **Auditory** makes sense but one can also *see* bells and whistles."

See, you're *too far into this*. Keep it **simple**. Bells and whistles is purely and simply **auditory**. If you said, "*See* the bells and whistles", *then* you're talking about something that you're *looking* at but you're *still* using a **synesthesia** pattern. In other words, you're *still* asking them to *look* at something that has *sound*.

Basically, if it fits more than one category it automatically is **unspecified**. Hopefully that helps with the elaboration that you've asked for.

CHAPTER TWO

Eliciting Higher Criteria

Number two. "When **eliciting criteria** I sometimes quickly encounter very strong *away from* **criteria** after only the first '*what's important about*' question or even without having to ask that.

"For example, a client will tell me that they need a management solution that keeps their projects from slipping, from losing money because of that, that signals them when things are going wrong and helps them keep more of a grip on their efforts.

"Would I need to go *higher* than that and **elicit *higher* criteria** or back up the ambulance right there and then?"

That's a question that's a bit. . . *artistic*. I would suggest to you that you *keep going* for **higher criteria**. I would say it much like this. . .

'*All right. That makes sense and what you're telling me is if you could have a good management solution that keeps your projects from slipping, you won't be losing money and the management* *solution will help you know when something's going wrong so that you can control your efforts more effectively. You'll know what to do when. So let me ask you a question. **If you had that in place right now, what would that do for you?***'

You could say, '*Ultimately* what would that do for you?' You could say, 'What would it *really mean*?' So you could stress the *really* and get them to dig in and give you something really profound.

Because, look, you *could* back up the ambulance with what you have there. That's true. However, I would say to you it'll *create more power for yo*u if you can go a little *higher*.

Now, **how do you know when you've gone *too* high?** And I know I've said this before but I'll say it again. They'll look at you like, '*Huh*?' You know, like if you asked someone, 'What's important about having a better grip on your efforts?' And they'll say, 'Well, you know because it'll let me run business efficiently.' And you say, 'What's important about running business efficiently?' And they say, 'Well, bottom line.' And you say, 'Okay, well what's important about bottom line?' They say, 'Well, if you have to ask *that* question you're not the consultant I need to talk to.'

There *you've gone too far*. Even when they start being **flippant** with their responses like that, then you know that you're probably *going too far* again. What I would do there is learn to *really watch* your prospect, you have to learn to really watch them so you can learn to see how they're responding. And if you feel like they're starting to be flippant then lean in a little bit and say, '**Well what would that really mean to *you personally*?**'

All right. You hear how to do that? Let's go to number three.

CHAPTER THREE

Eliciting an Emotional State

"I have a question about **changing/adding to someone's criteria**. It seems to violate the basic principle of why we elicit criteria in the first place."

. . . Ahh, this is going to be a *great* question . . .

"Correct me if I'm wrong, but we elicit criteria from people so that we can offer them exactly what they want. We use their words literally because that is exactly what they told us they want. However, *adding* to their criteria involves us *defining* their criteria *further*, adding words to it that are *ours*, not *theirs*, and makes us sell something that they did not ask for. Besides that, it is somewhat intrusive and condescending to tell someone that they only have a limited understanding of what they really mean with their criteria and that they have missed the fact that the criteria means *more* than other things that they have come up with.

"I have two questions. Am I correct that **adding to the criteria** *violates* some of the principles behind **eliciting criteria**? And what can be done to do this in a non-intrusive, non-condescending manner?"

All right. Great question. I love this. First of all, well, do you want me to be politically correct or do you want me to give you the answer? I'm just going to give you the answer.

This is like saying, is the law of two plus two equals four, is that a law? Is it never, ever able to be violated? Well, I can tell you mathematicians will tell you that that *is* a law but that you can *supersede* it possibly with *other* laws, with other forms of math. And that's *exactly* what we're doing here. So let's first go over this technique a little bit more and hopefully it will make sense to you. Let's start first with plain, pure and simple **criteria**.

Criteria's goal is precisely as you stated, to *elicit* what someone *wants* and *give* it to them. Or, you forgot the other one, **leverage** it. Leverage it meaning, I'm going to *elicit* it in your mind and make you *feel like* I'm giving you that. All right? So both can work really, really effectively. They're similar yet there's a considerable amount of differences between them.

All right. So you're correct in that. Two plus two equals four. It's like saying. . . I think I may have even used this example before with you, but you have someone come up with a jar and they fill it full of pebbles, like stones you'd skip across a lake, a quart jar. And they fill it right up to the top and they say, 'Is it full?' And you say, 'Well, yeah.' They say, 'All right.' Then they turn around and they get some gravelly rocks and they start dumping the gravel, and a whole bunch of gravel is able to go in there, filling the spaces between the pebbles, clear up to the top. And they go, 'Well *now* is it full?' You go, 'Yeah.' And they go, 'All right.' And then they go get sand and they start pouring sand in and they're able to fill up a whole lot more, clear up to the top. And they go, '*Now*, is it full?' And you go, 'Yeah.' And they go, 'All right.' And they get a bucket of water and they start pouring the water in and you can pour in a whole lot more.

At which point was it *really* full? Well it depends on what *rule* you're judging it by. If we take **criteria** plain and simple in its purest sense, **it's what enables us to *aim* our persuasive message**. It's what enables us to find out *precisely* what the client *wants* and to *give* it to them. It's what enables us, though, even more powerfully on a higher level, to **focus them on their criteria in the form of an emotional state** and when you do that, what you're doing is you are absolutely **eliciting within them a feeling**.

Notice that if I were to stop right now and elicit from you your **highest value of life** and I got you to really talk about it, it would in fact **elicit a feeling** and a strong one. When we go to *adding* to their criteria, what we're doing is we're now *working with criteria* instead of strictly as what they want, we're now *working with it* as we would an **anchor**, an **emotional state**.

So we've elicited a strong emotional state and what we're going to do that makes what we're doing acceptable to the person, the majority of times.

What you're doing on an advanced level is you are **eliciting an emotional state**. You're eliciting an emotional state of the **criteria** itself of their **highest value of life** and with that state elicited, you're able to then **leverage** it to mean additional things. For example, if I elicited within you a state of absolute *excitement* about *earning money this month with these skills* and I **anchored** it with a sound or a touch or whatever, and then I turned around and I said, 'Now, I'd like you to feel that feeling of *excitement* and think about, by the way, how much *further* you could become involved in my materials.'

Well, if I had actually **elicited the emotional state**, that new thought I'm asking you to think about, would begin to *blend* with that first emotion. In other words, *the emotion lends its power to the suggestion*, just like an attractive man or woman lends itself to the commercial for the purposes of influencing the viewer.

Ever wonder why they have the ring girls at fights? Or they have the good looking men or women in ads? Ever wonder why they get paid all those millions of dollars? It's because they're lending their physical appeal to the ad and the sheeple out there take one look at this ad and they go, 'Oh my goodness. I want a Mercedes just like that.' Because what they're thinking is, 'because I want that hot guy or girl that's in the car. And there's a **kinesthetic/visual synesthesia** there referencing the earlier question.

In other words, what we're doing with this pattern—and it's very advanced when you use it right—is we're *combining* **criteria elicitation** *with* **emotional state elicitation** and we're *leveraging additional information into someone's* **criteria** via the high level of **emotional response** that we've raised in them. And I hope that makes sense.

You're asking what can be done to do this in a non-intrusive, non-condescending manner. Number one, be *good* with it. So practice. Number two, get good at eliciting the criteria and make sure you've got *very high* criteria. Then when you ask them the question, 'What does that mean? If you could have that what would it be like? I mean tell me.' And when they get into the *emotion* of it and they're really *feeling* it, then when you say to them, 'All right. Let me tell you. I think it's all those things and I think maybe there's something even more there.'

And when you tie it right straight to that **high level emotion**, let me tell you it does *not* feel intrusive and it does *not* feel condescending.

Option two, don't use this. Just stick with the **criteria**. If you're more comfortable with that, go for it. But this is a far, far and away more powerful way of doing this. It's like graduating from simple mathematics to nuclear physics in one fell swoop. It's incredibly powerful.

Remember the key to this is you must have strongly elicited an **emotional state** for this to not feel intrusive and to not feel condescending. In other words, to be done right, **they have to be so strongly into the emotional state that they're just going along with it**. Okay?

I love questions like that. That's phenomenal. I really appreciate you asking such a well thought out question like this and I'm glad to have been able to present this here.

Let's go to question number four.

CHAPTER FOUR

Aggregating Criteria in a Group

"I frequently am in situations in which I need to sell to a small group of company representatives. Generally I do not know who will be in the meeting. They are often heads of various departments or divisions. Together they eventually decide whether or not to buy my product. There typically is no leader. Decisions are made by each division separately and only if enough agree they want the product, it is purchased, spreading the cost."

. . . Wow, interesting environment . . .

"My question is, how do I use **criteria** in this case? Since there is no leader, they are all basically at the same hierarchical level, I cannot mainly focus on eliciting criteria from the *leader*. I can elicit from *each* of them separately but I'm afraid that asking all of them consecutively the 'what's important about' question will then soon become recognizable. So what to do? How to harness the power of criteria here? I cannot assume that the criteria for a manager will be similar to that of manager two. They each run different departments. Similarly I have much difficulty in creating **physical rapport** since they tend to sit and move differently from one another. Another indication of a lack of a clear leader.

"I can only **physically pace** one of them at a time. I have experimented with **pacing** and **leading** one of them and then moving to the next, but have yet to figure out how to **maintain rapport** with the first one once I move to the second. Can you provide some useful tips here?"

I'll do my best.

Number one. When you **pace** the *first* person and **lead** to the *second*, you're **leading** person number one. If your **lead** *works*, person one **follows you**, so now person number one and person number two are **in lock step** together. It won't always show up as in *perfect physical symmetry* but often it can.

What I can tell you there is by definition, that's one way to do it. However, it's not my favorite way. If you had six or eight people in the room you probably might not be able to get through all six or eight in the timeframe of the meeting and there are far more powerful tools.

The biggest question I have to ask you is, what are the *similarities* between the departments that makes all of them, or most of them, want what you have? That's where you have to *focus*. All right? In other words, there is greater, grander **criteria** that *cuts across* all of these departments or *none* of them would be interested in this, or only one department would be interested and none of the rest.

So if you've ever made a sale to a place like this and you've ever had competing departments, or different departments, all of which or most of which agreed to buy it, then somehow *you* **hit their criteria** or *they* **hit their criteria**. Does that make sense to you? Okay?

You have to get good at *knowing the **criteria** of your market* without being able to elicit it on the fly most likely. What I would do is, after a sale I would go back into that place and I would talk to each of the different departments and I would **elicit their criteria** one after the other, and what I would do is I would write this information down, along with the department head, what kind of department it is, and then I would *aggregate these* after time. So in other words, after ten sales, I would have ten different departments, probably similar, a marketing department, maybe a sales department, maybe a human resources department, whatever, and I would start to **look for similarities between their criteria**.

Then I would figure out which are the *highest*. If you took those ten people together and made them one, what do you suspect would be the **highest criteria**? Then, when you go in front of a group like this and you know there's a marketing department represented and a sales department and a human resources department and whatever, you'll be able to talk knowledgeably about the criteria they probably have. That is *not* as good as being able to elicit it *directly* and *personally*. However, it's a *second best*. And that's what I would do.

The next thing you can do is begin to use *all the other kinds of patterns* I'm teaching you now, the **verbal pacing and leading** and all the **language patterns** to come. You can start applying those to what you're doing. For example, ever notice how you probably feel pretty persuaded when you read these books, you get pretty excited about them and you're going to go in and use them and that kind of thing, right? Well, why? I can't get *your* criteria one on one from you each time. I must be doing something *else*, right?

And I want to point you in that direction, and as we proceed with the learning and with these books, you'll see more and more how to do *exactly* what you're asking for. Focus on the **language**, focus on the **grander criteria**, the bigger criteria and **aggregate** the criteria of individual departments so you can start to figure out if I'm talking to a sales team, *this* is what they want, and a marketing team, *that's* what they want. And so you can take the five departments that are represented, or whatever, and you can present to them a little bit of information *for each one*.

You can say, 'For those of you in the sales department, what I'm going to say is probably going to make an awful lot of sense, and those of you in the marketing department will saddle up right along with this and it will probably interest you too, but I'll tell you in a second what will really excite you and hang tight for the rest of you because it's going to get even better.'

You can put in little suggestions like that all the way through your presentation.

I hope that helps.

CHAPTER FIVE

Telling Persuasive Stories

Now we're going to get into one of my *favorite* of all persuasion strategies and that is **telling persuasive stories**.

Telling persuasive stories in my way of looking at things is *the penultimate form of persuasion that exists*. People are **naturally wired** to be able to hear your stories. It's just a *phenomenal* way to communicate, it's a *phenomenal* way to persuade. You literally could do nothing but just **tell stories** and be very, very successful.

Isaac Dennison said, "To be a person is to have a story to tell," and I couldn't agree with it more, and if you *aren't* telling a story and telling it *persuasively*, you're *missing out* on a huge amount of persuasion power that you could have otherwise been having.

Stories put people in a place that lets them accept what's being said and they're *not* just fables and fairy tales, that's not all that stories are, they can actually be **mini-documentaries** of what you've *experienced* and that allows the people that are hearing it to experience those same kinds of things as well.

Here's a real key: **stories bypass resistance** and **touch the heart** and that's the key to stories. Everyone wants to feel proud of themselves and they want to feel that they're important. You can *tap into these things* very effectively with stories.

We're talking about **faith, not fact**. People need to have *faith* in you, to *believe* in you, and stories give you the chance to believe in you and to have faith in you. Facts, on the other hand, will *not* accomplish that.

People have well-trained B.S. detectors. They don't want to feel persuaded, they want to make up their own mind. I love it when people tell me that, by the way. I *encourage* them to make up their own mind, *my way*. I don't really say it exactly like that but sometimes I do.

Stories give them the ability **to make up their own mind the way you want them to**, to see what *you* want them to see. That's the beauty of stories. And it's really beautiful.

People need to have two questions answered in order to trust you: **who are you?** - which is what we're going to be focusing on, and **why are you here?** And once they know that, once they know those things, then they can *trust* you.

When you're sitting down in front of a client talking and they don't know who you are and they don't know why you're there, they're not really going to trust you. Yes, yes, yes. You are a car salesman and they're on the lot, so that's who you are and that's why you're there. Nope. That doesn't cut it.

You could say, on the other hand, I'm an adviser and they need help with their money. Nope. That's not it. They have to *really* know who you are and why you're there.

Imagine the power of this strategy combined with the **physical and verbal rapport techniques** that you've been learning. In other words, you can use *all* the things that you've been learning so far throughout these books and you can put them *all* into the **stories**. And we'll talk a little bit more about *how to do that* as we proceed.

But it's a beautiful thing to be able to add all these together and here is the perfect format for doing just that.

Stories speed up rapport. A story can *drastically* speed up the process of learning who you are and thus of your clients trusting you. Instead of having to discover who you are over a long period of time, a story can stimulate the clients into *seeing* that very quickly.

Stories *mesmerize* and *suck people in*. They fit into the **indirect permissive model**, not the **direct authoritarian model** and once again, therein is one of the most significant powers of stories. They *mesmerize* and *suck people in*. Look at it this way, when you go to a movie, for the most part, you go to a movie and you sit down to watch the movie. How much *defense* do you erect in your own mind against the movie? 'Ah, I don't know if this is going to be any good. I'll bet you I'm going to have to walk out within fifteen minutes. I'll bet you it's just going to not be any good at all.'

No. What you do is you go in and you *listen* and all of the sudden it's *done* and you think, 'Oh, my goodness, it's been an hour and a half or two hours already? Wow.' That is if it's good.

Let's talk about a *New York Times* and a *CBS* news poll. Sixty-three percent of the people they found believe that in dealing with most people, you can't be too careful. In other words, you must be *very careful in dealing with other people*. Sixty-three percent of the people believe that.

Thirty seven percent believe that *most people would try to take advantage of you if they had the chance*. Over one-third of the population believes that most people would try to take advantage of you if they had the chance. That means one out of every three people you talk to *believes* that *you're going to try to take advantage of them* and almost three quarters of the people you talk to believe that *you can't be too careful in your dealings with others*.

Wow. That same poll—if you want to get knocked off your socks— says, people taking the poll believe that *of the people they know, eighty-five percent would try to be fair*, that is **of the people they know**. How can we *immediately* turn up the pressure of persuasion on the people that we want to influence? Well, **get them to know us**.

How better to do so than a story? The best way in the world to do that is a story because all of the sudden we go from almost three-quarters of the people thinking you can't be too careful and well over thirty percent of the people believing that you'd try to take advantage of them if you had the chance, to *eighty-five percent odds that you would try to at least be fair with them*.

Is that amazing or what? So **use a story to let people know who you are** and **your trustworthiness almost triples**. That is an exciting number. You can triple the way in which people perceive you and trust you simply by using a story to let them know who you are.

That's pretty cool when you figure that just a little story about who you are can give you *that much* of an advantage. Will you be using them more readily from now on? I sure hope so.

CHAPTER SIX

The Hero's Journey

Let's talk about **creating your story** or **how you became a hero**.

We're going to talk about Joseph Campbell and his work detailing **the hero's journey** in his book that talks about *myths*. And that book is '***The Hero Within***' and it's an incredible book. I would highly, highly recommend you get it. It is not a simple, easy book. It's actually pulling apart the myths that are prevalent in our society, the biggest of which is the hero, the myth of the hero.

This *journey* that he details is found in almost every movie and in almost every television show and in the stories that move us. Isn't that interesting? That's how profound and prolific it is. The process of **the hero's journey** is to create a compelling story. Stories have at their core some *key aspects*. Number one, **they reduce resistance**. Number two, **they move those hearing it past**

critical thinking filters during the story. In other words, the minute I say something like, 'Let me tell you a story. I had a good friend back in college and he and I were rooming together. We were sophomores. . .' But the minute you hear, '*let me tell you a story*', **your brain just relaxes** and goes, 'Okay.'

Now I hope in the future your brain *won't* do that anymore because that's when you're *most easily influenced*. But the rest of the world, when *they* hear '*let me tell you a story*' or its equivalent when they go to a movie, the story just begins.

Let's look at some stories that were *designed* to heavily influence us. Take a look at Gore's movie that he won an Oscar for. Was that a *story* or was that designed to full out *influence* you through the medium of a movie, through the medium of a story? Yes. That's what it was *designed* to do.

The great thing about stories is **they move people past critical thinking filters**. They lead people to their own conclusion but it is a conclusion the story helped to shape, and in later books we're going to get far more into shaping the conclusion via strategies that we use within the story.

But first let's get great at using the story itself. Because this story, when you do it this way, is absolutely amazing.

We're going to jump right into it. I'd highly recommend getting the book and reading it if you haven't already called '***The Hero Within***' by Joseph Campbell. It's an excellent book. It will give you tremendous background on what it is that I'm going to be going over with you in this book and I can tell you that it's just worth the time to spend reading it. It will really help you understand this process and then once you *understand* it, you'll begin to *see* it in your day-to-day life. You'll begin to *see* it all over the place. It will be as if it all of the sudden you get it.

CHAPTER SEVEN

The Call To Adventure

Let's start with the *first step* the hero goes through and that is **the call to adventure**.

Often this **call** is *ignored* or *refused* until circumstances or a mentor encourage them to take the first steps. Let's apply this to *your* **call to adventure** in *your* life. We're going to apply this to *your* story that you're going to be telling in your business.

So to help you figure out your **call to adventure**, here are some questions that I want you to *stop* and really *go through this*.

- What was '*a*' or '*the*' **defining moment** in your life or career that put you on the path that you're on now?
- Did you have an '*aha*' moment? Did the light bulb come on all of the sudden?
- If so, *what was* that moment? Do you remember it? And if you had one, you will remember.
- Did you have a time when you went *seeking knowledge*, you went to *figure out something*, how to *solve a problem* or whatever and that led you into what you're doing today?

- Did you have an *emotional* event or time that pushed you to find an answer or the truth to *change your life* that relates to your business? Did you get a *divorce*? Did you have a *bankruptcy*? Did some *traumatic event* happen or a *time period* that was very difficult that pushed you to find an answer or to find the truth that changed your life that relates to what you do today?
- Did a *key figure* or *mentor* help you or cause you to change your way of thinking? Did someone tell you that you weren't doing right and that you need to be doing a little differently?

It's important. . . I want you to really *think those things out* and write it down. Write them down.

I want you to really think about the points of the questions. Which of them can apply to your story now? And now I'm going to give you a **key point** that I want to drill into your mind over and over again. I want this to become the Bible with which you live as it relates to telling stories. Do not, and I repeat, **do not try to remove the emotion from your story**. Don't gloss over it.

If you actually *suffer* a bit while you tell your story, all the better. You'll know that I frequently tell stories about my mother and when I do sometimes I have to choke back the tears. This is very good and very powerful for *influencing* an audience or an individual. It's also critically important *not to fake it*. You must *feel* what it is that you're talking about.

For example, imagine a movie that glossed over the emotion. Instead of imagining the main character suffer with difficulty in overcoming their problems, which really entertains us, you saw them shrug it off and go on with life as if nothing happened. It would make for a pretty *boring* movie, wouldn't it? And that's the point. And that's *exactly* what your story will make for too if you're just boring, if you don't actually have an emotion and **convey an emotion**.

Remember that people go into an *altered state* when they hear you begin a story. That *altered state* begins with the words '*let me tell you a story*,' or 'I'm glad to be able to meet with you today. I have a few questions I want to ask you about.' And then you proceed to tell them, '*Let me just tell you a quick story* by way of letting you know why I'm here today and who I am, who you're working with.'

The *minute* you say that, **their brain goes to sleep**. They kind of **listen without critical judgment**. Provided you don't put your foot in your mouth somehow, they're just going to *listen* kind of in a nice *altered state* **without critical judgment** of you.

You want to begin *right now* to build your story with your **call to adventure**. What happened? Did you have an 'aha' moment? Did you have a defining moment in your life or career that put you on this path? Did you flunk out of college? Did you get in trouble? Did you go to jail? Did you get a divorce? Did you have a bankruptcy after you told everyone how important you were? Was it devastating to you emotionally and in every other way? Did you care for a sick parent?

There was a person in my coaching program that they were caring for a sick father and during their college, their father was putting them through school and they were living an easy life, they basically just said, this is easy, this is good. And all of the sudden the father had a heart attack or a stroke or something and all of the sudden there was no more money. The father called the guy and said, 'Hey, I'm really sorry, son. I have no more money for you. I'm going to lose everything.' And that immediately put this person on the path to becoming a financial adviser. He determined right then and there that he would never, ever let another family go through this because of a lack of planning.

It was devastating to his family. And he went on, figured a way to put himself through school, it took him a couple more years, and became an adviser and now works to help people to not ever have to experience that kind of problem. Do you think when he's sitting there telling this that he can keep his eyes dry? Do you think there's no emotion for him? Do you think he says, 'No big deal, and I was a kid. It was kind of bad at the time but then I got over it, I grew up and I went on my way'? No, he is **really emotional** about this. It *chokes* him to the point of not being able to speak.

And that's *exactly* what this should do for you. Please remember, **keep the emotion in your story**. *Don't* gloss over it. If you *suffer*, if you *cry*, if you actually break down and cry, *that's a good thing*. Not if you sob uncontrollably for the next half an hour, but if you struggle to find your words to get back on track because it has such an **impact** on you, it's going to have an *enormous impact* on your client and they will absolutely see this in a positive light.

CHAPTER EIGHT

Crossing the Threshold

The next step is called '**crossing the threshold**'. There are several *thresholds* the hero goes through that you're going to learn. Crossing the *first threshold* causes the hero to *leave their ordinary world* and step into a special world where they must **learn the protocols and ways of passage**.

Within this world, they must *pass tests*, earn the assistance of *allies* and defeat or learn from *enemies*. This is very, very powerful, okay? So let's discover how to apply this to your story.

How did you **leave your ordinary life behind** in *your* story? Had you perhaps started in a particular direction studying or doing the predictable and expected? Or perhaps doing what *everyone else* did to get where you want to go? Did you discover a *special world* or find some *special knowledge* that you somehow knew was important and set off to figure it out?

I did this, when I began studying what it is that I teach you today. I was eighteen years old when I first got started and I knew there was something here. I didn't know what. And the first seminar I went to, I was *hooked for life*. I watched things happen that *I didn't think were possible* in the real world but I *saw them happen* with my own eyes and I determined there and then to do this. And I set about on a *course of action* to get this knowledge and I got it. And now I'm giving it to you.

What did *you* experience? What did *you* do? Did *your* new knowledge cause you to be *challenged* by your friends or your family or those who had been in your field, like experts, because it was *different* or caused a *different conclusion* or used a *different protocol* or went against the accepted methods? Did you develop *supporters* and *allies* and *people who understood what you were doing* even though they resisted you or your ideas?

Now you want to *stop* at this point and *really write this out*. Okay? I want you to **have this knowledge in your head**. I want you to write out what this **threshold** is for *you*. Okay? And as soon as you've done that let's continue on. But it's important. **You have to go through this step-by-step and write it**. Okay?

Did you write it? If not, why are you still reading? Let me encourage you to *stop*, please, and *do this work*, okay?

CHAPTER NINE

Entering the Innermost Cave

Entering the innermost cave, which is the *second threshold*. In time the hero must cross a *second threshold* and **enter the innermost cave**. Often this is the result of *time* pressuring them or they're simply *ready*. In this **innermost cave**, the hero must undertake **the supreme ordeal**. Upon victory, the hero *seizes the reward*. Those involved with the status quo are often *angry* and become their *enemy* and pursue the hero along the road back to their ordinary world.

What's *your* **innermost cave**? Here's where it begins to come together for you. *This* is where you cross your last threshold of *traditional thinking*. You discover that you're *unique* and you *find* this uniqueness and you also find *those that resonate with you*, like *clients* and *supporters* and *customers* and *followers*. So you go through the first cave, if you will, and because you seek a better life, a better way or to overcome a problem or to learn something, and then in your second cave, the second threshold is where things start to come together and it's where you *let go* of the last bit of your old thinking and you discover that you're *unique* and you find people that *resonate* with you.

Those that *were* in power and that have maintained the *status quo* now become your *competitors* and even *enemies*. They try to *discredit* and *attack* you, but when they disagree with you it simply reinforces that *you were right*. You use this, or you can use this, as **social proof that you were right**.

By the way, you can put that in the story just like that. These "experts", who I was unseating with ease, and whose businesses were hurting as a result of what I figured out, started doing exactly what I knew they'd do. They started *discrediting* me and *attacking* me, letting me know that I was absolutely on the right track. If I didn't bother them any, why would they bother to spend any time trying to hurt me?

Again, it's important that you **stop and write this out** so you can see the elements all coming together. Okay?

CHAPTER TEN

Finding Your Uniqueness

The *third threshold* is **death and resurrection**. As the hero is heading back to their ordinary world after undertaking the *supreme ordeal*, they cross the *third threshold*. Here the hero suffers a **metaphorical death and resurrection** as they *confront* and then *give up* any remaining patterns, behaviors, beliefs, and even possessions— home, country, friends, job—that stops them from making the **final transformation**.

Let's apply this to your story. Any vestiges of your *old way of thinking* is *let go* here in this third threshold. As you were reborn, you find that *single focus* that **lets you be who you are now** as a result of crossing these thresholds and experiences. So think about *when* that happened for *you* and *how* that happened. Also, notice how by doing these exercises, it helps you to **zero in on who you really are**, what you really want to be. In other words, what's *true* for you that you can **communicate with passion and power**.

Your **single focus** and **uniqueness** differentiates you from anyone else and draws those to you that *resonate* with you. And isn't that also the strategy? In other words, what could be *your primary focus* and your main *uniqueness* that *differentiates* you from anyone else and draws those to you that *resonate* with you? It will draw them if you find your **uniqueness**.

And maybe your **uniqueness** is just your *life history*, where you come from. There may be a hundred thousand realtors out there, or a hundred thousand people, or a million people out there trying to scoop up properties in foreclosure, but what makes *you* **different**? And with what you're learning here, you're going to be able to *know what that is* and *put it into your story*.

This now becomes your **truth** and you tell the world whether anyone believes you or not which leads you to . . . . But first, before you're led there, make sure you've **written out how this applies to *your* life as you build your story**, okay? So write it.

CHAPTER ELEVEN

The Elixir

And then let's go to *the final step*, which is **the elixir**.

When the hero returns from this journey with the **elixir**, they are no longer the person who started out on the journey. They have become *a new person*, changed, and they now can make a *positive difference* in their world.

Beautiful.

Let's apply the final step of the **elixir** to *your* story.

You share your *journey*, your *story* and your *truth* with those that want to hear what you have to say. What was that for *you*? What is *your* **elixir**? What did *you* return with in *your* story? How can *you* make a positive difference with that?

Your story captures their attention and generates powerful **rapport**. Your story allows them to taste your **elixir** which powerfully *influences* them to **draw their *own* conclusion that *you* have *influenced*.** Isn't that nice?

They become a loyal customer and your fame spreads far and wide. *That's* the goal. So how can you *apply* this? It's important that you **write it out right now**. How can you apply this final step?

Let me give you a tip on using **criteria** with all this. Now that you understand how the hero *became* a hero and are starting to *zero in* on *your own* story, here is something that you can use. And I personally use this and really enjoy it, really like it.

It's often useful if you can **elicit the person's criteria** that you are persuading *before* telling your story. This way if you're good at telling your story you can *adjust* it very quickly and on the fly as needed. In other words, you can *bend the story* that makes the point that *involves their* **criteria** right on the fly, and that makes the story all that much more powerful. In other words, *you* were living for the *same* kinds of things *they* live for.

Of course you have to make sure that it's **true** but you can take a bit of creative license provided that the *overall process* is absolutely true. Even the specifics are true. But I could just as easily be excited about really helping someone to make money as I could about saving money. So either way I could **adjust my criteria in the story to fit whichever kind of person I'm talking to and be completely honest with it**.

CHAPTER TWELVE

Figuring Out Your Hook

Here's a very important part called **figuring out your hook.**

What happened in your call to adventure that was incredibly *difficult* for you? Remember I told you, *do not spare the emotion*? Was there something very *emotional* that happened that was your call to adventure? Did something *shocking* or *surprising* happen? You need to dig deep and go back into your history and figure this out. It's really important, in other words, **you have to have a hook**. What's going to *keep people listening* to your story? What is the *most shocking thing* about what you do but especially about what got you started along this path?

Just asking you these questions I'm hoping will help you to generate what it is that you're looking to accomplish with the story. In other words, when I ask you what is the most shocking thing about what you do but especially about what got you started along this path? Well, there we go. If you can come up with that, you've got a **hook**. A powerful hook.

You know, I had the opportunity to have my mom ask me to come. She knew she was dying and she asked me to come be with her. And I did. I immediately left and came to see her. I was a good four or five hours away and by the time I got there she had lapsed into a coma. And everybody was around the bed there and I came in and I immediately asked everyone to leave. I said, 'I would like to spend just a few moments with my mom. You've had the opportunity and I would like to spend a few moments with her.'

And that was one of the *most powerful things* that ever happened to me in my life. I can tell you that. The nurse there said that she had just lapsed into unconsciousness, into a coma and she said, 'However, it's not a typical coma like you would normally think of.' She said, 'It's only been a few minutes, fifteen minutes or so, that she wasn't even able to squeeze my hand.' And she said, 'But the hearing is the last to go, so she is still hearing you and she will register as if she were fully awake and alert what you're telling her.'

And I had the opportunity right then and there to really experience some personal healing and an opportunity to talk to my mom in a way that I'll never, ever forget and as you can tell, this is *really painful* for me. It's *painful* and it's *loving*, I guess, all in one fell swoop. I absolutely worship my mother. She helped me become what I am today and she certainly set me on the path of good and right.

I remember as a teenage boy in high school I hated the world. I was a freshman in high school and I just hated everyone and everything. And I would come home and I would say, 'I'm going to get even with this teacher.' And my mom would say, 'Yeah, well I bet they really deserve it.' And I'd say, 'Yes, they sure do, they're jackasses.' And mom says, 'All right. What are you going to do?' And I said, 'Well, I don't know.' She said, 'Well, I'll tell you what. Why don't we get busy on some homework and let me help you so that at least they can't try to hurt you again because you haven't turned it in.' And she'd spin me right around and get me off of my anger and let me move forward in life dealing with my hormones and with every other thing that I had to deal with—the anger and the bitterness that I experienced because of the divorce that I went through, etc.

But what I can tell you is that she put me on that path of goodness and rightness and forever I will be *grateful*. There isn't a day that goes by that I don't thank her for that. And I can tell you that I used to be scared to death to talk about this because I can't talk about it without really tearing up and I thought I seemed weak when I did this.

One day in front of a very large group of people, several hundred people, years ago, I tried to tell this story and literally broke down into tears and I got through it and I called for a break and I must have had half the room come up to hug me and to tell me how much they appreciated me sharing that with them and I began to understand what I'm teaching you now back all those years ago. I can tell you that when I got it, when it made sense to me, I was stunned. It was exactly the *opposite* of what I *thought* this would be.

It's a *profound* tool of persuasion. When you see an actor on the movie screen break into tears, do you think they're really crying? And the answer is if you are *believing* their performance they're *really* crying. And that's the method acting where they train themselves to cry, to emote, they must emote anything—laughter, excitement, sexuality, sadness, whatever, respect, whatever they want to emote—but they must do it and do it profoundly and thoroughly or they won't transfer that to the people who are there in the movie wishing to influence.

Can you look back to the start of your journey and find **the defining moment**? Can it be told in such a way that it **captures someone's attention**, that it really gets their attention? Can you do that? I *know* you can.

Perhaps there is something about you that is really *unique*—where you come from, any struggles you had in your life, or things you've done or learned that were incredibly difficult.

What can your journey identify that *might save someone else severe consequences*? On my computer monitor is a little sign I made that says, 'What are we *really* selling?' and I would highly advise you to put that on yours. Or somewhere. What are we *really* selling? I'm reminding myself that people don't buy CDs and DVDs and paper from us. Nor do they buy information. They buy what that information will **do** for them. People don't buy homes from you, they buy a **lifestyle**. They don't let you take their home in foreclosure for $5,000 or whatever you have to pay, they do it to *solve a problem* that's so big and so embarrassing that they don't know where else to turn.

You understand? So **identify** what your *product* or your *service* or your *information* will **do** for people and then ask yourself what the **emotions** are that are *associated* with those things and see if this helps you with your **hook**. I can tell you it will.

CHAPTER THIRTEEN

Framing Your Life Story: Why Are You There?

If you can, add into the story **why you were there telling them your story**. This is extremely powerful. You can do it as a *separate* story and you should in fact have a separate story made for this so you can use it when you need to and you can also just add it into the story.

You can actually have a short paragraph or a sentence or two even that says *why you're telling them this*.

If you extol the benefits of what's in it for the person you are trying to influence long enough, they'll wonder what you're hiding. They want to know what's in it for *you*, so **why are you there?**

You're there *to help people not to experience the same kind of problems you went through*, or you're there *to save people the huge learning curve* because you saw a friend of your family go down in flames and you don't want that to ever happen to another person again and you've dedicated your life to that process. You need to be a bit **dramatic** here. What is it that you can do here?

You can't just *extol the benefits* of why they should buy from you over and over because they'll wonder what you're *hiding*. **What's in it for *you*?** Even if your motives are selfish, that's okay if you **frame** them so they are acceptable.

What is the reason you are here? Write it out. And stop reading until you get it written.

If you've gone through and done the writing then you have in front of you on several pieces of paper **your hero's journey.** *You* are now the *hero*. Isn't that cool? You've just **framed your life in terms of what the whole world responds to**. You're now Troy. You're now Cleopatra or whatever the hero is you want to be. But you've just **framed your life story as a hero**.

You don't have to *think* of yourself as a hero, but did you stop to realize how many ways it's *true* that you are?

Here you are and you have framed your life accordingly so that you can have the *impact* you want and now, instead of having to try so hard to gain **rapport**, they just actually *trust you as a result of your story*. You've *entertained* them, you've put them into a little *altered state* and their brain just *goes to sleep* and *stops critically evaluating* what you're doing and *accepts* what you're doing. Isn't that beautiful? Beautiful. This is persuasion at it's finest.

Better still, it's *your* story. Not one made up. Not just a little anecdote or quip or something else that you have figured out to say to try to sound tricky, although those work great too, but **this is your story** and you can tell it with *passion* and with *emotion*, with a *hook* that will get anybody to listen.

BOOK SEVEN

DEEPENING YOUR PERSUASION SKILLS

CHAPTER ONE

Advanced Rhythmic Speaking

Welcome to **Book Seven** of **Persuasion Force**.

I'm excited to share this book with you, because I found a number of *questions* that I hadn't seen before, and I'm going to go ahead and answer them for you. These should really **deepen your understanding** of the themes and strategies we've been talking about in this series so far.

The first question is a question about **rhythmic speaking**. It says, *"At 45 beats per minute you would speak like 'My. . .name. . .is. . .Joe. . .Blow'. This is a completely unnatural way of speaking."*

Yup.

"During the section in **persuasion** *you say to* **skip a beat**, *so would the format be more like, 'My. . . name is. . .Joe Blow.' I hope that this makes sense. I've been practicing every day since the beginning and don't want to mess this up."*

Okay. Well, good. **Keep practicing**. This is something that to this day I *enjoy* practicing and every now and then I do because it's **incredibly effective**. So, yes. Let's go back through the question in a little bit more detail now. Yes, if you're using *either* way you've actually outlined here like, 'My. . . name. . . is. . . Kenrick. . . Cleveland.' That *is* very unnatural and even really *two* words like that is unnatural. But I can **shift into** speaking in a rhythm just by simply **emphasizing** one of the beats from time-to-time. And when I do it like that you will *lock on* to the way in which I'm speaking, to the **rhythm** I'm delivering with the way I'm **using the spacing**.

Now, I'm not necessarily *stopping* on *every* beat. So a better way to look at this would be that from time-to-time, I actually *skip a beat* altogether, meaning that I don't actually make more pronounced what it is I'm doing at that particular beat. And yet as I'm speaking now, you can **begin to hear a beat** quite clearly if you're following along with this in the free audiobook.

In other words, it's like, if I'm hearing a *beat* like this, then from time-to-time, I simply **emphasize** one of the beats that I'm going to be using, or I pause. Okay? So in my head I *hear this beat* like this all the time and I don't really know what beat level that is. Sometimes I hear it a little faster and sometimes I hear it slower but it's actually quite easy to learn how to speak where you don't really emphasize *each and every one* of the beats but you simply emphasize *one from time to time*.

So hopefully that gives you kind of an idea. That's just an off the cuff demonstration for you, if you're listening along with the audiobook. The easiest way to think of it is that you **either *pause* or *emphasize* a word that falls on a beat**. So that's sort of an easier way to hear it. In other words, what you need to get good at with this skill is *hearing a beat in your mind* and then *from time to time* just *emphasize* a word that *falls on the beat*. And then what you're really doing is you're still **sending a beat in your message** and they can **lock on** to that.

Now, here is something that I'll just say that you probably *know is true* if you're a musician, it's probably pretty easy for you to hear a beat in your mind and I was raised in music my whole life. So it's kind of *easy* for me to hear it. However, to get good at doing it with my words, it almost was like as if it didn't make much difference. I could *hear* the beat in my mind but I couldn't *speak* on it. So it took some **real practice** and I did that by listening to evangelical type ministers.

And I don't mean a specific religion, I mean . . . Well, maybe that *is* the name of a specific religion, but what I really mean are more like the *Holy Roller* type of ministers or the *hellfire and brimstone* type on TV. Even the ones that aren't necessarily hellfire and brimstone, but that are rather **dramatic in their presentation**, so again, let me reassert that I'm *not in any way* putting down any religion whatsoever, and if you happen to be partial to one of the ones that do what I'm talking about, I hope you see that I'm simply **pointing out a truism** here, that they do tend to **speak in a very strong rhythm**.

And so they also tend to **repeat in threes**. And so as I was *emulating* these people, actually word for word what they were doing, and what I would do is I would *listen* to them and then I would *say what they just said* a second or so behind them and I would try to *emulate their tone*, the *effect of their voice*, the *speed of their speaking*, the way they *emphasized their words* and everything and the more I did that the more I was able to just go off and do it on my own.

And it works very, very well. I highly recommend that as a way of learning to do this better. It works like crazy actually. And why do you think *they* do it? You're not brought up in life speaking by making every single thing you say into a rhythm. Because that's the way He would want us to be.

No. We aren't brought up talking like that. At least I doubt you were. I certainly wasn't, even though I was brought up in a very religious family. But that religion didn't quite talk like this so I had to go out and **learn it** and then I had to **soften it down again** when I brought it into persuasion but I realized that *they're doing this for a reason*, a very important reason, and that reason is, they want to **alter the minds of the listeners**. In essence, like I've taught you with stories, they're *entertaining*.

When they're *bigger than life* up there and they're *entertaining* and they're using *strong effect in their voice*, well it's *entertaining*. It kind of **rivets your attention**. It *stops* you and **you have to listen** to what they're doing, don't you? That's what's happening is that they're in a sense *entertaining* you and through the rhythm **lullabying you** so that **your critical thought process stops** and you can be converted, you can **have an experience**. And they talk about having the experience of Jesus Christ.

In fact I was watching a TV show that I had recorded some time back called, I think it's called

"*Wife Swap*"—hysterical show. The name alone probably has gotten them tremendous viewership here, but if you haven't seen the program, you'd get a kick out of it. They generally pair up two families and then they switch mothers or switch wives, nothing sexual about this, by the way, but what they're doing is they're showing how one family is radically different than the other. And both families generally come away with quite a learning. It's worth watching a show or two and see if you like it. It's kind of a reality show and it's really fascinating to see the theatrics and what goes on. But I remember one family in particular that were raised a very devout Christian family and they paired up, they switched wives, if you will, with a mother from a very non-religious secular family who didn't believe in God at all. And she was appalled that the kids weren't allowed to go out and have fun, to date, to do all these things. And so at one point she asked one of the children, he was twelve or thirteen years old if I remember right, something to the order of, "Don't you like to go have fun?" And his response was, "We have fun in the Lord." And I thought much like the woman did personally, I thought, "How sad. The child has no clue what he just said. He's parroting what he's hearing his parents say and doing a good job of it. One day that may make sense to him. But at twelve, it does not. It genuinely does not make sense."

And if you think about it, even if you can just *step outside of whatever conditioning or processes you've been brought up with*, what does it mean to have fun *in* anything? To have fun *in* the Lord? To have fun *in* a friend? It's sort of nonsensical but in essence, there are a lot of **dichotomies** that are presented like this and again, those dichotomies are presented often as a method of **stopping conscious functioning** so that your brain is tied up going, "Huh?" You'll hear ministers even say, "Look. There are doubters out there who would say if God is real, let him make a rock so big he can't lift it." Then he'll go on with his statement showing the mindset of disbelievers.

Well isn't it interesting that **that statement alone stops thought**? It may have even done it for you *right here*. If you haven't heard that before, you're probably still thinking, "Huh. A God that makes a rock bigger than he can lift it. But if he's almighty and can do anything how can that be?" So it's a **dichotomy**, *there's no answer. How long is infinity?* There's another one.

My daughter told me today that mathematicians are studying infinity, so she tells me, I don't know that she's accurate on this, but she said that computers are able to get up to a million digits after the one or whatever and that there is still no *repetition* in the pattern and so they believe they have yet to figure out just *how far* infinity is, because they believe that when they do that the numbers will begin *repeating*. Of course I find that *very* amusing because if infinity as a concept is *real*, then we should *never* be able to figure it out, mathematically or any other way.

But it's a very interesting concept and it really makes your head think about it. So perhaps you're thinking about these things right now and if so, **I've succeeded in stopping your thoughts**. Now, if I were to launch into **a rhythm with my speaking**, oriented to get you to *experience something in particular* like an emotion, or just a logical argument even for that matter which would be a far second place to the emotion, **I could easily sway you one way or another**, *whichever way I'm pointing you*, simply because **your ability to defend consciously is now reduced or eliminated**.

So if you think back to **Book Six**'s lesson on **stories**, that's *exactly* what we learned to do. By telling *the hero's story*, you've also learned how to *entertain the conscious mind*. In other words, **stop its conscious processing**, stop its *resistance* to a large extent, and as you launch into a few of the *additional* skills that we've been studying, you can take advantage of the fact that you've *stopped* that kind of *conscious processing* and **expand on your persuasion message**.

117

And one of the ways that you can do that real efficiently is by **locking on to a rhythm** because that even further **creates a lullaby** and in the mind of the listener, they just simply **zone out**, especially when you use *commands* like I just did that just begins the process of **people altering their attention**. And as long as you're giving them *process oriented instructions* and as long as you're *guiding the directions of their thoughts*, then you're very much *in control* with the other than conscious.

I've answered a question that came about from potentially some time back, but with a *much more advanced degree of an answer* to it, enabling you to **utilize this far more efficiently**.

CHAPTER TWO

Repetition in Three

I also brought up the idea of **repetition in three**. And the second question asks if I would please *expand on that*. And I'd be happy to.

There are a number of reasons **repetition in three** works. Our society is indoctrinated with the concept of the Godhead being in its form of a *trinity*. Most every major religion on the planet talks about *three things*, God the *Father*, God the *Son*, God the *Holy Spirit*. Even in humanist psychology, they'll talk about the *id*, the *ego* and the *super ego*. The *conscious* mind, the *sub conscious* mind and the *super conscious* mind. There are all these different iterations of the same. There's the *father*, the *mother* and the *child*. There are all kinds of iterations of the number three in our society. And it's actually quite profound but if anyone who's ever been exposed to anything religious - and that's pretty much 100% of the population on the face of our planet today - has heard something from the Christian religion that deals with the Godhead being a *trinity* and even if they couldn't express it in those words, they've heard of *God*, his son *Jesus* and the *Holy Spirit*. Most likely they've at least heard those names. They may not *understand* it much but at least they have *heard* it.

That's one reason **repetition in three** works is it immediately is a *reference to religion*. It's a *subconscious* reference to religion. And if the people you were persuading were highly religious, repeating in three would have a *dramatic* impact on them, or it could. Okay?

You might even say, "*Today, there are a few of the things that I believe so strongly in that I want to emphasize so profoundly, that I believe in with all my heart, that I'm going to do my best to try to take the position of a **father** who's giving this information to his beloved **son** in such a way that he can **infuse his heart with the spirit** of the message such that it's really understood through and through and there is a resulting change, such that today, by the time we've gone through this process together, you will experience this information in a whole new way. Not only will you be excited about it, not only will you feel fantastic about it, not only will you have a sense of understanding that you've never had before, but you'll begin to experience how it will work in your life. Now I want you to understand that for me this is a mission, it's a mission that I live my life for every day. See, my **dad** taught me something important when I was young, he said, '**Kenrick**, if you love what you do for a living, you'll never work a day in your life.' And he also taught me that if you don't like what you do then every day will be a struggle and a fight. So I realized early on I* *had to love it and it's my mission to help people understand these principles just like I do so that they can have a change of life, they can completely **accept into their heart** a new way of understanding, a new way of dealing with this subject matter and that's my goal for us today as we talk.*"

Now, what have I done? Well *I've used all kinds of religious symbolism*—**repeating in three**, I used the *father*, the *son* and the *holy spirit* symbolism to *infuse you with the spirit*, blah, blah, blah, I'm talking to you as a *father*, meaning *God* and for any of you that have a Christian orientation or background, you'll have heard that very loud and clear and you'll understand the *power* this kind of language would have on somebody if you began using it like that.

On the other hand, if you were talking with *non*-believers, people who aren't Christian in orientation, it may not only *not* influence them positively, it may go the *other* way around. But, the **repetition in three** will work *everywhere* you use it.

Let's focus on one of the main reasons that it works and that is that *every single person* that you use a **repetition of three** on is *having your message repeated*. **Repetition helps install anything**. So **repeating in three** is simply a convenient way of remembering that you *repeat* the things that you most want people to *remember*. That's pretty simple. But it also has far additional *symbology* attached to it that works in a big percentage of cases.

So if you were a conservative politician and you were talking to your conservative base of religious people, well, my goodness, would you absolutely be able to use this to your advantage? Well, you bet you could. And it would probably make a very considerable impact on them.

Hopefully that will help. Let's move on.

CHAPTER THREE

Reinforcing the Unconscious Greeting

A question about the **unconscious greeting**. And it's written, "*If you know the **unconscious greeting** from a person from earlier, for example, earlier that day or that week or that month,*" - in other words, you've *interacted* with a person, you've *learned* their **unconscious greeting**, and now, you're seeing them again - "*Is it okay to do the **unconscious greeting** on that person first even before that person does it himself or herself?*"

The answer: *Absolutely.* You got the gist of that process. Yes. That's why we do it. We do it for two reasons, number one, we do it after they do it so they immediately **link us to themselves**, they go, "Hm. This person's just like me. In fact, even at a very profound level, they're just like me," and the **rapport** can be instant and profound.

Now when you see them again, if you fire their **unconscious greeting**, it simply *reinforces* that yup, sure enough, this person *really is just like them* and it's very, very profound what it can do. So by all means, you can and should do it exactly like that.

CHAPTER FOUR

Prospecting Vs. Selling

Next question, and I'm not sure if I've answered this before or not, but it bears repeating if I haven't. The person writes, "*Kenrick, you talked about the eliciting and use of **criteria**, but I'm curious if it can be applied to convince someone to set an appointment instead of the 'what's in it for me' reasoning over the phone. In other words, instead of using the **criteria** back at them over the phone. If so, how?*"

No. Not really. You *can't* really do it that way. Somebody could prove me wrong here and that would be great. I'd love to expand my own use with this but what I can tell you is this. You're in a sense almost *crossing hats* in a way that won't really be too helpful to you. Remember that *setting appointments* falls under the realm of *marketing* and in particular, we would call that *prospecting*. And **prospecting is different than selling**. In a sense, you can lump *everything* into selling if you so desire, okay? You can say, I'm selling someone on an *appointment* and then I'm selling someone on the *product* itself. And okay, but really traditionally, **marketing** is the act of getting people to raise their hands and say, "I'm interested."

Now, some companies *don't provide* that kind of service to their sales people and I think that's a very serious mistake. I personally would prefer to work on **positioning** such that people call *me*, and on **marketing** which I would define as a *one-to-many approach* in which my goal would be to have those many people, as many as possible, raise their hand and say, "Hey, me. Me, Kenrick. Talk to me. I'm interested." Okay? That to me is a very effective use of my time and energy.

Running through the phone book or going door-to-door and trying to get people to raise their hand is *intrusive selling* and I think that is definitely falling more and more by the wayside. There are some markets that have always and may always depend on this type of marketing. Stockbrokers and that kind of thing may build their book of business by calling cold on the phone. However, even at that rate I would very seriously recommend that you look at it like this. When you call to set an appointment, you're doing what would traditionally be thought of as a *one-to-many* kind of a process on a *one-to-one* kind of a basis. And so what you're doing is you're *suggesting* to people, you're trying to find out if they'll raise their hand and be interested. If not, move on quickly. In other words, **it's not worth it to sit and try to argue or convince someone who doesn't want what you have**, far better to go find a willing and open mind who is at least *interested* in hearing what you've got to say.

There are exceptions to this rule but if you kind of look at it like that, it will be helpful. Now the minute they *raise their hand*, go after them with all you've got with **criteria**, etc., etc. and even in the raising of their hand they may *spill* some of their **criteria** which you can *instantly* then say, "Oh, great. **What's *important* about that?**" And immediately get **leverage**.

Therein is a tremendous opportunity if that happens, but if it doesn't, *don't worry about it*, because when you get to the sale stage where you put on the sales person's hat, *that's* when you're going to go after the **criteria**, because at that point you now have *a mind who has indicated that it's open and ready to participate*.

CHAPTER FIVE

Making Your Skills Automatic

Let's move on. The next question is, "*Hi Kenrick. The question that I have spans across the first couple of books and is related to* **up-time**. *For many of the strategies that you have taught thus far, you indicate that it is important to* **stay in the up-time state**. *I was looking for some additional advice on how to maintain this state as I find myself continually just missing the opportunity to use the skills as I'm inside speaking to myself. Somehow both the* **unconscious greeting** *and* **physical pacing** *have become an automatic and unconscious act for me and I would like to get to that same level with both* **leading** *and* **criteria elicitation**. *Any strategies would be greatly appreciated. Thanks in advance.*"

All right. Here's the thing here. First of all I guess my first and foremost question to you and to everybody else who's reading this right now is a simple one: **How did you get to the point of making the unconscious greeting and physical pacing automatic and unconscious?** Because in *that same way* you'll make *every other skill* that I've been teaching you in this series of books automatic and unconscious. And that really is the answer. It's actually an easier answer than you might imagine.

First of all, what I hear in your question is **you're missing opportunities**. You say you find yourself *continually missing the opportunity to use the skills*. Welcome to the club. So do I. And what I do is I get upset at myself and I say, "Look, Kenrick. Stop it now. You need to use this skill." So if I miss it enough times I finally will take sort of *aggressive action* with myself and what I'll do is I will go out and I will dedicate a day or two or even three, on occasion, to *just that skill alone*. So I will say, "Okay, starting tomorrow, every interaction I have, I don't care with whom or what, I will first use this skill, no matter what. I will use this skill. One way or the other I'm going to use this skill." And then I *do*. I write out note cards to keep around me so that I have to see them all the time, that *remind* me of what the skill is that I'm focusing on and every presentation I make before I begin it, I *remind* myself of the skill and how I'm going to use it. And then I find that I start missing that opportunity less.

I would recommend that as a way to help you with it. But it's really as simple as, **what have you been able to make automatic and unconscious in your life** and whatever it is you did it by *rote practice*, maybe some *memorization*, and *doing it over and over and over* and watching carefully to find out where it would work and where it wouldn't and then using it where you know it will and pushing the envelope. That's how you'll do it with each and every one of the skills.

CHAPTER SIX

Dealing With a Procedural Perspective

Moving on, "*I **elicited criteria** from an individual. It was very easy. I did the 3-2-1. She couldn't give me a word for one. The best I could do was try and get her to sum it up. Still not one or two words to describe the highest criteria. Mind you, I've got a very detailed description. Is this normal? Does it come up much where there's no specific word but a whole lot of detailed explanation? By the way, she favors **visual** words.*"

I would ask you is she also **procedural**, meaning, did she give you *a number one, a number two, a number three*? Was the explanation in the form of a *story*, "Well the first thing that happened is, and then this happened...." And was it *sequential*? If it was, then she is very **procedural**. So what happens at her highest levels, she *converts into a procedure* that needs to be followed which is why you are unable to get a **criteria**.

However, there are several things you can do. Let me give you a few of them. Number one, you can **synthesize** it for her. You can say, "So is what you're telling me *this*?" And you *describe* it in a word or two. When you can get her to agree with your one or two words, it will work. But I'll tell you this right now, that's *not* the best way to do it. Why? Because *you're putting words in her mouth* and I try not to do that as often as I possibly can, but it will work. And it will work quite well.

However, if you *miss*, if she goes, "No, no, it's not quite like that," then you say, "What *is* it like?" and if she *repeats* the whole process again, just know that she is *very procedural* at that point and I would **shift your speaking** to a procedural point of view and say, "Okay. So it's not a particular thing necessarily. What I think I'm understanding is you're showing me that there's a series of steps that need to be taken, the first thing is this, then this, then this, and then that. Is that correct?" And then she'll probably say, "Yeah. Absolutely."

However if when you **synthesize**, she goes, "No, not quite like that. It's more like this..." And *she* synthesizes as well but just changes it ever so slightly, bingo. You've got it. Then use *those* words and move forward. Okay?

CHAPTER SEVEN

Realizing the Purpose of Rapport

Let's go to the next question. Isn't this good? I hope you're seeing the *distance* that you've come since reading some of this material, and how it can be *applied at higher and higher levels*.

"*Is it possible to have such a deep **rapport** that not only do you disarm conflict in the discussion, but something else can be gained, like respect, an equal, some persuasion ability, etc.? The reason I ask is that I had a major agenda meeting with an owner of the business I manage and my specific **outcome** was to **gain rapport** through **mirroring**, **pacing**, using his **key words**, and* *sticking to him motion-of- motion, eye movement, tone of voice, speed of communicating, etc., etc. My only outcome was to really **mirror** everything."*

And unfortunately the questioner doesn't go on to say what happened but I will assume based on the information that begins the question when they ask if *something else can be gained*, that something *was* gained, that they maybe ended up with additional *respect* or to be seen more of as an *equal* or they had some *persuasion advantage*, etc.

The answer is very simple. Yes. Not only yes, but *absolutely* yes. That is **the whole point** of deep **rapport** and the minute you enter into it all those things come flooding over to you—greater respect, seeing you more as an equal, maybe even as a superior, and incredible leverage when it comes to persuasion. So yes, yes and yes some more. *That's why we do it*. The point isn't just to be able to **lead** them, we need to *analyze* why we do **rapport** skills like this to begin with and I have said to you previously, it's so that we can *lead them to our way of thinking*, but it's also so that we get them to *trust* us and *believe* in us. That's one of the key and primary reasons that we're doing what we're doing.

I hope that makes sense because it's so, so, so profound.

It's important then that we use **rapport** skills all the time and assume that all of that's going to take place, in other words, that as we gain **rapport** through the *physical movement*, through the use of their *criteria*, through *breathing* like they are, etc., that we are absolutely having them transfer to us, *respect*, *belief*, we're completely *eliminating resistance* if there was any, etc. And that's why we do it.

CHAPTER EIGHT

Knowing When to Stop

Next question: *"When asking the **criteria** question, what do we do when the answers you get are not quite strong enough and subsequent questions only get you* lateral information *as opposed to going up their* values? *Is that an indication for lack of* rapport *and what can be done there?"*

Let me answer the questions in reverse. Yes. It could be an indication of **lack of rapport**, meaning that they may now be *uncomfortable* really digging in deeper and so they may not be willing to. However, there is another possible answer which we'll talk about in a moment, but let me stay with the first one here. So you have to *know* whether or not that's happening *by your own feelings*. Do *you* feel **rapport** for this person? Do *you* feel like they're in **rapport** with *you*? Do *you* feel that they're **trusting** you and **believing in you**? Do *you* feel that process kick in?

If you *do*, then you're experiencing the *second* answer I'm going to give you shortly. If you do *not* feel that **rapport**, then what I can tell you is, you need to **start learning what rapport feels like more** so you can *transfer* that to other people more effectively and if *you're* not feeling it, *they're* not feeling it and you've probably reached the limit of what they're willing to tell you.

Another reason that you'll get *lateral answers* is that they simply *don't understand* the question and/or they're *incapable* of going higher. So if I said to you, "*What's important about. . .?*" Well, let's use the stupid question that there are people out there actually training, "*What's important about money?*" I mean they just come out off the top and *say* this if you can believe that. Knowing what you know today, you know *so much more* about how to do this, don't you? I mean it's absolutely amazing why anybody would try to shove someone down a rabbit hole and force them to answer a question like that, but they do. So you're *light years ahead* of many, many, many people out there that have been trained to talk like that.

Okay, so, "*What's important about money?*" Well, that I have **more** of it. "*Okay, what's important about having more of it?*" Well, with enough of it, I guess I can be happier. "*Okay, and what's important about being happier?*" Well, dummy, I guess everybody wants to be happy, right? "*Yeah, that's true. And let me ask you this, what's important about everybody finding it important to be happier?*" Isn't that what life is all about? "*Okay. And what's important about that that's what life's all about?*" Uhhh...

You see what happened here? I mean, several questions ago this got *ridiculous* and you weren't paying attention. So what happened is you've taken them *up to the top*, like if I said, "*What's important about life?*" Well having someone to share it with. "*And what's important about having someone to share it with?*" Well, because companionship is so important and to me that's just very, very fulfilling. "*Okay. And what's important about then having your life fulfilled with companionship like that?*" Well, I think that's what I'm on this planet to experience.

You see, that's pretty high. Now we're talking about the planet itself and your total experience of it. How much higher than that are we going to get? Okay? Well, let's try.

"*What's important about that?*" And the person goes, Well, you know it's what my existence is about.

We're now at the level of existence. First of all, you're *not* going to get people to tell you that very often unless they've been psychoanalyzed for a long time or in therapy and they know how to talk like this.

So what's going to happen though is they're going to say something like this, they're going to try to tell you something like this, and if you said, "*And what's important about existence?*" Well, you're just being a fool, okay? In other words, it could be that they've gone *so high* on their **criteria** tree that they're simply unable to express more. . .you know, how do you answer a question, "*What's important about existence?*" Well I guess because I don't want to not exist? I don't know. What do you say, right? So you're *badgering* them. At that point, you're **way beyond what this is designed to do** or oriented to do and you need to **stop**.

CHAPTER NINE

Keeping It Honest

Here's a question that goes back to **intention** and **honesty** and the question is, "*If you tell a metaphorical story with an intention to persuade, but the story itself is not real, but you imply that it is, does that have an impact on your will?*"

I'm going to answer that question indirectly. I'm going to suggest to you that you *stop*, and *think* about that. Does it have an impact on your will? And I want you to think about it like this. First of all, when is a *metaphor* only a *metaphor* and when is it a *lie*? And I would have to say that that's going to be a very personal interpretation, not one I have a right to give you, but I will give you some guidelines you can choose to think about. I do not suggest that you blindly accept them but I would suggest you think about them. And the first guideline is, or thought process is, I would say more accurately, does your story or metaphor have any **selfish motive** to it? If it *does*, and if your story *isn't true* but you say it *is*, I would suggest to you that it's possible that could have an impact on your will in a negative way.

If the story is 100% about *helping* that person in some way with you not even having a secondary gain, and you tell them a made up metaphorical story, I would suggest that you think about this but that may have no impact whatsoever on your will. I would also suggest that you learn **not to say something is true when it isn't**. In other words, if you're telling a *metaphor*, why not preface it with something like this, "*As the story goes. . . In an ancient time. . .In the land now long forgotten. . .There were people that were talked about, never was it proven conclusively as to whether or not they even existed. But the story goes. . .*"

Now, what have you just said? I'm saying to you this is a *story* that's designed to *entertain* you and it's going to have some *analogies* or *symbologies* here that may be very *helpful* for you but I'm **not** telling you it's **real**. In fact, I'm telling you the exact opposite, aren't i? So if you're going to tell a metaphorical story, why not just be **honest** about it. I would say that when you learn to be brutally and completely honest, your life will soar forward. You'll have less junk and clutter in your life than you've ever dreamed possible before and I think you'll truly love your life even more.

And if you're doing all those things right now, see if you can't work to do it even better, but I applaud you for any progress along those lines that you've made and encourage you to continue on with it.

CHAPTER TEN

The Benefits of Adding to Criteria

Next question: "*Hi, Kenrick. I know you don't like features and benefits so you probably won't like this question. When you **add to someone's criteria**, aren't you just pushing the features and benefits of your product or service? In the example you gave the client wanted a home of 5,000*" *square feet or more and in a neighborhood where all homes cost one million dollars or more. You didn't have such a home to show so you told them about a home that you didn't have. Features and benefits, this home is 4,500 square feet but it is written up in a local newspaper that it feels larger. The benefit to you is you get to feel like you are in a 5,000 square foot home without paying full price. The home is also in an undervalued neighborhood. The benefit to you is that when this neighborhood because fairly valued, your house will be worth in the range of what you want it to be worth and maybe even more."*

This is very interesting, isn't it? And I have to really applaud you for asking this question. This is a powerful and very well thought out question, and the answer is, yes and no. Aren't you just pushing the *features* and *benefits* of your product or service? Yes, you are. But are you doing it in a *very specific way* that simply **leverages *their* criteria towards *your* uniqueness**? Yes, you are. So it's not *just* a features and benefits presentation, in fact, it's *far* from that. What you've done is you've **elicited the criteria**, you know *precisely* what they want, and then what you've done is you have brought up a feature, but that's almost irrelevant. In other words, at the time I was giving the example, if I remember correctly, I'm simply bringing up the fact that what they're looking for is the **feeling**, not just the actual thing itself. If you've actually gone out and told a realtor, hey, I'd like to have a 4,000 square foot home, or whatever square feet you want, and you go look at ten like that, you will see that every single home is vastly different than the last. In other words, what *looks like* 4,000 square feet to you the first time you see it, the next home may *look like* it's 6,000, the next home may *look like* it's 2,500. And even though they each have the number of square feet, the *space utilization* is absolutely amazing in the difference that it can create.

So all I was really going after there is giving them the **feeling** that it was what they wanted. In essence that's called **leveraging their criteria** and I leveraged it. I couldn't give it to them. For example, if someone says, *"Man, I want a fish dinner."*
And I don't have any fish, I could say, *"Really, wow. I bet that would be good. And after you've had a really good fish dinner, **how do you feel?**"*
"I just feel good. I feel light and I feel energetic and I just know I did the right thing for my body."
"Yeah. Excellent. You know what? Tonight I don't have any fish, but I was thinking I should have exactly that. A light dinner that would be very nutritious and would be just perfect for our bodies to the best we possibly can with what we have. So that we feel really energized afterwards. And I was thinking that chicken done very lightly and in small portions might really fit the bill, what do you say? I've got chicken."

Okay? So, does that help make sense of this for you a little bit? Yes, what we're doing is we're first **eliciting the criteria** and then with that we're **adding** in the form, and if you want to look at it this way, you can look at adding some of the features of *your own* criteria that only *you* can provide. That is what you're doing, but it's really not like spewing features and benefits at people and that's all I'm opposed to. I'm opposed to being lazy. Instead of asking someone for their **criteria**, you just start pounding away with your features and benefits. See, that's *not at all* what we're doing here. We've done the right thing. We've **elicited their criteria** and then we've simply **shaped** that criteria somewhat by *adding in* the features or the benefits of our particular product or service such that they only can see their value in light of our offering them.

CHAPTER ELEVEN

Framing Your Legal Obligations

Next question: "*Hi, Kenrick. If you are in* **healthcare** *part of informed consent is telling patients the bad things that can happen if you do the treatment or don't do the treatment. If the patient is towards, how do you go over this without pissing them off?*" I think that's a medical term, right? Just reading them like you write them.

First of all, you're not, necessarily and it doesn't really matter. Here's the thing, **the law is the law** and I would highly recommend you follow it. So if you're in healthcare, by all means, you've got to tell them the bad things that can happen. However, you can **frame** it a little bit. If they're a *towards* person you can say, "*Look, I'm obligated as your doctor,*" or whatever you are, "*to let you know that in this coming procedure there are things that can happen. Obviously you could get the results that you want, that's one thing that can happen, but now my duty is to tell you the things that could go wrong. And I probably hate having to do this as much as you hate having to hear it but nonetheless, this is the time where it's my* **obligation** *to do that. So please bear with me for a moment while I tell you the things that could potentially go wrong. And once I've done that you can choose to do with it as you see fit. You can choose to move forward or not. You can choose to put it into a different perspective and say, but the value outweighs the complications or what have you, and there I'll defer to you. But here's what can go wrong. This and this and this and this and this. All right. Now having said that, many people choose to say, all right, well now that I understand, I know that I'm not unrealistic, things can go wrong but hey, I actually really want to do this and I think I should and I've had the recommendation to proceed so let's proceed, doc.*" You could do that if you want.

"*It really is your call so now I've gone over it. Do you have any questions about what I've gone over?*"

See? So you can do it like that and I suspect that what I've just done is legal but you'll want to double check it unless you know yourself whether or not it is, but even if what I've done right there doesn't fit your particular instance in terms of the legality of it precisely, you'll easily be able to use what I've just shown you and make it work for you.

CHAPTER TWELVE

Reviewing Criteria Quickly and Effectively

"*When we are turning to a client after having obtained their* **criteria** *by asking 'What are we here for, what's important about that, and just so that I better understand you, what does that mean to you?' Upon the next meeting as I review the* **criteria**, *how much of a criteria review should I do? Should I start from the top or is there a better method?*"

Great question. And really you can start from the *bottom* and work your way to the *top* or you can start at the *top* and go back to the *bottom*, but I wouldn't necessarily do a lengthy review at all. It would sound something like this, "*Look, when last we talked, you told me that you really wanted me to* **focus in on your particular scenario,** *so that we would be focusing on solutions that you can implement for your investing, and that as a result of that it would make you feel like you are absolutely* **learning something** *that is* **profound** *and* **viable** *and that would give you an advantage in life that you couldn't really get elsewhere, and that doing all this would let you work with an adviser that you would trust and feel good about, and so that's what I've oriented myself towards since we've been apart and I have been working diligently to come up with what I'm going to go through with you today, that* **will help you to have those kind of advantages and the knowledge and the relationship that you've been talking about.** *With me, I know that it's important that I do it for all those same reasons, because* **I'm** *motivated exactly like that as well. So let me show you what I brought you today and I think you'll really begin to enjoy how this will unfold and how we can together make things work.*"

All right? And with all the knowledge you have to this point, I think you probably followed **exactly** what I was doing there. And if you didn't, go back and read it again and again. But some little **suggestions** thrown in and some **pacing** statements, etc., etc. So, there we go.

CHAPTER THIRTEEN

Rapport Comes First

"*What do you do eliciting criteria when what you normally do eliciting criteria doesn't work at all?*"

That's an interesting question. I'm going to have to make this up in my mind. Are you asking me what do you do when you are trying to **elicit criteria** when what you **normally** do to elicit the criteria **doesn't work**? If that's the question, my answer is **you probably don't have rapport**. So you need to be getting **rapport** first and foremost, you don't have to spend a lot of time on it but you've got to do it.

Then they'll be willing to give you the information you're looking for. And if I did not understand the question well enough, please send it again.

CHAPTER FOURTEEN

More Practice: Less Theory

Here is the next question: "*If someone is strongly* **visual** *and after having* **paced** *it I throw some* **auditory** *or* **kinesthetic** *words in my sentence, the person will go into a tiny bit of a trance...*" Okay, well let's say they'll alter their attention slightly. "*However, what does it actually do to that person since he or she is most conscious of the* **visual** *modality, are the other modalities equally processed as well, or less so, or do we aim those less conscious modality words towards specific levels of thinking and behaving, like, I want him or her to act, I use the less conscious words?*

Whereas I want the person to have a conscious understanding of something so I use the most conscious modality?"

Wow. Okay. I'm just going to go ahead and provide the rest of the question and then we'll kind of dive into it.

*"I would presume the **unspecified** words are at a higher logical level,"* …
uh oh,…
"and since the higher logical level controls the levels below it, it is much stronger. Is this correct?"
Careful there. You're going off into another little **rabbit hole**.
*"And since the higher logical level controls the levels below it, it is much stronger. Is this correct? Shouldn't we be using the **unspecified** modality most of the time?"*
No.
"When to use it and when not?"
I'll tell you in a second.
*"What to do with a person who is most of the time talking in **unspecified** words?"*
Call them the engineer that they are. . . .No, I'm just kidding. Then talk **back** to them in **unspecified** words. By the way, then **lead** to the use of **specified** words to **sensory specific** words.
*"Do we use **unspecified** words with him since he will have to fill in the right sub-modalities himself?"*
And let's say the right **modalities**, not necessarily sub-modalities, in other words, the **visual**, **auditory** and **kinesthetic** words. I guess . . . boy someone here has had too much training in NLP. **Too much theory, not enough practice**. But that's okay. I'm not naming names and you know who you are. But **more practice, less theory**. Okay?

Work with my stuff and you won't have these kinds of issues, I promise you. You wouldn't believe the number of people that come to me and say, I am certified at the level of a practitioner and trainer and blah, blah, blah, and I *still* don't feel like I know what I'm doing, can you help me?' In fact, I had one of those guys come into my elite program last year, and immediately, within like 60 days, rise to the top of a 50 or 60 person sales staff, and immediately rise to the top and has been there every month since, or at least in the top three and has cut back his work to about one and a half to two days a month. And his *biggest* question was to me, 'Hey, I'm certified at all these different levels from all these different people and I *still* don't know what to use and I'm *still* not sure when to use what I do and can you help straighten me out? If so, I'd like to be in your program.' And I said, not only yes, but absolutely yes. Get in the program and almost immediately he started getting straightened out.

That will happen to you too as you go through the material *precisely* as I present it and don't try to go so strongly into the theory of this because it's confusing you. You're all over the place with this question.

So let's go back through it.

Your first question is, if someone's **auditory** and you throw in some **visual**, you're saying they'll go into an *altered state*. However, what does that *actually do* to the person? It **expands their consciousness**. Meaning that we're capable of holding in our conscious minds seven (plus or minus two) pieces of information simultaneously. Meaning five to nine pieces of information we can kind of juggle. That's about the length of an average phone number depending on where you are in the world. So you can hold those digits sort of in your mind, at least for a few seconds.

We can work with that many variables simultaneously is another way to sort of look at this. And if the variables *increase* beyond our conscious capability, what's happening to them?

Well, the next question I have for *you* is, *what aspect of you is **controlling** which of those variables you're paying attention to to begin with?* In other words, while you're paying attention to the *conscious variables*, there are *other* things going on as well, such as the feeling of your *clothes* on your body, but you probably weren't thinking about that until I brought it up. How about the feeling of the *temperature* around you? You probably weren't thinking about it unless it was too all fired hot or cold. How about whatever *humming* or *buzzing* is going on in the background with your sound system right now? Aha. How about all kinds of things? How about *noises* and *creaks* and *groans* around you, from floors or faucets or what have you that you weren't paying attention to until I brought them up.

So what I can tell you is that **your unconscious mind is really the one that is dictating what you're paying attention to and what you're not**. Does that make sense? That's what's really happening here.

Being that that's how it is, it's dictating what it is you're supposed to be paying attention to more so than anything else. So what's happening when you *expand someone's consciousness into more things than they can hold at any one point in time*? It's dropping off into the realm of the **unconscious**, meaning **you have greater ability to influence them**. Okay? Then you go on and ask, 'Since he or she is most conscious of the **visual** modality and . . .Okay, are the other modalities equally processed as well?'

All the modalities are processed. However, they will be *more conscious* of the **visual** ones. And yes, you can learn to orient your language such that the things you *want* them to be conscious of, you could use the **visual** modality for, and the things you *do not want* them to be conscious of, you could use the **kinesthetic** submodalities for, or modalities. Meaning, you can **talk about what you see** when you want them to be conscious, and talk about the other things, in other words, **hearing** or **feeling**, when you want them not to so much know about what you're talking about. That does really work well. And you can prove this to yourself in a number of interesting ways. For example, if you're talking to someone who's highly **kinesthetic** and you walk over and you touch them all the time while you're talking, they will *notice* it and it may disrupt them. They also may like it. Actually, a **kinesthetic** person will probably like it.

But, here's the interesting thing, if you're standing really, really close to a **kinesthetic** person and you're touching them, that may be just fine. They will notice it. They will be *aware* of that touch. But it's no big deal. And of course if you're standing real close to them, that's fine too. But *now* try that with a **visual** person.

Visual people want some *distance* between you and them. So if you're standing really close to them, like a couple of inches from them, you're going to *disrupt the space around them* that they use to put their pictures in. Now their pictures are going to be muddled and befuddled and they won't be able to maneuver them with ease and speed and so they're going to be a bit *confused*. They *won't like* you standing so close and they'll probably back up. So you can sort of see this demonstrated in that way as well.

*"So shouldn't we be using **unspecified** words?"* I assume you're saying that because that forces people to come up with their own understandings. No, we don't want to force people to do it that way unless we're giving **process oriented instructions** and those need to be *separate* from your everyday speaking, otherwise, you'll bore people to tears and they simply won't be influenced by you. So the goal is that I'm talking to you like this, I'm talking *clearly*, I'm using **visual**, **auditory** and **feeling** words, I'm wanting you to hear me *consciously*. Right now, read what I'm saying, and listen with the audiobook if you can, and let's look at **how this is used in your life**, because as you do you'll begin to find certain and specific methods and ways that you can implement this really strongly.

Now, one of the great things that you can do is you can begin to **repeat** this in your mind *over* and *over* right now, about exactly how you're going to be using these ways to get this to work better for you. And that's fun.

So look, let's be **specific**. With the training you're getting, there's all kinds of ways that you can do this. Okay? I just did it to you. I used very **specific** words. I called you. I said, *'pay attention'* and then I slipped into **process oriented instructions** telling you to find specific ways to make this stuff work better and to go out in the future and make it work. Blah, blah, blah.

But I did that **consciously** and **purposefully** while to you delivering the equivalent of **unconscious suggestions**. Meaning, you had to probably alter quite a bit there to *hear* that. And if you wonder what I just did, if you don't know what I just did, it's probably time for you to take a break and come back to this when you're fully conscious again because this is some heavy, heavy duty stuff I've been telling you so far in this book. I mean, this is **heavy duty persuasion material**. Hard core, 100% applicable to what you're doing. And when I'm **shifting in and out of consciousness** like this it will take its toll and you will kind of be feeling a little fuzzy sometimes. So what I would like you to do is just maybe it would be good for you just to *stop* and take a minute or two to *think about what I've just told you*, and then continue on.

All right, if you're continuing on, I assume you stopped or you're extremely conscious and are paying attention to every word, but I guarantee you, when I feel *myself* starting to slip in and out like that, I know *you* are.

CHAPTER FIFTEEN

Recognizing the Strategy Exit

Let's go to the next question. *"Let's say I **elicited the decision strategy** and the customer has used for this **visual** and **auditory**. Would it still be a good idea to put a **kinesthetic** at the end?"*

First of all, let me just stop you. I don't believe that a strategy is complete until you get to a **kinesthetic**, so if the client hasn't gotten to a **kinesthetic**, *you haven't gone far enough into their strategy*. It may loop a bit. Loop-de-loop. It may go **visual**, **auditory**, **visual**, **visual**, **kinesthetic**. It may go like that. It may go **visual**, **auditory**, **visual**, **auditory**, **visual**, **auditory**, **kinesthetic**. It might go like that. We don't know how it will go, but I would keep asking until it feels right.

131

When you get a **feeling** statement, they're **exiting from the strategy**. So for example, I would **future pace** at the end, giving right after I use the **visual** and **auditory**, a good **feeling**, linked to the **criteria** of the customer to the product or service I deliver. You're assuming that their whole strategy is **visual** and **auditory** to begin with. You're in error in my opinion, right off the bat, because that strategy has *not completed* in their mind so you don't know how that strategy exits. You don't know how they exit and you don't know if that's enough to actually insert the **kinesthetic** at that point. So if you're really going to go true to a strategy, I would ask them, "*What happens next? So first you **see** something, and you **see** X, and then you **hear** something, and you **hear** X, and then what happens?*"

"*Well, then I **look** to see if it's right.*"

"*Okay, great. And after you **look** to see it's right, then what do you do?*"

"*Well then I know it is because it **feels** right. I know it is.*"

"*How do you know?*"

And you see them looking down or they say, "*Well, I know because it just **feels** right*", and they **touch** their stomach, or their chest and they say, "*It just **feels** right.*"

Okay, then *that's* the exit of the strategy. So then just **use it right back at them the way they said**. Okay?

CHAPTER SIXTEEN

Synesthesia

Next question: "*What does it mean when a person is using a certain modality a lot in his speech and at the same time, the **eye accessing cues** show something different? Which modality is the person really using?*"

Well, this is a pattern used as **synesthesia**. I *hate* using technical words, I don't find much use for them as a general rule, but here's the time when it's worthy of breaking it because this is a good term for you to know. **Synesthesia**. It means *where one modality drives another*. You see what I'm saying? Do you **SEE** what I'm **SAYING**? How do you *see* what I'm *saying*? I guess you could see my lips move. But right now you can't. So if I were to use a statement to you like, '*Do you see what I'm saying?*', that's a **synesthesia** pattern, meaning that the first thing that happens is some **picture** happens that *drives* an **auditory** component, that drives an *awareness* of an auditory component.

It goes into a lot more technical detail here and it's not really necessary. Let me just tell you that the *only* thing you really need to do with **synesthesia** patterns to keep this simple is just **do the same thing they do**. So if you hear someone say, '*Do you see what I'm feeling?*' You want to do the same exact thing. '*Yes. I see exactly what you're feeling. Yes, that makes sense to me. In fact, the other day, it's like I had this image flash in my mind and I immediately felt...*' blah, blah, blah, blah, blah. So just concentrate on doing what *they're* doing and that will be just fine.

So another way to look at this is instead of which is the *real* strategy, or the *real* modality, it's what's the **lead** modality and then what's the **next** modality that follows, the following modality. That's another way to look at it. And often the *lead* modality may be out of consciousness but not always, and it takes a lot more lengthy discussion to really go there, all of which is sort of not all that useful for persuasion, but when you see this, just know that the person is rather unconscious even at that point. In other words, there's something going on with them as it relates to that information or that part of your discussion that is *relatively unconscious*.

If they **see** something to have a **feeling**, and they describe the feeling at length, then probably the *image* that *started* the feeling is *outside of consciousness*. So *you* could then describe a picture briefly by way of saying to them, '*Let me just **show you an image** that will be kind of interesting. And in this **image** it's bright and it's close and it's you having more success than you've ever had before in your life and as you **see** it, it **feels** good. In fact, in like a millisecond, it's like the image isn't really that **visible** but you know it's there in your mind but you just have this persistent **good feeling** that lets you know that the picture is really there. Do you know what I mean?*'

So you could do that. All right? And *that's* the way to use **synesthesia** in persuasion and at this level, the easiest.

CHAPTER SEVENTEEN

Linking Everything in an Expanded State

Next question: "*If we **overload the consciousness** of a person by **using all the modalities** at that same time in one sentence, make the sentence really long, linking everything, throwing in lots of **unspecified** stuff, we create a blank in the mind of that person. What's the use of this?*"

Great question. I think I've answered that really in previous questions to a certain extent. But what it's doing is it's **creating an altered state** or an **expanded state** in which we're **shutting down their critical functioning**. There is *so much going on* that they're stuck back at the barn back at the bakery somewhere, not really knowing exactly what to do, sitting there in more or less of a stupor, *taking in everything that we say*, so when we begin then **linking everything**, well, what are linking to? Hopefully **emotions**, which we're going to talk about here now. And what are we talking about in an unspecified manner? Hopefully we're talking about **processes** that they're going to be following. **Ways of thinking or feeling** about what we're there doing. So that it **guides** them in general but we leave the **specifics** to them.

Nonetheless, it's like taking a train and putting it on a track and giving it a shove. Where's it going to go? Where the *track* goes, right? The engineer thinks he's in control but all he's really doing is starting and stopping the thing. He's really not steering it anywhere.

In essence, *you've provided the rails* and *suggested that the train move down the track*. They think they're in control because they're in the engineer hat. They think they're in control but in reality they're going down the rails that you laid down. So that's what it does.

CHAPTER EIGHTEEN

Talking the Same Language

Last question: "*With regard to the impact of using different **representational systems**, don't we all encounter the different systems every day in the various people we meet? If we are used to hearing other rep systems, why would changing the systems up when talking to someone cause confusion? Thanks.*"

Another excellent, excellent question. And here's the answer to that. While we are used to doing it ourselves, or hearing other people do it, rather than listen to them for what and who they are, we're immediately interpreting what they're saying and doing into *the language that we most understand and like*. This is what took people so long to figure out that human beings were doing this in the first place. Okay? Because the minute I say to you, "You know, the other day I was having a feeling about this job that I had to do and it felt really good to me," and I go off into a description about it. Well all of the sudden, *you're* going to go off about one of *your* jobs that you're doing.

In other words, **my words remind you of your experience**. That's *how you make sense* of my words. But as such, you begin to *lose* a whole lot of the meaning of the other person's words. So because we're *always in our own head* reinterpreting and doing it our own way, we're not *nearly* as flexible as you might imagine by your question. In reality, we're quite **inflexible** and that's really sad. So by using the system that I'm teaching you, you're going to dramatically *increase your flexibility* with the representational systems and with all things persuasion, and you're going to be able to **speak back** to the person in a way that they **don't have to reinterpret** unless you want them to begin the process of interpreting because you're giving them **process oriented suggestions** and you want them to make sense of it any way they want to, provided it's the way you tell them to.

The reason that it can *cause confusion* is because it's *not in the same system* or the same organization that the person is traditionally used to doing it in their own mind. Like I told you very early on, using these representational systems like this, it's like speaking *four or five different languages*. The language of the **visual**, the **auditory**, the **kinesthetic**, the **unspecified**, even the **taste and smell**. So it's like speaking a bunch of different languages. Yes, it's all within the realm of the language that we speak, you know English, French, German, whatever, but within that it's like a *sublanguage* and so really we all make sense of what we hear based on our own model of the world and that's what we're constantly doing, is *comparing other people's words to our model*. And that's why two people see or hear or experience something, the exact same thing, and yet it's two wildly different events if you were to hear them tell about it.

Okay?

All right. And that brings us to the end of the questions. And I most sincerely hope that you are beyond excited and thrilled about this additional information in this book and taking the time to really **make sure you have as much information and knowledge on this as I possibly can**. I very much enjoy helping you to personalize this and bring it right up to speed and make sure that you are understanding this at the levels that I would like you to.

BOOK EIGHT

USING EMOTIONS TO YOUR ADVANTAGE

INTRODUCTION

Eliciting Emotions

In this book we're going to talk about **using emotions to your advantage**. It would be best if you could listen along with the free audiobook, as described on the previous page.

I'll start with a statement that I believe encapsulates what this is about and that is that **all persuasion is benefited to a large extent by eliciting the type of** *emotions* **you want your prospect to experience and** *leveraging* **them to get the results you're after**. Now in fact, this is one of the core concepts that will make a giant difference in your ability to persuade and then in your life.

What we're going to talk about today is useful in persuasion but it's every bit as useful in your day-to-day life. It's really, really powerful.

Eliciting the emotions can take several forms. You can elicit the desired emotions *directly*. So for example I could ask you *what was it like* when you felt X? And you can elicit the emotion by *using emotionally charged words* that will get you the response you're looking for. So if I wanted to *raise your level of excitement*, I could start talking about something that you were very *excited* about. I could use words like, *excited*, I could be *dramatic* in my speech, I could use other words, like *phenomenal, amazing, unbelievable*, you know, the people were running around *so excited they could hardly stand it* and I could start describing using **sensory based terms** what that *excitement* was like which would begin to *convey* it to you.

I could just *ask you directly*, what's it like when you feel excited, or I can use **emotionally charged words**. It will get the response too. And both work really, really well and of course a third way we can do it, and a really powerful way, is you can **tell a story** to elicit the emotions.

CHAPTER ONE

Eliciting Emotions With a Story

Now, in the **story**, you can **elicit the emotions** *directly* which still really takes on an *indirect* form, and the way you could do that is you could be talking, telling a story about these people or what have you, . . .Well, let me give you an example. Just a little bit earlier when I was telling you about how my cousin knocked me out of my job by exploiting a weakness that I had created mainly within myself, but certainly would not please an employer, but when he *took advantage* of that and knocked me out using that stratagem, when I told you that, did *you* also feel a sense of betrayal? I used the word betrayal, but did **you** feel it? You probably did. You probably felt like, "Huh. I hope no one does that to me," or "I remember a time when somebody did that to me and it wasn't fun." Or, "Wow, I would never do that to someone else. I'd just quit, but I wouldn't knock out my cousin or my friend. That's just not right."

So isn't that kind of interesting? *You* *felt it*. Why? Because the **story** *stopped your critical functioning from happening* and you just kind of *got into hearing it*. That's the power of the stories.

Another way you can do it with a **story** is getting the listener to **bond** with one of the characters of the story and thus *experiencing the emotion the character is experiencing*. Again, by way of *stopping their critical processing*, and they're simply *bonding* with this character who is going through these good or bad times, whatever, and they begin to **feel** it. Is that not *precisely* what movies and books do for us?

CHAPTER TWO

Emotions, Not Logic

Now your ability to **utilize emotions to your advantage** will take you from being an *average* sales person to being a *great persuader*. I've said this before but now we're going to put some *power* behind the words. **People buy based on emotions, not logic**. If you think that persuasion is *out-arguing* someone, nope. That's not it. If you think that persuasion is having *a more powerful logical argument*, nope. Wrong again. That's not it.

I could give you the greatest logical argument in the world and if I'm *not* **appealing to your criteria**, it may well fall on completely deaf ears. If you can't afford something, for example, let's say I want you to buy the Empire State Building, just for sake of discussion. I don't know why you'd want it but let's just say that I did. I wanted you to buy that. And let's say you don't have whatever it would cost, a hundred million dollars to buy it. *It doesn't make any difference* how logical of an argument I come up with, it's probably not going to work.

People buy based on emotions not logic and it's *critical* you really get this because that is part and parcel to this book's lesson. That's what I want you to get, is **people buy based on emotions, not logic**, and therefore I want you to **begin to *use* emotions powerfully**, really,

really powerfully. If you've been structuring your presentation around making it *logical* instead of *emotional*, you've been missing the boat. Implementing these strategies will immediately put you in an entirely different league in terms of results.

If, for example, you watch the movie *Fahrenheit 911*, (now again, whether or not you buy into this or not doesn't make any difference to me.) But if you saw that movie, at the end of the movie, there was the guy who made it who was following around a U.S. Senator, for real, asking him. . . and by the way, this was basically, for those of you that don't know what this movie is, it was basically an expose of how the government screwed up on 9/11 and how the whole thing is sort of a scam and he basically set out to prove it. Whether he did or not, I'll leave up to you. But at the end of this movie, he was following this senator who has loudly yelled at the top of his lungs that we need to support the military and the military is great and invading Iraq is wonderful and we're doing the right thing, yada, yada, yada. He came up to this senator on film and said, "Senator, you've stood in support of this war and I'm just curious, I don't believe that your son is in the military and he's of age to be able to serve. And so I brought for you here these papers so that you can enroll him in the military and I'd like to sit down with you so we can do that. Since you support it so much, let's make sure your son gets right in."

Oh, you should have seen his face change. This senator was not about to hear one single word of what the movie producer was saying. He was like, "Uh, yeah. Okay. I've got to go." He goes, "Wait, wait, wait. Senator. We haven't got your son in here. You're so in favor of this war, come on, let's get this thing filled out and let's really show the American people where you stand. Since you believe so much in this war, put your son in it. Come on."

I mean this guy was. . . if you want to ever see the definition of *evasive*, I mean, it was this senator trying to *make haste away* from this guy and his cameras because he was looking like a complete fool. Oh, it's okay for *everyone else* to be in the war, but *not* his son. And the producer made it perfectly crystal clear that that's *exactly* what he was saying. He just brought the world down on the heads of these people and I certainly think it contributed to the stance of the United States being so adamantly against this war at this stage of the game.

And our leadership being completely out of touch because they have an agenda. Okay? So in any event, this is all for you to determine, not for me to say, but I want you to see how this works and the **emotion** that was brought to bear here.

So many sales people think through the **logic** that would be needed for *them* to buy their own product, and then they structure their presentation accordingly. Look at any sales presentation you've ever been given. Like a verbatim or a written out sales presentation. What is it? Well, it's **nonsense**. What it is, it's a *logically based presentation* of, well, if you want this, it's basically an '*if... then...*' kind of a thing usually. *If* that, *then* this. *If* this is your situation, *if* these are the things you need to do better at in life or you need to solve these problems, *then* this is the answer and we provide it and now that we're here talking to you about it you want to go ahead and buy it, right? No.

Thinking through the **logic** that would be needed for *you* to buy your product and then structure your presentation that way as you give it to *everybody else* is akin to an advertiser *telling* you that they've hired an especially attractive spokesperson that they've had dressed rather provocatively so that you'd be more influenced by their ad, but *not showing you* the spokesperson, just *telling* you that this is what they've done.

So the question then becomes, is it a male or female spokesperson they've hired? *You don't know*, do you? *You don't know* by what they've said so far. So **how much real impact** is this *supposedly* attractive, provocatively dressed spokesperson going to have? None. Imagine a voice on the TV coming across and saying, "We would like you to buy this car and to do that we've hired an especially attractive spokesperson and we've dressed them very provocatively because we know that this works so we've done that and they're standing right here by me and they'd like you to know that they would like to use their attractiveness to lend credibility to this car and they want you to go buy it now. Thank you so much for paying attention to this ad."

It may work just because it's *humorous* but it certainly *wouldn't* have the effect of the beauty being used to pull you to the ad, would it? Because **you can't see it**. You can't tell that they've done it. They've just *said* they've done it. Okay?

On the other hand, as you probably know, studies show that if you *see* a very attractive person in an ad it *does* have a positive impact in most circumstances, in a lot of circumstances. In other words, **the *emotion* of the experience is what causes the results**, *not* a logical description of it.

If I were selling you a house for you to live in and I'm telling you it's 3,500 square feet, 3 bathrooms, two floors, blah, blah, blah, statistics, that wouldn't necessarily impress you too much. But if I said I've got a home that **equals the criteria you told me about**, you said you wanted one to do *this* and *this* and *this* because of *that* and *the other thing*, and **as you see it** you're going to have a **feeling** that you're at **home**, it **feels really good**. Really, really good. And then you take them to the house and show it to them, they may well go, "Oh, my God. This is it. You hit it right on the money. That's it. That's what I want. Give me this house."

If you're an adviser and someone comes in to see you and you say, "Look, I'm going to recommend the following portfolio. This stock we're going to recommend because of that, and this mutual fund we're going to recommend. Here's the specific performance over the last ten years." And you break out your charts and graphs and blah, blah, blah, blah, blah, you'll probably put him to sleep within seconds.

But if you're telling them, "Look, you're probably *tired* of risking your money with no name advisers who sit behind a big corporate veil and don't interact with their customers. Well here you are today in the exact *opposite* situation sitting belly to belly with me. My name is Kenrick Cleveland. This is what I do. I do it because I'm *proud* of it. And I do it because I can *help people* just like you never again have to be afraid of losing their money. I'm telling you that when you work with me *you have me on your side helping you*. I'm not saying I'm perfect always. The market's not perfect always. But by careful thought and planning and having someone on your side watching over it, to whom *you're not just a number*, to whom you can *pick up the phone and call* makes all the difference in the world. It makes you *sleep easy* at night. You know what I'm saying?"

Well there we go. There's **emotion** being delivered to help you with the sale. And I know that as I'm speaking these words right now many, many people who are reading this book are selling based on *logic*, not on **emotion**. And I'm telling you that **emotion is the majority of what makes the sale**. The logic must *back it up*. You have to *be* logical about it. But by the same token, it's the **emotion** that you're going to use to get them.

Archimedes said, "Give me a lever big enough and I can lift the world." Well let me tell you,

emotions and *using* them well will *extend the length of your persuasion lever* significantly. So with this you can lift sale after sale the way you want it to go if you do it really, really well.

CHAPTER THREE

Eliciting an Emotional State Directly

So let's talk about *how to use* the emotions really powerfully. Let's go through the steps of how to **elicit an emotional state directly**.

Number one, you must **go into the emotional state yourself** and this is the *missing piece* for most people. This is where they miss it. Okay? You've got to go there *yourself*. And you've got to **feel** it. And if you don't, how do you think you're going to convince anybody else to do it? If *you're* not even willing to feel it, why should *they*? Ever think about that?

There are a number of reasons to go into the **emotional state** yourself. First of all, you should be in **rapport** with them, if you're not you don't deserve to be talking much about emotions anyway, you *need* to be in **rapport**. So if you're in **rapport** with this person and you **lead**, what do *they* do? Well if you're truly in **rapport**, they **follow**, right? Right. What does that mean for you? Well, what it means is if you are in let's say a relatively *non-emotional* state as you gain **rapport** with them and then you *go into* an **emotional state** of being absolutely *convinced* or into *strong belief* about something or into real *excitement*, etc., and they **follow** you there, can you see how that would be an advantage?

Step two, once you are *in* the state, and this is why, by the way, you must get *good* at this - you have to get good at *going in and out* of emotional states *quickly*. You have to learn to be a method actor where you can learn to cry at the snap of your fingers. Not cry really. I don't expect you to do that. I don't do that either. But I can certainly get *happy* real quick. I can certainly get *convinced* real quick. I can certainly feel *passionate* real quick. And one of the ways I've learned to do that is to *speak that way*. So when I'm *passionate*, I speak with *passion*. When I'm *excited*, I probably speak with a lot of *excitement*. When I'm *serious* and I'm *committed* to something I speak that way. So start looking at. . .there we go, here's **synesthesia** coming out of my mouth, start figuring out for you what those **sound** like because maybe by *adjusting your sound* you can help yourself get *in* and *out* of these **emotional states** when you need to. And second, **practice** going *in* and *out* of those emotional states.

So, you've made it there *yourself*, you're *in the state*, now you're going to ask your prospect *questions* about the target state. Such as, "Can you remember a time when you absolutely had to have something and you bought it? *What did it feel like* right at the instant when you made the decision to do it?"

Isn't that a great question? Now, you can also ask them, "What's it like when. . . ?" And then follow up with whatever emotion you want to know about because then they're going to *describe* it to you.

Now I want to stop and do sort of an aside for a second because there are some of you that are thinking, "Ah, Kenrick's going to get to **anchoring** finally." Nope. Not going there. And you say, "But why not? It sounds like you're headed towards **anchoring**." I'll tell you why not. It's because when you try to learn this **emotional state usage** and **anchoring** all at once, what you end up learning is *not much of either*. And over many years I've figured out that **it's really the emotion that has the power**. The **anchor** is the special sauce. I'm going to teach you how to do **anchoring** but it will be in a later book. Okay?

In other words, if you have the meat, you still got a good dinner. If you can add the special sauce down the road, hey great, add it. I'll teach you how to have it, but I want you to **master the emotional state material** first and foremost because here's what I found happens. Unless you know how to do *this*, when people start talking about the **anchoring**, those learning end up instead *tricking themselves* into *believing* that they're using an anchor when in reality they're not doing squat, they're not doing anything.

So they're going, "Oh yeah, I'm anchoring this, I'm anchoring that." And in actuality, they're not doing anything. They're getting *no results* from it whatsoever. But because they think they're making some tricky little movement or some tricky little sound, they're going to do something, they are simply *led astray* and so on the one hand they're questioning, "Hey, why aren't my results better? Because I'm using anchoring and all these other things?" But in reality they're *not* using them well at all. And so for all practical purposes, they might as well *not be using them* because really, that's the effect and so if the **results** are what you can **see** and **hear** and you're *not seeing* any results from it, then you're *not using it*. It's that simple. I want to make sure that when we do this together, you're going to get results from it and I'll tell you, 80%, 90% really of the results you're going to get will come from *this*. If you were to lump **emotional states** and **anchoring** together, it's just *logical* to teach them together, but it's *not practical*.

So I'm going to go for **practicality** as I always do and *make certain* that you can do the **emotional state** part first. So even if you've been exposed to **anchoring** at some time in your life, please *disregard everything you know about it right now*. I want you just to *put it out of your head*. And just focus on what I'm teaching you with **emotional states**. Use *this* and *only this* and when we're ready I will proceed to talk with you about how to do the **anchoring** portion of it as well.

Step number three, **be congruent**. If it's an *excited* state you want them to go into, *be excited yourself*. Now I said the *first* step is to go into the state yourself, but you've got to *stay there*, don't you? And that's another mistake people make. They go, "Okay, I'm going to go into *excited* so. . .I'm getting excited, I'm getting exited. Okay. Now I'm going to get *them* to be *excited*, so let's just talk about, so 'if you were *excited* right now, *how would you be feeling?*' What does that do? You just **blew it**. So **go there and stay there**. So number one could be called '*go into the state yourself*', number two, '*ask questions about the target state to elicit in them*' and *stay there yourself*. And number four, it's really important that you have the person you're persuading **associate into the experience** of whatever you're talking about in step two.

So if you're talking about *excitement*, you've got to *put them into excitement*. If you're talking about *desire*, you've got to *put them into desire*. Talking about *buying*? You've got to *put them into a time when they've bought*. So notice that in the second question I asked, "*What did you feel. . .?*" So I said, "What did you feel like right at the instant that you made the decision to do it?"

CHAPTER FOUR

Associated and Dissociated Emotional States

Let's talk about these *two important distinctions* that I just started to allude to, because these are distinctions that will help you **control emotions** within yourself and others more effectively.

1. Number one is the concept of **associated emotional states**. And this is when you or the person you're persuading *actually feels* the emotions. It's simple. It's just a word that means *you really **feel*** it.
2. And number two is **dissociated emotional states**. And this is when you or the person you're persuading is *thinking about* the state but *not experiencing* it. You're thinking about it but not experiencing it.

This would be like *talking about* an emotion. Make sense? So if I said, "The other day a friend of mine was really upset and they were raging actually and they were going on and on and it was really difficult for them. They were talking about how they put a hole in their wall and they had driven over here and their car was still hot and blah, blah, blah." Okay, well *am I angry* as I tell this to you? Am I all *emotional* about it or am I *talking about* that emotional state? And if you said talking about it, you're right.

I'm **dissociated** from the **emotional state** I'm telling you about. It would be like saying, "The other day in the store I saw this kid and he wanted . . . it was very funny, he wanted this box of cereal and so his mom said, no, we're not going to get Cap'n' Crunch and he started screaming and he was yelling and screaming and throwing the biggest fit I'd ever seen and man I was just laughing about it. He was kicking his feet in the cart and then he reached over to the isle where the boxes of cereal were and he started pulling them all down onto the floor until his mother raced over and stopped him." Am I talking to you about that experience in an angry state? Am I throwing a fit and knocking cereal off the shelves myself as I tell you about it? No. So I'm **dissociated** from it.

Now let's analyze that very carefully. If you were **dissociated** from the **emotional state** you're trying to **elicit** when you're talking to your client, the one you're persuading, *they too will talk about it* from a **disassociated** state and you will not have much of a persuasion lever. It won't do *anything* for you at all. It's only when you **associate** them to the **emotional state** and they **feel** it that you have one giant persuasion lever.

I wrote, "In order for emotions to work in your favor, to leverage them to your advantage, the person you're persuading must be **associated**, meaning, they have to **feel** the emotion. And in order to get *them* to feel the emotion, *you* must feel it first. Don't expect *them* to go there if *you* haven't or if *you* won't." And again I see so often in people that I train, I see so often that they start off *thinking* about the emotion and taking a long time to *get there* and by then they start to go out of **rapport** with the prospect. That's a mistake.

The second thing I see is that they *go there* and then when they begin talking about it with the client, they *leave* that emotional state, thinking they have to go back to talking professionally to their client. Again, a huge mistake. Doesn't work. Okay?

CHAPTER FIVE

Breaking the Poker Face

Now there's a **challenge** in **using emotions to your advantage**. Since everyone knows they can be *swayed* based on their emotions, prospects often try to deal with you by putting on their best **poker face**. You've experienced that if you've sold for more than a few months.

I remember going to a really nice high end audio store here and I walked in the store and I didn't know what I was going to find for sure but I knew I wanted a better stereo. This is a few years back. And so I walked in and here was this nice lady who asked if she could help me. And I said, "I'm interested in some high end stereo stuff," and so she said, "Okay, here. Let's go into the high end room." Well, okay, that was nice. And there were all these beautiful speakers and she showed me one, she played it for me, and okay, it looked pretty, sounded nice. I thought, that's better than what I have. And she said, "But if you *really* want to hear high end, I mean if you *really* like music, you've got to hear the Martin Logans." And I said, "Okay." And they're stunning, beautiful speakers. She sat me down in this chair, she went to their best stereo system in there, and she flipped the switch to engage them and she said, "First, tell me, *what kind of music do you want to hear* with these? Could I recommend. . . " and then she starts recommending a few. I believe the song she played was, 'You Lift Me Up.' I forget the artist's name but it's a beautiful song. And so I said, "Okay, fine."

So she stuck in this CD and turned the system on and oh, my goodness, I was transported straight away to the most beautiful place in my mind, surrounded with this singer and his band. Oh, my goodness. I thought I'd pretty much died and gone to heaven. I couldn't believe how *good* that sounded. Oh, my goodness, it was *amazing*.

As you can imagine I have that pair of speakers sitting in my living room. I told my wife the other day I'd like to get their much higher end speakers one day but they're spendy and I'll wait a while. But it's just *amazing*. But when I walked in that store I had my best poker face on. "What are you looking for?" "I don't know. Kind of a nicer stereo. Kind of a high end stereo. But I don't really know. I'd like to just kind of look around and see what you've got." "Okay, sure. Come on into the high end room."

Well, look, by the time she had gone through her little spiel about the Martin Logan speakers **I was already ready to be sold**. Man, I was sitting in that chair. I was **excited** to hear what she had to say and I was **excited** for the treatment I was getting and for this tremendous sound I would soon be hearing. *Unbelievable* is a better way to put it.

You've probably put on your best poker face and *how far* did the sales person get? And I'll tell you that if you didn't want them to get very far because you kept your poker face on, well then, you probably walked away without buying and they without a commission. **What breaks the poker face?** Yup. **Rapport**. The best way around somebody's poker face and being *unwilling* to have those **emotions** is to **gain strong rapport** with them. And that way you **disarm their resistance** to you and your message, so this enables you to get them to be *comfortable* having emotions.

Now there's *another* way to do it. What is it? **I just did it with you**. I hope you got it. **I told you a**

story. A story. Were you right there *with* me in the chair? Were you *listening* to the Martin Logans *with* me hearing the song 'You Raise Me Up' if you know what that song is? Did *you* feel like *you'd* died and gone to heaven too? Are *you* interested in going out and hearing a set of Martin Logan speakers?

No, I get nothing from the company if you do. But let me just assure you they are incredible sounding speakers, though, let me warn you in advance, unless you're getting their very, very high end which are somewhere in the neighborhood of $7,500 and up, you do need to get a sub-woofer with them and I actually ended up getting two, one for presence, and one for slam. Yes, I know, those are words I would have never thought of before in my life either until a few years back, but presence is that low end pressure in the room that you feel when you're hearing a very good sound system. It's not super, super. . .well it can be very low but it's on the low side, that's for sure, and it's called presence. You feel the room you're in as a result of presence. And slam is like you hear at the movies when there's a big crash or a slam, an explosion of some sort. And so I have yet another sub-woofer that just handles the slam. And that's also a Martin Logan, but the presence one is not Martin Logan, it's another one. Even higher still as sub-woofers go.

It's a great system. By no means, do I have the highest end, but *were you there hearing it with me?* I'll bet you were to at least some extent. To the extent that you like music real well, I'll bet you were right there with me. So, did that *drop away your resistance*? You bet it did. And that's exactly the point of **stories**.

When you gain **rapport** with someone especially through a **story**, you're **disarming their resistance**, you're **stopping their critical thinking** and I can **leverage** that to my advantage and you to yours. I could have said, "And it's that kind of *symphony* in our minds, that *sound* of perfection that we're going for in persuasion. And I want you to hold that ideal. And I want you to *let my words reinforce it* as we go through this course together such that with each book we *build this reality* into your mind *stronger* and *stronger* and stronger, such that you get more *excited* with each book to come and you *understand* how much you're learning and just how *excited* you are to learn it and to *continue* the process."

Now would that have been to my *advantage* to say? Yeah, it was. Uh oh. Was that a little *sneaky one* again? You get the point, right. See, every time I launch off into a **story** I can **leverage** it any old way I want, can't I? And so can you. And that's the key to this. You can **leverage these stories** every which way but loose and you can **leverage the emotions** even more powerfully still.

The stories allow you to invoke the emotions without any resistance. Now that *doesn't* mean it's not effective to just go straight for them and I'm going to show you how to do that in just a second.

It's so well known that *emotions can sway us* that for many purchases the law requires, at least here in the United States, a three day right of rescission, so when your emotions *subside* you can change your mind if you want to. That's true for every state in the United States. Did you all know that? When you sign a big contract here in the US, you have *three days to change your mind* on almost everything.

Stories, **rapport** skills and eliciting and using the person's **criteria** *disarm that resistance* so that they'll have the **emotions** and in a later book, I'm going to also show you what to do to help the emotions to *never subside and change away* from the way you got them to go. It's a fascinating study in a very practical skill.

CHAPTER SIX

Some Useful Emotions to Elicit

Let's talk now about **some useful emotions to elicit** so you can be off to a fast start with a skill that will absolutely add to the very core competencies you're building in persuasion.

Here's a list of some of the *most useful* emotional states you can use to sway your prospect to your advantage. **Criteria** and **high values**. I list them as number one because they *are* number one. Everybody has a **feeling** about their **values** and their **criteria**. So once you've **elicited their criteria or values** you can always ask, "*And how does that feel?*" A person comes to you and you say, "So why are we here today?" And they go, "Because you know what, I need some help. I need an adviser who can help me with my finances and who I feel like I can *trust*. I mean, I'm tired of being worried." And you say, "Boy, do I understand that. Let me ask you, *what's important* about not having to worry anymore?" And they say, "Well, because if I don't have to worry anymore I guess I'll just make more money. That's what it is. I think I'll make more money." And you say, "Okay. And *what's important* about making more money?" And they go, "That's what my money's supposed to do for me. It's supposed to be making me money. I worked hard to get it, now it should work hard, and that's what it's supposed to do."

Therein is what he says. That's his **criteria**. Now, here's what I want you to know. With that knowledge I can simply say, "*How would you feel* if your money was working hard for you and if you just felt great about your adviser, you didn't have to fear anymore, *what would that be like*? *How would you feel*?" "Oh, I'd feel so good."

Could *that* be useful? I think so. That's the kind of power that **emotions** will give you when you start to use them to your advantage. We go after **criteria** first and foremost because we want to know *exactly* where to aim our persuasion message and second, because we can **elicit the emotion** from it.

Right up front you're doing two hugely powerful things when you get that person's **criteria** and **values**. And boy does it have an impact.

All right. Let's talk about another thing you can elicit. **Decisions**. And this would be especially *ones that worked out well* for a person. Unless you're trying to walk on the dark side a bit and then you can elicit decisions that *didn't* work well. And you can probably imagine how to aim those. But if you elicit the decisions of times when a person made a decision that worked well for them, could you use your language to **link it to you** and **deciding to work with you**? Yeah.

Wouldn't that be interesting? And I'm going to give you some very specific examples in a minute. How about *buying*? A time when a person *bought* something and felt really good about it and it worked out well for them. How about *excitement*? What's it like when you're really *excited* about something and you know that the advantage is huge for you? There's excitement. How about *passion* or *desire*? When I say passion it doesn't have to be the sexual version, it could be you're

144

passionate about something you believe strongly in. Or you have a lot of *desire* to do or accomplish something. Those are *very powerful words*.

How about *something you absolutely must do*? Let me ask you, what's something that you *absolutely must do* in your life? I'm serious right now. I want you to think about it. **What's something you absolutely must do?** Think about that. Maybe you absolutely have to get up and go to work tomorrow. Maybe you absolutely need to pay your mortgage payment next month. I mean, if you don't, you're going to lose something, right? So if you want to not lose, you're going to have to pay it. If you want to build your equity and keep it and do better, you got to pay it, right? Think about something you *absolutely must do* and I want you to **lock in** to the fact that you *must* do it and whether you like it or not, I just want you to experience that you *must* do it, for a moment.

You might ask why I've asked you to think about that. Well, I'll tell you. As you hold that in your mind, and read my words carefully (or better still listen with the audiobook) because I'm showing you how to do this. I'm telling you, I guess. My **synesthesia** is leaking out all over. As you hold that in your mind that you absolutely must do it, would it be useful to you to begin to **think the same way** about following through with the work that I'm assigning here in these books?

Now you can add some *excitement* and *good decisions* and all these things, your **high criteria** and **values**, add all that stuff to it, but **if you absolutely believe that you *had* to do it**, and you *began* doing it, would it be *even more valuable* than you're already experiencing? I think there isn't one among us that wouldn't agree that this is several packed books of extreme value. But *if you used it even more*, **if you absolutely believed you *had* to do the homework** and even more *completely* and *thoroughly*, would there be *even more value*? And I think you know the answer would be yes.

What am I really doing? I'm simply **leveraging** *something you must do* into *doing more homework*. Now because I'm *calling your attention to it consciously* like this so much it may not be quite as powerful as it could have been had I *not* called your attention so powerfully to it. And that's okay because the point is simply, I want to show you how to do it with language. All I have to do is **elicit** it within you and say, "*Isn't this useful to apply over here?*" And that does it. You don't have to be real slick about this. You can just do it like that.

Let's talk about a really big one, **something that is no longer true for you but used to be**. I love this one. You might say to me, "Kenrick, you're talking about **emotions** here." Well, I'm kind of going *beyond* it now with 'something you must do' and with 'no longer true but used to be', I'm going into the realm of **strategy**. And I'm **eliciting a strategy** that I can apply to my advantage.

It's not just an **emotion**, it's really more of a **strategy** and if I can get you to *imagine* the strategy, then I can **leverage** it like mad. For example, if I have you think of *something that's no longer true for you but used to be*, most people have a difficult time coming up with this unless you *prompt* them. So if I wanted you to do this, I would probably say something like this, "Hey, let me just show you something kind of interesting and useful. . ." And by the way, that's like a **softening frame**, I'm *prefacing* what I'm saying so that I *get you to do it*. You go, huh, interesting, useful, okay, I'll try that.

"What's something for you that's no longer true in your life but it used to be? I mean, like for example. . ." And now I've got to give you some *examples* because otherwise you won't *get* it. A lot of people don't. So I would advise you to do what I'm doing here. "Like, for example, you used to live at one place but you don't live there anymore and you'd never go back either. You lived in an older, small apartment when you were younger but you don't live there anymore, that's for sure." They go, "Yeah, yeah, that's an example." Or you say, "Or you used to have a really bad habit that you just wouldn't even consider doing anymore. Maybe you used to smoke and now you don't and you'd never go back in a million years. Or you used to drink and now you don't. You wouldn't start up again no matter what. Or you used to swear like a sailor and now you don't at all." Whatever. "You used to believe in God, or you used to not believe in God and now you do." That's a really powerful one. You're kind of playing with fire there, so be careful with that one a little bit, but wow, is that ever powerful.

So you say, "So *it's no longer true* that you don't believe in God anymore, right?" "No. No, it's not." Or you say, "So it's no longer true that you live at that older apartment, right?" "No, it isn't."

Okay, now. Say, "The reason I had you think about that is because I'd like you to stop and *think about it the other way around*. What's something you *absolutely believe in*. . ." Now, by the way, at this point I'm really more or less just **camouflaging** what I just did. I'm simply *switching their attention* away from what I just did. I'm presenting **a quasi-logical argument**. In other words, "Oh, and it makes sense that you have to know both sides," is really what I'm saying. "So what's something that is *true* for you? What's something that's *true for you now*?" Whatever. And they'll go, "Well, I'm 46 years old." "Okay, great. Forty six years old. Okay, perfect."

The reason . . ."And by the way, that's *absolutely true*, isn't it? No getting around it?" "No getting around it, that's true." "Well look, interestingly, I brought this up for you so that you could *compare* something that *isn't true anymore* for you, that's just *not who you are*, with something that is *true* and *is who you are*, because as I talk with you about this material today, **you're going to find yourself having a particular feeling**, like knowing that you're forty-six and it's like you have a way of knowing how to deal with it already and there's another part of you that can just go, yeah, but that's like that old apartment. Those things don't matter anymore. I'm not there. I'm forty-six. So as I talk, I'd like you to begin to think of these things like that so you can clearly see how this applies to you. And I like to help my clients with this because it just makes it easy for them to begin to understand what it is I'm really doing for them in a more profound and personal way. Do you know what I mean?"

What I'm really doing there is a lot of **camouflage** because all I really wanted to do is get to the point of saying, so when I talk about what I do, *you have a way of thinking about it, just like the fact that you know you're forty-six*. In other words, *you know it's true* and I'm aiming *no longer true* at **objections**. So the guy goes, "I don't know. I just think I want to think about it." And you go, "You know, you wouldn't *think about* going back into that old apartment, would you?" "No, not really." "Yeah, you know. You know how to think about what you just said to me and I think that you begin to realize right now that really what I'm talking about probably feels more like, 'I'm forty-six. It really is useful and it really is something I should move forward and do.' Do you agree with me?"

This is rocking powerful. I didn't need to set any little **anchor**. I didn't need to make any noises. I didn't need to wave my hands. I didn't need to do anything. I could have done all of those, but all I had to do was bring it up and that's all it takes.

Another emotion that you can elicit: **fear**. Now you've got to be *careful* with negative emotions, you've got to really be careful with it.

146

When you **elicit negatives** what will happen is that it can *backfire* and hit your product or service or company and you don't want to do that. So be careful, very careful. But if you have an *away from* person, okay, then go ahead and elicit it. Back the ambulance up to the door just like I've taught you and there would be an example where you could elicit *even more* fear.

As I said before, you can *ask* about these states *directly* to **elicit** them and you can use **emotionally charged words** about the emotions to elicit them, so I mean to tell you that you have a really power packed way of going about this. You can also, of course, tell a **story** about any of these and use them effectively.

I want you to begin, though, asking this question: "What's it like when you **feel**? What's it like when you feel? What's it like when you feel really *excited* about something? What's it like when you feel *passion* and you feel passion burning inside you and you want it? What's it like right at the moment that you *make the decision* to buy something? What's that like?" And by the way, that sort of *combines* decisions and buying into one big thing, one big emotion.

CHAPTER SEVEN

Adding in Other Emotions

I'm going to give you another strategy you can do. A little bit more advanced, very easy to use

I can *ask you a question* about your emotions and you start answering me and I can simply **add in other emotions** to that and it will *combine* a new hybrid more powerful emotion making it more *unique* within you and thus potentially affecting you even more powerfully. For example, I could say, "What's it like right at the moment, right at the very moment when you *make a decision to purchase* something? What's that like for you?" And the person goes, "Well, I don't know." And you go, "Well think about it. *Think about a time in which you bought something* and right at that moment, right as you decided, yeah, I'm going to go ahead and do it, even before you said anything, but right in that moment inside you, *what did it feel like*?" "Well, I was a little *nervous*, kind of like *butterflies in my stomach* but in a good way. And I was a little *scared* but *hopeful*. I guess, kind of *scared* and *hopeful* and just *determined*, I guess then. Just *determined*."

And you go, "And you know what? I'll bet you if you were to sprinkle in a little bit of *excitement* into that as well, you know, *scared*, *hopeful*, *determined* and *excited*, that might have **made it even better**, wouldn't it?" "Yeah." See. So you can just **add in an emotion** by saying, "And if you added in a little X or a little Y, **wouldn't it feel great**? I'll bet that would even add more, wouldn't it?"

No, that's *not* features and benefits. No, it's *not* changing criteria, exactly. It's literally **adding to the emotional state**. It's **stacking emotions** one on the other to get more leverage out of them.

Very interesting strategy. "What's it like when you. . ." blah, blah, blah, blah, blah, and **name what you want to elicit from someone** and then simply *talk about it in your presentation*. "You told me that you just feel when you're convinced that something is right for you, that you just feel like, wow, like you found home, like walking along a twisted underbrush path, fighting your way through and all of the sudden emerging into a clearing with clear blue skies above and crickets softly singing in the background and the sound of a stream nearby just over the hill there, nice big rocks warmed by the sun that you can stretch out on and just soak up the sun and the warmth and all the good vibes of that valley. Doesn't that feel good?" "Yeah, it really does." "You know, *as I talk with you* about the subject matter that we'll be talking about today, *just reflect on that from time to time*. Let your thoughts wander to that beautiful rock with the sun drenching it with its warmth and comfort and *allow that to spread here to us today* and I think you'll begin to put this in the proper framework of really making you feel good about you and about all of these skills. . ." or all of the products that you're selling, or whatever. That's how you do it. It's just that simple.

In other words, **you're using your words to leverage the emotional state you're eliciting**. It's that easy. It's not hard. And notice that it's *logical*, it *makes sense*, but we're really using **the power of the emotion** to do it and that's why it's so profound. That's what we want to continue to do is just make this really profound for you in a way that is really easy to use. I'm telling you, this will increase your persuasion skills enormously.

CHAPTER EIGHT

Homework

Here's what I'd like you to do for homework with this book. I want you to work on *extending the length of your persuasion lever* through **the use of emotions**. So determine which emotions would be most useful to you in your presentation and *begin working them* in very early on. Ask, "What's it like when you. . . ? Here's why I ask." In other words, after you've **elicited** them, *tell* them "Here's why I ask." I want people to begin to understand a way to think about what I'm talking about and you know when you start talking like that, especially in general words like I'm doing using **process instructions** like I'm doing, people just kind of **zone out**. They're like, "Okay. Cool. Wow, yeah. Makes sense to me." They will. It's amazing. I want you to begin to *think of emotions as giant persuasion levers* and carefully study how you can **leverage** the mind of your prospect more effectively through their use.

Keep wrestling with these skills, most importantly. And take several moments every day to be grateful for what you have and for this learning because it will help, it just keep right on coming. It will help you keep getting even more of the good things of life and help you to progress the way I know you want to.

I hope you're exited about the contents of this book and you're beginning to find more and more ways to *use* it and *apply* it and it's important that you just *work* with this. You've got to **work with the emotions** and *make them yours*. Start in with your friends, with your family, start **eliciting emotional states** everywhere you go. Realize that it's about *capturing the mind of the person that you want to persuade*. You do that through **emotions**, you do that through **stories**. And I want you to begin to have *emotional* presentations, not just *logical* ones.

All right. It's been great giving you all of this information. I've really enjoyed it and I can't wait to talk with you again in the next book. Take care.

BOOK NINE

THE ORGANIZING PRINCIPLES OF PERSUASION

INTRODUCTION

Understanding Context

Welcome to **Book Nine** of *Persuasion Force*. We'll start off this book with a questions and answers session to help clarify some of the strategies we have learned so far.

*Can a person be **toward** on one thing and **away from** on another?*

You bet. They sure can. In fact, let's just take an example. Let's say a person has a **very high value** as it relates to their finances to be **a good provider** for their family. Let's just say that's the case. Let's say that they are moving **towards** being a really good provider. And let's say in another context, let's say about their car, they might want to have a new car because the one they currently have is *old* and they *don't feel it's as safe* for their family. So that would be an **away from** there. So they're looking to *get away from a lack of safety* and you'll see this play out all over the place.

Here's a way to look at this. A person can be *towards* on one thing, *away* on another all day long. However, whatever they are, they'll tend to stay that way in that particular context. A better way to look at this is *contexts* will fall into whatever they are in that context so if they're *towards* in a particular context, they'll pretty much *stay* towards in that context.

Trying to get a context to *change*, even over time, it just generally *doesn't*. There is certain change work you can go through to try to switch that around but that's a pretty tall order. Whatever they are, they tend to be, but for each different *context*, they can be a different one, *towards* on one, *away* on the other, etc.

CHAPTER ONE

Starting to <u>Do</u>

*Apart from **EFT**, what could I do to shut up, stop thinking and start doing what I know I should be doing? Thanks.*

Ahhhh. Great question. Well, I'm going to give you a simple answer. You asked me a very straightforward question, I'll give you a very straightforward and simple answer. Start doing *anything* and start doing it *right this minute*. Whatever it is. In other words, demand of yourself every day that you **do something**, not think about something, but **do** it. And if you do this every single day, you're going to find that in a month's time you'll have done *a lot*. It reminds me of the joke, my mother in law started a walking program here recently. She walks a mile every day. Now she's approximately 200 miles from home.

So the idea is that you want to get 200 miles from home by doing a little bit every day. And what I can tell you here is that the **key** to actually **doing something** is whatever *thinking* you're going to do regarding it, let it be **global**. In other words, say to yourself, I've got to accomplish the use of these skills. I want to start using these skills more effectively. Then say, what's the first skill I'm going to learn, I'm going to start doing? Well, let's say you choose the **directing of your intention**. Then simply write down on a three by five card that you're going to **direct your intention** every opportunity you possibly can all day long. Carry that card with you and before every presentation, before every time you meet with someone, pull out that card, sit and relax for a few moments and instruct your other than conscious mind what you want it to do in that interaction.

That will help you to **start to do**. And then after a month or so, or a week, or a day, however long you want, then *add one skill to it* and then keep *adding* and *adding* and *adding* and if you're doing that, you've really come a long ways, you've walked 200 miles.

CHAPTER TWO

Tapping and Swishing: Eliminating the Negative and Installing the Positive

Next question: *You talked about the **swish pattern** that could help us to **eliminate negative emotions**. As I understand, **EFT**, **tapping**, can also be used to eliminate the negative emotions and it seems much easier. Could you please give us more application when we should use **swish patterns** and when we should use **EFT**. Thank you.*

Let me tell you how *I* do it for *me* and I'll give you some ideas for *you* and then you can kind of take it from there.

First of all, I like **EFT** for working on negative stuff and the reason for that is that *it's so easy to do*. In other words, **EFT**, for me, is *quick*, I don't have to try to stay in a positive state, I don't have to try to manage my emotional states like I would with more traditional techniques, such as the **swish pattern**.

That said, where I personally love the **swish pattern** is *directionalizing* something. So I found **EFT tapping** type stuff to be best at *removing negativity*. It doesn't really *install* anything. It doesn't really do much else except kind of *neutralize the negativity* which is, of course, brilliant in and of itself for what it's for. But let's say that I am consistently avoiding making cold calls, if that's something I needed to do and of course, if it was, I would probably find myself either doing something different or creating more referrals or in some way eliminating or lessening that supposed tactic of selling. However, let's say that I was avoiding this because I felt a knot in my stomach and it made me nervous to pick up the phone and call somebody cold.

The first thing I would do is I would use **tapping** and I would use it to *eliminate those negative things*. The next thing I would do is I would use the **swish pattern** then *to give me a direction of action* on that cold calling so I would actually *directionalize* through the **swish pattern** that cold calling is going to be making me money, making me feel good, it's going to be propelling me towards my goals in a very cost effective manner, etc., etc., to get me to feel better and actually *take action* on it. So I would *start* with the **tapping** and I would *follow up* with the **swish pattern** and that's something that I do frequently.

So since I've found that **tapping** doesn't really work that well on anything unless it's negative, and there it works brilliantly, and that's just, by the way, my interpretation of it, meaning, some of you may have found ways to use it to *install positive things* but really it was originally created as a **therapy** to overcome fears and phobias and that kind of thing. And therein is where it works really, really well.

If you're using it that way for yourself I think you're right on the money. The **swish pattern** is used to *generalize* your thoughts and your behaviors about something. In other words, you want to *do more* of something or *feel more positive* doing what it is you're doing. That is where the **swish pattern** can come in really handy. And so that's how I like to use that.

CHAPTER THREE

A Persuasion Checklist

As we start the main material of this book, I'm going to share with you *what to keep in mind as you start to persuade*. What I'm going to give you here is a little checklist, if you will, and you can use it as you begin any interaction with someone so that you have kind of a *cheat sheet* or something to consider as you begin your persuasion. And this will help you to prepare for any persuasion situation that you undertake.

First of all, if you have time, **learn as much as you possibly can about the person or company you'll be persuading**. The more you know, the better you'll be able to persuade them.

Next, let's deal with the realm of **intention**. And here you need to *set* it. So **set your intention** by making sure you are *very clear* about what you want to accomplish. Then you want to give real clear directions to your other than conscious mind. If you start off a persuasion situation and you have *not* set your intention, the odds of it working well for you are slim to none.

Now, another way to think of this, if you'd like, is you could **set your intention** right this minute for *every* possible persuasion situation to follow. You could do that by setting your intention as to *global* ways of thinking and outcomes. However, if you have the opportunity to know that a persuasion situation is imminent, it's coming momentarily for example, then you have the opportunity to just kind of stop and *be very specific* about what you want your intention to do for you.

If you have time, again prior to the interaction, then **imagine the interaction flowing perfectly** and you ending up with the results that you want.

Next, you want to **put yourself in a peak emotional state** to persuade and really feel it. The next step is, you want to make sure you gain **rapport** quickly as you begin. That is, make sure that you're not using your peak emotional state to *run over the top* of your prospect. You probably experienced that before. And it's important that you don't do that, you make sure that you **develop rapport quickly** but **manage your emotional state** so that it works on your behalf.

As quickly as you have **rapport** or even in the process of gaining it, **elicit the person's criteria** that you want to persuade as quickly as possible and **leverage** it to your advantage the whole rest of the time.

Those steps are about as much as I would put into my mind prior to beginning. I wouldn't try to think through 100% of everything but I would think through at least that far. That will get you off to a very solid start and enable you to *use your unconscious mind* to help guide you as a result of programming it, in other words, *telling it what your intention is*, for that interaction.

CHAPTER FOUR

Harnessing Intention

All right. I am going to be sharing with you in this book about **the organizing principles of persuasion**. We're going to examine **the underlying organizing principles of persuasion** and the **core principles** that we've been studying and that we'll be using as we proceed.

The idea that I had in preparing this book for you was to help you **put all the skills you've been learning into perspective** so that that helps you in understanding and using them to your advantage. You sort of see the big picture, and not the big picture in terms of just techniques, meaning, okay, first step do this, second step do that. But more in terms of *the organizing principles* that comprise persuasion. As we go through this I think that maybe it will make a lot of sense to you.

We'll talk about **harnessing intention** as the first step in the process. *Everything begins with our* *own intention.* To the extent that it's working on our behalf, our intention *amplifies* what we do well and it helps us to *change* with effortless ease the negative into the positive. Meaning, it helps us to *flow with whatever comes up* and it still keeps us on track. So **our intention guides our behavior and our words**. It helps us understand and anticipate what is going to be needed to make persuasion happen and create the results we set out to create.

You can see why I put **harnessing intention** as the very first of the organizing principles because if your intention isn't solid as a rock, if it isn't *organized* and *oriented* towards what you need, if it hasn't *directed your unconscious*, then your results are going to go all over the place and that's a problem.

So **intention is a two way communication with our other than conscious mind**. Intention allows us to instruct our other than conscious so it can follow our guidelines during an interaction and it *communicates* with us during interaction helping us to *adjust to the changing circumstances*. So **harnessing intention** is step one of the **Cleveland Method** and it is the first thing that you need to focus on and concentrate on getting and doing well. Everything else will flow easily once you can do the harnessing intention really, really well. And I suspect by now you're probably getting pretty good at this, but like I said, my goal here is to give you a bunch of the pieces of the process of persuasion and in so doing, I think you'll discover the kind of *overall process, the overall system, the overall strategy* that we're aiming at.

CHAPTER FIVE

Trust and Rapport

At the heart of every persuasion interaction **trust must exist**. Persuasion without trust, there's a word for that, it's simply *coercion*, and that doesn't work. Fortunately gaining someone's trust is a skill set that can be learned. Techniques and strategies can be used to engineer **rapport**. Let's talk about that for a minute. When I say *engineer* rapport it sounds pretty doggone manipulative and not all that positive and yet nothing could be really further from the truth.

As a sales person one of the things that's absolutely true is you've got *minimum time* to make *maximum results* happen. Now why do I say you have *minimum time*? Well, your time is valuable. You've got to get things done. To the extent that you can get things done, you're going to make money. To the extent that you're *not* getting things done, I don't care how fast or how long it takes you, you're still *not* making money.

We need to *engineer*, to *create*, to *manufacture*, if we need to, and **jump start rapport** so that it will lead us to **trust** and fortunately this can be done. And it can be done very powerfully. All **trust** and **rapport** starts with *being like the other person*. Okay? So this is genuinely a set of skills that's dependent upon the persuader's **intention** in order to be used with **integrity**. In other words, the exact same things that a con-artist would do to gain trust and establish rapport, may be very close if not identical to what *we* would do. The difference is in our **intention**.

Let me go to a field of study that seems to be so prevalent today and it's the field of **seduction**. Here what I'm talking about has some significant bearing. If you're going after a person, a man or a woman, and you're *saying what they want to hear* in order to get what you want, well that may be extraordinarily manipulative bordering on evil. Yes, sure, I'll love you in the morning. The classic, right? And yet, if it gets the job done, you may think that that's smart. However, I like to paraphrase the old saying and change it ever so slightly by saying, "Hell hath no fury than a person scorned." Maybe it's more true substituting the word woman for person. I don't know. But I can tell you that *anybody* who gets *lied to* to get some end result or outcome is *not* going to be very happy about its result. **Trust** and **rapport** truly depend upon the persuader's **intention**, *your* **intention**, in order to be used well.

Ensuring the presence of **trust** in any interaction should be highest on every persuader's mind as they begin. **Rapport** facilitates **trust** and can be done *physically*, with *words*, *rhythmic speaking*, *stories*, finding common enemies, observing and using *unconscious greeting* strategies, *eliciting the emotions* of trust directly, *language patterns* and many, many more things some of which we've covered already.

That's **the organizing principle of trust and rapport**.

CHAPTER SIX

Criteria and Values

The core of **The Cleveland Method** deals with how to very quickly **elicit and utilize the prospect's criteria and values** for whatever it is you sell. This completely eliminates, gets rid of, destroys, makes useless, features and benefits selling and as you know, my opinion about this, *features and benefits selling epitomizes typical and old-fashioned sales methods*, branding you as a sales person. You might say, "What's so bad about being a sales person? I'm proud of what I do." And you should be. Nothing's bad with being a sales person. However, when you're *branded* that way, that's not a pleasant way of referring to you, "Oh, well, that's a sales person." Yeah.

In fact I drove up today to the store to pick up a few things that I needed and on the way in there was a woman standing outside the door with a table. I didn't really look at what she was selling in that moment and she said "Hi". I said, "Hi." She said, "Is the top of your car there black for some reason? Is there something about that?" And I said, "Well, yeah. It's glass." I have a Lexus, the new ES350, their high end version of it which is all glass on the top, glass moon roof in the front over the passenger and the rear as well. And it's black when you look at it, especially at a distance.

As you get close you can tell that it's glass but it does look like it's kind of black from a distance. And I thought, well, how interesting. How interesting of her to ask me that. That's fascinating. And she said, "Oh, great. I was just curious." She says, "Well, stop by and check out what I'm doing on your way out." I saw then that she was selling Girl Scout cookies. I smiled. I went in the store, got what I needed and on my way back out she said, "Come on over." I said, "Not today, thanks though." And was impressed with her use of strategies. Wow. I mean, find something about the person that's *personal*, that you can bring up without appearing to come on to them in some way and she did that very well, brought up something about my car, and made it *a personal statement*, **elicited** from me a discussion about something I'm *proud* to have, and then *invited* me to check out what she's doing.

I thought it was very, very powerful. Very powerful. And then *invited* me to stop over. Everything was very understated and no pressure. I was very impressed with that. No need to use features and benefits. First of all, she was simply *appealing to my human nature* to come on over and check this out. And to the fact that we had a *previous relationship* based on what she created as I walked into the store. I was very, very impressed with that.

Now, had she immediately started in with features and benefits, well, it would have branded her a typical and old-fashioned sales person, but she didn't do one of those. I mean really, I almost stopped just to give her the courtesy of a discussion simply because she had done so well and if I weren't in such a rush today I suppose I would have. So the thing is it will brand you as a sales person and worse it makes you appear unprofessional and someone to be afraid of in case you don't have your prospect's best interest at heart. And the fact is, if you're the prospect, that's right. If a sales person can't figure out *how to determine what you really want and need* and quickly, at that, they deserve the label.

My system was the *first* to bring this to the world of business in an absolutely duplicable way. It was available in the field of therapy long before, but making that transition is something I'm proud to have brought to the world of business.

CHAPTER SEVEN

Language Strategies

Another one of the core organizing principles is **language strategies**. Once one understands how to get **criteria** then they must learn how to **link it to their product or service** in such a way that the prospect's *values* and *beliefs* become *synonymous* with the products or service the sales person wants them to buy. Wow. I mean, really, stop and think about that. I know I've said it to you before, but as I'm giving you these overarching strategies of persuasion, **stop and think about the power of what I just said**. You're *linking* your product or service to *their values* in such a way that **their values and beliefs become synonymous with your product or service**. That's quite an accomplishment and that's the power of what *language patterns* and *language strategies* can do once you have their *criteria*.

You're learning in these books specific **language strategies** to create these results. We have many more to go. Once this is mastered, it enables you to *differentiate yourself* in the mind of your prospects because the prospect will see the product or service *through the filter of their own values*, thus making it far more *personal* and *understandable* to them. So we have a whole series of **language strategies** that we'll be getting into even in more depth that will enable us not only to hook people's **values** and their **criteria** to our products or service but to **presuppose** their criteria and values in ways that are absolutely un-defendable. They'll simply have to go along with it. They are some really powerful and amazing things.

CHAPTER EIGHT

Appealing to the Other Than Conscious Mind

Let's go to the next organizing principle, and that is **appealing to the other than conscious mind**. At the core of everything we do is the understanding of the need to appeal to the *other than conscious mind*, some call it the *unconscious* or the *subconscious* mind, of our prospects. This is a primary orientation of **The Cleveland Method**. We recognize the *other than conscious mind* to be the *real boss*.

We have to *placate* the conscious mind, because it *thinks* it's the boss but the *real* boss is the *other than conscious mind*. It's like going to work with a couple and the alpha male of the two juts forth his hand and shakes yours vigorously and acts like he's the dominating one but when it comes time to make the decision what does he do, looks over to the wife, maybe, huh? Who has the *real* power? That's sort of like the relationship between the conscious and the unconscious or other than conscious mind. And as I said, it is a primary orientation of everything we do and everything you should do as you apply this method profoundly to increasing your sales.

This stems from the fact that people's **values** and even often their **beliefs** are *outside of their conscious awareness* yet these things *control their lives*. Important to keep that in mind.

CHAPTER NINE

Subjectivity Has Structure

All right, let's go to the next step along our journey here called '**Process Orientation**.' Also at the core of what we do is the understanding that **subjectivity has structure**. Now, let's analyze that a bit. For the most part you don't ever really hear it said like this. You hear it said that *objectivity* has structure and that's the basis of the scientific method. In other words, I'm going to come up with a *hypothesis*. I'm going to create *supporting arguments*, I'm going to *research* it. I'm going to do an *experiment* that's *replicable*, and I'm going to come to a *conclusion*. And that whole process can be *duplicated* by anybody else who chooses to do it. That's *objective*.

However, human nature is anything *but* objective. It's all based on our *subjective* responses to everything. So therefore people have, since the dawn of time, been able to get away with saying things like, "Well, it's just how I feel" as if it's not logical, it's feeling and as such, we can't be responsible for it or we have the ability to not be responsible in some way because we must not be able to control our feelings. How convenient.

A principle part of what we do is understanding and using processes to our advantage and that has to do at the core with understanding that **subjectivity has structure**, meaning, the way you fall in love has *structure*. I can figure it out very quickly and *use* it to make that happen if that's what I desire to do. Same with buying. Same with buyer's remorse. Same with almost any activity you can possibly name.

All of this has **structure**. It's just that we're *not aware* of it. So once we understand that **subjectivity has structure**, then we can learn to be oriented towards the processes that people run at the *other than conscious* level and *use them to our advantage*. By learning how to understand specifically what our prospect is saying, we can quickly derive their *model of the world* and from that, our words and actions are directed to get the result we're looking for. **Process orientation** thus becomes a major focus and a major portion of what we do as we're thinking of organizing principles.

CHAPTER TEN

Suggestion Patterns

Let's look next at '**Suggestion Patterns**.' Another core element of what we do is learning to use language *cleanly*. In other words, to make sure our language facilitates what we want to happen. Another way to look at that is that this falls in the realm of **suggestion patterns** and how to get the mind of our prospects to *accept our suggestions* and *act on them*. And taking the clue from the first part of this what I'm saying is if our language *isn't clean*, meaning, if we're not in total control of the **presuppositions** of our language, then what happens is, we're *installing* and *suggesting* all manner of things, some of which are what we want, some of which are *not* what we want.

By learning the process of *delivering suggestions powerfully*, we're also *cleaning up our own language* such that it all aims in the same direction or at least in the way we want it to and as such, it facilitates what we want to happen much more quickly. It also relates back to another one of the organizing principles of recognizing the power of the other than conscious.

CHAPTER ELEVEN

Setting the Frame

Yet another core element of our processes centers around the concept of **framing**. Central to the understanding of **framing** is *understanding logical levels of thought*. With this understanding we can easily move into and around these different logical levels with ease. This in and of itself can significantly give one the advantage. **The Cleveland Method** teaches you to focus on **setting the frame** in a way that gives you the advantage.

I was watching the Reverend Al Sharpton today and someone asked him a question and he said, "What we're talking about here is . . " I forget what he said, something like acceptable social behavior, or something like this. And so *he framed the whole interaction*, the whole discussion about being what's right for society, I mean, in other words as if he's somehow the *spokesperson* for society. Hardly. I mean, I found that to be a very amazing and ballsy statement on his part and yet it really iterates *the power of framing*. Because *nobody challenged* that frame it became the de facto *standard* for the discussion and he kept coming back to the fact that what happened was not societally correct and the person deserved punishment. Wow. So somehow he **set the frame**, became judge, jury and then executioner all in one conversation and *nobody even challenged him*. It just goes to show the power of that.

I've come up with some *phenomenal* strategies and languaging regarding this and have been very seriously considering continuing on going into more advanced material. And very seriously considering doing that in which we would cover these kinds of things very extensively.

Framing includes *setting the frame first* and the knowledge of how to *change the frame that another person has already adapted*. It includes a lot more than that but for sake of thinking of it as an organizing principle, let's leave it at that.

CHAPTER TWELVE

Social Influence Skills and the Elimination of Resistance

We incorporate and study **social influence skills**, a la Dr. Childini, such as *liking, commitment* and *consistency, authority* etc., as well as **the elimination of resistance**, a la Dr. Knowles strategies. And again, I'm very seriously considering a very in depth analysis and study of these strategies to *eliminate resistance* here if we were to proceed on into more advanced materials. Let me tell you the net result of that. **Social influence skills** of this magnitude give us the *alpha strategies*, like what we're learning, in other words, *how to positively impact people to get them to buy*. If we look at this in terms of earning money, that's like *earning more money*. And the **elimination of resistance** strategies, are like learning to *save money*. So if you're both *saving money* and *increasing your earning*, what's happening? Your wealth is growing very, very fast.

I put these under the category of **social influence skills** as well as here we incorporate everything from the **mind control techniques** generated in the U.S. Military, and I've got a lot to say about that, by the way, Hitler's **mass control techniques**, Mao Zedong's **political influence strategies**. Of course, the Chinese stratagems as well as **cult indoctrination techniques**, which is one of my personal favorites and something I have spent a significant amount of time studying and working and would like to bring some very advanced cult indoctrination techniques to you as well, another thing I would like to bring into a more advanced set of books.

Of course, we *apply* these **social influence skills** with an application towards *ethics* and *integrity* and if you bear with me, I find this to be so *absolutely important* that when I think of organizing principles of persuasion, I give this a chapter all to itself.

CHAPTER THIRTEEN

Ethics, Integrity and Congruity

Ethics and integrity along with **congruity**, and we can't leave out congruity here, it forms such a *key component*, like I said I gave it an entry to itself. Why **congruity**? Well, if we're *not* **congruent** but we're *acting* like we have **ethics and integrity**, then we're still *not* really having ethics and integrity. So **congruity** is like someone making a mistake and being *genuinely* sorry they made it. Where *saying* I'm sorry doesn't necessarily cut it if *they don't really mean it.*

Ethics and integrity allow us to use these kinds of power skills and do so with *a good clean conscience* because we know that we're using things on others that we're comfortable having used on ourselves. And as you know, by reading these books, it's something we will constantly discuss. I constantly *encourage* and *promote* good uses of **ethics and integrity**, however, I try to *use* good ethics and integrity in *talking about* ethics and integrity and not *force* them but *bring them up, constantly* showing why it's *helpful* and *useful* to use them.

My belief is, that **without ethics, integrity and congruity, a sales person will never rise above the mediocre**.

CHAPTER FOURTEEN

Understanding Our Own Unconscious Drives and Motivations

Another core element of **The Cleveland Method** deals with **understanding our own unconscious drives and motivations** and I'll bet you that you have significantly learned about *a lot* of your drives and motivations as you've gone through these books so far. There are a lot more to go. It's only in the understanding of *our own* that we can genuinely understand that of *others*.

It is true that we're a *mirror* and we see in others that which we have inside ourselves. When you see ugliness out there in the world, it's because you've got it in *you* as well. When you see beauty out there in the world, it's because you've got it in *you* as well. We recognize more and more what's in the *outside world* by recognizing what's in our *inside world* and then **choosing what we're going to pay attention to**. So understanding these and **making them conscious** is a big part of what we do such that we can gain more and more mastery.

CHAPTER FIFTEEN

Core Drives

This is some groundbreaking work I've been doing lately in which I have been studying a lot of the work that's in the field right now on **core drives**. In fact, I've recently spent literally thousands and thousands and thousands of dollars to avail myself of all of the latest research that I can possibly buy in *psychology*, in *linguistics*, all manner of related fields and every known persuasion course on the planet because I'm determined to bring you the very best of the best. And if there's anything out there that I don't know or don't understand, I work diligently on bringing it into my own existence so that I can bring it into yours.

One of the things that has fascinated me my whole life has been the concept of **core drives**. Freud talked at length about these as have many psychologists, psychiatrists, philosophers, etc., since the dawn of time and I view incorporating *drives that are beyond even the other than conscious mind* as reaching right into the DNA of an individual. It's as if we're going with **core drives** even *beyond* the subconscious mind or the other than conscious mind right down into our DNA. And I'll name four or five of them right here for you.

We have **a need to sustain ourselves**—to *eat*, to *be alive*, to *continue the fight* another day. We have the need to *escape*, for *flight*. . . You've heard it called **fight or flight strategies** and we have the need to escape into security, away from problems if the need arises Or, if we can't escape, to fight. We have the need to *reproduce* ourselves. The nice thing here is that our unconscious mind can't tell the difference between our need to reproduce ourselves and having sex. And so this is a major, major drive. When we're young, our minds *present it to us* as simply the need to have sex. As we get older, we realize we want to *replicate* ourselves in so many ways. In business, Bill Gates, for example, in his foundations, etc. So we can have *baser* drives and desires and we can have more *elevated* ones but it all boils down to the same thing which is **reproducing ourselves**.

There are many, many more that you'll recognize and that you'll realize that we're going to be exploiting to our advantage and the advantage of those that are working close to us as we delve into that topic more and more. So the whole concept of **core drives**. . .So I would ask that you stop and consider how core drives play a part in your life and in those lives of people that you're persuading because that is in essence, if you want to look at it, almost a separate field of study that we'll bring into the realm of persuasion to add power to what it is that we're doing with our persuasion.

CHAPTER SIXTEEN

Metaphor

Metaphor can be thought of as *the ultimate delivery system*. And **The Cleveland Method** teaches many strategies to making and using **metaphors** and helping them to be easy and powerful. You can do anything from *isomorphic metaphors*, which means equal to in structure, but the content is different, to quick little *analogies* to full blown *hero's journeys*, to *why am I here*, to teaching *tales*, you can use them as literally **the ultimate persuasion delivery system**. We'll be spending even more time on **metaphors** as we proceed.

CHAPTER SEVENTEEN

Spiritual Truths

A lot of my personal focus is on **spiritual truths** and I bring this to **The Cleveland Method**. Let me be real clear here with you that I'm *not* preaching, nor am I teaching any specific dogma but to simply share those **principles of success** that are rooted in antiquity and thus have passed the test of time. It's similar to the work of Napoleon Hill and I certainly draw from that source and many others from that genre.

The outgrowth of this is the **universe** system, incorporating **tapping**, and *a deeper understanding of human nature* that I've been bringing to you to help us to move forward with balance. I view that as an *integral* part of persuasion and as a key organizing principle.

CHAPTER EIGHTEEN

The Underlying Organizing Principles

So what I've done in this book is to give you the **underlying organizing principles** of all of persuasion as I see it and I've thought on this for a great many weeks, this specific book, to bring you this process and I've written and rewritten and added and added and added some more and I think I've got the main core of the system down here that I use.

And I call this **The Cleveland Method** because that is at the core of everything I do and it is a formal method that takes into account these **organizing principles**. These **organizing principles**, as you give thought to them, will help you to understand more about why I view persuasion skills to be *the fire that underlies selling*. Typical sales training I consider to be the smoke. However, as an intelligent individual, I knew very early in my life that where there's smoke there also had to be at least some amount of fire or there would be no smoke and I set out and made it my life's journey to figure out where that fire is.

What I've presented to you here is the fire but described as **underlying principles** not as *specific techniques*. The *techniques* that fall out from these organizing principles are the techniques that we're *learning* in this series of books.

Now, it's interesting because over the years I've studied a number of specific disciplines and one of them said in particular that what they were teaching us is that even though we were learning *techniques*, there was **an underlying set of principles** or what have you, but those principles weren't really spoken of too directly and I figured that for you I wanted to *speak* of these underlying principles very *clearly* and *directly* so you have an understanding of how these techniques spill out from this mindset and this orientation.

You've been given, in essence, a **psychology**, a **mindset**, of what, when you adopt it, *enables* these techniques to spill out from you as a natural consequence. And there are all number of techniques that can be created and generated and brought forth as a result of this mindset interacting and intersecting with what it is that we do on a day-to-day basis.

BOOK TEN

LEARNING TO BE ARTFULLY VAGUE

INTRODUCTION

What is Process Orientation?

Welcome to **Book Ten** of *Persuasion Force*. I think you're really going to like the material in this book. It's very extensive. And so let's jump in and I'd like to get started with some questions and answers to begin with. And the first question really is comprised of quite a number of questions that I have received, all surrounding **process orientation**, so I can *summarize* the questions by saying, '**What is process orientation?** What is the *point* of process orientation? How do we *do* it? Etc.'

So I'm going to answer that kind of question *generally* because we're moving much, much deeper into **process orientation** in this book.

Alright, **process orientation**. So the best way to understand this is, **process orientation** is the '*how*' not the '*what*'. **Process orientation is the process of learning to become *artfully vague*.** The goal of process orientation is *to allow the mind of the person or people that you're persuading to come to its own conclusion, but yet it's still the conclusion you **want** it to come to.*

I guess an easy way to explain this to you is if I detailed the '*what*' of anything to you, I would be talking about the *content*. And you've had this experience now since you've been working with **criteria** all this time and I'm sure you've had the experience of asking someone the **criteria** questions and they launch off onto a personal story around what one of their criteria is to help you to understand it, of course. And so they jump in and they start telling you this long involved story.

And after a while, especially when you're beginning with this, you may *forget* all about what their **criteria** was because you've been so *engrossed* in their story. What happened? Well, the '*what*' of their story captured your mind and you stopped paying attention to the '*how*' of what you should be doing and that ended up being kind of a problem. The problem is, **when you lose track of what it is that you're trying to do, you're going to end up *falling victim* to the content that they want you to hear** and . . . I mean, that's okay, but it's not really going to help you be a better persuader.

And by the way, right this moment, if you're thinking to yourself, man, I don't get it still. I'm still not getting this. It's because there's **an overriding frame about learning** that I want to call to your attention and what it is, is if *I'm* the guy or girl *learning* then I should be getting some kind of *specific information* that I can *learn from*. So if I as the teacher am not giving you that specific learning, or in other words, if it doesn't equal your **criteria** of *specific learning*, then you might be saying, "I don't get it. And Kenrick isn't giving me the specifics that I'm asking for."

But I want you to just stop for a moment and understand **that process is *not specific***. By its very nature, it's *not* specific. So when I talk about the skills of using **process**, I'm talking about the very *nature* of **process** which is anything *but* specific. As such, it won't sound specific and you won't necessarily feel like you're getting specific information even though it *is* specific. It's *specific* to the **process** which is *general* in nature.

Process orientation is guiding someone's mind through generics. That's one way to say it, it's not the *only* way to say it, but it's one way to say it, instead of *focusing* them through *specificity*.

And we're going to get into this in great detail in this book, so I'm going to not talk a whole lot more about it here because the fact that quite a number of you asked this question is really great. It means you're wrestling with this material, you're thinking about it and you're trying to figure out some *specifics*, in other words, **how do I do it?**

Well, I'm going to give you several of those specifics in this book so you're going to *get it* and get it really easily, but I will warn you that **process orientation** does require that you *discover* the means with which it affects the way people think. So, the best way to do that, like I've said all along, and have for many, many years, is you have to **do it to you first** or **allow it to be done**, so I'm kind of alternating back and forth between doing it *to* you and *for* you and teaching you *how* to do it to and for others. Okay?

You have to know what it's like. You have to be able to understand what it's like to have your brain *guided in generalities*. Like as if I'm kind of asking you to go into a general direction with me but not telling you the *method* with which I want you to get there. You can choose to walk, drive, fly, read, listen, whatever you'd like. Okay? In other words, *there are all kinds of means of getting things done*. I'm just telling you the *direction* to get there in. And the rest I'm leaving to you and this is what I call the process of learning to be **artfully vague**.

Yet, remember, people will interpret your vagueness *personally*. You can't interpret it in a vacuum. It *applies* to something. To what? *You* or the person listening. In this case *you're* listening to *me* so it applies to *you*. When *you're* speaking and doing this to *others*, it applies to *them*. That's the beauty of this skill. I'm going to give you much specificity, very specific tactics and strategies in this book, so I'm going to move on.

<u>CHAPTER ONE</u>

Mind and Body

Next question: *"Does my physical energy level affect my ability to build intention? I think I know the answer, however I wanted to hear from you and maybe get some ideas."*

Mind and body are part of the same cybernetic system, and what that means in simple to understand words are, what we *think* affects our *body*. What our *body* does affects the way we *think*. So you can prove this to yourself, if you were to engage your mind right now in a particular fantasy. Let's say, how you would like to spend the money that you're going to be earning as a result of implementing these skills?

Well, you may find your *breathing* change. You may find your *muscles* changing in the quality of they way they are holding yourself. All kinds of things could change. If we took it on into the realm of what you probably thought of when I said fantasy, I'm sure you were thinking of science fiction fantasy, right? Well, you were probably thinking of something a bit more *intimate* and if we were to let our minds run in *that* direction quite strongly, what you would begin to discover is, you would have *a physiological response*. That's probably nothing new except when you think of it in terms of this level you begin to understand that **the mind and body are part of the same system**. Okay?

So yes, absolutely, your physical energy level *does* affect your ability to think and thinking is what enables you to **set your intention**. Kind of reminds me of the quote, "I am that I am" from the Bible. The **ultimate intention** is 'I am'. I am *expressing me*, it's just a very highly trained and qualified me based on much experience and capability. I'm speaking '*me*' generically, '*you*' as you use these skills. Okay?

If you can't *think*, it's difficult to build **intention**. So if your *physical* energy level is prohibiting your ability to *think* then by that very definition, you *would* be having trouble building your intention.

CHAPTER TWO

Changing Your Own Values

All right. Let's move on. "*Hi Kenrick, I would like to ask a question about the **life values**. Freedom being my number one value, I feel I have lots of freedom in line with my meaning. However, the meaning itself is restrictive. Is changing your own **criteria** as simple as changing someone else's?*"

In a simple word, the answer is *no*, it is *not*. And when I say *changing someone's criteria*, that's the easiest way to help people understand what we're going to be doing when I talk about the subject. I should *actually* say, it's **adding** to their criteria. That's a bit more clear probably now that you understand what the technique is. And in your case, when we're talking about a **criteria**, or even a **value**, we're actually changing slightly the definition, or adding to the definition. Okay?

When you're talking about **changing the value**, like *substituting* one for another or *moving* one up or down on the hierarchy, no, that's *not* easy. And if so, is that what's happening when you work your **life values** into your **universe**?

No, not really. Although it sort of could. If your values are a bit out of order and you write into your universe and you make it absolutely compelling to make your number three value, let's say, the most important thing in your life, you could by *focus* and *conscious effort* and *will* and *determined repetition in thought*, you could probably bring it up though it would take some time, you could certainly make everything more pleasant in your life. Okay?

However, when you say 'change' your **criteria**, I actually call that **changing your values**. And you've said that *freedom* is your *number one* value, so we don't have to hypothesize there, as a general rule, I find that to be a mistake. When you put *freedom* as your *first value* you'll have a difficult time really getting ahead in life because you probably won't want to take action in a lot of things because by agreeing to take action, you will be *stopping* yourself from accepting other things that might come up or from even having that *sense of freedom.*

So as a general rule, I don't think *freedom* is well served as your *number one value.* Some things that *are* well served as your number one value, being the best husband you can be, the best father you can be, the best person you can be in some specific sense that matters to you. You could put money number one although you've got to be careful that you don't turn into a money-grubbing shark when you do that, but you know, that is something you could consider doing.

You could put social activism, number one, but then you have to worry that you'll never have any money, so it does take some **real considerable analysis** to do this and some *very specific techniques.* It is something that I do from time-to-time personally for people at quite great expense and basically I used to do it and stopped because I don't really like doing things therapeutic, I spend all of my time working, teaching these skills as it relates to business and persuasion.

Sometime I might create a program or something that addresses these issues as best I can, but I want you to know that even if I did that, you couldn't watch that program or listen to that program and *do it to yourself* real easily. It really does require **working with someone else** to do it and the more *trained* they are, the better. So if you really want to do this, find a therapist that you trust and believe in that knows how to do these kinds of things and ask them to help you.

That's my take on that.

CHAPTER THREE

What Happens If We Throw It All In Together?

All right. Last question: "*If we overload the consciousness of a person by using all the modalities at the same time in one sentence, make the sentence really long linking everything, throw in lots of unspecified stuff, we create a blank in the mind of that person. What's the use of this?*"

No, you don't. You make a fool out of yourself. I'm not suggesting in *any* sense that you throw all that into one sentence. And if you do. . . for example, one might say, "*Kenrick, how come you teach so many strategies of persuasion, it seems like I pretty much use five or six or seven or eight, all the time? Why don't you just teach those?*"

Well, that's fine. Those five or six or seven or eight would work really well in a good percentage of the time. However, a good percentage isn't ever good enough for me. I want *all* the time. I want to be able to do this *every* time. So I keep working to understand **the overriding principles** so that I can evolve **techniques** and **strategies** that will give us greater and greater odds of doing things.

So it's not enough. In my mind it's not enough, to try to throw everything into a sentence. That *isn't*

strategic. If that were the case I could simply list twenty techniques and tell you to put them all in one sentence, have you utter that one sentence and everybody would do your bidding. And if that were the case, you couldn't buy this book. I'd be selling it for millions of dollars and there would be maybe five people that own it in the world and I'd be on top of the world somewhere as a king.

So **it doesn't work like that**. All right? Start to understand this for what it really is. What it is, is **we will get what we want in life by** *helping* **other people get what** *they* **want**, *not* **by tricking them or maneuvering them in some way that goes against what it is they want**. And believe me, I don't think you're thinking that you're going to trick people when you ask this question, I'm just calling attention to some of the possibilities of those that are reading this could be thinking. Okay?

Influence and persuasion skills are **not a formula** that when you do A, B, C, D, E, F, G, everybody says, "Yes, master" and does what you say. There are a great many **strategies**, as you know, you're learning them. And there are ways of understanding human nature that will help you to learn how to use them more *effectively* and as you learn to use these more effectively, you become *artful* and *skillful* in their use and you see your skill skyrocketing. You learn how to *organize* them more effectively and more profoundly so that you get more of what you want. Okay? All of which are exactly the point of what we're doing here. The point of what we're doing is not in any way to try to use *one set* of strategies to make *everything* work because there is no one set. If there was, I'd have already taught it to you. There's a whole *bunch* of strategies that as you begin to learn them and make them yours, wow, your abilities will skyrocket and we're getting into, in this book, stuff that's going to knock your socks off along these lines. In fact, I almost consider it that we had to do a lot of the things up to this point that we've done just to get to the point of *really understanding where we're headed now* so you could use it really well.

That's sort of my take, I guess, on your question. The point is *not* to create a blank. When we *do* want to create a blank, what we're attempting to do is to *stop for a minute*. And *put in* what we want. Now if you're listening to the audiobook version, notice when I said '*stop for a minute*' and followed that congruently with *silence*, your brain probably *stopped for a second*. So if I needed to *put a hold* on some kind of judgment that was being made, for example, that I didn't like, that's one way I might do it. There are times to create a blank in the mind of the person, but *not* by throwing everything but the kitchen sink at them all at once, you know, in other words, all the things that you mentioned. That's not the answer. That's not the purpose.

So let me speak to what I think you're asking. Why do we *want* to **create a blank** in the mind of a person? So that we can **install** what we want to install. That's why we do it. If we can **eliminate the resistance** to what we want the person to do, then there won't be anything *stopping* them from doing it. In other words, they will be *doing* it. Our goal is to **eliminate resistance in their mind** first and foremost to our ideas.

And once we've done that, our next goal is to create a situation in their mind where we are making it *very desirable for them to work with us*, they want to move forward and do what we want them to do. So therein, if we create mechanisms that **eliminate resistance** and **insert our ideas**, what you're going to find is that all of the sudden they'll start going along with you. Now it isn't always instantaneous. It may be an hour later. It may be at the end of the presentation. It may be the next day. These are **suggestions**, in essence, that we're artfully **inserting** into their mind and as we do so, their mind makes it their own and acts on them and what we're going to be learning in this book, actually, is a major **strategy** of doing exactly that. So I think you're going to really like what you're going to read in this book because it's going to completely open up your mind to show you *how* this is done and give you a **strategy** for doing it with ease.

Well, and I also want to say that it's also important to have the ability to **lullaby people into complacency** where they are *dependent* upon what you're saying. That is just flat out fun and creates really powerful results. So I'll be showing you more about that as we proceed, okay?

CHAPTER FOUR

Structuring Reality

All right. Here we're going to begin talking about **structuring reality**. Now, this is a really powerful lesson, okay, as we move forward today. It all blends together especially in this book's lesson, also with the **process orientation**, etc. and so we're going to *chunk up* real big now, meaning we're going to move to a much higher logical level and talk about **structuring reality**.

Would you like to be able to **structure reality** for other people and even yourself? I don't even have to ask, do I? Okay, that's why you're here so let's learn to do just that.

Reality consists as much with *the structure that's defined* as it does with the **assumptions** we make about that structure. Wow. Read that again, would you. Just stop everything for a minute. Just read that again.

Reality consists as much with the structure that's defined as it does with the assumptions we make about that structure.

That is pure brilliance if I do say so myself. I'm reaching around and patting myself on the back. This one sentence, if you can get this, your persuasion skills will skyrocket forward as it begins to come out into your **behaviors** and **language**.

That statement is even more true when it comes to **words** and what they **imply** or **presuppose**. I want to give you now a two part major persuasion **truism**. This has formed the basis of my work for many, many years, or it forms a root, shall we say, one of the roots of my work, for many, many years clear back before I could even articulate it. And that is, here is a truism almost to end all truisms: **People *might* believe *what they are told*, but they will** always **believe *their own conclusions*.** I'm going to say it again: **People *might* believe *what they are told*, but they will *always* believe *their own conclusions*.**

You may be able to tell someone something and they may go along with you, but they will *believe* what they conclude on their own. And part two of that is, and they will form those conclusions as much from what you *don't* say, as what you *do*.

I want you to *memorize* this and *live by it*. I'm going to write it again. **People might believe what they are told, but they will always believe their own conclusions and they will form those conclusions as much from what you *don't* say, as what you *do*.**

Wow. I want you to write it down, print it out, carry it with you, rehearse it over and over and over, make it a part of everything you are and everything you do with your persuasion.

CHAPTER FIVE

Hearing Your Own Punchline

So a major key then is to learn **how to structure what you say such that what you *don't* say communicates more powerfully than what you *do* say** and makes people come to the **conclusion** that you want them to have on their own.

Again remember, people *might believe* what you tell them, they *might believe* what they're told, but they will *always believe* **their own conclusions** and they will form those conclusions as much from what you *don't* say as what you *do*.

Okay. I have an example for you and it is an off color example. So my intention in telling you this is not to offend, not even hardly. My intention in telling you this is to make a point, I just don't have any ones that come to mind right off the top of my head that make it without it being an off color one. I'm sure there are plenty, but in any event, reading this is quite illustrative of this point that I'm wanting to make which is, people will **form the conclusions** as much from what you *don't* say as what you *do*.

These two jokes may actually be much more offensive to women, so if for any reason you're offended with anything sexual in nature or off color, please just skip ahead to the foot of the next page. My intention, again, is not to inflame anyone or anything or to be disgusting, but simply to make a point, so I hope that's understood and clear.

Okay. So I've said to you, people *might* believe what you tell them, but they will *always* believe their own conclusions and they will form those conclusions as much from what you *don't* say as what you *do*.

So here are a couple of jokes. These fall into a linguistic category called **Spoonerisms** and the person I heard say these was a very old man in his 80's and not doing real well health-wise, but a very brilliant man, I have tremendous respect for him. And this guy wanting to show what **Spoonerisms** were, in a very mixed crowd, said, *"Here is an example of a **Spoonerism**. What's the difference between a chorus line and a group of prostitutes standing on the street corner? One is a cunning array of stunts."*

All righty then. So. . . let me give you the second one. Hopefully you got the first one. Here's the second one. *"What's the difference between a woman in church and a woman in the bathtub? Ready? One has hope in her soul."*

Okay. Well, when I heard the first one it took me a second, you know, and all of the sudden, I mean, realizing this was an eighty some year old man, and he just said it with the straightest of face. I laughed so hard. I mean to tell you, I never laughed so hard in my entire life and the whole room was just splitting up with laughter. I just thought it was hysterical and the second one, I

169

mean, I was going hoarse with laughter. It was one of the funniest things I think I'd ever heard.

Boy, did it make the point that I'm wanting to make to you here. And I recalled wanting to really hold on to those jokes because I knew one day they would serve me very well and that day is here. So **what's happening** in those jokes? Well, obviously you *hear my words* but **your brain goes to the opposite**. But *I didn't tell you to do that, you did that on your own*. In other words, the nasty thoughts are *your own*, not *mine*. Right?

However, **you had to hear the opposite**, you had to *hear* that, and *you did it on your own*. And that's what I'm saying when I say people *might* believe what you tell them but they will *always* believe their own conclusions and they will form those conclusions as much from what you *don't* say as what you *do*. Do you get how you just did that? **You came up with the punch line of that joke**. *You* did it. And that's what makes it so funny because *you* heard the *opposite* or the *inverse* or however you want to say that. You had to *hear*, instead of 'cunning array of stunts', you had to *hear* 'stunning array of . . .' we don't need to get any more specific than that. You had to *hear* 'hope in her soul', you *heard* 'soap in her. . .' and so you obviously **came up with your own interpretation** there.

And I'm only being even that blunt just in case anybody missed it, I want to make sure I'm not leaving anybody hanging too far.

CHAPTER SIX

Structure: Creating Conclusions

Let's again repeat, people *might* believe what they are told, but they will *always* believe their own conclusions and they will form those conclusions as much from what you *don't* say as what you *do* say.

As we progress, you're going to see how we're going to be able to use the work we've been going through to teach you how to **bring your intention to bear** in every situation you're in. So let's explore a bit more about **structure**. Another way to look at this is we are talking about *how* and *what*. '*How*' equals the **structure** or **process** and '*what*' equals the **content** or **specifics**.

You could think of **process/structure** as the *freeway*. It will dictate the *general direction*, such as north or south, for example, and the *general mode of travel*, such as car, motorcycle, bus, whatever can travel on the freeway. So if I said to you, "I was on the freeway the other day, I was on I-5 the other day", well for anyone who lives in the greater Northwest, or anyone in Oregon, Washington, or California, will know I-5 is the major thoroughfare that runs from north to south. It runs all the way up to Canada and it goes south all the way to Mexico. All the way through Washington, all the way through Oregon, all the way through California.

When I say "I was on I-5 the other day", you know I was either headed north or south. You know I wasn't going west or east if you know the area at all. The other thing is, you know that I wasn't in a jumbo jet. See, I'm causing you to **create conclusions** from what I'm *not saying*. I'm *directing your thoughts* and you're *coming up with a whole bunch of conclusions* that I want you to come up with. You know I wasn't in a jumbo jet. You don't normally hear me talk that much about riding the bus. You could probably **assume** I was in a car or motorcycle, but it could have been a truck, it's most anything that could travel on that freeway.

In other words, I'm allowing *you* to **come up with the conclusion** of how I was getting down the road. Okay? But I'm *not* telling you what that is. I'm being **artfully vague**.

Content you could think of as *which lane* you chose to drive in. Or *what specific car or bus or truck* or what have you that I was perhaps in or driving.

CHAPTER SEVEN

Leading Through Artful Vagueness

You're going to be learning how to be **artfully vague** and yet still **lead** and **guide** a person's thoughts *precisely* to where you want them to go. And you'll learn to do this in such a way that **they think it's their own idea**. See how that fits in with the idea that people *might* believe what they hear, but they'll *always* believe what they conclude, and they'll conclude more easily what they make of it based on your **structure** than they will based on what you say based on the **content**.

You'll learn to do this in a way that **they think it's their own idea**. The power of these strategies, even what you've read so far in this book cannot be overstated. It bears re-reading over and over again so that you ingrain this into your mind and really, given my choice, if you asked me, "Kenrick, what's the best way to get the material that you're teaching me in this book?", I would tell you to stop right now and read again from the very beginning, all the way through the stratagems of this book's lessons, because those stratagems also talk about what we're doing here. All right? So I would suggest if you really want to *maximize* your learning just stop now and go through it again.

I'm probably more excited about this book than I've been about a lot of the others. Well, actually, they're *all* really good, but this one really rises. But we had to go through a lot of the others to get to the point of being *able* to do this one.

CHAPTER EIGHT

Defining Presuppositions

I'd like you to give me the *definition* for this word: **presupposition**. So stop for a minute and I want you to think of what is the definition for the word **presupposition**. Just think about it for a minute. Something is **presupposed**. What does that *mean*?

All right, come up with an answer? Well, I hope so. The dictionary defines it like this. "*To suppose or assume beforehand, take for granted in advance."* Hmmm. That's pretty interesting, isn't it? *To suppose or assume beforehand.* In other words, before you *know*, you're *assuming* or you're going to *take something for granted* before you know it to be so in advance.

The second definition, "*of a thing, condition or state of affairs to require or imply as an antecedent condition, an effect presupposes a cause*". I love both of these. What if we could *assume a mental position or thought* that the person has to take for granted? In other words, the **core concept has to be taken for granted** just to make sense of what you're telling them *without* you having to name it.

That is powerful. I would define **presupposition** as, **that which must be accepted as true in order to make sense of the sentence**. So think about that definition for a moment. In other words, if it is that which must be *accepted as true*, it has to be accepted *because you didn't say it*. In other words, it's **assumed**, or **presupposed**. My definition again: **that which must be accepted as true in order to make sense of the sentence**. If you *say* it, it doesn't have to be *assumed*, you've *said* it.

So start to wrap your mind around the idea that *you're going to learn to start to talk in ways that* **presuppose** *what you want someone to think*. They have to **assume** the core of what you want them to think just in order to make sense of what you're saying.

See how we're getting closer to getting people to think what it is that we want them to think *without* us having to say it.

The idea is, we want to get massively to the point of **not having to say the ideas**.

CHAPTER NINE

Patterns That Allow Us To Structure Reality

Okay. Let's talk about **patterns that will allow us to structure reality**.

By the way, this is just a really heavy, packed lesson in this book. Sitting down and devouring it all in one fell swoop, that's fine, I mean, you can read it like that, but boy, I'm just really encouraging you to *stop and break this up* and read it over and over and over. This is a really big lesson. It's just jam packed with wisdom and strategy all through it and it's going to take some contemplation time on your part and some writing and work to implement it and I can tell you that whatever you do, implementing these will make such a *huge* difference in your life, especially when you combine it with everything that's come before and all that will come after. Wow, you're going to be amazing to say the least.

There are **six linguistic patterns** that we're going to be working with that will allow us to guide people's thoughts as we've been describing. And that's six in the next short period of time, few books, etc. Four of these patterns give us the ability to *guide the minds of others* powerfully via **presuppositions**. The two remaining patterns allow us to *bypass conscious resistance* and **directly install** ideas we want acted upon . . . well, they allow us to do a lot *more* than that, actually, but that's certainly a *minimum* of what they allow us to do.

All right, we're going to work our way steadily through these patterns over the next few books as I've mentioned and rather than rush through them, I'd like you to work to *master* each of these and *combine* them with the other patterns that we've been studying. So these patterns aren't necessarily an island to be used all by themselves. They work best when you combine them with everything else and that's where you start seeing huge jumps in their ability to influence other people and ourselves.

CHAPTER TEN

The Adverb / Adjective Pattern

We're going to now talk about the **adverb/adjective pattern**. And as we do, by the way, don't be concerned with the fact that this sounds like it's English grammar. It will be intuitive to you the minute you start to understand what it is. So here's a strategy for using these types of words in this pattern. You want to put the *adverbs* before the *verb* and the *adjectives* before the *noun*. And that's a fancy way of saying, put the *descriptive* words before *what they describe*.

Let me give you a *bad* example and show you why this is so important. "I was walking along the beach and it was a very cold day. The rain was pouring down on me and I was walking along this beach having a great time, just a really wonderful day."

Now, I said I was walking along the beach and you probably had *your* example of whatever beach was in your head. *Now* I go on to describe my beach, I was careful as I was walking across the little rocks and the big rocks that I knew could easily cut my feet, and the debris throughout the water was very interesting.

Now, when I said 'beach' originally, you probably had an idea of a beach. And most people, when they think of a beach, they're thinking of a nice day and they're thinking of a big sandy beach and they're thinking of a nice warm experience or whatever. And here I said, it's a cold day and it's raining. Well, if you had thought of *your* beach being a nice warm beach, well then you were **interrupted**. You had to *stop* and you had to try to *change* your beach around to be a beach that was a very cold day and rainy and then with my tone I said it was a really cold day and it was raining, like that, but I said, "I was having a great time." So I **confused** the situation again. It's like, well, *how* are you having such a great time on a wet, rainy beach? It's cold. And then I talked about the aspect of the beach that it was rocky.

Well, I bet on *your* beach it was sandy, maybe, and then I said, "the debris strewn water". Whoa! Good grief. I have a pretty *awful* beach compared to probably what *you* started thinking about when I first said beach.

Now let me give you a different example.

"The black-robed, pointy hat wearing, deep-speaking wizard stretched out his hand indicating he had nothing up his sleeve. As he began to speak, the deep, rich warmth of his voice began to envelop your mind in beautiful sounds. He invited you to sit for a spell and he would chant a magical incantation that would create worlds of wonder in your mind showing you realities of how people will come to their own conclusions by words that you're using strategies that you're layering. He indeed was and is a wise and powerful magician."

Okay. Now, think about that. So did I say, "Well, there was this middle aged magician who . . .let's see, the guy was wearing black and he had a pointy hat. Let's see," and so I start going on. *No*, I said, "Black-robed, pointy hat wearing,. . ." so you *had in your mind* a black robe and a pointy hat. It has to go on somebody but you don't know what yet. All of the sudden I said, 'magician', and blammo!, the robe and the hat all fell right upon that magician. There it was and *the picture formed in your mind*.

The new tan leather seats, the beautiful white pearl exterior paint, and full roof as a sun roof, on the new Lexus ES350 is breathtaking. See? I didn't say, 'The Lexus ES350, it has tan seats and white pearl paint.' See? That doesn't help build a picture in your mind. It isn't **guiding your mind by the process**. It's giving you the **content** first. It's giving you first *what* I'm going to describe and *then* the descriptive words. And you're far better off using the **descriptive words first.**

This large, lushly appointed, strategically landscaped bungalow is perfectly situated, blah, blah, blah. Well, all of the sudden, all those characteristics of that house landed on a house in your mind and you began to *visualize*.

Here's one of the reasons this is so powerful. Note that the above examples could also be considered **framing** examples. So by stating the **descriptive words first** and not saying *what* they describe, it's like we're *defining the road but not the destination*. When we finally state the destination, it becomes very difficult for the person to object as *the pathway in their mind has already been created*. That's the beauty and value of this. You see, it forces their mind to stay open. Okay?

Imagine a guy going up to a woman in a bar, they're both single, both attractive, and the guy says, "Let's just cut right straight to the point. We're both probably single, you're certainly attractive, I view myself to be the same, people come here for a number of reasons but certainly to find someone to spend time with is one of the highest reasons and to spend time in a particular way is even more of a reason that they would do that, and you know what I'm talking about and I just want to skip to the chase and say, hey look, I'd rather kind of skip dinner and all the expense involved in that and just take you home and make wild, passionate love to you."

Well, may not fly. Might. Might not. Okay? Why? Well, for a whole host of reasons. Not the least of which we're probably *violating the person's idea of the way this should be done*. They probably have in their mind the idea that this should happen, 'naturally'. Well, what does naturally mean? Well, in other words, that their brain kind of *comes up to this conclusion* and it *naturally progresses* instead of some guy just lays it out on the line clear as day. I'm sure that makes sense.

CHAPTER ELEVEN

Three Words in the Pattern

And here are **three words** that fit into the category of **adverb and adjective pattern**. These are a part of this pattern and they're three of my *favorite* words in the pattern so we'll start with those and I'll give you more. **Naturally, easily** and **unlimited**.

Now, here's a major note for you: *everything that follows* one of these words is **presupposed** in the sentence. In other words, when you say these words, the listener *must accept everything that follows as true* in order to make sense of the sentence. People *may* believe what you say, but they will *always* believe what they conclude.

They'll always believe their own conclusions and they *form* those conclusions as much from what you *don't* say as what you *do*. Now we're getting to the point of how do we actually *do* this, how do we get them to come to those conclusions and how can we learn to do it kind of easy? Right? And that's exactly what this is about.

So, you may begin to discover **naturally** as you listen to this **pattern**, you begin to insert your own personal examples of how they work such that you can begin to use these in your own life, adapting these to your own style and that's going to feel really, really good.

Now, rather than deconstruct that one I just did one to you, let's look at a few examples.

- Have you discovered how **easily** you can make the decision to refer your friends to our company?
- Have you asked yourself if the **unlimited** potential of this information is what is making you so excited?
- Have you **naturally** discovered how persuasive you are becoming?
- Many people begin **naturally**, Mr. Williams, to create an idea of owning this just prior to making the decision to buy.
- **Naturally**, you'll find more than enough reasons to go ahead today if you understand even a little bit of what I say next. (I love that one.)

All right. I want to **deconstruct** these for you now. Let's look at *why* these have the power that they do.

"Have you discovered how **easily** you can make the decision to refer your friends to our company?" Am I asking you if you have *made* the decision? No. So am I asking you a question that you can answer yes or no? Well, yes, I am in a way, but it's a very special kind of question because it uses this **pattern**. I'm *not* asking you if you *will*, I'm asking you if you've discovered how **easily**. . . In other words, I'm not even just *suggesting* that it's easy, but that you can *discover* how easy. You don't even have to work at it. Okay?

So, I'm not asking you, 'would you' refer me. I'm **assuming you will**. The **conclusion** that you will come up to if you can make sense of this sentence is that *you're going to refer your friends*. That's

175

the **conclusion** I want you to come up with.

"Have you *discovered* how **easily**?" If they say, "No", my response would be, "Not yet, huh?" How do polite people *argue* with that? Well, no. And I might continue on by saying, "Well, you might *discover* just how **naturally** the right people to refer us to pop into your mind from time to time as a result of feeling the feelings of satisfaction as a result of what we're doing here together today."

All right? So in other words, there is *no way that you can lose* when you do this. Let's analyze the next sentence.

"Have you asked yourself if the **unlimited** potential of this information is what is making you so excited?" Man, this is just *loaded*, but let me pull it apart for you a little bit. First of all, am I *asking* them *if* they're excited about this material? No. Am I *asking* them *if* this material has unlimited potential? No. I'm asking them if it's the *unlimited potential* that's *making them so excited*.

Do you see what I'm doing here? What is the **conclusion** I want them to draw? That they're going to be *excited* by this, but I'm not *telling* them they have to be excited or they need to be excited, I'm simply **creating a cause and effect relationship in their mind**. In other words, understanding or even asking about the **potential** of this information will make them, in fact, *excited*. How cool that *they* come up with this all by themselves. It feels like by answering that question *they* come up with *excitement* and that's pretty doggone cool.

"Have you asked yourself if the **unlimited** potential of this information is what's making you so excited?" If they say, "No", say, "Excellent. See, for each person it's some other feature, some other process, something else that *leads* to that and I'll leave you to your own resources to *discover* that by the time we're here today." *You just don't lose* when you implement this.

All right, next one: "Have you **naturally** discovered how persuasive you are becoming?" Did I *ask* you if you are more persuasive? No. Did I even *ask* you if you've *discovered* if you're more persuasive? No. I've asked if you've **naturally** discovered. I love it. I just love this stuff. Can you tell? I'll try to contain my excitement here. Have you **naturally**. . . as opposed to what, pray tell? *Unnaturally* discovering? But see the minute I say 'naturally', you're *locked on to that word*. Now you could have a jerk, once in a blue moon but you won't if you have any **rapport**, but you could have a jerk go, "I don't think I'm becoming more persuasive", and then you say, "Might you be really amazed as you **easily** discover what you're learning that you *didn't know* you were learning?" And look knowingly at them.

And they'll go, "Aha." They can't argue with it. Not if they want to not look stupid. Okay?

"Have you **naturally** discovered. . ." In other words, I'm not *asking* you if you've discovered, I'm **assuming** you *have*. I'm not *asking* you if you're becoming more persuasive, I'm **assuming** you are. I've only asked if you've **naturally** discovered it. If the person says no, I can also say, "Sometimes that dawns on a person not so naturally but as a result of study and application, do you know what I'm saying?"

This is **implanting the roadway to the destination**. The *destination* will dawn upon you as you travel down the *roadway*. You'll *get* it, but it's not because I necessarily *said* it, or not in so many words.

Okay, next sentence: "Many people begin **naturally**, Mr. Williams, to create an idea of owning this just prior to making the decision to buy it." This one's good. Okay. Many people. . . who's that? Well, Mr. Williams, *that's* who it is. Remember when I said, when you're **artfully vague** people have to *apply* it to someone somewhere so *they apply it to themselves*. It's just a typical rule of thumb. Okay? "Many people begin **naturally**, Mr. Williams. . ." What is '*begin naturally*'? It's a **command** to begin. So you're telling him, hey, get started. But *how*? Starting *how*? Well, **naturally**. Meaning, *it's of his own volition*, not of mine or anyone else's. It's of his own. Get started to do *what* naturally? To create an idea of owning this. So you're telling him *to begin creating an idea of owning this*, when? Just prior to making the decision to buy it. In other words, this is also a very sophisticated **cause and effect logical sequence**. Let's reverse it altogether, let's say, what you're saying here is, "When people make a decision to buy this product, the first thing they do is they imagine owning the product and if they make that idea of owning the product in their mind, **naturally**, in other words, if they do it just *of their own volition*, it assumes something about the end of the process, like that it's going to be more enjoyable or it's good, or there's something better about it because it's natural. That's why I like '**naturally**'. Okay?

So what we're saying is, "Many people, in other words, *you*, Mr. Williams, begin now, *not* because I told you to, but because it's the **natural** thing to do, to create an idea of owning this." Now, how do you hear me say 'to create an idea of owning this'? For example, I'm writing this book you're reading right now. Many people begin **naturally** to create an idea of reading one of my books just prior to making the decision to do it at their earliest opportunity.

Well, okay, *how* do you do that? I'll pull it apart. Many people. . . in other words, Mr. Williams, *you*, start, to do *what*? Well, make an idea of owning this. Well, when you name something people if they're going to understand it, they have to be able to figure out your words so they *make an idea of owning this* and then you're telling them within deep **rapport** that they do that *just prior to making the decision to buy it* and so what happens is, **they start to feel compelled to buy it**. And they go, oh, well, I'm making an image of owning this, I guess it makes sense, it's logical for me to go ahead and buy it.

The *power* in that sentence. By the way, feel free to use this in your own work, not in the teaching of this, but in your own work, in other words, *use* this to sell whatever you're selling, to *persuade* whatever you're persuading. Okay?

Write your examples based on my exact wording like this. **Naturally**, you'll find more than enough reasons to go ahead today if you understand even a little bit of what I say next.

Am I asking *if* he found enough reasons to go ahead? No. Am I asking you *if* you understand? No. I'm *suggesting* that you could **naturally**, again sort of meaning *on your own*, find more than enough reasons. In other words, *more than* enough means *at least* enough. So in other words, *all that you need*, to do *what*? To go ahead. So if you understand even what the words are, your mind races ahead and finds those reasons and if it doesn't, then you're going to get an objection from the person, but that's good, you want to know so you can help them find the reasons.

And here's the kicker. *When* is this going to happen? *Today.* *If*, and that makes it so that it **eliminates resistance**, in other words, "Oh, I'm not necessarily sure I'm going to do that today." Well, *if* you understand even a little bit about what I say *next*. In other words, it makes it *conditional* on what happens next.

Now I'm going to say something *very simple* because I want him to understand *even a little bit* of it, right? "See, people learn these skills because they want to make more money and convince more people or be more powerful and persuasive in their life. Do you know what I mean?"

Okay. Are you starting to see how this works? Very, very, very powerful stuff. In and of itself, it has power, but when you start combining it with **rapport** and **VAK** language and **pacing** and **leading** and on and on and on, oh, my goodness, you're developing nuclear weapons of persuasion, in essence.

CHAPTER TWELVE

More Words For The Adverb / Adjective Pattern

The three words you have been given so far in the **adverb/adjective** category are, as you've probably figured out by now, representative of a whole class of descriptive words that will have the *same* impact when you use them.

I gave you, not necessarily the most important three, but three I *use* all the time. And here's a more complete list that you can choose from. *Some, naturally, obviously, finally, all, readily, still, many, infinitely, already, truly, begin, unlimited, repeatedly, most, easily, accordingly, usually, immediately,* and on and on.

That isn't exhaustive by any stretch of the imagination but it's more than you'll probably ever need though feel free to come up with as many as you like.

Now, look, all of these may not even fit depending on *how you use them* into the **adverb/adjective pattern**. In other words, into that *exact* way of talking about this, but what it does do for sure is it has the same impact, so don't worry about the technical language classification, this all works.

CHAPTER THIRTEEN

Combining the Pattern

Now let's **combine** these so that we can add a whole lot more power to the equation. Here's the rule. Put *as many of these words as possible* in your sentence, just don't sound strange. So put as many of these words as possible in your sentence but just don't sound strange doing it. Okay?

Now you're going to ask me, I know, my brain just went there, "But wait a minute, Kenrick, in the question and answer section of this book you said, *don't* necessarily put everything in there. You said that's *not* the way to go." All right, I did. You're right. What I'm suggesting *here* is that you're going to be **strategic** about what you put in and you're going to use a number of the **adverb/adjective words** to *build up the strength* of your sentences.

Now, what I'd like you to do is *write ten sentences each* modeling those example sentences exactly so that you can get how these work. So write ten sentences for each example using *those exact formats* so you can begin to get how this works. Sometimes people don't get it right up front, they just think you can throw in these words any old way, that's why I'm saying, **follow my pattern exactly**. Just put in your *words*, your *content*, but **follow the pattern**.

Okay. Here are some combined examples:

"You've **probably** started to become aware of **some** of the **many easy**, yet **powerful** ways you can use this information. **Naturally**, the most **readily available** and, more **importantly**, **competent** person to deal with is me. **Finally**, the most **reliably accurate** system of persuasion is within your grasp. Once you **begin** to **easily** absorb this information, you'll **naturally** discover how **easily** it works for you. Most of the reasons why people succeed with this information have to do with the truly **unlimited** power of the skills that you can **easily** put to good use in your own life, don't you think?"

These are bloody brilliant. All right? Let's go through them.

"You've probably started to become aware. . . ." well, if you hadn't before, you *will* now. Okay? "Started to become aware. . . of **some**, of the **many**. . ." That means there are *more* than what you've even become *aware* of. "**Easy**, yet **powerful**." So this is just *layering it in thick*. Some of the many easy, and it's saying they're *easy* and *powerful*, "ways you can use this information." In other words, this is implying that you can *use* the information and that you've *become aware* of just how easy and powerful it is. In other words, you're **drawing the conclusions** that it's *easy* and *powerful* and there are *many* of them. I don't have to **tell** you, "Hey, guess what, I'll teach you more ways to use this that are easy than anybody else possibly could and you're going to find it's really powerful. I know because I'm telling you so."

Well, okay. That wouldn't have a *tenth* of the impact as the example.

"**Naturally**, the most **readily available** and, more **importantly**, **competent** person to deal with is me."

"**Naturally**. . ." In other words, as opposed to *what*. So *it's in your own mind*, it just happens that the most **readily available**, meaning, *I'm here for you now*, and more **importantly competent**, is competent the *only* issue? No. I'm *both* readily available *and* competent. Okay? And it's *implying* that it's **natural** that that's *important* to you. The person to deal with is *me*. If you are a real estate agent or broker, could you use that to your advantage? Absolutely. If you were an advisor, could you use that? Absolutely. It doesn't matter *what* you do, you'll find you can *use* that.

"**Naturally**, the most **readily available** and, more **importantly, competent** company to deal with is us." It doesn't matter what you're doing, you can make this work.

"**Finally**, the most **reliably accurate** system of persuasion is within your grasp." **Finally**. What does that **presuppose**? Well, that you've been really *looking*. And *here it is*. The most **reliably accurate**. Well, says something about *proven*, says something about *no fuss*, no muss. It says *all kinds of things*. I'm being **artfully vague** and letting *you* put it in but you can get an idea of what that is, what's actually happening. "It's within your grasp", meaning it's not quite there yet but you're getting your hands around it and now *just buy this new thing*, or whatever. If I were on TV

179

doing an infomercial, or if you were on a TV doing an infomercial. "**Finally**, the most **reliably accurate** system of body building is within your grasp. Just call 1800-BIG BODY NOW and you too can have giant bulging muscles just like this." Okay?

Well, see, it's all of the sudden, it's **layering that stuff in**. Of course, as always, you've got to have **rapport** to make this really, really work well.

Once you **begin** to **easily** absorb this information, you'll **naturally** discover how **easily** it works for you.

All right. This is amazing. So I'm suggesting to you that what I really want *you* to *come to the conclusion of* is that it works for you. How? **Easily**. In other words, this is easy. Okay. And how did that happen? Well, because you *absorbed* it. But not through difficult, laborious means, actually, you **began** and it was **easy**. Then, it's not going to be *work*, it's going to be *a discovery process*. Okay? And how will that happen? Well, of course, on your own **naturally**, it will just come into your mind. It just does.

See? Isn't that amazing? Most of the reasons why people succeed with this information have to do with the **truly unlimited** power of the skills that you can **easily** put to good use in your life, don't you think?

Am I *asking* you if you can put this to good use? No. I'm *suggesting* that it's easy to do. So I'm focusing you on the word *easy* and I'm *not saying* all of the reasons that people succeed because I don't want to *create resistance*. Most of the reasons. And you may well then go, yeah, sure, that's true for me too. Okay. Great. Succeed with this information. . . well, am I *telling* you to succeed with it? I'm *not* telling you but *that's* what you're going to hear. And *why* will you succeed? Is it because it's powerful information? Powerful skills? Well, yeah, but it's **truly unlimited** power. So it *expands your framework* to include **truly unlimited**. You see?

I mean, these things just rock. They rock. They really do.

CHAPTER FOURTEEN

Some Thoughts On This Strategy

If you do what I've just done with every sentence, you're going to sound *ridiculous*. You want to do this *occasionally*. You're going to **naturally** slip into using this and **easily** create this kind of **powerful** wording scenario for your customers so that they will **naturally**, just as you are right now, follow along and then you'll want to just kind of stop and stop using it and just go right on back to talking normal again. It's that kind of *going in and out and taking them with you* **powerfully** like this and just sort of being there with them is the goal that you're going to do. So you're going to do this *occasionally*, but you will be surprised to learn that you can do this more than you thought you could and still get away with it. So I'm going to encourage you to *stretch the boundaries of what's possible* here. And as you start to increase the use of these patterns in your language, you'll find people zoning out as you talk. So purposefully *bring them back to consciousness* by redirecting their attention from time to time and how do you redirect their attention? Just start talking normally. Stop using those words all the time.

Or point to something on their desk and say, "Wow, that's really cool. Where did you get that?" or say to them, "All right. Are you with me so far? Are you understanding what I'm talking about here?"

Okay. Here is a real **power packed pattern**, it's kind of fun, I know you'll find uses for it. "Have you asked yourself recently how many services your present broker, (or whatever service provider you're talking about,) *should* be providing but *isn't*? Since I brought that up, *does it make you wonder* how much *more* you could be getting when we provide . . . (name whatever it is you do)?" No you don't even have to really wait, you can just go, "You know, *most people* I talk with *begin* thinking like that pretty darn quick. I guess it shouldn't surprise me."

Well, I could talk a *lot* more about that. That's an adaptation of a pattern I came up with that's been highly used in another market much to my chagrin, based on a conversation I had with a person in which I created a way to end relationships, more because I was goaded into saying, well, how *would* I, because I first said I *wouldn't*. I don't think it's necessarily a good thing to do and then I did. And that pattern got widely spread, but this is a way to **insert yourself**, if you will, *into* a scenario where you have *an opportunity to compete*.

And yes, the same thing *would* hold true in a relationship, the only thing is, I guess in my mind I view relationships as being a bit more *sacrosanct* if it's a committed relationship or a marriage, or what have you, I would say, *leave that alone* and *don't* show them why you would be better, just walk away and find one of the millions of other people that exist out there that don't have that situation that you'd be interfering with.

I would highly recommend you write at least ten of those sentences out so you can begin to see how you could use that to your advantage as well.

CHAPTER FIFTEEN

Adding Massive Amplification

So what I've taught you so far in this book has been good but. . .actually, no 'but', it's *awesome*. I love this stuff. This will absolutely take you to new realms in persuasion, but what I want to do now is take this to a much different level altogether. You can follow and *model my examples* and create extremely powerful **patterns** for whatever it is that you do and however you'd like to use these skills, but I'd like to teach you how to think to **maximize these skills**.

You'll note in the examples I've given I'm being **artfully vague** yet still *guiding the person's thoughts* where I want them to go. This is powerful and you should do the exact same thing. Follow my examples, okay?

A few years back I began to notice that I was doing something really special with these patterns that was giving me results way beyond what others were getting and I tried to figure out what it was and it took me some time and some effort to figure it out but all of the sudden I really got it and wow, what a difference it's made in my life and the lives of the people that I've been training.

I realized that I was **aiming** these in a really powerful way. And soon you're going to be able to. And in fact, I want you to know, I have *never* heard this taught anywhere else, period. Though, as usual, now that *I've* said it, you'll soon see others "emulating" my work. That's all right. Not really, but. . .

This is a breakthrough. This is really a breakthrough. So what did I do early on that enables you to **aim your persuasive message**? How did I aim it? Well, if you said it had something to do with **criteria**, you'd be right on the money. And so what I taught you early on that enables you to **aim your message** of course has to be **criteria**.

Remember I said that you have no business talking to somebody really unless you have their **criteria**. Why? Because *you don't know where to aim it* and now all you're going to be doing is using *features* and *benefits*. Blah, blah, blah. Okay? You need to use **criteria**. **Criteria** aims all your persuasion solidly where it needs to be aimed, right through their filters of **desire** and what they **want**.

So what if you **presupposed** their own **criteria** itself by *putting it into the structure* that I've been teaching you here in this book?

You guessed it. The power goes right through the roof. In other words, instead of just aiming at things in general, what if we aimed at **presupposing** their **criteria** so it becomes a given that they *get* that when they do business with you?

I will tell you, if there is such a thing as an ultimate skill, this certainly is right up there as one of them. And we're going to expand on this over the months to come unbelievably.

Here's the rule: Use these **linguistic patterns** to **presuppose** the **criteria** of those you are persuading. It's hot, hot, hot. Let's do a few of these so you can get the idea. And here are some **criteria** from clients I just made up. So an advisor asks the client, "Why are we here together today?" And the client says, "Well, I thought I'd look and see if maybe I could be a little more effective at my investment strategy." The advisor says, "Okay. And *what's important to you* about getting better at your investment strategy?" "Well, so I know my money's working for me as hard as it can."

The advisor says, "Okay, and ultimately, so I really understand what's going on with you so I can help you the best, ultimately, *what will that do for you*?" And the client says, "Well, I don't know. I don't feel like my money's working real well for me right now and if it was I guess I'd just have financial safety. I'd feel good about that, like that would change a lot in my life."

The advisor says, "You know, *that makes a lot of sense to me*. **A lot of my clients** say things like that. In fact, I'd have to say, a lot of clients come to me with that very thing in mind. What I'd like you to **begin** to think about is that **naturally** as a result of us working together, and even just talking here today, you'll **begin** to discover how some of the **tremendous** benefits I offer to my clients can **readily** be yours simply by having me as your advisor and the reason I say this is because as you **begin** to understand even a little bit of the kinds of skills and abilities I bring to the table **just even** by recognizing a little of what I say next to you, you'll **begin** to understand how this *can **completely*** change a person's life giving them the kind of thing that they need and want *the most.* Let me get into your situation a little bit more deeply now. And let's talk about the way in which we can bring *financial safety* to the forefront in your life."

Do you see what I'm doing there? Let's give you another example.

A realtor asks a person, "What is it that you want?" And they go, "Well, we want to sell our home." "Okay, *what's important about selling your home*?" "Well, that we get the most money for it as we can." "All right. And so that I can really understand you, **ultimately** *what's important about getting as much for your home as you can*? In other words, ultimately?"

The person goes, "Well, we're ready for a bigger home and we can afford a bigger home, but the more money we get from our house, the more home we can afford or the less it's going to cost us to get that home." The realtor says, "Absolutely. That makes really good sense. I can see *a bigger home* in your immediate future and **naturally**, as you **begin** to understand all the value and reasons why people work with me to accomplish those things, you **begin** to understand why people have such a **relaxed** attitude about it. They just **feel confident** knowing that I'm on the job because of all of the success I've had. In fact, in this area, by the way, I just want you to know I've just sold four of the *biggest and most expensive homes* in this area and I did it in record time. But I guess you may already know some of that, but these are the reasons that **naturally** people work with me on doing this kind of thing. Now, before *you make that decision to do that right now*, I'd like to just go over a few things with you about the way you want this home to be so I can both be looking at helping you sell the current house that you have and finding you the *bigger house*. So first, tell me a little bit more about what neighborhood this new house is going to be in and let's talk about that."

So off we go. But see how that works? Let's say you do coaching and you say to someone, "All right, well, *why did you choose* to have this introductory appointment with me today?" "Well, you offered one for free." "Okay. Excellent. And I know that there's a lot of things offered for free including underarm deodorant and you probably don't waste your time to go and try to get it. So let me ask *why you chose today*? Why *now* to set an appointment to talk with me?"

"Well, it's just time to *move up in my life*. It's time that I move up and I know that you've helped a lot of people do that, or at least that's what it says on your website and I thought I'd call and find out if it's really true and if you could help me."

The coach, being well trained in this material, says, "Fantastic. Well, I think those are all very important things and to make sure I'm really understanding you well, let me ask you this. **Ultimately**, what will making sure this will be good for you or helpful to you do for you? In other words, what are you *really* looking to do with it?" The person goes, "You know, if I could move forward right now in my life, I'd have *better status* in my life. In other words, when you are *accomplishing more* and *your business is worth more* and you can drive *a nicer, better, more expensive car* and *dress nicer* and take your *wife* and *family* places and do things you've always wanted to do, it just feels good. You have *more status* in life."

The consultant says, "Excellent. That makes good sense. And **as you become aware** just how **naturally** *you can have that kind of status that you want*, by working with me in this system, you'll **begin** to understand why people seek me out from far and wide to be able to provide this to them. In fact, it's interesting that you bring this up. I had a guy. . . In fact he reminds me a bit of you. He *also* wanted *status* in his life and interestingly has a kind of a similar tone. I don't know if you might be from the same area, but anyway, he was saying to me the other day, 'You know, I've really been looking into what you do for some time. I've watched you on your website, I've watched you grow and it just seems like you're getting more and more expensive and I see the reason is you're able to document proof of helping more and more people and I figured I'd better get in there so you can help me too before you go to the point where I can't afford you.' I thought he made a valid point, you know, but *he too wanted to have status*. He too said, 'You know, it's important to me that I begin to develop everything I do such that I turn everything to my strategic advantage because what I really want is I want to reap some of the rewards of what I'm doing now. I'm willing to work hard. I'm willing to go for the long term, but I'd also like at least some of the things now. And I feel like *status* is one of the things I could really have more of and pretty quickly.' And he's right. So tell me a little bit about your business, would you?"

Now if you're following these, you're probably **zoning right through the floor**. And that's good because this is going to help you to really learn this and use this to your advantage and that's my goal, of course. All right? And by the same token, not only are you learning how to do this, but it's probably dawning on you that this is going to take a little bit of work and effort on your part. Well, yeah, it sure does.

To use these skills *powerfully* you are going to have to *write* them, you're going to have to *wrestle* with them and *think* with them. You're going to have to get good at making them come out of your mouth **as part of who you are, just as part of your nature**, okay? And to do that, you need to *write*. You need to *write them out*. Saying them alone isn't enough. I don't care if you write on a computer or you write with paper and pencil or pen and paper, I don't care. But **you need to write them out** and I'm telling you, this book is so jam packed. If you read it six or seven times between now and the next book, I would say you'd only *begin* to scratch the surface of what's here. There's just so much.

BOOK ELEVEN

SHAPING AWARENESS

INTRODUCTION

Shaping Beliefs and Structuring Reality

Welcome to **Book Eleven** of *Persuasion Force*. We will be covering **shaping beliefs and structuring reality** part two.

I'm glad to be able to offer this new volume to you. We have a jam-packed book. I hope you're holding on to your seats because this is really going to be fun. And as you read through this book, I want to encourage you to stop reading on occasion and *review* any particular area that goes by you a little too quick.

It's really important, just always feel comfortable to stop, take a breath and then pick right back up.

There is so much here. I'm just not kidding. I probably could have spread this out over a number of books but I'm always bringing you as much as I possibly can.

CHAPTER ONE

Looking For Evidence That Will Support What We Want To Believe

I got a call from an acquaintance of mine a short time ago and I'd like to tell you about that call. It went something like this: "Hey, Kenrick, how you doing?" I said, "Good." He said, "You know what? I'm just stunned." I said, "Why?" He said, "Well, I was thinking just today about our conversation we had sometime back about Africa and everything, just feeling really good when I checked my e-mail and *you won't believe it*. **I won an international lottery**. In fact, it's one that originated from Africa. Can you *believe* that?" He said, "You know, **I'm just convinced everything happens for a reason**, doesn't it?"

He said, "You know, I'm so lucky. This is just *amazing*. So I've written back and I'm looking forward to hearing from them. I sent them my personal info so they know who I am and I can't wait. But it's a lot of money and listen, I want you to know, that as soon as it comes through, you know, I won't forget you. You've really been a great friend." I said, "Well, thank you. That's very kind."

So I thought for a few moments and I responded something like this, "You know, I think you're right. Everything *does* happen for a reason and really *it's a good thing that we're talking right now!*" And I went on to explain that I personally 'win' probably three or four international lotteries a day, many of them originating from Africa and **none of them are real**. They're all fake. And that he should be understanding that this is nothing but a con thing and that soon what he's going to receive back is a reply and they're going to ask for all sorts of personal info like bank accounts, yada, yada, and if he were to submit any of that, *he would promptly have all of his money wiped out*. Or the alternate route is, they're ready to send the millions of dollars he's won, but he has to *pay some bank fees* to get it to clear the bank that it's in and if he'll just remit $500, they'll have the funds quickly on their way to him.

So I got to thinking about this conversation and I realized that **people look for supporting evidence for what they want** in their environment. So in this case, here he was remembering our conversation, receiving an e-mail talking about winning a lottery from Africa and somehow he kind of *put two and two together in a way that wasn't really appropriate* and began talking about everything happening for a reason and so lucky and on and on.

Unfortunately I had to burst the bubble in order to keep him safe, but the point of it is is that, *why did he use that language?* And those are the kinds of things I'd like to look into with you now. And I'm going to give you a couple of **language patterns** that are going to knock your socks off and enable you to really influence for very deep and profound reasons.

Let's talk a little bit about *why* people look for supporting evidence for what they want in their environment. Oftentimes they do this because our world is very *unstable*. And whenever there's a tremendous lack of stability, everything kind of up in the air, people start turning to religions and they start turning to God and they start turning to spirituality and they also become more superstitious. And you can look back at history and see these trends over and over as you see difficult things in the world happen.

By the way, before I say another word, let me interrupt my train of thought to explain something very important to me. If you are a spiritual person, if you're a Christian or a Muslim or if you are any faith, I applaud you and I think that's great. My writing here right now is *not* oriented towards getting you to think or not think anything, it's simply going to *pull out things that human beings do*, such that you can use them to your advantage. That's it. And it so happens that these are very profound things. Very, very profound things. So as I tell them to you, please understand, my goal, my job, is to break things down in a way that gives us **tremendous power with our language** and our words and persuasion and in so doing, help you to have more success in your life. That's the purpose for this discussion. If you *don't* believe in God, or you're *not* a spiritual person, my point today is *not* to influence you towards or away from anything except towards a **language pattern** or away from not being as successful as you like, that you'll be able to use these patterns for your benefit and for the benefit of your clients.

Fair enough? Okay? Got it?

All right. So let's analyze my response just a little bit. When I said, 'everything **DOES** happen for a reason' - you'll note the word **DOES** is capitalized and bold for emphasis - what does that really mean? Well, it means that probably *I'm alluding to something more* than simply what he's just referred to and that's really important that he understood that and then I want on to say, '**GOOD** thing we're talking'. Again, this implies that there's perhaps *something more* than what he was just thinking about. That set the stage for me to *have entry into his mind* and to help him to understand the difficulty that he was about to face.

Before we go any further, let me repeat again, **people look for supporting evidence for what they want in their environment** and I believe it's *our* job to give it to them. And there are **language patterns** that are in the popular lexicon right now that we can *use to our advantage* very powerfully.

CHAPTER TWO

Telling Secrets

Let me ask you a question. How do you know that something has really made it? That it's in the consciousness of the public at large? Well, I'll tell you one way, it's on *Oprah*. *Oprah* features it. And I want to talk with you a little bit about the movie '*The Secret*'. I imagine that you've probably seen it, you've probably certainly heard of it, if not perhaps own it. Let me give you a few thoughts about this movie. I absolutely **love** this movie. It's a *phenomenal* movie. And I'm sad to tell you that there are a number of people, that in an attempt to make a name for themselves, and parlay off the success of it, have decided that it's appropriate to put this movie down.

Why? You might ask. And you're probably also thinking, what does this have to do with **shaping beliefs**? Well, you're about to find out. Oprah takes this movie and runs a couple of shows on it. If *that* doesn't put something right into the consciousness of the public at large, at least within the United States and probably much further, I don't know what will. If you have anything that you're selling or promoting or anything else, and you can get on the Oprah show, you probably have an instant huge hit on your hands.

So *why* would people want to put this movie down? And I'd like to write just a few words about that. First of all, I want you to know that to me, it's *embarrassing* that I'm involved in any way, shape or form in an industry where people have joined together to do that. A typical way of trying to **promote oneself** these days is to *piggyback* what you're doing along with *something that's happening in the news*. Well, '*The Secret*' is certainly in the news and I have no issue with doing that, in fact, I love to do that kind of thing myself when I get a chance. And I guess you have to *take a stand* one way or another on things so this group of people chose to take a negative stand.

Well, let me ask you a simple question. **Do you agree with *everything* that you hear from any source?** Any one source? I don't and I doubt you do either. Okay. So I guess we could then turn and ask, do you agree with everything that you've heard about '*The Secret*' or as a result of watching '*The Secret*'? I can tell you that I don't.

But that would be like saying, you know, *money* can be used wrongly and so I'm going to just do the right thing and never try to earn another dime as long as I live and make sure that if ever anyone gives me money, I'm going to give it away because after all, I don't want to be involved with something bad. That genuinely is the definition of **throwing the baby out with the bathwater**.

If a person *objects* to positive mental thinking, positive mental attitudes, and the sage advice that has shaped our nation and most all of the successful people in the world today that have followed along the footsteps of great thinkers of our time, then I guess someone could genuinely be upset with '*The Secret.*' But in particular, what did these people pick on? I'll just point out a couple of the things. One is that '*The Secret*' talks about being **responsible** for our lives, being **responsible** in every way. And '*The Secret*' says something to the order of, "Well, after all, the poor people in India, or wherever, or Darfur, *chose*, consciously *chose* their plight in life."

All right, so the people that stood against this movie basically said, "That's nonsense. '*The Secret*' is a cult." There's that **big, bad word**. "And so it's saying things that are blatantly not true." All right, so you might ask *me*, do *I* believe that the people in India or Darfur, or anywhere else for that matter that are hungry and having problems, did they **consciously choose** to be there? And I would say to you, *no*, of course they didn't consciously choose. And I think in the attempt to entertain and be dramatic, '*The Secret*' went a bit too far.

However, do you know that there's a *huge* group of people out there, I mean, many, many, many millions from what it appears to be, that actually **believe** at least along those lines. I don't think anyone would say they consciously **chose** it, but let me ask you a question like this. Let's say that *you* **believed** that we are here on planet earth for a reason. That reason is, it's a school. And we are here going to school to *learn*. What are we trying to learn? Well, we're trying to learn all the lessons this school has to offer.

Let me break away from that for a moment and ask you, in the school called high school or college, are *all* the lessons *positive*? I dare say not. I'll bet you would agree with me. Some of them were very difficult. Some of them hurt a lot. You probably broke up with a number of boyfriends or girlfriends during that time and it was probably quite devastating. You probably thought your whole life was coming to an end and then all of the sudden you were saved by something else going well for you.

All right, so you *learned the lessons* of your schooling, good and bad. Well, there are a lot of people out there who believe in reincarnation. Now once again, I'm *not* going to ask you to believe in this, not for a second, I'm not going to ask you *not* to believe in it, not for a second. What I am going to say is, I think you would go along with me that there's *a huge number of people*, a huge number of religions out there that *absolutely* **believe** in this. And from *that* perspective, if that's so, then they might believe that we **choose** our parents, we **choose** the country we're going to be born in, and we **choose** to live the lessons that earth has to give us such that one day we don't need to come back anymore and we can evolve to a higher level. Whatever these things are, is up to them. I don't know. But I'm just sharing with you some of their basic **beliefs**.

Now, if you're a reasonable and intelligent person, you know that I'm speaking the truth, that there *are* groups of people out there who **believe** this and there happen to be a huge number of them. All right? So if all of this is the case, then would it be *reasonable* if you were the creator of the movie '*The Secret*' and *you* believed in these things, that you would make a statement such as, "The people in India that are starving, have chosen their plight in life so that they could experience these difficulties to learn how to overcome them or simply to experience a life of poverty", and I think the answer is absolutely yes. They *didn't* choose them *consciously*, they chose them *before* they came into this earthly experience.

All right. In other words, if you choose to take on the **belief system** of a huge percentage of our world, then this would make complete sense. Is it still said a bit *dramatically*? Absolutely. Do I agree with it? In other word that they *consciously chose* it? No. And I'm not quoting '*The Secret*' very well here, either. Do I agree that they *consciously chose* it? No. But I will not argue that they *perhaps* chose it at some other level. Although, how could we ever *know* that? Well, the answer is, we probably can't. Okay?

So the big question I have for you is, why should we knock it? In other words, yes, I have my *own* beliefs about this, I have my own thoughts about this and I believe that we need to be **responsible**, I believe we need to be careful, but to throw the baby out with the bathwater, I just can't fathom. To me, that's cult like behavior and absolutely ridiculous, inexcusable, even. But I guess, if the goal is to **promote** something, well, '*The Secret*' did a darn good job and I guess those that want to stand in *opposition* to it *also* did a good job because they apparently got some press somewhere and here *I* am giving them more. So I suppose they did a good job.

CHAPTER THREE

Using It To Your Advantage

I think, though, that we can look for some deeper things. And one of those is, '*The Secret*' is talking about how to **set our intention** very, very powerfully. Okay? And if your **intention** is set strong enough, then are there such things as accidents? Well, realistically, heck yes. There sure are. Tell the woman (my wife, actually) who sat at a stoplight and had a utility truck ram into the back of her new car that she did something wrong. I don't believe it. That's an **accident**. Yes, it *could* be argued that somehow at an ethereal level or energetic level, she needed to learn something about chiropractors and so she *chose* for herself to be at the wrong place at the wrong time, and I pretty much say, *hogwash*. I don't think that's the case. I think it was a genuine accident. And if it *is* the case, okay, that's fine. I don't care.

But here we have a movie that talks about how to **put ourselves in alignment with good**. I like that. But around these kinds of discussions come **statements** like, '*Things happen for a reason, don't they?*' or, '*There are no accidents.*'

My point being, that when we *hear* these things, or even if we don't hear them, we can **use them to our advantage powerfully**, and I mean, *really* powerfully. So, for example, saying "*Things happen for a reason*" or "*There are no accidents*" **supports what you want to happen**. Let's say you're an advisor and you're talking with someone, and they say something positive like, "Wow, it's a good thing that I'm talking with you here today, because I feel like I'm really getting somewhere in my learning, in my understanding of how all this works." And your *response* could be, "Fantastic, after all, **there are no accidents**, right?"

Or let's say you're talking with someone and they say, "Wow, thank you so much for helping me get my house sold. I mean, your advice, your knowledge and your help is spot on the money. This is really good stuff." And your response is, "**I absolutely believe that things happen for a reason**."

And now, is that a stretch to say? I don't think it's a stretch for anybody, no matter what our belief system is. After all, everything happens for a reason, it's just a matter of whether or not it's a reason you *like*. Okay?

The accident to my wife happened *because* the guy that was driving the utility truck wasn't paying attention. That's *why* it happened. She can't be blamed for it. All right? So **you can use these kinds of language patterns when someone says something that you want to reinforce**. And this is where it starts getting really fun. See, '*The Secret*' does this really, really well. They *use* this kind of **language pattern** all the time. They imply things that are bigger and greater than us are happening left and right in our lives. And is that so bad? I don't think so. I think our **consciousness** is greater than we'll ever consciously understand. I believe that. You don't have to believe that, but I believe that.

I don't think it's so bad to believe that when we **set our intention** for something, *we can accomplish great, great things*. And that's what it is that they wanted us to *know*, apparently, and I just think that that is absolutely *phenomenal*. Unbelievably phenomenal, actually.

CHAPTER FOUR

Assigning Blame

All right, now, let's talk about the **flip side** of this, and that is **assigning blame**. Better hang on here if you are religiously oriented because I'm going to shake the tree just a little bit here. Okay?

So the next thing is, **assigning blame** and let's talk about that for a moment. In group theory, there's a lot of discussion about *enemies*, common enemies, etc. Why? Well, because **one of the greatest ways you can ever** *bond a group* **is to have an enemy**. Now let's talk about two of the biggest religions—they're *sort of* opposing each other—but let's just talk about this so you can see how it works, let's talk about two of them, Muslims and Christians. So using good group theory . . . let's say you started your own religion, actually, what would be something you could do? Well, you could figure out **a common enemy**, someone that you wanted to have as an enemy or some thing that you could have as an enemy. Let's start with Christianity as an example.

What's the **common enemy** of Christianity? Well, you probably know right off the top of your head, it's *the devil*. How do we **leverage** this for huge benefit? Well, we start saying things like, *the consequences of sin is death*. We say things like, *we as humans are born into a world of sin and the mere act of being born causes us to not be able to get into the life hereafter until and unless we accept Jesus as our savior.*

So let's look at the **enemy**. The enemy is, well, just *being born*, for Pete's sake, because we're *born into sin*, **who's responsible** for that? **The devil**. Okay? This is a *great tool*. I heard someone say many years ago, "*The devil is the best friend the Christian ever had because without him, there would be no need for a savior.*" Think about the word '*savior*'. Savior implies **someone** *needs* **saving**. And if *you're* born into sin, *you* in fact do need saving. And again, I'm not debating any of this. In fact, I'm kind of being the devil's advocate here, inadvertently, I suppose, because I'm literally standing back, removing my own beliefs here, just to point out to you *what's going on* so you can see this.

Now does it mean, by the way, having a common enemy isn't a good thing? No, I think common enemies are great things. What I can tell you is, one has to be *careful* and *responsible*. Is it responsible of a Christian to say that the devil's a common enemy? Absolutely. Absolutely. Also **note the advantage** of pointing at a common enemy that you can't *see*, you can't *hear*, and in fact, even humanity's basic *drives* and *desires* can be attributed to the influence of this being? It's pretty amazing. Again, I'm not debating the *truth* of it or the *lack of truth* of it, I'm just simply pointing it out.

All right, so we **assign blame**. We have an inherent need to assign blame. In fact, it's so fundamental to the core of who we are that *everybody* does this. Let's take the Muslims, for example. I recently saw a special talking about some of the things that are going on right now in Great Britain. Here we have a guy who's an attorney and a Muslim who is, what appears. . . unfortunately, I don't know as much as I'd like to know about that religion, it does seem quite fascinating in many ways and certainly I would say that the majority of people that practice that are far from being the terrorists that everybody thinks they are, but this gentleman that was being showcased was quite radical and basically believed that *anybody* who did not follow the law of the Muslims was going to be overthrown or overrun and that one day, could face military action, a Muslim military that would actually go and *force* religious things to be made right.

Well, this special went on and showed those that practiced the Muslim faith and asked them what they thought of this and they, without question, said, "Wait a minute now, what about our free will? You can't just enforce this on everybody. That's not right."

So I'm **contrasting** '*things happen for a reason*' with '*blame*.' So at our core, we look to **assign fault**. Remember being back in grade school or high school and you and a buddy or friend get in trouble? What's the first thing you say? "Well, I was misbehaving because I was laughing and I shouldn't have been because Billy made me laugh. He told a joke and he said it real quiet so nobody else could hear, but it's his fault." As if *that's* going to save you from your inappropriate behavior. Who's at fault? Who's wrong?

Well, let me tell you something, as it relates to *you* personally and to *me* personally, I would rather **look for the solution** to issues than to **point out the blame**. And I recommend that you take a serious hard look at this. This blaming of everything and everyone causes *lots* of problems, BUT there *is* a golden side to this and here it is. Let's say that someone says to you, "It's a good thing that we're here talking together today because my advisor, I think, hasn't been doing right by me. I'm very concerned. My investments have just not done well lately and I don't like that. I want to retire before long and they're not doing well." And you ask or state, "Well, **you just have to wonder whose fault that is**, don't you?" And most probably, the person will say, "Well, I think it's my advisor's." And you might, if you want to feed the fire a little, you might say, "Well, and I think really **that's just sort of the tip of the iceberg**. I mean, I don't know your advisor so I can't really comment, but I would say that's probably just the tip of the iceberg." And they go, "Yeah, it's probably their company too. Actually letting people get away with this is really bad. And here I am suffering and paying the price." And you say, "Yes. That's exactly right."

I wouldn't dwell there because if you dwell in the land of **negativity**, it's like a double edged knife. It's going to come right back and cut you. It cuts going *and* coming. Be very careful.

So another way you could do this is when they start talking about how bad things are, you could say, "You know, you just have to wonder why someone would let things get so bad. **I'm sure glad you decided not to let it continue.**" What have you done there? Man, have you **driven a wedge** between that person and what they currently are doing or what? Yes, you absolutely have.

So **things happen for a reason, there are no accidents** and **assigning blame**. *Two sides of the same coin* and they're incredibly powerful and I mean, knock your socks off, blow you away powerful, and you can *slip these little guys in* anywhere in your conversation.

CHAPTER FIVE

Superstition

Let's take this just a little further. Let me go and explain a little bit more about **superstition**. Doesn't this sound a bit **superstitious** to you? If it does, you're really not alone. What is the *meaning* of superstitious? Well, **superstition**, if you think about it, is **ways of looking at things that are relatively disconnected from reality or from facts**. For example, let's say you've heard, well, it's not wise to walk underneath a ladder. It gives you bad luck. Okay, well, I suppose there's *some* truth to that. I'll bet you would agree with me. Where did this come from? Let's say that you decide to walk under a ladder and it so happens there's somebody up on top of that ladder and they're painting and as they're painting they happen to slop some paint out and it hits you and there go your very nice, new clothes, and they've just gotten paint all over them because you stepped right where their paint was falling carelessly.

Well, when *enough people* do that kind of thing, or worse yet, the paint bucket tips over and drenches you and smacks you on top of the head and you fall down and you're hurt, well, *when this happens enough times* throughout life, **it becomes sort of bigger than life**. It becomes a **superstition**. But I mean, really, you have to admit it's kind of wise, I suspect, not to really put yourself in a position of danger any more than you have to, unnecessarily. But then we start going into things like, step on a line, break your mother's spine; step on a crack, break your father's back. Are *those* based in reality? Well, I'll bet somewhere in antiquity, we would find someplace where those existed? How about a black cat crosses in front of you? Does that mean you're going to have problems? Well, I don't know. I mean, there might be a time when that's the case. I don't really know. But what I *can* tell you is, that **the more our world becomes unstable, the more people look for stability and look for ways to explain things**. They want to have things explained. And so you, as a persuader, have **the ability to offer explanations**, just the same way that they do to make sense out of their life. I consider it to be largely junko logic but so what?

So in the same way that people look for **supporting reasons**, even nonsensical ones, **to explain their reality**, and they look to **assign blame**, *we* can do the same. So we now have two sides of this same coin that we can deal with any time we want to and we can do it in a way that is very, very profound.

When there's problems, we can ask, "You have to wonder **whose fault** that is." Or perhaps you even say, "You know, if you aren't getting at least X return on your investment, you have to **wonder whose fault that is**, don't you?" And wait and listen. He'll probably go, "I hadn't thought about it that way." And you go, "It's high time, don't you think?" And they go, "Oh, yeah." You say,

192

"What would be the **consequences** of hanging on like that, of letting time go by, years maybe?" "Well, things would really go downhill." And you'd say, "Well, **you'd have to really wonder why someone would let things get so bad.**" And they go, "Yeah, you're absolutely right. I don't want that." And you say, "Well, you know what? **I believe there are no accidents.** It's a good thing that *I'm* here today to talk with you." See the *power* in that? Do you see how *powerful* that is? It is really profound.

But just be careful that you aren't *buying into* the world of nonsense to look for explanations that don't exist. Does that mean I *don't* think that things happen for a reason? No, I personally believe they do. I believe that my **consciousness** is able to create results simply by **setting my intention**. I believe I can get results that way, if nothing else, within my own head and that's good enough for me. More than that, we don't have to go to.

Do I believe there are no accidents? Well, if *they* believe it, *I* believe it. I *actually* believe there *are* accidents, but really it's more of a euphemism, it's a way of saying something, a way of **communicating that I'm here for a reason**.

So I think that all of these things are things that persuaders should be *looking at*, *examining* and *using to their advantage* provided that they can do so in a way that's helpful to themselves and to their clients.

So the **two sides of the coin**, '*things happen for a reason*' and '*whose fault is that?*' or '*you'd have to wonder why someone would let things get so bad*'. And '*there are no accidents, are there?*' Pretty much, you can throw these out almost anywhere. You want to be careful about overusing them, but this is a very, very powerful technique, an extremely powerful technique, and you can put them to use right now. Once again, let me just remind you, I absolutely believe in and practice a spiritual system and a way of thinking that I think has helped me profoundly and whatever your belief is, I'm thrilled, whether you don't believe in anything at all except what's here and now and seeable, that's fine, or if you are a Christian or a Muslim or any religion, that's fine. This isn't about picking apart our beliefs to make you change them, it's about picking them apart so you can *see how people move through this world* and we can find handholds that will help us to have an entry into their world and to be able to **persuade** them to do the kinds of things that would be good for them based on their **values**.

So we have tremendous **ethics** built in to everything that I'm talking about here. Yes, it's true that people that have them as a client already, if you're *displacing* them, they probably won't be too happy with you, and that's certainly your call as to whether or not that's appropriate, but I can tell you that as you get better and better at *reading people* and *understanding the way they tick*, you'll see how **this fits right in with their belief systems**, with the way they are and enables you to really *influence* them at a profound level. There is so much communicated when you say, '*Things happen for a reason*' and it's in keeping with what I taught you in the last book about being **artfully vague**. '*There are no accidents.*' **What does that imply?** Ohh. . .last book's lesson was even *more* profound than you've given it credit for, which is true, but you see the point.

I can say this *anytime*, *anywhere*, as can you and I've found tremendous personal advantage using this pattern. So I'm excited to bring it to you.

By the way, I get so passionate about this material because I see how *dramatically* it changes people's lives and I'm so excited to share it with you that I just find myself getting really carried away and telling you these wonderful **stories** that to me really help *illustrate* the point so I hope you are enjoying this method of learning and how you can benefit from it and make these skills a part of who you are very quickly.

CHAPTER SIX

A Quick Overview About Structuring Reality

As we begin this chapter, I would like to do a quick review of what we went through in Book Ten, just a quick overview about **structuring reality**.

Reality consists as much with the **structure** that's defined as it does with the **assumptions** we make about that structure. In other words, if you are in a supermarket and you see a number of lines and tellers, or baggers, or whatever they are, standing there, you know that in order for you to leave with your food, or with whatever you've come there to buy, that you pretty much have to go and stand in one of those lines. In other words, you can't start waving your arms, sit down in the middle of the floor and throw a fit as to why someone won't come and help you out right there while you're sitting on the floor crying and screaming. In other words, **the structure is important** and what we're learning to do is to **build structure with our language** and as we learn to **build structure with our language**, we can put any **content** in it that we want to put. That's a really beautiful thing because we can guide people then, **structurally**, *anywhere we want them to go* and **our content just flows in naturally**.

So this is even *more* true when it comes to words and what they **imply** or **presuppose** and remember in Book Ten we talked about a major persuasion truism: **people *might* believe that they are told but they'll *always* believe what they come up with themselves**. If you can get someone to **come up with their own conclusion**, well, they're *always* going to believe that. And, they *will* form those conclusions as much from what you *don't* say as what you *do* say. Wow! And now you're remember, I'm sure, from the last book, that when we talked about the **adverb/adjective presuppositions**, that it's the fact that **they have to be accepted as true**. In other words, the **structure** is **everything that follows one of those little guys has to be accepted as true in the mind of your prospect**, that's why it's so powerful.

CHAPTER SEVEN

'How' and 'What'

As we progress, you're going to see how you're going to be able to use the work we've been going through to teach you how to **bring your intention to bear**. There's that **intention** word again. Well, you know, I'll tell you something. When you begin to gain control over your own mind, and you *are* as a result of really applying yourself in this material, you are able to bring *a higher degree of awareness* to what you do and this higher degree of awareness does make all the difference in the world about your reality.

So I'd like to explore a bit more about **structure** with you. And by way of review, another way to look at **structure**, or actually **reality**, is talking about **how** and **what**. **How** equals the **structure** or **process**, **what** equals the **content** or **specifics**. So remember from Book Ten, we talked about **adverb/adjective presuppositions**, which really is more about the '**how**'. How? *Naturally, obviously, really.* The '**what?**' is **what follows**. **Naturally,** *you want to learn more about how this works so you can apply it powerfully and effectively.* So the **structure** is *shaped* by the **presupposition** and the **content** is thrown in there to give the person something to hang on to.

And I mentioned to you in Book Ten that you can think of **process** or **structure** as the **freeway**. It dictates the *general direction*, north or south, and the *general mode of travel*, such as a car, a motorcycle or a bus, and the **content** you can think of is *which lane* you choose to drive in or *what specific car*, in other words, instead of a *general concep*t of car or bus or what have you.

The *goal* of what we're doing is to learn to be **artfully vague**. That's the goal, and yet still **lead** and **guide a person's thoughts precisely to where you want them to go**. That's the biggest goal, right? And you'll learn to do this in such a way that **they think it's their own idea.** So we're going to make them *come to the conclusion on their own* and we do this through the artful use of **presuppositions** so that they simply go along with what we're saying.

The *power* of these strategies, even what you've learned in this review, can't be overstated. It really does bear reading over and over again so that you ingrain *this into your mind*. And remember we defined **presupposition**, which is **that which must be accepted as true in order to make sense of the sentence**. I also define it a bit more broadly by saying, **that which must exist prior to something taking place.**

In other words, you probably need to be reasonably *convinced* before you buy. That would just make sense, wouldn't it? But if we just think of the definition, **that which must be accepted as true in order to make sense of the sentence**, it *has* to be accepted because *you didn't say it.* In other words, it's **assumed** or **presupposed**.

So this is how we're getting people to think what it is we want them to think to come to their own conclusion, in other words, without us having to say it.

CHAPTER EIGHT

Awareness

So let's go on to the **awareness pattern**. This is one of the most powerful patterns you'll ever learn. This qualifies as one of my absolute all time favorites. I love this. And we're going to really get into this pattern and take it to a very profound level.

Let's talk about the *three words* that I tend to like a lot in this category: **aware, realize** and **experience**. By the way, I'm just *flying* through this material in this book so, like I said earlier, please just stop any time you need to review something or re-read it, there's just a lot here and I would highly recommend you read this over and over and repeatedly. Okay? It's *dense.* You could read it, I guess, in one sense and just go, okay, yeah, yeah, that's good, that's good, or you could really get into it and start to *understand* where the real power is and *apply* it in your own life. Okay?

All right, this is the **awareness** category and this is one of my personal favorites because simply *saying* one of these words **makes the person start the mental process that you mention**. In other words, to become **aware**, to **realize** or to **experience**. These words are very important in your persuasion arsenal because like the **adverb/adjective** words, *everything that follows them is presupposed to be true*. These words also force the issue of not, *will you do*, but instead, *are you aware of*, which is far more powerful in persuasion.

By the way, as you gain skill in being able to use these words powerfully, you might think that someone may respond to the question, "*Are you aware of?*" by saying, "No." I assure you when done properly this doesn't really ever happen but if it ever did, all you need to say is, "Not yet, huh?" It's pretty nice. In other words, if you said, "Are you **aware** of the growing feeling of excitement that you're beginning to have as a result of hearing how this material can apply to you so powerfully?", and the person goes, "No." Well, number one, you're *out of* **rapport**, right, because otherwise that wouldn't be happening. Number two, you probably came on too strong, too fast. Again, you're out of **rapport**, I guess is a good way to put that, but it's pretty slick to be able to say something like that because the minute that they say, "No", you respond, "Oh, not yet, huh?" And they'll probably again say, "No." And you say, "Okay. Good." That's an example of asking a question where you're **eliciting** a *no* but *no means yes*. Very, very powerful, very smooth.

Let's go through some examples. Is the **awareness** of the power of these patterns starting to sink in? The more you begin to construct in your mind the ways you'll be using these patterns lesson by lesson with me, the more you'll begin **realizing** the explosively profitable techniques you are learning. Are you starting to **experience** the growing **awareness** of what being involved in this course brings you as I tell you about it and as you go through it?

And of course, you can *combine* them to create super powered suggestions and you can do this anytime you want, it sounds something like this: Becoming **aware** of the potentials of this policy, allows you to start to **experience** the inner sense of **realizing** how completely this program fits your needs. Do you know what I mean?

And boy, am I telling you, now, if right now you're sitting there going, "Ummm. . . huh. I'm not sure what he just said", that's because we're talking about **process**. We're **directing people's minds via the process of the awareness pattern** and when we talk **process**, there's not a lot of **content**. What is the **content** in that sentence? Here, I'll analyze it for you, let's go on and we'll analyze each of these.

Is the **awareness** of the power of these patterns starting to sink in? Now let's go through this real carefully. **Awareness**. So I'm *not* asking you if these patterns have power. That would not be a **presupposition**. Do you think these patterns have power? That's not helpful. Okay? So based on that, what *am* I asking you? Well, I'm asking you '**are you aware**'. In other words, if you're *not* **aware**, it **presupposes** you *need to be* **aware**. And if you *are* **aware**, you'll state such that you *are* in fact **aware**. If you say, 'Yes, I'm aware,' then you *know* the power of the patterns and you *agree* they're starting to sink in and if you're *not* **aware**, then by hearing the question asked, **you begin to *become* aware**.

So **awareness** is like **dawning**. Dawning of the Age of Aquarius. There we go. I guess that's dating me quite a bit, isn't it?

So in other words, in that song, it's not *whether or not* the Age of Aquarius is valid, it's has it **dawned** or it is **now dawning**. If you said, "No it's not," the person could say, "Well, that's just only because you're not **aware** of that *yet*. We're trying to bring **advanced awareness** to people such that they're ready for the Age of Aquarius." Such mumbo jumbo, but wow, the power of it, huh?

CHAPTER NINE

Realization

Let's go to the next one. The more you begin to construct in your mind the ways you'll be using these patterns as you proceed lesson by lesson, the more you'll begin **realizing** the explosively profitable techniques you are learning. Now let's stop right there. So I used *another* pattern which you're going to learn in the books that follow that deals with *a specific way to get people to put something into their head* using another one of these **presupposition patterns** but we'll just kind of go past that and we'll talk about **realizing**. In other words, I *told* you to construct in your mind ways to use the patterns as we proceed and that as you do, you'll begin **realizing** the explosively profitable techniques you're learning. What am I really doing? Am I *asking* you, let me ask you a question, do you think these techniques are profitable? Let's switch the example. The more you begin to construct in your mind the ways you'll be using the advice I have to give you about your finances as you proceed, the more you'll begin **realizing** the explosively profitable advice and how you can profit from this as a result of working with me.

And by the way, that wasn't very grammatical, but that's okay, you still get the idea. And as a result of that, people will look at you kind of dumb and go, "Uh-huh or uh-uh". If they go "Uh-uh", you say, "*Not yet*, huh?" If they go, "Uh huh," you go, "That's right." And then we go on.

CHAPTER TEN

Experience

Are you starting to **experience** the growing **awareness**. . . So now I'm *doubling them up*. Are you starting to **experience**. . . Well, how can you *not* start to **experience** when I *bring to your attention* that you can start to **experience**? So in other words, **just *saying the words* causes it to *start to happen* in the mind of the person**. Amazing. Are you starting to **experience** the growing **awareness**. . . Okay, so now we're asking you to **experience** the reality, in essence. Whoo hoo. You're **experiencing** the growing reality. Really? I mean, my word, *just from my words alone*. But you're starting to understand, this is the power of persuasion. In the hands of those that know how to do it, look out.

The growing **awareness** of what being involved in this course brings you as I tell you about it. The only answer you're going to get to these kinds of things is, "Yup". What also it does, is it *seeds these things into the mind of the listener*. That's what's happening. Make sense?

All right, let's go to the third one. **Becoming aware** of the potentials of this policy. . . Now, so **becoming aware**. Am I asking you, does this policy have potential in your life? Is *that* what I'm asking you? No. I'm saying, **becoming aware**. I'm *not even asking* you if you're **becoming aware**, I'm simply stating that you are **becoming aware**. So now all of the sudden you have **awareness** of the potentials of the policy, allows you to start **experiencing** the inner sense. . . Well, where's the inner sense? As opposed to what other sense? In other words, I'm telling you to **experience** it on the *inside* and if it's on the *inside*, who *put* it there? Well, *you* must have. Of **realizing**. . . **Realizing**? That implies a degree of *truth*, doesn't it? How completely this program fits your needs. Oop. There's the **content**. Links back to policy. All right. **Becoming aware** of the potentials of the quick sale of your property allows you to **start experiencing** the inner sense of **realizing** how completely this offer fits your needs right now.

So you can aim this at *anything*. I can make up a thousand examples right on the spot. And now, **as you're beginning to understand** these techniques, so can you.

CHAPTER ELEVEN

Further Words For The Pattern

The three words that you've been given in the **awareness** category are, as you've probably figured out by now, representative of a *whole class* of **descriptive words** that will have this *same impact* when you use them. I gave you three that I use all the time. Here's a bigger list. You can add tons more to this too if you like, but at least here are a lot of additional words for you. **Realize. Think. Speculate. Accomplish. Weigh. Weigh the benefits. Aware. Feel. Perceive. Fulfill. Consider. Know. Wonder. Discover. Grasp. Assume. Understand. Puzzle. Experience. Reconsider. Conceive.** These are words that you can use to have this same **awareness** effect.

CHAPTER TWELVE

Combining the Awareness Pattern With the Adverb / Adjective Group

The *real power* of these words comes when you use them *in combination* with the **adverb/adjective** group. Aha, now it all starts to fit together, huh? Remember, **no pattern is an island**. In fact, by definition, **a pattern is something the unconscious mind recognizes**. It's like a special form of *communication* and the unconscious goes, oh, he or she is talking to me now. How great.

It's like a *clue* that it figures out and it starts **piecing together a deeper sense of reality** as a result of the *clues* you're leaving behind and when you do this right, what you're going to be doing is using all sorts of these things at high speed, I mean really high speed, you're going to be using the **language of awareness** and **adverb/adjective**, to create **patterns**. . . In other words, these are **patterns**, and you're going to be **embedding the content**, you're going to be kind of sticking the content in, in other words being **artfully vague**, and as you **combine the patterns** together, they're all going to be aiming in the same direction.

When that happens, you're leading a person down the freeway towards what you want them to do. It's almost *impossible* to go against this. It's almost impossible.

Let me give you an example of linking the **adverb/adjective** example with an **awareness** example.

Naturally, as you start to **realize** the **unlimited** ways you can **easily** become **aware** of how joining this team will help you to **truly** accomplish your goals more **rapidly** and **effectively**, you'll start **imagining** the success you can **actually** achieve with my help and guidance. **Now**, are you starting to **experience** the possibilities?

Let's pull it apart, shall we? **Naturally**. . .Well, let's just start right off with a **presupposition**. In other words, *everything that follows* in this sentence that I'm going to say, *everything*, has to be **accepted as true** to make sense of it. If you first conclude it's *true*, it's harder to get to change your mind that it's *not true*. Oh darn. So **naturally**, in other words, now everything that follows is going to be accepted as true, as you start to **realize** the **unlimited** ways. . . *Realize the unlimited ways*, so as you have **awareness** of the **adverb/adjective** word, **unlimited** ways, so you have **awareness** of *what*? Of a whole bunch of ways that you can, *what*? Not just become **aware**, but *easily* become **aware**. In other words, your brain is just going to do this **easily**. Of how joining this team. . . oh, there's some **content** that they can lock onto, will help you to **truly** accomplish. . . in other words, it doesn't just accomplish a goal, it *truly* accomplishes it. And it doesn't just accomplish a goal, it does it more **rapidly** and **effectively**. . .you'll start **imagining**. . . wow, is that a great **awareness** word? So you're telling them, in other words, **dream**. Dream of *what*? The success. That you can *what*? **Actually**. In other words, *everything that follows that word* is **presupposed** to. . . achieve, with my help and guidance. In other words, **it's all about you imagining what will happen as a result of working with me**. What a great thing to say to people!

I'm using the equivalent of an **embedded command** with the word '**now**' which you're going to learn about in the books to come. . . And by the way, I've got some *hot, hot* stuff for you on **embedded commands**. Are you starting to **experience** the possibilities? **Experience** can also be thought of as a **command** here, but in reality when I say '**experience**' you have to start *feeling* it, *experiencing* it, somehow, *seeing, hearing, feeling*, some way of **experiencing**, correct? Well, if you're **experiencing** my words as *reality*, are you *objecting* to them or *not following along* with them? No. Thank goodness. Starting to see the power?

Okay? This is just *two* of these patterns, by the way.

All right, I want *you* to **write an example** like I just gave you using the following words and I want you to use them in this order: **naturally**, **aware**, **unlimited** and **experiencing**. Let me give you an example of it myself, all right?

Naturally, as you become **aware** of the **unlimited** power of following the advice that I map out for you, you'll begin **experiencing** success after success in ways you never dreamed possible before.

There's one. Let me give you a real estate example. **Naturally**, you have goals and dreams. As you become **aware** of the situation that you're genuinely in, you begin to **realize** it's important to listen to somebody who can help you to make some changes, get out of this property and move on with your life, to move on with the **unlimited** potential of what you have available to you, that this house is robbing and stealing from you since it's simply sitting there doing nothing and sucking away every last dollar that you have. You could be **experiencing** a life of success after you clear up this problem. Now, let's move on and let me show you exactly how you can do that.

That would be like, for example, if you were an investor and you were trying to get someone to give you the equity in their home. Okay? I mean, I can put any number of examples to this as now you start to see this. I suggest you start the sentence off with '**naturally**'. Follow up with the rest of them at your convenience, but use as your gauge, does it *sound* like what I do when I say things like, "**Naturally**, as you start to **realize** the **unlimited** ways you can **easily** become **aware** of how joining this team will help you to **truly** accomplish your goals more **rapidly** and **effectively**, you'll start **imagining** the success you can **actually** achieve with my help and guidance. **Now**, are you starting to **experience** the possibilities?"

You should make a list of the **awareness** words and the **adverb/adjective** words such that you can begin to just kind of pick and choose as you come up with examples.

To that end, I'm going to give you some. As you **think** about the things that I've been presenting to you during this process of **learning** that we've been going through together, you can begin to **perceive** some of the **incredible** power that people who understand these skills have but you also **realize** that it's not enough to **simply** understand. **Naturally**, you have to **integrate** these into your life. And to do that, you can **simply** read them over and over again. And, you'll **immediately** begin to **discover** advantages in your language that you didn't have before. But **of course** if you'll stop and go through these patterns together with me **now** as you're reading them, if you'll write out the exercises as I tell them to you **repeatedly**, you'll begin to **discover** just how **easily** you can make these patterns your own and that feels really good. **Of course**, you might have to stop and ask yourself why on earth you didn't know about these things before. But I can **simply** tell you this, **everything happens for a reason**, doesn't it? And **now** here you are, **experiencing** the power of these patterns in your life, using them and beginning to **understand** them and put them to work in such a way that you can go to that next level and **look forward** to your **ongoing** journey with me.

You see how I'm doing it? Do you see. . . I'm just literally going back and forth between lists of **awareness** words and **adverb/adjective** words. It's literally about that simple when you start getting the hang of it.

Some people begin **repeatedly** reviewing the successes in their mind that they're **already anticipating** having as a result of becoming **aware** of all the things that they could have been having as a result of working with me but hadn't been until **now**.

So if you were talking to a *group* of people, could you say something like that? You bet. All right. It doesn't matter *where* you're trying to persuade people, these skills are just incredible and they'll pay dividends over and over again. **Repeatedly**. Another **adverb/adjective** thing thrown in there.

Accordingly, you'll find yourself beginning to grab onto and utilize these words, **understanding**

how they fit into the puzzle of your **experience**, **realizing** that what used to be a puzzle is **now** becoming crystal clear. Still, you'll **discover** that as you become **aware** of how these words **really** work, you'll **naturally** find yourself using them more and more and getting the kinds of results you've always **dreamed** of.

CHAPTER THIRTEEN

Adding Massive Amplification

Now I want you to remember to **add massive amplification** like we talked about in our last book. Two ways to do this, be **artfully vague**. So you'll note in the example that I've given you that I'm being **artfully vague** yet still **guiding the person's thoughts to where I want them to go**. This is extremely powerful and you should do the same.

You should also **presuppose** their **values** using these **language patterns**. So you're going to **presuppose** what you've already **elicited** in terms of their **values** and now you're going to *add awareness presuppositions* along with the **adverb/adjective presuppositions**. That's pretty impressive. And when you do, you'll be stunned at the results.

Here's the rule, you use these **linguistic patterns** to **presuppose the criteria**, or you could say **values**, of those you are persuading. Hot, hot stuff.

So let's do a few of these so you can get the idea. Here are some **criteria** from clients that I just made up off the top of my head and I'm just going to show you how to do some of this. Let's start with *financial safety*. Let's say that's a very high **value** for a person that you're talking to.

As you **realize** how important it is that you have the kind of financial safety that you've **always dreamed** of having, you can begin to **become aware** of some of the many reasons why working with me will bring this to you. **It's possible** to **easily** implement the kinds of things that I'm going to be suggesting to you and as you do, you can **see** your life **automatically** begin to change. Look at the pictures now inside your own mind and **wonder** why it is that nobody brought you these kinds of things before. The fact is, **I don't believe there's any such thing as an accident** or a mistake because **here we are together today** helping you to gain the **awareness** that you need to make the changes that are so important to you. So let's talk about **now** some of the specific things that we can do to make your life have the kind of financial security that you've always **dreamed** of.

Do you see what I've just done? Pretty cool. Bigger home. Let's go there. So the person says to you, "Ultimately, if I just had a bigger home, I'd just really be happy. We need the space, you know?"

And you say, "**Naturally**. A bigger home will bring you so much and I think it will bring you so much more than you're even **aware** of now. You **assume** you understand but I think there's a **deeper** part of you that may be right now beginning to **search** quickly through your memory banks **finding**, **locking on**, to things that you haven't thought of in so long, maybe you haven't **even** allowed yourself to **dream** at that level in a very long time. Yet, as you do, you begin to **realize** just how powerful a bigger home is, what it **really** means. It's also nice to **realize** that you're dealing with someone who understands what this **really** means because that helps me in finding exactly what it is that you're **looking** for. This is something that I think we'll enjoy doing together as we go through our **experience** in this process of getting it for you."

And let's say that a person says: "Status". That that's what they want. Maybe they're buying a new car and they are telling you that they want to have a lot more status in life.

A person begins to **consider** that they've reached a **particular** level in life and some people begin to **wonder** how they could demonstrate that a little more **effectively**, **not necessarily** for the benefit of others, but **naturally**, that they themselves are a **living** example of what it is that they believe and I've found that **a lot of times** people, when they do that, they buy **this kind** of a car. I've just seen this over and over in the people that I've worked with. They buy the car because they **naturally** become **aware** of what it means in their life, the symbology that it contains. And they begin to **perceive** a **real** joy, a power, in being able to **self-actualize** their dreams and their goals. Yes, I think it's great that other people see us as successful and that we've achieved a **certain** status but I think **probably deep down** inside we all **know** that other people see that **already** and we are enjoying that we can finally **experience** something like this in our lives for ourselves as well.

So there's *another* way that we can use this kind of thing any time we want which is really, really nice.

So many examples we could go through, so many we have, and you can re-read this and just see them left and right.

BOOK TWELVE

TEMPORAL PATTERNS

CHAPTER ONE

Increasing Your Stable of Adverbs and Adjectives

Welcome to **Book Twelve** of *Persuasion Force*. We're going to cover part three of **structuring reality** in which we're going to be going much, much deeper into this process.

But first, let's go through a few questions. Here's a question. The person writes, "*Hi, Kenrick. Thanks again for this infinitely powerful program. I'm truly grateful. By the way, thanks so much for writing. I always love to hear from you and know that you appreciate the material.*" That's really nice. Thank you. "*On the **adverb/adjective pattern**, I'm wondering if there is a general rule of thumb for knowing which other ones are also falling under this category of **adverbs and adjectives**. If so, can you please share with me in more detail how to <u>naturally</u> discover just how <u>easily</u> we can know which other ones we can <u>also</u> begin to use <u>immediately</u> so we can have an even more <u>unlimited</u> amount of choice of words to use that also fall within this category. Thanks, Kenrick.*"

Wonderful. You're doing pretty good. I'm impressed. You know, there are a couple of rules I covered with you. First let me just tell you that any '*ly*' word, any word ending in '*ly*', general<u>ly</u>, as in *there's* one other one, falls into that category.

Quite often you can look at **adverbs** and **adjectives** and use most *any* of them for that kind of thing. However, being more specific than that, I don't know how useful that will be because really I gave you *so many* choices to choose from that *any* of those will work, and then of course, any '*ly*' word will work. And most *any* **adverb** or **adjective**. The **key** to it is to *follow the strategy* that I've been laying out for you. So take the examples I give you in each lesson and if you have a word that you'd like to work in, **test it against the examples** that I've given to see if it works.

CHAPTER TWO

Determining High Level Criteria and Direction

Okay. Next question. "*Let's say I have the following conversation. I'm a realtor. Me: 'Why are you selling now?' Seller: 'My ex and I just had a nasty divorce and I got the house, but there are so many bitter memories that this house reminds me of."* The person asking the question writes, *"I assume he just gave me a really high level* **emotional criteria** *with this answer, right? I can't imagine asking 'Well,* **what's important** *about getting rid of the bitter memories?'"* Okay, you're right on the money there. But let me tell you something. What you got is **high level emotional criteria.** You're right on the money with that. However, that may not really be the *sole* **criteria** I'd want to go after.

I think in a situation like this I would personally be inclined to say something like, "Wow. I'm really sorry to hear that. I know these kinds of things happen. Let me just ask you, *other than the difficulty of the divorce, etc.,* is there *any other reason* why you want to sell the house?" Now, at that point, if they say, "No, I don't want to live there anymore, I just want out and that's it. That's what I'm trying to do." Okay, then you know you're right down to the fact that maybe it's a big house, there used to be two or more of them living there, they got a divorce, the guy got the house, now he has to get rid of it because he doesn't want to live there on his own, he wants to move somewhere else. It may not be the *highest* answer. It is a **high level emotional criteria** and you're right, you should *not* ask what's important about getting rid of the bitter memories. The person writing the question continues by responding to the statement of the bitter memories by saying, *"Wow, that's horrible. I can really see you decided to make this choice. So as we begin the process of selling this house, and along with it, all these unwanted memories, what will that ultimately do for you?"* And then he writes the word *'directional'* as in he's attempting to look for the direction of **towards** or **away.** *"Seller: 'I'm hoping this will give me a chance for a new start, some healing, maybe even I will move out of state and get a new job as well.'"*

Okay, so he wants **a new start.** In other words, in a sense, he wants a new start because he *doesn't like* the start he has *now.* He's trying to get **away from** a bad start. Does that make sense? So it's definitely **away from.**

Let me go through a couple of things that I'm hearing though as I read this part of your question. First of all, you say, *"Wow, that's horrible."* And that's good. You're **pacing** what's going on with that person. I like that. Then you say, *"I can really see you have decided to make this choice."* Okay. I've got an issue a little bit with those words. First of all, I'm not sure if this is *mind reading* on your part. The person says they want to sell the house because they went through a really bitter divorce and it brought up bitter memories. I don't have an issue with it. . . rather than call it mind reading, let me call it this way. You're **implanting a suggestion** there. But I don't like the way it's done. *"I can really see you have"* **past tense** *"decided to make this choice".* Make this choice could either be **present tense** or **future tense.** It really is a bit towards the **future.** It's not exactly right in the now.

In other words, *"I can now really see you have decided (in the* **past***) to make this choice".* So you're saying he's *decided* to make the choice in the **past** but it isn't *known* as to whether or not that decision's been *made.* If you wanted to make that suggestion I might recommend you say, *"I can see that you* **made the choice***"* blah, blah, blah. In other words, you're saying, that choice was **already made.**

And by the way, the lesson today is going to deal with issues of **time** and how we can **structure** this to our advantage so it's a really timely question if I do say so myself.

All right, so in other words, I'd like to see that *tightened up* quite considerably. So you say, *"As we begin the process of selling this house,"* that's good **suggestion,** I like that. *"And along with it all* *these unwanted memories"*, okay, that's a **sentence fragment**. I like **sentence fragments** like that. However, in this case, I chuckled just a bit because you're *linking* it to beginning the process of selling the house. So you're saying that you're going to sell the house *and* sell the memories. It could be interpreted that way. And that's not such a bad suggestion. I might have been a bit more *direct. "So as we begin the process of selling this house, as well as you begin the process of unloading all of those memories as a result, **what would that ultimately do for you?**"* And you asked that part of it perfectly.

Okay? So then he explains his **towards** or **away**. In this case, he's aiming *out* of this situation, **away** from it, but he *wants* to kind of move **towards** maybe a new job. Okay. That's where I would have gone right there. So I would have said, *"Oh, move out of the state and get a new job. Very interesting. Why out of the state?"* If he comes back to bad memories, because he doesn't want to stay here. Okay. Wonderful. *"But tell me about it, a new job. What makes you want a new job?"* Now you're going to hear a *lot* of information there that you're going to be able to **leverage**.

Okay, the questioner goes on to write, *"I don't know. It looks like I have a lot of info to seed and attach to my product, however, at this point if I wanted to **change the criteria**, how might I do it with this example? Or will that even help me in this example?"* Yes, it will absolutely help you. And here's how you would do it.

So assuming that I didn't want to continue asking about why out of the state and why a new job, I might say something like this, *"Well these sound like really appropriate things to do. In fact, I have to hand it to you. For someone who's gone through such a difficult and traumatic thing as a divorce and then discovered that they must sell the property to the point now of finding me to come in and handle it for you so you can move on with your life, I've got to tell you, I'm impressed. But it seems like that isn't really enough. It seems like all of those are very, very important. But right up there, along these lines, would also be the importance of making certain that we do this in a way that gets you as much money as possible for it. And maybe that's why you chose me, I don't really know. But a lot of people that I've worked with in this area that have gone through similar kinds of problems, have looked into my track history a little bit because of it, and were excited to work with me because, hey, the worst thing in the world is to take an asset that you have and because you have a mental disruption, an emotional disruption in your life, to then also throw away the financial asset that you have. So in other words, with me on board, we're not going to throw the baby out with the bathwater and I think that's kind of an important thing too, don't you think?"*

Now when he says, *"Yes, it is,"* he's **agreeing** to *all of the above*, including **you being the guy to take care of this for him**. Okay? So you can see that there is lots of room to **add things** that will help you in this example. Lots of things. That's just one. There are many, many more you could do. Anything you want him to think at this point. For example, if you wanted him to realize the property prices were *depressed* in that area and that what he really needs to do is to fix it up, or whatever you want him to do, you could start **framing** those kinds of things into your conversation at that point. So it would help and you're right on track with it.

CHAPTER THREE

Ulterior Motives?

The questioner continues this train of thought by saying, *"The main example of **changing criteria** was for a trainer/trainee relationship which of course was there for a sneaky reason, I suspect."* Well, not really. I mean, I suppose in a sense you could say my unconscious mind has an **ulterior motive** for everything. And to a certain extent I suppose that's true, but in reality it's because it was simple for me to come up with. It was easy for me to talk about and that's why I did it. As a general rule I suppose I could say, that isn't really a part of what I do.

This kind of gets me to an interesting point. It's kind of interesting in life how when people know that you're an expert in *persuasion*, or *influence*, or *selling*, even, you know, that **they assume you're doing it to *them* all the time**. That's been something that I've struggled with my whole life is people saying, *"Well, you know, I don't know if I can really trust him, because after all, he's one of the top persuasion experts."* And it always kind of made me mad until finally I just kind of got used to it and went, well, okay, whatever. They're going to think whatever they think.

Still, I've worked to remain un-jaded such that I really *am* just genuinely myself. To me that's part of operating with a lot of **integrity** and *not* always having an **ulterior motive**.

Now, an **ulterior motive** that is *supportive*, I have no problem with and an **ulterior motive** in a sense means something *sneaky* or *behind the scenes*. And for each of us using **persuasion** skills. . . For example, if I were to use skills to help people to stay involved with me, provided that I'm really giving them *value*, I find no problem with that whatsoever. However, I also find that people just *find* that value regardless of me attempting to *install* it or not. And you'll find the same is true for you.

But it is kind of a humorous topic so I thought I would show you a little bit about the inside workings of my mind and how I've dealt with some of those kind of things and how it affects me. I know there was no slight intended, nor did I take any, I just wanted to share with you a little bit about kind of what goes through my mind when I hear that kind of thing.

And by the same token, I too would find myself early in my career, asking those that I was studying with, the same kinds of things because I wanted to see *where does their mind really go?* At *what level* have they thought this through? So just so you know where my mind goes, I *have* thought this through. I've thought it through at *every* kind of level.

It doesn't mean, though, that because I think it through, I'm actively attempting to do it, though I know full well that my **intention** is to not only provide *information* but *entertainment*. Not only *information* and *entertainment*, but *longevity* for my clients and me to be together and working together. And so, that's going to come out. These are my **intentions**. And my **intention** is to *help* and *help* and *help some more* and as long as that's recognized then I feel really satisfied and I think this is something you might want to examine in your own life for each of you reading because it will be something that comes up from time to time in your life and it's nice to have thought it through so that you know where you stand on it.

CHAPTER FOUR

Affecting Whose Reality?

Let's move forward to the part on **presuppositions** now that I'd like to talk with you about. We're going into part three now of **structuring reality**. Structuring *whose* reality? Well, the first thing I want to tell you is, please, stop reading this and go back through Book Eleven and read that again. All right? Starting with the 'structuring reality part II'. I really want you to have that as the basis of how you move forward.

First and foremost, ***whose* reality are we structuring?** Well, you could say, "That depends on your point of view" and I would agree with you, and if you said that in your head then you're absolutely learning how **persuasion** works because the *reason* you got into this program was to **structure the reality of someone else's head**, but I think you're beginning to understand that it's *even more important* to structure *your own* because as you become facile with these skills, as you become easily able to **language** what it is you want, you're going to find it's even easier still to get people to do what you want them to do.

Change comes first from the inside. All right? If we take the old adage, "As above, so below", as within so without, however you want to look at it. In other words, what we see on the *outside* is *a reflection of who we are* and if you're so competent at the **structuring of reality** the way I'm teaching you then this is going to be **sliding right by people's minds and consciousness** left and right and you're going to be **accomplishing near miracles**.

Something, by the way, I recall Tony Robbins saying when he first got started, and I've always loved it. I just thought this was brilliant, he says, "*If a miracle happens within fifty miles, take credit.*"

Well, I'll *expand* that for you. **If a miracle happens within 200 miles or within ear shot of anyone who knows you, or anyone you've ever talked with, take credit.**

Or look knowingly and say, "Aha. Yeah."

So **structuring reality, creating near miracles, take credit**. All right?

It's really important you *understand* how we're **affecting the reality of those we persuade** with this type of persuasion and to that end, you have to know **how it affects you** first. I won't go through it again here. I'm going to trust that you're stopping now and going back through Book Eleven.

CHAPTER FIVE

The Temporal Pattern

And in this book, we're going to be going deeply into **patterns that utilize time**. I want you to hang on, it's quite a ride. And I'm going to give you *bite size* at a time here because I want you to gain a degree of *mastery*. Please, gain a degree of mastery with this. That means you have to not just *read* about doing it, you've got to **do it**. You can't just *read* this, you've got to *write* it. And I mean, it really *depends* on you writing this out. No kidding. *You've got to write it out.*

So please, start writing as I give you the exercises as we continue and let's move on to discuss '**The Temporal Pattern**'. This category of words deals with **manipulating time and/or numbers to your advantage** both in *your* mind and in the minds of *the people you're persuading*. The three words that I look at in this category that remind me always of this category of words, are the words '**before**', '**during**' and '**after**', also, '**first**', '**second**', and '**third**'.

Before, during and **after, first, second** and **third**. This is truly **the temporal category** as you can hear.

Time and *numbers*, by the way, are so linked that I can't really separate them. **Before** number two comes number one. The words '**before**', '**during**', and '**after**', **presuppose a numerical sequence** so they're just *inextricably linked* and so you won't see me separate them here. I put them together because it's easier to learn that way. Sometimes it's easier to learn more by adding more things in at the same time. This is a good example of it.

In all communication, time is presupposed. Now let's take that sentence: in all communication, time is presupposed. Okay? How about in *that* communication? Is time presupposed *there*? In *all* communication . . .**ALL**. . .does that mean **past**? Sure. Does it mean **present**? Sure. Could it mean **future**? Sure. So in *all of time*, in all the ways in which and all the time in which communication can take place, **time is presupposed**.

It makes sense when you start thinking of it that way. In other words, communication is talking about some *thing*, some *actor* and some *action*. That's the basic construct of a sentence—a *noun* and a *verb*. Some actor is acted upon or some someone is acting upon the actor or however you want to say it, but some *verb* is doing something to some *noun*.

And as a result of that very simple **truism, the language presupposes that it happens *some time***. It happened in the **past**, it happens in the **present**, it will happen in the **future**. And so this is what we're going to learn to maneuver in what we're going through now and this will open a world of possibilities for you.

This pattern teaches you to *turn it to your advantage* and gives you further advantages in **installing information really easily**. Here are some examples. "***After*** *you work with me, you'll understand.*" So what's up with that sentence? Well, that *you're going to work with me*. It **presupposes** you're going to work with me. And the mere act of working with me will cause understanding. Interesting. You're suggesting they make meaning out of something that may or may not contain meaning.

Let's go to the next one. "**Before** *you decide just how easy this decision is to make, let me tell you a few things that might help, okay?*" I love this stuff. Oh, my goodness, this is great. All right. So what are we doing here? "**Before** *you decide*". . .what does that **presuppose**? That *you're going to decide*. But I can name it in so many words now, can't I? "**Before** *you decide*. . ." Decide *what*? Well, just *how easy this decision is to make*. All right?

In other words, **you're telling them** this decision is going to be easy and you're going to decide to make this easy decision. But **before** that happens, let me tell you a few things that might help. Now, if you hear "*a few things that might help*", I'm **telling** you, **after** hearing "*a few things that might help*", you are going to make an easy decision.

Do you see how **I'm installing the suggestion that activates itself based on a number of criteria being met**? In other words, I or you *meet* that **criteria** and the **suggestion** *must* fire in your head.

Don't you love it? I think these are the most grandest kind of suggestions in the world. I love these things. I can't remember it happening to me, but I mean, it's *possible* somebody says to you, "*Oh, you're using a **temporal based presupposition**. I don't choose to make a decision or to choose if it's easy or not and I don't really want to hear you tell me anything.*" I've *never*, ever had anyone do that to me. Ever. The only place I've even seen this done is on forums where little wannabes are fighting over who knows the most amount of material. Let 'em fight. I left that silly arena many, many years ago because if you have all day to sit and look at a pattern, you can tear it apart. Try to do it *real time*. Okay?

So here we have a wonderful, wonderful **installation** process. "**Before** *you decide just how easy this decision is to make, let me tell you a few things that might help, okay?*" You say, "okay" to that, you've *given me permission* to tell you a few things. That's another added benefit. So **now** I'm telling you a few things. **After** I've told you a few things, **now** you will *automatically* have that **suggestion** kick into your head, especially if I'm using more than one of them. Especially if I'm using more than one of the **presupposition** patterns.

Let's go to the next sentence. "**During** *our time together* **today**, *could you be* **applying** *the benefits* **you will be discovering** *about this product or service to your life? I think you probably could.*" Let me use it at the material I'm teaching you. So I'm **suggesting** that *meaning is made out of time*. You're going to **make some meaning**. *What* meaning? Well, the value or benefit of applying. . .*What* benefits? The ones that I'm asking you to assume are present.

Do you see how deep this goes? So I'm *asking* you for **a period of time** that we're together, you're listening and I'm talking, that **during** that time you're going to *apply* benefits, that you're going to be responsible to *create*, to *make up*, to *imagine*, to *remember*, and *discover*, actually, about these skills of persuasion and you're not only going to do that just at some particular place like for your business, but about your whole life.

I'm *asking* it in a question. Could you? If you say, "*No*", I'll say, "*All right.* **Not yet**, *huh? Well, hang in there a little bit because* **while**. . ." another **temporal word**, "*I talk with you, new ideas will* **begin** *flooding to the surface, ideas that have great meaning for you and I don't know which of those will cause you to understand how you can apply even more benefits just like that to your life, but I know it'll happen.*"

Oh, my goodness, this stuff turns me on. All right. So imagine using that out of your mouth in your business. It is *profound*. Now *add* to that the use of **rhythmic speaking** and you can speak with a rhythm, as you use these skills and really **embed** what it is you want the other person to understand very powerfully.

So, remember when we started I told you to get a **metronome** and to begin to *practice with your metronome*. Do you have it? So *start adding all this together*. You're at the point **now** in your learning where you're going to start doing some real **combining** and you're going to go to much, much higher levels.

CHAPTER SIX

Before, During and After

One way of using this **pattern** is to **write down what you want the person to think or do and preface that with one of the words in this category**. So you can use my examples from the previous pages and I want you to *write three of your own examples* of how this is going to work for you. All right?

Now, moreover, let me just give you a couple of examples of the kind of thing I wrote here and **then** made your note. And that is, let's say that. . . what's something I want someone to do? List their house with me. So I say, "**Before** you **list your house with me today**, *I want to go over a couple of the things that I think will make selling it even easier. Fair enough?*" And they go, "*Yeah, okay.*" Well, so what did I do? I followed the **suggestion** I told you. I said, "*One way of using this pattern is to* **write down what you want the person to think or do** *and* **preface that with one of the words in this category**."

Okay. So now we're saying, "**Before** you **list your house with me**," so "*list your house with me today*", that's what I want you to do, and I just say, '**before**' and then I say something else that makes sense. "**Before** *you* **list your house with me today**, *I want to go over a couple of things that will help making selling it even easier. Okay?*" They say, "*Okay.*" Well now they've *agreed*, okay, you're going to go over something to make it easier, they've *also agreed* to list their house with you today. So don't be surprised when they just say, "*Sure, where do we sign?*"

The nice thing about this is, you're **installing** it so profoundly and so *outside of consciousness and out of their awareness*. As an advisor, you want someone to *let you do their planning for them*. "*So* **before** *you* **bring me on as your planner**, *let's go over some of the real specific goals you have so I make sure we work out the right kind of plan for you, sound good?*"

See?

"**During the time that we're working together**, *and* **after** *I've done my initial consultation with you, you'll be able to pick up the phone and call me any time you want to review the plan and of course, I'll be calling you no less than two times a year as well, to give you an update and to make sure that we're all on the same page and that we're getting the kind of results you're looking for.*

Does that sound like the kind of advisor you want to work with?"

All right? See? So now, right now, stop reading and *write three examples*. You can use any of the ones I've just told you or you can use any of the previous examples and so go ahead and follow my example by *writing similar kinds of sentences to what I've just done*. Write at least three right now so you can get in the groove of doing this and come back as soon as you're done, all right?

CHAPTER SEVEN

An Analysis: How the Pattern Works

I assume you've done that and you've got your sentences. Let's analyze each of the sentences so that you can see a little bit more about *how they work*. All right? "**After** *you work with me. . .*" **presupposes** *what*? That **you're going to work with me**. "*You'll understand*", understand *what*? Well, at a minimum, probably *why* you're working with me.

Is the word '*understand*' an **awareness presupposition**? Oh, yes it is. So we have a **temporal presupposition**, we have an **awareness presupposition**. Okay? We have a **suggestion** in there "*to work with me*". Are you starting to see some more of the power of this?

"**Before** *you decide just how easy this decision is to make. . .*" So, "**before** *you decide*" that *you're going to decide*, that it can be easy or not, and is *decide* an **awareness presupposition**? Yes. In a way. It is a decision which is *akin* to **awareness**. It's right in there. All right?

"*Let me tell you a few things that might help*" . . .all right, so in other words, this is also like an **X causes Y pattern**. In other words, **before X, Y**. That's really the format I'm using there. "**Before X**", **before** you decide, decide *what*? You *tell* them *what* you want to decide. **Y**. That would be what you want to happen or what you are going to do prior to it happening. "*Let me tell you a few things that might help.*" In other words, once you've *told* them a few things that might help, they'll turn around and want to go ahead.

"*During our time together today. . .*" what does that **presuppose**? That we're going to spend time together. "*Could you. . .*" When? Today. "*Be applying the benefits*", what benefits? Well, *whatever you think* they should be. . . In other words, your **values**, your **criteria**. "*Could you be applying the benefits you will be discovering. . .*" Is '*discover*' an **awareness presupposition**? Yes. Awareness of *what*? Discovering *what*? Benefits. Benefits of *what*? Well whatever you're there to talk about.

Do you see **how removed** it is? How **indirect** it is? *About what?* And then you could even *tell* them, about your product or service, name it or whatever, and then applying where? Well not just in that one area you're suggesting, but you're going to apply it to their whole life. Wow. Man, that rocks. That just rocks. That's my idea of an absolutely good time. This is the way to persuade and you're really going to persuade people something fierce when you do this. All right? You're stacking in so much stuff that you might be saying at this point, how do I do that?

Follow my examples. Do exactly what I'm doing and write them out accordingly and you'll get it.

CHAPTER EIGHT

More Temporal Words

The three words you've been given in the **temporal category** are, as you've probably figured out by now, just like the other categories we've done, *representative* of a *whole class of descriptive words* that will have this same impact when you use them. I gave you six, actually, of the most important three. The most important three are **before**, **during** and **after**, but actually I like **first**, **second** and **third**, and **one**, **two** and **three**.

And here's a more complete list so you can choose from them: **before**, **during**, **early**, **second**, **chief**, **former**, **after**, **along with**, **latest**, **later**, **highest**, **another**, **was**, **were**, **when**, **until**, **while**, **continue**, **other**, **earliest**, **currently**, **foremost**, **first**, **second**, **third**, **eventually**, **in addition to**, **more**.

These words *all* **presuppose time and numbers**. There are many, many more like that, but this is all you'll ever need. And of course if you have a good vocabulary you probably know lots more and you can feel free to make a list.

CHAPTER NINE

Temporal Pattern Loops

I now have an incredible pattern to share with you called '**Temporal Pattern Loops**'. We're going to talk about **loops**. And this is another incredible way to do this. What are we talking about? Well, we're going to **create *loops* in the mind of the listener**. This is a favorite pattern of mine. In fact, if you go back through the *Persuasion Factor* titles, you'll see I've been *doing* it to you from time to time. In fact, you might want to go back and re-read and challenge yourself to discover where. It'd be a big process, but boy would you learn a lot in the doing of it.

There are *three really powerful things you need to know* in order to do this.

1. Number one, **people need to have closure**. All right? They *can't stand* to have balls up in the air. They need to have the balls *land*. They need closure, they need a yes or no. What's one of the biggest things you *hate* if you sell anything? "*Well, I'll think it over.*" And in essence, that's a "*No*" but "*I'll think it over*" doesn't *end* it. You want to either end it or don't end it. Either say *yes*, or say *no*, but *don't* tell me you want to think about it. So **people need to have closure**.
2. Number two, when they don't *get* it, **their response potential is increased**.

Okay, now let's move on to the next thing about **loops**. You can use **loops** to **increase response potential**. What? What are you saying there? Am I hearing you say "*What's the third thing?*" I told you that there's *three powerful things* you need to know in order to do this and I gave you *two* of them, didn't I? **People need closure**. And **when they don't get it, their response potential is**

increased. And then I went on.

What's the third thing? Well, you're just **waiting** for number three, but you know what? Let me ask you **how much do you want to know** what number three is? Do you *really* want to know?

All right, I'm *playing* with you, because *there is no number three.* I just said *"There are three powerful things you need to know"* and I gave you *two.* Why? Because there were only two that I wanted to tell you about. I could have made up four out of five or five out of six, or one out of two, or whatever, but the fact is, I used three, I like three, and I gave you two of the three. *I purposefully left the third one blank.* I don't *have* a third one. There *is no* third one.

Why would you do that? Because **it increases response potential**. *Don't close all the loops.* In fact, you want to leave *most* of them *open*. You want to use **loops** all the time. Let's look at it this way.

If you think about something you really know well, for example, maybe how to wash dishes, and somebody comes along and says to you, *"You know, there's a novel new way of washing dishes that will really help you."* Well, you kind of probably already think you know most of what you need to know about washing dishes. You may not be a bit interested in their *"How to wash dishes faster"* program. Because **your loops are closed** on that. You *already know* how to wash dishes quickly and if it saved you five seconds a day, or whatever, big deal. Even if it saved you two minutes a day, probably you think, big deal. It's not worth the three hours I'll have to spend to learn to save three minutes.

So you can use **loops** when you want to **increase response potential** because if you *leave* a **loop**, it makes people want to like sit forward and try to figure out what it was that you just didn't tell them. In other words, they're *missing* something. Like when I said, *"There are three powerful things you need to know to do these loop patterns"* and I told you *two* of the three. For many of you, you're like, *"Well, what's the third one?"*

Now if you weren't reading with full attention, it may not have had that affect on your conscious mind, but it *will* have had it on your other than conscious mind. So what happens is, when you **open loops** and **don't close them**, people become of the belief that *they don't know all there is to know* about the subject. And if people *know* all there is to know about the subject, they go away and don't come back.

Why deal with a financial advisor if *you* know as much as *they* do? Why use a real estate agent if *you* can sell the house as good as *they* can? But asking questions like, *"Are you aware of the thirteen biggest reasons that cause people's homes not to sell?"* No. *"Well, I tell ten of them to people before they become a client of mine even. I save the three for those people who I'm going to actually work with because it's those three that can really help make a difference that nobody else knows. Let me go through what those ten are."*

Now what did you do when you read that? If you were in the *least bit* wanting to sell your house, you were like, *"Well, what are the thirteen? What are those special three? I want to know those three."* See?

So **loops increase the response potential**. If you *close* the **loops**, if you *say* there are thirteen things and you *tell* them all thirteen things, then *they know* the thirteen things and *they don't need* *you anymore.* If you close people's **loops** like mad, they'll think they know it all. If you leave the **loops** *open,* they'll think they need to keep learning, they need to keep understanding, keep working with you in order to learn.

I use this in my teaching all the time because, let me ask you a question. . . Let me tell you a story. A teaching story. I think it's a Sufi teaching story.

There's a student walking along the road with his master and the master says to the student, "Are you thirsty?" And the student says, "Well, yes, master, I am." The master says, "Please produce your cup." So the student pulls his cup out of his pack and the master filled a pitcher of water and began to pour it into the student's cup. And the cup filled with water more and more until it reached the top and the master kept pouring. And the water is pouring out all over the cup and over the arm of the student and the student looks at the master and says, "Master, it's full. And no more will go in." And the master says, "Yes, that's true. In order to fill more, you have to get rid of some that's there."

So if the student would have had a drink of some of it, there would have been more room for the master to put more water in it.

Well, it's easier for me to teach a mind that *wants* to know. It's easier for you to learn something you *want* to understand. **Increasing your response potential** to that end, makes it much, much easier. So if you're teaching anyone anything, in what you do in your life, **leave loops open**, all kinds of places, because it's going to help them learn the material faster because *it keeps their* **response potential** *high.*

In fact, there's even another way to use a different kind of **loop structure** within **stories** in which we work with **looped emotional states** to create even more powerful acceptance of our message. And we'll get into that in later books. And by the way, is *that* a **loop**? Well, yes it is.

Remember that a job of a teacher is not only to *educate,* but it's to *entertain.* So if you make people believe they know it all and you still have to try to teach them, it's like pouring water into a filled glass. All you're going to do is get everybody messy.

CHAPTER TEN

Examples of Loops Using Temporal Patterns

And here are some *examples* of the **loops** using **temporal patterns**.

"Before I give you the most important strategy today, let's review what we know so far." Then *don't* talk about the most important strategy.

So you say to me, *"Yeah, but Kenrick, what if they say to me, 'Well, wait a minute, you said before we talk about the most important strategy,' we're nearing the end of our time, I want to make sure you can give it to me."*

"Oh, you're absolutely right. I'm sorry. I forgot all about it. I'll try to get to that maybe at our next meeting and remind me if I forget. All right?"

What are you doing there? **You're making them keep their loops open**. You're keeping them hooked and engaged. Good things.

"There are three things I want you to know about how to work with me." Then tell them number one and number two only. In other words, you're leaving the third thing out. And this can drive people insane. You can often hear, *"And what's that third thing?"* *"Oh, I told you."* And just go right on. They'll go, *"No, no, you didn't. No."* You say, *"I'm sure I did. Well, all right. I'll think about it and tell you after a bit here if I remember it. All right?"* And then just conveniently forget. Don't remember.

Now some of you, this bothers worse than others. For some of you, this drives you insane. You hear this and you're like, *"What in the hell is the third thing? I want to know."* All right, and that's because you exist in a particular way in your model of the world that **necessitates closure**. You *must* have closure. So I want you to know that when you find people like that in your life, *they're* going to be the ones asking you to please tell them what it is that they want to know. That's okay. You can live with that. You know?

And what you're going to do, though, is just find ways *not* to close all the **loops**.

Here's another one: *"After you hear me describe this spatial pattern, you'll find yourself blown away with all you're learning in this program."*

Then, you can present what you said you'd do to **close the loop** and thus make your **suggestion** come true. So *"After you hear me describe this spatial pattern"*. In other words, at that point, I would describe this spatial pattern. And *then* what? And then the **suggestion** says, *"You'll find yourself blown away with all you're learning in this program."*

So you see how this **installs a suggestion** very covertly? Remember, remember, remember, people *might* believe what you *tell* them, but they'll *always* believe what they *conclude on their own.*

So you're **installing a suggestion** that they have to *hear* and *experience* on their own. They'll not even recall that you said it. That's the power of these things.

All right. I'm going to ask you to stop reading again right here, right now, and *write three of your own*. Three patterns just like I just did. I just gave you three. All right? And I want you to write three of them on your own. So go ahead.

I assume that you have done that, and you're back, ready to continue forward, so you've got some good examples now of how you can use this **temporal pattern** in your life. The real power is in *combining* these patterns of **presupposition** and **suggestion**.

CHAPTER ELEVEN

Combining the Patterns

Now you have *three levels* of **presuppositions** to use to **install** things into the mind of those that you're persuading and this is where you start having real power with the **language of influence**.

I want you to use the words you've learned to come up with *high powered sentences* such as one like this: "**During** our discussion today, **naturally** you'll **begin** to **experience** the excitement about what the **future** holds for you as you **begin** to **understand** how **easily** leveragable this information is for you."

Whoo hoo! I mean, listen to that. That is like a **mind wipe**. It's like you probably *don't recall* much of what I just said even because it's very **artfully vague**. "*During our discussion today, naturally you'll begin to experience the excitement about what the future holds for you as you begin to understand how easily leveragable this information is for you.*"

Wow. Let's analyze. "**During** our discussion today. . ." in other words, we're going to be discussing. "**Naturally**. . ." meaning everything that happens after that word is **presupposed** as well. "*You'll begin to* **experience**. . ." and **experience** is what kind of word? **Naturally** is an **adverb/adjective** word; **experience** is a what? **Awareness** word. **Experience** *what*? "*The excitement. About what the* **future** *holds for you.*" But not just in *any* old future, it's "*what the future holds for you as you* **begin** *to* **understand**. . ." another word. **Begin** is a **temporal** word. **Understand** is an **awareness** word. "*How* **easily**. . ." which is an **adverb/adjective** word. "*Leveragable this information is for you*. . ." bringing it right back to them personally. Not someone else, not someone else you've known in life, but to that person.

Wow.

To move yourself towards mastery, *write 100 sentences* using different combinations of **presuppositions**. And look, you may say to yourself, that's *overwhelming*, Kenrick. There's *no way* I'm going to write 100 sentences. All right. Then don't. I'm just telling you, if you want to really move yourself towards *mastery* of this material that we've been talking about over the last couple of books, it's **important** you *write sentences*. A hundred of them will really get you started in the right direction.

So if you would, please, *write the sentences*. All right?

The **second** thing that I'm going to cover today, as a result of **beginning** to **realize** the profound impact that this training is having on your life is that **naturally**, one of the **early** things that you want to start **focusing** on is how you can combine these skills for maximum advantage. It becomes a wall of persuasion **like** a wall of water, that just washes over the person listening. There's no real way to defend it. Not in real time.

So therefore you don't want to go too long so as to elicit some kind of nervousness or what have you, but you don't want to go so short that you miss the point either.

Notice how I just did that. Okay?

So right now, I want you to stop again and I want you to *write ten examples of sentences* just like the example I just gave you that used **temporal**, **awareness** and **adverb/adjective presuppositions** in it.

So stop reading and write it.

When you're ready keep going.

I assume you've done that. It's important that you remember to **add massive amplification**. And remember, there are *two* ways to do it. **First** you want to be **artfully vague**, and in the example I just gave you, you read me being very **artfully vague**. In the examples you see written in this book, you see me being **artfully vague**. Yet I'm still **guiding the person's thoughts where I want them to go**. It's really powerful. You should work on learning to do the same.

You can **presuppose** their **values** using these **language patterns** and that's the way to get giant benefit from this lesson.

All right. Whenever you're talking about a person's **values**, you're really connecting with them. Whenever you're doing so by using **presuppositions**, you are making enormous inroads into their mind.

BOOK THIRTEEN

SPATIAL PATTERNS

INTRODUCTION

Further On Structuring Reality

Welcome to **Book Thirteen** of *Persuasion Force*.

Let's get right on, 'way down into the rabbit hole', as we continue looking at **structuring reality**.'

We're dealing here with **structuring reality in the mind of the listener through language patterns that are oriented to persuade**, and I do mean persuade *powerfully*.

So I suggested it in the last book and it would really be a great idea if you'd *stop reading* now and go back a couple of books, and read them again. It would really help you, I promise. Even if you have already read it four, five or six times, please go back and read it again. It's just   that important.   It will really put your mind into the mind space that you need to be in to really gain value from what it is that I'm talking about. All right? So please, stop reading this book now and go back and read what came before again real quick. It won't take but a few minutes.

It is important that you *understand* how we are **affecting the reality** of those that you're persuading through this type of   persuasion strategy.

And again, you know, I covered it last time and in Book Eleven so I'm not going to go through it, but I'm just going to suggest you go back there because in this book we'll be *going deeply* into **patterns that utilize space and spatial relationships**. And this gets really heavy.

Heavy, meaning, it's *confusing*. **It will put you into an altered state in a flash**. Okay? Trust me on this. It's really powerful and it's really trippy.

Okay? I call it, '*heavy*'. It's just *heavy*, it's kind of hard to get your mental arms around a little bit.

I'm not trying to *suggest* that, I'm just saying that this has been my *experience* over the years, so you've got a really hot session this time and I want to suggest you just *read* it, *absorb* it and begin to *get* it. All right?

From that will come tremendous *skill* and *ability* and *talent* but I guarantee you it's going to take you *doing the work*. Fair enough?

CHAPTER ONE

Spatial Patterns

This category of words deals with **manipulating space** which is *closely linked* with **time** and can be *used with* **time**, by the way, to your advantage. The three words that represent this pattern are, 'among','expand' and '**beyond**.'

Now **spatial words are used to create some** *relationship* **between things**. These could be *thoughts, ideas, products, services,* and other things. These words **evoke powerful imagery in the mind of the listener**. You can't help but **make pictures** when people start using these words. **They force the issue.** And they're **smooth**. They're **effortless**. They simply **create magic** in the minds of those that you're doing them to.

Let me give you some examples.

From **among** *the positive thoughts that you're already starting to realize you have about working with our firm, will come the most obvious yet overlooked reason to bring us on board now.*

Now, here's the thing. You don't have to stop there and look at them with this big pregnant pause waiting for them to jump down your throat and tell you how excited they are to work with you and beg you to please use your pen to sign the contract. I mean, you can just look at them with kind of a knowing look and say,

So **when that happens,** *you be sure and let me know.*
Or,

As that is happening now, *let me continue to tell you about some of   the really exciting things that I think you'll focus on.*

And then go off into something that you think they might want to hear. What might that be? Do I hear you already thinking their **values** and **criteria**? Yay. If you are, you're on track.

Now, as you read that sentence, I'm sure you also could read the plethora of additional **presuppositions** that I was using. Right? I hope so.

By the way, have you ever heard someone trained in NLP and they're like an *NLP monster* and they're doing the '*do you not, could you not, are you not, should you not*'? Do you want to know *how* to do that? All right, well, I'm going to cover that in a later book. I'm going to cover ways to do it really **slick**, **ways to do it** *without* **doing it** and I'm going to cover *how and how   often to do it* and *how to use it more effectively.* You generally don't hear *me* sounding **clichéd** like that, I don't think, and it's because **I work at** *not* **sounding like that**.

So the strategy is effective when you do it *right* and *occasionally*.

Okay. Here's another sentence.

*To **expand** on your **ever growing** ideas that **contain** the essence of your good feeling regarding using this information powerfully, think of the money you'll be making.*

Let me tear that apart. *To **expand** on your **ever growing** ideas. . .* Well, there's *two* of them. '**Expand**' and '**ever growing**'. *What?* **Ideas.** We're expanding ever growing ideas. So we have ideas that are *already* **ever growing** and now we're going to **expand** on those.

So *to **expand** on these **ever growing** ideas that **contain**. . .* now we're going to tell them what the ideas themselves are going to **contain**. Well, isn't that handy? I mean, you know, so here we can **suggest** to them **what it is that we want them to think**. . . so *that **contain** the essence of your good feeling.* The essence of your good feeling. What in the heck is that? Well, it would be the good feeling encapsulated, I guess. Right? But I mean, **what's the picture in your mind?** *regarding using this information powerfully. . .* finally we land. Remember my description, I think, in earlier books I talked about **adverb/adjective**. . .maybe I said this.

You put the words to **describe** the nouns *first* and the words that **describe** the verbs *before* the verbs. In other words, **the descriptive words first**. So that way we *don't* have *the magician in black robes carrying the wand in his twinkle toe boots dancing around like an idiot*, and you were starting off thinking he was a serious magician and all of the sudden he became a nonsensical figure. And in so doing I'm *making your mind change the way you had the picture* and **that's not good for persuasion**.

Here, if I say to you, '*The black robed, serious, wand carrying magician walked slowly into the room, or slowly walked into the room,*' you can't *land on anything* until you hear *magician* and then all of the sudden **it makes sense**.

So here I say, '*to **expand** on your **ever growing** ideas*' and they're thinking, '*what ideas?*' '*That contain the essence of your good feeling. . .*' So we're **expanding**. I'm going to now **expand** on their **ever growing** ideas that contain the essence of their good feeling *about what*?

'*Regarding using this information powerfully.*' Oh. So all of the sudden, in order to understand '*using this information*' and then '*powerfully*', what do they have to do? Well, they have to immediately *have good feelings*, and have an *essence* of that, that has *ideas* about it that are *growing* like mad that we're all of the sudden *expanding* on.

In other words, **they cannot defeat this language**. They can't do it. It's too fast. The only way they could possibly defeat it is if it was in writing and they could sit and study it. Then, it's *possible* that they could. But they'd have to really *try*. And they'd have to have **training** like this. And then, *maybe*, they would be able to but I can guarantee you it is the few of the few of the few that have this analysis capability.

So regarding using this information powerfully, '*Think of the money you'll be making*' What is that about? Well, *that's* the **expanding** part, right? So in other words, the way in which I want you to **expand these ideas you have that are growing**, that contain your ideas that contain the essence of good feeling of using this information powerfully, **the way to expand it is to think of the money you'll be making using them.**

That structure is pretty much indefensible. Nobody can come back at that and break it apart, certainly not in real time. And I mean, not anyone **trained** in this. You'd have to be *incredibly* talented and gifted to be able to break that apart. Now, **you're going to be able to do that** so you say to yourself, 'Well, *somebody* can.' Yes, people like *you* that have gone through this much, but I guarantee you, this is **unique** and you're learning things in ways that are making you **far ahead of the pack** that are out there. I mean, way, way, way ahead.

So now think of the money *you'll* be making.

Isn't that cool?

CHAPTER TWO

Leveraging Positive Statements

Let's say a person makes a **positive statement** about what you do or about you or anything of the sort, basically some relatively **positive statement**. You might respond with, '*That's a great observation.* **Let me suggest** *that* **as you start** *to* **experience** *the* **realization** *of what you* **just** *said, you can* **begin** *to* **realize** *that the full, positive ramifications will go* **beyond** *even your expectations. In fact, can you* **imagine** *how much* **further** *they'll go?*' And just wait. They'll **nod yes** eventually, or they'll go, 'I think so.' And you go, 'Absolutely. That's great.'

So if a person makes a **positive statement** about you, that's a way you can **leverage** this. All right? And I like that a *lot* actually.

CHAPTER THREE

Using Spatial Patterns in Sentences

I want you to write ten sentences using this **spatial pattern**. And really, you can write ten sentences just focusing on the **spatial pattern** first. Sentences like, '*Along with the ideas that I'm sure* **you came in with**, *there existed some hope that maybe you hadn't even yet identified, that this would be the* **place** *and this would be the solution that would most quickly help you get what you want, and as you identify that, and* **find it** *linking itself up to what I'm saying today, I think you're going to* **find yourself** *really excited by the time we're through, just how completely accurate that statement is.*'

Now, let me pull that apart just a little bit for you. What did I really just do? Well, what it did is **it put something into their head that they had to act on**. In other words, **I'm seeding now for a later result**. How much later? Well, probably the end of the sales call or the next sales call if you do a two or three call kind of presentation. So it would be like quickly though, but you might not see the results for three or four or five minutes, or ten minutes, or a half an hour or an hour or until the next time, but what you're doing with these kind of **patterns** is you're **putting in a suggestion that is designed to be acted upon at a bit of a later date.**

I mean, you've probably heard that in the past referred to as like a **post-hypnotic suggestion**, and this *isn't* exactly a post-hypnotic suggestion though it does carry some of those same similarities, it kind of shares some of the features of that.

Now, '*From **under** any resistance that you might have had prior to talking with me today will come the truth that will absolutely **steer you into the direction** that I've been **suggesting** and before that becomes obvious to you, let's take a look one more time at exactly what you said you wanted and how this will accomplish that for you.*'

See what I'm doing? That's a really good statement and '***towards** this working in your life every bit **the way** you want it to, let's **look around the corner** of the future and peer into what life will be like with this product in your life. And as you see that, just notice how **underlying** everything is a sense of, yeah, this is just right. This is mine and I'm happy about it. Notice that?*'

All right. And you can laugh or whatever you want to do but just move on. Okay?

Now, a person says, 'I don't know if this is working for me. You know?'

'*Well, **piercing through** all of that are the original reasons why you did this, **surfacing** at blinding speed now, comes the thought of (their value, their value, their value) that **roots a hold** of your consciousness now and begins to **encircle** any remaining doubt and burn it up, **dismissing** it, **letting it go**, realizing that what you need is exactly what you determined (their value, their value, their value). And that's why this is the right thing for you. Make sense? Wait a minute.*'

They'll go, 'Yeah, it makes sense. I get it now.' Pretty slick stuff, isn't it?

'*As you **come nearer and nearer** the decision to **move forward**, notice how you feel **pulled like a magnet**, **pushed like a gentle wave pushing in a boat**, and **up through** all of that, is a sense of yeah, it just is the right thing to do. Do you know how many of my clients tell me that? I mean, it's just amazing every time I hear it. Do you know what I mean?*'

Now, if right this minute you're saying to yourself, 'Well, Kenrick, I don't know, I don't feel good when I hear that.' It's because you're imagining saying that if they were having an **objection** but if you've eliminated those and you've simply got them following you, there will be no objection when you say that.

Now how about '**without**'? '*You've mentioned (their **value**, their **value**, and their **value**) and **without** those, it would sort of feel as if you're a ship **without** a rudder, or a sail **without** the wind, not really knowing how you're going to **get to where you want to go**. Knowing that we created the XYZ model because this gives **direction** to the boat, **wind** to the sails, and enables you to **move** through difficulties and **sail into the calm seas** and that's exactly why I love doing what I do. And before you immediately **become aware** of exactly how this applies, let's go through some of the details that I think will help make sense, okay?*'

See how that works? I mean, it's just so simple.

An **objection** is sent at you and you say, '*You know, oftentimes I like to **suggest** that people **separate** those kinds of things from who they are at their core because it really **doesn't belong there**. It's simply some kind of an attempt to hallucinate some potential that **doesn't even really** *exist* and ***through*** all of this, ***bring up*** a sense of stability and strength so that ***in place*** of those doubts, now they have a sense of this is right, it's ***mine***, and then ***encircling all of that***, they have a sense of rightness, joy and happiness, ***come circling around*** and it all of the sudden ***overtakes*** them as if ***from behind***, making them feel absolutely phenomenal. Let that process work as I talk ***with*** you a little bit about how you can really accomplish (name their ***values***) right now with me.'

Let me tell you, these are **persuasion magic**. I guarantee most anyone reading these words that I'm writing now is doing one of several things: blanking out, going 'Oh, my God, will I ever learn that?', enjoying it, going 'Wow, this is pretty good, I'm liking this,' and maybe there's a few of you that are going, 'Huh, I wonder if *I* could do this better.' Well, good. Okay. But probably the *majority* that are reading this are going, 'Oh, my word, this is really *trance--y* sounding.' Writers are probably going, 'Oh, my God, how do I use so much of that in my writing?' You *don't*. Make it *simple*. But I'll cover that in just a minute.

For the rest of you, look, this is kind of **spacey material**. Okay? It just is. And as you **uncover** the real power that it **brings** you, you'll **move closer and closer** to persuasion mastery. I guarantee you that this will **expand** your persuasion abilities **beyond** anything you've ever **seen**, or **done**, for that matter.

So I can tell you this, it will always **support** you, it will always **give** you abilities, and it will always, always help you and you'll **get much further with** these skills.

Now, notice that even just now in my supporting statements to you, I just used a *ton* of these, didn't I? Lo and behold. Isn't that cool?

All right. That's how this stuff works. That's how this **spatial pattern** works. I've given you example after example after example because I'm telling you the easiest   way to learn this is to have example after example after example given to you. All right? You'll easily be able to morph these examples into examples of your own.

CHAPTER FOUR

Some Spatial Words

Now I want you to put together some statements, and you can do them in paragraph form if you like, using the following **words** in the order given. By the way, there's no particular reason for this order. I'm just giving you an order to practice with so that you have a place to start. It makes it a little easier.

I want you to remember to **aim this pattern at something important** that makes sense in your life or your business. So in other words, maybe you're talking to a client. Maybe you're talking to a spouse. I don't know what you're doing. Maybe you're talking to yourself in your own head. Maybe you're creating a script that you want to run in your own mind to make learning this even easier. Whatever you're doing, it's okay. Just do it. Okay? Just practice with it. And how about you do five examples of this **pattern** in this order.

So for example, the words in order are: **realizing**, **after**, **beyond**, **easily**, **effectively**, and **realizing**. So **realizing**, **after**, **beyond**, **easily**, **effectively**, **realizing**. So we *start* and *end* with **realizing**.

Make some notes here for the above exercise so that you can easily do it. You might even want to make a brief outline first, like '*what's the objective?*' Now, every time you create an objective when you do your work like this, **you're compounding the results you can get**. I mean, you're really making it better for yourself. Why? Because **you're teaching your unconscious**, your other than conscious mind, your gentle giant, **you're teaching it how to follow your intention**. You're teaching it through your intention. **You're teaching it that when you assign it something to do, it is to carry it out**. So I want to highly encourage your use of that kind of skill from this point on as we continue in the program.

Let me give you just an example, kind of off the top of my head here, in which I did the same thing, I made a couple of notes just kind of following the format and then I'll see if I can put it all together.

'*As you start* **realizing** *the power of what you're learning in this program and* **after** *you consciously make the decision to look* **beyond** *what you thought was possible with these skills, you'll* **easily** *and* **effortlessly** *begin* **realizing** *just how excited you are to be part of this incredible opportunity to make these patterns yours.*'

Okay? There's an example and you can do the exact same thing. It's pretty doggone easy if you'll just kind of write a brief outline of where you're headed, a **statement of intention** maybe, would be a good way to put it, and then go ahead and write it out. So it's pretty much that easy.

So I'd like you to stop whatever you're doing right now, if at all possible and write this out. And again, you know I've given you these instructions from the very beginning, but if you would follow when I say stop now and **do the exercise**, you won't believe it. It'll be so much easier to get this. You'll get it so much faster, it'll make sense to you. And let me just share with you a big mistake. A **big mistake** would be to read this and go, 'Huh, interesting. Wow, yeah, okay. That's a pretty powerful pattern and Kenrick's pretty good at it. Wow, in fact, he's really good at it. But okay. I'll come back another time and try to go through it and hopefully we'll make some progress. All right. Next. Let me get on now with setting some appointments,' or whatever else you got to do.

No. No. No. No. No. **That is one humungous mistake**. That is the surest way I know to make it such that you *read* the material but *don't get* the material. Okay? Really, please, just, whenever you can as you're going through this, *stop* at each point and **do the work** because it will make it immediately make sense as you move forward into the next piece. So that'll really help you.

CHAPTER FIVE

Some Directions For Practicing

I want to give you some **directions for practicing**. And this is the part that I'm *so excited* to give you. What you're going to get right now has never been given before, ever. I have never seen this anywhere, nor have I taught anyone this in so many words. I've demonstrated it. I've used it. But until I **elicited it from myself**, I sort of sat down and tried to really figure out a strategy, like, what am I doing, was I actually able to come up with this for you? So you're the first to read it. I'm excited, really excited to give it to you actually, and I realized that as I was working with myself to come up with this, over a period of time, that there was quite a number of things I was doing.

I've identified some *big ones*. And I'm going to tell them to you now. These are solid gold. These are worth the price of admission, right here, and much, much, much more. If you'll practice with these, I guarantee you, your language skills will jump above anyone else out there.

I call this '**Directions for Practicing**'. Work with the different strategies below to improve your skills. None of these are etched in stone. They're just a way to learn these and things to get you started.

They are, however, the way I do it. I use these patterns like this all the time. So I'm going to go through them with you, read them all in one fell swoop and then we'll go over them in a little bit more detail.

1. Number one strategy: this isn't the most important one, it's just the one I listed first. Practice starting your **language patterns** with an **adverb/adjective presupposition**.
2. Number two: Liberally sprinkle in **awareness presuppositions**. These things are magic.
3. Number three: leave **open loops**, all over the place, like, '*I'm going to tell you three things you need to know today to really be successful*' and then only tell them two.
4. Number four: **Use their words or statements** to leverage into the **spatial presuppositions**. I'll come back to that and give you an example under that.
5. And number five: Work in **temporal presuppositions** before **awareness presuppositions**. And if you want, throw an **adverb/adjective presupposition** in first for good measure. And that's a power, power, powerful pattern, man.
6. Now, number six, use *all* these patterns and strategies to most importantly **presuppose** that **it's you or your products or services, etc., that is the answer to their criteria**. In other words, presuppose their **criteria** full out.

In other words, one of the things I'm saying here to you, this is critical.

****IF YOU IMAGINE THAT THEIR CRITERIA ARE QUESTIONS THAT YOU ARE ANSWERING, YOU'RE FRAMING IT RIGHT.***

In other words, they've *asked* you an *unspoken question*. They've directed their mental attention and energy at you and asked you to *solve* or *fix* or *give* them their **criteria**, their **values**. And you're *answering* that unasked question with, **how specifically what you do fulfills their values and criteria**.

Man, those are words of gold right there. I don't know that I've ever said that quite like that either. So wow, we are on a big roll.

CHAPTER SIX

Breaking It Down

Let's go back to number one. Practice starting with **adverb/adjective presupposition**. This is easy. **Naturally** you'll want to practice starting with an **adverb/adjective presupposition**. Did I just do it? Yup. You'll **readily** find that **becoming aware** of some of the **most important** aspects of what we're doing is easy when you focus on *answering the unasked question* that is directed at you by way of **eliciting their values**.

Now that was a sentence that was trippy, trance--y, zone--y. Okay? You probably are sitting there going, *huh*? So it's okay to go back, read it again. Notice the rhythm in the words.

Now, number two, liberally sprinkle in **awareness presuppositions**. All right. **Awareness presuppositions. Aware. Realize. Understand.** *Be careful* of the word '**know**' because it has a **phonetic ambiguity** '*know*' and '*no*' sound the same but they mean radically different things. One means to understand, one is a negation, one means not, one means, I don't want to. But you can use it. I used to be radically against it. I'm not anymore as I have grown in my understanding, for I could tell you right now that you want to *limit* it. Be careful, especially when you're learning like this.

Awareness presuppositions. Let's say we're going to do number one and number two. **Naturally**, you want to become **aware** of the need to **liberally** sprinkle in **awareness presuppositions** in all that you do. **See** how I'm doing that? Not too tough, but it **really** is effective. So there's that. Okay?

Next, **leave open loops** — *three* things you need to know, tell them *two*.

Or, there are two things that are the most important aspects of what I do, let me talk to you first about the one I think is the most important right after I   tell you what I like the most. Or let me just tell you the most important one, and then never get around to telling them the second one.

Why do we leave **open loops**? Because **it makes them dependent on our words**. It makes them feel like they don't know everything and that's useful because the minute they close down all their **loops** and they think they know it all, their mind snaps shut and they're no longer interested in talking to you because they think they know it all.

So it's useful from a persuasion standpoint to make sure that they want to continue. Okay?

Number four, **use their words or statements** to leverage into the **spatial presuppositions**. For example, you say, '*From **amongst** the thoughts you just had will come a new **realization** bringing with it **satisfaction** and a **feeling** of, yes, this will work the way you want and need.*'

See? So someone says whatever, and you say, 'Well, from **among** those thoughts will come a new **realization**.' Well, if you think of that, it's just funny, isn't it? From **among** those thoughts will come a new **realization**. That is pure **linguistic magic**. You are **creating** something from **among** the thoughts that **didn't exist before**. And you're *willing it into existence*, you're **languaging** it into existence such that doing so *makes it so* in the mind of the person you're persuading.

Remember, I have said this over and over, 'And Adam named the beasts of the field and had dominion over them.' He **named** them. He **languaged** them. And **had power over** them. You ever notice online that people sometimes don't want to give their name when they post? Why? Because   you could ridicule them. You have some power over them. If you know their name, you could track them down, try to follow them, right?

All right. All right. It's true they're also chicken probably, right? But nonetheless, you know what I'm talking about. So when we **name** things or **language** things, we **create** them. God *spoke*, and human beings *became*. Right? Again, I'm not trying to get religious on you, but just trying to go back and show you that in some of the greatest religious texts even, **the power of the spoken word is paramount**.

CHAPTER SEVEN

Speaking It Into Existence

When we *speak* these things, we're *speaking them into existence* in the minds of our customers. Oh, my goodness, does this give you some serious power or what? And either you're getting this or you're brain dead. Well, maybe you're in an altered state and you're going to get it in a few minutes. That's okay too.

But I'll tell you right now, it's hot, hot, hot.

Okay, <u>number five</u>, work in **temporal presuppositions** before **awareness presuppositions**. Before you **begin** to **become aware** of just how powerful this material is, you can have the thought that, wow, I wonder if I'm **getting** this and doing all that I can, **whereupon** everything I just said **will start** to **make more sense. Go ahead**, do it **now**.

That also follows the format of a **bind** which I'm going to get into with you in some really sophisticated ways of using them. You guys are getting the full on, hard core deal here.

Languaging it makes it so. Words call it into existence. As you speak, they picture, the pictures are coming from *within* them, they must be so. Get it? Now imagine doing all of this surrounding their **values**. Whoo! That's *hot*. That's hot. Stop right now and read that back. Read it *again*. Wow. This is the way persuasion works. It works just like this. You are reading the real deal.

Now, do you have to have **rapport** and everything to make this work?

Of course you do. Do you have to be good and knowledgeable of what you're doing to have some effect? Sure. Absolutely. Do you have to be able to provide customer service — yourself or your team? Yes. I mean, all the standard things have to be in play. We're talking about how to leverage the mind of the person you're persuading to get what you want.

How about if you put all this inside of **rhythmic speaking** such that as you speak, it affects their brains even more powerfully and then when you start putting the **temporal** before **awareness**, throwing **adverb/adjective** in front, **open loops**, etc. you are knocking the ball out of the park. And right now, I'm hoping that you're thinking, 'Oh, my God, how am I ever going to be able to do this? How am I going to remember to do it? Will I ever get it that good?' Yes, you will. Yes, you are.

CHAPTER EIGHT

Combining the Skills

All right. I've got more hot stuff for you. As if this weren't enough. I'm going to give you here some strategies of **combining the skills**. As I've said already, with this pattern and the others, you have the makings of huge power as a persuader. **Your language can create miracles in your life**, it can *also* wipe out benefits causing you to lose sales and make people not trust you. It's all in the language and your behavior, both in combination.

Language is the part people will *key into*. It's funny, I'll talk to certain people and they'll go, '*Yeah, well, I'm feeling that you're thinking, blah, blah, blah.*' Well, in other words, what happened is, as I'm talking they're making pictures and hearing my sounds and it's *creating feelings* and then they believe that their feelings are an explanation, or prefacing even, my words. In other words, they had some *psychic sense* that all of the sudden came upon them, but in reality it's the other way around. *It's based on my words that they had their feelings,*and their feelings didn't just come wafting along through the air and whack them upside the head. Okay? **My words cause it**. And *then* they had feelings about what it is that I'm saying. Interesting, isn't it?

All right, so you have to watch it because **your words will create feelings, pictures, and sounds in their head** and it will make them *come closer to you* and do what you want or *repel them*. It's all up to how you do it. All right?

Here are some keys for you that will help you to be more powerful at persuasion and using these **language patterns** in particular. You need to be in integrity. You need to be persuading *for the right reasons*, for honorable causes. Okay? That's critical. If you're not, you're going to be *broadcasting* like mad. They're going to see that you *lack integrity* and your **language patterns** will *magnify* what you're doing and who you are and it will *magnify* the lack of integrity and they'll run.

Right off the bat, *if you don't feel good about what you do, you better stop it and you better find a way to feel good about it or you better go do something else.* I'm telling you, we're right down to the nitty gritty now and that's the bottom line. Either find a way to feel good about it or go do something else.

Next, **keep your intentions simple**. People pick up on trickery. Don't be slick or all knowing when you use these **language patterns**. I've had a lot of exposure to people who have been trained by Anthony Robbins.

I hate to name names but I will tell you this, the guy is absolutely brilliant at a lot of what he does. This is not to knock him in any way, shape or form but simply to point out something I've witnessed.

One of the ways, I believe, this is just my own interpretation, that he helps people to learn some of the patterns, and he's not teaching nearly the level of sophistication that we're going into here as a general rule. . .well, in my opinion, he's not period. What he does is he gets them to feel a bit *superior*. . . Well, first of all, he does this to them, he models a bit of a superiority complex, like, '*See? I'm really slick. I just did something to you. And so you are experiencing that I'm doing something to you and as a result of that, you're feeling that I did something to you. So now I'm doing this, and that's that. And so hopefully you'll get it. I think you're going to get it. I'm going to show you how to get it.*' See, well then pretty soon, the people when they're learning like that, they then do it to others like that so when they start selling and using this, they start going, '*You know, as you **naturally** become **aware** of that **growing desire** within you, to feel **really** good about everything I say, you'll **just marvel** at what we can do together as you **experience** the effect of this **now**.*' And they have this all knowing smile and nodding head and all these things, okay? And the people having it done to them are going, '*Well, you think you're smarter than me or better than me? Do you think you're pulling something over on me?*' But see, that's how the people learn to do it, so you can't really hardly blame the persuaders because they don't really know better.

You, on the other hand, reading this book, learning the most sophisticated strategies that exist, you know better. All right? **Keep your intentions simple**. They'll pick up on a tricky, slick, all knowing attitude, so lose it. Okay?

Next, you need to really *care deeply about others* when you use these **language patterns** because it comes across. And if you *don't* care deeply, *that's* going to come across as well.

Next, **combine the patterns**. There is power in combinations. There is power in combination. Should I say it again? Power in combinations.

There is *power* when you combine the thirty--six stratagems. There is *power* when you **combine these language patterns**. I'm telling you, there is *power* when you combine what I've taught you and where you're going and what you're learning. Power, power, power. Keep combining.

Next, **keep it relatively simple in writing**. Don't go too far in writing.

Make your sentences relatively *short*, your paragraphs relatively *short*. You can string three or four sentences together that will have the same impact as a great big long group of them that you might do live, by speaking. So just keep that in mind. It isn't necessary to do a huge amount of length in these.

You want to clean them up by doing them as well, so even as you write them for your exercises, you'll start with them being unwieldy and big and long and meandering so, you know, just work on cleaning them up. Rewrite them. Clean it up. Get your language clear and concise and powerful.

Next, **alternate** between using the patterns and redirecting to "normal, logic-style language" In other words, *this* helps with *that*, *this* creates *that*, now you can understand easier. In other words, bring them back to normal language. So you slam into their brains some of these very strong patterns that make them visualize and it does all these cool things and then bring them back to simple language so they're not off in the ozone for too long.

Next, use **rhythmic speaking** and put the patterns in when doing it. So practice this month **speaking rhythmically** and put in the patterns while you're doing the **rhythmic speaking**.

There's a lot of practice here this time isn't there?

Next, watch the other person carefully and keep their attention. **Watch for buy in**. What does that mean? Watch that they're *going along with you*, that they're with you, they're getting it with you, you know, they're happy, and really go for it. All right? I mean, **commit**, fully **commit** to getting the results, but if you see that the other person's drifting off to sleep on you or getting completely bored, well then you're not. Bring them back so then say, '*Well, let me just ask you this, can I? Do you understand what I'm saying? And are you with me?*' Or, '*Let me ask you something. What's the most important point I've covered with you so far?*' In other words, get their attention. Make them feed back. Get them to where you're keeping their attention.

Don't let them just drift off and out to sleep.

Next, **push the envelope** when doing the patterns. In other words, you need to push yourself. You're going to sound silly at first. You're going to sound exaggerated, unwieldy. That's fine. Push yourself. Push the envelope until you can do this with ease and smoothness. But it does take practice.

Where we're heading is in the next book we're going to learn specific strategies of **manipulating logic** to add to what you know, and let me tell you, there are a few strategies that when added to what you know, will superpower what's possible. We're *laying the foundation for them* right now and one of the next steps is **logic**, also **commands** and a few other really cool things. Also, **framing** and all sorts of **reframing strategies** and then some **higher level language strategies**. I mean, these things build *momentum*.

So that's why it's so important that you read this book over and over and write out the examples as much as you can. I mean, listen, even if you can't write it out, or you refuse to, or whatever, at least read over and over and over. Ten, twenty times reading if you can.

CHAPTER NINE

Homeplay

All right, let's go to your homeplay for this book.

Model the patterns in the examples I gave, primarily for the **spatial patterns** and *write twenty-five sentences* using **spatial presuppositions**.

Next, write the high **values** of five of your clients and *write twenty--five sentences* in which you **presuppose their criteria** by using *all four* of the **presupposition patterns** in combination that I've taught you.

Okay, what a jam--packed, powerful book. I'm telling you, solid gold here. Much meat. Huge substance. So, *practice, practice, practice*. Do your writing. Please, do the writing. You're going to *love* me for pushing you to do it, okay?

All right, until the next book, persuade lots. Take care, I'll talk to you soon. Bye bye.

BOOK FOURTEEN

EMBEDDING COMMANDS

INTRODUCTION

Embedding

Welcome to **Book Fourteen** of *Persuasion Force*. If you've been following along faithfully with every book, I think that you'll have to agree that this is one incredible series of lessons, certainly I think the finest I've ever created like this and I'm really glad to have you with me.

All right, well let's jump into this book in which we're going to learn the concept and strategy called **embedding**, as in **embedding commands**, **thoughts**, **emotions** and more.

What you're going to be learning in this book can *amazingly transform your results in persuasion* if, and it's a big if, you really **understand it and know how to use it the right way**. So many people that I've met that have been exposed to this, have been exposed to it as it relates to *therapeutic* stuff and **it does not translate into business like that**. They also have a complete *misconception* and *think they can command people to do anything* from give them their wallet to buy ridiculous items that the person doesn't need, and then they wonder why they're not getting any results. So I hope you will take all of this learning to heart and as a result, **really learn how to use it powerfully** because it is very, very powerful.

And once you learn *how* to use this the right way, you're going to feel real good and you're going to know exactly **the parameters of how it works and where it doesn't** and I think maybe sometimes knowing where a technique *doesn't* work or where its *limit* is, is maybe as useful as knowing what it does.

CHAPTER ONE

Bypassing a Person's Conscious Filtering System

In this book, let's learn how to **bypass a person's conscious filtering system**, enabling you to **implant ideas, thoughts and instructions at will**. Now let's just stop right there. Does that sound pretty cool? I think it does. In fact, I'll give you some *examples* of ways I've seen these used and they just blew my mind. I think it's amazing.

Let me ask you something, let's just take your very best friend, *would you do 100% of what your very best friend asked of you?* Like let's just take the next five years of life and over that time, do you think it's possible that there may be something that your best friend asks of you that you don't or you won't really want to do and you probably won't do? I know for me that's true. I don't do everything *anyone* asks of me really. I mean, if it doesn't work for me, I'm quick to say so.

So do you think that you're going to be able to get another person into the mindset where no matter what you want them to do, even if it's not in their best interest, they're going to do it anyway? And *if you think that, you're wrong* and it'll slow you down. So let's get right now that the way these skills work is   that **as long as you're operating in the client's best interest**, and they *know* that to be the fact, they *know* that to be true, and you're **appealing to their values**, you can *probably* get them to do most things that make sense.

However, you probably will *not* get them to be able to do things that don't make sense. For example, you probably will not, using this skill, be able to get someone to change sexual orientation, not that I think you'd try, but just so you get an idea, I mean, that's just sort of *ridiculous*, isn't it? **You're not going to cause those kinds of changes with this.** What you're going to be able to do is **get people to do more of what they *want* to do,** more of what their **values** would, could lead them to do and more of what *you* want them to do in terms of **leveraging the trust that you've built up with them.**

So **there are limits to this** and I'll try to explain them as we go.

You'll be able to covertly give instructions that will be carried out by the other person, often later without the person being conscious that you caused it. That sounds pretty slick too, doesn't it? And it really is.

In fact, it's *really* slick.

The thing is about that is it sounds really **manipulative** and *it doesn't have to be quite as manipulative as it sounds*. For example, *you're* doing things today that somebody **embedded** in you many years ago and *you do them all the time*. And you don't give it a second thought and it doesn't seem manipulative. I'll bet you *your parents* gave you a set of **values** and **morals** that to this day you adhere to, think about, or it affects you, maybe even on a daily basis. Maybe some of them you've changed, but I believe probably a lot of them you haven't. In fact, there's an ancient writing about that, a Biblical one, I believe, that says, '*Train a child in the ways of the Lord and he shall not depart from them.*' Or something like that. Basically it's simply saying, **what you teach a kid, they're going to do.** The kind of **morals** and **values** you teach them, they're going to stay with.

So, yes, **you will be able to give instructions like that**. You'll be able to **teach people things, install things**, and **get them to act on them at a later date**. And in fact, there's a specific strategy for that that we'll be getting into later on as well in an upcoming book.

It sounds really hot and it *is* really hot. Just understand where it works. We'll also be able to have you **do your persuading on an unconscious level as well as conscious** so we're looking now to start having multiple levels of consciousness. So for example, right now you're reading my words, you're probably **focused on the overall concepts** that I'm getting out to you here, and there we are. All right?

234

However, I could start to **structure my language** such that **another level of communication began to take place**.

Now, let's look at this on an *interpersonal* level to begin with and let's take the dating scene. So let's pretend that you are out on a date.

Could be a date with your spouse or a date with someone that you'd like to be more intimate with or like to get to know better or what have you. If this date is going successfully **there are multiple levels of communication going on**. For example, let's say I'm talking to you and you're a man and you're out with a woman and you're talking about what the woman does, but as you do that, maybe she's playing with her hair, crossing or uncrossing her legs, changing her way of sitting towards you, fiddling with a button or something like that. What's she really doing? Well these are probably *flirting gestures* to let you know she's interested. So **there are several levels of communication**.

Let's say you're a woman, you're talking with a guy and you're sending off all the right signals, in other words, you're **communicating on a secondary level** while talking about what he does for work, for example, and he sits with his legs crossed, his arms crossed, and sitting back. Now, I really hate to ascribe too much meaning to those kinds of things, I prefer a different way of doing it, but for now let's just say that that has a valid meaning of he's not interested. So there's the **conscious level** stuff going on, you know, well here's what I do for a living and here's how long I've been doing it, etc., etc. and there's the **other level** going on, which is still *somewhat* conscious, probably, of well, is he interested in me or not.

So **there can be many, many levels of communication going on simultaneously**. And one of these levels can be **hidden directives** and that's what we'll refer to them as from here on out is **hidden directives**.

CHAPTER TWO

Hidden Directives

Hidden directives are **suggestions** or **commands** that fit into the normal structure of a sentence but are **marked off** in a way to **call the other than conscious attention to them**. So *they fit into a normal sentence*, into the normal structure of a sentence like I'm using right now, but when you use them, you **mark them off** so that **the other than conscious is able to recognize that something is being sent to it that it should pay attention to**, which makes it pretty cool.

All right, here's an *example* of this.

If you learn this material, you will be able to use it powerfully and that will allow you to feel good about your increased sales.

Okay? So that is an *example* of this kind of communication. So what I want you to do is *write down the* **commands** *I just used*.

What were the commands? All right, now if you said, '*learn this material*' is the first one, you're right. If you said, '*use it powerfully*' as the second one, you're right. And if you said, '*feel good*' for the third one, you're right.

You're going to learn that when you first start, you're going to have *mangled* and *malformed* **commands**. I'm going to write about what **a good, well formed command** is, but you know, the *mangled* ones don't work very well so you want to learn to put in **really tight commands** like you see here. So let's read these three commands just on their own. Supposing I said to you, '*Learn this material, use it powerfully, feel good.*' **Those make sense all by themselves**, don't they?

Now the **structure** of this sentence, the **meaning** of this sentence is those **commands**. So when you **command** them, **you're just enforcing, or reinforcing the purpose of that sentence**. However, you could also say a sentence that is *less* about this but *still* with *those same commands* and have the *same effect*. But the idea *isn't* to be too awful tricky, all right? It's not to go too awfully far.

Now, this though is an example of **communicating on multiple levels**.

And we'll get really into this. Here's another example, '*I'm wondering, by now, if you can, John, feel great inside by understanding the value of what you've learned so far and this is just the beginning.*'

Now, this is a sentence like I was talking about a minute ago. This is the kind of sentence where *I'm talking, not necessarily just about the commands*. I'm really talking about the **value** of what you've learned and this is just the beginning and all these things, but **I've stuck in two commands** that I want to take effect inside the mind of the people that I'm talking to.

Okay, *what are the two **commands**?* The first command is, '*by now*'. Let's go to number two, the second command, '*feel great inside*'. So let's read the two **commands**. '*By now, feel great inside.*' Hey, those are pretty slick commands, aren't they? If you can get someone to *buy now*, in other words *purchase your product now*, and *feel great inside*, wow, that's pretty good, isn't it? While you're off talking about understanding the value of what they've been learning and that this is just the beginning, blah, blah, blah.

Okay. I did a few important things that you should be aware of. First, I used the **directive** '*by now*'. Now, this is what's called a **phonological ambiguity**. In other words, *read, reed, read*, anyway, you know what I'm talking about. *Right* and *write*. You know? So these are **phonological ambiguities** where **a word can have more than one meaning but it *sounds* the same**. So the mind actually translates *all* the possibilities of what the word sounds like and chooses an appropriate one, but **it interprets *every one* of them**. Isn't that interesting? That's the way our mind works at the deep structure. It figures out meaning.

In fact, you could say, your mind is the greatest meaning maker ever.

It far surpasses the computer's ability to do.

You *hear* me say, '*b--u--y now*.' *Purchase now*. You *also* hear me say, '*as of now*', in other words, *that* way of looking at by now. Isn't that interesting? So you can use **phonological ambiguities** to your advantage. This is why I always say **be careful of the word *know***.

How's it pronounced? *No.* So if I say, '*Know the value of this product*,' well one way of looking at that is '*understand the value of this product*'. Another way of looking at that is, '*no*', as in '*don't the value of this product*'.

I'm careful as a general rule, not all the time, but as a general rule, not to load up too much of what I say with negatives or negations like that. It can really cause problems. Okay? It can **cancel out** a lot of what you're trying to do. This is quite subtle. It's not gross. It's quite subtle.

So you want to be careful. I would much rather hear you say, 'understand' blah, blah, blah, instead of 'know'.

All right. I also used something called, if you want the technical term, a **noun substitution**. A big technical term, huh? All right, so read the example above and leave out the name John.

Here we go. '*I'm wondering, by now, if you can feel great inside by understanding the value of what you've learned so far and this is just the beginning.*' Does it mean the same thing? Yes, it does. It means the same. However, **adding the name makes the directive stronger** because **it focuses the person's attention**. It's like drawing a target on them, or it's like you've seen in the police shows, someone flashes a laser on the guy's chest and all of the sudden **gets immediate compliance**. It's like he knows he's been **targeted**. So this is like, '*I'm talking to **you**, unconscious mind of John.*' And it adds a lot of power when you do that.

Now, you can't do it too many times. I'll never forget a few years back, taking my kids to the dentist close by here, and there's a husband and wife dentist team, and the wife deals with the children and she's a very, very good dentist, you know, I think the kids actually really like her. I, on the other hand, was more irritated than I could imagine because she called me into the office, she goes, 'Dad', she hollers into the waiting room. Fortunately I guess I was the only man out there so I stood up and headed in that direction and when I got in, she goes, 'Hi dad, I just wanted to tell you a few things, dad. Okay, dad, one of the things that I noticed, dad is that Victoria is brushing her teeth quite well, dad, but dad, one of the things, dad, that I want to point out to you, dad, is that...' I was like,   *ugh*. I mean, literally, it was probably worse than that, but within about three or four minutes of hearing *dad*, I must have heard dad a thousand times in three or four minutes and my head started hurting. Literally. I told the staff, I said, 'Please, a little training here or something, but this is really hard to hear.' So all right, **you will increase the power of the directive, though, when you add a person's name but you can only do it once in a great while**.

All right?

Now sometimes you can't use the person's name because it would make the sentence sound strange but often you can and you can put the name *before* or *after* the **directive** and still get the same results. It doesn't matter. It's not better one way or the other.

Another thing, if you think you're going to get *caught* using **hidden directives**, think again. I will tell you right now, it just simply isn't going to happen. I don't know that I've *ever* been caught using this **language pattern** and neither will you. It just doesn't happen. So by all means, feel free to use it for all it's worth and in fact, let's talk about that. The *more* you use **embedded commands**, the *better off* you're going to be, **embedded directives**. Why? Well, **they function because they establish a pattern in the mind of the listener**. It's a **linguistic pattern** and they often kind of fall into a **rhythm** as well.

And then **you use these patterns in a rhythm**, what happens is, people, it kind of **lullabies** people. What we're looking for here is **pattern recognition** and as I mentioned, your brain is the greatest **pattern recognizer** and **meaning maker** that exists, period. And what you're looking to do is have the unconscious mind of the individual you're doing this with **recognize the pattern** of, *this is an instruction for me*. Wow, somebody's talking to me. I better pay attention.

That's what you're looking to create. So this goes way beyond normal communication and it adds another element, you know, like the flipping of the hair, etc. that the unconscious mind of the person you're communicating with will pick up on and you want them to, but you want it to stay, more or less, **outside of awareness**. You want it to stay at the level that is a bit, shall we say, **subliminal**. And to do that, you need to use a lot of them so that there's a **pattern** that the unconscious can recognize.

Interesting, isn't it?

Okay, I want to give you a third example so you can begin to understand this even more as you read it.

'I had a client come in the other day and ask me if I thought this would be a good product for him to buy. I told him, 'If you want a good investment, by all means, buy it.' I said, 'Take my word. It will do what you want.' Finally I said, 'You are the only person who can convince yourself that it's right.' Then I asked him if he felt it was right to go ahead and get it. He said he was. I get asked a lot for my advice, and I'd love to be of service in any way I can.'

All right, I want you to write down the **directives** that I used.

All right, what are the four **commands**? And if you said, number one, *'buy it'*, you're right. Number one is *'buy it'*. Number two, *'take my word'*. Number three, *'convince yourself'*. Number four, *'go ahead'*. Er. . . and number five, *'get it'*. So there's a *fifth* one there, I guess, all right.

He said he was. And on I went with the sentence. So there are the **commands**. There are a number of sentences and a number of commands, but let's read the **commands** all by themselves. *Buy it, take my word, convince yourself, go ahead, get it.* Isn't that slick? I mean, that has a meaning all   unto itself, can you see that? And yet **wrapped around that meaning** are words talking about clients coming in asking me their opinion, is it a good investment, you know, and I get asked a lot about my advice and love to be of service. You know, but at another level, I'm saying, *'Buy it, take my word, convince yourself, go ahead, get it.'* Pretty slick, isn't it? So are you starting to see the **multiple levels of communication** that this causes? And if you are, you are getting it.

CHAPTER THREE

The Command Structure

Okay, I want you to look back over the three examples that I just gave you and note that **they follow a specific format**. Each one of them used a *different structure* for **embedding commands**.

So what I want you to do is *write down the structure*. What is number one? What did I do there? What kind of format did I use?

Number one uses commands in a **statement format**. Plain **statement format**.

Example number two, that one uses commands in a **question format**.

And number three uses commands in a **quote format**, using quotes of what you or someone else says.

So those are **three different formats** that you can find yourself using commands in — **statements**, **questions** and **quotes**. All three can be very, very persuasive.

All right, let me give you a couple of things here to understand in addition. There are a few easy ways to learn **embedded commands**. In other words, a few **linguistic mechanisms** that will make it easier to use. Often I **embed a command** *after* the word 'to'. It's important *to . . . feel good* as you read this material *so that* you can *learn it quickly*. And there's the next one, the next **linguistic mechanism** is **modal operators**, *can, should, must, have to, need to, will*. **Modal operators** in general can be used to **embed commands**. *So that you can. . . feel good as you learn this material powerfully*. And *as you do that* you'll *incorporate it* into your work *in such a way* that you *begin to make more money*. I know that for me *when I begin to use these skills* it really helps me a lot and I'm able *to advance myself and my clients* in many very useful and powerful ways.

Interesting, isn't it? Getting the idea? So I just used a whole bunch of them there, one after the other after the other. Go back and read that one again if need be. And you'll see how exactly they work.

CHAPTER FOUR

Analogical Marking

Analogical marking is a fancy way of describing a way in which **hidden directives** are **marked off** with a *tone*, *gesture* or *touch* to **draw attention to them unconsciously** and you can use any of those.

There are probably more ways that I haven't thought of, but at least those.

All right, here is **specifically how to mark off commands**. Number one, **pause** before giving the command. I'd like you to think how you can. . . *learn these skills*. Now I'm not suggesting you go too long. I'm just suggesting more that you make a **pause** before giving the command. And number two, **change your tone**, preferably making it **deeper** while giving the command.

Now let's talk about **why that works**. Remember that we learned in a previous book, I believe, that there are **three types of tones**. There are tones that *turn up at the end*, that *stay level at the end* and *go down at the end*. Tones that *go up* at the end are tones that are indicative of *questions*. Do you know what I mean? Right? Is this making sense? *Questions end in an upturn* with your tone. *Statements* just *stay flat*. They just stay like this. They're simply kind of a matter of fact, and that's how they sound. And **commands**, well, they end sharply *down*. So you can imagine for a minute a drill sergeant, if you will, since we are a world at war. And let's imagine this drill sergeant. He's going to say the following: '*Clean the mess hall?*'

Is *that* what he's going to do? He's going to say, '*Give me fifty pushups? Soldier, drop and give me fifty pushups?*' What's the message he's sending there? You wouldn't know. '*Like, ummm, okay. Now?*'

See? So *a question is an upturned tone* and when you turn your tone *up*, you'll make people question *you*. You'll make people question whether or not you really want them to do what you're suggesting. All right?

A statement just stays flat and that's better at least, for a lot of things in persuasion. Let's say I'm an advisor, I'm talking to somebody and I'm saying, '*Yes, I've been an advisor for twenty years? And during that time I have helped people to save money? And I have helped them to structure their finances so that they're more content?*' It sounds weird, doesn't it? I mean, it just doesn't sound right. Because it's *not* right. **It's not congruent**. I mean, you either did it or you didn't. If you did it, it's a *statement* or if you want to make a point, it's a *command*. So *how* would the command sergeant major, *how* would he say this? He would say, '*Do it now! Drop and give me fifty! Clean the mess hall! Ten hut!*' Okay? This is more what he's talking about. He's not wishy washy, he's getting the job done. And *that's* how you have to use a command.

Now, you're going to have to get over the idea that **it's not *polite* to use commands**, that people don't want to be commanded around. In fact, they don't. Nobody wants to hear you come along and say, '*Get off your ass! Drop and give me fifty!*' Nobody wants to hear that.

However, they will be more than happy to hear you use a command in your sentence in such a way that helps them to understand. See, I just did it, '*use a command in your sentence*'. So as long as you **don't end on a command**, and that's another major thing. As a general rule, **don't end your sentence on the command**. You want to keep going after that. Why? Because **it calls attention away from the command** and you can get away with more.

Number three, **increase or decrease your volume** when giving the command. This just further **marks it off** in the mind of the listener.

Four, **make a specific motion** when giving the command.

Five, **anything else** that **marks off the command**, you could *tap on the table* with each command, you could do *anything* as long as it's **consistent**, but **you have to do it consistently**, okay?

If you *really* want a very, very powerful impact, then you'll **use numbers one, two and three together**. They really make a powerful impact when you use commands. So you'll want to **pause before giving the command**, you could do it *after* too, but generally I pause *before*, **change your tone**, preferably making it *deeper*, and **increase or decrease your volume** when giving the command. Okay? If you want to also add a **specific motion** when you give the command, you know, a *hand movement*, a *lift of your finger*, any of those things would also help **mark it off** effectively.

All right, hold on to that question, I can just hear you thinking about a question, I'll answer it in a second.

So what does it **sound** like? Well, let's say I wanted to say to you, '**Analogical marking** is a fancy way of *describing* a way in which you can **mark off directives** in order to get people to do more of what you want them to do. And when you want to get people to do something, you'll want to begin to use a lot of commands, such that when you do that, they're just kind of going right along with you while their unconscious mind is paying attention to the secondary meanings.

Now see, because I *didn't stop* on the command, I just *kept on going*, it sort of *drew your attention away from it*. That's how you make sure you're not caught.

CHAPTER FIVE

Strategies For Success

I'm going to give you some strategies that you can use to make this really easy on yourself and so let's do that now. And here's how I want you to do it. You're going to **choose five commands that you can use in your day--to--day business. You** want to make them **short**. Okay? These should be like two to four words each. No more.

These should follow the basic following **format** and this is what all good suggestions follow. Number one, you want them to be **present tense**. Notice that all of the commands I've issued are **present tense**.

This is where I see a *lot* of people fall down with this stuff is they start using **past tense** to command. 'And you *wanted* to do this.' *Nope*. You just **completely eliminated** the power of that one. Also, **they used too many words**. Yes, you *can* do six and eight words, okay, but they should be the *exception*, not the rule, because they're **too long**. What you want is *short, punchy, powerful* fragments of commands to go into the mind of the person that you're influencing. That works far, far, far better.

So **write down five commands that you can use in your day--to--day business** like, '*Buy now. Feel good. Move forward. Follow my advice. Act now.*' Anything like that, okay, that you want people to do.

Now here's the strategy that I want you to consider. Consider that these five commands should **start with the mental and maybe end on the physical** like, '*Get started*' or whatever. You always want to **go after the mind first** and I'll talk just a little bit more about that later, but the bottom line is **make sure you're going after emotions and mental things, not after physical things**. Okay? That's important because you won't get anywhere if you're binding right off the bat with physical things.

So write them down and then what I want you to do is you're going to *write five statements that consciously don't call attention to the commands* and I want you to write them down using the commands that you just wrote above, you want to start off with at least one command in a sentence. In fact, really you don't need a whole lot more than that, you'll just want one command and you'll want to use a lot of them. So this takes some training to teach yourself how to think about the commands. That's why you're going to write them out first, and you're going to write the commands you want to start teaching yourself to use in your day--to--day persuasion life.

And then, I want you to *use these same commands in questions that don't call attention to them*. Use these in **quotes form**. So use the commands in quotes. So I want you to do all of that. All right? And then you'll have the basis for the homework for this lesson, for this book.

Now, using what you've learned so far, I want you to write one sentence that uses **pacing and leading**, several of the **most powerful words**, and at least two **commands** all in combination. Now, by the way, this can actually be *more than one sentence*. This could be three or four sentences, but *do all those things* in this group of sentences. And that's really hot.

Here's another powerful way to use **hidden directives**. You can **quote yourself talking to yourself in your own head**. So for example, '*You know what's really neat? When I talk to you, I get excited about what the possibilities are for our future. I even say to myself, 'Be open to really be of service here.' I really appreciate our relationship.*'

So I could have **marked it** any way, but you know, any number of things or actual **commands** there, but see if you can look at that sentence and see maybe some other commands. For example, I could have commanded '*get excited*' . . . or maybe I did command that, actually. '*Be open*', '*be of service*', '*appreciate our relationship*', all of those things are things I could have commanded.

So notice how **they all fall into the normal sentence structure** and **they also are all present tense**. And that's very important that you learn to do it like that.

Okay, I want you to write one example just like this example, so where you're actually **quoting yourself**. So write one example like that.

CHAPTER SIX

"Now" and "Stop"

Let's look at the words 'now' and 'stop'. Now these are two of the words in the *eighteen most powerful words* that, to me, are representative of **commands** because **they're simply forceful commands on their own**. And I like them a lot because **they control the mental processes that are going on inside someone's head**.

Here are some examples. '*This is a great idea and I think you're beginning to gain the understanding of my ability to help you, are you not? I mean,* **stop**, *and* **start** *to begin to become aware of all the ways you can use just the few ideas I've given you so far.*' Pretty impressive isn't it? Do you notice the real **emphasis** I gave to the word '**stop** *and* **start**'?

There's a technical term I'll throw at you here, not that I think it matters, but for what it's worth, it's called **apposition of opposites**.

That's like, **stop/start**, **forward/backward**, and these things have quite an impact on the brain. So when you can throw them in they're useful but for our purposes let's just work with the word '**stop**' primarily or '**stop** and **start**'. And you can just throw these in anywhere.

Let's look at the next example. '*As you begin to realize all the power The Cleveland Method gives you to influence others effectively, you'll begin to discover your ever increasing enthusiasm for mastering this.* **Now**. *Let's keep practicing on putting more and more of the patterns together, shall we?*' So what are we doing? '**Now**' is very interesting in this context, isn't it?

Now, does the word '**now**' *end* the sentence '*ever increasing enthusiasm for mastering this* **now**'? Or does it *begin* the next sentence, '**now** *let's keep practicing on putting more and more of the patterns together*'? Which is it? And I would say the answer is yes. It does both. So if you work at it a little bit, you're going to see how you can use the word '**now**' to *both end sentences and simultaneously begin them*. In other words, **you're slurring what it's really for** such that they won't really get that **you're ordering them to do something now** but that you're simply bringing up the next point of what you want to do.

So I could say to you, '*As you learn these skills effectively, you'll begin to find yourself really loving how they help you in your business. In fact, the more you use them, the more you'll find yourself getting excited and I think that's one of the reasons that people get so thrilled to learn this material.* **Now**. *One of the ways I want to teach you to do it is to effectively get people off those commands by continuing on past it, just like I'm doing here, transitioning with the word* '**now**'.' So **now** I used it to even forcefully install the command harder. **Now**. And then I went on.

I could say, '*As you listen to what I'm saying,* **now**, *and then you'll also have things going on in your mind, so that as a result, when I'm saying what's going on in your mind it's like there's levels of communications with one reflecting off the other.*' Kind of interesting. See, I'm deflecting purposefully now into another train of thought so that you sort of get off these commands. I mean, when I say to you, '*learn this* **now**', I mean, that's pretty forceful, don't you think? And you can't really get away with that unless **now** becomes the first word of the next sentence.

It's just really powerful and I've got some additional really cool things to show you along these lines in later books.

Okay, what you want to do is throw in these words, **now** and **stop** and **start** even, as frequently as you can *without being ridiculous*. So that means you can't do it that often. You can do '**now**' occasionally, more so than you can '**stop**'. One of the things that you can use '**stop**' for is with *objections* or with *concerns*. People say, '*I just don't know that this is going to work for me.*' And you go, '*Well, you know, let me tell you, if you were to just **STOP**, go inside, and **start** to look at this from a few different vantage points the likes of which obscure what you were thinking previously,   because they point out to you the obvious reasons that people get involved in this program. You'll begin to understand just exactly the power of the kinds of things I'm talking about. And let me help by pointing out some of the really unique features that this uses along the way. Here are some things I like about this program personally.*'

Now make sure you're talking about their **values**, right.

So that kind of talking is really effective, really effective.

CHAPTER SEVEN

More Types of Directives

Here are additional strategies. You can **command emotions** like *excited*, **get excited**, *happy*, **you can be happy** knowing. . . blah, blah, blah. **Feel good, you can feel good** as a result of. . . and many more emotions. Any emotion that you want, you can use.

So that's another way. I mentioned earlier that you should go after *thoughts, emotions* and *values* more so than physical behavior. That's far more helpful for you. If you really want to direct *physical behavior*, commanding something be done **in the future** is better. And do it after getting them loosened up, meaning that you've been using some of these skills on them, you've been doing some of the **eighteen most powerful words**, the **presuppositions** and all those things and so their brain is kind of getting *loosened up* to experience this kind of communication. And then you absolutely can talk about them **doing things in the future**, like *to feel good about moving forward with this as you think about the reason why you got started* **in the future**.

So is it in the future that you *got started* in the future, or are you *thinking about it* in the future while you got started today? See, these are all **ambiguities** that I'm leveraging on purpose. This is a very powerful lesson and it's one that requires some effort, okay? But I'll tell you, if you'll follow the instructions on the homeplay, you'll really get this. You'll get it and you'll get it all day long. It just takes practice.

One of the best things that you can use as a **hidden directive** is their **values**. So you can always use their **values**. You could say, for example, let's say a person has a **high value** of *earning more money*.

244

You could say, '*As the result of following this strategy that I outline and you **begin to** experience what it's like to **earn more money**, you'll feel real good knowing that this strategy is leading you to victory, **now**, let's **stop** for a moment and **start** to imagine a future where all these things are taking place. And as you do, notice just how good it begins to feel. Isn't that nice?*'

I'm really layering that in. I mean, that's being slammed in at the other person's mind. Not negatively so, but just with machine gun fire it's just pounding away. And I know that you're thinking to yourself, and I told you I'd answer this question, '*Okay, but how do I use it in writing?*' All right, here's how you use it in writing. If you weren't thinking that question, how about you think it now? Because you probably would like to know, wouldn't you?

CHAPTER EIGHT

How To Use It In Writing

All right, so here's how you use it in writing. First of all, you use it the same as you do in speaking in the sense that you have to **mark off the command**. All right? However, what you're going to do is you're going to **mark it off in writing** in print a little different. You can't do it by **pausing**, exactly, although I use **ellipses** a lot, three periods, dot, dot, dot, I use that a lot to **indicate a pause**. A **comma** works. Okay? You can also **mark this off** by **changing the font slightly**, you can *bold* it, you can . . . I wouldn't underline it, I would only do that when you're practicing this. You could change perhaps the **color** slightly, so it slightly stands out, not much, you don't need much. You could make the points a half a point bigger so it stands out or you could change the **type of font** that you're using so that it stands out a little. You could **italicize** it. There's a whole bunch of things you can do, but make it subtle. What you need is **more commands** in your written piece, **not more blatant commands** that are fewer of them. Got it?

CHAPTER NINE

Homeplay

Okay, so you can use these kinds of directives to do almost anything.

How about '*trust me*', how about '*work with me*', how about '*learn this material*' or '*feel good about what we're doing*'. All those kinds of things can be done too. Don't be afraid to apply them selfishly for your advantage as long as the other person also has an advantage by doing so. In other words, if this is going to help the other person, then what are you waiting for?

All right, lots and lots here, isn't there? This is a really jam packed book, I'll tell you. Let's go over just a few of these ideas here. First, study the stratagems and come up with several ways you can use each one in your business.

Now, practice doing **marking off the directives**, the **analogical marking**, all the time, the more you do it, the better you get, the better you get, the better you feel. So **mark more directives** at every meal, or something like that. Literally practice it all the time. I would write out the five commands that are two to four words long each, put them in your pocket and take them with you. Wherever you go, put them on your car seat, okay? And as you're driving down the road, pick up the paper and say, '***Buy now**, Bill, one of the things I'm sure you're beginning to think is how we can **work together with me** to be able to **accomplish the things that you really want most**, and that's what I'm really here to talk to you about.*' There you just used a couple of them.

See **now** pick the next two and do it again. Or the next one and do it and do it and do it. But the more you can **mark these off**, get the **pause**, the strong **down turn**, the **increase in volume**, do all those things. All right

The **command** itself should sound relatively *stern*. The rest of your speaking should sound very light and polite and happy. Okay? That's what you're working to do and after you think you've got it down, write out a couple of sentences and read it to a friend that doesn't know what you're doing and say, '*Hey, give me some feedback about these sentences, I'm curious what you think.*' And if they go, '*Wow, man, what do you sound so funny for?*' then the odds are you're probably doing it wrong. Although if they're a real good friend, they'll be more inclined to think you sound funny than someone who doesn't know you. So don't give that too much weight. But at least, hopefully, they'll go, '*Yeah, it sounds fine. What are you trying to do?*' '*Oh, I'm just practicing something. But it just sounded okay to you, huh?*' '*Yeah. Sounded okay.*' All right. Then go back and keep working, you know you're on it.

Okay, next, write five two to four word commands and insert them into one hundred sentences each for **statements**, **questions** and **quotes**. So in other words, there are three hundred sentences to write.

I'm telling you, if you want to learn this, *that's* what you're going to do.

Not only that, but you're going to *start saying them all the time*. And you're going to push yourself to begin to say them any time you want.

I can literally throw a switch in my unconscious, that's how it feels anyway, and I can begin to use commands powerfully and I can do it all the time. All I have to do is say '**commands**' to myself and away they go. They start pouring out of my mind.

So I am also very clear about what I want with my **intention** so when I turn this over to my unconscious to my **intention**, it already knows what to do. It knows what I'm trying to accomplish and it goes out and gets it for me.

So practice using the different types of commands as I outlined for you in this lesson, you know, things like the **emotions**, commanding using the words '**now**', '**stop**', '**start**', commanding using their **values**, all kinds of things.

Have lots of fun. Celebrate your victory and a victory in this case would be using even *one* command with a client and feeling good that you actually did it.

Now, let me tell you something kind of humorous. I get people occasionally that have had some training somewhere in their past with this and they'll come to me and say, '*Man, Kenrick, you*

know, I'm really doing good. I used an **embedded command** *in my presentation the other day and I said,* **'Buy now'** *and I feel really good about that but I'm not really sure that it's working. You know, how do I tell that it's working?'* Well, it's **not**. Can you tell me **why** it's not based on what I've taught you today? Well, if you said because **there's only one** and therefore the unconscious has yet to **establish it as a pattern**, you'd be right.

So *that's why* we use a lot of **presuppositions**, a lot of **commands**, a lot of **directives** like this is because we want to **establish a pattern** at the level of our client's unconscious mind so that when they hear it, their unconscious sits up and goes, *'whoa, he's talking to me, I'd better listen up and do what I'm told here.'* That's how it does. Remember, it's very literal, it does what it's told. It's young, it's like a very small child and that's who we're appealing to.

Okay, well, that's this book's lesson. I wish you well and boy do we have some exciting stuff for you coming up and I will look forward to going over it with you next book. It's just getting better, isn't it?

You're starting to be able to put it all together, I know you are. Keep at it and we're really into some advanced and fun things now. All right?

Talk with you soon.

BOOK FIFTEEN

THE LANGUAGE OF BELIEFS

INTRODUCTION

Installing Whatever You Want

Welcome to **Book 15** of *Persuasion Force*. In this book we're going to study the **language of beliefs** and how to use this to **install whatever you want**.

Now, I'm going to keep this a little shorter than normal because I really want you to **realize** a couple of important things. First of all, **it's in the doing that you'll become skilled**, not just in the *reading* and in the *imagining*. It's in the **doing**. In particular, with these skills that we've been working on, it's in the **writing**. Now, yes, read this over and over and over again. But I don't care how many times you *read* it, you need to *do* it. Moreover, this is such an *important* lesson. I don't want to combine it with anything else because this just flat—this and the next one, actually, that we'll be studying next book—deserves your full attention.

So I really want you to focus on **doing the work** with this book. And to that end, I'm going to make this *a hard, packed in lesson*, I'm going to give you the **bottom line nuts and bolts** of exactly **how to do it** and lots of *examples* I've never given before, and I'm going to ask that you really knuckle down and *do the writing*. You *must* do the writing on this. I guarantee you if you will, your *results* will blow you away. This is one of the **super high powered strategies** that you're going to learn in this course. It's not all that hard in its simplified version. However, you can make it as bloody hard as you want it to be. You can really **get creative** and you can make this into a **dynamic pattern** that will blow away anyone who's ever even heard of this. They won't even *recognize* your use of it. It will not be some simplistic little thing, it'll be *mind blowing* and the results will just *amaze* you.

CHAPTER ONE

Implied Cause and Effect

So, we'll get into the **language of beliefs** and how to use them to **install whatever you want**. And I'm talking here about the **implied cause and effect** category.

Now, the power of this pattern comes from the fact that **the pattern imitates the way people**

speak when they are telling the "truth" of their belief.

Now, all **beliefs** either **state directly** or **imply** that **something causes or equals something else**. *ALL BELIEFS*. Yes, I mean *all* beliefs. Either *state directly* or *imply* that *something causes or equals something else*. I want you to think it through. In fact, we'll get into it here but think this through for a minute. Think these two statements through. **The power of this pattern comes from the fact that the pattern imitates the way people speak when they're telling the "truth" of their belief. And all beliefs either state directly or imply that something causes or equals something else.** This is important.

I want to give you some *examples* of this kind of language. Here's the first one. '*The early bird gets the worm*.' Now that just sounds like a simple statement. It doesn't sound like anything with **cause and effect**, does it? It's **implied**.

Okay? And *how* **is it implied?** Well, to learn how it's implied, we're going to simply ask '***because***?' So if you were to say to me, '*Kenrick, the early bird gets the worm, you know?*' I'll say, '*Because?*' And you might say, '*Well, because if you're late, someone will have beaten you to whatever you were wanting*.' Duh.

So this is interesting. It *starts off* with a simple statement but it *sounds like* a **belief**. The early bird gets the worm. In other words, I could have easily said, '***I believe** the early bird gets the worm*' or '***It's commonly believed** the early bird gets the worm*.'

Now, when you hear a **belief** and **it doesn't represent both sides**. . . In other words, they *don't* say, '*Well, you know, the early bird gets the worm because if you're late someone will have beaten you to whatever you're wanting so you better be there first to make sure you get it*.' That is a **full expression of the belief**. *Both sides* of the equation. *Both sides* of the **cause and effect** are listed. Okay? The **something that's causing something else**.

Now here's another one for you. '*You have to work hard to get ahead*.'

Now that sounds like a **belief**, doesn't it? It would be easy if I were just to say, '***It's commonly thought** that you have to work hard to get ahead*' or '***most people believe** you have to work hard to get ahead*' or '***you know**, you have to work hard to get ahead*'. This sounds like a **belief**, right? But we're **missing the other side**. In other words, it's a statement of what the person *believes* but *no justification* behind it. Boy that's really good. Wow, I really like that. That just popped right out. **No justification is listed**. So with **belief**, you want the **justification**. I love this. Okay. Now we're talking. So I just learned a new **distinction**, just figured out how to *language it* for you. So in this one, '*you have to work hard to get ahead*' it fits the pattern of a **belief without justification** and we want them to **justify** it. We want to see how they came up with it, so we say. . . remember what I told you to say? One word? '***Because?***' And they say something like, maybe, '*Well, you know, because everyone knows that lazy people are not successful*.'

Who knows what they would have said. There's *lots* of things you could say to that. '*You have to work hard to get ahead because everyone knows that if you don't do anything at all, odds are nothing will have happened and if nothing happens, you won't really be successful*.' '*You have to work hard to get ahead because you have to make things happen somehow and if you're going to do it, you might as well hedge your bets and make them happen by working hard and making as many of them happen as possible*.' Any of those qualify.

In other words, *whatever* they say, *you don't really care*, because all you want is . . . Oop. There's that word again, isn't there? So now *I'm* speaking to you in the language of a **belief**. Because **anything they tell you is fodder for your persuasion cannon**. All right? And down the road, we may get into **how to overcome objections** and this is one of the first steps. When people **object** it's in the form of a **belief**: '*I have to think it over.*' In other words, they could say, '*I believe that it's only prudent for me to think things over before I do anything.*' And of course, **what's missing?** The **justification**. You say, '*Because?*' And they say, '*Well I think it works out better for me. I don't make bad decisions that way. And I'm sure I don't have to cancel things, I'm sure that I have made a good decision this way.*' There's the **justification**. There's the **both sides** of the equation. We're going to talk more about that in our next book, how to get **both sides** and another strategy that *uses* both of these sides.

So you can always ask '*because?*' after any statement of **belief** to uncover the **other half** of the belief and it works like magic. Start using it and watch what happens. You'll <u>naturally</u> find yourself <u>instantly</u> able to outmaneuver someone's **objections** when you <u>start</u> asking the word '**because**'. Yes, that was a bunch of **language patterns** I just threw at you there. I'm glad you recognized them and if you didn't, please review previous lessons and you can really enjoy this one, however, it's also very true. It's just a true statement that I just made.

CHAPTER TWO

Beliefs Are Not Necessarily Provable

Beliefs are funny. *They aren't necessarily true*, yet wars are fought over them. *They aren't necessarily provable*. Let me say that again. **Beliefs are not necessarily provable**. Think about that one just for a moment. Just stop and think about it. Can you tell me *why*? Well, I'll tell you. If a belief were **provable**, it *wouldn't be* a belief, would it? It would be a *truth*. So is there a *difference* between the words *belief* and *truth*? And if so, *what's* the difference in your mind? Let's stop and think about that.

This will really help you in persuasion. **What's the difference between belief and truth?** So for example, I *believe* in God, but I *don't* believe in my couch. I *don't have to* believe in it, I can just go to my living room and sit down in it. Okay? So it's there. The couch is a *truth*.

Now, listen, I'm not trying to tell you God's *not* true. Far from it. I believe he is. I'm just saying to you that it takes **belief** to believe in God because you just can't go sit on his lap like I can go sit on my couch.

Make sense to you? So I'm talking about **the difference between belief and truth**. Now if I'm pushing your buttons a little bit, I'm trying to.

Please allow me the opportunity to teach you by doing this and hang with me because it's really going to make a difference in how you see this and how you are able to understand it.

We are **trained** *not to argue* with other people's beliefs. It is politically incorrect, no matter what they are. Someone says to you, you know, the democratic system of government is superior to anything else.

Well, what if you're in a communist country and you've been trained *that's* superior? But, you know, what we're trained to do is not necessarily argue directly but to say '*Well, it seems to work better in some countries than others.*' We sort of want to **skirt the issue** and get around it, right?

Sometimes we'll argue but, I mean, for the most part, if people say, '*I have a right to be gay*' for example, let's say you hear that, well, yeah. You're absolutely right. And of course, from a humanity perspective, that's true, and who are we to argue and try to change someone's belief? In other words, we're **trained** to simply say, '*Well, of course, everybody should be treated equal as human beings*' regardless of your personal stance on it. You may not like it, you may love it. It doesn't matter. I'm trying to get across to you the idea that **when we speak using the language of beliefs, people are trained not to argue with it**. They're trained to be more *accepting* of it. And they're trained to simply *go along with it*. And that's how this works.

So when we speak using the **language of belief**, others tend to be *more accepting* of what we have to say. It *fits a pattern* that they understand at a very deep level. It does an awful lot, and I'm going to get into some of the things it does so you can evaluate it for yourself but for right now, let's examine some beliefs and this is meant to *stretch* you, not to *offend* you. See? When I deal with **beliefs**, even *I* have to use a disclaimer. This is meant to *stretch* you. Okay? Let's take a belief that God is the supreme being. Think about that for a minute. God is the supreme being. Now let's say you **believe** that. I certainly do.

Whether you do or not doesn't really matter, just think of that **belief** that someone issues. Okay? So we could follow up and say, '***Because?***'

And now we have *lots* of things we could say, '*Well, the bible says so.*'

'*Well, I don't believe in the bible,*' the person goes. You go, '*Well, it's just simply convenient to believe that. It's convenient, it keeps us in check, it makes us humble.*' And whatever your answer is, or whether you don't believe it, the fact is, when someone says it, you're trained *not to really argue with them*, correct? Correct. I mean, now maybe you're very jaded. Let's say you **really** don't believe that and you've been hearing it your whole life and you're **tired** of hearing it. Well, you may start fighting with people just to say you did, but let's say that a good *friend* of yours says, '*God is the supreme being*'. Well, if you want to *keep* that friend, you probably won't really jump in and start arguing with them.

What is one of the **reasons** that you wouldn't? Well, **it's because they speak with** *conviction* **when they speak their own beliefs.** So what we know is, we're at a *heightened state of awareness* when we are speaking our **beliefs** because they're *our* **truths.** Okay?

Next, '*Sin causes death.*' And if you're a Christian, you know this one real well. And is it *true*? Well, you know, I don't know. I mean, let's put it this way, it requires *faith* to really accept that as a **belief** because **we can't totally prove it**, it would depend on the *definition* of the word '*sin*' also the *definition* of the word '*death*'. Is it eternal death? Is it death of an idea? What is it? So all these things, when you hear them, you **intrinsically** know that **this is a belief and shouldn't really be argued wit**h.

How about, *'It's important to respect your parents?'* Well, what if someone asked the word, *'**Because?**'* And you say, *'Because it's the start of the rule of law. It's where we learn the rule of law in our world, by answering first to our parents, we learn later to answer to authority and to the extent that we have a good relationship with authority and with our parents we'll probably tend to have a better, easier life.'*

That *doesn't* mean *submission* to authority always, it means that we need to have a *good relationship* with it. For example, my dad and I can *disagree* now that I'm an adult, but I'm still very *respectful* of him. But we can *agree to disagree* and have an intelligent discourse and conversation, in which both of us come away more enlightened about the other's perspective. So again, it is a **belief** and the beliefs pack a whale of a punch when you start talking and saying them.

CHAPTER THREE

Increasing Our Use of Belief Patterns

Our goal then is to increase the amount that we use belief patterns when we speak and write. This gives us more credibility and portrays us as a person of conviction and it also lessens the amount we are disagreed with. Most importantly, using this pattern activates a sense of acceptance in the person hearing it. It subtly shifts the frame of things your way. Why does it activate a sense of acceptance? Well, because they see you as a person who is convinced about things, that you're speaking your truth, your beliefs, what you have faith in, and the minute you start doing that, you are more congruent. So this increases your congruency level, it therefore increases your level of believability. If you're more believable, are you more persuasive? The answer to those is yes.

It also allows you to use a way of speaking that **gives you the ability to install things you want the other person to accept as true and believe in**. And the real power here—and this is a big one—is in **combining numerous instances of this structure along with the other patterns you've been learning** and that's where we're going to go to as we proceed. All right? So I hope this has given you a real understanding of the power of **belief** and why it's so important and what it will actually do for you and why it **increases the perception that people need to go along with you**.

CHAPTER FOUR

Implied Cause and Effect

Implied cause and effect is the pattern. This is a *giant* of a pattern. This is a *powerhouse*. It's so *powerful* that we're literally taking it on its own. It is just that powerful. And **this pattern implies, not states directly, but implies that two things are linked together**. The basic pattern for you to learn is: *'As X happens, Y naturally follows.'* And we can break it down further by saying, *'As X* which X is a **pace** *'happens, Y* which is **what you want them to believe** *'naturally follows'*. So again, we're doing the **verbal pacing and leading** here in a very simple, easy way, and we're using **pacing and leading** to add yet still more to this structure.

So let's go over some examples together. And I want you to really *stay alert* here. This kind of pattern is a bit on the *trance-y* side. It'll *zone you out* much like listening to a song with a very steady beat or some such thing, so stay alert and really get this consciously. Okay? In fact, it would just be so helpful if you'd re-read this five or six times over the next week.

So, here are some examples for you. '*As you learn this pattern and start using it, you will have a certain sense of accomplishment.*' Next one. '*As you start to assimilate this information, you will instantly begin to find ways to use it.*' Next one. '*As the realization begins to sink in of how easily, rapidly and efficiently your profits will go up as a result of using my help, you'll naturally get more and more excited.*' By the way, notice the **repetition by three**, etc. etc. as you read these sentences.

Okay. Now. Each of those followed the format of '*As X happens, Y naturally follows.*' What I want to do now is to pull each one of these apart a bit and show you **how** it does that. And let's simplify. So what I've done is I've **obfuscated** what I'm *really* trying to do here by using rather sophisticated languaging. Let's simplify. Let's take the first one. '*As you learn this pattern and start using it, you will have a certain sense of accomplishment.*' So what is this really saying? This says that using a pattern makes you have a sense of accomplishment. So using a pattern makes you have a sense of accomplishment. That's what I'm saying. Pretty simple, but it **implies** it by starting off with '*as*'. '*As X, Y.*'

Let's go to the next one. '*As you start to assimilate this information you will instantly begin to find ways to use it.*' Okay? What is this saying? Assimilating information will allow you to use it, or find you ways to use it. The **implication** is, *you're going to use it*. And yet it sounds kind of nice, doesn't it? '*As you start to assimilate this information you will instantly begin to find ways to use it.*' So words like '*instantly*' and '*begin*' **obfuscate**, you know, **hide**, **conceal** if you will, the *actual* thing I'm trying to accomplish here.

All right, let's go to the third one. '*As the realization begins to sink in of how easily, rapidly and efficiently your profits will go up as a result of using my help, you'll naturally get more and more excited.*' Now this is a bit of a **reverse**. So let me just do it the way it's written. *Realizing how I can help you, gets you excited.* That's basically what's being said. I just added a whole bunch of other stuff in there to sort of **distract your attention** away from the *real* **cause and effect** that's going on and I **implied** it and then I added a bunch of stuff to **conceal** what I'm doing and that's a heck of a powerful sentence and pattern. Okay? So they all follow that format.

What I want you to do is to pause reading right now and I want you to *write three of your own* and the way I want you to do it is to be very careful. It's really better if you stop reading now and just follow my suggestions, okay? So I'm going to give you the suggestions and then I'm going to ask you to stop and then continue on with me. I'm only going to have you write a token number of three sentences so that you can get the idea but here's how I want you to do it. I want you to take each of *my* example sentences, and I want you to *follow my strategy*. So model what I'm doing.

Follow my strategy. Use my exact wording. Just alter it to fit your particular circumstances. Okay?

But I want you to *actually write out three sentences* that are just like mine that follow my strategy.

All right? And in so doing, you're going to get to figuring out real quick, real easy, actually, **how to make this work**. It's going to make it real easy for you. So please stop reading now and do that work real quick.

CHAPTER FIVE

Combining With Other Patterns

Okay, did you do it? I hope so. Let's *combine* these now with other patterns that you've been learning already to really increase their power. Now this is the beauty of these patterns. Now is when your study is going to start *paying off*. Now is when you're going to start seeing some *really significant results* because now I'm going to have you start *combining* everything. You've been combining as we've been going, but now we're really into full tilt, full tilt boogie, I guess I should say, on combining things. So let's start with an **implied cause and effect** with **adverb/adjective pattern** thrown in. So there are three examples, let's go through them together.

'**Naturally**, *as you begin to realize just how effective these strategies are, you'll find yourself doing what it takes to move forward.*' Now let's pull that apart. What am I really saying here? *As you understand how effective the strategies are, you'll just begin doing what it takes to move forward.* What does move forward **imply**? Well, *with me*. With *this product*, with *this service*, with *whatever you're selling*. Do you see how that works? So I'm being **artfully vague** and I'm **obfuscating** hiding, concealing, a whole lot of things here, but you get the gist.

All right, I also threw in the **adverb/adjective** to begin with: '*naturally*'. So if they buy into '*naturally*' they simply **go along** with the entire rest of the sentence. The rest of the sentence deals with things from the perspective of **applied cause and effect** so it further **obfuscates** what's really going on in their head, it further hides it. In other words, you're speaking now with such *congruity* and *power* and *ability* that it's just sliding this stuff into their head and there's very little to argue with or fight with unless they're highly trained like you're becoming now.

All right, let's go to the second one. '**As** you **easily** *absorb the deeper meaning of what I'm saying, the reasons become* **clear** *why people choose us to help with issues like this.*' Wow. What is this saying?

Well, first let's look at the **awareness presuppositions**. '*Easily*' is the **presupposition** there that I wanted to point out to you. Well, what is this sentence saying? It's simply saying that *as you understand the deeper meaning*, as opposed to *what*? The shallower meaning? The surface structure meaning? So this is really **sending the unconscious on a search** to figure out *what's* deeper than what I'm saying. That's a big, big **obfuscation** or a hiding mechanism there.

So *as you absorb the deeper meaning. . .* In other words, when you understand and internalize the deeper meaning of what I'm saying, *you'll choose us to help with issues like this*. But I said to choose us by way of putting it into almost like a **quote pattern**. All right? The reasons become clear *why people choose us. . .*So notice here also I'm using a **visual predicate**, '*the reasons becoming* **clear**' as if they *weren't* **clear** before. So in other words, I'm **presupposing** that currently, or before I began talking, you did *not* have reasons that were clear that would help you to choose us, but *now* that you're easily absorbing an even deeper meaning than what I'm saying, you all of the sudden *have* clear reasons why you should choose us, which I'm **commanding**—*choose us*—to help with issues exactly like you've come to me to help you with.

I mean, this is really, really powerful. Let's go to the third one. '*As you **listen** to the thoughts inside your mind, you'll **naturally** begin to **hear** them steer you towards working with us for all the obvious reasons.*'

Now, let's pull this apart. The **adverb/adjective presupposition** is '*naturally*'—'*you'll **naturally** begin*'. Okay? That's it. But let's pull this apart because there is **obfuscation** going on all over the place.

'*As you listen to the thoughts inside your mind...*' Now, let's first of all just do it the way it should have been written. '*As you listen to the thoughts inside your mind...*' Well, so the first big tactic I'm using right up front is I'm starting with an **implied cause and effect** '*as*' and the next thing I'm doing is, I'm doing a huge **shift** from the *external* environment to the *internal*. This is the equivalent of **altering someone's consciousness**. That's why I told you, stay present, stay conscious, really listen here. This is powerful stuff.

So I immediately and powerfully **shifted** them *internally*. All right? Because they were seeking out the word, the meaning of the words. . .when I said, '*your mind*'. Now on the one hand they're going to hear and think you said, '*your mind*' M-I-N-D. But I would really say, '*You're mine*' M-I-N-E. So what's the thing that's happening there? I'm **commanding** '*you're mine*'. In other words, I *own* you. I own your mind.

It's kind of funny but it can make a subtle **shift** power play almost in which they begin realizing that the net result is already foregone. It's a **foregone conclusion** that they're going to do what you want. That's the **shift** that it makes. All of that in the first nine words of that sentence. Okay? Before the first comma, we've got all this going for us.

Next, '*you'll **naturally** begin to **hear** them steer you towards*' ... So now these thoughts are *not under your own control*. You'll *naturally* begin to *hear* them as if you're only a participant, you're not the actor thinking them. So here you are listening to thoughts you're not controlling. *Why?* Because *I* am. *I'm* controlling them. And what are these thoughts? What's the purpose of these thoughts? Well, they are to *steer you towards working with us* and for what reason? Well, *all the obvious reasons*. In other words, **presupposing** that there are many that are very obvious to everybody including you. Do you hear, see and experience the huge amount of **obfuscation** that I've packed into that sentence? I mean, that could be a study in and of itself, that one sentence, in massively powerful persuasion.

So . . . And I'm also introducing to you now another type of a **command** which is a very powerful **ambiguity** in which **you say one thing, they think they hear another and you just look at them as if nothing is weird or wrong** and you look at them and say, '*As you listen to the thoughts inside **your mine**, you'll naturally. . .* ' They'll just think you slurred '*mind*', like you have an impediment or something and so as a result, they're going to just go right on . . . I mean at that point, you're **obfuscating** things so powerfully anyway that they won't be able to be stuck on that and even remember that you said it.

256

Let's go to the **implied cause and effect** of that one. What is this saying? This is saying, *as you become aware of your own thoughts, these thoughts will steer you towards working with us.* In other words, *your thoughts cause you to work with us. Your own thoughts cause you to work with us.* So there's **another level** here in which I'm telling them, in essence, it's *not me* that's persuading you, it's *your own thoughts* that are persuading you. And again, how much resistance do people have to their own thoughts? Basically none. If I'm telling you that *it's your own thoughts* that are causing you to do what it is, to work with us, but I'm **implying** the sale. I'm not stating the sale in so many words.

This is really worthy of a significant amount of effort on your part to really *learn* and *understand* what I'm doing here. I've pulled it apart for you word for word. Now re-read it ten times. And the very next thing I want you to do now is to stop reading and follow my examples there and *write three of your own*, just a token three, I'm not asking you to do a lot right this minute, just *write three* and **follow my exact strategies**. Just change the content enough. That last one, of course, you could lift directly. But I'd rather you change it slightly so that it becomes more meaningful to you and write it out. So stop and do that now and then continue as soon as you've finished.

CHAPTER SIX

Implied Cause and Effect With the Temporal Pattern

So let's move on now to implied cause and effect with the temporal pattern. Here's the first example, '*And while we talk, another part of you will be putting two and two together, coming up with the same conclusion on your own I'll be going over with you after which you'll understand why you are feeling so good about this.*'

Okay. **Obfuscation** coming up the yin yang here. All right? This is one big pattern of **obfuscation** where **I'm saying one thing and I'm doing another**, exactly like hiding in the open.

So let's first look at the **temporal pattern**. Starts with '*while*'. '*While*' made it **temporal**. That means it's **an ongoing sense of time**. And the **implied cause and effect** is because we started with the word '*and*': and XY. **And, as, while, during, since.** . . All these engage the **implied cause and effect** pattern. Okay? And second of all, now what does it mean? Well, first of all, let's just look at the **implied cause and effect**. *Talking to me* **makes you come up with my conclusion yourself** *and that makes you feel good and even understand why you feel good.*

So notice that there's really *two* **causes and effects** in this sentence. The first is that *while we talk you'll come up with the same conclusion on your own and that will allow you to understand.* So *coming to the conclusion will help you understand and understanding will cause you to feel good.* So there's all those **causes and effects** in there. The next thing is, let's look at what's really being said now. . . or at another strategy.

Another strategy, and this is really trance-y stuff, is that we did a **parts** thing in which **I separated you into a number of parts**. I said, '*And while* **we** *talk,* **another part of you** *will be putting two and two together.*' Not *you*, but *another part of you*. Wow. Which part? I don't know. But you did it. As will everybody when you use this kind of pattern. Nobody will object to it and go, '*Wait a* *minute, I don't have any parts. I'm just me. I'm just one guy. I'm just one person.'* They won't do that. They'll go, *'Oh, okay.'* And it adds **a sense of urgency** or **deeper meaning** to this, like, *'Oh, another part of me. Wow!'* And people just go along with it like as if you're making sense.

This is, again, an extremely power packed and advanced pattern.

Let's go to the next example: '**While** we talk, **another part of you** will **naturally** begin putting the big picture together in such a way to help you understand at a deep level why this fits so well.' Note that starting with the word 'while' makes this both an **implied cause and effect** as well as a **temporal pattern**, doesn't it? Isn't that interesting? So we really knocked two birds out with one stone there.

And what else are we doing? Well, again we're **splitting into parts**. We're also talking about putting the big picture together meaning. . . what's the big picture? Well, it's *what will control the details* and so we're asking them to see the big picture of them going along with us, in essence, and we're asking them to do that not just by going along, but at a deep level. Well, where's the deep level? *They* have to go and figure all this out. Talk about **obfuscating** again. Okay? So a deep level that does what? Helps them understand why this fits so well. Why what fits so well? What I'm selling them. What you're there to do. It's all **implied. Implied, implied, implied. Presupposed, presupposed, presupposed.** You get it? Do you understand that?

Let's go to the third one: '*The second aspect to* **understanding** *why this is the way to go will make more sense* **as you** **start** *to internalize how this works.*'

This one is really **complex** in a sense. I **reversed** the **implied cause and effect** strategy to be like this: **temporal**, first, then *why* **lead** as naturally occurring event happens. See? The second. . . And I also did **temporal** the *second* aspect. Well, what was the *first*? *They don't know.* To understanding. . . Oops, is *understanding* an **awareness presupposition**? I believe it is. So the second aspect to understanding why this is the way to go. . . In other words, it's **assumed** this is the way to go, right?, will make more sense, in other words, it isn't making sense yet, but it's about to, as you start to internalize how this works.

In other words, the reason it wasn't making sense is it wasn't internalized, but now that you've internalized it, well, duh, it makes sense.

This is *massively* **obfuscating** and **presupposing** at level after level after level. So what I want you to do is stop right now, stop reading and *write three sentences exactly like I'm doing*. If for any reason you're confused about this, and I suspect you will be until you really work at it some. Now you can see why I just wanted to really *zero in* and *focus* on this pattern. But what I want you to do if that's the case is just write the exact sentences that I wrote, that I gave you, just write those.

Write each one of them even five or ten times until you start to *get it*, until you start ingraining this into your neurology. This is how it works. Okay? And then modify my sentences slightly by rewriting them, changing a few elements of them until you can actually write them on your own.

This is really, really strong.

Now, when you're done with that, continue on, but stop reading now so that you can do it.

CHAPTER SEVEN

Implied Cause and Effect With the Awareness Pattern

And let's go to **applied cause and effect with the awareness pattern**. '*As you start to become aware of the added benefits we haven't even spoken of yet, you'll discover even deeper reasons to support you in feeling good with going forward.*'

So in this sentence '*awareness of benefits*' causes going forward, which is pretty darn powerful. I mean, it's exactly what you want, right? They become aware of the benefits, boom, they move forward. What a great **cause and effect** statement again. But I'm **obfuscating** with words like '*start*' which is also a **temporal presupposition**, '*aware*' which is the **awareness presupposition**, '*added benefits*' in other words, more than we've even spoken of or will speak of, probably, benefits that we haven't spoken of yet? Wow. In other words, **presupposing** we're going to speak of some but in the meantime, you're still going to *imagine* some, and **become aware** of them. And those imagined reasons will allow you to **discover** even more and deeper reasons to support you in feeling good.

Of course, *doing what?* Going forward. *Means what?* To buy, to purchase, to hire me, whatever it is you are wanting them to do.

See how this works? Let's go to the second sentence. '*As you **understand** the process, you might **consider** this understanding in **light** of how it will help you in your situation.*'

So understanding the process causes you to apply it to yourself. The **implication** is that this is why you'll *do* it too. You'll actually *work* with me too with the process. Very much **presupposition** within **presupposition**.

'*You can, Bob, **be convinced, as** you **naturally internalize** what we're talking about.*' Okay? This is another interesting use of the pattern.

First, a **command** then the pattern is **reversed** as you **internalize**, you're **convinced**. Well, it's kind of reversed and not depending on how you want to look at it, but bottom line, the explanation is less important than the effect and as you read that to yourself out loud, and just quietly a few times now, you'll feel that effect.

In other words, **you're commanding him to be convinced**. You're *telling* him to **naturally internalize** something, as opposed to what? I guess. So you're going to be convinced about what we're talking about as they naturally internalize what we're talking about. I mean, this is just **leverage** upon **leverage** upon **leverage**. Really profound.

All right, you want to again follow my examples in this and *write three of your own*. Also, note the **commands** I'm using as well and do the same in your sentences. You can use *any* **commands** you want or you can use the one I'm using, whatever you want to do, but make sure you're starting to put **commands** in there as well, from Book Fourteen's material. So go ahead and again stop reading and *write the three sentences* that you need to do. And if you're doing this, you're doing this session exactly like I *meant* you to do it if you're stopping and doing the writing. You're going to see how one adds upon the next and the next and the next to build an enormously powerful session here for you.

So go ahead and do that now and come on back.

CHAPTER EIGHT

Homeplay

Now, let us get to the homeplay for this book. I want you to write fifty simple **implied cause and effect** sentences this month. Fifty simple **implied cause and effect** sentences. That would be '*as X, Y*'. So '*As you listen to what I'm saying, understanding ensues.*' '*As you understand what I'm telling you, you feel compelled to buy or you sign the contract*', whatever it is. Okay?

Next, I want you to write ten sentences for each **presupposition** category we've studied *combining* them with **implied cause and effect**.

Go through each of the ones that you've studied and *combine* them with **implied cause and effect**. Put **commands** in everywhere you can. You should really be **using** this material now in your day to day life. And each time you're victorious or you even have a small success, I want you to really **celebrate** it because it does so much, it teaches your unconscious mind that you want *more* just like this and that's really powerful. It does so much more than that even but at least celebrate your victories.

We're really getting into the good stuff here, folks and I'm so excited to be presenting it to you. The next book will be absolutely as powerful and I'll have more really advanced material for you and we're starting to get into some really hardcore stuff that's going to just make you just light years ahead of the rest of the world anywhere. I mean, nobody can teach you how to do material like this. You're getting it right here from the source and I'm telling you, this will really change your life if you begin implementing it.

Make sure you do it *frequently*. In other words, don't just do one pattern. You've got to do a bunch in your talking, but don't use so many that people think you're just sounding altogether stilted and strange.

That brings us to the end of this book. So you've got lots to do between now and the next one so get busy and really hold yourself to doing this, really hold your feet to the fire and make sure you're actually following through with the homework because doing so is going to **internalize** this really, really quick for you.

All right, until next time, have a great one. Persuade lots. Bye bye.

BOOK SIXTEEN

CAUSE AND EFFECT

INTRODUCTION

Installing Whatever You Want, Continued...

Welcome to **Book Sixteen** of *Persuasion Force*.

Here we move into the **language of beliefs** and how to use this to **install whatever you want**, *continued*. And in this book, we're going to move into the second strategy for doing this. In the last book, we studied **implied cause and effect**. This time we study **cause and effect**.

And this is really some pretty cool stuff. When we think about the *power* of **cause and effect**, you will recall in Book Fifteen we talked about what it does based on **belief**, that it really **impacts a person's belief** and that's why this has such power. So *this* pattern along with the **implied cause and effect** pattern is powerful because **it imitates the way people speak when they're telling the truth of their beliefs**. Again, this is really **speaking in the language of beliefs**.

So when you start **speaking in beliefs**, you cause people's brains to kind of shut off and go to sleep – not shut off in a negative way, you cause it to shut off in a way that causes them to defend against you – they just sort of **open up and let it pour in**. Now, **all beliefs either state directly or imply that something causes or equals something else**. So in this book we'll study how to do it using a *variation* of the pattern you learned last time. In order to increase your power even more, you can *interchange* these at will, you can *interchange* **cause and effect** and **implied cause and effect**.

CHAPTER ONE

Some Examples

So let's look at some examples of this and actually if you'll note too, that the strategy is '**X causes Y.**' X is a **pace**. Y is a **lead**. So X should be **something that's true**, and Y should be **something that you want them to believe**. All right? So given that, let's look at the examples.

'Sitting there causes you to completely absorb what I'm saying and as you completely absorb it, it will cause you to immediately accept it at the deepest levels.' So there we have really *two*

examples of it. Also, 'and as' starts off looking like an **implied cause and effect** but sort of **shifts** when I go, 'it **will** cause you to'. There's not much *implied* there. It states it quite *directly*.

All right, the next one, '*Thinking your next thought causes you to agree with me that you need to really master this material.*' Now that's pretty slick because how can you *not* think your next thought? Do you notice that **I look for things that I can *force* to be true**, that there's no real way to defend against being true so that if *that* part is true, well then, gee, the *other* part must be too? Or, for example, someone says something and I say, '*And simply saying that excuse causes you to understand why you already don't believe it.*' I love that, that's a real mind scramble.

CHAPTER TWO

Taking Back Control

Now remember in Book Fifteen I taught that you can ask '**because?**' after any **statement of belief** to uncover the *other half* of the belief. Consider now that should you ever *hear* a statement like you're learning to use here, like any of the examples I just did, you can ask the word '**because?**' to **give you back control**. So if someone says to you, '*Sitting there causes you to completely absorb what I'm saying. And as you completely absorb it, it will cause you to immediately accept it at the deepest levels.*' And you go, '**Because?**' And they go, '*Well, . . . uh. . .*' and you go, '*Right. Okay. Moving on.*'

So someone who has *minimal* training in this, someone *unlike* yourself who is getting quite a bit of it, would be flustered with that kind of a statement and you will have sort of **caught them red handed** trying to do what they're doing. If they're slick and they go around and say, '*Well, because it's obvious. You know?*' You'll go, '*Really? Okay. Because it's not making sense to me yet.*' And they'll go, '*Well. . .*' And pretty soon they'll just sort of go away or go on to something else, but you'll really cause them grief if they're trying to use this to persuade you.

So therefore, **what do you need to know?** Well, you need to know that when you use this, if the person has been *trained* in this, which the odds are what? One in a million? Okay? But if they have, then you want to be able to have a '**because**' and remember, since *any* X can cause *any* Y, then the statement that was just made is the X, their **because** is the **causal link**, and your Y is *anything you want it to be*.

So let me give you an example. Let's go back to the first one. You say to a person, '*Sitting there causes you to completely absorb what I'm saying and as you completely absorb it, it will cause you to immediately accept it at the deepest levels.*' And the other person goes, '*Yeah? Because?*' And you go, '*Well, because I just said it, right?*' And they go, '*Well, I'm not sure if I really get it. You're saying that because?*' And you might say, '*Well, because this is what you want to hear. It's the way that the mind works, right?*' And about that point, jump in again, '*And, listening to me now helps you to understand what it is that you're missing to make sense of this a lot more effectively. So let's move on, shall we?*' And that's the way you can really get this to work effectively.

So that's a powerful use of the word '**because**'. You can use it to **interrupt other people** or you can use it to **get them to actually give you more of what they're trying to accomplish** or you can use it on somebody to **break up their pattern of persuasion** and if *they* do it to *you*, I've just shown you **how to get around it** as well. We're kind of playing chess with ourselves but it's a powerful way to integrate this material. Like I said last time, this stuff works like magic. Start using it, watch what happens. You're going to be blown away impressed.

CHAPTER THREE

Cause and Effect Words

All right, now, let's look at some **cause and effect words** to choose from. This is a larger list that you can use in formulating your suggestions. It's only a sample listing. You can easily generate a much larger list if you want to, but this will work pretty well for most anything you want to do.

And here are the words: *kindles, invokes, justifies, forces, brings to pass, makes, verifies, allows, constitutes, creates, generates, stimulates, derives, settles, determines.*

So simple **X causes Y**. Making a statement like that is *derived from* your need to be right. Listening to me *generates* even more reasons to project yourself into the future and *create* vivid images of what I'm suggesting. Thinking that next thought *stimulates* you at a very deep level to just sigh a sigh of relief; you've finally found the answers you've been looking for.

X causes Y. *Any* X causes *any* Y. It's just that simple.

And before we go even one bit further, I'd like you to *write three cause and effect sentences of your own* following my examples. And this is going to help cement this in your mind so please stop reading, take a few minutes and just go back and look at my examples and write three of your own. You can pattern them right after mine so that it makes all kinds of sense for you and it's real easy to do, but get this going by *combining* reading and writing and action all at the same time so that you're really **indelibly etching this into your brain**. Do it now and I'll meet you back here in just a minute.

CHAPTER FOUR

Combining Patterns

All right, now, let's **combine these with other patterns to increase the power**. Now, here is where this stuff gets powerful. We did it in the last book on that pattern and we've done it before. Now we're going to do it with this pattern. This work that you're going to do right now is where you're really going to progress and I mean, *really* going to progress. Okay? So please take the time to do it.

Cause and effect with the **adverb/adjective** pattern. Let me give you some examples. '*Learning this material **permits** you much greater access to the unconscious mind of your prospect which* *easily enables* your confidence to build.' Can you detect the pattern? What's the **cause and effect** word? Well, there are *several* but '*learning this material*' is X, **permits**, which is the **causal word**, '*greater access to the unconscious mind of your prospect*'. . . so learning this material permits greater access to the unconscious. That's the **X causes Y**, '*which easily enables. . .*' so '*which*' is another **causal linking** thing, '*enables*'. . . so all of what was just said before '*enables confidence to build*'. So see, I did **one upon the other**. Okay? As well as '*easily*' which is the **adverb/adjective** word thrown in there. See how it works?

Let's go to the next example, '*Reading the books **repeatedly enables** you to generate significantly better sentences **which obviously enables** you to gain even more from this program.*' Let's pull that apart. '*Reading*' X. So '*reading the books repeatedly*', that's the X, '*enables*', there's the **causal word**, '*you to generate significantly better sentences*', so there's the Y. **X causes Y**. Reading enables better sentences. '***Which obviously***' and *obviously* therein is the **adverb/adjective** word, '*enables*' another **cause and effect**, '*you to gain even more from this program.*'

These are powerful sentences. I'm going a little more advanced on you here. Okay? It's probably not quite as obvious to you when you read them. They scan a little *smoother*. I'm **increasing the gradient** each book as we go. I'm expecting that you're really keeping up and I'm telling you, even if all you can do is just read, if that's *all* you did, preferably repeatedly, you're going to get it. But I really want you to *write*. So right now, follow my example, I want you to **increase the gradient** a bit, just like I did, and write three of your own **cause and effect** with the **adverb/adjective** pattern put in. Go ahead and do that now and then join me back here.

Okay, and let's move on. **Cause and effect** pattern with the **temporal** pattern thrown in. So here we go, '***Before*** you **conclude on the inside** that everything you're hearing **causes** greater integration of this material, you might **imagine a way in which you can use these patterns successfully** even if for only a fraction of a second.' That's pretty hot. What are we doing here? Let's look at this. '***Before***', is that the **temporal** word? Yup. '. .. *You conclude on the inside*', that's a **suggestion**, '*that everything you're hearing* **causes**', so in other words everything you're hearing **causes** greater integration of the material. **X causes Y**. So there is the **temporal** followed by a **suggestion** as to where that's to happen (on the inside), you might imagine a way in which you can use these patterns successfully.

Okay, so I'm giving them another **suggestion** '*imagine a way in which you can use these patterns successfully even if for only a fraction of a second*'. Now remember, the only way to **make sense** of what I'm saying is to **do** what I'm saying. Right? So how do you make sense of me suggesting you imagine on the inside a way in which you can use the patterns successfully? And how do you do that for even only a fraction of a second. In other words, you'll quickly see it. Now if you see it, that these patterns are helping you, then are you concluding on the inside that what you're hearing gives you greater integration? See how that **suggestion** then sinks in?

This is pretty sophisticated language. Okay? We're getting up there now. All right, here's another one. '***Some people*** imagine that they've heard what I'm saying **repeatedly** only today in a way that makes complete sense which **naturally causes** them to feel fantastic. **Before** you remember what you imagined, take a moment to sigh a deep sigh of relief that finally what you've been searching for is at hand.'

Now this one is *really* complex. I really loaded this thing up. Okay?

'*Some people imagine. . .*' so who's some people? You. The person you're talking to. '. . . *Imagine that they've heard what I'm saying repeatedly. . .*' by the way, what's the rule that makes it so that '*some people*' means them? It's because **everybody will apply it to themselves** as they hear it. So when you say '*some people, Mary*' then Mary's going to apply it to *her*. If Mary's the one listening, or if there's a room full of people listening, they're *all* applying it to *them*. That's the beauty of that kind of pattern.

'*Some people imagine that they've heard what I'm saying repeatedly. . .*' So what are you suggesting that they do? Imagine that they've heard you repeatedly. Now why would we do something like that? Well, we're going to get into those kind of patterns right away, but for example, that is the pattern called the **convincer** pattern and I'm going to lay it out for you step by step, but one of the things that happens is people have **a length of time** or **a number of times** that they will need to do something in order to be **convinced** about it and so when you have people start *repeatedly imagining* that they've heard what you're saying over and over, it's going to start firing that kind of thing off. So you're saying, '*some people*', meaning them, '*imagine they've heard what you're saying repeatedly, only today, in a way that makes complete sense.*' In other words, they've heard it before and it didn't quite settle in, but **now** it all of the sudden makes complete sense. '*Which naturally causes them to feel fantastic.*' **Naturally** is what? **Adverb/adjective**. '*Causes*' is the **causal** word, the Y—'*Feel fantastic.*' Then we follow up with a **temporal** pattern. '***Before** you remember what you imagined*' so you're asking them to remember an imaginary thing. Okay? Or what they just imagined seconds before. '***Before** you remember what you imagined, take a deep sigh*' (sigh) and you **want** to do it, just like that, okay? Because that way *they* are going to do it *with* you. It's like if you do it with full on conviction, you know, if you're being **congruent**, it's like yawning. Everybody wants to do it with you. So if you do it in that same way, deep sigh of relief, '*that finally, what you've been searching for is at hand.*' So what are we really saying? Let's kind of paraphrase this. You're asking them to imagine that they've heard you repeatedly, as if you are familiar to them, but now to hear you in a way that makes sense finally. Okay? And it doesn't just make sense in a vacuum, it makes sense in a way that makes them feel fantastic. We're talking about **suggestions** that are very difficult to defend against because it's very hard to understand and pull it apart. And then you're saying, '*And before you go back and remember what you imagined milliseconds before, a few words before*', which they had never done anyway, so you told them to imagine hearing you before, they may never have, and now you're telling them to *remember* remembering you. '*Take a deep sigh. . .*' so you're **leading** them again into a particular behavior, '*that finally what you're searching for is at hand*'. Well tell me, if your prospect believes that what they're searching for is at hand and you're the one that's there talking, would they be inclined to buy from you? I've really stepped up the gradient on these. If you want to emulate them, just use my words and put in some of your content. You can even use these sentences directly if you'd like until you get the hang of it. But this is a very sharp increase in gradient. I'm telling you right now, this whole book will have been of tremendous value to you if you can just step up the gradient by patterning after what I'm doing right here. This is hot, hot stuff. I get excited teaching you this. I mean, I could never have taught this to you back fifteen books ago, you simply *wouldn't have even heard me* and I'm finally getting to the point where I can start kind of pulling out the stops and giving you some really heavy duty things. But to do so, what I need you to do is to really go through and **write the patterns** so that you're getting it.

So right now I want you to *write at least two sentences*. If you can, pattern them after mine. And if you want to, just write the exact two sentences I did so you can begin to implant in your neurology how this works. And I want you to read my explanation of that over and over again. It is very complex. I assume that it's confusing to an awful lot of people reading it. Okay? We've really stepped up the gradient. That's powerful material. Just write it in your own hand.

Type it. In fact, you know what you really should do? Type my exact words twenty-five times. That would *really* help you to ingrain this. You'd start to get it. Say it 100 times out loud. Say it twenty-five times a day for the next ten days. But get this into your neurology and then begin to *adjust* it and *modify* it and *add your content*.

Slick, slick, slick patterns. Stuff I have never written anywhere else like this. So you're getting a real treat here.

Okay, once you've written those patterns at least a couple of times, rejoin me. So stop reading now so you can do that.

CHAPTER FIVE

Cause and Effect With the Awareness Pattern

'**Starting** to **become aware** of the added benefits we haven't even spoken of yet, **enables** you to **discover** even deeper reasons to support yourself in feeling good with going forward.' Now, if you want, take a quick break and go open up Book Fifteen and compare the sentence I just did with Book Fifteen's **implied cause and effect** with the **awareness** pattern and you're going to see that it's similar and I want you to *contrast* the two. Okay? At this level, you actually have to do a little bit of work to really build your competence. So do that and *contrast the two sentences*, okay? See a lot of similarity. You're just going to see a slight *adjustment of the tenses* and a *shift* to the *full on* **cause and effect** instead of the *implied* **cause and effect**.

Now let's evaluate it. '**Starting** to **become aware**' so in other words, what does that do? It *limits* the amount of **awareness**. In other words, it's saying that it's *just beginning*, it's only to start. It's not to complete. It's to enter into a process, to start it. To do what? *To become aware.* ... so there's the **awareness** pattern right off the bat, '*of the added benefits*'. . . what added benefits? We haven't even spoken of them yet. Well, *how* are they going to start to become aware of added benefits if we haven't even spoken of them yet? Well, they're going to do it by **imagining** them. Their **mind** is going to **create** them. This is the power of persuasion. Okay? This is where we get their mind to become our friend and do what we're telling it to do. This is where they imagine what we suggest and they're persuaded. This is full on influence and persuasion skills. All right?

So '*these benefits we haven't even spoken of yet. . .*' so in other words, '*starting this* **enables** *you*', so there's the **cause and effect** word, '**enables**'. . . '**enables** *you to discover even* **deeper** *reasons to support yourself.*' Now, '*even deeper reasons*' **presupposes** they've *already* found some reasons. Okay? '*Deeper*' is a **spatial presupposition** as well. '*To support yourself*', how do you support yourself? Don't you just love that term? Actually, I can't stand it when psychologists or psychiatrists say that. But in any event, isn't that just hysterical? '*To support yourself in feeling good with going forward*'. What in the heck are we telling them to do? Well, we're telling them to begin a process of what? Of '**becoming aware** *of added benefits*'. Well, what kind of benefits? We haven't even spoken of them yet, so you go ahead and **imagine** whatever ones you want. So they're now imagining benefits, not consciously necessarily, but they'll be flashing in their mind nonetheless, and starting this process '*enables*', there's the **cause and effect** so we're speaking in the **language of beliefs**, '*you to discover even deeper reasons,*' as if they've found any so far, but now we're **assuming** they are and they will, okay, '*deeper reasons to support yourself*'. How do they do that? Well they've got to figure out how to do it. '*In feeling good with going forward.*' So in other words, just stating this, in essence, makes them move forward. Wow. I mean, dense. This is really seriously increased gradient. I mean, this is a very increased gradient.

Let's go to the next sentence. '*Focusing* on what you want *brings to pass* a deep connection with this material *along with* an *awareness* of ever increasing ease in its implementation.' Now be honest, if you heard that in normal conversation, doesn't that just sound good? Especially if it's about something that you want to learn like this. Sounds good, doesn't it?

And the last thing I want is for anyone to say, '*Oh, my god, you're so good at this, Kenrick. I'll never get this good.*' Oh, hooey. You will too. That's exactly **why** you're doing it. All you have to do is read it over and over again if nothing else. But start writing, even if you just write my own exact words. Okay.

And let's tear it apart. '*Focusing. . .*' so what am I doing? When I'm asking you to focus, am I asking you to increase and see a bigger picture, or zero in on something? Well, I'm asking you to zero in on something. '*Focusing on what you want*', in other words to zero in on something that you want, '*brings to pass*' there is the **connection** word, the **causal** word, '*a deep connection with this material.*' Now stop for a moment. How does focusing on what you want make any kind of connection? Well, technically it doesn't, does it? But when you say it like that, it just makes sense, it just feels good. Because it's in the **language of beliefs**. And it's **bringing it to pass**. When? Well, you didn't *say* when. The **assumption** is *now*. So it '*brings to pass* a deep connection with this material *along with* an *awareness*.' So '*along with*', again, is a **spatial presupposition**, '*with an awareness*' which is the **awareness** pattern, '*of ever increasing ease*'. Well, I guess what you're saying is if it wasn't easy before, it's to become so now, '*in its implementation.*' So I'm suggesting to you that you are connecting with these skills in a very profound way. And that in so doing, it makes the implementation of them easier. Great suggestion, isn't it? It's kind, it's nice, it's also extremely slick.

Okay. Next one. '*Coming today* **invokes** an even **deeper** desire to bind these skills with your highest aspirations, the understanding of which spurs you forward.' Imagine saying that to a group of people that come to listen to you in a seminar, for example, if you were teaching them, I don't know, investment advice or how to get loans, or whatever you might be doing.

So a statement like that after achieving a degree of **rapport** sounds like butter. It's just smooth. It rolls off the tongue and it makes them go, '*Oh, yeah. Wow. That's good.*' Hard to argue with that. Lots and lots of suggestion power.

Okay. Follow my lead, *write three of your own* **cause and effect** with **awareness** patterns. I loaded these things up. I really went all out. The gradient is really getting steep. So just enjoy it. If you feel a bit bogged, stand up and shake it off. Okay? And then sit down and *write my exact words*, ten times each sentence. Believe me, you'll start to get it then. All right? Even if you can't do it yourself yet, you will soon and if I don't push you to do it like this. . . In fact, a great strategy I've always used and I've been using it on you, is I just keep adding more and more and more and demanding that you keep getting this at higher and higher levels, all of the sudden the basic levels just drop in. A few more months, *this* will feel like the basic level and it will just be dropped in. See? Great strategy, it works well.

With that, we'll bring this book to a close. I look forward to seeing you in our next book.

BOOK SEVENTEEN

MILITARY PATTERNS OF PERSUASION

INTRODUCTION

Refining Your Skills

Welcome to **Book Seventeen** of *Persuasion Force*. Well this is a really exciting book, actually, it's a very compact book. It's jammed full of strategies that you can use to take your persuasion skills to a much higher level.

In fact, I'm excited because in this book, you're going to actually take one of the *earlier* skills that you learned in this course and take it to a much higher and more refined level.

This is going to be a lot of fun. Like I said, it's jam-packed. This one will *really* make you stop and think and in fact, that would be the **best** way to consume this book. I recommend that you *stop* from time to time to let your brain rest and then, jump right back in and continue.

CHAPTER ONE

Military Patterns of Persuasion

Okay, let's look at '**Military Patterns of Persuasion**'. This is some really fun stuff. I love these patterns. And what happened is a number of years ago top military recruiters were evaluated to determine what they did that made them able to recruit effectively and I became privy to the information and as we proceed I'll give you their best patterns.

But before we go any further let me just tell you a couple of things about these **military patterns**. First of all, it's really easy to find yourself going, yeah, yeah, okay, *there's* a pattern, there's *another* pattern, okay, that's great, a couple of patterns, wonderful.

I want you to know that that's really *not* the way you should think of **military patterns** like this. What you want to do is **say the pattern over and over and over in your mind** using *every possible variation* that you can. The goal would be that you're going to become so *adept* at that pattern that you will so *ingrain* it into your repertoire and into your behavior that it just pops out all the time, any time, wherever it could be most useful. So if you think of these patterns like that, you'll be right on track. You must practice with them. You can't just write them down and then look at a little note right before you want to use it and go, *'Okay, let's see now, I'm supposed to say, oh, yeah, like this'*. You know, you can't do that. That isn't going to help you.

CHAPTER TWO

Have You Found...?

So let's look at pattern one, and here it is: **have you found . . .** and then state whatever your *outcome* is for dealing with them.

So here are some examples. **'Have you found** *that more and more people like yourself are looking to improve their persuasion skills?'* All right, you know what I'm going to say now, be the devil's advocate for just a second and tell me, *'No, I haven't found that'.* Okay. So I say, *'Oh, not yet, huh?'* So it's **hard to lose** when you're using this pattern. It just works that well.

'Have you found *that people who are really interested in securing their future increase the amount they invest whenever possible?'* See? Once again here we have a very interesting sentence.

Okay, let's go to the next one, **'Have you found** *that the more you consider going ahead now, the more you feel compelled to do it?'* And I don't think I've talked about this much yet, we will, but this would follow the format of a **bind**. So you're literally **binding the mind of an individual into compliance with you**. Very fascinating, very powerful.

Okay, next sentence. **'Have you found** *that people who want to get ahead act decisively?'* Napoleon Hill certainly discovered this about the most successful people he interviewed.

So it's a very simple sounding pattern. **'Have you found. . .** ' state your *outcome*. Okay?

'Have you found *that more and more people are turning to the advice of a really competent real estate agent when navigating the treacherous waters of the real estate world in these days?'* Now, let's say they go *'No'*, say, *'Well, I think you'll be surprised and will soon find yourself understanding why so many people do.'* Notice that **both** of the things I just said are really **framing** kind of skills. That's where this stuff really gets good. You're **framing** and putting people in a position to understand exactly what it is that you're wanting, literally by **framing them** with these kinds of language things.

CHAPTER THREE

What Would Happen If...?

All right, this pattern is very cool. Ready? It sounds like this, **'What would happen if . . .** ' fill in the blank, **'because. . .'** here you **leverage their values**. So that's why I said earlier that you absolutely *must* get their **values**. Or if I didn't say that, I should have, but I'll talk about it a little bit more here before we're done.

Okay, let me give you some examples of how this sounds. '*I appreciate that you feel you can't make your decision right now.* **What would happen if** *you did make a decision* **because** *the more you wait for something different to occur, the more you miss out on being able to take advantage of opportunities available now.*'

Now, it won't always end up where the person will instantaneously go along with what you're saying but what you're going to see when you use a pattern like this is it's going to **rock them off of their objection** or off of their statement. This isn't always just in response to an objection and you'll see here for example. '**What would happen if** *you started to think now about the opportunities you are not aware of for using your new skills and* **what would happen if** *as a result of that, you began to unconsciously increase the use of the skills? Would you enjoy life more or would it become more profitable?*'

Now there's a lot to that sentence. There's a lot of stuff crammed in there. But that's what these patterns *enable* you to do. It's like I'm giving you **templates** here that you can just *memorize* or *learn* and then *apply* to your own ends.

Here's another one. . . '*By the way,* **what would happen if** *you purchased this option and then immediately felt good about having done so* **because** *you want to take advantage of every opportunity you can to make money?*'

Okay? These patterns, to me, are flat out fun and they will really help you. Let's just say, for example, that as we've been proceeding through this material, you haven't put in quite the amount of practice that you might have. And you know what? That would probably apply to *everybody* including myself. *I* practice this as well. So let's just say you haven't done quite as much as you could have. Well the nice thing about *these* patterns is it starts **organizing your thought processes** such that you can begin using what you've been learning much more effectively.

So if you just start using *these* kinds of patterns, you're going to find that all of the **presupposition** formats and all the other kinds of things that I've been teaching you, start to make a lot more sense and it works really, really well.

CHAPTER FOUR

Just Suppose, For Your Own Good Reasons...

Okay, now, this last pattern, pattern three, is especially useful when a person expresses **necessity**, like, I *can't* do this or I *have to* do that or I *must not* do something else or I *shouldn't* do this. That is where you'll find an immediate application.

However, I like to go way beyond that immediate and obvious application. For example, the third example in that which was '*By the way,* **what would happen if** *you purchased this option and* *then immediately felt good about having done so **because** you want to take advantage of every opportunity to make money?'*

Okay? Now, you may be hearing these right now and thinking to yourself, *'Hmm. .okay. . . That's okay. But it isn't really thrilling to me.'*

Well, if that's the case, it's because I'm not **leveraging your values**. In other words, I haven't **elicited your values**. Okay? Now, as a result, obviously, it won't have *near* the power on you that it would for the person if I had **elicited the values** that you're hearing and I used it accordingly. So what you're going to discover is that as a result of **eliciting their values**, you now have a language format that organizes your thoughts and your mental resources in a way that stimulates persuasion. And that's the real value of these patterns. Okay? So it's why I like these so very much and have found them to be extremely useful.

All right, let's go on to the next pattern. And this pattern is a really interesting one and I'm going to give you both the *simple* and the more *complex* version. The simple is, '**Just suppose. . .**' and you can optionally add, '**because**'.

Now, I'm going to give you the first example and then I want to discuss this pattern with you a little bit. It's simple and very, very profound. '***Just suppose** that you made the decision to go ahead with this and transferred your account to us **because of your own good reasons** that only you are just becoming aware of.'*

Before we even get to the '**just suppose**' part, let's talk about what this is *doing*. First of all, notice that I'm using here an **assumption of values**. Now, I'm not going to suggest that you do this often, but I do want to introduce the concept to you.

You've heard me do it throughout the course so far, now you're really beginning to probably *become aware* of what it is that I'm doing. So I said, '**Because of your own good reasons**'. . . '*your own good reasons*' are the critical words here. In other words, I'm saying, because of your **criteria**. When you say that, **you make the person focus in on their criteria**.

Now, it's *not* as good as if you had **elicited their criteria** and you were using it on them *directly*. That's *far* more powerful. But notice the power that you can use even if you don't yet know their **values**. Or you have, for some reason, forgotten to elicit them on that day. Maybe you were sleeping a little bit. And so now, you're going to go ahead and you're going to run some patterns anyway to loosen them up and make them feel more compelled to do business with you.

Okay, so let's go to a little bit more analysis and that is, of **your own good reasons that only you are just becoming aware of** . . . Now, '*only you*'. Who else are we talking to? But notice that it **heightens response potential**. Those words will start to **heighten response potential**. I know there's someone right now that's thinking '*So should I do that all the time to make response potential even higher?*' The answer is no. Do it rarely.

But I want you to begin to see what I'm doing. I'm dissecting this piece by piece. '*Are just becoming aware of'. . .*' meaning, that they *aren't even aware* of all of their own good reasons. They're *becoming* aware of more of them. So that's a great use of a **presupposition** there too, but now let's go to this pattern and you can see how it all fits in.

Just suppose. All right? This is like me saying to someone, '*All right, I'd like you to imagine that I'm a wizard and you're in need of something profound and I have my little pointy wizard hat on and my magic stick, and I'm going to wave it in just a moment to help you to get what it is you want. Before you tell me about it, I'd like you to* **just imagine it** *because that will start the process profoundly. So what I'd like you to do is just* **think it through, imagine it, hear it, say it to yourself,** *what is it that if I could wave my wand and create for you, you would most want? And, after you do that for a minute, go ahead and tell me so I understand.'*

And so what's going to happen at that point is they're actually **going inside** and they're *imagining, hearing, feeling,* all those things, perhaps. This is a short version of it and can be used in language.

Again you can't **just suppose** someone all the time, '*just suppose, just suppose, just suppose, just suppose, just suppose*'. Okay? You're talking to the person of the opposite sex, of your dreams and you say, '*Well,* **just suppose** *you found the perfect person that would absolutely fulfill you in every way. As you look into my eyes, and* **imagine** *that happening, perhaps you could share with me what it is you're most looking for.'* And I'm going to show you a way to **amp that up** even stronger in just a minute.

In other words, now you can't turn around seconds later and go, '*Well,* **just suppose** *that person is me, and* **just suppose** *you decided that you were going to fall in love with me immediately. . .'* on and on like that. Okay? You can't keep on with '**just suppose**' but you can certainly use it occasionally and when you do, it can be very profound.

What does it really do? Well, we're using **neutral language 'suppose'**. We're **disarming resistance** with the word '**just**'. In other words, we're not asking them to take action, but just to **imagine** something or **suppose** it. Okay?

So '**just suppose**' *disarms resistance* to the process and helps them to move forward and to **imagine**. And as I taught you when we first began, when you begin talking about getting someone to *imagine, think through, visualize,* that kind of thing, boy, a huge percentage of your persuasion is already done for you. If you can get them **imagining** your way, you're really, really doing something very profound.

All right, so now, the next thing is that we're going to do is let's **just suppose** that you had the ability to use these patterns powerfully **because** you're studying them and you want to become even better at persuasion and this is really fun. So if that were the case, and that were me, and it is, I would want to read more examples. So let me give you some. See how you can do that?

'***Just suppose*** *that you can have our service,* **now***, how would you use it?'* All right, now go back and read that sentence again. Notice how I said the word '**now**'. **Now** took the form of a **command**. '***Just suppose*** *that you can have our service,* **now***, how would you use it?'* So you can start throwing these kinds of things in. We're getting to a more advanced level of explanation here and I think you're going to really enjoy amping your skills up even further here.

All right, let's go to the next one, '***Just suppose*** *that on your own you discovered the reasons why you need to share the excitement of what you've learned in this course,* **because** *you identified* **what's really important to you** *and want to help others to be their best as well. How would that positively change your opinion?'*

273

Now, if you say that kind of thing, you're going to find that people are going to simply sit up and take notice. It will kind of put them into an **altered state** a little bit so you can't go on and on forever, but you can go on quite a little bit and that is very, very nice.

CHAPTER FIVE

The Bonus Pattern

Okay, now, just for the fun of it, I want to introduce you to a pattern, and you may have heard this before, it's not original to me, but I've certainly made great use of it as will you. It's not a **military pattern** but it does fit in very nicely to what you're learning right now. And so that would be something that I think you'll enjoy. So let's look at that. It's called the **bonus pattern**, and here's how it sounds.

'When would now be a good time for you to . . . ' and then say whatever you want them to do.

Some people will catch you at this and kind of chuckle. Some people will look at you kind of silly and go, '*Well, I guess now.*' In any case, if they chuckle, you chuckle and move on as if it were nothing. I found though, that it's a pretty good thing to say but you have to do it judiciously. This is why I didn't give it to you earlier in the program, because you'd have probably been saying it all the time and not coming across real professionally.

Let's say you've gotten strong **rapport** and you've **elicited people's criteria**, and you've been **leveraging their criteria** during the presentation and you've been using **presuppositions** and you've said, '*It looks to me like probably this is a pretty good match.*' And they go, '*Well, yeah, I think it is.*' And you go, '**Well, when would now be a good time** *for you to go ahead and get started?*' And they may go, '*Well, yeah, I guess you're right. Now.*' You go, '*All right.*' And get them started.

So it's a nice question, a gentle question, it does advance your position. So be very careful. You pretty much want to use this question when *you already have agreement* more or less unconsciously. In other words, they're pretty much *going along with everything you're saying* and now you need to advance it to a conscious recognition of 'let's move'.

Okay. So here are some examples, '**When would now be a good time** *for you to make the decision to go ahead with this?*' '**When would now be a good time** *for you to enjoy the benefits of ownership?*' '**When would now be a good time** *for you to start to enjoy discovering what you don't know about persuasion* **because** *that would make you more money, would it not?*'

By the way, that sentence will cause a little mild confusion which is a bit of an **altered state**. And you'll find that your **suggestions** will enter into their mind even easier and more effectively. So you'll enjoy that.

'**When would now be a good time** *to consider who will benefit from learning about this course in such a way that will cause you to get them the information they need?*'

274

Now, by the way, that reminds me of the '**just suppose**' pattern, the third one I gave you, the one where '**Just suppose** *that on your own, you discovered the reasons why you need to share the excitement of what you've learned in this course because you identified what's really important to you and want to help others to do their best as well. How would that positively change your opinion?*'

Now, when I say that, of course you know I'm talking about actually talking about people with the skills that you're learning. If you, for example, take some sales person, maybe junior to yourself, and say, '*Hey, let me just teach you a quick pattern I've been playing with, I think you might like it. Don't overuse it, but here's how it is. The pattern is '**just suppose**'. . .'**because**'. . .* ' and so you go and talk about the pattern with them. When you do that, you'll actually find *your own* use of the skill *increasing*. I have no problem with that at all. Of course, you want to keep your materials to yourself and encourage them to go get their own and I think you'll be excited about how it will be helping you as well in that process we'll be telling you about shortly, but in any event, the idea here is it's important as you advance to higher and higher levels, pick a person and from time to time share a pattern with them. Sit down and teach it to them. It will help you to become more skilled at what it is you're doing. And I highly recommend that.

So that's why I'm giving you patterns like that because I want you to actually *go out and teach somebody* one or two of these patterns and watch what happens to your skill. You'll get more value from what you're doing here and it'll become more second nature to you. There's something about talking to someone else about what you're learning that helps embed it deeply within you.

Okay, so '**just suppose**' *creates a mental picture* in their head and '**when would now be a good time for you**' too **moves an unconscious agreement into the more conscious realm** of things. And I think you'll find it fascinating and extremely beneficial. So practice with both of those.

In fact, what I would recommend is that you begin **combining** these as much and as fast as you possibly can. That would help you a lot.

All right, I said this is *condensed* this month and it really is. I'm just rapid fire giving you strategies and patterns that you can begin to use. Now reading them, and seeing me explain them, will help you considerably. However, what will *really* help you considerably is when you *write them out and practice*. Okay? So practice, practice, practice.

And to that end, before you go to the next one, and we go through it together, I would like you to go back to the beginning of these **military patterns**, and I'd like you to do some writing. So first of all, start with pattern one, '**have you found**' and then state the outcome you're hoping to accomplish for them. So why don't you write five of those right now and then come back and continue reading. Just stop what you're doing, take a quick minute, and jot down five examples of this. This should come pretty easily for you.

Okay, great. Hopefully you did that. And let's continue on. So now to the next pattern, '**what would happen if**'. . . ' fill in the blank, '**because**. . .' and then **leverage their values**. Okay, so take five minutes, or less, and write out five of those patterns. All right? I'm not looking for them to be perfect right now, I just want the pattern to begin to get into your brain. So please do that now, stop reading and jot those down right now if you would. And then pick back up with me.

Okay. . . You already did '**just suppose**' and '**when would now be a good time for you to**'. . . so you should be pretty much up to speed now and having at least jotted down a few of these for each of what we've covered so far which would be absolutely perfect.

CHAPTER SIX

Don't ... Unless You Want To

All right, I want to cover one more **military pattern of persuasion** in this section for you. And in the next book we'll cover a few more.

This pattern is a bit more complex. And I can tell you that one of the best ways to *learn* and *use* these patterns that I'm giving you, in particular the ones in this book, is to simply **memorize** them and *start using them* with people. So they're not that hard and they are extremely effective and it's probably actually better just to **memorize** them and **use** them that way. Now, I can tell you that as a general rule, I *don't* like memorization. Okay? I don't think that's the way to go. I think ingraining **the pattern in through massive repetition** is much, much more powerful. However, in the meantime, this is the way to go. And so **memorize** it for these few patterns and begin using them. You're going to find it's going to really take your persuasion skills to a new level because it puts your mind and your words into a proper kind of **persuasion mode**. That's one of the reasons I like these so much.

All right, here's the pattern that we'll end on for the **military patterns**. '**Don't**. . .' and then state an action or what have you, '**unless you want to**. . . ' and then state an outcome. '**Don't**' action, '**unless you want to**' outcome.

Now, this pattern has the equivalent of a **bind** in it. A **bind** is '**the more you X, the more you Y**'. I know we've touched on that a bit if not gone through it entirely. We haven't gone through it in great detail, I will, as I think you'll really enjoy learning more about that, but even for now, if you understand '**the more you X, the more you Y**' there are many *variations* of that, but '**the more you X, the more you Y**' is a **bind**, a **bind format**. The more you listen to what I'm saying, the more deeply embedded these skills become.

So it's like, in other words, when the *first* thing happens, the second thing is *guaranteed to happen*. It's like that's the effect in the brain. And this pattern has that. But it's an interesting *twist* to the **bind**. So listen to the first example, you'll start to understand.

'***Don't*** *give me any objections* **unless you're sure you want to** *buy this.*'

Now, you may be saying, '*But Kenrick, that's really blunt. How do I really use that?*' Good question. So first of all, you again would want to say that kind of sentence *when you have someone pretty well on board with you*. In other words, they have yet maybe to express 100% that they're going ahead, but they do *want* to go ahead and just get it done. So in other words, at that point, you would want to . . . you could say that by way of *getting conscious agreement*. Okay?

'***Don't*** *give me any objections* **unless you're sure you want to** *buy this.*'

276

Okay, let's go to the next one. '***Don't*** *disagree with me **unless you already recognize that doing that will cause** automatic agreement with me at the deepest levels.*' I again hear someone saying, '*Yeah, that's really blunt*'. Yes, it is. How could we make it less blunt? Think back to what I've taught you before. How about if we said, '*I had a person who was helping me and teaching me and working with me to advance and he said to me when I was just about ready to make a purchase to bring him on at an even deeper and more powerful level, and certainly more expensive, he said, "Look Kenrick, **don't** disagree with me **unless you already recognize that doing that will cause** automatic agreement at the deepest levels." It took me a second. I realized he was right.*'

So what are you doing when you give a metaphor like that? Well, you're making them think about it *for them*. You're making that person you're saying it to think about it for them. You could also say, '*I told someone who was sitting right where you are one day, in fact he looked a lot like you, I said, "You know what? You'll understand this and you'll thank me later, but I want to suggest now that **don't** disagree with me **unless you already recognize that doing that will cause** automatic agreement at the deepest levels." I saw kind of a funny blank look pass his face and then he looked at me and said, "Yeah, I got it." Now you know, I guess that's the kind of customers that I work with all the time. Anyway, let's move on.*'

So you could talk to them like that, and this just slams in a **suggestion** that has very little way of defense if you do it smoothly and elegantly like I'm teaching you.

Here's another good one. . .Now you can see, by the way, why I say this is a little bit more complex. '***Don't*** *even think of a thought that is in any way contrary to going ahead with this **unless you want to** immediately discover how powerfully that thought can convince you right now to do it.*'

Let me tell you a way I've used this before. I've said, '*You know, I know that within every problem is the seed of a greater and better situation, is the seed to the answer. Every problem contains a solution. Knowing that I've often suggested to people, "**Don't** even think of a thought that is any way contrary to moving forward with this **unless you want to** immediately discover how powerfully that thought forming the seed of the solution, can convince you right now to do it." It just makes sense. And when you think of it like that, you think, huh, I get it. I thought I'd just share that with you.*' And then move on.

So you see, there are very *elegant* ways of structuring this. You don't just have to beat someone over the head with one of these patterns. You can structure them with great elegance, a profound nature as you do that.

Okay, next one, '*I often tell people that they **shouldn't** tell me that they can't afford this **unless they are** already committed to finding a way they can.*'

Think about that sentence. First of all, it's kind of a **lullaby effect**. In fact, I just found myself **lullabying**. And what else? It's because it's rather **unspecified**, and the only thing specified is '*can't afford*' and finding a way that they can. So it's not specified in terms of . . . well, '*telling people*' is **auditory**, I guess, but it just kind of rolls off the tongue. '*I often tell people that they **shouldn't** tell me that they can't afford this **unless they are** already committed to finding a way they can. See, I know when I look in someone's eyes, Mary, that you really want this. I can tell.*'

*And **when would now be a good time** to just take a deep breath, a breath of relief that you've gone ahead and decided you are going to put you first. You know it's like (deep breath) . . . it just feels good. Do you know what I mean?'*

Okay, so can we **combine** these? Oh, yes. Within metaphors. With the other **military patterns**. I mean, the world is your oyster here.

All right, the last example, *'You might wonder what would happen if I told you, "**Don't** think another thought in disagreement **unless you** already understand that doing so will have bought you **naturally** into agreement with me."'*

Now, there's many ways to deliver this. First of all, if you stop after the word *'thought'*, it's the equivalent of a **pattern interruption** in which their brain is sort of put on hold for a minute. This is heavy stuff, folks. I love it. I love it. I'm so happy that you're able to read this now because we have a few books left in this series, a few lessons left, and let me tell you, man, this is hot. This is really hot. You're getting more and more advanced to be able to understand and hear this and I'm really thrilled to share it with you.

So if you pause after the word thought, *'**Don't** think another thought'*, all of the sudden, it's going to spark their brain. . . it's like pulling a plug. Okay? And then they'll move on in the way you're aiming them, you're **setting the direction**.

Now, when I say *'following that in disagreement unless'*, it could be argued, well yeah, but aren't you *causing* them to be in disagreement? Let's say that the person was disagreeing a little bit, not majorly, but let's say there was a little bit. And you laughed and said, *'You know something, I had a guy tell me that the other day and I looked at him, I looked him right in the eyes and I said, "Bob, you might wonder what would happen if I told you **don't** think another thought in disagreement **unless you** already understand that doing so will have brought you **naturally** into agreement with me" and he started cracking up and he goes, "You know, you're right. That's how I feel," and on we went.'*

Now if you do it that way, see, you can get away with murder if you're doing it to what you told someone else. So that's how I would phrase a number of these. This one can be very blunt. And it can be like batting someone over the head but then again it is a much more complex pattern and so you can begin to apply all of your other skills to this pattern and you can start using it with great skill.

I hope you really enjoy the **military patterns** I have brought forward for you in this book. They are spectacular. They're really fun and there are some new slants on these that I've given you that will help you to put them to use very, very powerfully and combine them with what you already know.

Further, one of the biggest reasons for learning these skills and using them in your day to day life is the fact that they automatically put your brain into the mode of persuasion that's most helpful and most effective. So I just wanted to let you know that so that you can kind of see them with the eyes of the power that they really contain. Does that make sense to you?

CHAPTER SEVEN

A Powerful Pattern to Convince

Wow. A lot of material in this lesson. Again, I want to warn you because it would be very, very easy for you to make the mistake of just reading the patterns and going, '*Okay, that's cool. Wow, that's some cool stuff. All right. Well, that's this lesson, let's move on.*' No, no. You must ingrain **this into your behavior**. You must practice and wrestle with it to make it your own. Okay? And that's *especially* true with the pattern that's coming.

On the one hand it's. . . how do we put this? I guess it's simple but not easy. That's kind of my *motto* for this book, okay? Simple, but not necessarily easy. It will absolutely take you *getting good at it*. And to get good at this coming pattern, you're going to have to *use* it quite a number of times and get the hang of it.

All right, this strategy is absolutely amazing. It is one that has served me extraordinarily well. You know, it's funny, **the only reason this pattern *doesn't work* is if you *don't use it*.** When you use it, you're going to find yourself benefited significantly. It can, in and of itself, single-handedly, add money to your bottom line. It's that powerful. Even without doing it in combination with anything, it's just that good. I'm going to suggest, though, how you can do it really, really well as we go through, and elegantly.

So first of all, let me ask you to go back and remember our early books in which I talked with you about **visual** words, **auditory** words and **kinesthetic** words and **unspecified** words. So you learned lot about those words, right? Here's the deal. Those words have *far greater ability* than what I told you back then. But if I would have taught you this, back then, you would not *understand* the power that you're actually wielding. I know because I've taught people early on in their learning this pattern and they just ran off and started using it and when it didn't work well for them, they couldn't figure out why. Now it's going to be far better for you, far different. Okay? So that makes me happy to know that that's the case.

What I want to do is look to see how this is actually going to work for you by giving you the examples and having you **imagine the effect**. Okay? Let's first learn the **elicitation question**. This is going to be the **elicitation question**. Now, as always, I recommend that you do this *after* you've already **elicited criteria**. Why? Because doing the **elicitation of criteria** amounts to so much more than simply you having communicated to you the **criteria** of the person you're persuading. What it *also* does is it establishes very profound **rapport** *without* doing any non-verbal stuff, without doing any **VAK** stuff, without doing any of that thing, just simply **eliciting criteria** will strongly gain **rapport** for you.

Now if you're good and you do all the rest of the skills combined, in other words, if you've just been following along like I've taught you, well this is already a very powerfully engrained thing for you.

So here's the pattern. '**How do you know that. . .**' fill in the blank with whatever you want to know about or persuade them about. . . '**is good?**' Okay? It's *that* simple, '**How do you know that. . .**' whatever you want to persuade them about, '**is good?**' So for example, '*How do you know that* *a financial advisor **is good?*** '***How do you know that** a realtor **is good?*** '***How do you know that*** *a course **is good?***'

You can literally ask how they know that *anything* you want to sell or persuade them about is good. Now, there are some limitations. You want to be careful with this. You can't necessarily say, '***How do you know that*** *violating your own morals **is good?*** Because they'll say, '*Well, it's not.*'

What you're asking them to do is to **contrast in their own mind** what it is you want to persuade them about to discover good. All right? Now, you first have to *hear* and *understand* the first question, '***How do you know that*** *(blank) **is good?*** So let me just do this with you on something I know you'll understand.

'So ***how do you know that*** *a course **is good?*** So you can apply that question to the *Persuasion Force* books right now. **How do you know that it's good?** And you'll come up with whatever answer you have, but I want you to **say it out loud**. Did you do that? Say it. All right.

Where we're going, by the way, is profound. I'm going to show you, if you've ever heard of any of these patterns, I'm going to show you in the next couple of books how to **link them together** so that *one* question gets you *multiple* answers the likes of which nobody will even understand that you understand. In other words, this is so deep and profound that *they won't know* what you know and you'll know instantly how to turn the key in their lock to get them to do what you want. It's about that good.

CHAPTER EIGHT

How Do You Know...?

So now that you've answered the question I want you to note the answer to your question here, because what I'll tell you is, the answer you're going to hear will be **phrased in one of these four ways**—what they **see**, what they **hear**, what they're going to **do** or **feel**, or what they **read**. Those are the four ways you're going to hear this done.

Now let's go back to **knowing what we know**, and let's look through how this might sound.

'***How do you know that*** *a financial advisor **is good?*** you say. And the answer comes, '*Well, I **look** at the skills that they give me, and I know they're good. I **see** their strategy and I think, this is going to be really good.*'

So which one of those four answers is that? Well, duh, it's the first one, **see**, right? So they need to '**see**' that the advice the advisor is going to give them, is going to be good. Let's do it again, '***How do you know that*** *a financial advisor **is good?*** and the answer comes back, '*Well, I **listen** to what the person tells me and if it **sounds** right, I guess I know. I mean, I guess I'll trust them. I'll **listen**, and I'll know.*'

Okay, and so with that answer we know that **hearing** is the one that they're doing. Now let's do another one. '***How do you know that*** *a financial advisor **is good?*** And the person says, '*Well, I* *guess I have to kind of **follow** the advice they give me for a short period of time and if it **works**, I guess it's good.'*

All right, what is that? That's the 'do' of the 'do feel'. They want to 'do' first and then they'll know. All right? Let's do it again. Let's do the **feel** one. So, '***How do you know that*** *a financial advisor **is good?**' 'Well, I just **feel** it. You know? I guess I **connect** with the process and it just **feels** right to me.'* Well, obviously you know that's the **feel**. So **do** and **feel** are lumped into the same thing.

And lastly, '***How do you know*** *a financial advisor **is good?**' 'Well, I **read** the things that he shows me and I know he's good.'*

Perfect. Excellent. Now we're on track.

So there we go. That's the first half of this pattern. Okay? Now, there are some very specific ways I want you to practice this. Don't go any further ahead. Follow what I'm going to do.

I'm going to suggest you stop in just a minute. Please do, because I want you to get this part first or you're just going to confuse yourself. All right? I want you to go back and answer the question, '***How do you know that*** *a course in persuasion **is good?**'* All right? And answer it. So state your answer again now out loud. Go ahead.

Can you *identify* one of those four categories? **See**? **Hear**? **Do/feel**? Or **read**?

Okay, and by the way, would you please note that the way the course is delivered to you, the experience of the books, **enables** you to **see** it, **enables** you to **hear** me if you acquire the audiobook from the Power Ark app, I ask you to do the exercises so you have a **feeling** and you ingrain **it within yourself**, and there's the book to read. The whole thing is there. Okay? Not bad. Not bad at all.

So you're seeing or experiencing, would be a better way for me to say it at this point, that I'm aiming it all for those **modalities** all the time. By the way, could you do the same? Yes, of course you could.

All right, next, what I want you to do is I want you to go out and I want you to ask five people about something. Now, this could be as simple as going to the grocery store and you're looking in the fruit section and there's someone there and you ask innocently, '***How do you know if*** *a melon **is good?**' 'Oh, well, you **shake** it like this and if you hear water, then you know it's good.'* Okay, so what is that? That's the '**do/feel**'. They want you to **do** something to tell it.

How do you know that a banana **is good?** Well, you **look** at it and if it's nice and yellow, not green, but nice and yellow and not too many brown spots on it, then that's how I make my decision. For example, here's one that's too green. Here's one that's too brown. Here's one that I would say is really right. So they need to **see** something. In particular, by the way, you know they also need to **contrast**, they're quickly contrasting.

Now let me just stop for a moment and explain to you that where we're really going is **we're learning to create a key that fits into the lock of our prospect's minds**. We're creating a key that fits into that lock. Okay? By their *answers*, they show you how to shave that key. By your *understanding*, the key is shaved, inserted, and the lock is turned. Okay? That's where we're headed and with a great many more to come. I'm going to get you started with this one in this book but there's a whole lot more that we're going to be doing together. The net result. . . well, I'll save that for a later time.

But anyway, when you get good at asking this, and you'll have the gist of it if you just go ask five people, go ask how they know anything is good. Go to the manager of that grocery store and say, '**How do you know that** a checker **is good?**' you know, the people that check you out. You know, go to a bank teller and say, '**How do you know that** a customer **is good?**' Go *anywhere* and ask how someone knows how something is good. And in so doing, it'd be preferable, if you could ask about something that you're selling or that you want to persuade about, but just for now to learn it, I want you to go out and get the hang of it and get this in your mind as to the **four categories** so that you can quickly engage and know which of the categories.

To take it to the next step what I'd like you to do is the following: I would like you to *respond back* in that **modality** that *they* have used to answer your question. So if they go, '*Well, you know, you* **look** *at the banana and if it's not too green and it's not too brown. . .* ', say , '*Okay, I'm* **looking** *at them and it* **appears** *that this one* **looks** *right. Is that correct?*' And they would say, '*Yes.*' And then you say, '*Great.*' And so that completes the exercise with that person. Thank them and move on.

I mean, you can find *anything* to ask about there in a store. So just keep asking and/or go to different stores and ask. Or go to a coffee shop, they're famous here in the U.S. and ask '**How do you know that** a latte **is good?** If I were learning, **how would I know that** a latte **is good?**' And they'll probably go on and on telling you. But they may say, '*Well, it's just up to how it* **tastes**.' '*Okay, but if you would just tell me, let's say I'm going to try to understand the quality better,* **how would I know** *the latte* **is good** *based on a quality standard?*' Now they're going to have to go beyond **taste**, probably, and say, '*Well, it should use two tablespoons of espresso per whatever amount of water and it should be at X temperature*' and all these things. So say, '*But* **how would I know** *those things?*' '*Well, you'd* **look** *at it, you'd* **measure** *it.*' You may be able to easily *assume* but it's better to get them to *tell* you.

So that's how they would know and that's how I want you to proceed. So please stop reading now before you go on. I'm telling you, it's important that you do this. There are two reasons, one, I want you to *get good at it* **before** you hear the next part so that you don't confuse yourself and number two, I don't want you to read further until you've had a little *experience* with this, so that what you're installing in your brain is something that you already have done a little bit of. That's real important.

CHAPTER NINE

How Often Do You Need To...?

Okay, after you've completed the work that I've told you to do, we'll pick right back up.

Once they answer you, you're then going to ask them the *last* part of this sequence. And you're going to say, '**How often do you need to . . .** ' and then you're going to put their answer in. Like if they said '**see** *it*', then you're going to say '*see* *it*' '**in order to be convinced?**' '***How often do you need to*** *see* *it,* **in order to be convinced?**' '*How often do you need to* hear *it* **in order to be convinced?**' '*How often do you need to* do *it or feel* it *in order to be convinced?*' '*How often do you need to* read *it* **in order to be convinced?**'

I want you to go back to the exercises that you've just done, you've gone out and you've asked people the question and I want you to remember the answers that you got, and what I'd like you to do is to just go real quickly and say this sentence and then **combine** that sentence with what it is that I want you to ask here, so let's say they said, '*Well, you have to* **see** *the banana.*' So I want you to say out loud right now, '***How often do you need to*** *see it* **in order to be convinced?**'

I know, I know, you're saying, yeah, but Kenrick, you only need to see the banana *once*. I know. But I want you to *get used to saying it* just so you can say it. Okay? That's really important.

So do it now, remember the answers that you got and I want you to say it right now. Go ahead.

Okay, so you said a couple of them? I hope you did. It'll make it far easier. So now the next thing is, we're going to hear **four choices** again. So it's really important that you are *good at the first ones* so that these are clear for you. And here are the four choices. You're going to hear an answer that is a **number** of times, a **length** of time, what we call **automatic**, or **consistent**.

So you have those four choices, you're going to hear them in those four choices. So let me go over with you exactly what these mean.

If they respond in **a number of times** manner, it's just as it sounds. For example, you say, '***How many times do you need to*** *see it* **in order to be convinced?**' and they say, '*Well, I guess about four times.*' So they'll name a **number**. It's just as it sounds. That one's easy. They'll name a **number**.

If they respond in **a length of time**, here they need to hear something **over a period of time**. So they'll say, '*Well, maybe if I saw it for* **a month or so**, *maybe I would probably feel convinced.*' So they're looking to have something cover **a period of time** to convince them.

Now, the **automatic** one is our *favorite* one. You'll like that one a lot. And this is the equivalent of someone saying '*One time*'. In other words, if you *say* it's so, it *must* be. So here you say, '***How many times do you need to*** *see it* **in order to be convinced?**' and they go, '*Well, if you* **show** *me that that's the way it is,* **it is**', or if they go, '*Well, just* **once**. *I mean, I* **see** *it and* **I know right then**.' So the **automatic** is the *good* one. I mean, that's the *great* one. **Number of times** is really good too. I like less the **length of time** and **consistent** personally, but they're still all persuadable.

So let's go to number four, the **consistent** response. This is where *every time* you want the person to be convinced, *you have to do it all over again*. And it sounds like this. '*All right, so* **how many times do you have to** *see this* **in order to be convinced?**' '*Well, I guess* **every time** *you want me to move forward again, you're going to have to* **show it all to me** *and if I believe it's the right thing to do* **at that point,** *I'll do it.*'

What they're saying to you is, if you convince me *today*, it *won't* mean I'm going to be convinced *tomorrow*. You're going to have to *keep doing it*. And that is, of course, my *least favorite* kind of person to deal with, but, on the other hand, if you know it in advance, then it makes it so much better. Like all the skills I'm teaching you, once you understand, you can deal with it.

Instead of just walking away going, '*I don't know why I didn't get that*' or '*Well, they went for it, I don't know why.*' I mean, here, at least you start to understand what's really going on so you can make it work for you the way you need to.

So **number of times**, they name a **number**; **length of time**, they name **a period of time**; **automatic** it's like they say **one time**, or **if you say so, it must be**; and **consistent**, which is they'll imply that they're *never* really convinced, that **they'll always have to be convinced more**, and **every time** you want them to be convinced again, **you have to do it all over again**. You have to go through and explain it all to them again, or show it all to them again, or do it with them again, or whatever the case may be.

All right, now, to use it, you simply put the two questions together and do whatever they tell you. It's easy. The results might just bowl you over. Okay? So what you're going to do is you're going to say to someone, preferably after you've **elicited criteria**, you're going to say, for example, '**How do you know that** a realtor **is good?**' and they go, '*Well, I guess if I can **see** things that they've done it will let me know that they're good.*' And you go, '*Great. **How many times do you need to see it in order to be convinced?**' 'Well, I guess if I saw **a few** examples, you know, maybe **two or three**, I'd be convinced.' 'Fantastic. Well that's great. I like to know because it's useful as we work together to be able to understand each other well and I think that's just a good thing to do for us both. And by the way, before we go any further, let me just **show you an example** of something that's kind of like what you're asking me to do that I did and it worked really well for everybody concerned. Let me go over that with you. . .*' And away you go.

So that is *one time*. Now, you're going on a little bit further, a little bit longer in the presentation, and you say, '*Hey, just reminded me of something. Here **let me just show you** a house that I just sold for someone. Again, there's a lot of similarities between what you're doing and what you're asking for. Let me go over that with you real quick.*' That's *two*. They said *two or three*. I'd do another one. And a little farther into the presentation or a little later on, show them the *third* one and you'll see them, just. . . their eyes will just light up.

Now, if they say **length of time**, let's go over that. '*Well, I guess if I could **see** something and I **saw** that it worked over a **length of time** I guess I'd be convinced.*' '*Okay. How long are you suggesting, for example?*' They say, '*Oh, maybe a **month**.*' First of all, I would do your best to **go back a month** and show them this is what you were showing people, telling people, doing for people a month, two, three, four months ago, these are the results you were getting and these are the results they can expect.

'*So **imagine** that you came to me **a month ago** and you said, "I'd really like to see that this works **over the period of about a month** and then I'll be convinced" and now today we're meeting and **it's been a month** and you see that it's still working exactly as we said it will. Feels pretty good, doesn't it?*' So you can do the '**just suppose**' in a sense, although I didn't say, '**just suppose**', but you can do the '**just suppose**' technique here, to get them to **go backwards in time the length that they named**, and you show them evidence, or tell them evidence, or whatever, so that they will go and **experience that length of time**. If it doesn't work, if they go, '*Yeah, yeah, that's then and I'm talking about now*', all right, well at least you know what you're up against. Okay? I would also say to you that if you can let 20% of the time go by it may trigger enough in their mind that they'll go ahead and move forward. That is just what I found to be so as I've been doing this kind of thing.

So let's say they say '*a month*'. I would try to get back in front of them in about six days, about a week. Okay? And I would then say, '*You know, it just feels to me like it's been quite a while since our last discussion. It **feels** like **a month** has gone by but I wanted to just go over with you a few things that I didn't tell you at the time when we talked*' and then bring up something new to go over with them and they may be triggered to move forward. Worse comes to worse, it's going to take a month. All right?

Let's go to the **automatic** one. This one is just really easy so if you ask someone, '***How many times do you need to do it in order to be convinced?***' And they go, '*Well, I guess I've just got to do it **once** and if it works, then I'm convinced.*' '*Okay, great.*' So go do it with them, whatever it is. Maybe it means they want to go through, be stepped through, and it's just language, a plan that you've come up with for them. Or what you're advising them to do or the steps you think they should take. So maybe it's just a matter of them feeling like they're stepping through the process and actually **doing** it.

My daughter came home the other day and she said, '*Dad, I have to write a persuasive essay on cloning.*' And I said, '*Okay, great.*' The next morning she said, '*Dad, you wouldn't believe this website I found. There's a website that I was able to go and actually do the process of cloning. I cloned something.*' I said, '*Really?*' She goes, '*Well, you know, it's just online, but they showed you how you have to take the nucleus out and so you take the nucleus out and then you take it over to this other thing and you incubate it and you mix it over here with something else and then you end up with a monkey*' or whatever they were doing. And she said, '*It was really cool. I really understand the process better now.*'

So that's what that kind of '**do**' person is wanting. And if they're the **automatic** type, well then all of the sudden you just **do** it with them **once** and they're convinced.

Now the **consistent** type. Here you have to go through it with them in whatever their **modality** is, let's say it's **hearing** or **seeing** or **doing** or **feeling** or whatever, until they're convinced. With this person I would especially go into a time in the **future** and make them **imagine** that this is working for them exactly the way it should and I'll be going through those strategies in detail with you and some new ones on that too that I think you'll really like, in future books, but in any event, that's the **consistent** one is just make sure they're thoroughly sold when you take the order. Okay? And that will be fine. And know that when you go out to sell them something *else* in the future, you'll have to do it all over again probably although you can use what you've done the first time as a foundation. However, you'll need to do really thoroughly from start to finish in order to make that work.

Okay. So you're going to love this pattern as you start putting it to use in your life. And you just simply **put the two questions together**. And that's it. *Do* whatever they *say* at that point. What you're actually learning here, what you're eliciting from them is **what kicks off their ability to be convinced**. That's what it is. Let me just share with you a personal story that happened to me a number of years ago now.

I went to an event, it was a public conference, and at this conference I was known to be pretty much the top persuader there. And they broke up into little groups, different groups like people that were interested in different applications of what was being taught, and of course I went into the group that was interested in the business application and there was quite a number of people

285

there. And it was nice, as people were saying that they had my materials, and lots of accolades, etc., but pretty soon they asked my opinion about a few things and I started telling them, and then they asked this other gentleman about something. And he said, *'Well, let me just show you,'* and he demonstrated with me.

I'm telling you, it pretty well made me fall over myself. I was just *stunned*. I was like, what did he just do? I had not heard that kind of thing done quite that way. And so pretty soon I came back and threw a bunch of language at him and he sat there sort of in a stupor and I went on and did my thing and took the group to where I wanted them to go, and after fifteen minutes or so, he kind of recovered and he did something else and it kind of had the same impact on me again. I'm like, what in the dickens is this?

Afterwards he and I came and met. And he said, *'I've just got to ask you, what are you doing?'* He said, *'I've worked with people that are phenomenal at language patterns but I've never seen them at this skill.'* And I said, *'Well, listen, I've got to ask you the same thing because I've been in this a long time and I've never, ever had someone be able to make me feel like this and just to kind of put a dead stop to what I'm doing. What are you doing?'* And he kind of chuckled, and he goes, *'I'll tell you what, I'll share with you if you share with me.'* I said, *'All right. Fair enough.'*

Well, little did I know, he had this pattern he was about to pull out on me and he goes, *'Here, so that I know how to talk to you better, let me just ask you, first of all,* **how do you know that a course is good?'** And I told him. And he heard my strategy which I will share with you. It's **auditory** three or four times, with a few **criteria** thrown in for good measure. And he said, *'Okay, fair enough.'* And he discovered that it was **auditory**, that it was three or four times, and so he said, *'All right, let's do this, let's reconvene here before the end of the day and let's you and I sit down and share a little bit.'* I said, *'All right.'*

Pretty soon he brought over someone to me, he says, *'By the way, Kenrick, since we have this thing we're doing together now, let me just introduce you to a student of mine. He has just got my new course where I teach these strategies. He'd like to tell you a little bit about it.'* So the guy obligingly tells me a little bit about the program. And I listen. And I'm impressed and I say, *'Okay, great. Whatever.'* Fifteen minutes later he brings over person number two. He said, *'Here's another person here. I didn't realize he was here but I found out that he is, I asked him if he'd just come speak to you real quick for a minute and he'll tell you a little bit more about the program'* and so he did. And I'm starting to feel now like, *'Well, maybe I really need to know this.'* Then he brings the third guy. And he says, *'Look, I want you to know, I still have a couple of these left, but they're going fast.'* He said, *'I wanted to bring you this friend of mine that has my program and let him tell you a little bit about it'* and when he did this, he met the rest of the **criteria** that I had mentioned to him and when this guy finished talking in about two or three minutes, I was salivating. I had to have that.

Well, listen, at the time I didn't have nearly the resources I do now, and I had about in my pocket enough to buy that thing and wondered how I'd get home. And by the time the fourth person came, I was hurting myself to give him the money to make sure I had one of those courses and he obliged and gave it to me.

It was just that powerful and I absolutely knew what I was doing and was very, very capable with the other skills. When I learned this one, my life changed. I went, all right, now we're talking. And I went and began to refine them and make it even more useful and began to combine them with other things and it just had that dramatic of an impact in my life. So I share it with you with excitement knowing that it's also going to have a dramatic impact for you.

So let me just tell you a couple of additional thoughts on this. You should *not* use this pattern in lieu of **criteria** unless it's a last straw and you're just throwing something else out there. But I wouldn't do it that way. I mean, in general, you need to **elicit criteria**, you need to elicit it first, and it's important that you do it that way. Okay?

This pattern can work really fast. If it's a **number of times**, you may be able to make it work right on the spot. If it's a **short length of time**, you may be able to make it work right on the spot. And if it's **automatic**, you'll probably be able to make it work right on the spot. It's really fast. So it's useful in that way.

So in other words, don't keep talking if they're ready to go, if they're ready to buy.

Now next, here's what I'd really like you to do. I'd like you to *have the experience* by sharing this pattern with somebody, writing out your notes, maybe, and say, '*Look, I want you to do this to me.*' And just have them do it, even ever so clumsy. Say, '*Just give it your best.*' Point out what you want them to do and then have them do it to you.

Even though you know it's coming, even though it's crude and they don't have near the skill that you will, still I think you're going to be shocked at how you feel. It will engender that **feeling of being convinced**. Imagine if you *didn't* know what was coming. Imagine if the person was *skilled* like you'll be as you implement these. Imagine if all that were the case. **Just suppose. . .**

CHAPTER TEN

Homeplay

All right. So what I'd like you to do now is consider your homeplay, and it's simple. Write the **military patterns of persuasion** until they become second nature. Okay? They're just so profound at putting your mind into the right place to persuade, you're really going to like it.

Next, *teach two people* how to do the pattern that can be used to convince people, the last one I've just been talking with you about, and have both of them *do it on you* and be prepared to be amazed.

All right. What a wonderful book, jam packed full of stuff. I told you it's going to be dense and packed and I think you see now that it is. I'm looking forward to your thoughts about this as you begin to implement it. Just enjoy the results. Okay? In order to do that, you have to be *using* it. In order to *use* it, it would be really helpful if you *write out* the material so that you can start to *make it yours* and it feels like it's yours.

All right. Take care, I'll see you in our next book.

BOOK EIGHTEEN

BINDING THOUGHTS

INTRODUCTION

Overview

Welcome to **Book Eighteen** of *Persuasion Force*. I'm lining up some of the most incredible material you've ever read, now that you have a very significant foundation, you're going to love it. You've got an awful lot to look forward to.

All right, in this book, we're going to be talking about **binding thoughts** and we're going to learn the last half of the **military patterns of persuasion** that we started in our last book and something I call **making a notch in the key more apparent**.

CHAPTER ONE

Binding Thoughts

Let's move on to **binding thoughts**. And this is a fascinating strategy that we're going to study in this lesson and I'll tell you that as you gain competence with it, you're really going to find yourself able to **direct the thoughts of others** even easier.

The strategy you're going to learn in this book, this part of it, is *not* something you're going to do with a high frequency count. You're going to do it *from time to time* and I'll kind of guide you along those lines here as we continue.

Here's the pattern: **the more you X, the more you Y**.

Now, this has a number of names that you may hear, one is **'bind'**, the other is **'single bind'**. This is like **one thing binding another**, one aspect binding another. And as a general rule, the **X** will be a **pace** but it can also include a **suggestion** or a **challenge**, and the **Y** will be a **lead**, how you *want* them to think or respond but they're not currently doing, necessarily.

So the pattern is **'the more you X, the more you Y'** and this is a **cause and effect** pattern so when we studied *causes, forces, makes, and, as, while, during, since* and all the **implied cause and effect** patterns, etc., this is sort of a takeoff on those, it's a little bit more advanced. All right?

So you already have a *general* idea about using **cause and effect** and now we're going to study the *specific example* of a **bind**.

So let me give you some examples of **binds** and how they operate. You'll catch right on to this and it'll make sense to you real quickly.

Here we go. '*The more you listen to what I'm explaining, the more you'll understand the power of using it.*'

'*The more you look into how this works, the more you'll find applications that will excite you.*'

Now let's stop and pull this apart a little bit. You see **the more you X, the more you Y**. It's very blatant. **The more you. . .**let's take the first sentence. . .*listen to what I'm explaining. . .* Now, am I explaining something to you right now? Yes. You're hearing me. Is that a **pace**? Yes it is. Okay? And so what I'm saying is that the **more** this **pace** happens, the **more** this **lead** is going to happen. So what am I suggesting? *The **more** you listen, the **more** you'll understand.*

Now the rest of it is **presuppositions** and being more specific. But the strategy is the way I'm telling you, the more you listen, the more you'll understand.

It also makes **logical** sense when you think of it that way. Although **binds** do not have to in any way make sense or be logical. All right, *the more you look into how this works, the more you'll find applications that will excite you.* Doesn't that stand to reason? But it's also pushing that **suggestion** into the mind of the listener which is why it has such power.

Let's go to the next one: '*The more you hear about this piece of property, the more you will be compelled to buy it.*'

Now, is that logical? Well, not necessarily. In other words, hearing a lot of things doesn't necessarily compel people. Hearing the *right* things does, but here you're suggesting that there's a logical link between hearing about the property and being compelled to buy it. So **you're creating** that link, **you're creating** the truth. . . you're making it so in their mind.

Now here's where we start to get into some really interesting ways of doing this. *The more you try and object, the more you will find yourself going along with these ideas.* Aha. So here what are we really doing? We're **issuing a challenge**, in essence. The more you try and do something we *don't want* you to do, the more you'll find yourself doing what we *want* you to do. Now, you can just say this sentence like this, but if they're *already* objecting, what are the odds that this is going to turn them around in real life? Well, probably not real high. However, what if you were talking and you used this as a **quote**? So early on in a presentation, near the beginning, maybe you say, '*You know, I was talking with a guy the other day and I was laughing with him, I said, "You know something, you know you want this. And in fact, the more you try and find reasons why you don't, the more you're going to be compelled to get it anyway." The guy chuckled and he goes, "Yeah, you're probably right." Anyway, I thought that was kind of funny.*' And then go on with your presentation. So you could do that earlier on, let's just say. You could find a way to work that in.

And you're having quite an impact on the person that you're telling it to because they're not really objecting yet. See how that might work?

All right, here's another one. *The harder you try to find reasons why this won't work, the more you'll be forced to admit that it does.*

So when would you use that? Well, let's say a person goes, '*I don't think this is really right for me here. You know, here's an example where I don't think it would work.*' And you let them talk and they go, '*Well, actually, I don't know, maybe it really would work here in this situation.*' And you laugh and you go, '*Well, let me just tell you, the harder you try to find reasons why this won't work, the more you'll be forced to admit that it does, and when that happens, now, you'll all of the sudden say to me, "Kenrick, I need to do this."*' See how you can follow up with that?

At first blush this sounds like, oh, my god, I couldn't use that, but you can. All right?

Here's another one: '*The more you want to feel good about yourself, the more you'll need to act now on this proposal.*' And again, you might say, well, you can't just say that to people. Well, yes I can. And I do. And it works great. Okay?

So a person, if you were selling something that would lend itself to this kind of a statement, if they go, '*Look, I just want to do better in my life, I want to feel like things are moving along the way I want them to.*' And I go, '*You're right. In fact, the more you want that, and the more you want to feel good about yourself, the more you'll need to act now on what I'm talking about. This will help you accomplish all those things, you know?*' And they'll go, '*Well, yeah, you're right.*' '*Okay, well let's do it.*'

See, you can **work this in**. I'm trying to give you the simple pattern so you can begin to see how to do it, but here I'm also guiding you in how you might make it a little more sophisticated.

CHAPTER TWO

Three Helpful Strategies and Temporal Binds

I'm going to show you three strategies I use all the time that will help you formulate these. Now I want you to use these three strategies more like as a **template**, okay?

These are more like a template.

So here's one: '*The more you don't comply, the more you will find yourself complying anyway.*' So you could say things like, '*Look, the more you think you're not going to take advantage of this offer, the more you're going to find yourself wanting it, and just saying, what the heck, I guess I really need to do it. But don't take my word for it. Just watch and see how it comes up for you as I talk, all right?*'

All right, here's another template: '*The more you do what I want, the more you will do even more of what I want.*'

That's basically another template. And that you've heard a lot of in the examples I've given you already.

'The more you think that this really will work for you, the more you're going to find that it really does. It's going to be spectacular.'

All right, so **the more** you do what I want, **the more** you will do even more of what I want. So it's a **template**, you don't want to use that sentence *exactly* like that, it's a template.

And here's a third one: *'The more X happens, the more you'll know. . .'* and whatever you want to say.

So the more thoughts that come up in your mind that might make you question this decision, the more you'll begin to know that your thorough thinking has caused you to find all the right reasons to go ahead and do this.

Yeah. I mean, that one's a good one, right?

The more something happens, and you name it, **the more** you'll know whatever you want them to do is going to happen.

So these are three templates that I use a lot. Now, I'm going to give you a **twist** on these. And really, this one is an **X causes Y** pattern but we can call it more like a **temporal bind**, okay. Because we're throwing the word *'when'* in, it makes **time** enter the scene. And here's an example. So the pattern is, **'when X happens, you'll Y.'**

*'***When*** you reflect back on this conversation, **you'll** begin to understand even more why what I'm suggesting is the way to proceed.'* In other words, the **bind** happens, the **bind** will engage them, I should say, **sometime in the future** when they do the **X**. What is the **X**? *Reflect back on this conversation.* And by the way, here's another fascinating thing about time. **When** will they do that the first time? That's a trick question. **When** will they do that the first time? Let me tell you the sentence again: *when you reflect back on this conversation, you'll begin to understand even more why what I'm suggesting is the way to proceed.*

When will they do that the first time? **Right now**. Why? Well, in order to make sense of my words, they have to imagine it, hear it, feel it, etc., they have to somehow use their five senses to make sense of my words. Okay?

When they do that, what's really happening? Well, they have to *reflect back on the conversation* **immediately** and *then* understand even more **immediately** because the **bind** kicks in. So the first time this will happen is **right when you say it** which lends further credibility to what you're doing. Now that's some pretty advanced thinking about **binds**. So I want you to go back and read this several times to really get the hang of what I'm saying. All right?

The *next* time that they could do this is some time off in the future when they reflect back on the conversation. Then they'll begin to understand even more. In other words, like I told you when I talked about **'just suppose'** and what that really does. . . so when we say **'just suppose'** we're making people *visualize*, *hear* and feel something, whatever it is that you're asking them to suppose.

In other words, **we're training their brain on how we want it to behave and act and think in**

advance. And that's what this does. That's what this pattern does when you use it like that. Let's use another one.

'**When** *you lose your next employee,* **you'll** *wonder if you could have avoided that loss by implementing these strategies. And in the back of your mind, you'll know you could have.*'

When will that *first happen*? Well, **right now** as they **imagine** losing their next employee. All right? When will it happen *again*? When they *actually* lose an employee. If you want to look at this as **projecting into the future**, and **setting up a bind that is time triggered**, that's *exactly* what we're doing. We're just adding quite a bit of sophistication to it.

Here's another one. '**When** *you hear the next piece of bad news on the TV about the markets,* **you'll** *rest easy knowing we have together created a plan to get through these tough times and* **you'll** *rest easy while others out there might not be so fortunate.*'

This is a really good one. Think about it. When *first* will this take effect in their brain? Yes. **Right now** as they **hear** it. And then *again* the next time they are watching the news or the TV and they hear something bad about the markets, they'll *already know* how they're supposed to behave. The brain will click into place what it is they've already rehearsed. *Resting easy*, that a plan has been created to get them through these tough times. Okay, now if times were really good, you could still say the same kind of thing. You could switch it around a bit. It doesn't really matter. These kinds of **binds** are incredibly powerful. So that would be more like a **temporal bind** or a **time enhanced bind**, okay, when we throw the word, '**when X happens, you'll Y**.' But you'll notice it doesn't follow technically the format of '**the more you X, the more you Y**' it jumps more into a **temporal** format, but it's close enough and I wanted you to be able to have that as I think it's of extreme value.

CHAPTER THREE

Binding Criteria

I've outlined these four strategies and what I'd like you to do is to *write ten sentences for each of those patterns* so that you can create actual examples that you can use. Now think about it, based on what I just explained to you about the **time bind**. So when I ask you to do that, what are we really doing? Well, and if you said, '*Well, Kenrick, I get it. Sure if I do my homework, I'm going to be more capable with these skills.*' '*Yes you are.*' And if you went on and said, '*But Kenrick, that's how learning works. If you rehearse something and repeat it, you'll learn it and then you'll do it in the future.*' And I would say, '*Yes, you're right.*' So what are we doing when we're getting our *prospects* to **rehearse the behavior we want them to demonstrate**? We're **teaching them the behavior that we want them to use**. And they'll have *a tendency to do it* because that's the practiced behavior.

Isn't that cool? So yes, we're educating our prospects, but educating them what? Well, very strategically in the way we want them to think and behave. Okay? In other words, we're educating them more based on a **process** we want them to follow instead of just . . here, we want you to know how to add one plus one and come up with two. What we really want them to do is to **think the way we tell them to think** such that they'll **take the actions we want them to do**, i.e. buy our products or services.

So I want you to *write ten sentences for each of the patterns* so you can create actual examples that you can use and that will help you significantly. So my suggestion is, just stop and write these patterns and then continue on with me, okay? So go ahead and do that now and we'll pick back up in just a minute.

Okay, hopefully you've done that. And by now, you can ascertain one of the biggest things that you can put into the **bind** format, I'm sure, and that is **criteria**. If you said, '*One of the biggest things that I can* **bind**, *Kenrick, is the person's* **criteria** *that I'm working with*', oh boy, are you right on track. Again, these are things that you're not learning elsewhere. A lot of people, they're trying to say things like, '*Well, there's a limited value to* **criteria** *and selling based on it,*' etc... well, they're wrong. Yes, there's a lot of other skills we can use, however, **criteria** is like a flashlight coming out of people's heads. And it shines the light of their focus on **what it is that they're looking to find and what it is they're looking to do**. And so if we can *seize control* of that flashlight and aim it where we want it to aim and give it supporting reasons and things around that, well then we're really on the right track. So this is just incredibly important to be able to understand and do.

Let's look at **criteria** and let's say that we have a person with very high **criteria** of *not having to worry*, to have a plan I'm comfortable with. Let's say that's the next one. Okay? So let's take a look at this. '***The more** you don't have to worry, **the more** you rest easy in the coming months, right?*' See how we can **bind their criteria**? **The more** *you don't have to worry,* **the more** *you can rest easy* in the coming months, right? **Now** that you have a plan that you're *comfortable* with, you'll find it *easy* to *relax* and pursue your life instead of always reacting to what you hear on TV about the market.

All right, now, again, that uses time '**now**' and it's really kind of more of a **cause and effect** than it is a **bind**. However, you're seeing here where this sort of *blends*, where **binds** and **cause and effect**. . . it's hard to tell where one begins and the other leaves off. But you can see also how they're *interchangeable* and extraordinarily powerful.

Okay, so we can use the four basic patterns, **the more** you don't comply, **the more** you'll find yourself complying anyway; **the more** you do what I want, **the more** you'll do even more of what I want; **the more** X happens, **the more** you'll know; and **when** X happens, **you'll** Y to accomplish all kinds of really, really powerful things.

CHAPTER FOUR

Military Patterns

All right, let's move on. We've got lots to cover. Let's get with the **military patterns** right now. And we're going to cover the balance of them in this book that we didn't do in **Book Seventeen**. And so let's go through those right now.

And the first pattern: '**Don't (action) unless you want to (your outcome).**' Okay? Now think about that for a minute.

'*Don't (action) unless you want to (your outcome).*' This pattern has the equivalent of a **bind** in it, as you're going to see. . . by the way, that's one of the reasons that I taught you **binds** earlier in this book. . . So let's take a look at how this might work and what this does to the brain. Knowing what you know about **binds**, listen very carefully to some examples.

'*Don't* give me any objections **unless** *you're sure you want to buy this.*' Isn't that a mind scramble? '*Don't* give me any objections **unless** *you're sure you want to buy this.*' Okay? That's a very, very interesting pattern.

'*Don't* disagree with me **unless** *you already recognize that doing that will cause automatic agreement with me at the deepest levels.*' Now you're saying to me, '*Kenrick, I don't see how I'm going to really be able to use that.*' And I disagree with you. I think you could use that. In fact, **don't** even think anymore along those lines **unless** you're ready to recognize that somewhere you're going to be able to find ways to put it to use.

Okay? See how that pattern **works**? I mean, you could just *sneak* this thing in anywhere. And like always, you of course could absolutely use it with **quotes**. You could talk about how you just told someone this earlier in the day and you're kind of chuckling about it and so were they, but you saw that it absolutely had the results that you wanted.

Here's another one: '**Don't** *even think of a thought that is in any way contrary to going ahead with this* **unless** *you want to immediately discover how powerfully that thought can convince you right now to do it.*'

Isn't that an interesting sentence? There's all sorts of *don'ts* and *nots* in there canceling each other. Read this one and also you'll see how this one works. Okay?

Let's go to the next example: '*I often tell people that they* **shouldn't** *tell me that they can't afford this* **unless** *they are already committed to finding a way they can.*' Very, very interesting way of doing this.

You can see how this pattern works though. You might wonder what would happen if I told you, **don't** think another thought in disagreement **unless** you already understand that doing so will have brought you naturally into agreement with me.

Now it's interesting, if you say, '**Don't** *think another thought*' and then you pause. . . at that moment, they're **starting to think another thought**, and you say, '*in disagreement. . .*' It really is sort of pulling the plug in their brain and you'll see when you actually go and practice with that kind of pattern what it does, but it has quite a powerful impact.

Let's go to our next pattern. '**I appreciate (intent of objection) and what would happen if (new behavior) because (reason) and if you do that, I'd be willing to (concession).**' Okay?

So this is a *heavy duty* pattern. Let's hear a couple of examples. This is in response, by the way, to '*Can't afford it*'. '**I appreciate** *that you want to spend your money wisely.* **And what would happen if** *you went ahead and got this because of the wisdom of doing it as well as you've really waited long enough to have this, and as you know, things don't get less expensive.* **And If you do that, I'd be willing to** *guarantee delivery by X date. How would that work for you?*'

Now, this is a really powerful way of doing things. Re-read that example a few times. You'll realize just how powerful it is. Let me give you one more in response to '*I want to shop around*'. '*I appreciate that you want to be sure and get the best price and service for your money. And what would happen if you went ahead and bought this now because of this comparison chart that shows you that we do give you the best price and service? And if you do that, I'd be willing to personally provide the service for you whenever you need it in the future. How would that work? Would that work well for you?*'

See? This is a really fascinating pattern and this pattern comes directly from the military and they were *signing people up* left and right with them. It's an amazing pattern. It uses **cause and effect**, the word **because**, and it's starting right off with **naming the intent of the objection**, and giving a **concession** or an **apparent concession**. I mean, this is a very, very powerful pattern, I think one that you'll come to love a lot, but probably the best way to use these is just to memorize it and that will help you to put it into play even more for you.

Okay. And here we have another pattern somewhat like that. And this pattern goes like this: '**Yes** (*negative feature objected to*), **but** (*positive feature of your proposal*) and **if you're committed to** (*emotion* or *value*) then *you must be committed to* the proposal).' So that's how this works and it's a fascinating way of using this. It's not, again, something you would use constantly or all the time, but it is something that you would use from time to time when you're finding the need. Okay?

And this would be another method of **handling an objection** and it's extremely powerful.

Okay, so here we go: '**Yes**, I can't give you any discount. **But** I can give you all the service you'll need when you need it. And **if you're committed to** improving your standard of living **then you'll want us to** go ahead with the work. When would be the most convenient time for us to begin?' That's persuasive. I really like that. Okay?

Now let me tear this apart a little bit for you. '**Yes**, *I can't give you any discount. . .*' What's that doing? Well, it's **pacing** their reality. Okay? '*But*', what does that do? Well, '**but**' cancels **everything that comes before**. So already we've **paced their reality** and now we're just sort of *dismissing* everything and moving on. '*I can give you all the service you need, when you need it. . .*' **reinforcing** what it is that they want. This could be aimed at their **criteria** or **values** as well. '**And if you're committed to** *improving your standard of living. . .*' So in other words, that would be where you're **leveraging a value**, '**then you will want us to** *go ahead with the work.*' Very powerful.

Let's hear another one. '**Yes**, *it is a lot of money* **but** *there is even more value that you'll receive when you attend, value that is crucial for you to have in your life now. And* **if you really are committed to** *the kind of life that this will provide you,* **then you must be committed to** *attending this now.*'

That's a strong pattern.

And let's do the last example of this: '**Yes**, *it is a lot of time to take from your schedule,* **but** *the time it will provide you with after you have this knowledge as well as the added power you'll have to persuade people powerfully will make it worth the time it takes to learn this and* **if you're committed to** *mastering this type of ability,* **then you must** *make the time to be in this program.*'

I'm sure that makes sense.

Now, I mean, that's *very* persuasive. It can handle a simple objection and it can handle it quite powerfully.

Okay, I'm going to give you one bonus pattern from these patterns and then you'll have them all.

So this pattern is really only useful if you're *already* working with someone and doing business with them. It can be used to overcome a hiccup along the way if something goes wrong once they've committed to working with you as well as long as it's like the second hiccup. So primarily this would be for people that you're already working with. Here it is.

'*(You state your objective)* **and I appreciate** *(future obstacles).* **Imagine** *for a moment that* **together,** *(we or you)* **overcome those future obstacles as we've or you've done in the past**. *Don't you feel good now?*'

So here's how it might sound. '*I want you to give us your business now* **and I appreciate** *that you're concerned about meeting your financial obligations in the next few months, but* **imagine** *when* **we've overcome the future obstacles just as we've overcome difficulties in the past**. *Don't you feel good now?*'

So in other words, let's say you've already done business with someone and you've helped them overcome some obstacles or whatever, and they've said to you, '*Look, I just don't know if I can continue on with you*' and you say, '*I want you to give us your business now* **and I appreciate** *that you're concerned about meeting your financial obligations in the next few months, but* **imagine** *when* **we've overcome those future obstacles just as we've overcome difficulties in the past**. *Don't you feel good now?*'

So this is a **temporal shift** of things as well. Okay? So you're **shifting between the future and the past and the present** and it creates a very powerful, compelling argument. Again, this isn't something you're going to use every day or all the time, but it's very, very powerful and when you get the opportunity, now you'll have the ability to do it.

CHAPTER FIVE

A Notch in the Key

Let's move on. I'm really excited to present this to you in this book. I think you're really going to enjoy it. I call it '**making a notch in the key more apparent**' and the reason I'm calling it this is because I've *already given* you this **notch in the key**, to a certain extent. I've taught you a little bit about it. But now I'm going to make it explicit and very clear for you.

Early in the course, I taught you a strategy to **open up a conversation**, to start a presentation. You learned to ask '**Why are we here today?**'

Now, this question, as we've discussed, can't *always* be asked. Depending on why you're there, how the appointment was set, if it's a follow up appointment, if it's the second time there, you may not be able to ask **'why are we here?'** because it may be blatantly obvious and that'll sound silly. Okay? But when you *can* ask a **'why'** question, you should. And here's the reason. Now we're going to make this very explicit for you and you'll start to understand even more.

'Why' forces a person to choose between **'what'** and **'how'**. . . so they have to answer a **'why'** question with either answering in terms of **'what'** or in terms of **'how'**. **'What'** is **criteria** and **'how'** is **procedures**. Okay? In other words, if I said, **'*Why* are you in this program?'** you would have to tell me the **criteria** that made you choose to be here or the **procedure** that you went through in your mind to do it.

That's how **'why'** is dealt with in the mind. It **forces a choice between 'what' and 'how'**. So answer this question. **Why** did you choose your current job or career? And I want you to answer that before you go on. Just answer it the way you normally would. **Why** did you choose your current job or career?

And when you're ready, we'll continue on.

Okay, I assume you've answered the question, **why** did you chose your current career or job? Here are the four ways you could have answered this. First, you could have answered with strictly what we would call an **options response**, meaning, all you spoke about were **criteria** or looking for *other ways* or *possibilities*. So in other words, you could have said, '*I chose my current career because I wanted much more from life, more money, more opportunity. I wanted to be able to control my future, and I wanted to earn what I felt I was really worth and I knew I would never be able to do that working for others.* So there's **options**, **options**, **options**. In other words, **criteria**, **criteria**, **criteria**. *All the person talked about* is **criteria** there.

Now, I'm going to skip the second one, I'm going to go to the third one called **procedures** because I want to *contrast* the two. Okay? So if you answered more like in terms of *necessities*, *facts*, or you *described the way* you did it or you *started counting*, the first thing, the second thing, the third thing, then you'd be dealing with **procedures**. So if I asked you, '***Why* did you choose your current career?*'** You might have said, '*Well, I don't know that it was really a choice. I mean, I was unemployed. And I had to have money so I was looking in the paper and I found an ad that said call here if you have a college degree. We're looking for financial advisors and I called and the guy said, do you have a college degree, I said, yes, and he said, okay, well I'd like to schedule a time for you to come in and see me. And we did. I went there. He told me about the things. He suggested that I give it a try, and I did, and well, I've been here ever since.*'

Do you see how I'm giving you *the way I did it*? I'm giving you a **procedure**. I'm telling you step one, step two, step three. '*Well, I was looking in the paper, then I did this, then he said do that and I did, and then we did this and then we did that*', I'm **counting**, one, two, three. . . I mean, this is a very **procedural** approach.

Now, *contrast* that with the approach you heard before that, the **options** approach or the **criteria** approach. The person wanted to **fulfill these different criteria** where the person telling us a **procedure** had **a number of steps they had to go through** in order to get what they wanted.

Okay. Now, let's throw in the **shades of gray**. So let's say when I asked you, '***Why* did you choose** *your current job or career?'* you answered with *mostly* **options** but *some* **procedures**. Here you're going to hear an *emphasis* on **criteria** but also *some* **procedures** or **counting**. So maybe you said, '*Well, I wanted to get ahead. I wanted to control my own life and give myself the opportunity for success and I was looking as to the industry that would do that for me and I found the field of financial advising and I thought, this looks interesting, and I got on the phone and I started talking to a few people and one of the guys said to me, he goes, "Look, there are a few things you've got to do. The first thing we've to do with you is. . ."'* (Notice I said, *first*. Now we're into **procedures**.) '*"First thing we need to do is have you fill out our test because we'll be able to tell just how good you're going to be." I thought, all right, and the guy said, "Come on in, let's set an appointment and we'll do that". So I did and I filled out his test. And he suggested to me that I had what it takes to really be a good financial advisor. So I went ahead and I took the job and I've been here ever since. I mean, it worked out very, very well and I am accomplishing the things I set out to accomplish.'*

So you heard them start off talking about **options** and then you heard them kick into some **procedures** so another way I look at this really is it *starts* with **options** and then it *moves* to **procedures**. That's sort of the *mostly* **options**, *some* **procedures** way to look at it. All right, let's do the other way.

If you answered the question I asked you, '***Why** did you choose your current job or career?*' with *mostly* **procedures** and *some* **options**, then you would have put an *emphasis* on the **procedures** but probably *ended* with some **criteria** so it might sound something like this, '*Well, I was looking in the paper. I found an ad. It said to call, I did. They said they were interviewing people in groups and to come on either Thursday night or a Friday morning. I had missed the Thursday night already so I went on Friday and at this meeting, they asked us what we really wanted from our lives and I realized what I wanted. I wanted to have more control over my life.*' Control, by the way, is a **criteria**, right? '*I wanted more control over my life and so they suggested that this could be done here, and I kind of saw the light. I saw what they were trying to get across and they said, "All right, we're going to only hire three people out of this group and I want you to all fill out your applications." I did. I went and did it and I was picked and, well, it worked out really well for me.*'

So they *started off* with **procedures** but they kind of *jumped into* a little **criteria** and they pretty much kind of *went back* into **procedures**. So they're *mostly* **procedures** but they had a *little bit* in the way of **options**.

Now, that will take some time to learn how to determine what people are doing. All right? But you've already had some practice with this from the beginning I taught you how to ask, '***Why are we here today?***' Now you can make the '**why**' question, *any* question. You can ask '**why**' of *anything*, really. But it needs to be about the subject matter that you're trying to persuade in. In other words, it needs to be in the realm of what you're trying to persuade in or it won't necessarily be valid information that you're getting.

So what do you *do* with this? Well, I bet you already know, but let me explain it. When the '**why**' question produces primarily **options**, you're going to give them all kinds of **criteria**. In other words, you're going to **use their criteria**, you're going to talk about their **criteria**, you're going to aim everything you say and do into their **criteria**, just like I've taught you all along. Let's say that your '**why**' question, you discover that they're very **procedurally** oriented. What you're going to do there is you're going to go *first, second, third, fourth*. You're going to show them a **specific process** of how you're going to do it. And if it's *mostly* **options** and *some* **procedures**, you know what to do. And same with the other way around.

So I just wanted to kind of make this a bit more apparent as to what's really happening when you ask a **'why'** question. Now you understand why I like asking a **'why'** question very early on. You've got to be careful with them. I think I've already told you that they make you sound like you're whining if you don't do it right, but done like I'm showing you, they immediately identify whether the person is oriented towards **options** or towards **procedures** which allows you to quickly adjust your presentation style to take advantage of it.

If someone is very **procedurally oriented**, you want to give them *a number of steps to follow*. And here's a big key in dealing with **procedures oriented** people, make the *buying step* happen in the *middle* of the **procedure** you tell them, *not* at the end. This makes it much easier for them to follow through. Okay? Because people that deal with a **procedure** have to *go to the next step*. Now I've talked about this off and on throughout the program but I wanted to give you a little more deeper understanding of what's really happening with this.

For example, I can identify real quick **procedural** people that are listening if I say it like this. Look, I want to give you now *five steps* that'll help you understand this, *five specific steps* that will really make this clear. Number one, here's what I want to do. . . . You might want to jot this down.

As an aside, I really don't have five steps. Do you feel *disappointed*? If you do, you were thinking very **procedurally**. You can do this in a group or even one-on-one with people. You can say, look, there are *four things* I want to show you today. Number one, . . . If they start listing the 1, 2, 3, 4, ... and you see this happen a lot. People start *writing numbers* on the pages. They're going to *fill in* those numbers. Okay? You're literally **opening up holes in their brain**. Now we talked about this when we talked about **leaving loops** in their brain. Opening holes in their brain by saying, '*Look, there are **three things** I want to tell you today. .*' and you tell them *one* and *two* but you leave *three* out.

That works on **everybody**. But here you can really *identify* when someone is a **procedures oriented** person and **they want to follow through the procedure**. So when buying is step *three* of *six* or *five*, they have to go *through* the buying part to get to number *four* and number *five*, so they **haven't completed the process** until they buy. If you put buying at the very *end*, they can go all the way up to that point but then they *don't* really go through the end one because they already know what it is and there's nothing *compelling* them on to the next step.

So deal with **procedures** people by **putting buying in the middle**. Okay? With **options** people, you just need to **keep giving them their criteria**, feed it back. Now does this mean that **procedures** people *don't* use **criteria**? Not at all. They *absolutely* use **criteria**, it's just that they'd like to have a **procedural** way of going through things and you've got to give them things in a **procedure** and it makes them happy when you do.

CHAPTER SIX

Homeplay

All right, I already told you to write ten **binds** for each of the three strategies I listed plus ten for the bonus strategy. That's a *bare minimum*, folks. That's just a *bare minimum*. That's if you just want to kind of get brushed up on them, okay? If you really want to *master* it, you'll probably write a *hundred* for each of the strategies, all right?

I've written many, many, many, many, many times more than that. I mean, if you do it, you're going to see just how powerful this is for you and it's going to really help. In fact, the **more** you do it, the **more** you're going to love doing it.

Next, write the **military patterns of persuasion** we covered in this book until they become second nature. Really, I would say **memorize** these. These are some of the few patterns I would recommend memorizing but I would memorize them. All right? And practice honing your skills with **options** versus **procedures** pattern. Make that **notch in the key** that I've given you all along very, very clear and apparent so that you understand it and you can use it with ease. This will just make it easier when you're working with people to hear what they're really doing and why.

All right. Have a wonderful time writing this homeplay out and persuade like mad. And until we speak again, go out and make it happen. Talk to you soon.

BOOK NINETEEN

THE ILLUSION OF CHOICE

INTRODUCTION

Overview

Welcome to **Book Nineteen** of *Persuasion Force*. I want to thank you for joining me in this course of books it's really been a lot of fun so far. And can you believe it? We only have about five books left. That's it. We're almost through the entire program. But these last editions will be *incredible* as we increase the complexity and get to even deeper and more powerful strategies now that you have some background to understand them with. So I'm really excited to present this information to you and this lesson is going to rock. We're now into some of my most favorite territory and I think you're really going to like it.

In this book, we're going to be talking about **creating the illusion of choice**: more ways to **bind thoughts**.

CHAPTER ONE

Double Binds

I want to talk with you about **double binds**. We've talked about **single binds** which is, '***The more you X, the more you Y***'. We've talked about **implied** kinds of things, '***As X, Y.***' We've talked about '***X causes Y.***' Now let's talk about **double binds**. And we're going somewhere with this so hang tight, because in this book I'm going to kind of open the kimono a bit. . . that's kind of a *bad image*, isn't it? To show you why I'm going there. Okay? So you'll see.

Now, this pattern uses **two alternatives** where *either* **one you choose creates the** *same* **basic choice only they're worded differently**. In other words, it's like, '*Would you rather do A or B tonight?*' but A and B is **the same thing** and whether you do A *or* B is just fine with the person asking because **they both mean the same thing**.

So a good example of this is Milton Erickson who would say when trying to get a young child to get ready for bed, he might suggest you say, '*Do you want to get ready for bed now or brush your teeth?*' Now, note that *either* choice they choose got them in the direction of heading to bed, whether they're doing the prerequisites of bed or they're actually getting dressed and ready for bed. So that's a great example of the use of a **double bind**.

Let's talk about **how to do it**.

So what you want to do is *think about something you want someone to do and write that down*. Now this is how I learned it and it made it really easy for me. Find *two ways* to language it and then deliver it.

Okay? So, for example, '*Would you like to go out to eat tonight or maybe we could explore some new restaurants in the area that we just haven't been to yet. What do you think?*' Well, either way, you're going out to eat, right? Okay? '*Would you like to go out tonight or would you enjoy going bowling, perhaps?*' There's another example where it *sounds* different and the word '*or*' creates. . . you know, most people when they hear '*or*', '**this or that**', it sounds like there are *two*. . .In other words, we're **trained**, we're **conditioned** that when we hear '**or**' you're going to hear *two different things*, maybe even *opposite* things. Or two very different things.

Would you rather go to the movies or to dinner? Would you rather go bowling or to the movies? Would you rather have an appointment on Monday or Wednesday? Okay? **So what we're doing with this is finding ways to say the same thing using the word '*or*' to make people kind of trigger that there's something different, but in reality, there is no difference.** Shall we get you started or shall we just fill out the application first? Okay? Have you decided to go ahead with this or are you contemplating just what it will mean to you in your life when it's yours? Really, **either way works**. And it works really, really well. It's just that, you want to make sure that you're doing it, I guess, with *sophistication*.

'*As I talk with you, you're going to begin to probably imagine what this would be like in your life and feel a sense of real happiness and contentment **or** you might just begin to become curious about what it would be like if it were yours right now and you already had the protection that we're talking about. Either way, I think that this would be a good time for a conversation for us.*' See? That's **the illusion of choice**, you've made it *sound* like there may be something different, but there really isn't anything different. It really is the same thing.

So that's the gist of this. That's how this works.

And the *old fashioned* way to do this was, '*Would you like to use your pen **or** mine to sign the contract?*'

And nobody, not even really back then, was fooled by that. It was just a slick way to close, but look, the idea of
trying to *trick* or *slick* someone into something like that where it sounds *too* smooth, that's not really helpful. That won't work real well. Nobody back then really believed, oh, well, let me think. Okay, yeah. I'll use your pen. Sure. That **never** really did get people to buy, or at least not very many times and not with people who were very bright anyway.

So I guess what I can say to you is, really *think* about this because **you want it to *sound* very different**. And whether you make it sound really different **or** come up with a completely unique way to say it, it doesn't really matter to me, but you'll figure out how to do it. See? That is another. . . I just did it. Okay? Whether you choose to hire our company to go ahead with this project, **or** you say to me, '*Kenrick, just help me. Would you? I want you to be the one to watch *over this because I think you really know what you're doing.'* Either way, it's totally okay with me. I'll go along with you. So let's talk about it.

See? Again, **it sounds better**. It sounds like there's some kind of a **conclusion**. Now, if you were ever *caught* on it, if they go, '*Wait a minute, isn't that the same thing?'* '*Well, I suppose it is I guess. I was just thinking more about you just being happy with our service or you actually want my specific help, but yeah, sure.'* And just act like it was nothing. Like, what they just said was nothing.

And let's **put it into practice**. The thing I'd like you to do is to *write five things that you want someone to think*. Now you can do this about behavior, but it's far better to do it about what you want them to think, and then *phrase each one of those five things in two different ways* and *practice delivering them so you sound natural*. That's the key to this. You've got to **practice** delivering
it so you sound natural. Okay?

Now this one will **not** work just by you reading it here. **You have to write this out and practice it**. So practice it. They have to sound natural. They can't sound like your pen or mine. That's not going to work.

CHAPTER TWO

Installing Future Thoughts and Behaviors

Let's go on to talk about **installing future thoughts and behaviors**. We're getting into real profound things here as we get into this one. In fact, the strategies we're talking about now have been responsible for more deals going my way, more money earned, and more success in my life than you can hardly imagine. Truly, this strategy alone is worth its weight in gold. And when you understand its far reaching implications and you begin to implement it, let me just tell you, you're either going to be absolutely thrilled **or** you'll wish I'd spend even more time talking about it. It's just that good. . . Hmm was that a **double bind**? Okay. See how you start to *use* these things. That's a way to do it. You know, I kind of hate it because as I give you all of these strategies that I've been giving you in these books, now, occasionally, I'm hoping you're spotting me **using** them on you. It's fun.

As you catch me, by the way, let it sink in even deeper, because that way you'll *get* it and you'll *learn* it and it'll become even more available to you. Now *right there*, if you go back and read it again, I just *did* what I'm going to be writing about here. I'm starting to kind of call your attention and your awareness to what I'm doing because I really want you to start to notice it.

So a lot of the strategies that we've been talking about up to this point have been oriented towards getting people to go along with you. And really, this one is too, though this one has very special properties to it. It can make sure that once you *get* a commitment, the person that gave it to you **won't ever change it**. And **it can stick things in their mind that will be remembered** without you having to be there to remind them. This one . . . this one is just brilliant.

All right, the reason I'm teaching this to you now is that you've been learning about different ways to **bind thoughts**. What I'm teaching you now is perhaps **the ultimate type of bind**. In essence, it's **the bind a person does to themselves through rehearsal**. That one is one of the most *brilliant* lines I've ever written if I do say so myself.

***All* persuasion is really *self* persuasion.** The only way it wouldn't qualify is if you're holding a gun to their head or if you've used the first stratagem of using a woman to ensnare a man or a man to ensnare a woman, whichever way you've done it, where you've photographed somebody in compromising positions and used it against them, but that's not persuasion, that's coercion or worse.

So we've been talking a lot about **binds** because they are a **cause and effect** type of pattern that are incredibly powerful. You learned about the word '*because*' and *causes, forces, makes,* and *as, while, during, since. . .* those kinds of words. And you learned the **single binds, the more you X, the more you Y**, and you've learned **double binds** now in this book. Okay? And by the way, if for any reason this feels like it's *flying* by, it *is*. We are *jamming in* the information. So **stop**. Whenever you get a feeling like that, just **stop** and **go back** and **re-read**. Okay? It's really important. That's why I break these things up into short sections, because you can kind of go back over any section that you want to whenever you want.

But it's really important that you *understand* that this now is rather like **the granddaddy of all binds**. This is the **ultimate**. Okay? And **it can use the others within it**.

Let me demonstrate by talking about this course of books with you for a minute. Okay? This will help you to understand better. So first thing I want you to do is to just stop for a moment and remember *why* you bought these books. Think about that for a moment. Think about what *convinced* you to do it. Think about your personal **values**, the things that you are looking to accomplish more of and to be better at and to maybe get away from, etc. And I want you to think of a few of the *strategies* that most impressed you, or that most stand out to you. Just identify a few of the strategies that you think, *wow*, when Kenrick talked about that, that was pretty cool. And I'd like you to think about any **wins** that you've had since beginning reading the *Persuasion Force* books, any successes, okay? Or places where you know you should be using it and are beginning to.

Now, we're only a few books away from finishing the program, as you know, as I told you earlier in this book, and you've been with it now from the beginning, and I imagine you would really like to have the last few books of the program, so you will have the *whole course* with no gaps or missing sections, is that right? I suspect you said *yes*. Now suppose that a family member or friend tried to convince you to quit. What would you say to them so that you would be able to *finish* and get the last few books? Really think about it and come up with what you would say.

Now let's suppose that another friend tried to convince you to stop, what would you say to them so that you would *really feel good* about getting the last few books here?

And as silly as this is, suppose that you began to doubt your decision. In other words, you began to doubt the decision to continue and finish out the program. What would come up in your mind just *before* the doubt could enter, *knocking it out altogether*, that would *convince* you to finish the last few books? Answer that question very specifically.

Okay. Now, I want you to just think about **how you feel right now**, because if you went through that process with me, you probably feel pretty good and pretty strong about finishing the program. Now the question is, *why*? Well, you **rehearsed in detail** what you'll do if anything comes along that tries to change your mind. So right now, you have **a sense of certainty, a sense of knowing**, and that's *desirable* by humans. Humans would like to have **sureness, certainty**, that they know what's going to happen in their life. Okay? And now you *do*, as it relates to this. You probably had before this, but nonetheless, now you have more of that as well. But there's a real key part, okay? You **rehearsed in detail** what you'll do, so **you already know what you're going to do**. That is key. That's paramount. It's incredibly powerful. Remember, I told you that **it's a *possibility* that people *might* believe you when you try to convince them of something, but they will *always* believe what they *conclude on their own***. Remember that? And you just went through a **process** in which **you concluded how you would behave** under conditions of people trying to get you to quit the course. You **rehearsed how you would act** even if *you* tried to convince *yourself* to quit. Now are you getting why this is so powerful?

This is . . .oh, my goodness, I'm telling you, this stuff, it rocks the world. Now you can use this to help you **remember things** as well as to **make other behavioral changes**. In fact, for example, if something's really important and I have to remember it, sometimes what I do is I imagine a big neon sign on the door, the door to the front of my house, and so when I'm getting ready to leave, and I imagine it's turning on and it's flashing the message at me, in really big letters and everything, colorful, and I tell myself that when I get ready to leave, I'm going to look at that sign flashing and I'm going to be reminded that I have to bring that with me. And so what happens is, I get ready to go and while typically I might have forgot it, or I'm fifty-fifty, I might have remembered, I might have forgot, now I see this sign flashing in my mind and I remember.

Now you could imagine that another part of you steps forward at the door and says, '*Excuse me, sir, are you remembering to bring your. . . ? Excuse me, ma'am, do you have your papers?*' Okay? So you could do it in what you see, you could do it by what you hear, you could do it by what you feel. You know? For example, you're going to have an image come into your mind of you weighing your briefcase, and if it weighs too little, you know that you've forgotten something and what you've forgotten is the exact papers for the contract that you need to bring, or what have you.

So you can use it to **make behavioral changes**. You can do *all kinds of things* with this. We'll get into some of that.

So in fact, have you ever tried to **pressure yourself to do something** and told yourself how you could *get out of doing it* if need be? You ever done that? In that instance, **you rehearsed failing** and I'll bet that's what happened. Okay? So this is why, by the way, when people sell and they go, '*All right, look, if for any reason Mr. Smith, you've gone ahead and signed up for this health spa membership today, but look, if you don't like it, just cancel. Really. Any time. Just cancel.*' Or, '*You know, listen, we're going to go ahead and sign you up for this program to get your roof replaced, but if any time within the next 72 hours you want to cancel, just do it. No problem.*' Well, what do people do? They **rehearse** it, they **imagine** it, and then they **go and do it**. They *quit*.

So **we tend to do what we rehearse in our mind**. Always remember, **people *might* believe you when you try to *convince* them of something, when you *tell* them something, but they're *always* going to believe what they *conclude on their own***. And what's a way to *get* them to conclude it? **Get them to believe it's their idea**. Get them to **rehearse ownership of it**. If you do that, it's a **bind** of the most inordinately powerful strength.

CHAPTER THREE

Self-Fulfilling Prophecies

Now think about how this is related to **binds** and **double binds** and **cause and effect** language. Here's the thing: if I say to you, '*The more you think about this, the more you begin to find it's true.*' Well, what am I getting you to do? At high speed, I'm basically **instructing** your mind **on a process level**, to *do* something. '*The more you think about this, the more you'll find it's true.*' So you'll start thinking about it and if you think about it a few times, it becomes **familiar**. As it becomes familiar, your brain goes, '*Wow, it **must** be true.*'

So it's sort of like **self fulfilling prophesies** and we'll talk about that in just a minute. You can use *all* of the **bind** types of language to make the process of **installing future thoughts and behaviors** even more powerful if you want to, meaning you can *combine* all of that. But now I hope you understand why I am teaching you this now. It makes sense, doesn't it?

Now just recently you learned about '**just suppose**'. Now let's get right down to it. Think about what that's *really doing*. You understand how when you say '*just suppose*' you're getting someone to throw open the doors to their mind, allow you to march your soldiers right in, and **get them to do exactly what you want**? If you can get them to **imagine** it, they'll be far more inclined to **doing** it. Remember the saying, **if you can conceive it and believe it, you can achieve it**. I think that's Napoleon Hill. Well, if you can *conceive* it, that just means *imagine* it. And *believe* it, how do you *believe* something? Well, it could be a gut instinct, but it could be you **rehearse it over and over**. You **imagine yourself doing it**. You imagine that you could do all the steps and all the parts and pretty soon if you can **rehearse** it enough, you'll **believe**. And if you can get to the point of *believing* you can and will *achieve* that, whatever it is. So you start with '**just suppose**' and in order to **just suppose**, you're in essence saying '**imagine**' in all of the **modalities**. *Imagine, hear, feel. . .* Okay?

And they throw the doors of their mind open to your words, your soldiers, which march right in and get them to believe that this is the right thing.

Think about how when you get people to believe that *they* came up with an idea, it far more powerfully affects them then if *you* have the idea. If it's *their* idea, it's even more powerful, isn't it? And that's in keeping with the whole theme of what we're talking about here in this book.

Can you use *that* strategy within *this* one? *Aren't* we?

So that's the whole basis of this is that **we're getting them to bind *themselves* with *their own imagining***, talking, of the way they're going to handle something, their own **rehearsal** of the way it's going to work.

Now let's make this more concrete. What we're really doing is we're **linking** to something that's *real* or *known* or *expected* or *true* or *verifiable*, or all of those. Okay? So you're going to understand what that means in just a minute. This strategy is in and of itself incredibly valuable and powerful because you can use it to do all kinds of **installation** things with people.

So for example, you can suggest that the person you are persuading is going to *think* or *remember* or *do* – but *thinking* and *remembering* is better – something when the *real* or *known* or *expected* or *true* or *verifiable* thing happens. For example, imagine you're driving home. What road do you always pass or what sign do you always pass just a few minutes before you get home? Do you know what I'm talking about? So you're driving home right now, okay. What road, road sign, or sign, do you always pass just a few minutes before getting home? Pick one. Got it? Okay, **imagine** as you pass that sign right now it **signals your unconscious mind** to *combine* what you're learning in this course into your thoughts, behaviors and speaking in a way that causes you to get even more of what you want. Can you **imagine** that?

What just happened? Well, first of all, answer this. What is it that *causes* that signal when you're nearing home? So imagine you're going home, and now you're *signaled* to *combine* what you're learning in this course into your thoughts, behavior and speaking just like I just told you. What *caused* that? And if you said, '*Oh, well, I passed such and such a sign. I passed the sign that says whatever. . .*' Okay? Or '*I see this road sign...*' So that's the *signal*. So look up where it says **linking** to something just a page back. Look up where it says **linking** to something *real, known, expected, true* or *verifiable*. All right?

That's what I'm talking about here. So it's a *sign* and they pass it all the time. It's *true*, it's *verifiable*. It's not something they have to *believe* that they're going to pass this sign, they're *actually* going to pass this sign every time they go home. And you're **using that as the signal to trigger the suggestion** that you just gave. Okay?

Now, just **imagine** that you're on your way home right now and you see that **signal** and *what happens*? How does it *feel*? Well, some people say, '*Well, you know, I don't have much of a feeling.*' Well, that's okay. I didn't elicit much of an emotion with it. Some of you, though, will go, '*Well, yeah. I have this thought that I should be. . . that I'm like integrating this stuff a little better.*' Or what have you. It's subtle, but it doesn't have to be blatant. Subtle is absolutely fine.

I'd like you to list some things that you can **link** to and these things need to be like *real, known, expected, true* or *verifiable*, something like that. I'm going to give you a few of them here. And I've used these.

- Flushing the toilet and seeing the water spin.
- Turning on a faucet and hearing the water run.
- Shutting your car door and hearing the sound it makes.
- Catching a glimpse of yourself in the mirror.
- Seeing your house as you pull up to it.
- Hearing the sound of your breathing.
- Feeling your right shoe as you put it on the morning.

For example, you might. . .well, here, I'll just do it to you now. For example, you know, every day, throughout the day, we all end up *flushing a toilet* one or more times, usually several times. And we do that for a *reason*. We want to *get rid* of something. And I'd like you just to **imagine** any possible *reservation* you might have about this program or what you're learning and I want you just to **imagine** that for all the obvious reasons, that the next time you *flush the toilet*, there goes all of those things right along with it and you see the water swirling. Now, I don't know what part of the world you're in, but I know it swirls *different directions* in *different places*. So which way is the water swirling? And you might just make a note of that for the next time you flush it, which way does it swirl, clockwise or counter-clockwise? Okay?

Now, have I just **installed a future thought or behavior**? Well, yes, to a certain extent. Okay? So that's all it takes. It's just real simple. Now they *can* resist it. People *can* resist it, but typically if they're basically going along with you, it just kind of *goes in one ear and out the next*. It's like, okay, whatever.

Now, if you're wondering if any of this has anything to do with **anchoring**, it does, and you are right on track. In an upcoming book I'm going to give you strategies that are going to blow you away that you're going to be able to use to gain *huge* advantage tying all this in with **anchoring**. I'm telling you, you're going to love it. So that's kind of where we're headed. You're starting to see some glimpses, I'm sure.

But what I'd like you to do now is to come up with as big of a list as you possibly can on your own of **things that you can use** that equal basically *real, known, expected, true* and *verifiable*--things like street signs, flushing the toilet, turning on a faucet--that kind of stuff, and I want you just to make as big a list as you possibly can. So stop reading and do that.

And then, what I want you to do is **practice languaging these so they're smooth**. You've got to practice languaging them so they're smooth. That's the key. You can't start cracking up when you do it. All right? Just make it smooth.

Now, you can use this as you start a presentation to have them *remember* something later on. You could say, '*Now, you probably have a real desire for why you came here tonight. You have a desire to accomplish something of importance for yourself. And you may have yet to come to the conclusion that what I'm going to be talking about is the right answer. But I'd like you to **imagine** that in about. . .well, in a little ways, in a little time period, I'm going to actually **show** you something that I think will make the point very clear. It's a slide that I'll be showing you and you're going to know this slide because it's purple colored. And when you see it, you may just immediately have the thought, 'All right, this really is for me. Now I get it.' I'll let you come up with your own conclusion on that, okay?*' And then go on.

Well, what have you done? You've just had them **rehearse** seeing a purple slide with something on it that is going to make them think, '*Wow, this is for me.*' So that slide, you'd want to put a purple background on it at the point in your presentation when basically you're giving some **proof** element that they would have to accept. . . if they accept it as true, then it will trigger what you've just programmed. So it's a way of putting into the figure what you want them to think or do. You can use it to recall a commitment to something, to stop **buyer's remorse**. I'm going to get into that in great detail in a minute. You can automatically get someone to think something when you're not there, to remind them when the trigger is present, like a road sign, the sound of water, or whatever. It doesn't even have to be an agreement, just, by the way, I want to make sure you remember to do X or Y, so for example, on the way home tonight, when you pass by Division Street, will that remind you to make sure and drop off the movie before you get home? See? That kind of thing.

Also, you can use this to **make predictions** about what you want someone to conclude that are **self fulfilling** just like I just demonstrated. So you can **predict** that they will **think X when you get to Y** point in the presentation. Saying it will help make it happen because they have to **rehearse** it even to make sense of that sentence. That's why it's so powerful.

CHAPTER FOUR

Stopping Buyers' Remorse

I want to talk with you now about **stopping buyers' remorse**. The first step to this is to **get a commitment**. Now, *before* you're asking for a commitment, I assume by now you should already have their **values**. You know that it's *critically important* to get their **values**. Okay? So you get their **values** and in the course of your presentation you **get a commitment** from them. '*Okay, I'm going to go ahead and buy this. Yup. I'm going to go ahead and do it.*'

Now, you pretty much want to do three things. You want to first suggest that someone like a friend might ridicule them for making this decision and ask them **what they would say** to them if that happened. So in other words, they've committed. '*Yup, I'm going to do it.*' Let me give you some languaging that I've used a lot to make this happen.

'*Fantastic. Well let's go ahead and get you started then. Great. Here's the application. Go ahead and get to filling that out. I'll start filling this other thing out.*' So they're going along. Okay? And now you get them to sign the contract and they're all happy. And you say, '*Great. Congratulations.*' And they go, '*Well, thank you.*' And you go, '*Look, let me just ask you a couple of quick questions. You're happy about this, right? Everything feels good?*' '*Oh, yeah.*' And by the way, I've **got the commitment**. And if I wanted, I could **reinforce it with their values**. '*You're happy right?*' '*Absolutely.*' '*Well, obviously, it makes sense because what you said is you wanted to have more security and you wanted to have more of Y and Z, so it makes sense.*' And they go, '*Absolutely.*' And you go, '*All right. Let's say that you're telling a friend of yours about this decision today. And let's say that they begin to ridicule you for doing this. Now, **what would you say to them** if that happened, that would **cause you to really feel good** and to **continue** to feel good about the decision we've made here?*'

And then shut up and let them answer. And they're going to go, '*Well, it's none of their business what I do. I mean, after all, . . .*' So the first one I start with is like a friend, a bit removed. Okay? You're going to see how I zero it right in. But I want to make the first one real easy for them to be able to do. '*Well, my friend doesn't have anything to say about whether I buy life insurance or how I protect my assets. I'll just tell them, really, this is my decision. It's a good one, and that they ought to talk to you too.*'

And you say, '*Absolutely. That's fantastic. Well, let me ask this. Let's say your spouse didn't understand or agree with your decision and let's just say that happened. **What would you say to them** if that happened so that you could **continue to remain committed** with the decision that you've made?*'

And just wait. Okay? Now, actually in the writing that I wrote for you it says, if that happened so that they could **remain committed to their decision**, but *actually*, you're saying it about the person that *just made* the decision. So **what would you say** to your spouse that would get them to understand that you would be absolutely rock solid, continue to be committed with this decision, you would feel really good about it? And let them go through it.

Now you may need to help them a little. If you do, that's fine, but try to let them come up with it all on their own. Usually they'll say, 'Well, no, they trust me on this. This is after all, how it works. I make these kinds of decisions and if I didn't feel good about it, I wouldn't do it. I mean. . .and they know it and that's the way it is.' Or something like that. Okay? If they say, 'Well, gee, I don't know what I'd do,' go, 'Well, think about it. Think it through for a minute. Think about what they might say and how you would handle that.' And literally give them the time to think about it and to make it happen. That's just really important.

Now, when you get *that* one done, then you say something like this. 'And you know, even though it's not something that I think a person like you would have any difficulty with, sometimes a person begins to doubt their own decision. So if that began to happen for you, just prior to that doubt surfacing, **what would cause you to remember the reasons that you decided to do this so that you would stay committed with your decision?** What would. . . just prior to doubting, what would immediately surface that would cause you to **remember** why we did this tonight?'

And they'll go, 'Well, you know, I think just knowing that I did the right thing. It just feels good.' And you say, 'Absolutely. That's correct. Perfect.'

Now let me tell you something. If you do those three things like I just told you, you will very rarely, and I mean so rarely you'll count them on one hand, find someone changing their mind. If you do it like I taught you how, it **locks** them, literally, into their decision. Now, this is so powerful I've often thought of just not explaining it quite this blatantly. I've had a couple of very powerful experiences with this and I'd like to share them with you, a couple of stories that I think will help you understand.

First, many, many, many years ago I was brought into a car dealership to teach them persuasion skills. Now, the people at this dealership, for whatever reason, weren't all that excited about actually spending time to learn how to do persuasion. I was shocked. I figured, well, management has spent a lot of money to bring me here to teach them how to do this and these guys are going to be thrilled. They're going to love every minute of it. Man, I could not get them to even sit still for five minutes to learn. I was shocked. But that's okay. I was going to do my part the best I could. So I taught and taught and taught. Nearing the end of the training, I taught them how to do this strategy and let me tell you that almost without exception, it stopped all of them dead in their tracks and you could see their minds at work, and they listened.

They role played it with me. They figured this one out. This was very early in my career and I didn't really understand what it meant that I was teaching. . . that's why I said to you, I almost decided later on not to be so explicit in the teaching of this or to teach it at all because it just really worried me. I've gotten beyond that now as you can tell, but this impacted me quite significantly.

I finished up my training and that was that. They were happy with me. The company was happy, the people seemed happy, everything was good. I left and went on about my life. Didn't think anything really about it. I think it was the better part of a year later, maybe more than a year, somewhere like a year or so later, I got a call from the guy that hired me. And he said, 'Kenrick, how you been?' I said, 'I've been really good. How about you?' He said, 'Well, you know, we've been well. We've been better, but we're doing okay.' And I said, 'Well, how can I help you?' And he said, 'Well, what do you charge now for a day of your time?' I said, 'Well, it depends on what I'm doing. What do you have in mind?' 'Well, we're currently encountering very significant difficulty and we'd like to pay you to come back in and do some negotiating for us and help us out.' I said, 'Well, tell me about what you're talking about and I'll see what I would charge you.' He goes, 'Well, *do you remember there was a strategy you taught my guys?'* He said, *'They really liked it, but somehow we've kind of run afoul with the bank.'* He said, *'The banks have pulled our funding and without this funding, we're going to go under like immediately, but we're certain that you can explain to the bank and help us and negotiate us out of this difficulty.'*

All of the sudden the light went on in my brain. And I said, *'Wait just a minute. You're talking about where I taught them how to* **lock people into a decision***, right?'* And he goes, *'Yeah.'* I said, *'Okay, let me just take a couple of WAGS. . .'* You know what a WAG is? Wild Ass Guess? I said, *'First of all, what's happened is, your customers have defaulted on their first or second or third payments and they're happening in large numbers. Is that right?' 'Well, yes. That's what's happening. How did you know?'* I said, *'Well, I'm just taking a WAG here. And let me just ask you, is the reason for that because they were sold a car that was* **beyond their ability to pay for***?' 'Well, you know, that's subjective, right. I mean, if they bought it, then nobody held a gun to their head.'* And I go, *'Well, you kind of* **did***, though. What you did is exactly what I told you* **not** *to do which is to go out and influence people* **against their will***. In other words, you took people that maybe had X budget, and it was* **real***, and you got them to afford X* **more** *in their* **mind** *and to go along with it and they were* **locked into the deal** *and they couldn't get out, right?' 'Well, I guess you could explain it that way, but that's a pretty negative way to explain it.'* And I go, *'But that's* **real***, right?'* He goes, *'Well, yeah.'* I said, *'Okay, I'll tell you what. I'll help you on one condition.'* He said, *'What's that?'* I said, *'You go back to every customer that defaulted on their loan, you go back to them, and you ask them, you just ask them, you do a needs assessment, you find out how much they* **really** *could afford for a car, you offer to put them in the right car, and you absorb the expense and then I'll go to the bank, explain what happened, that there was a little misunderstanding in a strategy, etc., etc., and that you've already made everything right.'* The guy says, *'No way. We'd go broke.'* And he said, *'We can't do that.'* And I go, *'Well, I can't help you unless you do because you've really been* **unethical** *with your customers.'*

I never did hear how that story came out. I don't know what happened to them. But I can tell you that I was *horrified* when I learned how they had used the strategy. I hadn't thought of using it real negatively. Now, once I kind of got past that, later on in my life, I was running a health spa and a kid came in, a young man, eighteen years old or so, and he wanted to look at purchasing a health spa membership. He had a thirty day free pass. And I was teaching my staff how to close, how to get this to work, how to turn people from a free pass into a paid membership, etc., and I was exceptional at it, personally, and so I was showing them how to do it.

So I had three or four people trailing and listening as I showed this kid around. So we went through a workout together and he was real excited about it and then after the workout we sat down in the office and I had already been layering it on thick and heavy about what I wanted him to do. And I went through the presentation and he agreed he wanted to buy.

So, because I was teaching everybody, I didn't need to, but because I was teaching everybody, I said to this kid, *'All right, well let me just ask you a question. You're excited about this, right?'* And he goes, *'Oh, yeah, man.'* The kid wanted to meet girls and stuff. *'Yeah, man. I met gorgeous women here. I'm going to be able to work out and get in even better shape. I'm excited.'* And I said, *'Great. Perfect. That's really nice. So,'* I said, *'let me just ask you a question. Sometimes, you know, when a person makes a decision like this, a friend of theirs hears about it and they go, "Dude, you're going to buy what? Why are you paying for a health spa? I mean, you could go out and have a drink and meet women. I mean, I can't believe you do something like this." And if that happens,* **what would you say** *to them that would cause you to really feel good about what* *you're doing and* **keep your commitment***?'*

He goes, '*I'd tell them to kiss my arse. I mean, that's my decision and I can do it if I want. And why don't they be cool and come join me.*' I go, '*Well, great. I'd love that. Just bring them in to see me and I'll help them.*' He said, '*Fantastic.*' I said, '*Sometimes a person's family doesn't like it. Mom or dad says, "I can't believe it, son, you're getting out on your own, you're doing your own thing, and here you are going to spend a hundred bucks a month for something you absolutely don't need." And if that were to happen,* **what would you do***?'*' And the kid says, '*Well, I'd just tell them, look, I'm eighteen, I can make this decision and I want it.*' I said, '*Well, that makes sense to me.*'

And I said, '*Of course, I know this wouldn't happen with someone like you, but sometimes a person begins to doubt their own decision and if that were to happen to you, what would come up just before the doubt enters your mind that would completely kick it out, knock it away and make you feel fantastic about what it is that you've done tonight?*' He goes, '*Man, the chicks. I want to be around the girls and this club has them and I want to get in better shape, and after all, that's going to be a part of my life. Wow. This is what I want.*'

And I said, '*Okay, great. Fantastic.*' Everything's good. Write up the membership and out he goes. That night, I get a call. It's his mom. '*May I speak with the manager please?*' I said, '*Yup, that's me.*' And said, '*Sir, tonight my son came in. He bought a membership from you and I'd like you to cancel that for him right now, please.*' And I said, '*Okay, well I can't do that on the phone. I need the paperwork back, but if you'll just have him bring it in, I'll be happy to do it for him.*' She said, '*Okay, no problem. I'm going to send him in in the morning.*' I said, '*Okay, great. No problem.*'

So the kid comes back the next day, he has his papers and he comes to see me. He said, '*Hey, you know my mom called, right?*' I said, '*Yeah.*' He goes, '*Well, look, I don't really want to cancel this, but she really wants me to. But look, could I just work out today? Would that be okay with you? Could I work out and hang out and then I'll just stop back by and give you the papers?*' I said, '*Absolutely.*'

So he went and worked out, but instead of stopping back by at the end of the night, he snuck out. So he didn't see me. I didn't think too much of it. I figured maybe he changed his mind.

That night, I get another call from mommy. Mommy says, '*May I speak with the manager please?*' I said, '*Speaking.*' She said, '*Sir, we had a discussion last night. My son bought the membership, his name is such and such. I instructed you to cancel the membership.*' I said, '*Well, ma'am, first of all, you don't instruct me to do anything. I understand what you said last night. I agreed. I told you to have him bring the papers in. And as far as I know he brought the papers in with him, but he asked to work out, I said absolutely. He asked if he could just stop by when he was done and give me the papers. I said sure. And he did, but he left. He didn't give me the papers. He didn't turn them in and he didn't ask to cancel it. So what do you want me to do? I expected that he would stop by and give me the papers.*' She said, '*Well, we're going to put an end to that. Tomorrow my husband and I are going to come in with him and you will cancel this.*' And I said, '*Okay. That's fine. Come on in.*' She said, '*Okay.*'

The next day, here comes in the whole family. This kid is absolutely dejected. He's looking down. He can't face me. '*Tell him*', the mother said. And he said, '*My mom wants me to cancel this.*' And I said, '*Okay. Did you bring the papers?*' He goes, '*Yeah,*' but he goes, '*but mom, really, it's my decision. I'm eighteen, I should have the right to do this. I don't want to do this.*' Mom said, '*You go

314

cancel that right now.'

I mean this kid was struggling, almost with tears in his eyes. It didn't hit me. All of the sudden though, I remembered, oh, my goodness. I did the **installation of the future thoughts and behavior** strategy that I just taught you. I said, '*Wait a minute. Let me sit down with you for a minute. Come all of you into the office. Come sit down.*' So we did. I told the boy, I said, '*Listen, remember us talking and I went through and asked you, you know, suppose a friend didn't like it or what have you?*' He said, '*Yeah.*' I said, '*You know, sometimes parents really do know best and sometimes a parent will look at you and they know what your circumstance is and your situation is, and they'll want the absolute best for you. Do you think your mom wants the best for you?*' And he said, '*Yes, I do.*' I said, '*Then you know what? Let's just **reverse** what you and I talked about. Let's just assume for a moment that this has nothing to do with your ability to make a good decision and it has to do with your mother wanting the best for you and wanting you to stop. Why don't we just cancel this?*' He goes, '*No, no, no, because I gave my word and I told you the way I would handle this and I don't want to do that.*' And I said, '*I understand. But what if we went ahead and did it anyway? You give some time to think about it. I'll let you use the club for thirty days. And if at that point, you want to go in and purchase it again, then you and your mom come and talk with me.*' He said, '*Okay. All right. I'll do that.*' And guess what, he didn't continue.

But I knew what I was facing. I realized that I had **locked him in** so hard the guy probably would have broken his arm to keep from having to cancel this. So I made it easy for him because I knew it was the right thing to do.

But I hope you understand why it's important to **use this technique with integrity**. Those two stories should show you. . .and the first story with the car dealer what happens when you use it *without integrity*, and in the second story, what happens when you use it *without thinking*. So that you actually **lock people in** that *shouldn't* be locked in.

It has *inordinate* power. When you use those three things that I went through with you—what would happen if a friend ridicules you; what would happen if a spouse or parent tries to talk you out of it; what would happen if you began to doubt your own decision—you do it with those three things and I'm telling you, you will **lock people in** so hard and so powerful, you can hardly believe it.

You might say to me, '*Kenrick, if I do that, and if they were going to cancel, maybe now they're going to cancel instead.*' If they go, '*I don't know, if my spouse doesn't like it, I guess I just wouldn't do it.*' Well, guess what? You **haven't sold them**, have you? Wouldn't you rather know about it right then than count your eggs before they hatch and think that you've got a sale when you don't and it turns right around and cancels on you? That's what I thought. So better to hear it right then and there than to think you got something done and didn't.

CHAPTER FIVE

Home Play

For your home play, write at least, and I'm just giving you minimal here, at least ten **double binds**. Most important, practice *saying* them to make them sound natural.

And then write up ten examples in which you **put future thoughts into the minds** of your prospective customer.

Write three examples of **stopping buyers' remorse** with this strategy.

So if you do this and you begin to implement this, let me tell you, you'll have a lot of victories to celebrate which I highly recommend you do all the time.

We have really exciting material in the final few books so look forward to them. I know I am looking forward to delivering them to you, and I would again, like I always do, recommend that you read this book many times. There is so much material here. If you'll read it over and again you'll really find even more value and it'll sink in deeper and it'll be more available to you when you want it. All right?

Go out and persuade lots and let me know about your successes, would you? Have lots of fun as you go out and use these skills. See you in the next book.

BOOK TWENTY

USING EMOTIONS FOR FUN AND PROFIT

CHAPTER ONE

Building an Image

Welcome to **Book Twenty** of *Persuasion Force*. I'm **Kenrick Cleveland** and I have a really exciting lesson for you in this book. In fact, I think it will become, as you look back on your learning, a very pivotal book in helping you to improve and enhance and grow your persuasion skills to levels that you had previously not even known existed.

But before we jump into this lesson, I'd like to go and answer some questions that were sent into me. Here we go.

"Hi, Kenrick. I'm a sales professional. All my sales are done on the phone. I'm what you call a 'one call closer'. My products are related to real estate and creative financing and range between $2,000 - 15,000. I know I can use **rhythmic speaking**, **pacing** and **leading** on the phone by listening and leading the conversation, but how do I know I have **rapport** on the phone and how can I **build instant rapport** on the first call when my intention is to get the sale?"

All right. here are some thoughts for you. First of all, **the more senses that you can bring into the selling procedure, the better off you are**, the more powerful it's going to be for you and the more control you'll have. It would be like trying to snow ski with one leg. It's certainly possible but you have to make some *adaptations* if you're going to do that. So too do people who are primarily working with just one sense need to make some *adaptations* and I'm going to describe to you a couple of them that I've learned to use that have worked very, very well for me. In fact, I really love them, I do it all the time.

In fact, let me tell you what I'm doing. I'm **imagining** that you and I are sitting, talking together. Now, I can't recall meeting you, but I just *make up in my mind* what you might be looking like. I'm **seeing a person** that is sitting across from me and I'm talking away and answering their questions. And as I talk, I *see* them nod, I *see* them smile or frown, and I'm actually **making an entire visual representation**.

Now, one of the things that I do, and I think this is really an important step here, is I teach my unconscious mind to **listen very acutely**. I *practice* having **tremendous sensory acuity**. And what I do is I tell my unconscious mind that as it **hears** the breathing, and any other sounds emanating from the phone of the person I'm talking with, that it's to **change the visual**

representation of what I'm seeing in my mind. So if what I'm seeing in my mind is the other person smiling and leaning forward and really going along with me, I *know* that my unconscious is telling me I'm right on track. All right, I'm sure you're asking, "Okay, how do I train my unconscious to do that?" And I would say the best bet there is **repetition, intention.** So **intend** that you're going to **repeatedly** get your unconscious mind to do this. And the nice thing is, you're on the phone all the time anyway, right? So before you start a call, **have a discussion with your unconscious** and say, look, this is what I intend to happen here. I'm going to make a picture of this discussion.

And you know what, Reggie? I'll bet you're doing this *anyway.* If you're real good on the phone, *you're probably doing some of this anyway.* I had a very high end phone sales person, they sold business-to-business, actually, and he was extraordinarily talented, he was in my coaching program for quite a while, and what he did is very similar. He would **make an image** of the person he was talking with in his mind. That image would be *adjusted* based on what he **heard** on the other end so that instead of just hearing a sound, he had *both* the **visual** and the **auditory** components as if he were live face to face with the person.

It's amazing how powerfully this works. So your first question is, how do I know I have **rapport** on the phone? All right, I'm going to give you the textbook answer to begin with, then I'm going to kind of elaborate. The textbook answer is, that you know you have it when you can **lead** them somewhere else and they **follow** you. That is the basic definition of **rapport.** So if you change the subject slightly or move in a different direction, or proceed with the presentation and they follow you and they're not resisting you, and they're more or less interested in going along with you, you have **rapport.** If you don't, if they don't, then you don't. That's a good way to put it. Okay?

Let me give you a little bit broader one. I told you to bring in the **visual** component as well. And the reason I want you to do that is first of all, it's just a logical crossover. In other words, you can **hear** what they're telling you on the phone and it's easy to **imagine** the two of you sitting and talking. So you have the **visual** component going. Now, if you have the **visual** component going and the **auditory** component going, would it stand to reason that you would have some **feelings** about what's going on? And the answer is, yes, of course.

And let me just break for a moment. This is in stark contrast to a presentation made on the phone where there is *no* **visual** component in your mind, there's only the **auditory** component and *you've walled yourself off from the prospect* simply parroting a presentation that was written out for you. So you're looking at the presentation and you're saying, "*Of course this makes a lot of sense, doesn't it, Mr. Smith? Yes, it does. All right, well let me tell you a couple of more reasons why our customers find this exciting.*" And you're just parroting this thing and you've done it 30,000 times.

The problem with that is that there's **none of *you* invested**, you're *not there* with the client, you're there with your pitch and unless you're there with the client you're *never* going to have **rapport**, the best thing you'll ever accomplish is rapport with your pitch, with your paper. That isn't going to work .

If you *do* have a pitch or something that you're following, at least use it only and strictly as a *guide*, *not* as something that you're actually reading word for word. If you have to read it word for word, at least memorize it.

All right, so you have the **visual** component, you have the **auditory** component, and now you're **feeling** as well. Interesting. I know that I have **rapport** when I **feel** it. That's how I've trained myself to do it. Because that way it sort of rests gently in and out of my consciousness. I'm paying *extraordinary attention* to what I'm **hearing**. It's easy for me to pay attention to what I'm **seeing** because the image I have in my mind is pretty big. I'm making a big picture. So the slightest movement, which of course is attached to any *change* my unconscious perceives in the **auditory**, is showing me a big picture change and I'm correspondingly having **feelings** about that. When I **feel** that I'm in **rapport**, I **know** that I **am**. And that's one of the main ways I would suggest you do it. You'll gain that by *repetition* and *practice* and *intending* to make it happen.

All right, your next question, how can I build **instant rapport** on the first call when my **intention** is to get the sale? The best thing you can do for **instant rapport** on the phone is immediately **match the tone**, tempo, the **speed**. In other words, *everything you hear* **instantaneously pace** all of it. Be *right there* with them. One of the top people in my coaching program today has been with me from the beginning for many years and he just keeps getting better. He does this without even trying. He simply instantly latches onto the **tone**, the **speed**, the **quality** of the tone, everything of the other person on the other line and *is* that person for all practical purposes. It's truly amazing to hear. And that is the fastest way that you can come close to the instant level of **rapport** on the phone. It actually works. It can be *instant*. The question is, if it's *instant*, will you *know*?

And the answer is, not necessarily instantly unless the response you get back is, "*Wow, hey, I'm so glad you called. What took you so long? How you doing?*" Okay?

CHAPTER TWO

A Question of Trust

All right. Let's go on to the next question. "*Hi. I have read both* **Millionaire Mind-Set** *as well as* **Persuasion Force** *multiple times. I have also been doing the homework. It's all great. I've been trying to* **integrate** *what I'm learning into my sales presentations although sometimes I forget to do it in the heat of the moment. And yes, I've also lost my* **intent** *on occasion because I have a lot of* **rapport** *with my prospects and then lost my focus,*" I can definitely relate to that.

"*However, I take notes after every presentation and try to correct my mistakes and to continue to do what's working. Kenrick states that if you want* **them** *to trust* **you**, *you must trust* **them**. *I have a hard time doing that and would appreciate your input. Perhaps if you knew more about my prospects you'll see why I find it difficult. I sell timeshare in Honolulu, Hawaii.*" Enough said. I understand.

"*I have returned to the company I previously worked for after a six month hiatus and read the current* **Persuasion Force** *books a couple of weeks before I returned.*" By the way, let me just say right there. I'm glad you did, but it's so often that I hear people that say, '*Hey, I'm getting this new job in sales and I need to quickly figure out how to get people to do what I want. What program should I buy, Kenrick, so that I can be up to speed next weekend when I begin, when I go for training?*' Well, for those of you that have been with me now for twenty books in this series, you know that I've barely scratched the surface. I could go 50 or 60 more and it just keeps getting deeper and more profound as you add one skill on top of another. If it were so simple that a weekend of study or a few lessons is all it would take to make the whole world bow and scrape at your feet, then I would charge a million dollars a lesson and you would gladly pay because a day later, you would have it all.

Now, after a couple of days of live training with me, for example, yeah, you're going to know a heck of a lot and you'll have an overview that will give you the basis from which you can proceed with absolute precision as to how you're going to do this, but the **integrating** it part, which is why people are studying these books, it's why *you're* reading *this*, right, the **integrating** part of it takes some time. We're talking about human nature and *changing* your human nature to take advantage and understand the human nature of others. This is what's outside of almost everyone's awareness.

As that happens, it becomes something that needs to be **ingrained** and it takes *time, practice* and *effort* and one of the best ways to do it is get regular and steady training. Anyway, I'm glad you got it at least a couple of weeks before you returned and I'm sure now you're probably going, wow, there is a whole lot here, more than you ever dreamed.

*"The vast majority of people that go to timeshare presentations have absolutely **no intention** of purchasing."* Very true. *"It is my job to sell them a vacation ownership program that costs from about $15 to 65 thousand dollars or more while they are with me and no ifs, ands, or buts, it is a same day sale. The logical premise of the sale is that if people are spending money on renting a hotel room or condo while on vacation, as owners they will enjoy larger accommodations in luxurious resorts for the same or less money then they're spending anyway."*

And by the way, let me just tell you that this whole book's lesson is going to **change the way you're looking at this** right now. You started with the **logical** approach. Bad idea. You go on to say, *"The **emotional** aspects of the sale vary from guest to guest but it often boils down to wanting to spend more quality time with the ones they love. This is an **emotional** sale backed by logic."* Good. I like the way you said that.

*"Part of the sales process is to **discover their needs and wants** shortly after building **rapport**."* I would say right there you're going to do the two simultaneously. *"All this comes after I requalify them. Most people go to a timeshare presentation because they are bribed."* Very true. *"With our company, a third party marketing company offers tourists on the street of Waikiki free dinner cruises, luaus, para-sailingg, et cetera, in return for spending a minimum of 90 minutes to two hours of their vacation time at a sales presentation. In order to qualify to attend our presentation, the prospect must earn a minimum income. The OPC's,"* that would be the people who are trying to get the people to come in for the sale, I believe, *"who solicit the prospects are paid for each tour they sell on going to the presentation."* Okay, so for each person that comes to the presentation, they get paid. *"And that's the root of the problem I have to deal with on a daily basis. Many of the OPCs are less than scrupulous and often wire their tours. They instruct non-qualified prospects on what to say about the income they make. My company is aware of the situation but it is and always has been a reality of this business, at least in this part of the world."* Actually, in all parts of the world, my friend. *"Although my company has tried to crack down, the problem still exists."* Yup. Whenever you find a situation that can be exploited, human nature will try to do it. You're spot on there.

"Therefore, shortly after I meet my guests and before I try to elicit their needs and desires, I must

ascertain if they are truly qualified. It is imperative that I do this because I only see one or two groups of people a day. It is a straight commission job and if they are not qualified, neither me nor my company win and if any do slip through the cracks, they often cannot afford to make the purchase even if they wanted to. Since buying Kenrick's books, I've attempted to put a pink love bubble around each and every one of my prospects before I meet them."

I'm going to stop right here for a minute. I've got to talk here. You're saying you're 'trying' to trust each one of the people that you're talking to. I say that's a mistake in this instance and here's why and here's how to change it. You're not necessarily going to trust *every person* that walks in the door, you're going to trust the people that are *qualified* to be there. In your industry, you're absolutely correct that you are going to find a good percentage of the people that sit down in front of you that don't want to be there, that shouldn't be there, that were pressured somehow into going by the excitement of something free and they're going to get their free deal. They're literally told, as you know, all you have to do is sit there for 90 minutes. Just sit there, tell them that you make this much money and this is what you do, et cetera, and they'll let you go para-sailing for free. Hey, what a deal that is.

Now, this is obviously a very, very unscrupulous sales person that's trying to get them into you. But they've learned how to beat the system and that's the case. Now, every time, by the way, you sniff one out, I would find out *which* sales person sent them to you if at all you can. That sales person is getting a commission for it so the odds are very strong you're going to be able to figure it out and then I would get the company to crack down on that particular sales person. But the long and short of it is, everybody, from the company to you, know this is happening, and yet they're still doing it. Why? Because it
works.

Also, I hate to tell you this, but it's because the company doesn't value you all that much. All they care about is putting bodies in front of you and seeing how many of them you can close. The company care how much you close and the more you close the more they like you and the more you're going to get paid and the more you are happy. However, it's more important to the company that they get bodies in front of you than every single body is qualified. This is simply a cost of doing business to them. And guess who bears that cost? Primarily you, because you have to waste your time with unqualified prospects. That is part of the job of timeshare sales. I wish it were different. I wish I had something really slick to say, but that is part of what you must accept. So what I would do personally if I were in your shoes is I would simply go along -- I would believe that every person can have some advantage through your services. I would believe that that's a possibility. However, I wouldn't necessarily go to the point of *trusting* them full out, especially since you're not doing it anyway and you're saying so in other words here in your writing. I just simply wouldn't go along with the full on trusting them until they're qualified.

Once you *know* they're qualified, and you probably even have a *feeling* if you're sitting with someone who's really good versus someone who's not, once you get that feeling, once it starts to click and make sense to you and things are looking the way they should for you, by all means, extend that pink love bubble and trust them with all you've got. Okay? And I think that's good.

When you say you 'attempt' to put a pink love bubble around each and every one of your prospects before you meet them, you could do that. You could even put a bubble of -- I don't know, you could hang a cloud in the door that they have to walk through that is going to turn those away that are attempting to scam you and bring those to you that need to be there and are good people.

You could also begin to project that more and more you are finding the people that you should be talking with. You could send out a bubble into the universe if you want, and have that bubble go and *find* people that need you such that the people that come to see you are more and more inclined to *want* to be there. I've found a lot of success with that kind of strategy too. I don't know why. I won't attempt to explain it here even though there are lots of good explanations, but I think that will help right there.

Okay, "*I've tried to remember to* **pace** *and* **lead**. *Some days I am more successful at what I'm trying to do than others.*" Lots of the word '**try**' throughout your writing. You better watch that. "*But the hard reality of the job is that often 25 percent or more of the tours I see are not financially qualified to sit in front of me.*" Yes, they're not only not financially qualified but they've been *lied to* already and told that all they have to do is sit there for 90 minutes and you're going to give them a present. So they're looking for a reward that they don't earn, that they haven't earned and they don't deserve.

"*So I found it very difficult to go into the qualification part of my presentation trusting them.*" So **don't**. Just qualify them and **then** trust them. "*I've tried to and in hindsight have gotten snowed.*" Yup. Exactly right because remember, when you start trusting them, then your guard gets dropped. So I would keep your guard up through the qualification process and then **when they're qualified**, drop it, put on full out trust and love coming from you and use every **rapport** strategy that I've been teaching you to immediately get them to come on board.

All right. That was a long question. I hope that helps and that probably also gave a lot of other people insight into the difficulties of the business that you're in. It is an incredibly difficult industry and it is a lot of pressure, but, you know what? If you just relax, let it happen, **intend** for the right people to come to you, **intend** that the people who *aren't* right find their way out the door immediately, that aren't qualified, that are there just for the freebie, and then get on to what you need to do, all the better.

CHAPTER THREE

The Unconscious Greeting

All right, next, "*Hi there. When I do the* **unconscious greeting** *with someone, they usually give you a nod or head dip, but without the smile; so you can still* **give it back** *to them, the nod or head dip, and still* **anchor** *it with them, so no smile. It will still work, won't it?*"

Yes, it still will. It sure will. I like to do the **unconscious greeting** by *immediately* sending back to them *the first thing that I saw* and then looking past their ear and using that as the **anchor**. Usually it works like this, whatever they display when they make eye contact and then you immediately do that back, they will respond, you do their response, and they smile. That's generally what you're going to see. Sometimes the smile happens faster. But you can absolutely still **anchor** it and it absolutely will still work. I'm going to talk extensively about **anchoring** with you here in this book, so hang tight.

CHAPTER FOUR

Adverbs/Adjectives and Rapport

Next question, "*Hi Kenrick, Here's a question about the use of* **adverb/adjective** *in relation to* **rapport**. *Let's say I tell a client one of the following after I got* **rapport**, *his* **criteria**, *etc.: one, 'you can* **easily** *find the budget to find this solution now' or two, 'you can find the budget to buy this solution now'.*" So you can '**easily** *find the budget*' and you can '*find the budget*'. "*Okay, now in reality the client can find the budget, but it will be very difficult for him. In that case, won't the first sentence elicit* **more** *resistance than the second sentence telling him to* **easily** *find it? Won't it also possibly break* **rapport**?"

Yes, it certainly can. Saying that *could* break **rapport**. In other words, that would be almost the equivalent of an **argument**, that you know the guy *doesn't have* the budget and you're telling him he can **easily** find it anyway.

You might instead say, "*You can* **easily** *find enough reasons to make room in the budget or piece out a part of the budget or take out a piece of the budget for this.*" So I would **shift** it from *finding the budget* to *finding the reason* or *discover the reason* to find the budget, so then the **presupposition** is, is there a **reason**. If there *is*, it **presupposes** he's going to automatically go find the budget. That's a deeper level of **presupposition**. I hope that helps and makes sense for you.

CHAPTER FIVE

Temporal and Spatial Words

Next question: "*Hi, I was going through the* **temporal word** *list and I saw that I did not understand why some of the words really fall into this category. Here they are:* **another, other, more, in addition to**. *Could you explain why these words fall into the* **temporal** *category? Also, is it correct that all verbs fall into this category because you can make them point to the past, present or future?*"

All right, this is great. I love your line of thinking and your questioning, it's great. And the answer is, it fits into that category because I say so. No, I'm just kidding you. All right, let me tell you that **temporal words** and **spatial words** are pretty much on a continuum. You almost can't have time without space or space without time and if you can, I'm unaware of how, at least in our dimension. So the words you're talking about could very easily fit into the **spatial** category -- *another, other, more, in addition to* -- these are **spatial** as well, but it depends on *how you're using them*, they could also easily be **temporal** words, '*another*', less so unless '*another*' implies that it's in time, you know, *in another time*, blah, blah, blah.

So, yes, all verbs can fall into that category but I'm talking in the **temporal** *things*, *things* that actually **specifically relate to time and/or space**. If you want, you can kind of think of time and space together. I break them apart because there's some very clear distinctions, the ones you pointed out are *not as clear* which is why you're confused, but if there's something that very *specifically* says **past**, **present** or **future**, then it is **time**, it is **temporal**, and to that end it would fit. Okay?

And I guess, to that extent, yes, '*He gave them a ball*', *gave* would be **past tense**, so it would be **temporal**. And if you're using it *deliberately*, then it will have an effect.

CHAPTER SIX

Group Convincers

"*Hi Kenrick, I found that the* **convincer** *strategy works like a charm in one-to-one sessions, however what can we do when we have a bunch of people in a sales meeting? Seems like pretty difficult to check the* **convincer** *strategy of everybody in the room.*"

All right, yup, that's absolutely the case. I remember one time I was sitting in a training with Richard Bandler and he taught a strategy and it was a strategy, for example, for one-on-one use, and the person said, '*Well, can you use this over here in programming yourself?*' And Richard goes, '*Well, no. Not really.*' And the guy says, '*Okay, well can you use it over here if you wanted to make a recording?*' Richard goes, '*Well, not really.*' And the guy says, '*Well, where else can't you use this?*' And Richard said something like, '*Well, you can't make coffee with it.*'

So, I guess I'm playing with you and saying, you're absolutely correct. You have found a *limitation* of the **convincer** strategy more or less. Meaning that if you were to try to go around the room and elicit *everybody's* **convincer** strategy it would look very obvious and very amateurish and it would not work for you. The same is also true about **criteria**, right? And I taught you a way that you could go and get **criteria** by doing it in a *generic* sense, and you could do the same thing with the **convincer** strategy if you wanted to. In a *generic* sense, it might sound something like this, "*Let me just ask all of you a simple question and you don't need to answer out loud, I'm just going to ask it and I'd like you to think about it, all right?* **How do you know when something is good?** *Is it something you* **see** *or you* **hear** *or you* **feel**? *I mean,* **how do you know** *that it's good? For example, how do you know that a co-worker is doing a good job, or how do you know that a product or a service is good? And let me ask you if you'd just nod your head when you have that answer --something you* **see**, *something you* **hear**, *something you* **feel** *-- just nod your head, would you? Okay, great. Mr. Bigwig there in the middle, would you share -- how do you do it? Is it something you* **see** *or something you* **hear** *or something you* **feel**?" "*Well, it's kind of something I* **see**, *I guess.*" "*All right, perfect. That sounds great. Now let me ask you,* **how many times** *do you have to* **see** *it in order to be convinced? Is it just* **once**? *Is it over* **a period of time**? *Is it* **a number of times**, *like you might need to see it six or seven times and then you're convinced or do you* **always** *need to be convinced? I mean,* **how do you know when you're convinced about it?** *And if all of you just take a second and think about it. Excellent. I asked you to do that today because as I talk with you, obviously I'm here to show you about something that will really change your life, in my opinion. However, it's not* **my** *opinion totally that counts here, it's really* **yours**. *And as I talk with you, I'd like you to be able to remember what it's like to* **know that you're absolutely convinced** *because if what I'm saying measures up to that, I want you to absolutely* *have that understanding now and as we proceed and as such, I think it will help you to understand what I'm talking about a little more effectively."*

I think that probably will help quite a lot, actually. There was one other way I was thinking of to do it, you could do it on one and let everyone watch that and knowing that if you're doing it on the big shot, in essence, that everyone else will sort of be going along with that at the same time, although the way I just did it is probably really good.

Now remember, you can't do very many of these. You kind of have to pick one. You could do the **convincer** or you could do the **criteria** -- but I wouldn't do them both, necessarily because it's going to add a lot of time to your presentation and it's going to sound like you're so **unspecified** after a while that nobody will make heads or tails about what you're saying. So to that end I would say just be a little careful.

CHAPTER SEVEN

Emotional State Manipulation

Okay, let's move on to where we begin the **securing, controlling and using emotions for fun and profit** section of this training and I think this is going to rock your world. I really do. I love this section. I've been dying to present it to you. And as we go through these strategies today, I'm telling you, this is just spectacular.

Now, if you'll reflect back with me, you previously learned about the way emotions work and the beginning of how to use them to your advantage. It would really be a great idea, I highly recommend just stopping reading right now and going back and reviewing that material in previous books in the series again. It would really be worth your time. You'll be far more up to speed and ready to continue with this if you do. I know you'll remember it as I go through it anyway with you, but it just wouldn't hurt to at least review that because in this book we're going to take your understanding of emotional states to a much, much higher level and show you some things to do with them that is going to rock your world.

To set the stage for you, I'd like to give you an example, a true example, a real thing that happened, of the use of **anchoring** and **emotional state manipulation** with a college professor. This really happened. I'm sorry I can't remember the university. It won't change the story any.

There were some college kids that learned how what you're going to be learning in this book works. And they decided they were going to do this to the college professor. So here's what they did. They all got together and agreed before class started that if the professor moved to the right of the classroom, to the students' right as they were facing the classroom, the students would sit up and pay close attention, be very quiet, smile and nod approvingly at the professor. But if the professor moved to the left of the classroom, the farther left he went, the more the students would cut up, act out, throw things, look away from the professor, at a bare minimum, and act disinterested. Got it? Okay.

Class began. It didn't take but about a half an hour or so and the professor was pegged into the right of the room, stood there for the balance of the class with the students absolutely gobbling up everything he said, excitely listening and nodding, smiling and showing their approval of all that he was doing.

The next day, they decided that they would do it different. What they decided they would do is to reverse it and do the exact same process but just reverse it. So class began and what they did is as the professor would move to the right, which he started right off towards the right of the room, they immediately would cut up and act up and act disinterested, et cetera, et cetera, and as the professor would go to the left of the room, they would act interested and they would do what they should.

It took not too long and the professor was pegged over into the left of the room. Now remember, the professor had no idea what was going on. The professor didn't know that they were doing this and had no way of knowing that they were doing this. He just simply was massively affected by what they did. Okay?

How would you like to be able to affect people in that same way and get them doing things and responding to you in ways that up to now has been happenstance? That's what this lesson is all about.

CHAPTER EIGHT

Persuasion Truisms Regarding the Use of Emotions

Here are some **persuasion truisms** regarding the use of **emotion**. Now, again, it would be very helpful if you had already gone back through the previous materials, but I'm going to assume that that's right on the tip of your mind and so let's talk about some **persuasion truisms** regarding the use of **emotions**.

First, **people are led to a decision based on their emotions**. All right? So it is **emotions** that bring people to **decisions**, it is logic that they hear that *cements* or potentially *breaks* that decision. Now here's the thing. When you think about this, the logic actually is very minor. For each person it's slightly different, but if I were to just grossly generalize, just to give you a way to sort of think about this, emotion may be as high as 80, 85 percent or more of the decision. Logic is only a very small 10, 15, 20 percent at most, to back it up. Now, yes, that's not always true 100 percent of the time, but you're going to find that overall, that's the way it works.

The *most important element* between **emotions** and **logic** is by far **emotions**. A person who makes their living persuading but can't use emotions well will most likely never make much money, at least the cards are stacked strongly against them. And similarly, a person who can make strong logical arguments but is not adept at manipulating emotion also has the cards strongly stacked against them. Make sense?

I'm coming at this from every which direction here to let you know that it's very important that you *understand how* and that you actually *do use* **emotion** to sell powerfully because that's really what's going to make the sale for you, that's what's going to *convince* people. That's the difference between people that say '*great speech*' and '*let's march*'. We want to be in the '*let's march*' variety of what we do, right?

Okay, we all want to believe that **we're doing the right thing**. We all want to believe that it makes the most amount of sense for our clients to act on what we tell them, just because we can back something up with **logic** does *not* mean the client will part with their money. In fact, your backing it up with logic is largely irrelevant.

If you get **emotionally involved** with your product or service and you **believe** in it -- if, for example, you're a financial advisor and you almost twisted somebody's arm to buy life insurance one day, and they did, and a few years later one of them dies and that life insurance pays off and saves the family, and the spouse calls you, in tears, crying, telling you that the loss of their loved one -- they don't know how they're going to get over it, but at least they don't have to worry about money, and that they -- when you were there, the person says, "*You know, I want you to know, I didn't like you very well. I told my husband I thought you were pushy and I thought that what you did was wrong, at the time. I just want to tell you, I was the one who was wrong and I'm so grateful that you did what it took to get us to be able to make that happen because at least now, I don't also have to worry about where my next meal's coming from. I don't know how I'll get over my husband's loss, but financially I'm all right.*"

See, if you get **involved emotionally** with your product, *you'll pass that on to your customers*, to your potential customers, to your current customers, to everybody, and they will know that they're dealing with someone who really **believes**, and that goes *so far* to help you sell powerfully, you can hardly imagine. Okay? Whereas if you **logically** argue the actuarial tables about they're this age and by that age, odds are they're going to die, and if they don't have insurance up to this point, it's a mistake, and blah, blah, blah -- it's just not going to work
for you.

Logical arguments, without laying the groundwork **emotionally** first, will fall on deaf ears. Let me give you a good example of this.

Before Richard Nixon became president, he was running -- I think vice-president, I forget under whom, but anyway, as the story goes, he was accused of having slush funds, of being given money somehow that was inappropriate, that he accepted gifts and created slush funds to help finance the campaign or something. And Richard tried to ignore it and the problem didn't go away. It kept getting worse and worse and worse, okay? Until finally he went public and he made a statement and what he said is, "*Look, folks, there's only one thing I've ever been given as a gift in my political life, and that was my dog Checkers. And I want you to know something, my children love Checkers. And I want you to know that even if it was illegal that I keep that dog, I'm not going to give him up. I don't care what anybody says. I'm not going to take the children's dog away from them. Other than that, I've never taken any money or anything else. I hope I've set the story straight.*" And on he went.

There was really no new information there except his **story**. And, from our previous lessons, you know how *profound* a **story** can be, right? Now all of the sudden, Richard Nixon, instead of being big vice-presidential candidate, is *human* Richard Nixon, the guy that's just like you are, that has a dog that his children love, and you know, you wouldn't ask your children to lose their dog, and you're not going to blame him for keeping his dog, for Pete's sakes. He went on to win and you know the rest from there, he went on to hold the highest office as well in the United States. So that strategy worked and it worked brilliantly. He was able to use an **emotional story** to completely get people to back him and to support him. He didn't make a logical argument by saying, *"Let me show you the facts and figures. I've laid before you my tax returns from the following years, my income statements and my bank accounts. Now you can see for yourself that I didn't do anything wrong."* People would just say that he hid it. So in the end it wouldn't have made any difference whatsoever, but doing a **story** absolutely changed the world.

In previous books, we talked about the following kinds of emotions: first of all, we talked about using **criteria** and **high values**. And we talked about the way to get them to **feel emotionally** about them, that is once you've **elicited the value or the criteria**, you can always ask, *"How does that feel?"*

I'm going to teach you something *spectacular* about that here in just a little bit but that's a way to get them to feel. For example, let me just do this with you right now. Think about **why** you are reading these books. Think about what **caused** you to get involved with them initially. And think about some of the **highlights** that you've found most **exciting** and have been most **helpful** to you.

Got one or two of them, specifically? Okay. Think about it for a minute and answer this question. **How do you feel** about those breakthroughs, those things that really made you go, wow, that's cool? **How does that feel?**

All right, now see what I'm doing is I'm **eliciting an emotion** from you, an emotion that is of your **high criteria and values**. Okay? Now we also talked about using **decisions**, ones that worked out well for the person and how *that* felt -- the feeling of buying something or the desire to buy something, excitement, passion and/or desire. I'm sure you can make your own mind up about how you might use that to your advantage. Something you must absolutely do. All right? **Something that's no longer true for you but used to be**, for handling objections, for example. Fear. We want to be careful about fear. It can backfire, but fear is also very profound in getting people to leverage it against competitors or what have you.

Now, remember I mentioned you can ask about these states directly to **elicit** them, and you can use **emotionally charged words** about the emotions themselves to elicit those emotions. Okay? So these are all things you can do to use emotions and the type of emotions you can use to your advantage.

CHAPTER NINE

Strengthening Emotions Through Elaboration

Let's talk about **strengthening emotions by elaborating on them**. If an emotion is like a wave, then let's say the emotion is traveling from the left to the right. And this is what emotions do. They're **waves**. They come along and you **feel** them and you feel the *profoundness* of them, and then they *recede* and you go back to your normal, everyday state of mind. That's the way you know you're happy. In other words, you may be *overall* happy most of the time, but if you're *really* happy, or something makes you *extremely* happy, then it kind of dies back down again. If it didn't, then it would become a normal, everyday state, and you *wouldn't recognize it* for being really happy, you'd just think of it as normal.

So **emotions by definition, are transient**. They come and go. So let's imagine a *wave* of emotion showing how it comes and goes. On the left hand side is your *everyday* emotion and then the *wave* of emotion hits, you know, you see the person's eyes well up or you see their chest swell with pride, or you see them become happy and excited or what have you, and then you see that emotion roll off down the other side, it *subsides* and goes back to the everyday emotion again.

Now, by **elaborating** on an emotion, you can **increase the power** of that emotion and thus what you can *do* with it. So here, I'll give you a story. Just recently, in another country, I got in a little fender bender. My fault, unfortunately. Where I was, you had to wait for the police to show up, or at least that's what you're supposed to do, if it's a rental car, which mine was, and the rental car agency requires that you have a police report.

Unfortunately, the police don't respond and they don't come. I didn't know that, so unfortunately, I had backed into a taxicab, crunched my car real good, only barely scratched his bumper. I crunched the door of my rental car and I had scratched only the bumper on his car. So besides being a real jerk, the guy just was very aloof and wanted nothing to do to talk to me. Later I learned why. What happened is, then, all of the sudden, I called the police and asked them to come, and okay, sure we're going to be on our way and we're going to come.

Well, all right, an hour later, no one's there, so I pick up the phone and I call again. Oh, yes, yes, yes, we're coming, lots of busy things going on here, but we're coming. Three hours later, nothing. Four hours later, nothing. Five hours later, nothing. I mean, it went on and on and on and nothing was being accomplished. My wife and I were sitting there in the car just waiting and waiting. And we'd get out and we'd look and then we'd get back in and we'd wait. We watched rush hour come and go and finally six hours later, nothing, seven hours later, nothing.

Finally, at seven and a half hours, I said, 'That's enough.' I went to the driver and I said, "Look, I'm supposed to wait for the police report to come, but . . . ' And the guy says, 'Yeah, I know, but here's the deal. When they come, you're going to be given a ticket. You're at fault.' I said, 'Yeah, that's true.' He said, 'When you go to court, then my employer is going to ask for my missed wages for the day. As a taxicab driver, I've missed a lot of wages today. And so you're at fault and they will automatically make you pay that and that's something your insurance isn't going to cover.' And I said, 'Oh, I hadn't thought of that.' And the guy said, 'All right, well, I'll tell you what. I'll take $200, it's probably going to cost me about $100 to fix the scratch and $100 for missed wages, and we'll call it fair.' And I said, 'Okay, let's do it.' My car I figured was probably about $450-500 worth of damage. It ended up being exactly what I thought it was going to be. I paid him $200. The deductible on my car was $1,000. Okay? So I saved money over the actual deductible by doing it that way.

All right, what's the moral of the story? Well, boring, boring, sitting there hour after hour, hour after hour. Nothing happening, nothing going on, just waiting for police that never showed up. In other words, I *stretched out boredom* and what I did is by **elaborating** on boredom, *you* probably got very bored. (Hopefully you're still with me, better be, hang in there.) But *you* got very bored and then I can **leverage that boredom into anything else I want to leverage it into**. All I have to do is bring up a topic and **link** it over to that story. Okay?

So you can see how this kind of thing could be very, very useful. Imagine if I had **elaborated** on *excitement*, or on what it's like to *really want to buy something* and you know, you *really* want it and you think, no, I better not. It's really not in the budget and I really shouldn't do it. I'm just not going to do it, but in the back of your mind it won't go away and you know that the *only* thing that's going to satisfy that urge is to actually go and get it, right? So finally you break down and you just go and do it. You know what that's like? I mean we all know what that's like.

All right, I just did it *again*. By **elaborating on emotion**, and by talking about a **story** in which it effected you that way, you're going to make the **peak** of that emotion in the other person *last longer*. It will give you more power with that person using that emotion.

CHAPTER TEN

Managing Emotional States

You must **manage the emotional state** of your prospective buyer *from the moment you begin*. In fact, your **reputation** that precedes you, that of any company that you represent, or any *research* your prospective buyer might have done, *all* will affect the **emotional state** of your prospective buyer when you sit down to talk with them, or you call them on the phone. And that's just for starters.

It's important to take into account the prospective buyer's **mood** as well. I mean, if the person just got in a fight, for example, before you sat down with them, they're probably *not* going to be in a very receptive state. So you have to **manage the emotional state** of the people you're talking to. This is incumbent upon *you*.

The second thing you need to do is think about your product or service. What **emotional state** would you love to find a prospective buyer in that would make them *want* what you have? So to the extent that you can, this state is an *ideal* state to **elicit** as you begin, or you can **elicit** it anywhere during your presentation.

So think about that, that's really important. **What emotional state would you love to find a prospective buyer in?** And if you said '*wanton desire*', well yeah, that would be wonderful, but you may not be *able* to get them to have wanton desire *instantly* as you begin. That may not be very appropriate, but there are other states that *are*. Maybe you can do that one. I don't know. Pretty much, your imagination is the limit here.

CHAPTER ELEVEN

Anchoring

We're going to talk about **anchoring**. **Anchoring** is based on **stimulus response conditioning**. Okay? And the psychologist, Pavlov, who you've heard of the dogs, you know with getting the dogs to be hungry and thirsty on command, discovered that our brain is capable of **one-trial learning** and what that means for the process of persuasion is that we can **create an emotional state** in someone and then **create a stimulus** that when *repeated* by us will *immediately* **cause them to experience that emotion again**.

So think about what Pavlov did. He put dogs in a cage and got them to salivate -- well, he would push a button or what have you and a light would light up, a buzzer would sound and food would come down the chute for the dog to eat. Well, pretty soon, all he had to do was make the sound of the buzzer and the dog would begin salivating, thinking that food was coming down. He realized that the dog's **emotional response** was **linked to the sound** and when he played the sound, **it caused the emotional response**. The two were **linked**.

So **anchoring** is based on **eliciting an emotional state** in someone and then **providing a unique stimulus** that makes an **association** in their mind between your stimulus and their emotional response and that association will be *automatic* for the most part. You don't even need to really say much about it but I'm going to give you a strategy, a method that is unbelievably *sneaky* and *powerful* that actually will cause you to speak about that **association**, but I will get to that in just a minute.

Let's look at **the procedure for creating an anchor**. All right?

1. The procedure is to first **elicit a state**, an emotional state, in another individual.
2. The second, at the **peak** of their **emotional response** you're going to set your **anchor**.
3. Three, you're going to **calibrate** closely to their state, you're going to *look* at it, and *listen* to it, so you can *see* if you did it right. In other words, if you tried to set an **anchor** and they *weren't* at the **peak**, you *won't* have set anything.
4. You want to **release the anchor** *prior* to their **emotional state** subsiding. In other words, when it's at its **peak** is when you want to basically let loose of it.
5. And five, you want to **test the state**. *Test* it, make sure -- **test your anchor**. Test that they *go back into* that state again and then **leverage the anchor** by firing it when you want them to have that response to whatever you're saying or doing.

Let's imagine the person is going along through their every day emotions, just living their life. You come along and you begin to **elicit an emotional state** in them -- tell a **story**, ask them about a **specific experience** that you know is going to get them to have an emotion. As that **emotional state** gets rather *intense*, you **apply the** anchor. And then as the state gets just near the **peak**, to *stop* applying the anchor. So in other words, you're **anchoring** it on the *increase*. Okay? And then you should have already **released the anchor** by the **peak** point and the person begins to *subside* and then they're back to their everyday emotions.

CHAPTER TWELVE

How to Set an Anchor

I'm sure you're asking *'How do I set an anchor?'* I'm going to tell you. **Anchors** are set in **representational systems**. Now what's a **representational system**? Remember back from many lessons ago? What you *see*, what you *hear*, what you *feel*, what you *taste* and what you *smell*. You can be **triggered to have an emotional response** in *any* of the five systems that humans have – *visual*, *auditory*, *kinesthetic*, *olfactory* and *gustatory*.

All right, right now I want you to think of something that you might *see* that *immediately upon seeing* it would create a very pleasant emotional state for you. You can imagine women, as they're putting on their makeup thinking to themselves, I want to look such that when I'm seen tonight, I'm going to immediately be considered beautiful, desirable, attractive, whatever. Men, maybe the same thing for putting on their makeup. So you can imagine that and then you can imagine that person out in public later on and being seen and being seen as attractive. They **created a response** with what they did. All right?

Now do that for each of the other systems right now. So *remember* something that you could *hear* that *immediately upon hearing it*, would invoke a very powerful emotion from you. For example, let me give you some examples, let's say that one day you got a phone call and it said that you got a raise or you got a promotion at work or you got the job you were looking for and you were *so excited* you couldn't believe it, and right at that moment on TV came a very specific jingle. And later, a few days later, you're sitting around and the TV comes on and that jingle comes on and you find yourself getting happy almost for no reason and you don't really know why. Well, that jingle, you **linked** it automatically to the state that you went into when you were told that you just got hired.

The unconscious, the *higher* of an **emotional state** you have, meaning the more *intense*, the *more* it will tend to **link** things in the environment to it. Very interesting.

So when I asked you, for example, to think of something that you might *see* that *immediately upon seeing it* would create a very pleasant emotional state for you, somehow you **associated** the positive feelings with what you were looking at. So you looked at it in your mind, you *remember* it, and it *brought back* those feelings again. And just *thinking* about it brought back those pleasant feelings, so it didn't even have to be in your ongoing environment, it could be in your mind. That's the power of **anchoring**, and it's a very powerful aspect of human nature.

What you want to do is **practice creating anchors**, especially in the *visual*, the *auditory*, and the *kinesthetic* system. So let's talk about a few right now that you could use. A *touch*, that would be in the *kinesthetic* system. And a *touch* could be used. So let's say you're talking about something that is *absolutely thrilling* to the other person and as you do that, as you see their eyes light up and their **emotional state** *increase in intensity*, you reach over and you *touch* them on the shoulder. Do it *specifically* so you can *repeat* that touch *exactly like* you just did every time you want to **create that state** again in them.

And you'll find that if you reach over and do it again, you'll see their eyes light up in that same way. Now if you have never had that happen before, you'll be blown away when it actually does when you do it.

What are some other *kinesthetic* type things you can do? Well, *kinesthetics* involve *touch*, right, *feeling*? So maybe the feeling of particular clothes against your skin does something for you. Maybe it makes you feel rich or successful or powerful and so if you need to feel that way in a meeting you're going to, well by all means, put them on. Do it that way.

What about some **visual anchors**? Well, you could *gesture*. You could *hold up a sign*, for example. Branding for corporations is all about a **visual message** that gets *repeated* over and over visually and/or auditorily, that makes you hopefully think about something in a positive way. So anything that a person can *see* that you can *replicate* would be a **visual anchor**.

Auditorily, well you could *tap* on the table. You could take your pen and you could *tap* on the table if you wanted. Or if you had something that sounded a rough noise, you could scratch it, for example. That would create something that would be rather *unique*. You might use two taps for yes, and one for no. You could do something like that. Every time you wanted someone to feel '*yes*' after **establishing** it, you could simply *tap twice*. If you wanted them to feel '*no*', you could just do it *once*. And if you could get some distinction to the sound, something that sounds a little brighter, for yes, and something that sounds a little duller for no.

If I had carefully **established** a *double tap* for *yes*, you know, I said to you, "*Think about something that you're absolutely in agreement with and I want to show you something. So think about something that you're absolutely in agreement with, for example, that you got your last pay check and you actually got it, so think about that. Great. So we know that that's true, we know that that's something that you actually did, is that true?*" **<Tap twice>** and they go, "*Yup*". "*All right. Great. Think about something that is not true, like for example, you're in 100 percent agreement with the political system as you know it today.*" And they go, "*No way.*" **<Tap once>** And you go, "*Right. That's not true, is it?*" And they go, "*No, that's not true.*" And as you're talking along with them you can say, "*Now, I'd like to show you some things that are pretty doggone powerful and could really affect the way you think about the kinds of services that we're talking about.* **<Tap twice>** *And as I do, I think you're going to find some unique ways to use them and to take advantage of what I'm going to be telling you about today* **<Tap twice>** *so that you can get ahead and become even more profitable.* **<Tap twice>** *Now a lot of our competitors think they have a better way, but they really don't,* **<Tap once>** *and I think as you start to compare that, you'll see the advantages of what I'm telling you about what we have* **<Tap twice>**.*"

Anchors can be set in *one* representational system or a *combination* of them. Here's a general rule regarding that. ***The more senses you use* when you set your anchor, *the more it might rise to the level of consciousness* in your prospective buyer**. Okay? So if I set an **anchor** that was me making a big gesture as I banged on the table, it might really get your attention versus if I just tapped kind of subtly on the table or even touched you subtly depending on what representational system you were mostly processing in at that moment.

In fact, to that end, if you want to **set anchors covertly**, use one of the representational systems that your prospect is *not accessing* at the moment. For example, if your prospect is processing *visually*, perhaps looking up or making pictures and blinking rapidly, et cetera, then *changing your voice tone* or *clicking the table* or *touching the person* might not be consciously perceived. But be careful, okay. Here's why. For all practical purposes, the best advice I can give you relating to **anchoring** is to simply **hide in the open**. Okay? I used to concern myself with trying to **covertly anchor** all the time and I learned that **if you are covert enough, you have *no* impact**. You covert yourself right out of the deal.

If I **anchor** so covertly that *you don't perceive* that I've shown you something, made a sound, or a feeling, if there's *no perception consciously or unconsciously*, then what have I done? That's right, **nothing**. So **the person at least has to perceive it**.

Okay, now, since nobody really knows what you're doing anyway, unless they're close friends or family, you're better off *not trying* to be so covert and focus instead on being *effective*. Okay? That will really help you.

That said, I'll show you some super sneaky and extraordinarily powerful ways to use this skill. What I'm wanting you to understand is that when I used to *focus* on *just* being covert and sneaky, it just *didn't work* real well. I could do it, I got really good at it, however, it took me forever until I figured out that it wasn't so much the covert nature of it, because it was the fact that *people aren't thinking that all these things are going on* when you're talking with them, and so by that, *already* they're not getting what you're doing. In other words, there's *no need* to be covert for you, there's a need to make what you're doing *work*. And I was trying to be more covert for me. In other words, because *I* wanted to do it more and more covertly, but I realized that my level of understanding of this was far greater than the people I was trying to persuade and so if I could make it covert for *me*, it was completely useless for *them*. Meaning, it was giving me no impact, no results.

Here are a couple of practical ways to use the skill we're talking about here. Let's say that you are talking with someone, this could be one on one, this could be with a group, and you gesture to one side and talk about something *irritating*. And you do it in an *irritating* tone of voice. Then you gesture to the other side and say, "On the other hand...", and you *lower your tone of voice* and make it *full and attractive sounding* and you gesture to the *other* side. Now, if you did that, what would you be able to do?

Well, let's say you're a realtor, just for sake of discussion and let's say that you're talking with somebody and they say, "*Well, I just have had such horrible experiences with realtors, I don't know why I would want to work with you.*" And your response is, "*Yeah, that must just really be terrible.*" And you're gesturing with your left hand off to the left. "*That must have been a bad experience.*" And they go, "*Yeah, it really was.*" And you go, "*Well, you know, I can tell you, some realtors aren't worth anything and it causes people a lot of problems.*" And they go, "*Yeah, yeah, it really was.*" And you could go, "*But on the other hand*", as you take your right hand and turn it palm up, for example, "*On the other hand, you know, there are some realtors that just have an innate understanding of people. And these realtors are what make the world go around. When you really need to get something done, these are the people you turn to.*" And you could also gesture toward yourself at that point. And they go, "*Yeah, you're probably right. But I just haven't really experienced much of that.*" And you go, "*Yeah*" and you use your left hand and point down again and go, "*Yeah, I know what you mean. All right, let's go ahead,*" put your left hand down and on your right hand you're gesturing to the right and you're saying, "*Well, let's go through and talk a little bit about what you'd like to do and see how I can help you.*" And now, if they bring up another realtor or the need to talk with other people or whatever else, you can start gesturing with your left hand off to the left and you can kind of speak in a nastier sounding voice, and when they talk about moving forward with you or you talk about moving forward with you, you can gesture with your right hand and speak in a very nice, attractive, full sounding voice. That would be a very powerful way to use this skill and a way you can practice with right now. You can get going on it right now. Okay?

Let's go to another way. You can also simply use *an irritating tone of voice* when speaking about what you *don't* want the person to like and *a pleasant tone* when speaking about what you *do* want them to like. This would be **auditory anchoring**. Okay? This would be the use of an **auditory** one. And **auditory anchoring**, by the way, is nothing more, really than **talking about**

different states and using different tones to anchor them with. It's really useful to only do a couple, by the way, you don't want to try to use a tone, then there's a tone, then there's another tone, and you're trying to use all these different things. I mean, you *could* do that, but it's kind of pointless for most business applications. You don't need to go that far.

If talking with a group, you can *walk to one side of the platform or stage* and **elicit an emotion** from the audience there. Let's say you choose the emotion of *being motivated*. Then you *walk to the other side of the stage* and **elicit 'go for it'**. You save the center of the stage for your main teaching and near the end of your speech, you may want to get the group to take action to set an appointment with you. And as you begin to talk about this, move to the side of the stage where you elicited *motivation*. Then, move directly to the other side where you have '*go for it*' **anchored**, and tell them at the break they can go to the back of the room and get an appointment with you.

So what have you done? Earlier in your presentation, you elicited on one side '*motivated*'; on the other side, '*go for it*'. You're going to use it now like a *slingshot*. So, you know, you pull a slingshot back and then you let it go and it rockets off. Later in your presentation, you want people to maybe sign up to come have an appointment with you where you can do a presentation for them, so now what you're going to do is you walk to the side of the room where you elicited '*motivated*' and you start talking about setting an appointment with you. You tell them, at the break you're going to make it so that they can set an appointment and you only have a limited number of spaces so you'd appreciate it if people would come right away to get one if they'd like to. And as you're saying that, you walk to the '*go for it*' side and then you give them a break. Well, you're going to **re-elicit tremendous feelings of motivation** and then, boy, **I've got to do it**. They've *got* to *do* something. What's that something? It's what you just **suggested**.

Now, it doesn't work on 100 percent of the people because you won't have been successful at **setting the anchor** on 100 percent of the people in the room, but it will definitely, and sometimes quite dramatically increase your numbers quite significantly. It depends on how good you are at eliciting the information. That would be by way of telling a story, by way of telling a joke, by way of giving an example that really brought out the emotion, or asking them directly to go and experience an emotion.

There are as many uses for **anchoring** as you have imagination to come up with them. I mean, it just almost doesn't stop. Okay?

CHAPTER THIRTEEN

Increasing the Power and Longevity of an Anchor

Let's talk about how to **increase the power and longevity of an anchor**. First, the *more* systems that you **anchor** in, the *more* power and longevity the **anchor** will have. It can become extremely powerful, however it also becomes *more conscious*, so based on your need for *covertness*, which I've pretty much already spoken to, you don't have much of a need to be covert because it's *already* covert by just the fact that they don't know it, but that's one of the ways you can do it, is you can, like, for example, I'm standing over on one side of the room, I'm using a bit of a different tone of voice. I'm gesturing off to *that* side of the room and then I go to the *other* side of the room,

I use a *different* tone of voice and gesture off to *that* side of the room.

So I'm using *voice tone, position in the room, gestures, all* of those things to **elicit** and **maintain** those emotions.

Another thing you can do to increase the power and longevity of an **anchor** is to fire the **anchor** *repeatedly.* In other words, keep going back and *using* it and *letting it work* on the people that you've set it on. That just makes it stronger and stronger and stronger. However, if you're applying it to something, in other words, you're talking about having them make an appointment with you and you're going over to the *motivated* side, what that's doing is it's *weakening* the **anchor** because it's **pairing** it with something they *wouldn't* normally feel that motivated about. If you fire it in a *pure* state, meaning, all right, now think about that **motivation** again. **How do you feel** now? Oh, yeah, I feel pretty strong. Okay, and when I point over here and you feel it *again*, you know you're *having* it, right? So see, when you do it *that* way, you're not **pairing** it against something else, you're just continuing to fire it and thus it's strengthening it.

Another way you can make them stronger is you can **anchor at the peak of the emotional state.** Now here's the trouble, emotional states are usually *pretty quick.* They come and go *quickly.* And so to that end, remember some of the tricks I've taught you. Speed up your own **vibrational rate** which will make the emotions *appear slower* to you so you can *use* them. But as you become **attuned** to them, first you'll just sort of note, oh, people are having emotions. Then you'll go, wow, I see the wave. And pretty soon you'll go, but it was too late, I forgot to **anchor** it. And then pretty soon you'll go, okay, now I'm going to do it consciously, I'm going to **elicit the emotion**, I'm going to **anchor** it. So the trick is **getting it as near the emotional peak as possible.** If you get it too near the *beginning* of the emotion, you're not really anchoring anything of strength. If you get it near the emotion on its *downward* curve, then you do it and the emotion comes up a *little* bit but it goes *right back down again.* This takes practice, takes a little bit of effort, isn't all that hard.

Fourth, you can **stack** other *similar* and *beneficial* **emotional states** together. For example, like in the room I was mentioning you can take *motivation* first and then *go for it*. These are **similar emotional states**. But you *couldn't* stack *happiness* and *anger* together as two emotional states because one *counters* the other. Okay?

CHAPTER FOURTEEN

Super Stealthy Spatial Anchoring

I promised to give you a really stealthy one, and here it is. **Super stealthy spatial anchoring.** And here's how to do it. First, **elicit the state** you want the person to be experiencing. You then ask them to **look at the picture that represents that state in their mind.** You want to ask them then to **point in space to where that picture is located.** As *they* point, *you* point at it as well, right to where they're pointing. And ask them if *that's* where it is. And that's the part I was telling you about, by the way, where you'll talk about that **emotional state** and you know, you're going to **link** it with your words to your **anchor**. So you're asking them if that's where it is.

Then you ask them if you point there, as you point, does it **automatically cause them to recall**

the picture and the feelings? They'll say, well yes. And you say, does it do it *every time* you do it? And you point there again, and they'll go, well yeah, I guess so. So what you're doing is you're using **words** to **connect** your unique **anchor**, the pointing at this picture, that **causes them to have the emotion**. This is a really powerful and very stealthy thing to do. Okay?

When you want to use this type of an **anchor**, tell the person to put that picture or thought here, and you point, and ask them how they feel, so for example, you can say, *"Imagine for a moment that you own the product that I'm talking about and imagine it right here"* and you point to where they had pointed about something they **absolutely must do**. *"As you think about it like that, how does it make you feel?"* And they go, *"Well, yeah, I think it might really help me."* And you go, *"Great, let's get you set up on it, all right?"*

It's extraordinarily powerful. The other thing is, you don't even have to ask them to *make a picture* about what you're talking about, and then ask them to put it in that location that they were visualizing earlier, **just point at that location** while you're talking to them. That's all it takes. And it will immediately **bring forth that emotion**. Okay?

You can use this **anchor** as you would any other **anchor**, only this one is way more powerful, way more powerful. So let me tell you something. If you were to read this over for a few minutes, about ten times, you'd be doing yourself a favor. This is one of the most powerful things you could ever want to do with **anchoring**. You can do this with groups, you can do it with individuals. It doesn't make any difference.

I've listed some *states* that I like to use with **spatial anchoring**.

Buying. *"What's it like when you want to buy something? You know you're going to go buy it, and how does it feel?"* *"Well, yeah, it just feels like you need to do it."* And you go, *"Right, make a picture of a time when you did that. Just look at a time in your mind when you did that."* You see them kind of look off in space and you go, *"Where is that picture if you were to just kind of point to it?"* Now, if they point at their head, you go, *"Yeah, yeah, I know, but if you were like a little bitty midget inside your own head, which way would you be pointing?"* And they'd point out in front of them somewhere. That's a great line by the way. And so they point out in front of them and you say, *"Okay, great. When you **point there** and you **see that picture** it makes you feel like, man, you **remember** that you wanted to go and **buy that thing**, right?"* And they go, *"Yeah."* And you go, *"Okay, so is it right here?"* and you point with your finger. And they go, *"Yeah."* And you go, *"So when I **point to it**, it can **remind** you of that **picture** and **you feel it again**, can't it?"* And they go, *"Yeah."* And you go, *"Does it do it **every time**, like if I **point** now, you **remember** it again?"* and they go, *"Yeah, it sure does."* Okay?

"By the way, I wanted to tell you a little bit about my course upcoming," and you point.

Another state I like is **being convinced to do something**. **Elicit a time** when they were **convinced to do something** and then get them to point, *you* point, go through that exact same process. Green light. Now, what I mean by *green light* is a **compulsion**. So imagine that you're sitting in your car and you're talking to the passenger. You're driving and you're talking to the passenger next to you. You're really paying attention to the conversation. You're stopped at a light. And all of the sudden you hear *honk, honk, honk*, and you look up and the light's green. What do you do? Yup, you **go**, don't you? You step on the gas. That's a **compulsion**. You feel **compelled** to go. You can't really just sit there. Not when you're being honked at, not when the light's green.

You can use for that matter *any* compulsion, like, for example, if you haven't seen the paper on a certain day, on that day, and you happen to see one on the corner at a newspaper stand, do you feel **compelled** to stop and look at the headlines? How about if you pass a doughnut shop? Do you **have to** stop and at least look inside or buy one maybe? Or some people have compulsions with chocolate. All kinds of things that make people **compelled**. But if you ask about a compulsion, that's really what you're doing. Red light, same kind of thing. You're driving down the road and you see the red light, what do you do? Well, you have to **stop**, right? And you can sometimes *pair* these, like a *green* light against a *red* light. So you can say, "*What's it like at a green light?*" and then you **elicit** that. And then you say, "*By comparison, what's it like when you see a red light? You're going down the road, lickety-split and bam, there's a red light in front of you. What do you do?*" They stop. Okay, so now you have **go** and you have **stop**. You use *stop* against the *competition*, you use *go* for *yourself*.

How about **something that's no longer true for you but used to be**? That one is *profound*. Okay? And you use that against *objections*. "*What's something that's no longer true for you but it used to be? Like for example, you used to live at a particular address and you don't anymore. Remember something like that? What is it?*" "*Well, I used to live over on such and such a street.*" "*Okay, and you don't live there anymore?*" "*No.*" "*So **it used to be true but it no longer is**, is that right?*" "*Yeah.*" "*All right, so when you think about it, you think, **no, it's no longer true for me**, right?*" And they go, "*Right.*" "*So, when you think about that, **point to the picture as you see it in your mind**.*" They point in the space where it is, and you say, "*Is it right here?*" And they go, "*Yup.*" And you go, "*Okay. So **when you point to it**, it makes you **feel that again**?*" And they go, "*Yeah.*" "*So when I point to it, **you** can **remember** it, right?*" And they go, "*Yeah.*" You go, "*So **every time**, like if I point to it right **now**, you **feel it again**, it's **no longer true**, you don't live there, right?*" And the guy goes, "*Right.*" Then they bring up that they want to look around, shop around, you just point, right to where you were pointing before. So you have to remember where you were pointing at, okay?

How about **an obsessing thought that led to action**? That's a really good **emotional state**. And **how do you know inside, what's it like inside, when you're going to get something**? That's another good one. That's like **buying**. And you can *stack* several like-minded emotions onto the same **anchor**, which is very powerful as I've mentioned. These are all really strong things you can do.

CHAPTER FIFTEEN

Taking Control

Okay, I've given you a world of information about **anchoring**, but there's a *trick* to this. You've got to start to *put it to use right away* and **it's done to you** all the time. You see an ad for a car on the television, and there walks right onto the ad this really hot member of the opposite sex. There they are. And you think, huh, wow, pretty good looking girl or guy, okay? Why do they do that? Why don't they put *ugly* people in to demonstrate their cars? Because they're hoping that **the model's attractiveness will rub off on your feeling about their car**. Does it? Yes, it absolutely does. Studies show that that affects us. It's done to you *non-stop*.

338

How about in a movie when it's getting really scary and you start hearing increasing sound effects, and you know, all of the sudden, you *know* something bad is going to happen, right? They're **conditioning you with music**. Later, all they have to do is play those sound effects and *you get scared*, because they've **anchored** that response.

There are so many things. How about the touch of a loved one that brings comfort and joy to you? How about the sight of an enemy that makes you livid just by looking at them? **This is done to you all the time**. Now you know how to **take control of it** and begin to do more of it *yourself*. Okay? And I'm telling you right now, **sales are made based on emotion** and they're *backed up* based on logic. And now you know how to gain tremendous power with emotion, both in terms of its **eliciting**, and now, when you *combine* that with the actual **anchoring** how to do it here as well, and how to do it even more profoundly and more precisely and more accurately with greater and more powerful results.

CHAPTER SIXTEEN

Homeplay

I want you to think about what **emotions** you would like your prospective buyer to be in and write them down. And practice **languaging the eliciting of these emotions smoothly**.

Determine what **anchoring** strategy will be most helpful and practice *putting together* the **elicitation** with the **anchor**. So in other words, first you have to get good at **eliciting the emotion**. Then next you're going to get good at **anchoring** that emotion.

You're going to have to *practice* with this **anchoring** strategy to make it effective for you, to make it second nature for you and to remember to use it, because it's so easy like with a lot of strategies that you just sort of forget about it and let it go do its own thing. So it's important that you practice and you get it to the point of *making it second nature*.

There's so much more to go through with this that I may devote an even more advanced lesson to the use of this,
or to how to do it, even in a more advanced way -- and I gave you *tremendous* advanced stuff with the **spatial anchoring**. I mean, that's just brilliant to do. I love doing that.

Put this stuff to use. And have a phenomenal experience as you practice with this. I would highly recommend you read this repeatedly so you can ingrain the languaging I'm using and you can make it part of your own vocabulary. All right?

Until the next book. . . I wish you tremendous success. Go out and persuade like mad. Talk to you soon. Take care. Bye-bye.

BOOK TWENTY-ONE

BUSTING FUZZY LANGUAGE

CHAPTER ONE

An Opposite Approach

Welcome to **Book 21** of *Persuasion Force*. Wow. Book 21. I'm surprised how amazingly fast these lessons have flown by, and what an incredible **foundation in persuasion** you're getting.

If *I* could have had this when I first started, I would have been light years ahead, literally cutting a good 10 years, maybe 15 years off of what it's taken me to get to where I am. So **congratulations** for getting this far. I applaud you. You obviously are serious about your persuasion skills and I think that's fantastic.

We have a really excellent lesson in this book and it's actually quite a *technical* lesson and so we're going to jump into that here in just a second. What we're going to deal with in this book is '**busting fuzzy language**'.

This is the most *technical* lesson I've given you to date, and before I even teach it to you, I want to explain some things about what you're going to learn. I want to tell you first of all, why I have *not taught this* until now. The primary reason is, that it's **the *opposite* of installing suggestions** into the mind of the person you're persuading, so it's kind of funny. There are some schools of thought here that say that you should *learn this first*, and when they *do*, the people *never, ever progress very far* in their learning. They use this as a **primary tool** and they wonder why they *get in arguments with people* all the time or they wonder why *they don't have the success* that they should have. So it's been my policy for many years that I *don't* teach this now at the beginning of any lesson, I teach it *at the end*, or much later, or to intermediate level students and above.

And by all means, going through this full series, definitely puts you in the realm of intermediate class persuasion level at a bare minimum. I mean, you're definitely really moving forward and that's a real milestone for you, let me tell you.

Here's the thing: when you learn what you're going to learn in this book, since it is **the *opposite* of installing suggestions**, of being *persuasive*, in essence; in other words – if persuasion is **the ability to open up someone's mind and get them to think your way**, and **arguing is challenging the person you're persuading at every turn and establishing that they're wrong and you're right**, you'll understand why I don't teach this early on .

And even when I *do* teach it, I'm going to teach it to you *in reverse*. I'm going to teach it to you the *opposite* of the way most people learn it. Why? I'm going to teach you **the valuable part first** and the *lesser* valuable part last. Okay? You have enough experience at this point to put what I'm going to teach you to excellent use and in fact, *without* what you're going to learn in this book, you would never go nearly as far as you could. However, it was critical to me that you learn **how to open up someone's mind**, i.e. **rapport**, **verbal pacing and leading**, the use of **cause and effect** language, the eighteen **most powerful words**, some of the **military patterns**, some of the different **commanding patterns**, all kinds of the different patterns that you've been studying, language pattern after language pattern that we've gone over. At this point, you can **open up someone's mind** and begin to **install suggestions**. But we all know that persuasion is not *just* about opening someone's mind and installing suggestions because from time to time, they'll have *questions* or *they won't really be going in the same direction we need or want them to go*. Then what? Then what happens? Are you stuck? No. Not with the skills you're going to be learning here.

These are very powerful strategies. And in fact, so much so that I see them again, like a **double edged sword** like I see **rapport**. Remember, with **rapport**, when we were going through that, I taught you that **rapport** can be used by you to **create trust in another individual** and with *trust*, they'll *believe* you, and if they believe you and they trust you, they'll follow you right into the sale or whatever you want them to do.

On the other hand, if you don't know *how* to wield that tool *with expertise*, then you'll go in bumbling your way through, trying to create **rapport** and in fact what will happen is, the person that you're trying to create **rapport** with will create **rapport** with *you. You'll* buy into *their* stuff because maybe you didn't have my class, you didn't go through what you've gone through, you didn't know how to do it. Someone gave you a couple of the ideas and you start using them, but remember, to have **rapport**, to get someone to have **rapport** with you, *you* have to have it with *them*. But you have to **lead** them to *your* way of thinking. Okay? Remember that, right?

So if you *don't* do that, what happens? Well, *you'll* be led to *their* way of thinking. And then what happens? When they look at you sorrowfully and say, "*You know, I wish I could do what you want, I just don't have the money*", **you'll immediately buy into it**. Man, do *I* remember doing that when I was young, selling when I was new at it. My goodness. It almost brings tears to my eyes to remember how much I had hoped I'd make that sale that night and I was walking away empty handed because I *didn't understand* the power of that **double edged sword**.

Now this skill is similar. They can *absolutely* lead you astray. They can turn you into a **monster** that **questions the living daylights out of people** and makes a *complete and utter nuisance* of yourself. Okay?

If I told you what I really thought, I'd have to be using language that's not very appropriate for what we're doing here, so I'll try to refrain as much as I can but let me just make it simple: **these skills can turn you into a jackass real quick**. Okay? So you have to be *careful* with their use. Another reason I've saved them until now. I thought I wasn't going to do that, but okay, I gave in. They can **lead you astray** *or* they can powerfully let you **direct a person anywhere you want them to be mentally**. All right?

CHAPTER TWO

Maps of Reality

These skills, for the most part, do the *opposite* of most of the kinds of things you've been learning how to do. You've been learning how to **put suggestions into someone's mind**, now you'll be learning **how to change the course or direction a person is taking within their mind**. You'll be learning how to **get more information** so you can **redirect the person to *your* way of thinking**.

And of course I have an entire program on 24 strategies to *completely* **redirect** a person, but this would be like a very useful *prerequisite* to that. With this, all those skills will come even easier.

It's important that just because you know that you *can* get more information from a person, in other words that *you have the tools to do it*, that you carefully decide *if* doing so will take you *closer* to your objective or *further away*. And I'll show you how to do it as we proceed and eventually this will become very second nature, and in fact, not even eventually, because I've created some strategies for you that will make this very *quick and easy to learn*. Yes, you will, as you begin, sort of make a fool of yourself. Not a fool, but you'll make a jerk of yourself, but you'll quickly see that you've done it and you'll stop it.

I can tell you that this is very quick to learn the way I'm teaching it to you and I think you'll really enjoy it. Don't overuse the skills. Practice on everyone, but not too much.

I'd like to tell you a quote from Leslie Cameron Bandler that I love. "*While I'm sure that you are familiar with the notion that the map is not the territory, I'm wondering if you have fully realized that as human beings, we will forever experience only the map and not the territory. We but alter maps. That is, we change people's subjective experience of the world and not the world itself.*"

I want you to come back and really *think* on that. When you *add* this lesson to what you've been learning, you will be able to powerfully and quickly **change maps**: *your* maps and *other people's* maps. So let's talk about it for a minute. **What are maps?** And **what does it mean to change our subjective experience of the world?** And this is going to get very deep and technical. Pause reading if need be as I go through this with you. If you want, just rip right through it to start with so that you get it, so that you've heard it once, and then *go back and read again*. It's a little technical, but it is extraordinarily valuable.

We do not operate on reality. This is what Leslie Cameron Bandler is saying. We don't operate directly on reality. What does this mean? Let's say that you're standing on a street corner and across from you is another person standing on another street corner. Just down the road a ways, a fight breaks out. Now you write up a report of what you saw, the other person writes up a report of what they say. You both saw the same fight. Do you think the report will be the same? Do you think the conclusion will be the same? It may well be very, very different. Why?

Well, you both saw the *same* fight, but from *two different vantage points*. So you have *two different perspectives* already as to what happened. Second of all, you both have *different world biases*. So what you saw was *filtered through your model of reality*, through your **world biases**, **personal biases**, upbringing, et cetera, **values** and **beliefs**, and the same is true for the other person that saw it.

So as you saw what happened, you will come to perhaps *different conclusions*. Interestingly, how do we *know* what happened? Well, you have what's in your **memory**, right? If you were to tell *me* about what happened, would *I* have experienced that firsthand? No. I would now be hearing *your thoughts* about what actually happened, but when you're **remembering** what happened, the best you can do is recall what was stored in your memory about that.

By definition, you're going to be **interpreting this in your way** as evidenced by us listening to the *other* person who saw this fight and how *they* went into it.

Now stay with me here. You may say, "*Yeah, so what?*" Well, you're about to see so what. We don't operate on the world itself, but there's a split second delay, meaning you *think* you're seeing something live and in real time, but in fact you're *not* because the only way you experience anything is through your five senses. So everything is **filtered through those five senses** and through all the other **filters** that exist in our brain, **filters** like I've been telling you about – your upbringing, your values, your morals, your beliefs, your socialization, your schooling, your friends. Now on and on and on it goes, and yet in the moment, you're making predictions about what will happen, you're deciding if you want to stay or go, you're imagining if it's good or bad. All these things are all happening in those split seconds.

So even though you're seeing what you *think* is in real time, it's still *only your perception* of what you're seeing. Even the light that's around you, there's a split second delay, infinitesimally small, maybe, between the time that it turned on and you experience it. But yet you *think* you're doing it in real time. Or *experiencing* it in real time.

So it's important you really understand that **everything that happens goes through these *filters* first**. Now, if we *change* our **map of reality**, will it seem to us that our *reality* has changed? Absolutely. Every single lesson I implore you at the end of the lesson, if you look at the homeplay, I ask you to please raise your vibration about what you've learned. And I ask you to be grateful for these learnings and for your ability to use them. To be grateful for the fact that you even got them to begin with. You're going through this series of books and you'll quickly have digested 20+ lessons of persuasion. Amazing.

Now *why* do I ask you to be grateful? Because it's a strategy that has *profound impact* on us. It **changes our view**, it **changes our map of reality**, it asks you to put in a **filter**, the **filter** of gratitude.

Now, when you're sitting there even now imagining how grateful you are for this information and your ability to interact with it, use it in your life, to gain nugget after nugget of value that you'll be able to implement. Is that *different* than if you were sitting in college feeling like you had to be there going through some boring course, whatever it is, knowing that if you don't pass it or you don't get a high grade, your whole GPA is going to be brought down and your whole world may change as a result? You don't like it, you're bitter about it, and you wish it wasn't so. Which one of those perceptions would you rather be in?

CHAPTER THREE

Surface Structure and Deep Structure

Let's go even deeper. Let's talk a minute about **surface structure** and **deep structure**. The **surface structure** is **what we're aware of in our lives**. If you said to me, "*I'm going to go to the store*" -- and I think I've given you this example in an earlier book -- you said, "*I'm going to go to the store in my car and get a gallon of milk.*" Well, that's the **surface structure**, right? Because *we all know* you're going to take a road to the store, but you didn't *tell* us that you were going to do that, unless maybe if you live in Alaska you're going to go four wheeling across something in order to get to the store, but I mean generally, when someone says that, you *know* that they're going to get in a car and they're going to go down a road and they're going to get to the store, that the store has a name, that the store sells food. We don't know what else the store may sell, but it may sell other things too. It may be the local corner convenience store that just sells little convenience things -- milk, bread, eggs, whatever. It may be a giant supermarket where you can buy all kinds of things. It may be a hybrid, sells clothes on one side and sporting goods elsewhere and food somewhere else in the store. We don't know what *kind* of store it is, all we know is that *this is what you said*. **In your mind**, all of those *other* things that you *didn't talk about* but you *knew that were there*, were at the **deep structure**, and the **deep structure**, we know, if someone *brings it up* to us consciously, but we don't really *pay attention* to it. We're *conscious* of what's on the **surface structure**.

Connecting people with the **deep structure** can be a real *eye opening experience* for them. And it's also a tremendous opportunity for us to persuade. *Connecting* people with their **deep structure** can and does **challenge long held beliefs**. And that's why you have to be *careful* with the skills I'm going to be giving you.

In other words, if I said to you, "*Look, I just don't know that it's so smart or it's just not so smart to move on something without thinking about it and I kind of need to give it some thought.*" You might come back with, "**What would happen** if you **did** move on it without so much thought? **What do you think the worst thing could be**?" And I said, "*Well, I don't know. I guess I could make a wrong decision.*" And you go, "*All right, **if you did** make a wrong decision, **what's the worst** that would happen?*" "*Well, I guess I'd lose some money.*" You say, "*Okay, and now on the other hand, **what if you did decide to go ahead** and do this. **What's the best** that could happen?*" "*Well, I'd learn something, I'd have a realization it could be good.*" "*And **if you did** have a realization and it **was** really spectacular like I'm telling you and it **did** change things in your business, **how much could that benefit you**?*" I might say "*It's hard to tell, but it could be significant. I don't know.*" And you go, "*I think with this knowledge in hand, we can **just put aside the fear or concern** because the **opportunity on the up side** is so significant.*" I might say, "*Well that's a good way to think about it.*"

It gave me a way in, but I'm going to show you *way* more profound ways of doing it than even what I just did there. Okay? It does **challenge long held beliefs** and you want to watch that.

CHAPTER FOUR

Consciousness Mapping Principles

We're going to talk about the three primary **map making principles**. When I say '*map*', I mean **the map of your consciousness**. And these principles are: **distortion**, **generalization** and **deletion**.

Now remember I told you I'm going to teach this to you in *reverse*. *Reverse* is **distortion**, **generalization** and **deletion**. Okay?

Distortion. Let's talk about that first. This is the process whereby we are able to **shift our sensory data** to **make different kinds of sense out of the same thing**. This is the way in which we plan. We take the sensory data that we have right now and **distort** it by **imagining what will happen in the future** if we do X or Y. **Distortion** is what allows us to *construct* things. And I'm going to teach you the three primary forms of **distortion**.

Next let's go to **generalization**. **Generalization** is the process we use to **create the structure that we have in our lives**. And believe me, we are *very, very, very* structured. All knowledge and science is based on **generalization** and it's **how we make sense of things we've never seen before** by **recognizing the things they have in common**. For example, let's just say that you are a child growing up and you notice that your parents have left the room and you'd like to find them, and you yell, "*Mom, dad where are you?*" And all of the sudden, the wall opens mysteriously and they appear. Isn't that interesting? And you think, how'd that happen? I want to be able to do that. Well, pretty soon you go over to the wall, where it was, and you see this little handle there and you push and you shove and nothing happens. There's no magic opening. And your parents watch you do it, and they go, "*No you have to turn the handle, see?*" You turn the handle and then you push. And sure enough the wall opens and there's a magic opening and you get through.

But let's go a little *deeper*. Now you're on the other side, in a different room, and your parents disappear and you want to get back. So you go up to the magic wall, you grab hold of the handle and you turn it and it turns and you push and nothing happens. And you think, well shoot. How come? And you push and you push and nothing happens. Your parents say, "*No, no, no, it only pushes this way, you have to pull it going the other way.*" Ah, you're beginning to see now. The light dawns.

Now one day you go over to a friend's house and they have a sliding glass door and you go to that door and you think, huh, this looks like one of those magic wall openings, I'll bet it works. And you look at it, and you try to figure it out. It doesn't push and it doesn't pull, but lo and behold you're convinced it will open. Well, there's a slider on that door, you slide it and you push it to the side and it slides right open and there you go. And you learned how to do that, *how*? Because you **recognize the elements that it had in common** with the regular door that you had in your house.

It's how we make sense of things we've never seen before. You're going to learn the two primary patterns of **generalization**.

And last we come to **deletion**. And **deletion** is the result of **paying attention to one set of**

information and as a result of doing it, it automatically causes a person to delete certain other information.

Now we all have seven plus or minus two *slots of information* available to us at any given point in time. Think about that for a minute. Science says to us that our **consciousness can hold seven plus or minus two things at any point in time**. Beyond that, *we can't remember it*. If I gave you say 15 random items real quick in a row, you'd probably be able to remember five to nine of them right now. Most of you couldn't remember 15, myself included. Now if I sat and tried to memorize it for a bit, I could. So could you. But we have these seven plus or minus two slots to *hold* things in our consciousness. What happens when that five to nine number *gets filled*? Well, when we orient our attention to anything automatically, it *causes us to be aware* of *how* we're orienting our attention or *where* we're orienting it and to **delete** what else is happening. And if it *didn't* work this way, we'd go crazy. We have so many things bombarding us for our attention all the time that we'd go crazy.

I was noticing this the other day. I went out with my wife. She'd get a call and we had arrived at our destination, and she was talking to the person. I had opened the door and said, "*Okay, honey, let's go.*" And she'd still be sitting in the car because it was like the multi tasking wasn't quite working like that. She needed to hang up the call, then she could go ahead and get out and shut the door and lock it, et cetera.

And I found myself doing the same kind of thing with her. I was looking at something and she wanted me to come look at something else and I couldn't really hold both in my attention simultaneously so I put down what I was looking at and went to look at what she wanted to show me.

Our consciousness gets filled all the time. It's *constantly* filling up, and yet what do we do? Well, once it's filled, **we're no longer paying attention to all the other signals and input** that's going on around us. For example, if you've been really tuned into what I'm telling you here, you probably have not been listening to the sounds that are going on around you. Maybe there are cars and horns or who knows what all, but you haven't really been listening to that. Why? Well, because you're reading my words. You're absorbed in what you're reading here. If you haven't been all that absorbed, you may well be hearing all kinds of things and realized all of the sudden, shoot, I forgot what he was saying. I don't remember. I better go back. And so you turn back a couple of paragraphs and re-read. Make sense?

You'll learn the four types of **deletion** and how to use them as we continue on here.

CHAPTER FIVE

Distortion: Lost Performatives

So now we're going to jump into **distortion**. Again, let's focus. **Distortion** is the process whereby we are able to **shift our sensory data to make different kinds of sense out of the same thing**. This is the way in which we *plan*. We take the sensory data that we have right now and **distort** it by **imagining what will happen in the future** if we do X or Y. **Distortion** is what allows us to

construct things.

And there are three types: **lost performatives**, **mind reading**, and **cause and effect**.

A **lost performative** occurs when *you talk like everybody has the same model of the world as you do*. If you say, it's wrong to cheat, or you should treat others the way you would like to be treated, you're violating the **lost performative** rule. The problem with this is that *people don't often realize* that **it is their model of the world that is causing them to make these statements**. In other words, they may be parroting what other people have told them in the past, but it's coming from *their own* model of the world. They're **dissociated** from what they're saying. In other words, **they're not taking ownership of what they're saying**. They don't realize it's coming from *their model*. They just are **parroting some truism**, so to speak.

The **challenge** for this is, '**according to whom**' or '**who says?**' Now you have to do this kind of *early* in a conversation especially in handling an *objection* so that they're willing to *take ownership* for what they say. They must understand that it is *their* model of the world they're referring to and *not* a general belief that the *whole world* believes in, therefore when you hear a person make a statement like, '*a person has to do what is right*' or '*it's always wise to think something over for a while before buying*'. These kinds of things can be **challenged** with a response like, '**according to whom?**' or '**who says?**'

Now, like always, you have to stay in **rapport** when using these skills and *especially* the ones you're learning in this book. So let's imagine for a moment that I say to you, '*you have to use these skills with integrity.*' You might say, '*well, who says that I have to do that, Kenrick?*' and I might say, '*well, I think it's best if you do it that way.*' You might say, '*okay, well I don't know that I agree*', but I hope you do agree, but you follow what I'm saying.

Or a person says to you, '*it's important that I think this over before I continue*' and you go, '*well, who says that you need to think it over?*' and they go, '*well, I do.*' And you go, '*okay, because?*' '*Well, because it's just known that you make better decisions when you think it over*'. And you go, '*Well, how is it known? Who says that?*' '*Well, I don't know. It's what I've always been told. It's what people believe.*' And you go, '*Well, what if that were wrong? What if that were right in the context that you heard it in, in other words, in the context of --* ' and then say something utterly different than what you're there to do with them. For an example, you're an advisor and you say, '*Maybe when you buy a car -- but what if your life is so important that it's better for you to seize the moment right now while it's fresh in your mind and so that nothing else happens? We know that you're insurable right now. Who knows what tomorrow will bring?*' They go, '*well, that's a really good point.*'

So you can see how learning to **challenge lost performatives** would be very, very helpful to you.

Now, I want to practice together with you on this. I'm going to **install** this quickly in your mind so that you'll always have it on the tip of your tongue. But before I do, I want to remind you of a very powerful point that you can use with anything that you're learning here.

Remember I taught you about **softening frames** in an earlier book? I want you to remember **softening frames**. You can always say, '***I'm curious if. . .***', '***I'm curious as to. . .***', '***I wonder. . .***', '***I'm wondering if. . .***', '***I'm asking myself and am curious. . .*** ' In other words, when you start saying **softening frames** like that, what happens is, it's the *equivalent* of asking them *directly* but just *nicely* and *they won't rebel* at being asked, at least quite so much. You also have to look at them with a very sincere look. If you look at them like a smart ass, like, you know what, I'm going to out logic you because you're just stupid and I'm bright. You're going to have a fight on your hands in two seconds flat, or someone storming out angry at you. And that isn't what we look to do with persuasion.

Well, you know what? There are times when it *is*. I was dealing with a bank recently and the guy says, "*Well, you know, we have to do the prudent thing here.*" And I wanted them to do *my* thing, and I go, "*Well, I think that's kind of interesting. And* **who sets** *what the prudent thing is?*" The guy says, "*Well, our committee.*" And I go, "*Well lord sure hopes here that they know what they're doing as they set those rules.*" And he goes, "*Well, whether we do or not, we still must follow them.*" And I said, "*That's true in the majority of cases. I completely understand. And in this instance, there's probably a lot of reasons why you won't want to, why you'll want to do things a little differently. I have a lot of things I could bring here, but I would be inclined not to if I couldn't get some consideration here. But then again, maybe that's completely irrelevant and it just doesn't matter to you but I thought I would do you the courtesy of bringing it up so that maybe another discussion could be had with the committee and you could rethink your position on it a little bit. I'll leave that in your hands. Is there anything else today we can complete until you review this one more time?*" And, by the way, they came back and made a small concession for me. Not a big one and not as big as I wanted, but it was *something*, especially when you consider that that went against their policy. It was very interesting.

So some very interesting thoughts here. Very interesting. Here is a way to learn this so it's easy, it's like a little *mnemonic*, it'll stick in your head, and to do it, first read it and then I want you to repeat it over. **It's right, it's wrong, according to whom? It's right it's wrong, according to whom? It's right, it's wrong, according to whom?**

And another one, **should, should not, who says? Should, should not, who says? Should, should not, who says?**

All right, now I want you to say it out loud. Just do it out loud. Why not do it out loud right now? Later, you can repeat it in your mind, all right. But for now, if you can, if you can repeat it out loud, go for it.

Can I say to you, "*Well, this is the right way to do this.*" And you say, "*According to whom? Who says?*" I go, "*You know, it's not right that you stay out past ten on a school night.*" And the person responds, "*According to whom?*" Now, if they did, they might be pushing it if they were my kids. "*According to me,*" I might say. But we begin to see how this can be used.

Now let's repeat the second one. Go ahead. We're going to say, **should, should not, who says?**

You can always put **softening frames** in like, **should, should not, well I'm curious, who says?** Or **should, should not, that's interesting, and I'm curious, where did you hear that?** You see?

All right, now, repeat both of them together one after the other. Repeat each one three times. It goes like this. **It's right, it's wrong, according to whom? Should, should not, who says?**

Perfect. That's going to start pounding this skill into your brain and you're going to get better and better at how to do it and your brain may right now be going, **yeah, who says?** And if it did, you're starting to get the hang of it.

Now you can imagine real quickly, can you not, that if you did this *too much* to a prospect, you'd sound like a donkey, right? The person says, *"Well, it's important that you be here on time because I'm running short on this day."* And you go, *"Well who says I have to be there on time?"* And they go, *"Well I do."* Okay. *That* wasn't too swift.

But if the person says, *"You know, in an economy like we're facing it's important to have our assets diversified."* You might say, *"You know, I'm curious, I know you probably heard that from someone you consider an authority, maybe even your own father, but I'm wondering if you really have stopped to think about today the strategies that make the most amount of sense. And I can tell you as one of the leading advisors in this field, that it's especially important to begin to question those things that we for so long held as truisms. Especially in this market. I can help you do that and that's what we're here to accomplish today and I'd like to ask you to hold in your mind a few of the thoughts that I'm going to be suggesting while we look to really find the truth behind some of the other things that we've long held as the way to go but maybe today, it just isn't."*

Now, if you tear that language apart, what I just did, I did this but without being so confrontive. Okay?

CHAPTER SIX

Distortion: Mindreading

In the **distortion** category still, we're now going to look at what's called **mindreading**, and **mindreading** is when **someone claims to know what someone else is thinking or feeling without having direct sensory evidence.** Sentences like: *'he doesn't like me'* or *'I know I'm not wanted here'* or *'the board won't like my presentation'* are the types of sentences we're talking about. And the challenge for this is: **how do you know?**

Now, of the three types of **mapping strategies** – **distortion**, **generalization** and **deletion** -- the most powerful and effective for purposes of persuasion, well it's the *mastery of all three*, but the most powerful of those three is **distortion**, and of the ones in **distortion**, **mindreading** ranks right up there with a pattern that you can *immediately* leverage to gain traction in your persuasion endeavors. This one, just star and underline it, mark it up. I mean, this one is a doozie. Okay?

Now, here's why, **this pattern can be used to challenge how a person "knows" anything**. If a person says, *"I think I should just wait before I make a decision"* you could say, ***"How do you know?"*** If they say, *"Well, it's just a feeling,"* you can say, ***"How do you know*** *that's a feeling that tells you to wait? Perhaps it's a feeling of anticipation of going ahead. As you recognize it for what it is, now don't you feel better? Can't you just stop, take a deep breath, and feel that sense of relief that you've identified this feeling and it feels good now?"*

Now that is powerful. That is effective. That does not make you a donkey.

So the practice for this one is, **he, she, they, do/do not, how do you know? He, she, they, do/do not, how do you know? He, she, they, do/do not, how do you know? He, she, they, do/do not, how do you know?**

The government says that it's not that smart to try to practice your freedom of speech while holding a gun in your hand in public. Okay? You might say, "*How do you know? How does the government know? How do they know? Maybe it'd be a great way to do it.*" Seems like how they did it in the Wild West, right?

Okay, so let's do the practice. This one is brilliant. Here's what you're going to say: **He, she, they, do/do not, how do you know? He, she, they, do/do not, how do you know? He, she, they, do/do not, how do you know? He, she, they, do/do not, how do you know? He, she, they, do/do not, how do you know?**

Now, I'm going to *add* something to this, okay? **He, she, they, do/do not, how do you know? I mean, maybe it's . . . He, she, they, do/do not, how do you know? I mean, maybe it's. . .**

So how would *that* work? They say that this isn't right. Well, **how do they know?** I mean, **maybe it's** not that they think it's not right, **maybe it's** just that they don't have the time to tell everyone else that's going to hear this how to do it in a way that will work, so they have to try to make something that will apply to everybody that will allow it to apply to them while you on the other hand, know how to do it in a way that works. In fact, I would say that's the difference between someone that has an adviser and someone who's trying to do it on their own. **Maybe** you'd make a blanket policy like that for the general population but not for those who have advisers and can actually get the help they need. Do you follow me?

This works for every industry. I don't care what you're selling. I don't care what you're persuading about. This is amazing. Even in the dating world someone could say, "*Well, I just don't really have a lot of time right now to go out.*" "*Well, how do you know? I mean, I know it probably feels that way, but in reality, it might just be that you're saving the time you have for a person who can really kind of make you think a little bit and if you think right now about what I'm saying, I think you'll find, huh, this guy standing in front of you is doing just that, isn't he? It might be kind of fun to hang out and see where this might go, what do you say?*"

It may or may not work, but at least you're still in the running, aren't you? You tried.

I love this pattern and can't speak highly enough about it. **He, she, they, do/do not, how do you know?**

CHAPTER SEVEN

Distortion: Cause and Effect

Let's go to **cause and effect. Cause and effect** is a statement that **some action by one person makes another person do, think, or feel something.** This is not a very easy pattern for people to get sometimes, you may even find yourself challenged by it. However, hopefully, since you've studied **cause and effect** in a previous book , this will come pretty natural for you.

Now, the reason that it's often difficult for people is that our society *supports* the belief that if a person says or does something to you, then they have **caused** you to have a particular feeling or response. And this also **presupposes** that you have *no control* over your own emotions and actions, that you simply *respond* to what's going on around you, and obviously, that's not true.

So sentences like, *they make me mad when they treat me like that*, or *I can't buy now because I have to look around more*, are the kinds of things we're talking about for the **cause and effect** pattern.

So the **challenge** for this pattern is, **how does X cause Y? How does some behavior or X person cause you to choose to Y?** And the practice for this is: **this causes that, how does this cause that? This causes that, how does this cause that?** One more time. **This causes that, how does this cause that?** Now I want you to say it out loud. **This causes that, how does this cause that?**

Now you can go through these practice patterns like this over and over and over and you'll just jam this into your head and make it really easy for yourself. **How will it make it easy for myself?** Well, it just will. **Who says?** Well, I do. Okay. Well **maybe it isn't that** it will make it so easy, **maybe it will** just make it really *compelling* and because I'm so interested, I'll get it faster than before. Yes. I agree.

But what we're playing with here is the way people **distort** things, the way they make things up in their head, the way they give *rules* or *meaning* to things. Okay? By **distorting**, we're *taking control* of **the way they imagined how things will take place in the future**, and instead of constructing things in the way they would default to naturally, they're beginning to default to *the way we want them to do it*. So you have to do it *early* in a presentation, *the earlier the better* if anything comes up that allows you to do that.

We've just covered one of the three major sections of **mapping strategies**. I highly advise you to stop now, stop reading, and go back over this section over and over and over and over. I told you, this is a very technical lesson. Okay? The abilities it will give you are *inordinate*, especially since you already have an understanding of how to put persuasion into the minds of the people you're influencing.

This gives you *the other side*. Okay? I very much recommend that there's very little reason to cram your brain *so* full of something that you're in a stupor. If for any reason you find yourself zoning out at this point, just stop and go back over this again and again. There's no rush. Give yourself some time. The nice thing about having these lessons in this book format is you can always go back over them again and again and again and I highly recommend you do so.

In fact, if I haven't told you this story, and I don't know that I have, I had a guy that worked for me many, many years ago. His name was Mike, I believe. Yeah, I think it was. Great guy, I really liked him. And Mike had an *earlier* set of lessons. It wasn't nearly as detailed as this. And Mike told me that by the time he'd started working for me, he had listened to the recording, I don't know, it was 25 times maybe, and it comprised maybe 20 hours. I mean, he had spent a *significant* amount of time listening.

Now, every day Mike would go out for a walk and as he would walk, he would listen, and he would go for long walks - hour, hour and a half long walks. And he would listen over and over and over. He told me he intended to listen to it that many more times and that every time he listened to it, he learned something new. Every time he listened to it, he got additional *ahas*. This guy was skilled, let me tell you. If he wanted to sell you something, he did, he would. He was very, very talented.

So I can't recommend enough to you that you go over and over and over it, and this would be a perfect breaking spot. Okay? All right.

CHAPTER EIGHT

Generalization: Modal Operators

Hopefully your brain is clear and refreshed and ready to go and we're going to now talk about the **mapping strategies** of **generalization** and first we're going to deal with **modal operators**. But before we do, again remember, **generalization** is **the process we use to create structure in our lives**. All knowledge and science is based on **generalization**. It's **how we make sense of things we've never done or seen before by recognizing the things that they have in common**. And there are two types of **generalizations** that occur: **modal operators** and **universal quantifiers**.

Modal operators are what we use to **express the rules that we live by**. And we're going to deal with two types of **modal operators** in this book. There are others, but we'll deal with two types. Now by the way, an even much more advanced strategy is using **modal operators** on the *other* side of persuasion, sort of, but again, very technical. Very fun , but at a later date.

All right. **Modal operators** of necessity are words such as *have to, ought to, should, need to, must* or *must not*, and of course *necessity* or *need*. So notice how **all these words have in common an element of necessity**. And remember, **we recognize things by the things they have in common**. All of these words *have in common* that they are part of a group of words that express *necessity*: *have to, ought to, should, need to, must,* or *must not.*

There are also **modal operators** of *possibility* such as *impossible, unable, can't,* and *can* and *will*. We can go on either side of the greater class of words that are contained in *possibility* words. *Impossible, unable, can't, can,* and *will.*

Now **modal operators** generally **remove choice from a person**. Now just reading that, can you *already* begin to imagine a benefit in knowing it? If people are speaking in a way that **removes choice**, what if *we restore it for them*? And/or what if *we speak in ways that remove their choice*?

Modal operators demonstrate the *limits* of the speaker's model of the world. Often you'll hear words like, *'just'* or *'it's only that'* in combination with these words. *It's only that* I *can't* do this. *I wish I could,* but I *can't. It's just that* it's *impossible* to make this happen. Okay?

Now, words like *can* and *will,* I *can* do this, *I will* do that, don't necessarily **limit choice** other than the fact that if you're doing *one* thing, you're *not* doing another by default. So you can see that in *that* way they **restrict choice** as well.

Okay, the **challenge** for this is, *just suppose you can*. Or *what would happen if you did or did not?* For example, take the word 'impossible'. You hear the word *impossible* and you're triggered, '*what would happen if you did?*' or '*just suppose you could.*'

These are really profound and here's the practice for you. **Could, could not, what would happen if you did, did not.** I'm going to write it again. **Could, could not, what would happen if you did, did not. Could, could not, what would happen if you did, did not.**

Okay. So can you see how this works? "*Well, I just **can't** come out tonight?*" "*Really? **What would happen if** you **did**?*" "*Well, then I'd be standing up this person over here.*" "*Uh huh, and **what would happen if** that weren't a big deal?*" "*Well, I think it is a big deal.*" "*I know, why do you think that?*" "*Well, because I just feel like it'd be wrong.*" "*Well, **what if** what you're feeling isn't that it would be wrong, but that it would be a minor inconvenience, but the major benefit to you in coming out would override that minor inconvenience, especially if you could eliminate it altogether by simply saying to the other person, 'hey, I have a tremendous opportunity. Could we reschedule?' What do you say? Come on.*"

Now you see how I'm starting to **line up** what I've taught you in the previous section. Do you hear how I just did that? Do you start to experience how persuasive this can be? I mean, this is really high level stuff. Okay?

Let's do the statement: **Could, could not, what would happen if you did, did not.** Ready? Let's repeat it out loud five times, here we go: **Could, could not, what would happen if you did, did not. Could, could not, what would happen if you did, did not. Could, could not, what would happen if you did, did not. Could, could not, what would happen if you did, did not. Could, could not, what would happen if you did, did not.**

You can say this over and over and over to yourself, like a mantra, **could, could not, what would happen if you did, did not**. And it'll just *train your brain* to get it. It will help **install** it, and reading this chapter will help you to get the power of what we're doing over and over and over. All right?

CHAPTER NINE

Generalization: Universal Quantifiers

In the realm of **generalization**, we have something called **universal quantifiers** which are **words that take an experience and *generalize* it into all other experiences**. For example, if a person tried to sell something *once* and it didn't work, he might **generalize** he could *never*, ever sell anything. Words like *all, every, never, everybody, no one*, et cetera, will tip you off to a **universal quantifier** being used. Okay?

And the **challenge** for this is, **use the *same word* as a challenge**. They say, "***All** the ways of doing this won't work.*" And you go, "***All?***" The other thing you can do is, you can **reverse what they say and put it in their words**. Okay? Examples: "***No one** pays that much for this.*" And you reply, "**No one**? You're sure that **no one** has paid this much, ever?" "Well, not that I'm aware of." "Okay, so they might have, you're just unaware of it?" "Yes." "Okay. And if they had, would that change your opinion any?"

Or, "**Everyone** knows that you shouldn't do that." You reply, "What is it that **you** know you **should** do?" So this really is **reconnecting them with their deep structure** and as such, it can be quite a blow, okay? It can be very aggressive and it can be combative almost, if you're not careful and you don't say this with **softening frames** and be careful.

Here's the practice. You say it like this. **All. All? All. All? All. All? All. All? And every. Every? Every. Every? Every. Every? Every. Every? And everyone knows. What is it that you know? Everyone knows. What is it that you know? Everyone knows. What is it that you know?**

So by *training* yourself with this, you're going to rapidly hear in other people's language when this is going on and have the option to **challenge** it.

Now, repeat each one of these aloud five times. First: **all. All?** Ready? Say it out loud. **All. All? All. All? All. All? All. All? All. All? All. All? All. All? All. All? And now, every. Every? Every. Every? Every. Every? Every. Every? Every. Every? Every. Every? Every. Every?** And now, **everyone knows. What is it that you know?** Ready? **Everyone knows. What is it that you know? Everyone knows. What is it that you know? Everyone knows. What is it that you know? Everyone knows. What is it that you know?**

See how that works? This is going to allow you to **challenge universal quantifiers** and quickly **redirect them to your way of thinking**. But remember, number one, it's *not* appropriate to challenge *everything* you hear. And number two, when you *do*, you *have to* **redirect them to your way of thinking**.

"**Everyone** knows that you have to challenge generalizations." And you go, "**Everyone**?" "Yeah, **everyone**." "Really?" "Yeah." "What do **you** know about generalizations?" "Well, I was told you have to challenge them." "Okay, great. Well, you believe what you hear then and I want to kind of raise this to a new level for you. You need to **challenge the ones that make sense**, that will **help** you if you challenge. Does that make sense?" "Well, yes it does." "Okay. How do you know it makes sense?" "Well, it sounds right." And I go, "Okay, well maybe it not only sounds right, but it sounds effective, like as if you can imagine already your skill level raising and you feeling a deep sense of contentment knowing that you're getting something of tremendous value, do you not?" Now. You see? Powerful stuff. Really powerful stuff.

CHAPTER TEN

Deletion: Nominalizations

Okay. Let's look at: **deletion**. And if you remember, we talked about **deletion** being the result of **paying attention to one set of information which automatically causes a person to delete certain other information**. We all have seven plus or minus two slots of information available to us at any given point in time and as a result, when we orient our attention to anything, automatically, it causes us both to **be aware of** what we are orienting our attention to, and to **delete** what else is happening. For example, right now, you probably *weren't aware of it* until I brought your attention to it, however, were you aware of the weight of your foot on the floor? Or of the feeling of your clothes against your legs? And by the way, this is also a very good kind of strategy for **creating amnesia**. Hopefully I'll have a chance to talk to you about that a little bit later.

There are four types of **deletion** that occur: **nominalizations, unspecified verbs, lack of referential index**, and **simple deletion**. These are the *least valuable* of the patterns. They're important that you know them, but using these very much will turn you into a donkey. Okay? Even worse. It's close cousin. You know to what I refer. You can get away with **distortion** and **generalization** all day long if you're *kind* and *careful* and *supportive*. You *cannot* get away with **deletion** very much. And if you do, you're going to sound like a donkey.

So let's go through it, starting with **nominalization** and that is what happens when **you take a process and turn it into a thing**. It's where **a process becomes static and unchanging**. *Processes* by definition are *changing*, that is *continuing to evolve*. So **nominalizations are verbs that have been turned into a noun**. For example, the word '*deciding*' is a verb, the word '*decision*' is more like a noun or at least masquerading as one. It is. One of the ways to tell it's a noun is that it ends in 'ion'. That's kind of a dead giveaway. **Nominalizations** will frequently end in 'ion'.

To **break** a **nominalization**, you have to **change it back into a verb again**. The **challenge** for this is, **how specifically** and then **state the noun as a verb**. Let me give you some examples. "*That **decision** is interesting.*" You respond, "***How specifically** are you **deciding**?*" They say "*Our **association** with our sales team needs to be changed.*" You respond with, "***How specifically** are you currently **associating**?*"

Now let's say that you're talking to a person and they say, "*I will give **consideration** to your ideas and then we can go further.*" And you say, "***What specifically** will you be **considering** so that I understand?*" Here's the issue. When you do that, you run a big risk. "*Well, dummy, what you just got done telling me.*" It's kind of what they're probably going to be thinking, or worse, "*Well wait a minute. I don't know why you're asking me this kind of question, but it feels like sales pressure coming at me and I don't think I like that.*" And that's like a death blow to a persuader. So you have to really *be careful* where you use this and I'm going to give you a way to make it better here pretty quick, but I've got to teach it to you the best way I can to teach you, and it sounds like, "**How specifically --**" and then **state the noun back as a verb**.

I'll give you two **tests** to *determine* if a word is a **nominalization**.

1. <u>Test one</u>. Ask yourself if the word *fits in a wheelbarrow*. If it does *not*, then it is a **nominalization**. For example, a rock, which is a noun, fits in a wheelbarrow. John, which is a noun, fits in a wheelbarrow. A relationship does *not*, therefore '*relationship*' is a **nominalization** and a rock is not. Make sense?
2. <u>Test two</u>. Say "*An ongoing. . .*" and put in the suspected **nominalization**. If it *makes sense*, then it *is* a **nominalization**. So an example: *an ongoing decision*. That *makes sense* and therefore it *is* a **nominalization**. But if you said '*an ongoing rock*', well that does *not* make sense and therefore is *not* a **nominalization**.

356

Here are some **nominalizations**: *decision, relationship, management, love, persuasion*. Okay? So if I said, 'an ongoing *persuasion*', that makes sense. It *is* a **nominalization**, but if I ask you, can you put *persuasion* in a wheelbarrow? No. And therefore, it does not make sense.

You might be able to get *Kenrick* in a wheelbarrow and then you have a persuad<u>er</u> in a wheelbarrow. It sounds like a bad joke, doesn't it? But you've got the *person* in there, not the *act*.

So you can see clearly that **things are things** and **nominalizations are *not* things but they're *masquerading* as things**. Okay? And when you **break** them, you are getting the person to begin to **challenge** or question the fact of whatever is *surrounding* that **nominalization**. And using some of the other patterns that I've been teaching you, you can get the direction changed back around to wherever you want them to be. Or at least you have more of a chance of doing it.

Now, I want to give you something fabulous. Here's a **persuasion strategy** for you. **Use nominalizations when you're persuading to fog the other person's mind**. And if *they* use them, selectively **challenge** the ones you'll benefit from. I'll tell you why in a minute but let's go back and let me just go through this a little deeper with you. If I said, "*The **ramifications** of your continued use of the material that you learn will assist you in coming to the **conclusion** that not only is there **value**, but there is a real **opportunity** for your life to be enhanced and for you to have more and more **realizations** of ways in which you can positively affect your life in the way you want to.*"

Now that probably started to *fog your brain*. You're like, uh, what? Okay? Now, that is a *very strong* persuasion strategy to **install** something in the mind of a listener. We practiced with this in earlier lessons a little bit. But let's say someone did this to *you* and as you heard it, you decided to **challenge** it and the minute they start in, you let them get a little bit, you say, "*Wait a minute, before you go any further, **how** would I be **realizing** this?*" "*Well, through your **practice**.*" "**Practicing of what?**" "*Well, the way in which you'll understand the power of how these can be used.*" "**How** *will I be understanding that **exactly**?* **What** *would I be seeing, hearing or feeling that would let me know that?*" "*Well, you'll be getting more results in your life.*" "*Through the use of what you're saying now?*" "*I don't know. Well, yes, that's what I'm saying.*" "*Okay, so you're saying that?*" "*Yeah.*" "*Okay, you're saying that but we don't know what other people, including myself even might say.*" "*Well, no, I'm saying that. That's what I'm saying.*" "*Yeah. Okay, well thank you for sharing. I appreciate it.*"

Now, you may not have established a lot of **rapport** there, but you've **broken** that person's rhythm and if you look at *why* you want to **selectively challenge** their **nominalizations**, look at the four bullets below:

- you'll break their rhythm,
- you can throw them off their game,
- you can take control of the conversation,
- and you can redirect their thinking to your way, or at least you have an opportunity to.

That's why you might want to **break a nominalization** like that. Furthermore, knowing this one strategy, you can always use it on you.

And let me just make a real break here and just say for a moment, all of these patterns you're using in this lesson can *always* be safely *used on yourself*. The worst that will happen is it will drive yourself a little insane. Not really. It might make you question reality a little bit but you'll quickly land with a more secure grasp on reality.

And you *can* and *should* **use these patterns and strategies on yourself**. You *can* and *should* do it all the time. However, as you do it, you're going to also see where you *should not* do it on others. You'll do it at first just to *learn* it and then you'll go, wow, I see what Kenrick was meaning.

CHAPTER ELEVEN

Deletion: Unspecified Verbs

Let's go to **unspecified verbs**. And these are **descriptions that do not supply enough information** and that's what we're going to be **challenging** here. It's real easy to go way overboard with this one.

Remember again, as I have been telling you repeatedly, it's most important to challenge **distortions** and **generalizations**, not **deletions**, but the **challenge** for **unspecified verbs** is: **how specifically?**

Examples: "*I was cheated.*" You reply with: "**How specifically** were you cheated?" Now let's say a person says, "*Man, this dumb cop stopped me and gave me a ticket. I was cheated out of this money that I'm going to have to pay.*" And you go, "*Well* **how specifically** *were you cheated?*" "*Like I just said, this dumb cop just stopped me and gave me a ticket and I feel cheated.*" And you go, "**Well, how specifically do you feel cheated by that?**" "*Well, because he gave me a ticket.*" "*Yeah, well* **how** *did he* **cheat** *you?*" "*Well, because he shouldn't have given me a ticket.*" You're going to be like, "*Well, if you had been driving responsibly you wouldn't have gotten a ticket.*"

See what I'm saying is you're going to be seen as a jerk if you keep it up. However, it's still useful to know and to use from time to time, just be careful.

"*I have to make more sales.*" You reply with, "**How specifically** *will you make more sales?*" "*I'm not comfortable with this.*" You reply, "**How specifically** *are you not comfortable with this?*" Okay? See how that worked? It's pretty simple. You want to be careful with it.

CHAPTER TWELVE

Deletion: Lack of Referential Index and Simple Deletion

Okay, here we're going to deal with a **lack of referential index** and **simple deletion**. **Lack of referential index** is when **a person deletes who is being referred to**. This also sounds *vague* and *ambiguous*. The **challenge** for this is: **who or what specifically?** You keep hearing this word '**specifically**', I'm going to talk about it in a minute.

Example: "**All our competition** is trying to get that account." You reply with: "**Who specifically** of our competition is trying to get that account?"

Or you hear: "**People** should respect the work I do." And you reply with: "**Who specifically** should respect the work you do?"

Or you hear: "**They** need to learn how to do **their** job." You reply with: "**Who specifically** needs to learn how to do their job?"

So you can kind of see that it's *argumentative* sounding, but still can be very, very useful.

And then let's go to the last, which is **simple deletion** and **simple deletion** is **a catch all category that is used to recover any other deletions that exist** and the **challenge** is: **who or what specifically?** Same as above.

And so for example here you might hear: "*I'm concerned.*" And you reply with: "**What specifically** is concerning you?" Or "*He hurt me.*" And you reply with: "**Who specifically** hurt you?"

Now, I want to give you an example of how to take this *way* too far and totally sound like a donkey, okay? You hear: "*I'm concerned.*" And you reply with: "**What specifically** is concerning you and **how specifically** are you concerned?" See? You're *overwhelming* the person. "*He hurt me.*" "**Who specifically** hurt you? **How specifically** did he hurt you? And **what specifically** got hurt and **why specifically** do you think he did it?" The guy goes, "*Forget it, I don't want to talk to you.*"

You can see that this turns you into kind of a monster if you're not careful. You can attack *anything* and *everything* that a person says. Anything? Yes. Anything. That **who specifically** says? That anyone says? Anyone? Yes, I just said that. Anyone. Well, **what would happen if** you didn't attack it? Then what? Well, then you wouldn't be recovering the deeper information. And, is that a problem? I guess not. Okay, I guess not. Let's move on.

You see? I mean, literally, with what I've just taught you, you can attack *any* part of *any* sentence *anytime* you hear it. **How specifically** will you be attacking it? **What specifically** will you be attacking? And that's why I'm telling you, and I warned you in the beginning and now that you have to be *really careful* of what's going on.

Now, I hear talk about the use of the word '*specifically*'. Now, I want you to know something. I'm using it to *teach* you, to help you to understand that the *point* of the question is to **become more specific**, to **get the person to be more specific**. In other words, we're asking them, please **stop and think about your *surface* structure that you just told me and let's connect that to your *deeper* structure**, and let's just see if we can't find something else there that will be of value to you.

So when you first learn this, you want to *use* the word, **who specifically, what specifically, how specifically, according to whom specifically**. But once you begin to *get* it, *drop* the word '*specifically*' and you'll sound much *nicer* and you'll find that you can use even the tools of **deletion** that I've been teaching you to help you when you need them.

CHAPTER THIRTEEN

Summary

Remember, the most *important* things to **challenge** are **distortions** and **generalizations**. Like **lost performative: according to whom?** "*Who says that distortions and generalizations are the most important things to challenge?*" "*Well, Kenrick does.*" "*Okay, well how do you know?*" "*Well, because I believe him.*" "*All right. Well, what if he's wrong?*" "*Well, he's not wrong.*" "*Well, what if he is wrong?*" "*He's not wrong.*" "*Well, what if he is wrong?*" "*Well, then I guess I'd believe something that I'm not real sure about.*" "*Okay, well how does believing something that you're not real sure about cause you to feel?*" "*Well, like I better test it myself.*" "*Perfect. So what you're telling me is, he's pointed you in what you think to be the right direction and now you're going to test it out for yourself, correct?*" "*Yes.*"

You see how I got them to turn that around? Okay? And I used **lost performative, mindreading** and **cause and effect**.

Of course, next, **modal operators. What would happen if you did/did not?** And **just suppose you can**, and **universal modifiers**: *all*, *every*, *never*. Do you see how using those can get people turned around in a really big way and how you can create a direction to get people where you want them to go? Nothing short of brilliant. Okay? **Challenging** the above list, **lost performative, mindreading, cause and effect, modal operators, universal quantifiers**, helps *establish the direction in their mind that you want them to be going*.

Challenging **deletions**, on the other hand, can be *really irritating* so don't go too far and watch the use of the word '***specifically***' specifically.

Wow. What a lesson. This is a lengthy book, a lot of stuff here. You know, you're ready for it but I can assure you that you will learn *more* and *more* and *more* every time you read this. Keep going over it.

Thanks again. Have a wonderful time until I talk to you again. Re-read the book lots. Persuade like mad. Talk to you soon. Bye bye.

BOOK TWENTY-TWO

AMPLIFYING AND DIMINISHING

CHAPTER ONE

A Question of Distortion

Welcome to **Book Twenty-Two** of *Persuasion Force*. Wow. Every time I do one of these I'm a bit blown away that we've covered so much and that we've only got a little left to go.

All right, well we have a really exciting lesson again this book. This is also a very *technical* lesson although in a much different way than the last book was. So we're going to just kind of jump right in to this book's lesson and there was a really good question that was asked about the last book, and as we start this time, let me jump in here and read you this question.

"Hi, Kenrick. **Persuasion Force 21** was sure a technical but also very interesting lesson. I've been going over it practically every day to truly understand it. There's just one thing that still confuses me a bit. Why does '**lost performatives**' fall under the **distortion** category and not the **generalization** one? It just seems more logical to me to put it under **generalization**. Thanks."

All right, let me go through that question for you. I think I can help you make sense of this a little bit more. Let's go back to the main *definitions* of **distortion** and **generalization**. A **distortion** is **the process whereby we are able to shift our sensory data to make different kinds of sense out of the same thing**. That's the key phrase there '*different kinds of sense out of the same thing*'. This is the way in which we plan. We take the sensory data that we have *right now* and **distort** it by *imagining* what will happen *in the future* if we do X or Y. **Distortion** is what allows us to *construct* things or *imagine* different types of things. Okay?

Now let's go to **generalization**. **Generalization** is **the process we use to create structure**. That's the key, that *we use it to create structure* in our lives. All knowledge in science is based on **generalization** and it's how we make sense of things we've never seen before by *recognizing* **the things that they have in common**.

Okay. Now as to **lost performatives**. **Lost performatives** occur when you talk like *everybody has the same model of the world as you do*. So that's the key. **Lost performative** is *not* about *making sense of the world* or *making structure*. It is a **distortion** of something. In other words, if you think that **everybody has the same model of the world as you do**, you're *wrong*. They *don't*. Not everybody does. And yet this is a very classic and common thing. We've all heard it throughout our lives as people saying, "*It's wrong to cheat*", as if *everybody* believes this, or "*You should treat others the way you would like to be treated.*" Well *not everybody believes that* and not everybody *needs* to believe that. I mean, it would be nice if they did to some extent, but this **lost**

performative rule is really about how we **distort** things and it's *not* about how we *create structure*. Okay? So creating structure would be a whole different kind of thing.

For example, if we talk about **generalization**, and we talk about '*ought to*' -- like **modal operators** -- '*have to*', '*ought to*', '*should*', '*need to*' – this is a **structure** that we're creating for our lives and that's a big difference between **distorting** something that *shouldn't* be true and *making* it true or visa versa. Now that's not the *only* form of **distortion** because we could also imagine if we took one road instead of a different road. Or we could imagine one skill being applied somewhere else, and that's a way to try to figure something out, but it's not a way that we're necessarily **generalizing** into all of our life. I mean, it could *lead* to that, that's for sure, but there's a distinct *difference* between trying to **create structure** and **distorting** something. And that's why **lost performatives** belongs with **distortion**.

I know that's a bit of a technical answer, but I'm hoping that that makes sense for you and that you get that. By the way, it's a very, very good question. I appreciate the study and the effort that you put into that question and the review that you've been doing everyday to get to the point of being *able* to ask that question. So I'm just really impressed with that. Thank you for submitting that question.

CHAPTER TWO

Altering the Intensity of Experience

We're going to talk about **amplifying and diminishing things in people's existence**. Like I said, this is a very technical lesson. Again, we're dealing with some very advanced things and the key to what you're going to be learning here, I guess really like an awful lot of the lessons, is in **your ability to *combine* them and use them at will** with many things. So we're going to spend some time integrating in this book that type of way of learning and using these.

Amplifying and diminishing is where we're going to begin. What if you could **turn up or down the intensity** at will on what your prospect or client is *experiencing*? Wouldn't that be cool? Well, you'll be able to after this lesson, I'll tell you that.

What if you could instantly **turn up or down the intensity** on what they *say*? What if you *don't like* something they say or something they say is even bothering *them* but you could **turn down the intensity** of it? Kind of useful.

Or what if you want them to be *more passionate* or *excited* about something and you could **turn up the intensity** on that? That's exactly what we're talking about. It's very, very powerful and very useful.

Let's go back and remember one of our first lessons in which you learned about *visual*, *auditory*, and *kinesthetic* words. You remember that we take in information through our five senses and they form the basis of a **bias** or a **preference** in our mind. Now, what does that mean? Remember when we learned that most people have a **preferred sensory system** that they like to deal with. That's what I mean by **bias**.

So you'll find a person that has a preferred sense of the *visual* or a preferred sense of the *auditory* or the *kinesthetic*, et cetera, and those are the big three that people will prefer. And you'll find that especially under stressful situations they'll resort to that preferred sense way more so than they will to some of the other senses.

Now we learned about these big chunks and yet there's a *smaller* chunk that we can work with so another name for **VAK** is **modalities**. The different sensory **modalities**. So if we kind of start with a **modality**, we could call a *smaller* chunk **submodalities** and we'll use that word as we go through our lesson today. **Submodalities** or *smaller chunks* of *visual, auditory,* and *kinesthetic* words.

Now, I want you to read what I'm going to tell you next really, really carefully. This is profound. You may not recognize just how profound it is until you go back through this lesson a couple of times or really give some thought to it. **The *meaning* that we give to an experience is directly related to and controlled by these submodalities.**

So information comes in through the five senses. Like right now you're *seeing* my words and reading them. However, the *meaning* that you give to the words that I'm telling you and to *any* kind of experience in your life is *directly related* to and controlled by the **submodalities**.

CHAPTER THREE

Visual Submodalities

Let's start with the *visual* system and we'll go through a list of the most important **visual submodalities** together. *Brightness, size, distance, location, color* or *black and white, focus,* whether it's *moving* or *still,* whether there's a *border* around it, and whether there's *one image or more.*

These are the most important of the **visual submodalities**. Now, let's go through these and let's think about what they *do*. What I'd like you to do right now is to *remember* something that happened really nice in your life. Just go back to a time when you had a very nice experience of something and I want you to actually just *focus* in on what that is. *Remember* it for a moment. I trust that you've got it. If not, pause reading for a moment until you can just find one experience that you enjoy.

Now, I want you to remember it and as you do, I want you to just *follow right along* and do what I'm asking you to do. As you look at this, or *imagine* that you're looking at it, either way, I want you to **increase the brightness**. Imagine that you have a *brightness* knob and you can just **increase the brightness** and make it *brighter* and *brighter* and *brighter*. And as you get it *really bright,* I want you just to *hold that in your mind* for a moment. Okay? Now I want you to **turn it back down** so it was where it was when we started, so reach up, grab that knob, **turn it down** to where it's back to where it was. And then I want you to go the *other* direction, I want you to turn it *down, down, down,* so it's *darker* and *darker* and it becomes *so dark* you can barely see it.

And just look at that very, very dark picture now. Okay. And now go ahead and bring it back up to where it was when you started.

Did anything *change* in your feeling as we did that? Did you notice for example that making it *brighter* made you *feel more strongly* about it, made you remember it more *vividly*? And when you made it *darker* it became *less important*, shall we say, or *less vivid, less impactful* emotionally? If not, that's okay. As we go through this list together, I want you to notice if *other* things in this list change. When we change *one*, you may notice that *others* are changing too. That's okay. Just make note of which of those there are.

Let's go to *size*. So now | want you to look at that picture again, remember the memory, this good thing that happened to you, and I want you to imagine now like you put your hands out in front of you to *as big as the picture is* and I want you to just **make it bigger** and *bigger*, just *increase the span of your hands* until it's *double* or *triple* the size, like as if you're *stretching* it and making it *bigger* and *bigger*. So make that thing *really big*.

Now look at it. How do you *feel* with the image of this being double or triple as big as it was before?

Okay now **shrink it right back down** to where it was and then with your hands **make it really small**, like maybe two inches by two inches or something. *Very little*. Even *littler*. And now how do you *feel* with it chunked *down*?

Now go ahead and *bring it right back up to where it was*. You can put your hands down, and think about it for a moment. When you did this, did anything *change* in your emotions? And did anything *change* in any of the others, like did the *brightness* change when you made it *bigger* or *smaller*? Did the *distance* change when you made it *bigger* or *smaller*?

Let's go to *distance*. So go back down and remember the image again. And what I want you to do is I want you to **bring it very, very close**. **Zoom that picture in** really, really *close*. Make it right smack dab in front of you. And how do you *feel*?

And now *zoom it back* to where it was and then **zoom it way out in the distance**. Put it *out there*, I don't know, half a mile away, just *so far* you can barely even recognize it. Okay, how do you *feel* when it's way out there? Bring it back to where it was.

For many people when you *adjust the distance* and you bring it really *close*, it also gets really *big*. It's hard for it not to get *bigger* when you bring it *closer*. Did you notice that to be true for you too? And when you push it *way away* it tends to get *small*. Now for many people, when you *increase the size*, it gets *close* and when you *decrease the size*, it goes *far away*. And for many people when you *increase the brightness* it also sometimes changes its *size* and its *distance*. Very interesting, isn't it?

If it *didn't* do that for you, that's okay, but I'll bet you that one of those had an impact of adjusting the others. There's a name for that, it's called a **driver submodality** and the **driver submodalities** are the *most powerful* and for each person it can be different, however I'm going to teach you a shortcut that you'll be able to use here pretty quick and you'll be able to use them at will and you'll know pretty much that you're probably hitting on at least one of the **drivers**.

Now, let's go to *location*. Let me talk to you about *location* for a minute before we adjust it. As you look straight out in front of you above the plane that your eye is on we'll call *above the horizon*, and below the plane your eye is on when you're looking straight out in front of you, we'll call *below the horizon*. Often images that you *feel very positive about* will be *at least level* on the horizon if not *higher*. And often images that you *don't feel that good about* will be *below* the horizon.

Now remember the classic pose of somebody who's *depressed*. Are they *looking up* or are they *looking down*? Generally they're *looking down*, their head is *down*, right? So where would that person be looking if they were thinking of something *positive*? Generally, at least at a *level* plane if not *above* the horizon line.

There's more to *location* than just *above* or *below* the horizon. *Location* is a fascinating **submodality**. So let's do the following, let's go back and remember this image of this nice thing that you had happen to you and just look at it for a moment and what I'd like you to do is *point to where this is located*. Are you pointing *left* or *right*? *Up* or *down*? *Far away* or *close*? So notice that *location* can have the elements of *size* and *distance* built into it. For example, if you're pointing to a picture that's very *near* to you, now we're talking about *distance* in that *location*. And the *closer* it is, maybe the *bigger* it is. Very interesting.

People tend to group things in similar places, things you feel really *positive* about may be grouped in similar places and things you *don't* feel very positive about may be grouped in *other* places. Not always true, not for everybody, but it's just sort of an interesting generality you might consider.

Remember that a *depressed* person may be *feeling depressed* when they're looking *down*. So let's think about this location. Well, it's going to affect often the *other* **submodalities** and therefore it can be a **driver**.

Now let's do the following. Wherever your picture is, wherever you're pointing, I want you to *change its location*. So imagine that your picture goes where your finger goes, so point out to that picture again and now *drop* that picture very significantly on the horizon. Drop it way *down*. Bring it down to around your feet, let's say, and just look at it down there. And as you hold it there, how does it *feel*?

What do you think about it there? Does it *change* your feelings? Now, let's also go to putting it way up *high*. Put it up *high* and bring it *close*. How does that *feel*? Now that might feel a bit strange if you bring it *too* close and it's *too* high so put it where it's comfortable but up *high*. Now bring it over to the *right* and then over to the *left* and *experience* what that does.

Now, by the way, let me address an issue. Some of you I know are thinking, *I don't feel anything*, Kenrick. What the hell's the matter with me or you, one or the other? Okay, fair enough. Well, when I first started experimenting and learning these, *I* didn't feel anything. They'd say make it *bigger*, make it *brighter*. I'm like, uh huh, *I don't feel anything*. Well, what I learned is is **I was consciously trying to do it too slow** so if for any reason you're *not feeling much*, **speed this up**. Just pause reading for a moment and go back to the beginning with *brightness* or *size* or *distance* or *location* whatever, and do it *quick*. Imagine it gets *bright*, or gets *dim*. Or it gets *big* or small or far away or *close*, but do it really **fast**. And you'll start to discern more.

I'm trying to go through this at a reasonably quick speed that will kind of keep you right along with me and give you a chance to pause reading and go back if need be.

So how you've noticed that *location* also has an impact, probably.

Now let's go to the next one, *color* or *black and white*. Imagine seeing a picture of something that you really like. Whatever it is, you can think of this in the privacy of your own mind. You never have to admit to what you're looking at. So just imagine that somebody took a sneaky picture of something you really, really like. Look at it. Now imagine it goes into *black and white*. Does it maybe feel *older*, like it may be an *old* picture? Or does it maybe *take some of the zip out of it* that you were experiencing before? Maybe it does *nothing* but it's something to consider.

The *focus* will often have a big impact as well. Let's go back to the picture that you really liked, or the imagining of the *experience* that you had that we started with, and what I want you to do is to *de-focus the image*. Make it *blurry* like as if you were looking through a camera that just wouldn't focus. Everything is *blurry* around you.

Now *snap it into strong focus*. Really bring it *clear*, like push the autofocus button on the camera and there it is in *full focus*. How does that make you *feel*?

Now let's go a step further. Let's look at it being *moving* or *still*. When we see a *moving* image, a *moving* picture like a movie, it has a different impact on us than when we see one that's *still*. Many people imagine things in full living color like as if it's a *movie*. Some people imagine things that are *still*. But if you were to go back to this experience, were you thinking of it as *still* or *moving*? And try *switching* it and just seeing what happens. See what happens to your *feelings*.

Then let's go to does the image have a *border* on it and you can experiment with this on your own. It's often a *lesser* **submodality** and whether there's *one image or more*. If so, which one is *central*, et cetera, et cetera, but that's a bit more arcane. Really the above ones will work just fine.

So what have you learned? Well, I hope you've learned that **by varying the *submodalities*, you can radically *change your feelings*** about something that you experience that you really liked. Now, you might be saying so what, I can do this on me, but Kenrick, this is a course in persuasion. And my first response to that is, yes, and **let's learn to persuade *ourselves* first**. Us first. Okay? And second, hang on, because I'm going to show you how it applies to persuading *others* very, very powerfully.

CHAPTER FOUR

Auditory Submodalities

But before we do, let's look at the important **auditory submodalities**. Now I'm not going to go through every one of these with you like I just did with the *visual*. Here I just want to *point them out* to you. *Volume* is a big one.

Let's go through just a couple of the ones that I find really important, *volume* being perhaps one of the most important. So look at this picture, if you would, of the thing we started out with in which you were thinking about whatever it is that you really like and I want you to **increase the volume**.

You've got a volume knob there, just reach up there and *turn it up* so it gets *louder* and *louder* and *louder*. And how does that make you *feel* about this image?

And now quickly go ahead and *turn it down* to where you can barely hear it.

Now one interesting thing is, most *still* pictures don't have much in the way of *volume*. Isn't that interesting? Most *moving* pictures will probably have something in the way of volume. Not always true for everyone, but keep that in mind as just a possibility. What was true for you? And what *happened* when you *changed the volume*? First of all, notice that just me bringing it up probably *started* or *stopped* your picture. Very interesting.

There's *pitch*, there's *rhythm*, and *rhythm* can be really important. We practiced extensively really getting down our ability to **speak with rhythm**, and I hope you're still working on that. I still work on it to this day. And also *tonality*. Now some people just have a really bad *tonality* and they sound like crap. Excuse me but that's just what it sounds like. Some people just sound like fingers on a chalkboard and when you hear people like that it can really mess with your pictures and it just sounds terrible.

Now, what does that do to your pictures? What does that do to your experience? So suppose I started describing your really good experience using this 'fingers on a chalkboard' *tonality* and I'm telling you all about what happened and I'm telling you, go back to the beginning and *experience* this.

Ew. You probably *don't like that very well*. If you have a *tonality* like that, change it. Stop it. Okay? It is *not* helping your ability to persuade. So get a real assessment from a good friend and say, "*Look, I want you to tell me the truth. How does my **tonality** sound? Do I have a rich, deep, wonderful **tonality**?*" And yes, if you're a woman doing this, you can too have a rich, deep, wonderful tonality.

Make sure you're working on your *tone*. Make sure it's *pleasant* to listen to. Now I want you to remember that again and I want you to go back as if I was describing this to you with a *beautiful, melodious tone* using the deep, rich warmth of a voice that guides you through this experience as you remember it again from the beginning and really think about it. How does this *tone* make you *feel* now? Different, isn't it?

A *melodic tone* versus a *monotone*. A good compelling *tempo*. The *duration* of the sound in the picture. Maybe the picture only has a sound in it for a period of time or maybe what you're remembering *auditorily* only happened for X amount of time. The *duration* is important. And often *where the sound originates from* is important. For example, think of the sound of a very close loved one, wife, husband, boyfriend, girlfriend, son or daughter. Think of *their voice* right now in your mind. *Where does it come from* when you hear it? *Above* you, *below* you, to the *side* of you, in *front* of you, *behind* you? Where? And you'll note that *location* will also play an important part here.

CHAPTER FIVE

Kinesthetic Submodalities

Let's go to important **kinesthetic submodalities**. I list these for you because I want you to know what they are. Not because you're really going to use them much. Let's go back to *the experience of the good thing* that I had you start off with and I want you to imagine this picture, *step into the picture* so you're seeing with your own eyes, and *how does it feel*. And wherever you experience those feelings, I want you to **intensify** them, make them *stronger*. Notice the *location* of the feelings in your body. *Where* are they? And are they *moving*? Which *direction*? *How* are they moving? *How fast* are they moving? *How long* do the feelings exist?

Where did the feeling begin in your body? *Where* was it? Focus on that for a moment, think about it, get in touch with it. And once you know where it started, how does it get from where it starts to where you are most aware of it? Powerful questions, aren't they?

Now, of these, *intensity* is very, very powerful and *where does the feeling start*. I generally find that those two **submodalities** in the **kinesthetic** system are probably the most important two. Again, you're not going to be using that system that much when influencing others but I want you to know about it and be aware of it and learn it real thoroughly.

CHAPTER SIX

Visual Submodalities in Everyday Language

Now let's have some fun. I want to talk with you about how **visual submodalities** sound in *everyday language*. So *things were blown out of proportion*. Now let's really think about that. *Things were blown out of proportion*. When you hear that, what do you think? If we study for example, the **visual submodality** of this, if you *blow something out of proportion*, what must happen? Well, it has to get a lot *bigger*, doesn't it? And probably pretty *quick*. So it's probably *really, really big* if it's *blown out of proportion*. It may even be *stretched* so it looks *distorted* or it may just be *bigger than life*. So when someone says, "*Oh, you know, this guy just blew it all out of proportion*" or whatever, well you know *exactly* what they're doing in their head with their pictures. You're going to come to really appreciate this in just a little bit here in this lesson.

I'm glad we see eye to eye. What is the **submodality** that we're working with here? It's whether or not we're *looking level at the horizon* basically or if we're *missing* somehow, we're seeing *above* or *below* the other person.

Moving seems overwhelming. Boy, does it ever. I've just done it. *Overwhelming*. All right, think about that. What does it *mean* to *overwhelm*? From a **visual** perspective, whenever someone says that they're *overwhelmed*, their pictures are *too close* and *up over the top of them* so it's literally like the picture is *right over their head, too close*, most likely *too big, too close*, and *up over the top of them*.

What does this get you to think about in your head? If I said to you, *"Man, I'm just overwhelmed with everything here."* Could you in fact say, *"Kenrick, for just a moment I want you to take that picture and* **zoom it way off into the distance**, *as you point, and* **make it smaller**. *And once it's out there, I want you just to attach a rubber band to it that also attaches to like a planet out there, so it can never come back in close until I tell it to. And now that it's out there, do you begin to feel like you have a bit more* **perspective** *on things, don't you?"*

Now if you're going right along with me on this you're thinking, *"Wow, I really have a lot more perspective."* Try it.

The word *overwhelm* I love it when I hear it because I instantly know how I can change that for somebody so as to **diminish that negativity**. All these choices are just *spinning*. If you take that good image of what you saw before and you start *spinning* it in your mind, what happens? Well, it's *hard to focus*. The *focus* is adjusted probably. It's changing its *position* and that's just weird when your pictures start changing positions.

A number of **submodalities** can be affected with the word *spinning*. These definitions are so *drab*. What does *drab* **presuppose**? Probably that the colors are *muted* in some way or *diminished* in some way, probably that the *brightness* may be a bit diminished as well. So it's just not crisp and sharp, the *focus* is probably not real good, et cetera.

How about, *"I can't seem to focus on the next step"*? Well, what is that? Well, we're stating it directly there. In other words, they're *focused* on *something*, like where they are, but they're not willing or able to *focus* on *the next step*. What does that imply? It's *out of focus*. My response might be, *"Of course you can't focus on it. In order to do that, we have to take what you're* **currently** *looking at and* **make it small** *and* **dark** *and* **push it way out into the distance** *while immediately* **bringing up that next step** *and* **making it crystal clear** *like you're looking through a telescope even maybe and it's* **perfectly locked on clear**. *Now when you take a deep breath, and just look at it, accepting it for what it is, how does it* **feel**?" And if you went right along with me there in your mind, you *know* how it feels. It *changed* it very distinctly.

All right, *I need some distance for this*. You may hear this in the form of an **objection**. *"I need some* **distance** *from this. I want to think about it."* All right, well if they need *distance*, you can *push it off into the distance* but not *too* far as to put it out of their mind. And you can combine it with some really cool suggestions. *"Sure, absolutely. If we were to just take it and* **push it out about 50 percent further away**, *just to the point where all of that content drops directly into the other part of you that knows this is the right thing to do and begins to adjust in your mind so that it feels really good. And as you do that now, and just contemplate for a moment the results of having something like this that's factual there in your mind, you can begin to think of it much like you would an anchor. It's just there and it feels really good. And as the* **brightness** *adjusts and the* **size** *adjusts, automatically becoming* **bigger** *and* **closer** *and* **brighter** *as appropriately so, to manifest in your life those things that you've already decided are true, now. It feels pretty good to understand how to get to our next step together."*

That cool or what?

"I have a vague idea of what to do." What does *vague* imply? Well, again, probably *dim*, *dark*, a *long way away*, *small*, all of those things could be *vague*, but something that's *vague*, is really

going to be *small* and *too far away*, probably. You can't quite see it. What if you brought it *zooming up close* making it *big* and *bright*? And what if you seed that idea with **what it should be** before doing that? *"Sure. I understand it's vague. And you know, out there as you look and you can't see it, but is the realization that what I'm talking about today absolutely fits perfectly. And of course we would know what that picture looks like and yet it's **so far away** we can't quite see it,"* and you put your hand like out in the distance from them, *"However, if magically something were to happen that..."* -- and you bring your hand in with a whooshing sound sound so that it's nearer to their face and you say -- *"...it brings that picture **close** and **big** and **bright** and you see all of what I was just talking about"* -- in other words, I'm referring to the seeding that I just did -- *"Wow, all of the sudden **it becomes clear**, doesn't it?"* And they go, *"Well, yeah."* *"All right, well leave it there for a minute. Let me tell you about a few things else that I want you to be aware of and we'll come back to that."*

Why would I do that? Because I want them to *get comfortable with it where it is* and I want it to *continue to convince them* which is what I just set up in their mind. Are you getting some idea of how powerful this is?

"This place has a colorful past." Okay, we know what that is, *color* versus *black and white*. So if this person sees a lot of *color* it holds a lot of interest in some way or a lot of significance in some way. We can *brighten* things up, we can make them *more colorful*, we can *dim* them down, we can make them *less colorful*.

"It's off in left field somewhere." This is usually a statement of it's often *to the side*. Generally speaking precisely like they said, *off and to the left*. Now usually when I hear something like this, I may be inclined to immediately say, *"Yeah, like where? Can you point? Off where?"* They'll point if you just act very congruent. *"Yeah, I know exactly what you mean, sometimes when things go **off in left field**, it's just crazy, isn't it? However, sometimes it's **out there** because we simply didn't know better how we could deal with this. You know how when someone hits a ball and it goes straight over the pitcher and it goes right **out to center field** and the pitcher catches it and drives it right into the pitcher and the pitcher is **fully in command of all that he sees**? Being able to go **right, left, straight**, whatever the situation calls for, now, as you **take a look at that**, doesn't it feel a little bit better? I think we're **zeroing in on that**, aren't we?"*

See what the power of this kind of language can do?

"That throws a little more light on it." Well, could that mean that we're talking about the *brightness* of it? Of course.

"That picture is etched in my mind." Okay. This is very interesting. This is really sort of making a distinction probably **kinesthetic** as well, and it's sort of crossing over between them because they're *seeing* something that's *etched*, so they're *seeing* it *engraved* in their mind. In other words, they're attaching a *permanence* to this. If you don't like that picture in their mind or your mind, what might you do? *"You know, when I was a kid I used to play with Etch-a-Sketches, you know? They were the coolest toy, weren't they? Have you ever had one of those? And you know, you'd kind of **etch** the picture right into the glass it looked like and then you'd turn the knobs **left** and **right** and the line would go **up** and **down** and you could make all sorts of cool pictures when you got better at it. The cool thing is that our minds sort of work just like that because when we don't want something there, we can **grab hold of it and shake it** real good. Now, and **watch** what happens. Yeah, it starts to change. All of the sudden those lines are simply gone leaving there a*

370

place for you to bring in what you always wished would have been there. Notice the picture --" and now you can get into all kinds of **suggestions** about what kind of picture should go there and zip it right into where that old picture left from. Makes it very powerful.

"*The last few months seem so hazy.*" This is dealing with *focus*. So here we can *adjust the focus* and bring the last few months *into perspective.*

"*I can't see myself closing like that.*" They've literally **blocked the picture**. They *can't see* it. And you go, "*Well of course you can't see it. The picture is probably not even out there where you could see. Where is it?*" You might gesture like it's **behind** them somewhere. And they point like it's **behind** them somewhere or way down **low** or way up **high**. "*Well of course. You can't see that, but watch this, let's just **grab hold** of that picture and bring it right around **in front of you** or **down** from up above or **up** from down below.*" Or whatever it was. "*Now that you can see it, wow. It's quite a bit different, isn't it?*"

"*I suddenly had a flash of insight.*" What's this? A bright, blinding light, so this has to do with *intensity*, has to do with *brightness.*

"*He's got me up on a pedestal.*" This has to do with *location.*

"*When people do that to me, I see red.*" Okay. Obviously they're talking about **anger** -- or at least that's what we can assume for a moment -- but it's the *color*. What if you were to say, "*Yes, absolutely. And if that **color** were to all of the sudden be permeated with relaxing blues and greens, and the red just sort of **drained away right out of it**, like, you know, like something that was bleeding and just dying, like it was just gone. And now in fact in its place is something blue and maybe green, peaceful, healing, calming. Wow. It's a lot better, isn't it?*"

"*That will cut him down to size.*" What are we talking about here? It's talking about the *size* of the image. *Reducing the size*. We can *enlarge* it, we can *reduce* it, and cutting is probably quite a -- it's a violent action.

"*Now doesn't that just brighten up your day?*" When they say that, what are they doing? You know that a very powerful **driver** for them is the *brightness*. You can use it to your advantage.

"*We're moving in the right direction.*" Right. *Direction*. This may have to do with *location* and it's *moving*, it's a *moving* picture.

"*This group has such a sunny look on life.*" Sunny would be *brightness*. Generally the sun will be *above* us on the horizon, so it may have to do with *location.*

And by the way, you know that that person, the *brightness* really affects them.

"*Things aren't just black and white.*" Interesting. *Black and white* has something to do with **clear choice**. That could be very useful to know.

"*That hits too close to home for comfort.*" That **hits** too **close**... now notice the *switch* in **representational systems**. *Too close* probably is **visual** because you can't *feel* closeness, but as something gets *closer* to you *visually*, it is increasing or decreasing their *comfort*, their *feeling*. So here you'll know that *distance* has a dramatic impact on this person.

"*Let's look at the big picture.*" What are they doing? Making pictures *big* or *small*. And here the *big* picture encompasses a lot of *detail* for them. There's a lot of detail in there. So make your images *big* and *detail rich* to show them the overview. *Over view.* Interesting, huh? Maybe synonymous with *big picture* for this person.

"*Let's bring this more into perspective.*" Interesting. Probably dealing with *size*, maybe *location*, maybe *clarity*, *focus*.

"*Put this top priority.*" This person assigns priority *top* to *bottom*. Now you can ask them to point to where this priority should be. You can say, "*Look, show me where this is in your mind,*" and they'll point *up high*. And you say, "*Okay, name a couple of other priorities in your life that are **lower** and point to those,*" and they'll do it. Believe me, people will point. They do it for me all the time. It's hysterical. It just takes a little bit of **rapport** and the absolute rock solid belief that they're going to do it, meaning that you have to act with absolute **congruity**.

Now, you know right where the *location* is of *top priority* to them. Do you think that might come in handy? Do you think you might slide in a picture of your own into that *location* if you want to? Getting it?

"*These experiences seem flat and meaningless.*" *Flat.* What if you take a picture that's in 3D and you shift it so it's *flat*. In other words, look out at a picture in your mind that looks *real*, it's *3D*, there's *distance*, there's *perspective*. And then look at that same picture as a photograph on a page that's *flat*.

When this person loses the *depth perception*, *meaning* is lost. If you want to *decrease meaning* for this person, make it *flat*, if you want to *increase meaning*, talk about the *rich depth* of the image. How there's so much *detail*.

How about, "*Well, when you frame it that way, yes*"? *Frame* it. Very interesting. When you *frame* something, okay, let's think through this for a minute. If you *frame* something, what are we really doing? Well, we're seeing it with *something around it* or from a particular *perspective*, from *above*, *below*, *left*, *right*, from the *middle* of it, but there's a *perspective*. So this is talking about *changing that perspective*. So you know that when this person *changes their perspective*, it *changes the meaning*. Very, very powerful.

Remember, let's go back where I told you that the *meaning* that we give to an *experience* is *directly related to* and *controlled by* these *submodalities*. Now you're probably starting to see what I'm talking about. Fascinating stuff, don't you think?

CHAPTER SEVEN

Auditory Submodalities in Everyday Language

Let's go on to some **auditory submodalities** and how they sound in *everyday language*.

"The right decision was screaming at me." Is *volume* something that affects this person? Oh, yeah.

"I understand loud and clear." Their audio is *loud* and there's real *clarity* in it. It's not like booming in a stadium where there's lots of echo and causing it to be unclear. It's *loud* and *clear*.

"Don't give me any static." This is the opposite of the former one. In other words, this one is *not very clear*, it's *static-y*, so what they're *looking* for is *clear*. Now you can *see* static as well but it's generally considered an **auditory submodality**, but you can *see* static on TV if you shut off the volume, you see the *fuzzy picture* and you know that there's static there too, so it can kind of go both ways there.

"Let's orchestrate our expansion." Orchestrate. They like a *full* sound, like an orchestra.

"A whisper in the back of my mind." If a person says that, that's very, very persuasive. They are *persuaded* by that whisper. You want to *seize control* of that whisper.

Someone says to me, *"It's like a whisper in the back of my mind,"* I think to myself, woo hoo, I'm going to get them with ease.

So how could you do that? Well, you could **become that whisper**. You could say, *"You know, I was talking with someone the other day and I said to them, sometimes it's like a whisper in the back of your mind so compelling it just doesn't quit, it doesn't let go, sort of like the things I'm talking about here with you today. Imagine that they turned into that whisper in that same way, that you just kept going over and over and it wouldn't let up, it was relentless. But it was comfortable like a friendly voice, do you know what I'm saying?"*

"My thought came to a screeching halt." So bad, *loud* sound, very much stops and starts their thinking process.

"If I just nag myself long enough, I'll do it." Probably relates to *tonality*. Remember that *bad tonality* I mentioned?

"I have to quit telling myself." So here they're talking to themselves. Okay? And that internal voice is affecting them.

"Eliminate the discord." Again discordant sounds, literally.

"And it's a real offbeat city." It's not a *harmonious* beat, it's not a *rock* beat, it's an *offbeat*, something *not quite right* about it, something a little *strange* about it. Now if they're a musician an *offbeat* could be describing a type of syncopation, but most generally when this is said it's because the person is experiencing something *off*, it's *off the beat*, not quite on the beat. Out of the beat, so to speak. It's interesting, huh?

CHAPTER EIGHT

Kinesthetic Submodalities in Everyday Language

Kinesthetic submodalities and how they sound in *everyday language.*

"*Quit acting so slimy.*" I'm just going to go through these quickly.

"*I've been weighing the consequences.*"

"*That's a hot idea.*" Hot, cold. Don't be so cold.

"*That throws me off balance.*" Balance is an issue.

"*Whenever I hear that, my stomach knots up.*"

"*I feel up to it, let's do it.*"

"*Let's meet our goals, the pressure is on.*"

You're getting the hang of this, I'm sure, by now.

CHAPTER NINE

Changing the Way People Feel About Things

Knowing what you've just learned, you can **change the way people feel about things**, especially those things that you want to affect. You can also **change the way *you* feel about things**. I told you, by the way, I was going to tell you a *shortcut* so you can do these real easily. Here it is. I found that in practice the following **submodalities** are the *most effective* to use when you're using them covertly: *brightness, size, distance,* and *location.* So try these with the **military pattern** '*just suppose*'. Here's an example: "***Just suppose*** *that you can accomplish exactly what you want and **as you imagine** it may get **brighter** and **closer** and really **feel** it. Now you know what to expect when we work together. It feels good, doesn't it?*"

Now I want you to think of another thing or pay attention to another thing that you've been reading me do, but I did it very blatantly there. Do you know what it is? Okay, I'll tell you next lesson... No, I'm just kidding, I'll tell you right now. Oh, and you know, since I've said that, you recall that **leaving loops open** really drives home the point. It **makes people continue to be curious**. It makes people continue to want to learn. I will tell you what this is.

Now let's go on to the next page. I'm just joking with you, but I want you to see what this does, to *experience* it. If you're like, "*Oh, come on, tell me,*" so one of the things I'm doing is I am **juxtaposing**, I'm *interplaying* between the **visual** and the **kinesthetic**. I'm, in other words,

presupposing that **by adjusting the *visual*, the *feeling* changes**. That's because it *does*. For *all* people, even if **visual** is not their preferred system, it works right across the board, for some more powerfully than others, but for almost everyone, very powerfully. That's why I tend to use a number of these all at the same time. It's sort of like using a **driver**.

Now if you're doing *therapy* with somebody, you could absolutely **elicit what the drivers are** and then just use those. Sometimes as you're watching people real closely you talk about *turning up the brightness*, for example, and you'll see them move back. Well, you know that that also is *adjusting the size*. So you can watch and learn how these work, but I want you to stop reading now and I want you to experiment with the '**just suppose**' pattern. Let's have you do it. Okay, go ahead and stop. What are you still reading for? You should have stopped.

I assume you've stopped.

CHAPTER TEN

Turning Down the Intensity

Now let's use this same kind of skill that I've been teaching you to **turn down the intensity**. So you want to practice on the following sentences.

"*I'm too **overwhelmed** to decide.*" Let's say you're hearing this from a customer or a prospect. How could you use your language to change this? For example, could you say, "*Well yeah, that makes sense, but let's do something for a moment. Let's just take this picture,*" and what if you were to gesture *up* over the top of their head and *close* to them, "*and what if it were to attach itself to my hand, and we were just to **back it off** in a way --*" and then you gesture *way off into their distance*, and you say, "*and we put it **way out there** somewhere and **lock it out there** so it has to stay. Now, as you imagine it **way out there**, so you have some real perspective on things, it probably feels a lot better, doesn't it?*" "*Well, yeah, that's true.*" "*All right,*" then you can go on and get them to decide.

"*I'm **too close** to the situation to figure out what to do.*" What would you do with that?

"*Trying to figure this out makes me really anxious.*" What could you do with that? Now there's no clear **visual** there but could you *use* the **visuals** (yes you can) to change this? Yes. "*You are trying to figure out what's happening here and it does feel like this maybe in part because it's **not real clear**. So let's do something, let's just **stop** the picture and imagine that we can look through a camera lens and hit **autofocus** and instantly all the pieces and everything comes **fully into focus**. We adjust the **brightness** so it's really pleasing. We make sure it's **not too close** so we have **perspective** on this. We can even see it with a certain sense of knowing that everything really is okay. And as we look at it like this, let's take just a moment to imagine some great big screws in each of the four corners being turned with an air gun. We know it's just really there now. It's always going to **stay** there. Like it's **indelibly etched** into your brain out in a way you can deal with it that's comfortable.*" See? *Where* it came *from*, the *way* in which you were looking at it, that place where things are *anxious*, see, *that* would be where I'd be putting things like not following the kinds of suggestions I'm giving you, images of trying to go to a *competitor*, you know, do something else that maybe *wouldn't* really be in your best interest. *"And now that we know how to look at this properly and you're seeing it there, how does it feel?"*

By the way, you can often get away with that because you already have such dramatic **trust** and you've been using **suggestion patterns** like you've been seeing me do this entire lesson. And you can get away with just a quick brief mention, zip, and then get right on by it.

"This costs more than I can afford to spend." So now you think about using the *brightness, size, distance* and *location* to adjust this thought that they just told you. And then do the same to, *"I'm too upset to think about this."* So stop reading again and I'd like you to **think through** or **write out** those two sentences so you really get it. Okay? Do it now.

CHAPTER ELEVEN

A Secret Way to Use the Skill

Here is **a secret way to use this skill**. This one is so strong you surely must have imagined it by now because now that you know how this works, you can use this strategy in your work and you can use it all the time. When you **elicit someone's criteria and values**, find the **emotion** behind the **value** and **crank it up** using the **submodalities** of *brightness, size, distance, location*, you want to throw in *volume* for good measure, go ahead. But let's say that you just elicited from someone that their **highest value** is *freedom* and so you ask them, *"What will having freedom do for you?"* And they go, *"Well, it just makes it so **I won't feel trapped** and I am certain about really getting ahead."* So you know that primarily it's an **away from** kind of thing and you go, *"Wow, **being trapped** just is horrible. I mean, talk about **confining**."*

Now notice even that word begins **adjusting the submodalities**. I'm *confining* the picture: *"It's confining and nobody could like that."* And they go, *"No."* Now could you **anchor** that right there? Yes. Yes, you could. *"In fact, as you think about having something like that, you know, where **you don't have freedom** and you're **confined** and you imagine it being -- well, just that, **confining**, and like **locked static into place**, like it's not changing. I know it can't feel good."* And they go, *"No."* And you **anchor** that.

Where are you going to use that? If you need to **motivate them to change**, there will be a giant motivation. *"Let's not be **locked into something** here, a previous behavior that didn't serve you well. Let's **move beyond that** right now, shall we? To **freedom**. So you can **go on to freedom**. So if you think about **freedom**, you know, imagine that **nothing's holding you back**. You see your life **clearly in front of you**, you **crank up the brightness**, you make the picture **big** and **compelling**. How does that **feel**? Feels pretty doggone good, doesn't it?"* Now **anchor** that.

So now we have a way of **controlling the intensity of the anchor** and **amping up or diminishing that emotion** quickly and easily any time we want to. Now is that really cool or what? I hope you said yes because to me we're talking about literally **how to adjust the way a person assigns meaning to things** through these **submodalities**.

This is a giant section. And we've really only scratched the surface of where we can go with these.

We could really go deeper still, much, and if you read this repeatedly, you'll begin to discover more and more ways that you can use these to your advantage. I told you this is a bit technical this time. Again, we're into some really advanced stuff. Heck, you've been with me for 22 books. I applaud you. And you're really getting this. So if you've read all these, you know that this is considerably more technical than some. The key to learning this is to re-read this book over and over. I'd read it a number of times. Just like the person who asked the question, okay, they're really wanting to *learn* this, they're really *experiencing* the material *over* and *over*.

Start listening even closer to **the way people speak**. Listen for these **submodalities**. Start **adjusting** them when you speak and watch how people *respond* to you. It's going to blow you away.

CHAPTER TWELVE

Creating Permanence

All right, let's move to the next section. Some more very cool language for you. I want to talk with you now about using your language to **create permanence in the mind of the people that you're influencing**. Here are words that you can use when you want to **create something as permanent in the mind of your customer**. So some examples of this: *keep the policy, be happy with your company*, the fact that *you're always with them* once they've bought from you, that kind of thing. Okay?

So here are **words that create permanence**: *enduring, persistent, persisting, remaining, staying, year after year, longstanding, long term, unending, forever, without end, everlasting, endless, perpetual, timeless, constant, nonstop, stay with it, continually, always, fixed, indestructible, it goes on and on, never ceases, locked in, steadfast, lasting, continuing, stable, extended, day after day, never ending, long lasting, eternal, ceaseless, in perpetuity, secure, staying power, keeps on.*

So you could language this in when you want to **create permanence in the mind of the people that you're persuading**. Very cool stuff.

CHAPTER THIRTEEN

How to Make Things More Temporary

Let's talk about **the language of temporary, how to make things more temporary in the mind of the people we're influencing**. And you can practice using these beliefs on *you* first especially on those that are not supportive of what you want. Do them on your own beliefs that you'd like to change or loosen up. Get the feeling for what happens.

Here are the words: *Impermanent, impermanence, even, transient, changeable, fleeting, brief, no time for, in an instant, immediately changes, fade away, fade like a shadow, vanish like a dream, burst like a bubble, go up in smoke, melt like snow, temporal, flitting, fading in, short order, fading out* as well for that matter, *short term, for a little while, short lived, for a short time, suddenly stop* or just *stop, changes with the times, suddenly gone, abruptly gone, in the blink of an eye, in two shakes, momentarily, in no time, in nothing flat, like a shot, vanishes, evaporates, replaced by, put in place of, make way for, halt, terminate, immediately changes, change one's mind, here today - gone tomorrow, final, at the speed of light.*

These are very, very cool and we're going to talk about why and how in just a couple of minutes, okay?

CHAPTER FOURTEEN

Language to Remember

Let's go to **language to remember**. So here are words that **presuppose remembering**.

Refresh your memory, recall, etched in stone, put in one's mind, prompt to remember, lasting impression, retain, bearing in mind, never be forgotten, indelibly inked into your mind, fixed in mind, keep in mind, persist with you, bring back to memory, like a boomerang it always comes back, remember to remember, snapped into your mind.

Practice using these kinds of words when you want people to **remember** things. You want to practice using this to **augment suggestions** you want to become a strong part of the person that you're influencing. These are really, really powerful and having a list like this - even *knowing* to create a list like this when I was beginning - would have changed my world, literally.

CHAPTER FIFTEEN

Language to Forget

Let's go to **language to forget**. Here are words that **presuppose forgetting**.

Dismiss, put out of mind, think nothing of, think no more of, forget about, let it go, turn away from, turn your attention from, put or set aside, forget to remember, unable to recollect, unable to recall, lose sight of, erase from memory, slip one's mind, drop from your thoughts, don't give a second thought to. And here's one of my favorites, *remember to forget to remember.* That one combines both *forgetting* and *remembering.* It's very cool. *Remember to forget to remember.* Very interesting.

Now, you can also use this with **suggestions** that are aimed at the conscious mind. For example, you can **remember to forget to remember consciously** what we've been talking about while the other part of you *continues* to dwell on all I've said making it a *permanent* part of who you are, now. And it just flows from your mouth easily and effortlessly until one day you say to yourself, this is amazing and you zero right in on your skill and your ability and it feels great.

CHAPTER SIXTEEN

Combining the Patterns With Presuppositions

All right. Let's talk now about some of the ways you can *use* these patterns, some thoughts I have on them. One of the most powerful things you can do is to *combine* these patterns with the **presuppositions** that you've learned. So I'm talking about *combining* **amplifying** and **diminishing** in the form of **submodalities**, **permanent** and **temporary** language and **remembering** and **forgetting** language with **presuppositions**. Remember **presuppositions** like **adverb/adjective**: *naturally, easily*; **awareness**: *aware, realize understand*; **cause and effect**: *causes, forces, makes, because*; **time**: *while, during, before, after*; **space**: *among, around, in, surrounding, throughout, from within, from without, outside*.

So imagine starting to language some of the things you want people to do by *combining* these things. **From within** the **enduring** thoughts you have, of the way in which these patterns are working profound miracles in your life, or are setting themselves up to do that **day after day** in a **ceaseless** manner, you find that your doubts, if any, have simply **gone up like smoke**. They've **evaporated**. And **from within** where they **used to be** comes a level of assuredness the likes of which you'll recall for the rest of your life. These patterns are being **indelibly inked** into your mind. You can **feel** the profound nature of how they're working. And it's like **during** this process you've **become aware of** some of the more profound things that are true for you and that help you to marshal your resources and organize your ability such that these skills become an **ongoing permanent** part of your life. Of course there are **other areas** and **deeper parts** of yourself that can **remember to forget to remember** the challenges and difficulties. They say it's one of the great things about childbirth and that is that if we as humans, if women in particular **remembered** the pain as much as they did on the day they experienced it, there would never be a family with more than one child. But you know, that pain just **fades into the back of their mind**. And what they **focus** on, just like you, is the child, the love, and their opportunity to have brought something into this world of such a profound nature that this excites them and propels them on in life and it's as if all of these skills are coalescing **within** you, enabling you to have a very profound experience of the ways in which you can persuade with power and ease and as you **crank up that brightness** on that image right now and bring it **close** and **big**, and make it so compelling and **step into it** and experience life from this **enormous perspective** of success, it's what **keeps coming back** into your mind **over and over and over**. And it's nice.

Now, see how I'm weaving these in? I'm weaving them in and through and around. Now you say, "*Yeah, but Kenrick, how much can I do that talking to a prospect?*" Hey, it depends on how much **rapport** you have. You can sure as heck do six or seven of those patterns, bam, bam, bam, in the space of two or three sentences. And if you've been talking to them for an hour or more, you can absolutely do it. And let's say you just sold them, oh, my goodness, could you language in a bunch of stuff to make this stick and make them excited? And by the way, I've got more stuff on making things stick. I believe I'm covering that on the last lesson, but we've got lots more. But I mean, look, could you language this in there after you've sold them? You bet. You could even start by saying, "I'd like to just tell you a couple of minutes worth of some things that I think will really make sense to you either **now** or in the **immediate future**. And then you language the kind of things like I just did only about your product or service. Imagine what that would do. **Imagine**. *Image in*. Interesting, huh?

That is the real power of what you've been learning in this lesson. Highly technical. However, incredibly powerful. It really does take some practice to get to a real good level of competency with these, but you can do it and you can do it quickly.

Isn't it great when you know what it is that I'm doing and it works anyway? Another great language pattern for you.

CHAPTER SEVENTEEN

Homeplay

I have a few thoughts for you about how to use this lesson with the greatest amount of strength. Begin using **submodalities** in your language and practice incorporating them *before* you practice with the balance of the lesson. And getting the hang of them really does mean *focusing* on them, *concentrating* on them for a period of time, so if you put *too* much together *too* fast, you won't be real good at much of it. So I want you to really spend several weeks just focusing on **submodalities**.

Now, even though I didn't write this down in the book as you read through it as I usually do, I want you to do this. I want you to *write out* at least ten sentences in which you demonstrate how you can use **submodalities** in your language to *increase* and *decrease* the power of things. All right? It's very important.

Next, *combine* **permanent** and **temporary**, combine those patterns, with the **presupposition** patterns and *write out ten examples*. So just focus on **permanent** and **temporary** language in with all the different types of **presuppositions** that I listed.

Then do the same thing but with the **remembering/ forgetting** patterns. Then when you're ready, *combine* **submodalities** along with as much of the other two as you can so you're combining **submodalities** with **permanent**, **temporary**, **remembering** and **forgetting** and the **presuppositions**.

This is going to sound much like what I just demonstrated in chapter sixteen. If you do the work that I've just said, your **suggestion** ability will dramatically *increase* and I'm not kidding you. You will find that you can just language **suggestions** like mad into the minds of the people that you're influencing. You'll find that if you're using this in a group, there are some really powerful strategies that you can do, especially if you know the kinds of things that I've taught you here that can just make group presentations go through the roof.

But in any event, the thing is about the way this works is that if you'll actually *do* it, if you'll *do* this work, your **suggestion** ability will skyrocket. This is fantastic.

Now of course you might also *recognize* the patterns that you're using and that would be great too. You'll also find, and I would highly recommend, that you listen to preachers on TV especially ones that kind who really get into it, you know the evangelist type. Again, I'm not in any way speaking poorly about any kind of ministry, I'm just simply wanting you to *hear* the way these language patterns operate and you'll hear a bunch of this type of language in really good preachers, especially the evangelist type. And so you'll -- by the way, I was watching one the other day that does the laying on of hands, actually, he didn't even have to do that, he just gestured at them and they fell, and hit the ground and stayed there for a long time too, it was really interesting, but the **suggestions**, the *physical* suggestions, the *language* suggestions that he did, I was so excited I was listening, I was like oh, the guy's about to go. Okay. And then he just barely started to lean towards the guy and you could see him start to quiver and he put his hand out towards him and down he went.

Of course there are many **frames** you could see that in. If you were a stage hypnotist, you could see it as really, really good hypnosis. If you were oriented towards that religion, you would see it as an absolute work of God. I don't know which it is, I'm open to both. But what I *can* tell you is that you'll be able to *duplicate* that with these language skills. That's very cool.

Most importantly, make this *fun* and *celebrate* the success you have. And what I mean by that is, hey, when you're out in life and you're talking along and all of the sudden you catch yourself using a language pattern spontaneously or you purposefully use one and the person goes right along with you, wow, you've really, really experienced a success. So chalk them up and feel free to relate back to them regularly and be excited about what it is you're doing.

This was a great lesson. I really enjoyed this. I told you I was going to give you another technical one and I think this certainly qualifies, so I hope you really enjoyed it and I look forward to the next time that we talk, on our next lesson. And I look forward to that. So in the meantime, as you go through your life, let your persuasion skills soar and take you to heights you've never dreamed of before. I've got lots more for you and we'll jam them in to the next book. Have a great day. I'll talk to you soon. Bye-bye.

BOOK TWENTY-THREE

CONNECTING STATES WITH YOUR OUTCOME

INTRODUCTION

An Extremely Experiential Lesson

Welcome to **Book Twenty-Three** of *Persuasion Force*. Wow, **Book Twenty-Three**! I've been working on this last lesson now for a number of months and I have some very, very special things for you. I think you're going to love it.

All right, this final lesson for **Book Twenty-Three**, is an *extremely experiential* lesson. For that reason, I'm going to do my level best to keep this just a little bit shorter than most of the e-books, or at least I'm going to try. However, I do want you to know up front that the goal of this lesson is very **experiential**. It's loaded to the gills. So join me for a really fun ride that will help you to persuade just amazingly more powerful and reading this book repeatedly will help you even more.

CHAPTER ONE

Question: Technique vs. Strategy

We have some questions from a very astute reader. And he writes, *"Hey Kenrick, Your stuff rocks. Hate to see it coming to an end. I have a couple of questions that do not relate directly to the recent content. The other day I was listening to some of Jay Abraham's material and he talks about the difference between sales courses that are based on* **technique** *and those that are based on* **strategy***. He doesn't really* **define** *that very well though and which of the two would you say your approach falls in?"*

Okay, really good question. Let me go into a little more depth here. I think it will help you. The *difference* between **technique oriented** sales training and **strategy oriented** sales training is this. **Techniques** are things like, here are *three ways* to shine your shoes, here is *the way* to hold your presentation book while you're making a presentation, here are *five opening sentences* that will tend to get people's attention. These are very **technique**-y oriented things.

Strategy is more about *why you do what you do. How to set it up* so that what you do has the effect you want it to have. It's a bit hard to define, but I hope that helps you. And you're asking which of the two would you say my approach falls in. Well, to begin with, we definitely talk about **techniques**, however, **the techniques are designed around strategy**, so this is why I have never really called what I do sales training. It's all based on **strategy**, how you *organize* what you're saying and what you're doing, how you *organize* the **techniques**, if you will, to really get into someone's head and make a difference quickly. So I would say mine definitely *deal with both* but it's very much *weighted* towards **strategy**.

Also Jay talks about **consultative** or **advisory** selling. You say, "*He speaks highly about that. What is your opinion about that? Seems to me that your approach is much **deeper** and **more directly addresses the client** than consultative or advisory selling. Would you agree?*"

Yes. Absolutely. I would certainly say that what I'm teaching is an **advisory** or **consultative** method, that's for sure, however even an advisory type method or consultative method could *still* be one in which the sales person thinks they know more than the client and knows exactly what the clients want and so begins advising them right off the bat and not really paying much attention to what they say. In fact, I've seen that happen many, many times throughout my career where someone *acts* like they're interested in what the other person says just so that they can let the requisite number of minutes or words go by before they can actually get into their "pitch" and what a shame that is. **That just doesn't work**. It never has, really, and it doesn't to this day. In fact, that would be the mark of an unprofessional sales person, someone who just doesn't quite get it.

Very, very good questions.

CHAPTER TWO

Putting Your Skills to Use

Now, there's a lot going on in this lesson. Before I get into what it is, let's talk about **finding, securing, and connecting states with your outcome**. Okay? We've talked about **anchoring** and **eliciting states**, and I trust that you've been putting this to use in your life, at least I sure hope you have. I'd like to go into this a bit further in this session. I've noticed something kind of *unusual*. Many people, once they've been exposed to the concepts of **anchoring** and **state elicitation**, will treat them as if they're like a *magic trick*. They get all excited about their potential but end up using them like a parlor trick. So either that, or they're very impressed in their own mind with the power of these skills, but they just can't actually figure out how to **put them into use** in their life.

I feel sorry for these people.

Sometimes they'll do them as a *demonstration* and they'll get a laugh or a wow from doing it and then move on, but they still aren't really **using them in their own life to get the results that these things can bring**. Is that true for *you* too? Are you actually *using* **anchoring** and **eliciting states** really fully? I mean, are you really doing them full out and taking advantage of the abilities that using these skills gives you?

I sure hope so.

There's a *big* difference between *demonstrating* these skills to others and *using* them to your advantage. My suggestion is that you do the latter. And there's a real trick to making this work and it's in your **mindset**. I want to talk about that a little bit with you here. It's *not enough* to be *technically* good at **eliciting emotions** and using **anchors**. You have to **strategically decide** how you'll use them to your advantage. This sounds like an obvious and simple thing to say, but the ramifications of it are deep, really deep.

So think back with me to the concept of **seeding**. Do you remember that skill that we talked about long ago, and more importantly are you *using* it? I sure hope so because it's really powerful.

Now go back and *remember* that skill, and with **seeding**, the idea is that after **eliciting the person's criteria**, you **tie it into your product or service** and to *you* directly and you **make creative suggestions that they're going to do business with you**.

All right, remember that? Let's talk about it just a little bit further. With your knowledge of how this works now, the idea of **seeding** is it's a *break*, for a moment. So you've **elicited their criteria**, you *know* what it *is*, you've *elicited* what it *means*, the complex equivalents, and you've been able to *change* it so that **you're the only possible solution in their mind**. And then you take all of that knowledge and you **seed** *doing business with you, using your ideas and suggestions, consuming your products and services*. So **you're tying you in and/or your product in to all of their criteria**. And what you're doing is you're using **suggestions**, eloquently, to get them to want to go along with you.

Now you remember that, right? And hopefully you're *doing* it. The advantage is that when you *do* that, you've **opened up a space in their mind**, a hole in their mind, with which you can **insert your suggestions** and they can't really defend against it. They don't see it coming and it's leveraged in with what they most value, their high criteria and values. So this is the same **mindset** that I'd like you to begin to use with **state elicitation** and **anchoring**.

Think about that for a moment because that's kind of a wild twist. The mindset of **seeding** used with **state elicitation** and **anchoring**. What does that *mean* and how can we do it effectively? Well, **boosting your credibility** is very important and if you boost your credibility you can boost your *effectiveness* quite a bit.

I'll help you do this more effectively in the next chapter.

CHAPTER THREE

Leveraging Suggestions

Let's talk first about **leveraging suggestions**. Now, I've demonstrated over these lessons that suggestions are very, very *malleable*. In fact, a person's *brain* is very malleable. Okay? You can *bend* it and *shape* it and *twist* it and make it do anything you want it to do. It's truly amazing.

Once you get good at the thought process that enables you to deliver **suggestions** quickly and easily, you'll discover that no matter *what* someone says, you can *twist* it to your advantage. Now, don't do it *too* much because it makes you sound funny, and frankly, I can't quite tell you *how* much is *too* much, just don't go to the point where you do this after everything a person says.

Here's how it sounds. A person says to you, *"This is something I've wanted to learn for some time."* And you say, *"Which is why you'll soon begin to experience some big ahas as we talk today leading you to the conclusion that it makes sense to take advantage of owning this yourself, now, let me ask you this -- "* And off you go with a question.

Why do we go off with a question? You know the answer. Can you tell me? All right, because **it redirects their consciousness**. It tends to start **creating amnesia**. You're going to hear a theme here pretty quick, okay?

So what did we do? Well, we *piggybacked* off of what they've said into a **suggestion** of what we wanted them to *experience* and *believe*. Not too hard when you get really good at it. Here are some more examples. I wrote these, but I *didn't* write my response to them because I want to show you, you can just wing it and it really works, really well.

So a person says, *"I'm concerned that I may not have enough insurance, but at the same time feel insurance poor."* What do you have to say about that? And my response could be something like, *"You know, I've often talked to people who feel insurance poor, but the one thing I've never talked to is a widow whose husband passed away and left her some life insurance. She never, ever looks back on those years as having been a time of feeling insurance poor, and as a result of that, you might just stop and consider your family and how they'll feel when you pass. It'll be hard enough for them to deal with the loss of their husband and their father, their brother or their friend, but imagine leaving them something so profound that at least they're not struggling financially while at the same time trying to get over and grieve over the loss of you."*

Just an example. Here's another one. *"It's hard to tell who to trust since there are so many companies that do what you do."* And you say, *"And that merits taking a deep and close look at what I have to say to you because as a result of doing that, I think you'll begin to find the idea creeping in from amongst all the things that we're going to talk about that pushes you in the direction of feeling really comfortable doing business together. And I think as that happens, you'll begin to understand why the discussions that we're having today are so salient for your future. It will make a lot of sense, I think."*

Or maybe the person says something like, *"This makes sense. No one has talked with me like this before, and I really appreciate it."* And you say, *"And as you appreciate that even more, it will allow you to get even closer in your mind with the strategies and suggestions I'm suggesting that you follow. And as you do and project down the road a few years, won't it be nice to experience the money and the success that following my advice and suggestions has given? I can tell you I have client after client after client that tells me that."*

Or perhaps they say, *"Could you explain again how working with you will save me money?"* And you say, *"And that question alone will stimulate from deep down inside the answer that you already know is there. The savings is a given. Working with me makes it easy, but I know that you'll come to that conclusion on your own not because I said so, but because you're saying so in your own mind. You might say, saying what? And my response would be that this is the right thing to do. It feels right. And as soon as you're ready, you'll know. Now let me ask you this --"*

So you see how I **piggybacked** on every one of those and I **leveraged** them to my advantage. Now if I did it with *every* sentence a person said to me, wow, I'd really be sounding funny and screwy, but I can sure do it every once in a while and it makes a really powerful thing when you do it. I mean, it just creates *huge* persuasion results.

Now, as you do this, I want you to remember the words, *and, as, because, which means, allows,* and *merits.* These words, when you use them to *immediately follow* a sentence that your prospect speaks, will put you in a position to immediately **twist** things to your advantage. Things should be so difficult, right? So you should absolutely use this strategy **because** it's extremely effective. It's a very effective way of bending people to your way of thinking.

CHAPTER FOUR

Effective Anchoring

Based on what you've been reading, how can you use this to make your **anchoring** more effective? You've read this in a little bit different form in an earlier book. What you *haven't* read is how to *blend it* with **anchoring.** So stretch your mind with me here, okay? How can you use the concept of **seeding** with **anchoring**? I want you to ask that question over and over as you read. *How can I use the concept of **seeding** with **anchoring**?*

What if you spoke of *great people in history* while pointing to *yourself*? Is that an **anchor**? Yes, it is, and let me explain how. There's a concept called **deep structure** and **surface structure**. When I *say* something, and I think I've talked a little bit about this before, but when I *say* something to you, in order to *understand* what I'm saying, you have to *think* about it. Your mind hears the word and you either have a *representation* of what I'm saying in your mind or you don't. What that means real simply is if I say, for example, a tree, well you've certainly had an experience of a tree in your life. You've sat by one, you've sat on a stump, maybe you've climbed a tree, maybe you've broken the branches or leaves off of a tree, maybe you've played in the leaves under a tree. I mean, you've had a *lot* of experience with trees. So when I say 'a tree' you *immediately* reflect at lightning speed to some *experiences* or some *construct* of what tree is for you. Immediately when you do that, you've *already* brought up the *construct* of tree. So you're already *experiencing* it. So if you begin speaking of *great people in history*, in order for people to make sense of it, they've got to have *their own experience*. They'll recall their experience of hearing this recording of a great person, or the quote of a great person or hearing the great person themselves actually speak.

If they are doing that *while you're pointing to yourself*, they could begin to get the idea that *you* are like that person. Interesting. It seems silly, consciously, doesn't it, when I write that. It sounds like, yeah, right, sure. However, *unconsciously*, it has a dramatic impact.

I've seen Anthony Robbins do this by saying, "*Jesus Christ*" while thumping his chest as if he were Jesus. Disgusting, perhaps, but it's extremely effective. Or he'd say things like, "*Buddha says*" and he'd thump his chest as he'd say this, "*Buddha says, blah, blah, blah, blah, blah. A great wise eastern master once was quoted as saying,"* and as he does that he's thumping his chest or pointing to himself.

Now, that's an **anchor**. But what do we *do* with it? Well first another example. You could mention you were reading about Abraham Lincoln or whomever, and as you talk about them, you can *point to yourself*. What is this exactly? I'm going to mention it a little bit later on again in a bit different terms that I think will make a big difference to you as you read it. What is that exactly?

We're **eliciting** -- though not with a giant powerful emotion – but we're **eliciting the construct** of these different things in people's minds and then we're **purposefully linking them to ourselves**. Another really great way to do this, and by the way this is done a lot in the world of dating, is somebody trained in these skills might ask a person that they're wanting to go out with, "*You know, if you just stop and think about the kind of guy that you want to go out with, if you just imagine the kind of mind this guy might have, the way he might use his body in ways that are really nice. The way he speaks to you, that makes you feel really good. Have you ever thought about the kind of things like that you might really like?*" And as they do, they're **looking right at you**. And so all of this is being **transferred to you** as if *you* were the person they were thinking about like that.

Think about it for a minute. What is that?

You could *quote great authors* and throw in one of *your own* quotes, so you know, you're talking about this author, *Dale Carnegie* said that and *Tommy Hopkins* said this, and *I* say this.

Now *what are you saying* when you do that? What you're saying is, *I'm* just like *you*. I'm *the same* as you are. *I'm in the same league you're in*. I'm *as important* as you are.

In a sense, this is **seeding** using **anchoring** to tie something to you that will help you get more of what you want. So what *do* you want? That's a really big key. In fact, it's *huge*. And to know what you want, it's good to start with the end in mind. Once you know what you want, you can begin to discuss and talk about things that would be of use for other people to think about you and you can **tie it to yourself** with something as little as a thump of your chest or a pointing to yourself or just having the other person look deeply into your eyes as they describe something near and dear to their heart. And guess what? All of that will *transfer to you*. And that is **the principle of transference**.

All of the sudden you become *more than the subtotal of your parts*, you become more in their mind, you become victory and success, or you become the wise sage and counselor or you become whatever, but the **rapport** is profound and keeps getting *more* profound as each moment goes by.

Now, you can determine some *interim outcomes* that you can use **anchoring** on to give you a boost. Here are some ideas. We talked a little bit ago about **boosting your credibility** being a real powerful way. And you can certainly use **anchoring** to do that. How about *the state of buying*? Or *the state of being convinced*? Or *the state of winning*? Or *the state of going for it*? Any of those ring a bell somewhere?

So when you think about things in terms of **seeding anchors**, then you begin to ask yourself, where can I use an **anchor** that I've already said or that I could easily *remind* somebody of and *set right now* that would make my presentation more smooth, more eloquent, more accepted in their mind. How could you do that? And as you begin to think that way, you're beginning to apply **the concept of seeding** to **anchoring** and **state elicitation**.

Seems maybe like a subtle shift on one hand, but on the other as you begin practicing it, you'll see that your mind -- well, it's what I used to call 'greased'. I guess I still call it that. People who have really studied these skills and they've been working on them, their mind is able to *flow from subject to subject*, they're able to not get jammed into a corner, and they're able to fluidly talk their way out of things and others into what they want with ease. Part of it is because of these ways of *strategizing*, so learning how to use **seeding** and *combine* that with **anchoring** so that you get that same effect with **anchoring** can really give you a decided advantage. I think that deserves a lot of talk, a lot of discussion in your own mind and a lot of work to implement.

<u>CHAPTER FIVE</u>

Stories and Nested Loops

Let's now start a discussion that is very near and dear to my heart called '**stories and nested loops**'. Now I'm going to try, I don't know how successful I'll be, but I'm going to try to keep this lesson just a little bit short because you're now about to have your mind blown, okay?

In this lesson, I'm going to expose you to one of the four or five *strategies* for using **nested loops**. In fact, *I've already done so* in this lesson. Do you know how?

In an earlier lesson you discovered that **you can use loops to keep response potential high** so that people are really hanging on your every word and to keep your listeners from believing they know it all so *their minds stay open* as well as to create mild confusion to make the **installation of suggestions** easier and to create a fertile ground to install suggestions where they won't be noticed.

So now you're going to learn how to take that to a much higher level.

All right. **Nested loops using stories** do *all* that I've taught you about **loops** but in a *much* more powerful way. In fact, think back to earlier in this book. *I did this very thing* to help teach you this skill before even talking about it.

Let's dive right into this strategy. **Nested loops** is a strategy of **using stories to capture the attention of an audience, or an individual, for that matter and to alter their consciousness so you eliminate resistance and then deliver suggestions that will be consciously forgotten but acted upon.** Sound powerful? Sound cool? Sound exciting? It sure is to me. I think you're going to love it. And here's how to do it.

You want to **tell three stories** as follows. You're going to *start with story one*, and you're going to tell it *until you are just at the climax*, and you're going to *stop*, you're going to *break* from that story and *launch into story two* and you're going to tell story two *until you're just at the climax*, and again you're going to *break* and *begin telling story three*. And you're going to tell story three just again –

you got it -- *until you're at the climax* but not having quite given **the moral of the story** and then *break* again.

And then what you want to do is **give suggestions for what you want them to do**. You can give as much as you want at that point because they are basically **zoned right through the floor**. Then you're going to **close in the reverse order**. You're going to *finish the last story* you broke in the middle of, story three, you're going to *finish story three*. And after you finish it, you're going to *go back and finish story two*, and after you finish that, you're going to *finish story one*. So you've opened them, story one, two, and three, stopping just before the climax of each one. Now *between* these stories you can do some teaching if you want, but I'd recommend going **at least three stories deep** before you do much in the way of talking or presenting, if you can. And I would recommend that you do the equivalent of **seeding** *after that third story*. You're going to load up on **suggestions**, you're going to load up on **state elicitation**, you're going to load up on **stories that make a point**, I mean, you're going to give **suggestions** hard and fast, even using *direct authoritarian type* suggestions, then you **go back** and you **close in the reverse order**, finish story three, finish story two, and finish story one.

By the time you've told the third story and broke off just before the climax, **you'll have their minds on full blown overload**. Their brains will be *tied up* trying to figure out how each of your stories ends, but they can't. They can't figure it out. You left them hanging. So at that point, you then have their minds **wide open and cooperative** so you can then give **suggestions** that you want them to think, to believe, or to do. Even direct suggestions as I've mentioned will work. But now, you know far more elegant ways of doing it as a result of all you've learned so far. You can just do all kinds of things, all kinds of *indirect* and *permissive* suggestions that you've been learning throughout the program – **embedded commands, presuppositions**, everything.

All right, *how many* stories can you use? I would say three is a minimum. You can and should regularly use at least five to seven stories in this exact same strategy. You tell story one, break at the climax, two, break at the climax, three, break at the climax, four, five, six, seven, break at the climax and then give your **suggestions** and then go right back through, seven, six, five, four, three, two, one, okay?

And you can go up as high as around 12 stories and this is especially true if you were giving a half day talk or longer.

Can you imagine that? Now the key is, **you've got to *remember* the stories and the *order* you tell them in**. It's *critical*. If you don't, you're just going to make a whole lot less of an impact than you could have otherwise. So let's say you were going to give a talk to a group.

Consider starting the talk and **opening the loop**. Then, at the end of the presentation, after you've *closed* all the other ones you've opened, you go back and *close the first one that you opened*. So the entire day of training would in fact be **nested inside of that story** that took all day to close. This is really profound. I love this so much I find myself doing it all the time.

Here's **the effect of closing the stories in reverse order**. It **collapses the content and/or the suggestion *into* the stories**. It's like the stories become a *bridge*, you go to story one, you just break, and you go to story two, and you break, and you go to story three, and you break, and now you just leveled both barrels of suggestions at people and they aren't going to be able to really understand or defend against it.

And then when you go back and *close* three, two, one, **it creates *amnesia* for the suggestions**. The importance of closing the stories is that **it creates a sandwich effect**. Your suggestions are *sandwiched* in all those stories. People will tend to remember the *stories* way more than they'll ever remember your *suggestions*. This *hides* what you've done from the conscious mind and promotes really fast and deep learning.

Now, let me tell you where I gained some real skill with this – watching stand up comics. One day I was watching one of them and I realized that he was doing *precisely* what I had been talking about. He kept going back to this one joke and finally he *closed with the joke he opened with* and people were just in stitches. Gallagher does the Sledgomatic, it slices and dices and makes julienne fries. It's just a basically a big stump on a lever and he swings it and smashes things. But if you can, I'll bet you could find a video of him on Youtube even, but I would go find that guy because he's *really good* at this. Really good at **nesting loops**. Many, many, many comics are. And in fact, the best ones you're going to be hearing him using this **nested loop** strategy.

CHAPTER SIX

Priming the Unconscious Mind

We're going to talk about this last concept today. As you can tell by what we've covered in this book, **stories can prime the unconscious mind**.

So **think about what you want your prospect to believe**. Then, **structure a story such that it gives them the answer**. In essence, you're *telling* them that this is how people like them solve issues like this. But you're doing it in a way that **doesn't cause resistance**. You're **giving them a track** for their unconscious to run on, and guess what, it's going to run on it. It doesn't know much else how to do it, so it's going to go ahead and take what you provided them.

Are you seeing some real powerful implications here for persuasion? And not just implications, solid hard core strategies? I think so, it's just so *exciting*.

Now there are ways of telling stories where they *don't* provide answers, and there are ways of telling stories where some of them *do* and some of them *don't*. But the fact is, is that it creates such a powerful structure that **their brain locks onto it in order to come up with the answers that you're going to ask them to come up with**.

Speaking of *exciting*, by the way, one of the things I want to tell you is, that that sentence that I just said is a way of **priming** as well, isn't it? In other words, **it's a way of framing you into a particular way of thinking about things**. By *prefacing* it with something like -- *by the way, speaking of exciting* -- well, you're going to have to hear the word 'exciting' and start to imagine what I'm saying in light of the word *exciting* and it will tend to **seed** that towards giving me a decided advantage in what we're doing.

I know some of you are saying, "*No, no, I saw through that. It didn't give you a decided advantage*", but I'm telling you it does. And not only that, you've had 23 lessons from me at this point. Okay? And at that rate, I mean, you're beginning to read and understand way more than average and that's all to your credit. Okay? So you really want to use the **priming the unconscious strategy**. You want to think about stories that will get your point across and tell them eloquently to your clients and it will create amazing results for you.

CHAPTER SEVEN

Homeplay

All right, let's go on our homeplay. Well, I wasn't able to keep this as short as I was hoping this book, but I suppose that's just as good as well. So let's go through the home play I'd like you to do. I want you to contemplate the strategies of **seeding**, but doing it with **anchors**. Where could you insert an **anchor** from time to time that you could gain control of quickly and easily that would boost you along the way towards getting what you want?

Next, I'd like you to *write out ten sentences* like I gave and practice **leveraging suggestions**.

I'd recommend you read this e-book at least ten times. I imagine by then, you'll probably get the hang of what I was doing. You'll probably start to figure it out. Like I said, *experiential, experiential, experiential*, that's what this lesson is all about. I guarantee you, you're going to learn more with each read.

Now, I want you to analyze the **nested loops** then jot down three **stories** you could use in your work and practice telling them and *stopping just at the climax* and then begin the next one.

I'd like you to consider how you can use **stories** and **suggestions** to **prime the unconscious mind** for the road you want it to run down.

The main thing with this lesson is to read it about ten or more times. You're going to find *strategies within strategies*. You're' going to find **suggestion** abilities and you're going to quickly gain those competencies yourself. But reading this over and over will be the ticket for you entering those realms.

All right, well this has really been a fun lesson. My head is off in the clouds just delivering it. I've been trying to stay grounded, but when you start doing work that gets profound like this, you'll find your own mind kind of floats off into the ozone as well and that, by the way, is one of the ways you'll know that the people you're talking to are doing the same thing. You'll learn to set up that kind of a signal for yourself.

A lot of refinements to things you've learned previously and some new things that are just -- well, are downright earthshaking in what they can do for you, so I want you to begin practicing quickly with using a *minimum* of three **stories** in a **nested loop** fashion.

I would be willing to bet most everybody reading this is zoned through the floor and struggling to even pay attention to the words I'm writing now, which is fine because it all of course is going, yup, you guessed it, **right into your unconscious**.

All right, well it's been great talking with you in this e-book. I hope you use it and prosper like crazy. I hope you've had a lot of fun in this, the final book in the **Persuasion Force** series. And it's been great working with you up to this point.

The Power Ark

https://goark.app/join

If you are ready to learn more about the cutting edge in persuasion strategy, skills, and training from a Titan of the Persuasion industry, scan the QR Code or click the link above.

Made in United States
Orlando, FL
17 April 2023

32187819R00217